# Street by Street

# EAST SUSSEX

## PLUS BURGESS HILL, EAST GRINSTEAD, HAYWARDS HEATH, ROYAL TUNBRIDGE WELLS

### Enlarged Areas Brighton, Eastbourne, Hastings, Lewes, Newhaven

C000173933

Ist edition May 2001

© Automobile Association Developments Limited 2001

This product includes map data licensed from Ordnance Survey® with the permission of the Controller of Her Majesty's Stationery Office. © Crown copyright 2000. All rights reserved. Licence No: 399221.

All rights reserved. No part of this publication may be reproduced, stored in a retrieval system, or transmitted in any form or by any means– electronic, mechanical, photocopying, recording or otherwise – unless the permission of the publisher has been given beforehand.

Published by AA Publishing (a trading name of Automobile Association Developments Limited, whose registered office is Norfolk House, Priestley Road, Basingstoke, Hampshire, RG24 9NY. Registered number 1878835).

Mapping produced by the Cartographic Department of The Automobile Association.

A CIP Catalogue record for this book is available from the British Library.

Printed by G. Canale & C. s.p.a., Torino, Italy

The contents of this atlas are believed to be correct at the time of the latest revision. However, the publishers cannot be held responsible for loss occasioned to any person acting or refraining from action as a result of any material in this atlas, nor for any errors, omissions or changes in such material. The publishers would welcome information to correct any errors or omissions and to keep this atlas up to date. Please write to Publishing, The Automobile Association, Fanum House, Basing View, Basingstoke, Hampshire, RG21 4EA.

Ref: MX019

| | |
|---|---|
| Key to map pages | ii-iii |
| Key to map symbols | iv-1 |
| Enlarged scale pages | 2-11 |
| Street by Street | 12-209 |
| Index – towns & villages | 210 |
| Index – streets | 211-227 |
| Index – featured places | 228-231 |

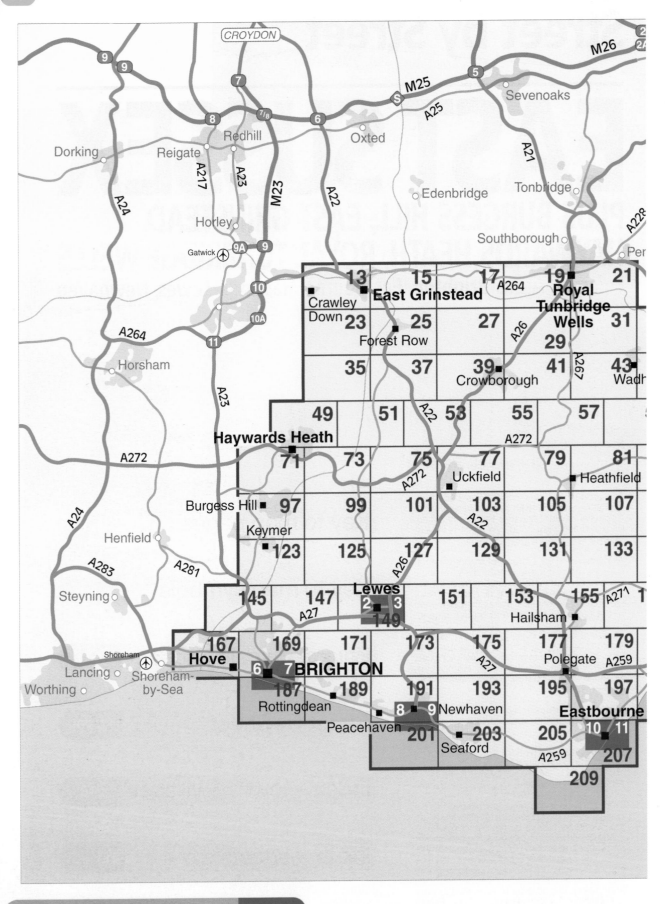

CROYDON

9 9

7

8 7/8 6

Redhill

Dorking

Reigate

A217

A23

M23

A22

S M25 A25

5 M26

Sevenoaks

Oxted

A21

Edenbridge

Tonbridge

Southborough

A228

Per

Horley

A264

Gatwick

9A 9

10

10A

11

A23

Horsham

A264

A24

A272

A283

A24

A281

Henfield

Steyning

Shoreham

Lancing

Worthing

Shoreham-by-Sea

Hove

| 13 | 15 | 17 A264 | 19 | 21 |
| Crawley Down 23 | East Grinstead 25 | 27 | Royal Tunbridge Wells 29 | 31 |
| 35 | 37 | 39 Crowborough | 41 A267 | 43 Wadh |
| 49 | 51 A22 | 53 | 55 A272 | 57 |
| Haywards Heath 71 | 73 | 75 A272 | 77 Uckfield | 79 | 81 Heathfield |
| Burgess Hill 97 | 99 | 101 | 103 A22 | 105 | 107 |
| Keymer 123 | 125 | 127 A26 | 129 | 131 | 133 |
| 145 | 147 A27 | Lewes 2 3 149 | 151 | 153 | 155 A271 1 Hailsham |
| 167 | 169 | 171 | 173 | 175 A27 | 177 Polegate 179 A259 |
| Hove 6 7 BRIGHTON 187 Rottingdean | 189 | 8 9 191 Newhaven | 193 | 195 | 197 Eastbourne |
| Peacehaven 201 | 203 Seaford | 205 A259 | 10 11 207 |
| | | | 209 |

Enlarged scale pages   1:10,000   6.3 inches to 1 mile

0          1/4        miles        1/2                3/4
0     1/4     1/2   kilometres   3/4        1        1 1/4

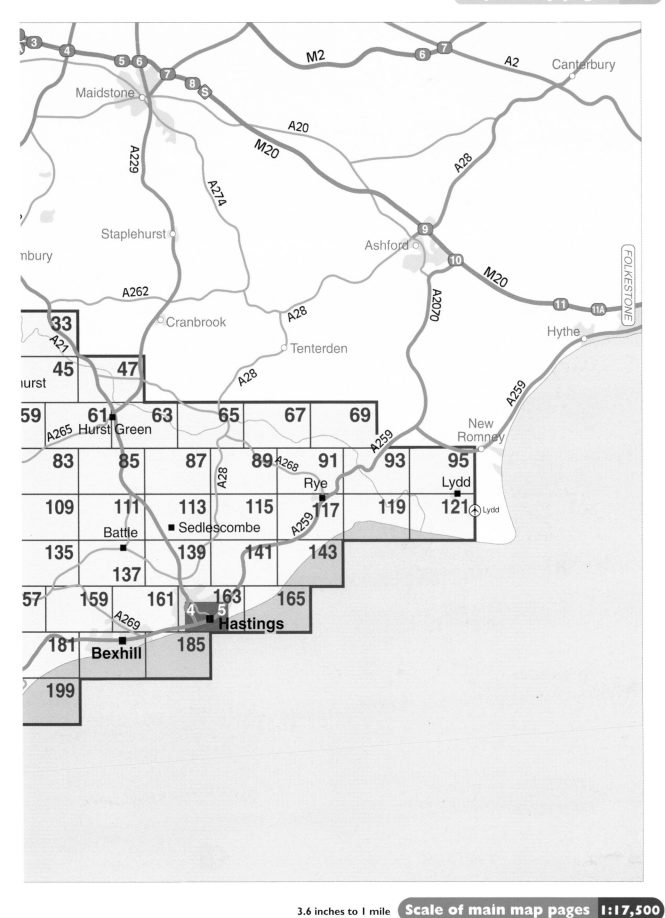

**3.6 inches to 1 mile** **Scale of main map pages** **1:17,500**

| 0 | 1/2 | miles | 1 |
| 0 | 1/2 | 1 | kilometres | 1 1/2 | 2 |

| | | | | |
|---|---|---|---|---|
| **Junction 9** | Motorway & junction | | **P+** 🚌 | Park & Ride |
| **Services** | Motorway service area | | 🚌 | Bus/coach station |
| | Primary road single/dual carriageway | | | Railway & main railway station |
| **Services** | Primary road service area | | | Railway & minor railway station |
| | A road single/dual carriageway | | ⊖ | Underground station |
| | B road single/dual carriageway | | ⊖ | Light railway & station |
| | Other road single/dual carriageway | | ++++++++ | Preserved private railway |
| | Restricted road | | *LC* | Level crossing |
| | Private road | | ●─●─●─● | Tramway |
| ← ← | One way street | | ----------- | Ferry route |
| | Pedestrian street | | ............. | Airport runway |
| | Track/ footpath | | —·—·—·— | Boundaries- borough/ district |
| | Road under construction | | ▼▼▼▼▼▼▼ | Mounds |
| | Road tunnel | | **93** | Page continuation 1:17,500 |
| **P** | Parking | | **7** | Page continuation to enlarged scale 1:10,000 |

| | | | |
|---|---|---|---|
| | River/canal lake, pier | ♿ | Toilet with disabled facilities |
| | Aqueduct lock, weir | 🅿 | Petrol station |
| 465 ▲ Winter Hill | Peak (with height in metres) | PH | Public house |
| | Beach | PO | Post Office |
| | Coniferous woodland | 📖 | Public library |
| | Broadleaved woodland | i | Tourist Information Centre |
| | Mixed woodland | ✗ | Castle |
| | Park | 🏛 | Historic house/ building |
| | Cemetery | Wakehurst Place NT | National Trust property |
| | Built-up area | Ⓜ | Museum/ art gallery |
| | Featured building | † | Church/chapel |
| ⊓⊔⊓⊔⊓⊔⊓⊔ | City wall | ♔ | Country park |
| A&E | Accident & Emergency hospital | 🎭 | Theatre/ performing arts |
| 🚻 | Toilet | 🎬 | Cinema |

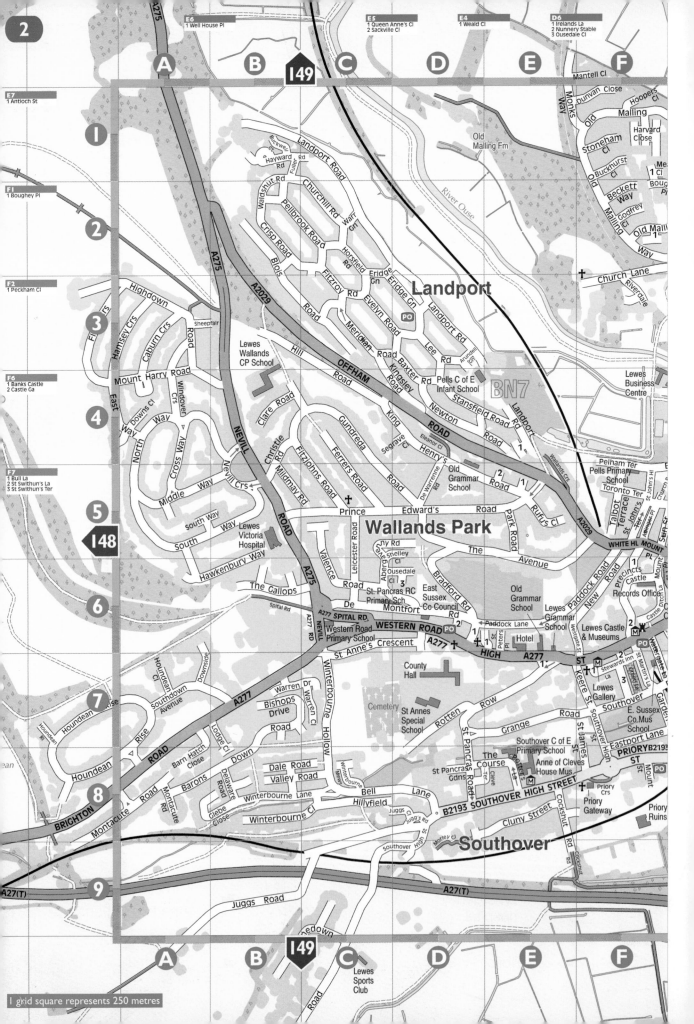

E7
1 Antioch St

F1
1 Boughey Pl

F2
1 Peckham Cl

F6
1 Banks Castle
2 Castle Ga

F7
1 Bull La
2 St Swithun's La
3 St Swithun's Ter

E6
1 Well House Pl

E5
1 Queen Anne's Cl
2 Sackville Cl

E4
1 Weald Cl

D6
1 Irelands La
2 Nunnery Stable
3 Ousedale Cl

Mantell Cl

Old Malling Fm

River Ouse

Monks Way
Old Dunvan Close
Hoopers Cl
Old Malling
Stoneham Cl
Harvard Close
Buckhurst Cl
Me Cl
Bougl
Beckett Way
Godfrey Cl
Old Malli Way
Church Lane
Riverdale

Landport

Landport Road
Buckwell Rd
Hayward Rd
Fuller Rd
Churchill Rd
Warr Gn
Waldshut Rd
Pellbrook Road
Horsfield Rd
Eridge Gn
Eridge Gn
Crisp Road
Blois
Fitzroy Rd
Evelyn Road
PO
Landport Rd
Baxter Rd
Lee Rd
Arundell Rd
Meridian Road
Kingsley Road
Pells C of E Infant School
BN7
Lewes Business Centre

Highdown
Fi rs
Sheepfair
Lewes Wallands CP School
Hill Road
OFFHAM ROAD
Newton Road
Stansfield Road
Landport Rd
Pelham Ter
Pells Primary School
Toronto Ter
Hamsey Crs
Caburn Crs
Road
Clare Road
King Road
Henry's Road
Old Grammar School
Road
St John's Hi
Talbot Terrace
St John's

Mount Harry Road
Windover Crs
Christie Rd
Gundreda Road
Segrave Road
Eleanor Cl
De Warrenne Road
Rufus Cl
WHITE HL MOUNT
PL
Castle
Records Office

East Downs Cl
North Way
Cross Way
NEVILL
Nevill Crs
Fitzjohns Road
Ferrers Road
Mildmay Rd
Prince Edward's Road
Park Road
The Avenue
New Road
Paddock Road
Castle Ditch La
Lewes Castle & Museums
PO
M

Middle Way
South Way
South Way
Lewes Victoria Hospital
ROAD
Valence Road
Leicester Road
ny Rd
shelley Cl
Aberdale Cl
Ousedale Cl 3
St Pancras RC Primary Sch
East Sussex Co Council Rd
Bradford Rd
Old Grammar School
Lewes Grammar School
Precincts
Lewes Gallery
Southover High Road
E. Sussex Co.Mus School

148

Hawkenbury Way
The Gallops
Spital Rd
A275
A277
SPITAL RD
De Montfort
Western Road Primary School
St Anne's Crescent
WESTERN ROAD PO
Paddock Lane
St Peters Pl
Hotel
HIGH
A277
ST
M stewards Inn La
3
Keere St
M St Martin's La

Brighton
Houndean Rise
Houndean Cl
Southdown Avenue
Downsland
ROAD
A277
Warren Dr
Warren Cl
Bishops Drive
Road
Winterbourne Hollow
County Hall
Cemetery
St Annes Special School
Rotten Row
Grange Road
St James St
Southover High St
Southover C of E Primary School
The Course
Anne of Cleves House Mus.
PRIORY B2193
Eastport Lane
ST
Mount
PO

Montacute Rd
Lodge Cl
Barn Hatch Close
Down Road
Dale Road
Valley Road
Winterbourne Lane
Winterbourne Mews
Bell Lane
St Pancras Gdns
St Pancras Road
Cleve Ter
Priory Crs
Priory Gateway
Priory Ruins

BRIGHTON
Montacute Road
Barons
Glebe Close
Delaware Road
Winterbourne Cl
Hillyfield
Juggs Rd
Juggs Rd
B2193 SOUTHOVER HIGH STREET
Cluny Street
Cockshut Rd
Cockshut Rd

A27(T)
Juggs Road
southover High St
Morley Cl
Southover

A27(T)

149

Lewes Sports Club

1 grid square represents 250 metres

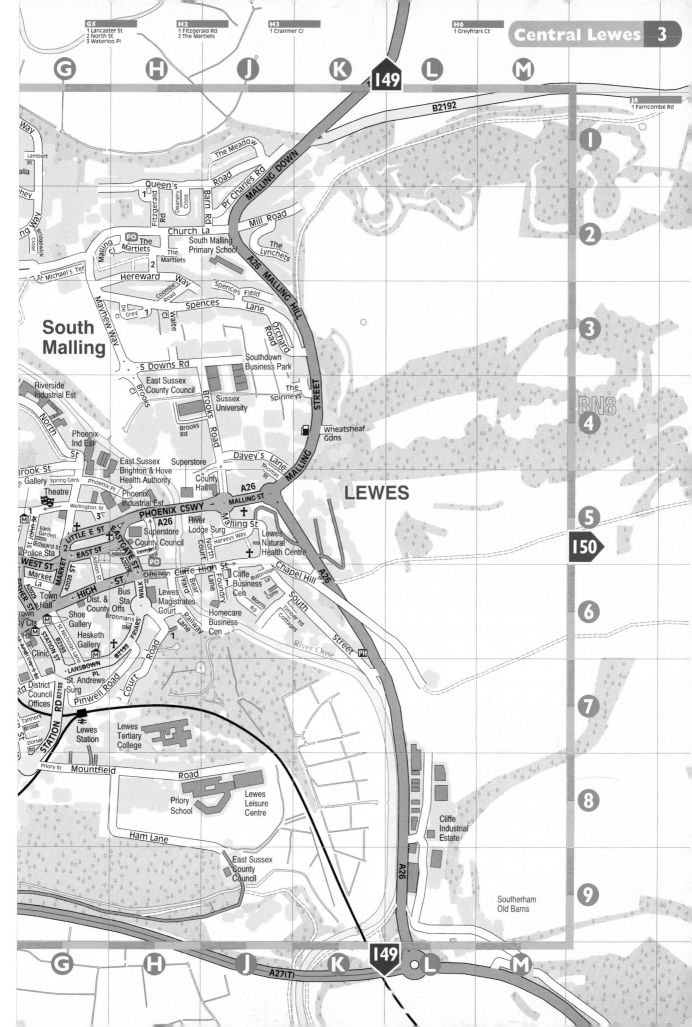

G5
1 Lancaster St
2 North St
3 Waterloo Pl

H2
1 Fitzgerald Rd
2 The Martlets

H3
1 Cranmer Cl

H6
1 Greyfriars Ct

J6
1 Farncombe Rd

G   H   J   K   L   M

149
B2192

1

The Meadow
Road
Pr Charles Rd
MALLING DOWN
Queen's
Fitzgerald Rd
Deanery Close
Barn Rd
Mill Road
Church La
South Malling Primary School
The Lynchets
2

PO The Martlets
The Martlets
A26 MALLING HILL
The Lynchets

**South Malling**

St Michael's Ter
Hereward Way
Coombe Road
De Grey Cl
Waite Cl
Spences Field
Spences Lane
Orchard Road
3

Mayhew Way
S Downs Rd
Southdown Business Park
BN8
4

Brooks
East Sussex County Council
Brooks Road
Sussex University
The spinneys
STREET

Riverside Industrial Est
North St
Brooks Rd
Wheatsheaf Gdns
Davey's Lane
MALLING

Phoenix Ind Est
East Sussex Brighton & Hove Health Authority
Superstore
County Hall
Thomas St
**LEWES**

Gallery
Spring Gdns
Phoenix Pl
Phoenix Industrial Est
A26
MALLING ST
5

Theatre
Wellington St
3
PHOENIX CSWY
A26
River Lodge Surg
Malling St
150

M
Earls Garden
Edward St
LITTLE E ST
EASTGATE ST
Superstore County Council
A2029
Harveys Way
Lewes Natural Health Centre

Police Sta
EAST ST
Eastgate whf
PO
Cliffe High St
Rusbridge S Cliffe
Chapel Hill
A26
6

WEST ST
MARKET ST
HIGH ST
Albion St
Cliffe High St
1 Cliffe Business Cen
Morris Rd
South

Market La
Town Hall
Dist. & County Offs
Bus Sta
Cliffe High
Bear Yard
Lewes Magistrates Court
Timber Yd Cottages
Street

Brown
Cts
Shoe Gallery
Broomans La
FRIARS WALK
Railway Lane
Homecare Business Cen
7

Clinic
St Nicholas Lane
Hesketh Gallery
B2193
1
River Ouse
PH

LANSDOWN PL
St. Andrews Surg
Court Road
8

District Council Offices
Tanners Brook
STATION RD B2193
Pinwell Road
Cliffe Industrial Estate

Dorset Rd
Lewes Station
Lewes Tertiary College
9

Priory St
**Mountfield**
Road
Lewes Leisure Centre
A26

Priory School

Ham Lane
East Sussex County Council
Southerham Old Barns

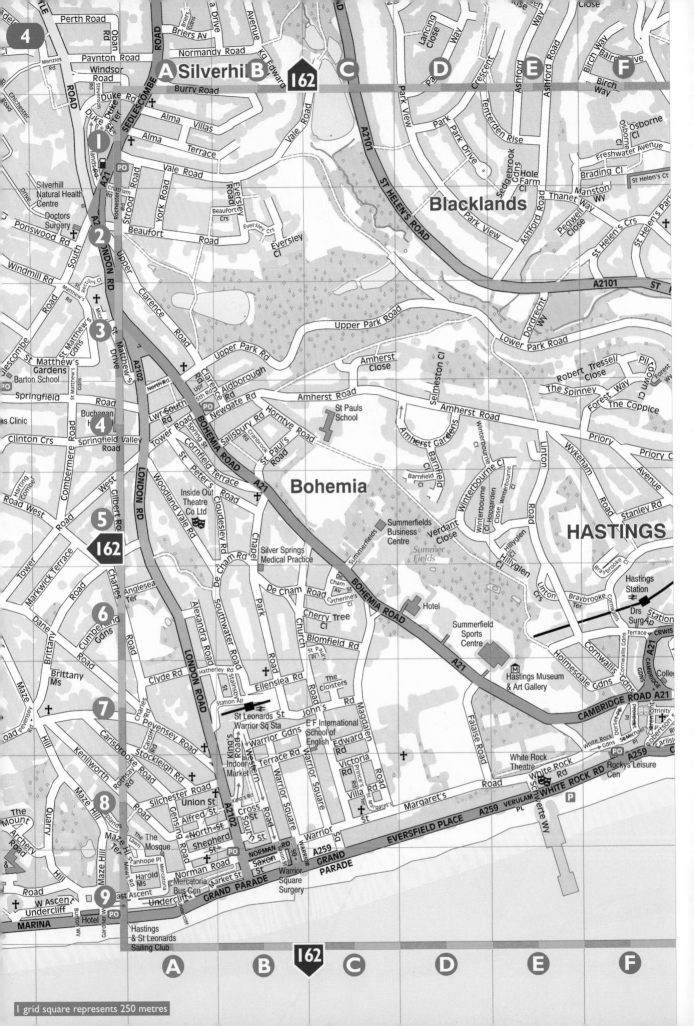

1 grid square represents 250 metres

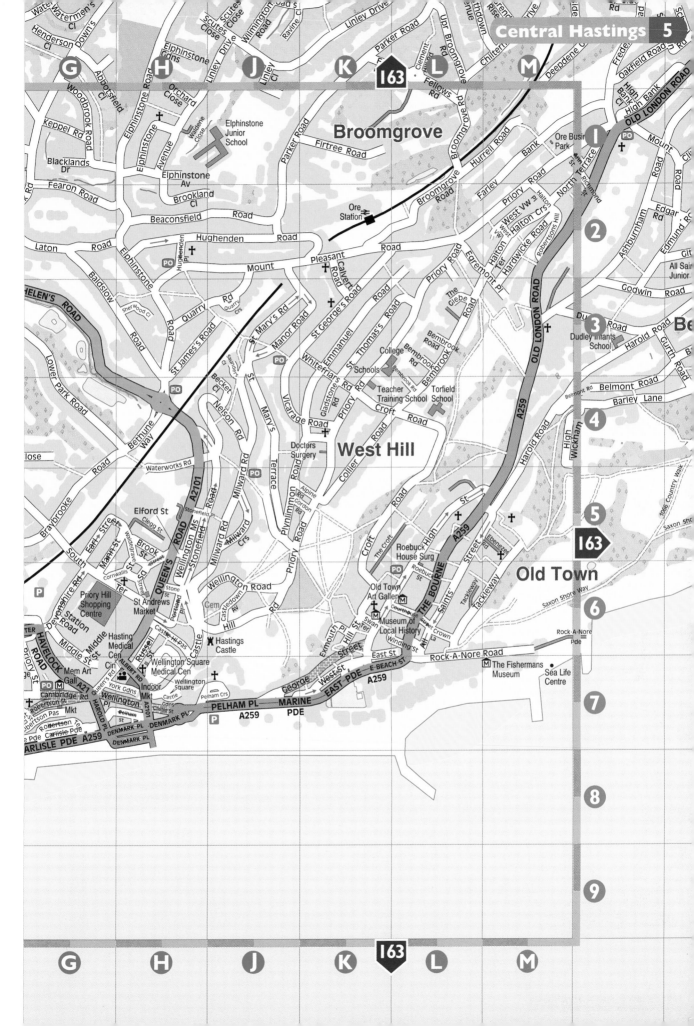

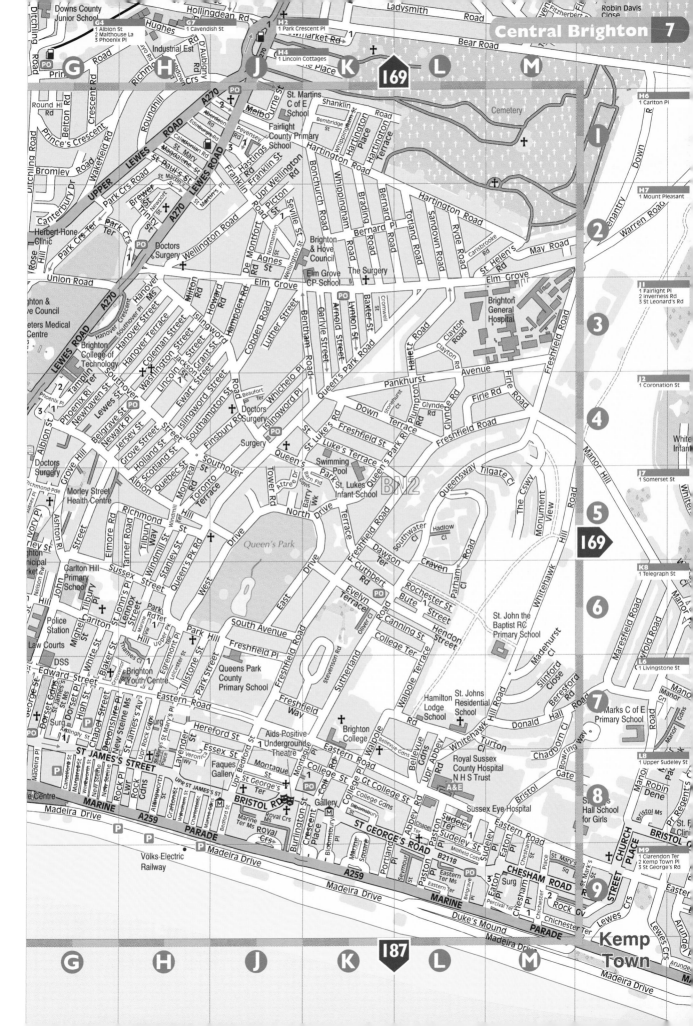

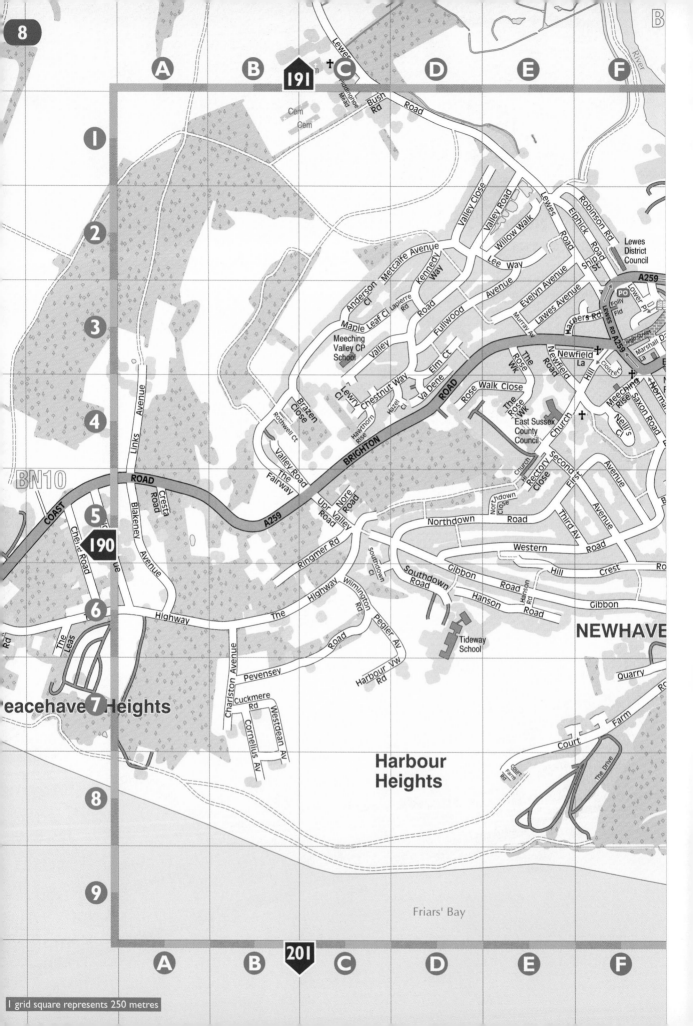

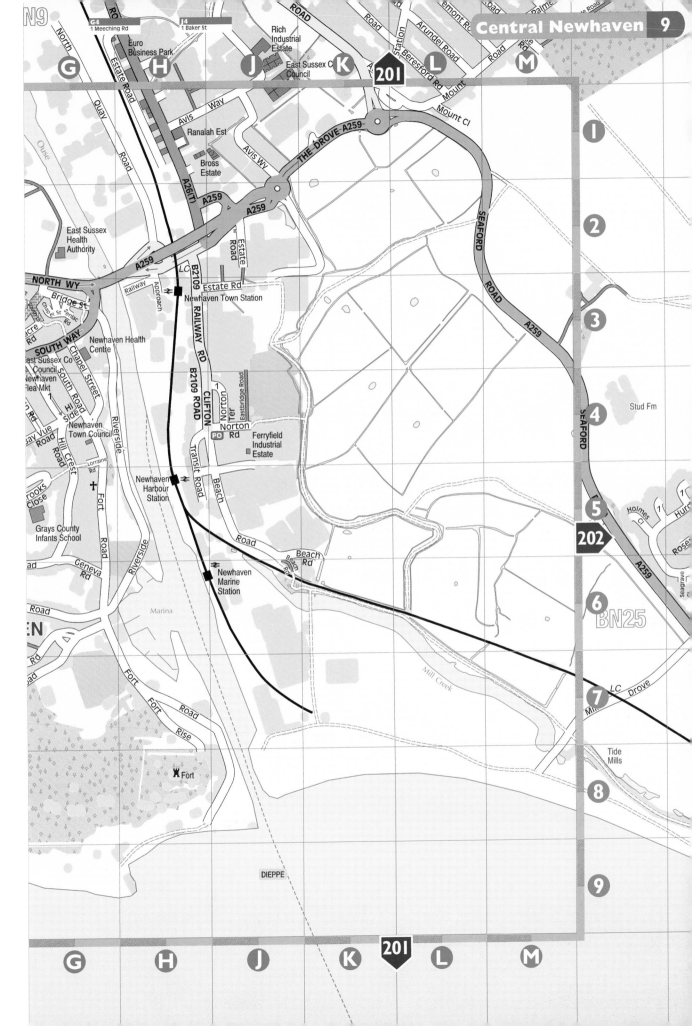

G4 1 Meeching Rd
J4 1 Baker St

Euro
Business Park

Rich
Industrial
Estate

East Sussex C
Council

201

Mount Cl

The Drove A259

G H J K L M

Avis Way

Ranalah Est

Estate Road

Bross
Estate

Avis Wy

A26(T)

A259

A259

Seaford Road

I

2

East Sussex
Health
Authority

A259

LC

B2109

Estate Rd

Railway

Approach

Estate Road

Newhaven Town Station

A259

3

North Wy

Bridge St

Chapel St
Seniac

Railway Rd

Seaford

4

Stud Fm

South Way

Newhaven Health
Centre

East Sussex Co
Council
Newhaven
Flea Mkt

Chapel Street

Newhaven
Town Council

Hill Side

South Road

Bay Vue
Road

Lorraine
Rd

Riverside

B2109

Clifton

B2109 Road

Transit Road

Norton Ter

Norton
Rd

Eastbridge Road

PO

Ferryfield
Industrial
Estate

202

5

Holmes
Cl

A259

Rose

Hurr

Brooks
Close

Fort

Grays County
Infants School

Geneva
Rd

Road

Road

Riverside

Road

Beach
Road

Newhaven
Harbour
Station

Newhaven Marine
Station

Beach Rd

Beach
Rd

BN25

6

Marina

Mill Creek

7

LC Drove

Mill

Fort

Fort Road

Fort
Rise

Fort

Tide
Mills

8

DIEPPE

9

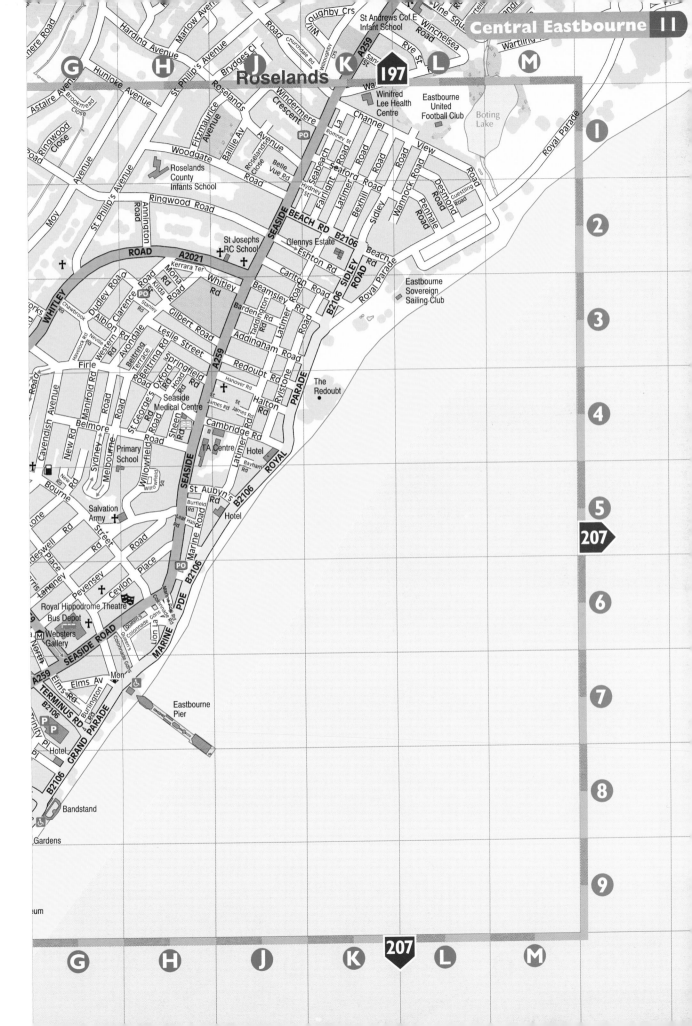

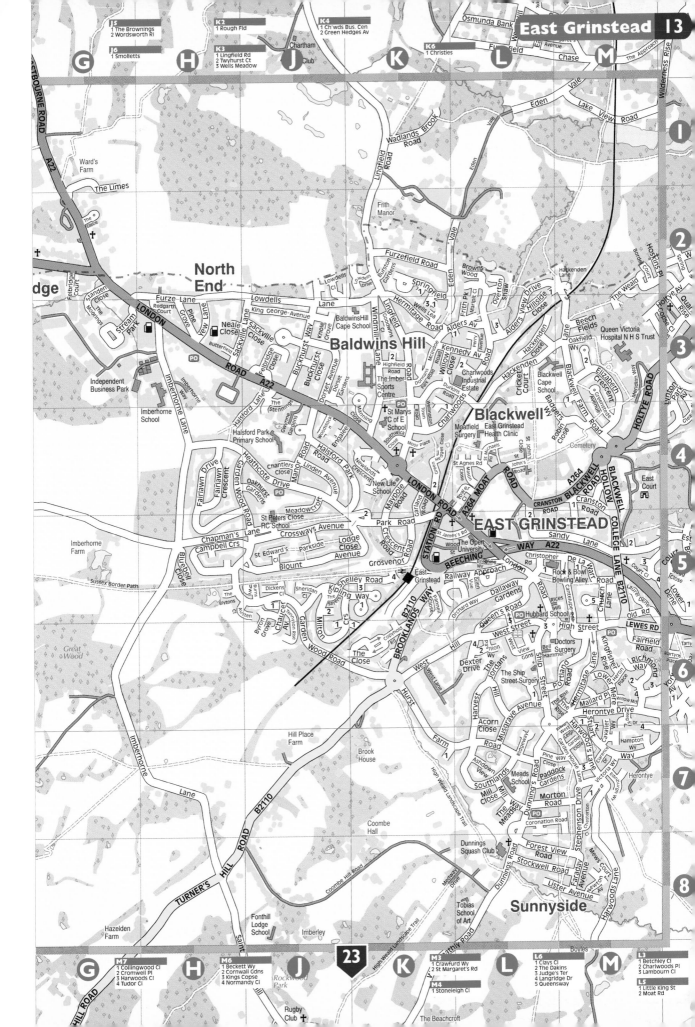

G H J K L M C

I

2

3

4

16

5

6

7

8

Basing Farm

Scarletts

Furnace Farm

Kent Water

Holtye Common

A264

† Hammerwood

Holtye

†

Brooklands

Hammerwood Park

Vanguard Way

Cansiron Lane

Little Cansiron Farm

Owlett's Farm

Great Cansiron Farm

Beeches Farm

Butcherfield

Thornhill

Surries

Pollard Wood

North Clays

St Ives Farm

High Weald Landscape Trail

Cansiron Lane

G H J **25** K L M

A    B    C    D    E    F

1
2
3
15
5
6
7
8

HARTFIELD ROAD

Kent County
East Sussex County

Sussex Border Path

Cowden

Chantlers Mead
Church Street
Cowden Mews
High Street
North Street

Holtye House

Sussex House Farm

Holywych House
Holywych Farm

Hethe

Cullinghurst Farm

HARTFIELD ROAD

B2026

A264

Edenbridge Road

B2026 EDENBRIDGE ROAD

Goodtrees Lane

Chantlers Farm

Tye Farm

Beech Green Park

Beech Green L

Bassett's Manor

Butcherfield Lane

Perryhill Farm

Butcherfield Lane

Hartwell

EDENBRIDGE ROAD

26

A    B    C    D    E    F

St Ives Farm

High Weald Landscape Trail

Chartners Farm

Forest Way

1 grid square represents 500 metres

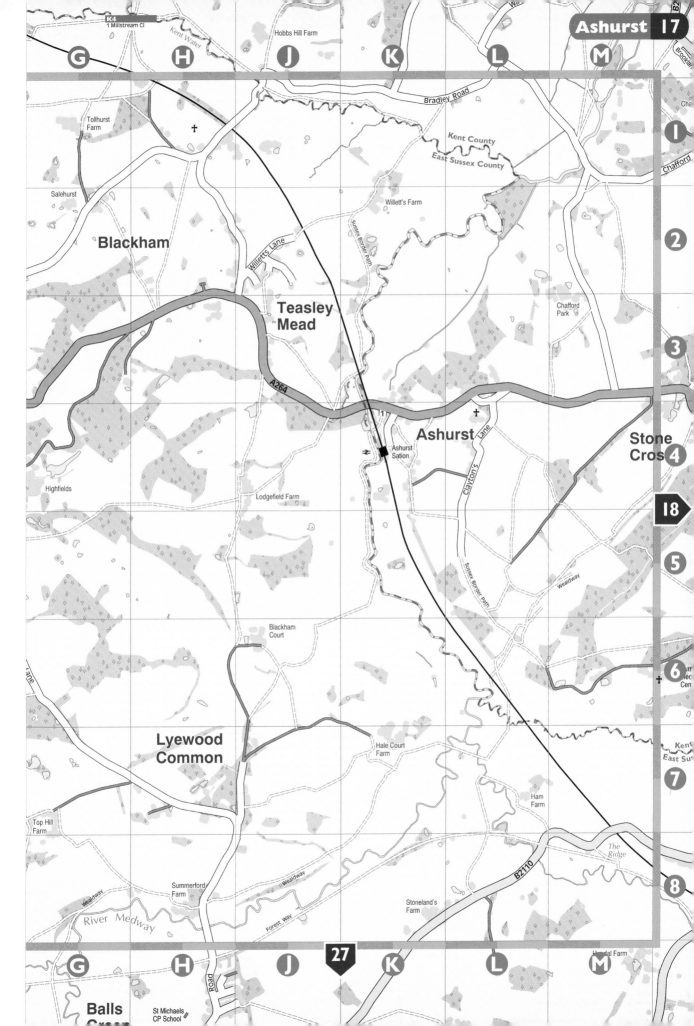

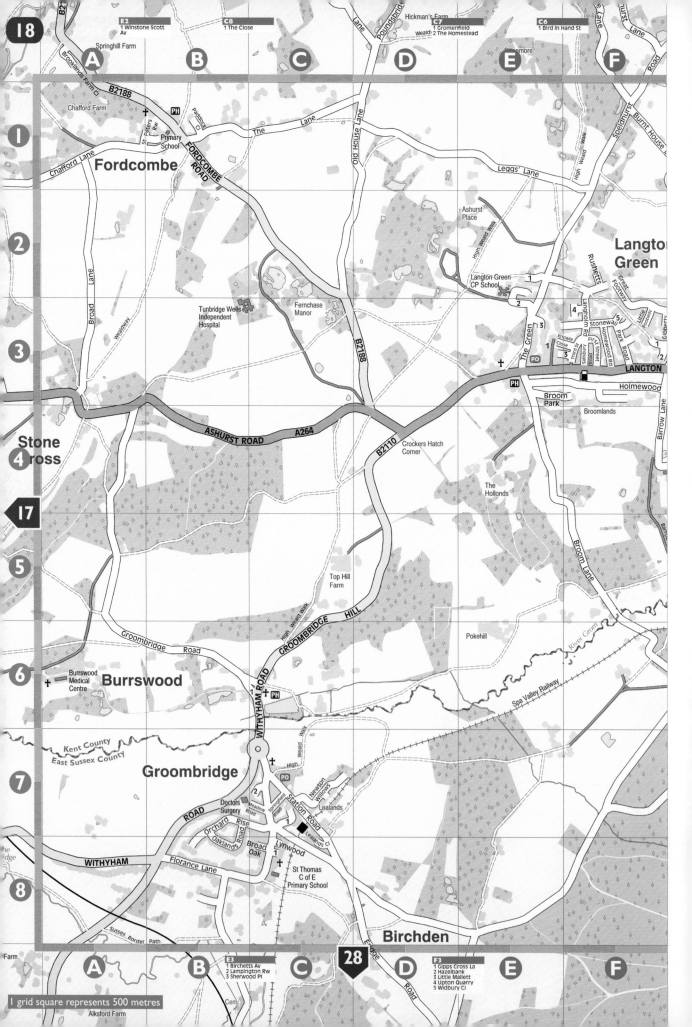

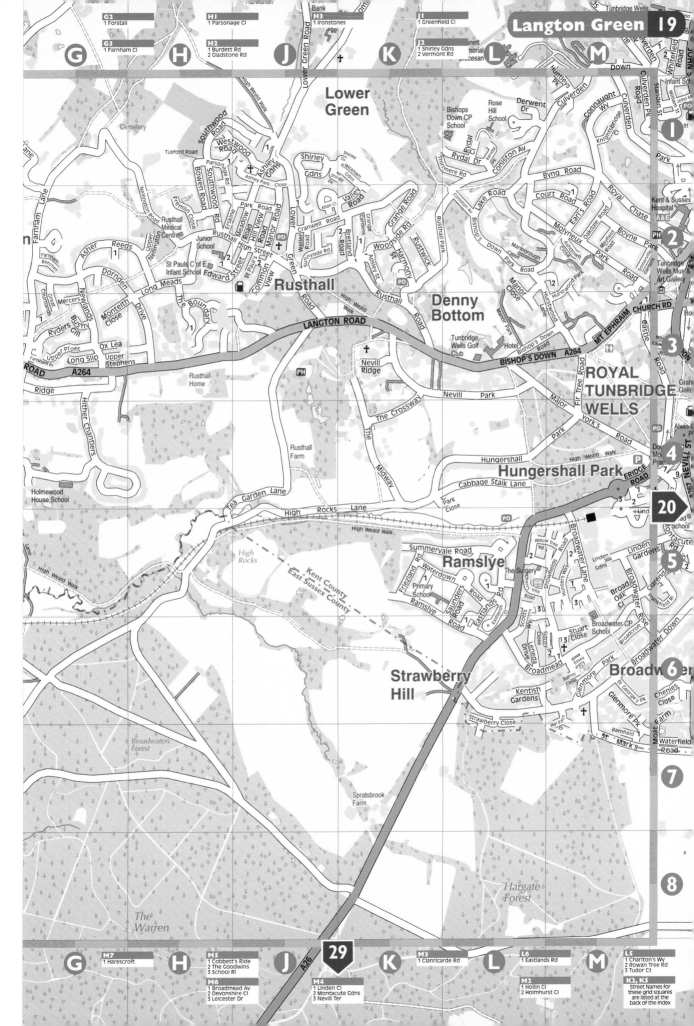

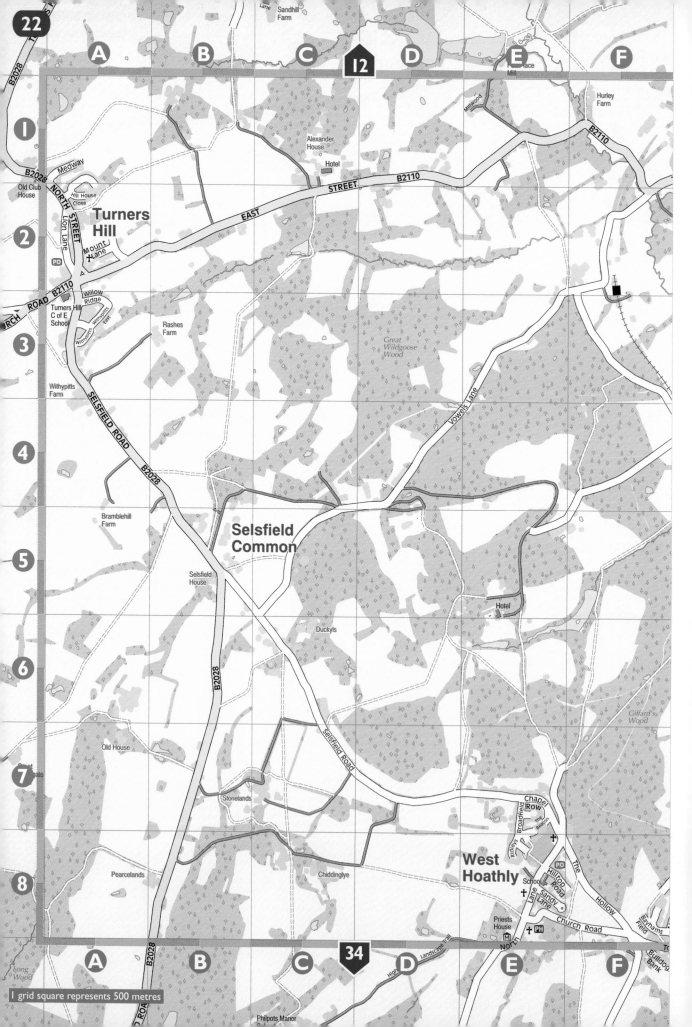

Sunnyside

G    H    J    13    K    L    M

I

Hazelden
Farm
TURNER'S HILL
Fonthill
Lodge
School
Imberley
Tobias
School
of Art

Boyles
Farm

Rockwood
Park

High Weald Landscape Trail

West Hoathly Road

2

Rugby
Club
East Grinstead
Sports Club

The Beachcroft
Towse

Sussex Border Path

Busses
Farm

Saint Hill
Manor

Standen House
& Garden (NT)

3

Ridge
Hill Manor

Saint Hill Road

West Hoathly Road

4

Bluebell Railway

Mill
Place

High Weald Landscape Trail

Admiral's
Bridge
Lane

Weir Wood
Resevoir

24

Birch
Farm

Charlwood

5

Neylands
Farm

Legsheath
Farm

6

Mayes

Plaw
Wood

Blackland
Farm

Grinstead Lane

East Sussex County

West Sussex County

Legsheath Lane

7

New Coombe
Farm

Coldharbour
Manor

8

Hamsey Road

Sharpthorne

Plawhatch
Hall

Marlpit Road

Station Road

Highcroft Road

Top Road

Home
Platt

Top Road

Tyes
Cross

Plaw Hill Lane

G    H    J    35    K    L    M

Courtlands

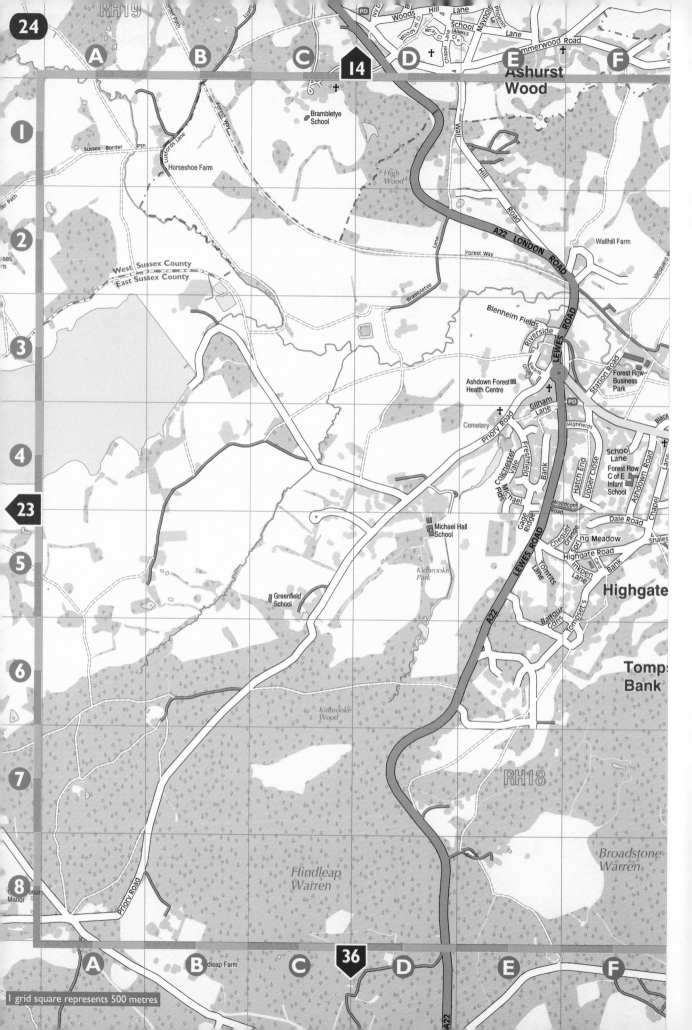

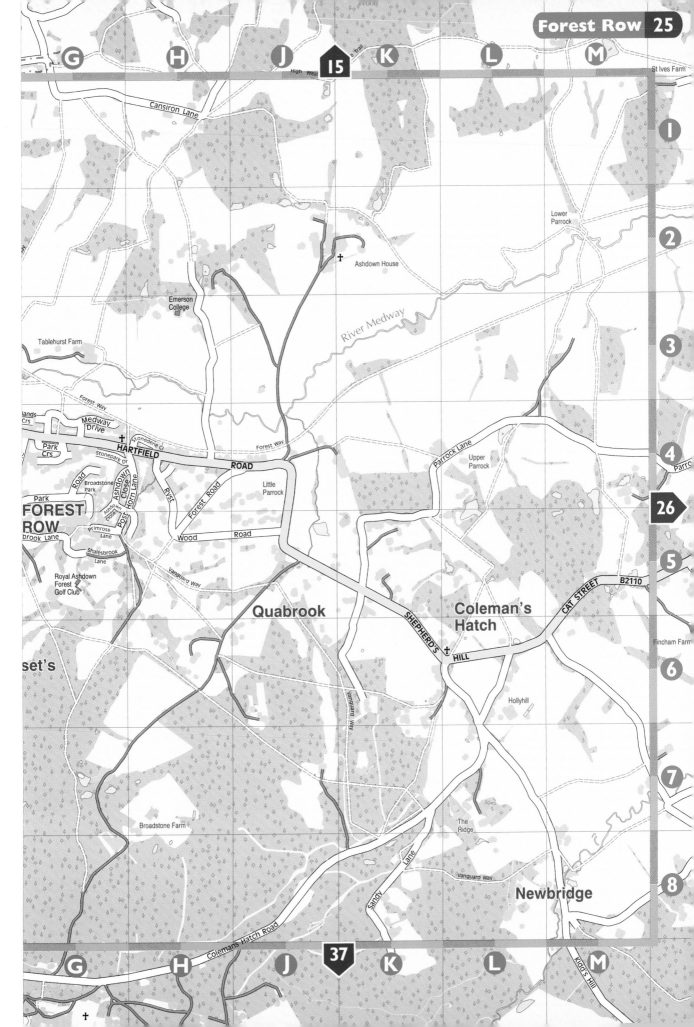

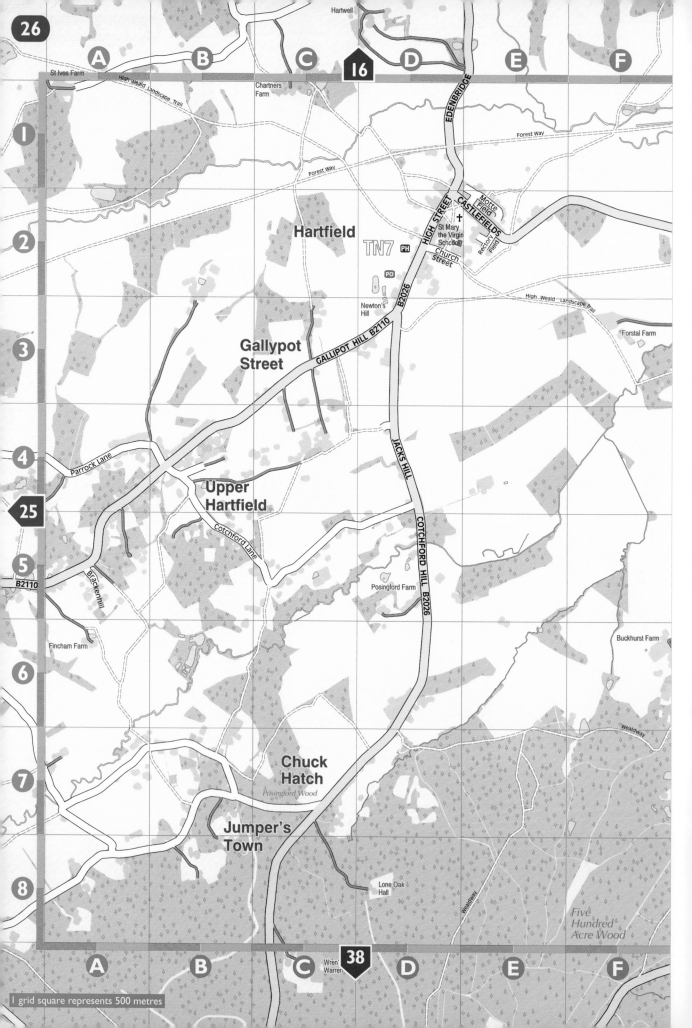

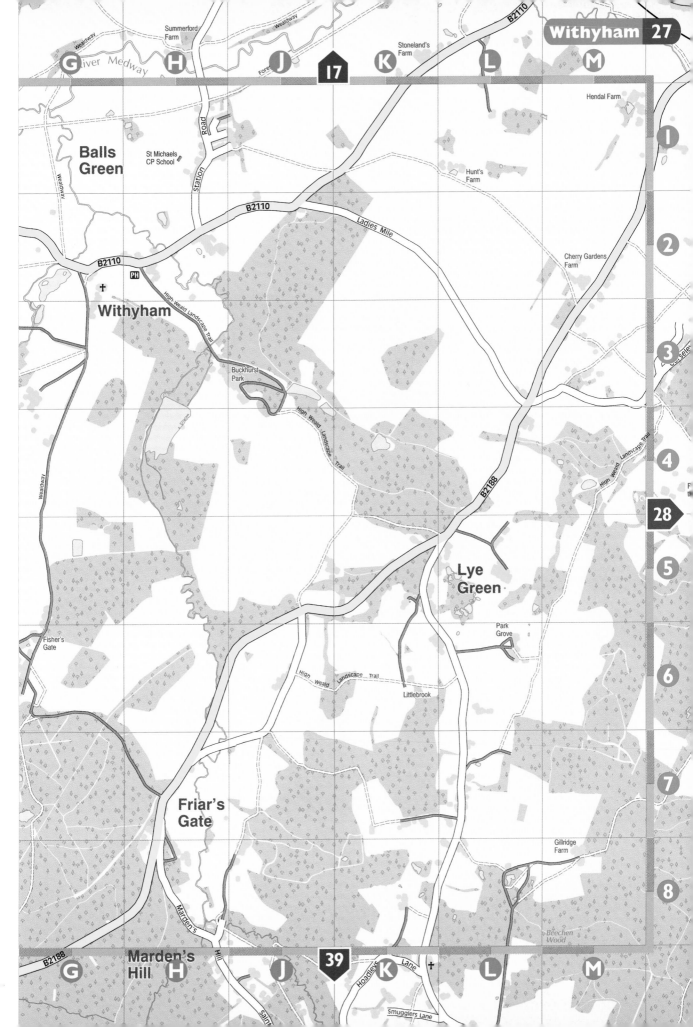

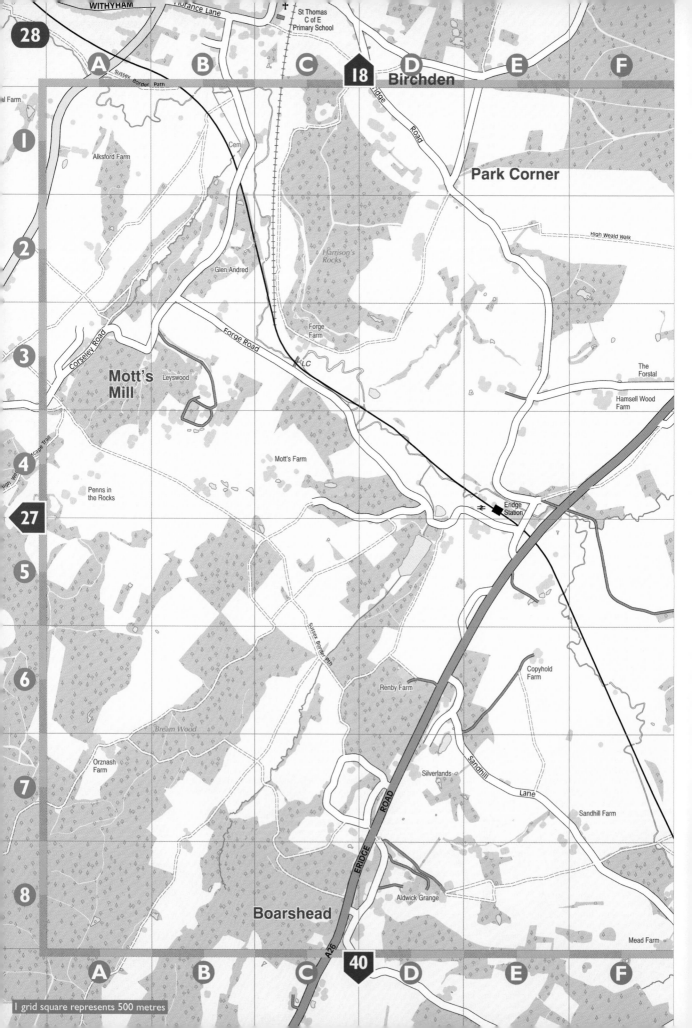

Hargate
Forest

G  H  The
Warren  **19**  J  K  L  M

A26

I

Warren
Farm

Warren
Farm Lane

Whitehill
Wood

2

**Eridge Green**

Eridge
Park

3

High Weald Walk

4

Forge
Wood

**30**

5

Hamsell
Manor

**Danegate**

6

Sussex Border Path

Stonewall

7

Sussex Border Path

Stitches Farm

Great
Danegate

Blackdon Hill

8

Redgate Mill
Farm

Green Hedges
Farm

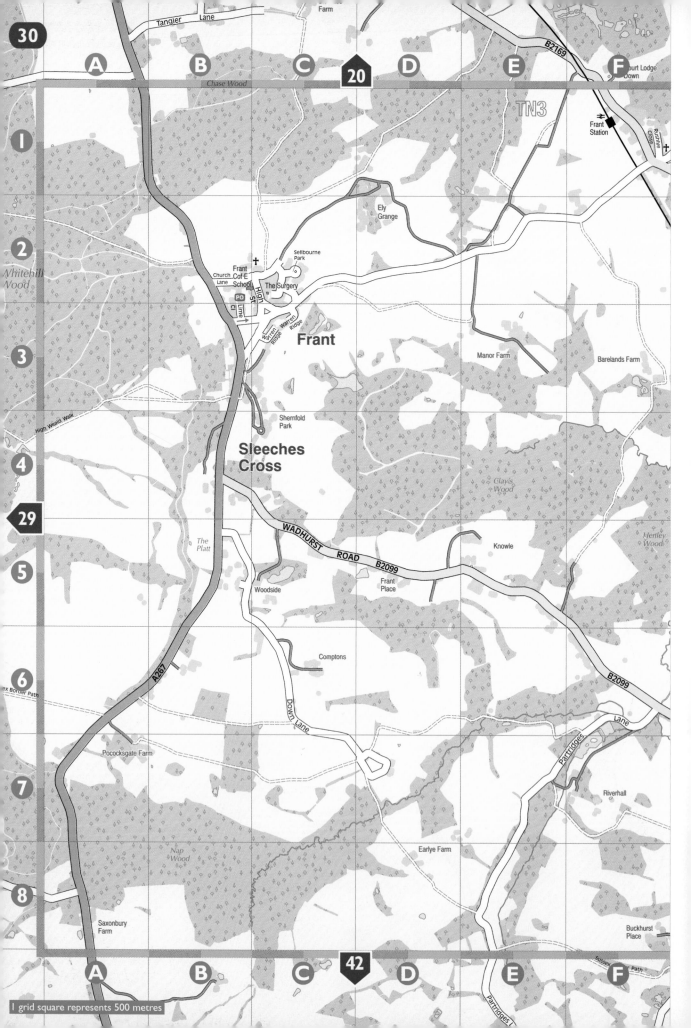

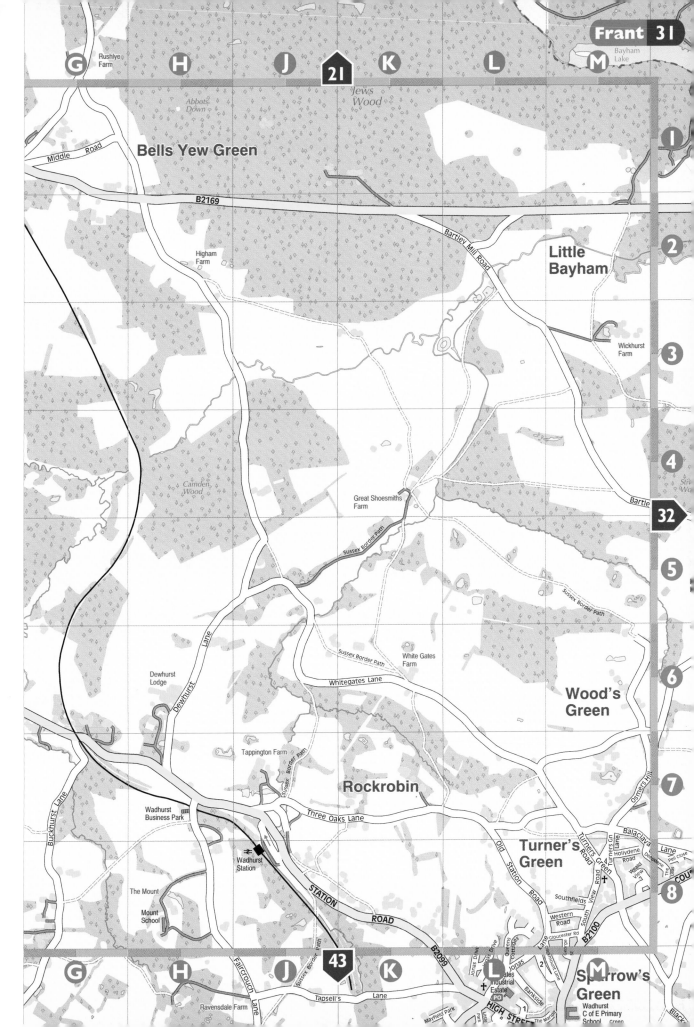

Bayham
Lake

Bayham
Abbey

Eise

Hoathly
Farm

Mount

**A** **B** **C** **D** **E** **F**

**I**

Wadhurst

B2169

FURNACE

Furnace
Mill

Free Heath Road

**2**

**Hook Green**

Clay Hill Road

LANE

Furnace
Farm

B2169

Furnace Avenue

Kent County

East Sussex County

Neills Road

**3**

T
D

**4**

Buss's
Green

Neills Road

Hoghole  Lane

Owls
Castle Farm

Stiver's
Wood

Free
Heath

Crowhurst
House

Sweetings Lane

**31**

Mill Road

B2100

**5**

Buckland
Hill Farm

Sleepers Stile Road

Markwicks

Hunter's
Hall Farm

Monks
Park

Newbury

Ladymeads
Farm

**6**

Monks Lane

Lane

COUSLEY WOOD ROAD

**Lower
Cousley Wood**

Windmill Lane

B2100

Sussex Border Path

Osmers Hill

Sussex Border Path

† 

**Cousley
Wood**

**7**

Butts        Lane

Balaclava   Lane

Turners Gn

Hollydene
Road

Pell Close

†

Great
Butts

**Pell
Green**

Little
Butts Farm

Bryant's
Farm

Weald
View

Diepdene

The Leas

COUSLEY WOOD ROAD

Sussex Border Path

**8**

Sussex  Border  Path

Yard's Lane

**A** **B** **C** **D** **E** **F**

mary
Green

Blackh

Little Pell

I grid square represents 500 metres

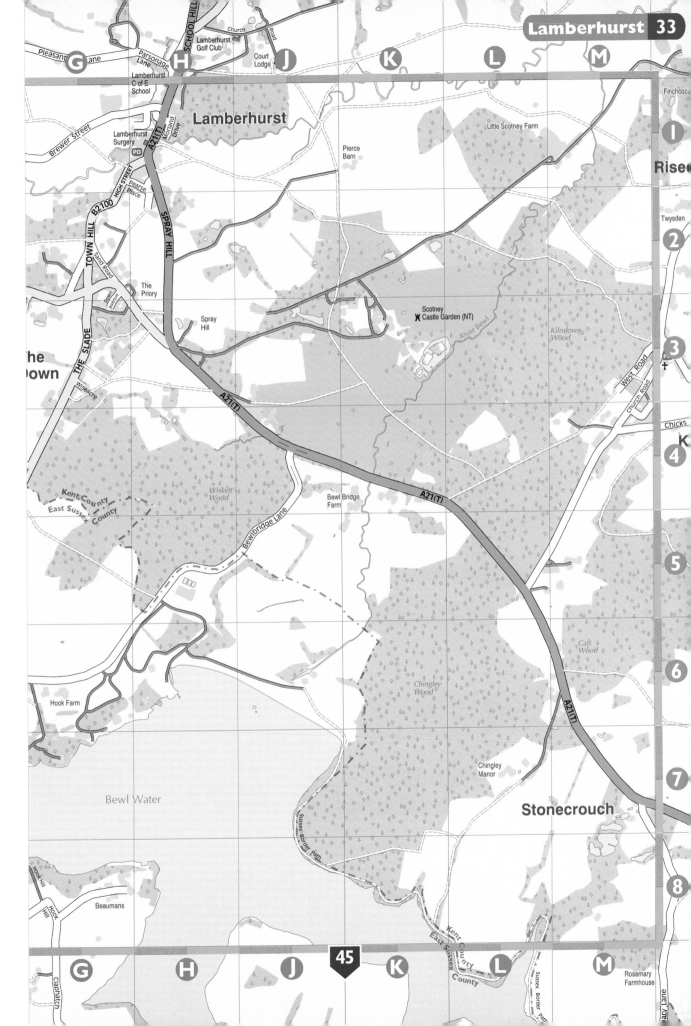

Pleasant Lane

G

H

J

K

L

M

SCHOOL HILL

Church
Road

Lamberhurst
Golf Club

Court
Lodge

Parsonage
Lane

Lamberhurst
C of E
School

**Lamberhurst**

Brewer Street

Lamberhurst
Surgery

PO

Morland Drive

A21(T)

SPRAY HILL

Pierce
Barn

Little Scotney Farm

Finchcoc

I

Rise

Twysden

2

HIGH STREET

Pearse
Place

B2100

TOWN HILL

Sand Road

The Priory

Spray
Hill

Scotney
Castle Garden (NT)

River Bewl

Kilndown
Wood

West Road

Church Road

3

+

Chicks

K

THE SLADE

Slade Avenue

Wiseacre

A21(T)

4

The
Down

Kent County

East Sussex County

Wiskett's
Wood

Bewl Bridge
Farm

A21(T)

5

Bewlbridge Lane

Cats
Wood

6

Hook Farm

Chingley
Wood

A21(T)

7

**Bewl Water**

Chingley
Manor

**Stonecrouch**

Sussex Border Path

Hook Hill

Hook
Hill

Beaumans

Kent County

East Sussex County

Sussex Border Path

Rosemary
Farmhouse

8

Claphatch

G

H

J

K

L

M

ary Lane

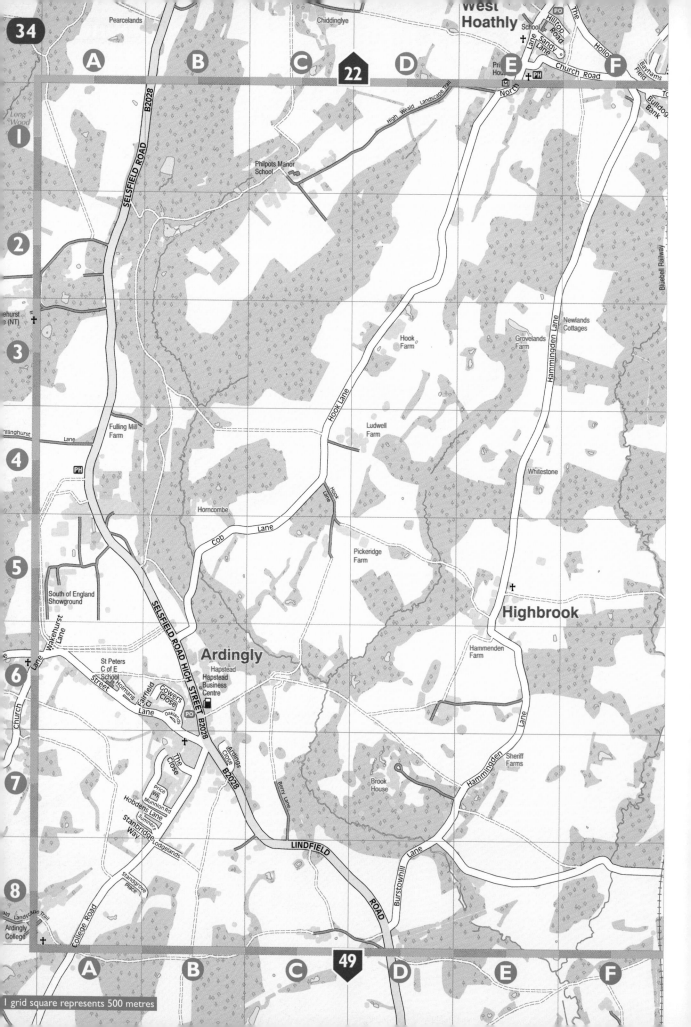

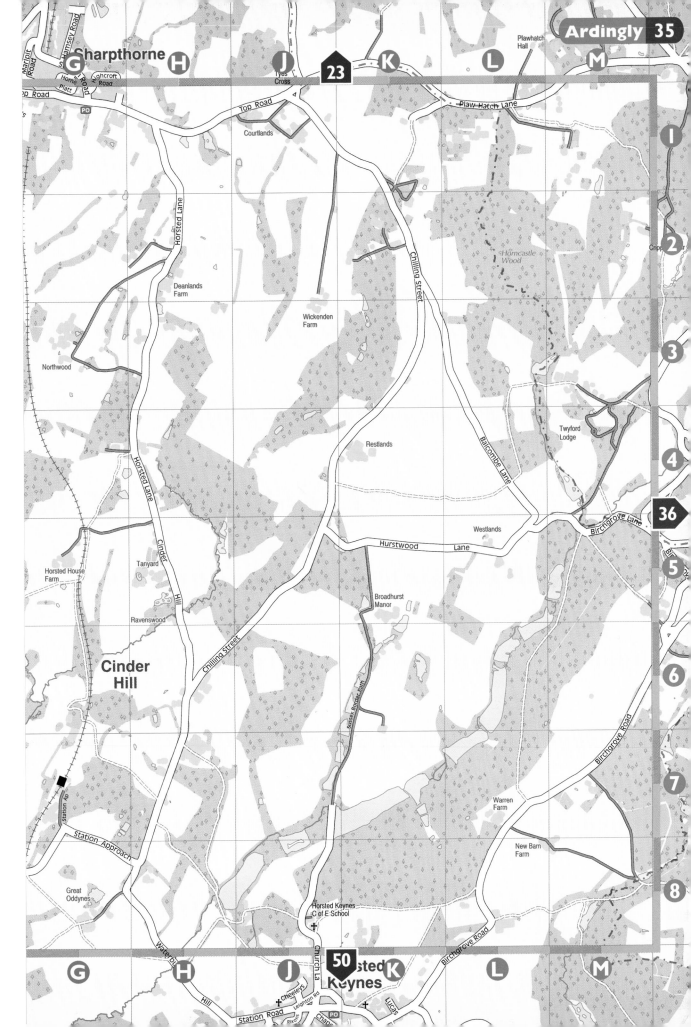

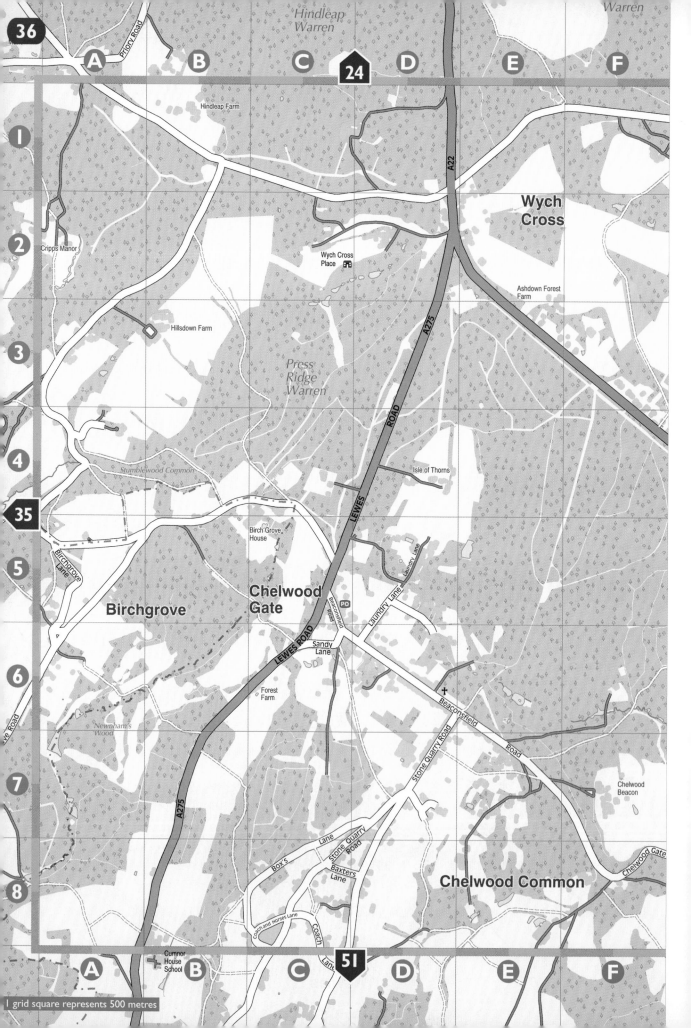

G
H
J
25
K
L
M

Colemans Hatch Road

Sandy

Vanguard Way

Kidd's Hill

1

New Lodge
Farm

2

Hotel

†

†

3

Ash Down

4

Pippingford
Park

38

Raven
Wood

A22

Chelwood
Vachery

5

Old
Lodge

6

7

A22

Londonderry
Farm

Marlpits

Road

Fairplace Farm

Crowborough Rd

8

Mill
Wood

Chapelwood
Manor

Ash Down View

G
H
Outback
Farm
J
52
K
Lane
L
M

Ridge Cl

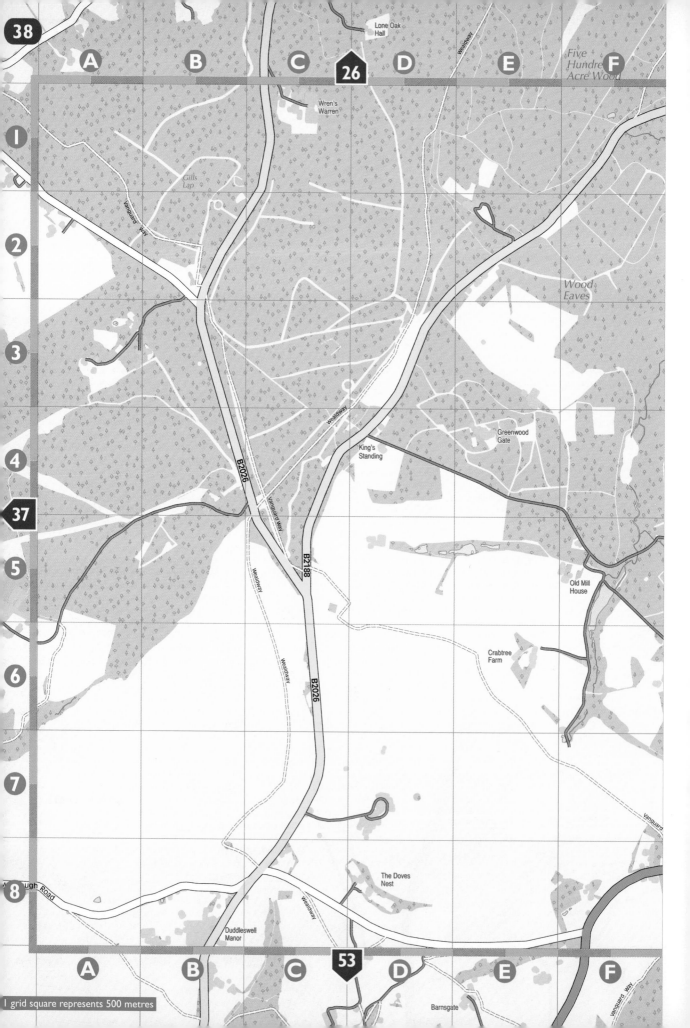

38

A  B  C  26  D  E  Five Hundre Acre Wood  F

I

Lone Oak Hall

Wren's Warren

Gills Lap

Vanguard Way

2

Wood Eaves

3

Wealdway

4

B2026

Vanguard Way

King's Standing

Greenwood Gate

37

Wealdway

5

Old Mill House

B2188

Wealdway

Crabtree Farm

6

B2026

7

Vanguard

The Doves Nest

8

ugh Road

Wealdway

Duddleswell Manor

A  B  C  53  D  E  F

Barnsgate

Vanguard Way

1 grid square represents 500 metres

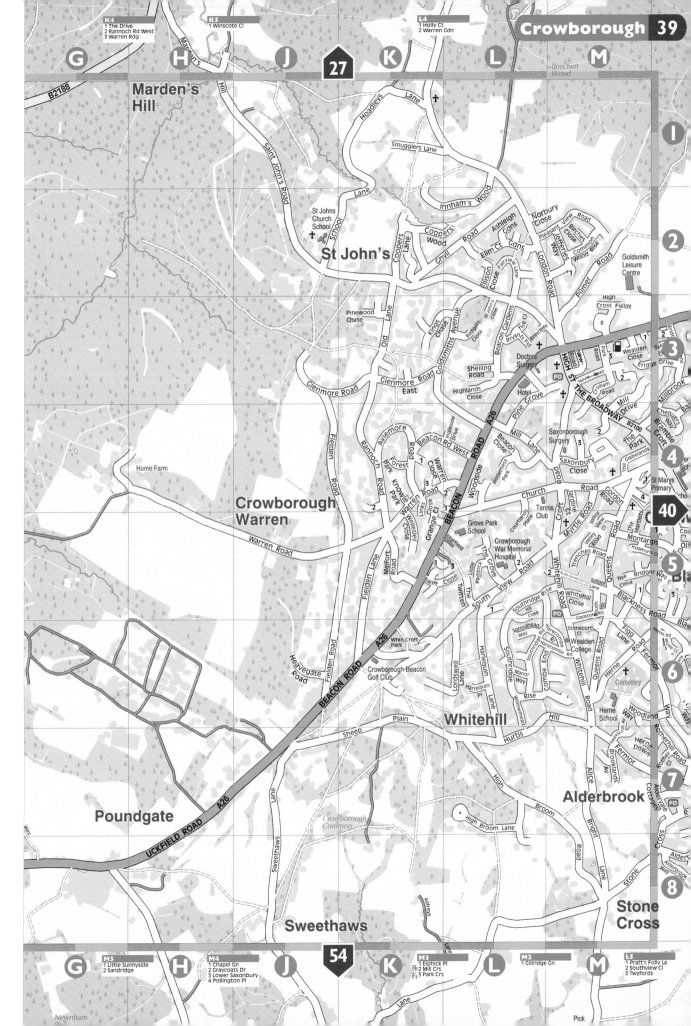

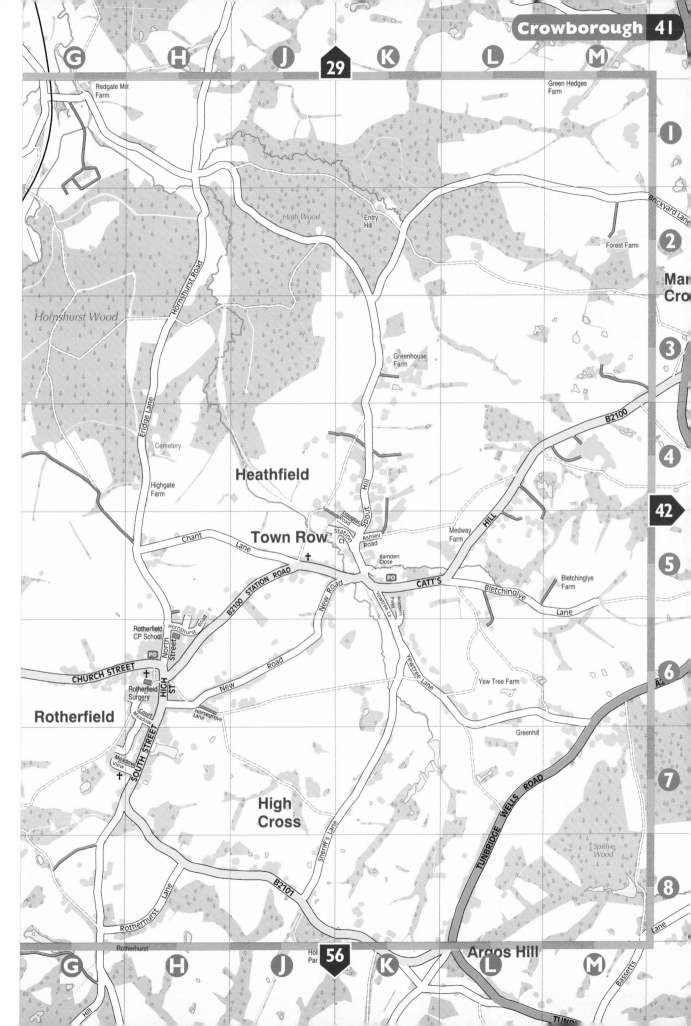

G H J K L M

29

I

2

Green Hedges
Farm

Redgate Mill
Farm

Forest Farm

Mar
Cro

3

Brickyard Lane

Hoth Wood

Entry
Hill

Hornshurst Road

B2100

4

Hornshurst Wood

Greenhouse
Farm

42

Eridge Lane

Cemetery

Heathfield

HILL

Medway
Farm

5

Highgate
Farm

Douglas
Road

Hill

Bletchinglye
Farm

Chant
Lane

Town Row

Station
Ch

Ashley
Road

Bainden
Close

Bletchinglye
Lane

B2100 STATION ROAD

New Road

PO

CATT'S

Rotherfield
CP School

Hornshurst
Road

North
Street

Yewtree La

Hosmers
Field

PO

Yew Tree Farm

6

CHURCH STREET

HIGH
ST

New
Road

Yewtree Lane

Rotherfield
Surgery

Court
Meadow

Horsegrove
Lane

Greenhill

**Rotherfield**

TUNBRIDGE WELLS ROAD

7

Meadow
View

SOUTH STREET

**High
Cross**

Sheriff's Lane

Spitlye
Wood

8

B2101

Rotherhurst Lane

Rotherhurst

Hill

56

Holi
Par

**Argos Hill**

Lane

Bassetts

G H J K L M

TUND

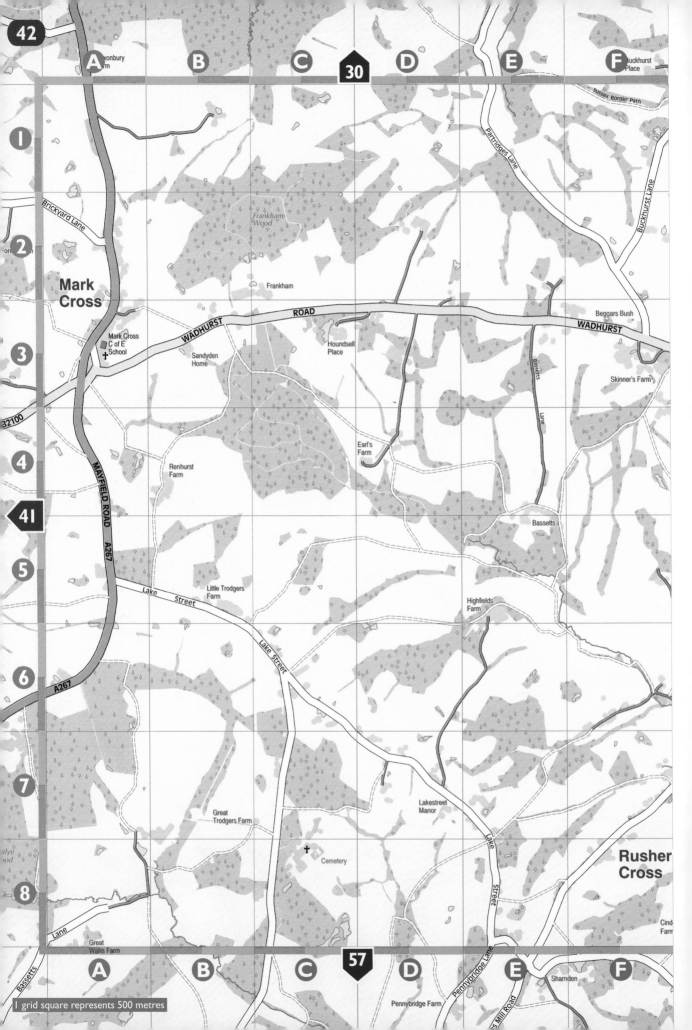

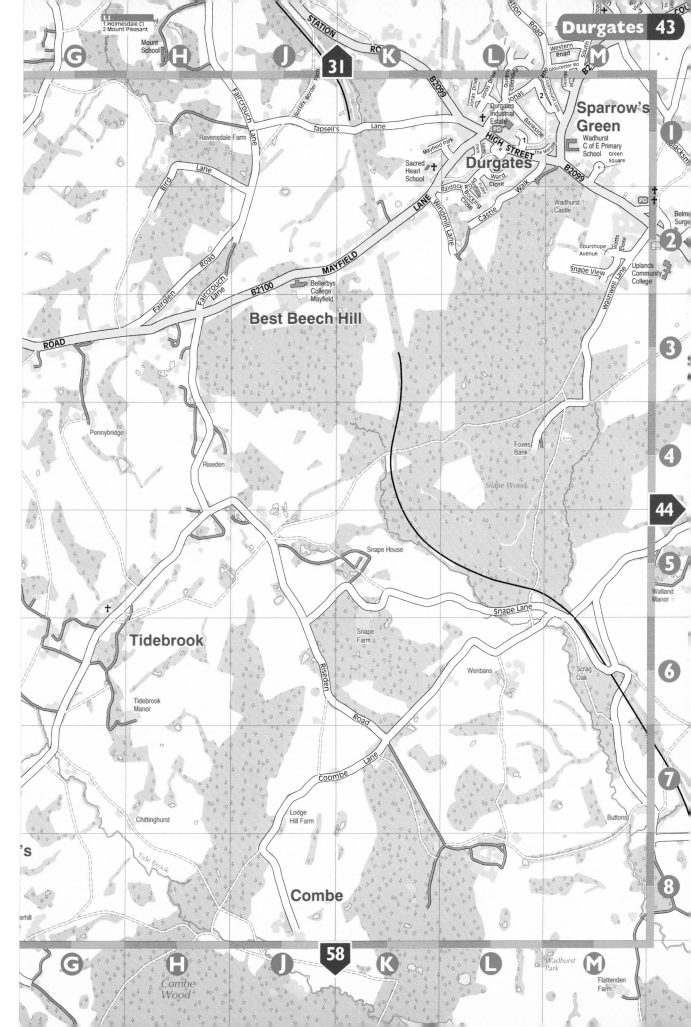

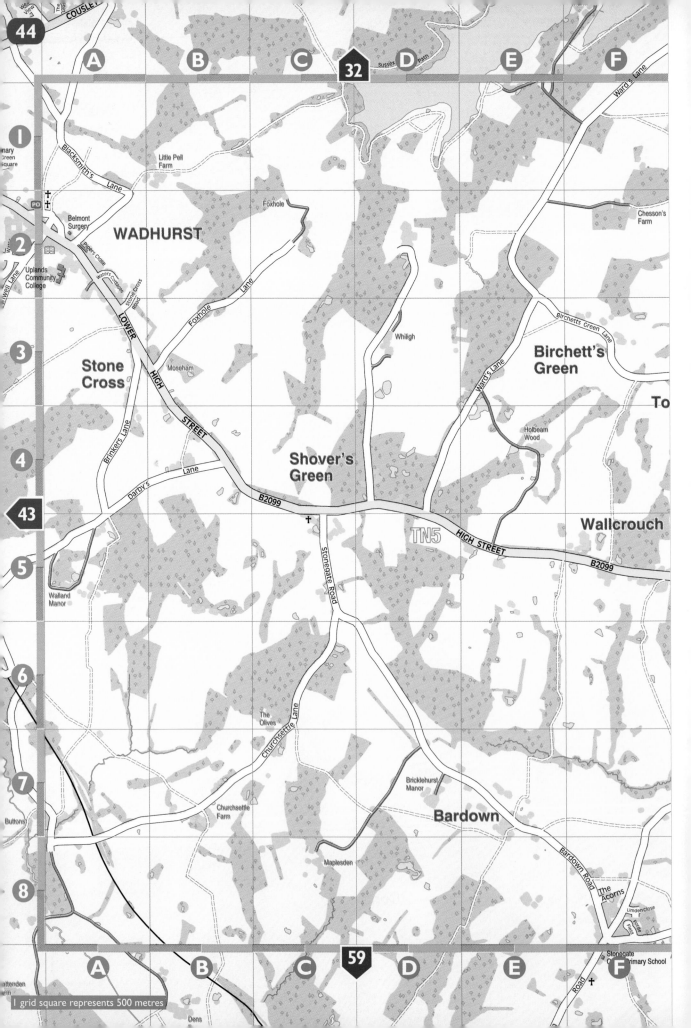

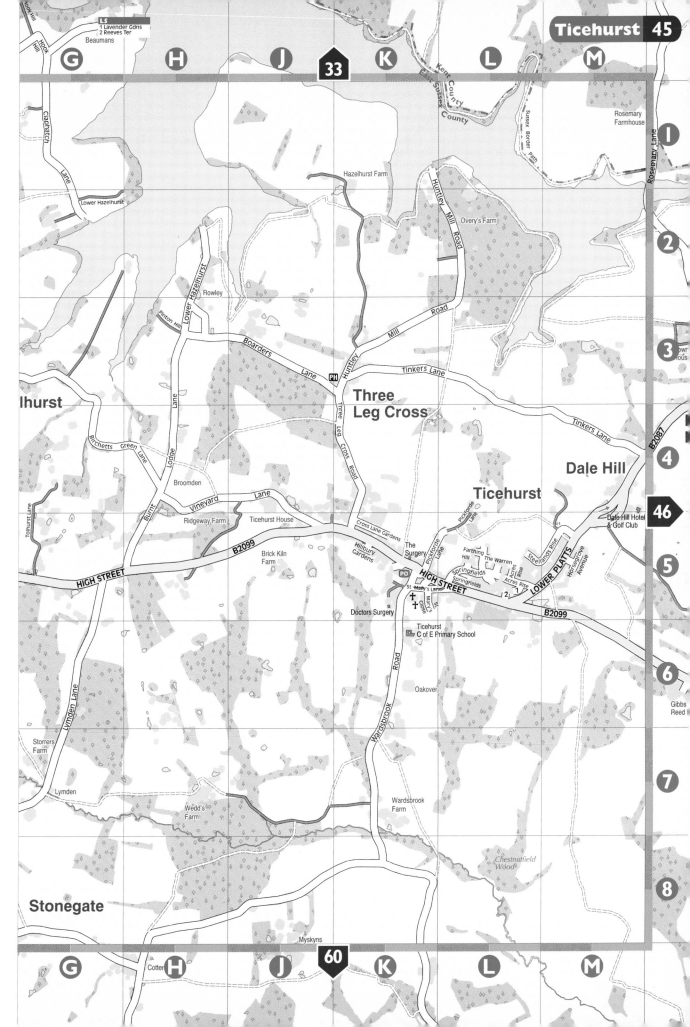

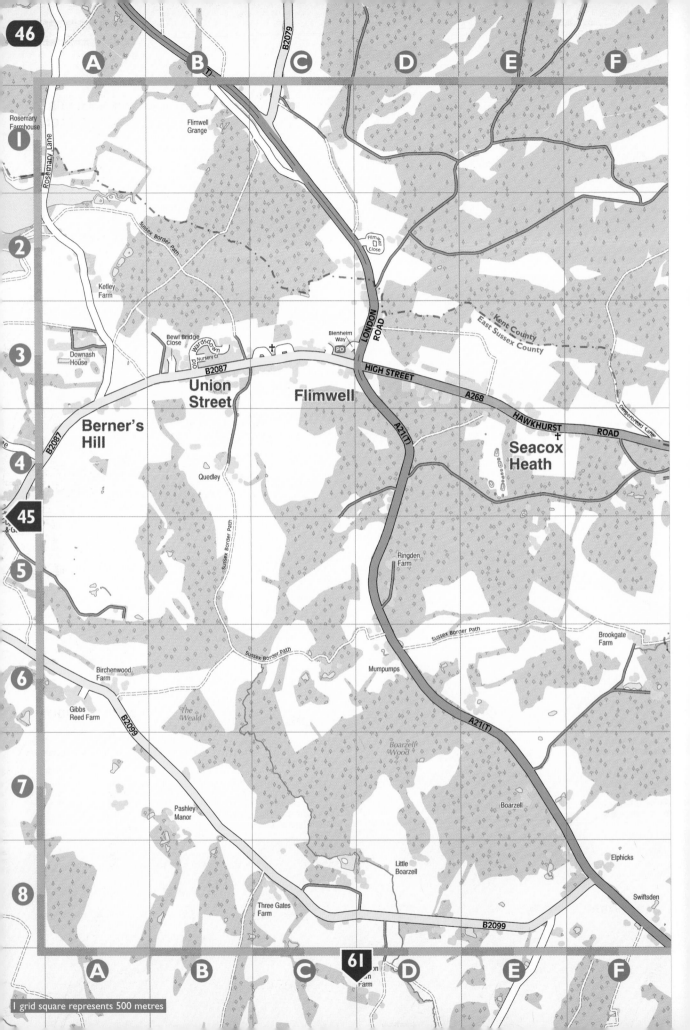

Gill's Green

**High Street**

**Hawkhurst**

**The Moor**

G H J K L M

I
2
3
4
5
6
7
8

M4
1 Northgrove Rd
2 Post Office Rd

Frith Farm

Trenley Farm

Tanyard Farm

Siseley Farm

Soper's Lane

Soper's Lane

Limes Grove

Slip Mill Road

Wellington Cottages

CRANBROOK ROAD

A229

Ockley

Ockley Lane

Slip Mill

Springfield Industrial Estate

Vale Rd

Woodbury

Winchester Rd

A229

Oakfield

Squash Club

Western Road

Terrace

School

Western Av

A229

PO

Queens Ct

Slip Mill Rd

Slip Mill Road

Little Pix Hall Farm

A268

Hospital

HIGH STREET

Marlborough House School

Theobalds

Fairview

HIGHGATE HILL

Doctors Surgery

Mercers

Highfield

Oaklands Rd

Copt

Haven

Elm Hill House

North Hill Road

Delmonden Road

Delmonden Manor

Sussex Border Path

Sussex Border Path

Hensill House

Wish Valley Surgery

MOOR HILL

Hall House

Hawkhurst C of E Primary

Delmonden House

Horns Road

Road

Sussex Border Path

The Chestnuts

Heansill La

Red Oak

Talbot

THE MOOR

PO

Avards Close

Cowden Close

B2244

Stream Lane

Collingwood House

Bokes Farm

A229

HORNS ROAD

Horns Corner

Cowden Lane

Cowden

Lillesden

HASTINGS ROAD

Kent County

East Sussex County

Cemetery

Ea
He

A21(T)

G H J K L M

62

Coldham

Merriments Lane

Merriments Farm

Stone House

Conghur

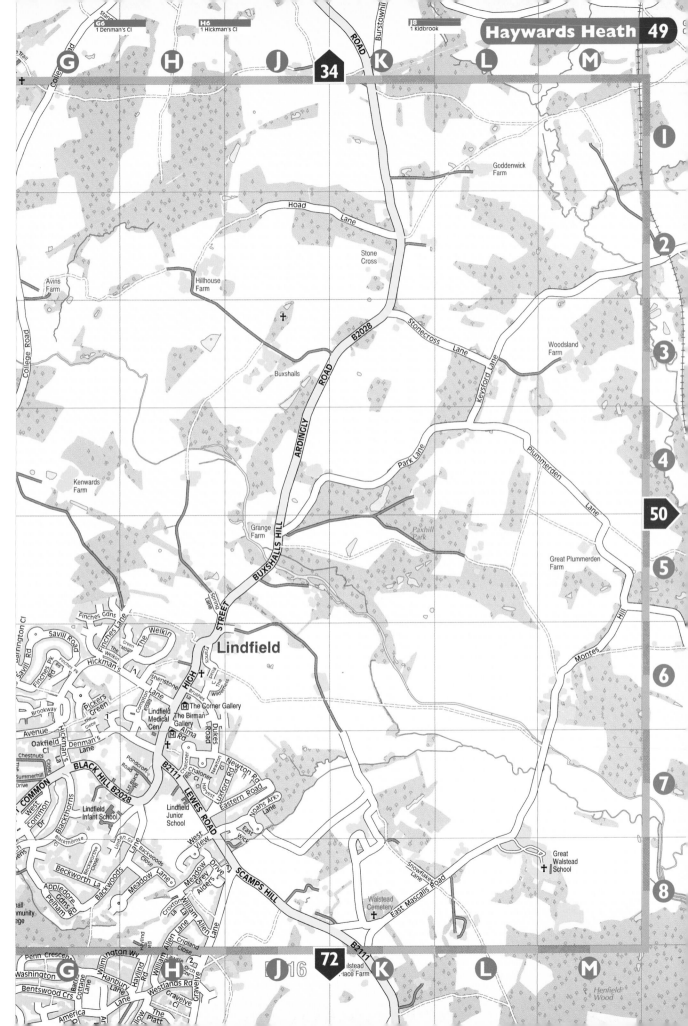

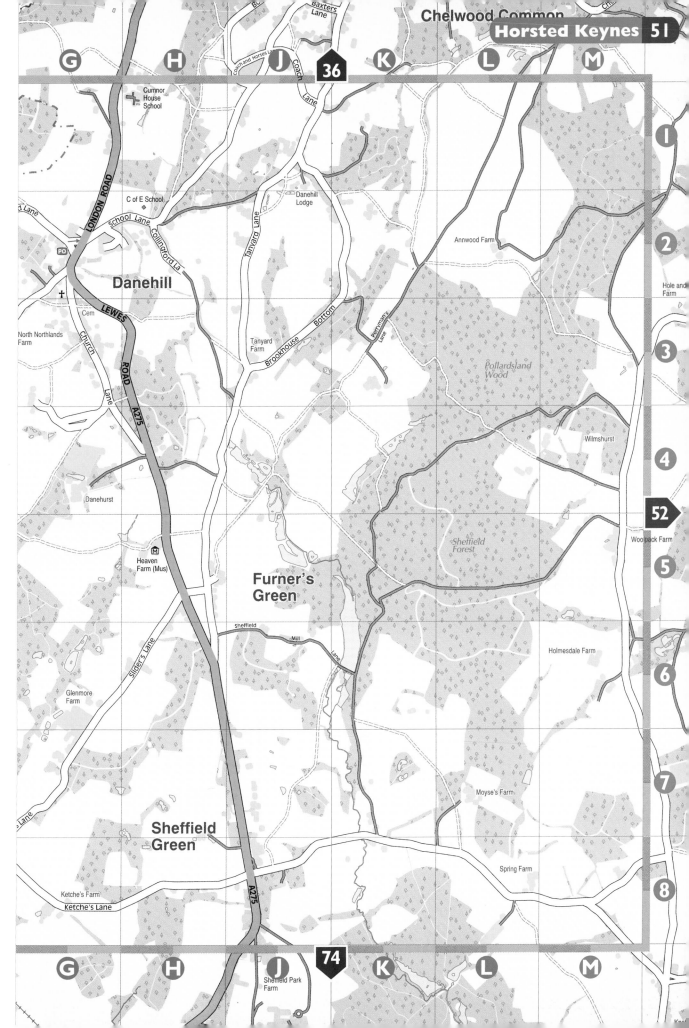

**36**

G   H   J   K   L   M

**1**

Cumnor House School

**2**

Annwood Farm

Hole and Farm

Danehill Lodge

C of E School

School Lane

LONDON ROAD

Collingford La

PO

**3**

Tanyard Lane

Pollardsland Wood

**Danehill**

Cem

LEWES

Church

North Northlands Farm

Tanyard Farm

Brookhouse Bottom

Perryman's Lane

Wilmshurst

**4**

ROAD

Lane

A275

Danehurst

Sheffield Forest

**52**

Woolpack Farm

Heaven Farm (Mus)

**Furner's Green**

**5**

Sheffield

Mill

Lane

Holmesdale Farm

**6**

Slider's Lane

Glenmore Farm

Moyse's Farm

**7**

**Sheffield Green**

Spring Farm

**8**

A275

Ketche's Farm

Ketche's Lane

**74**

G   H   J   K   L   M

Sheffield Park Farm

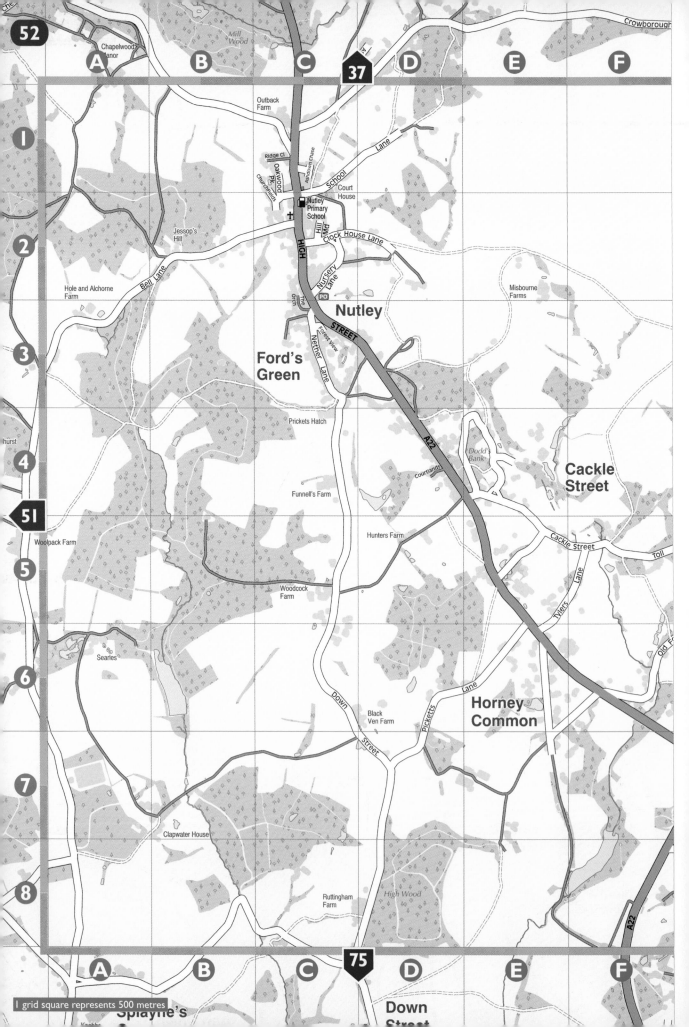

A     B     C     **37**     D     E     F

Crowborough

Chapelwood Manor
Mill Wood
Outback Farm

Ridge Cl
Oakwood Pk
Churchfields
Nutley Primary School
Court House
Ashdown Chase
School Lane

Jessop's Hill

Hole and Alchorne Farm
Bell Lane
HIGH

Clock House Lane
Nursery Lane
PO
The Porch
STREET
**Nutley**

Misbourne Farms

**Ford's Green**

Nether Lane
Forest View

Prickets Hatch

A22
Dodd's Bank
Courtlands

**Cackle Street**

Funnell's Farm

**51**

Woolpack Farm
Hunters Farm
Cackle Street

Woodcock Farm
Toll

Tylers Lane
Old Ford

Searles

Down Street
Black Ven Farm
Picketts Lane
**Horney Common**

Clapwater House

Ruttingham Farm
High Wood

A22

A     B     C     **75**     D     E     F

Splayne's

Down Street

I grid square represents 500 metres

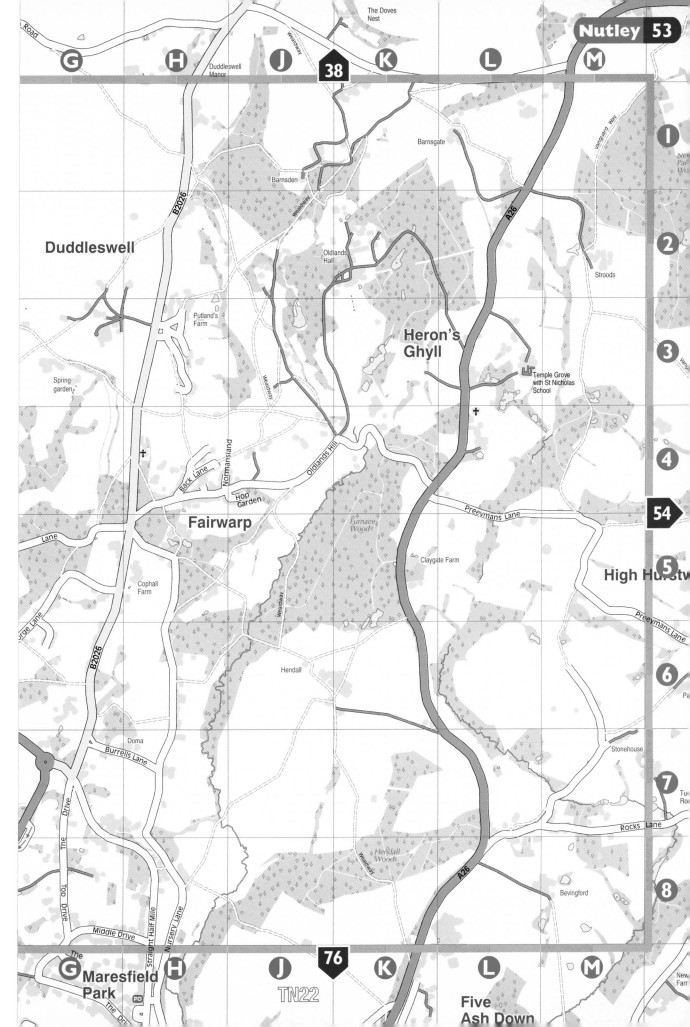

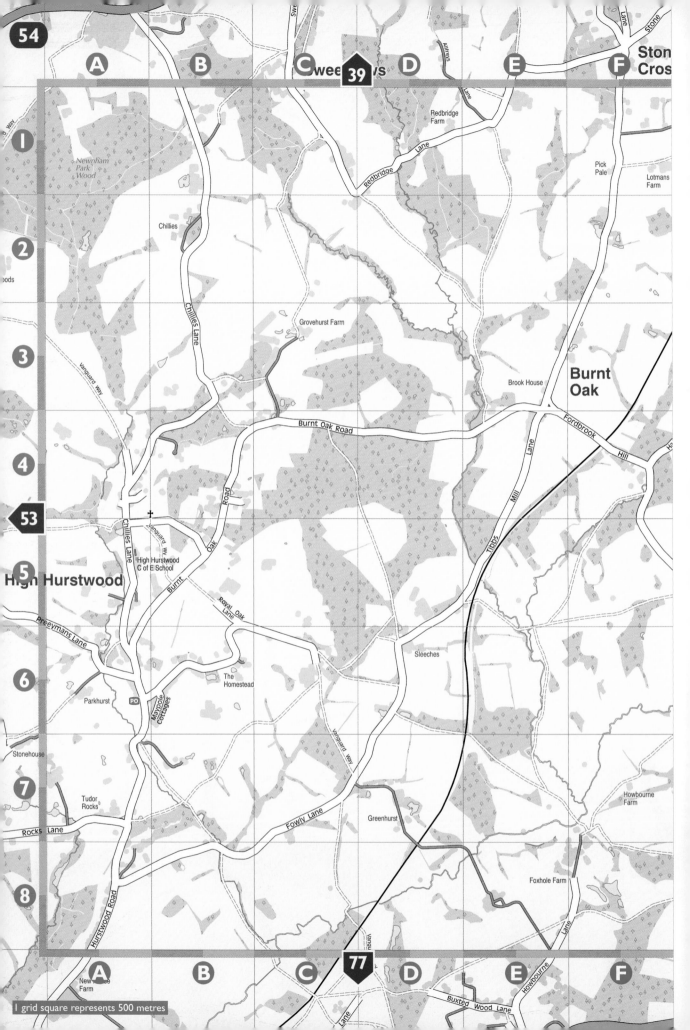

A    B    C    D    E    F

Swee...ows

Ston
Cros

Allreys
Lane

Redbridge
Farm

Pick
Pale

Lotmans
Farm

1

Newnham
Park
Wood

Redbridge
Lane

Chillies

2

oods

Grovehurst Farm

Chillies Lane

3

Vanguard Way

Brook House

Burnt
Oak

Burnt Oak Road

Fordbrook
Hill

4

Road

5

High Hurstwood

Chillies Lane

Vanguard Wy

High Hurstwood
C of E School

Burnt
Oak
Road

Royal Oak
Lane

Sleeches

Tibbs
Mill
Lane

Ha

6

Preeymans Lane

Parkhurst

PO

Maypole
Cottages

The
Homestead

Vanguard Way

7

Stonehouse

Tudor
Rocks

Rocks Lane

Fowly Lane

Greenhurst

Howbourne
Farm

Foxhole Farm

8

Hurstwood Road

A

New...ee
Farm

B    C

D    E    F

Howbourne...

Buxted Wood Lane

Lane

Vangu...

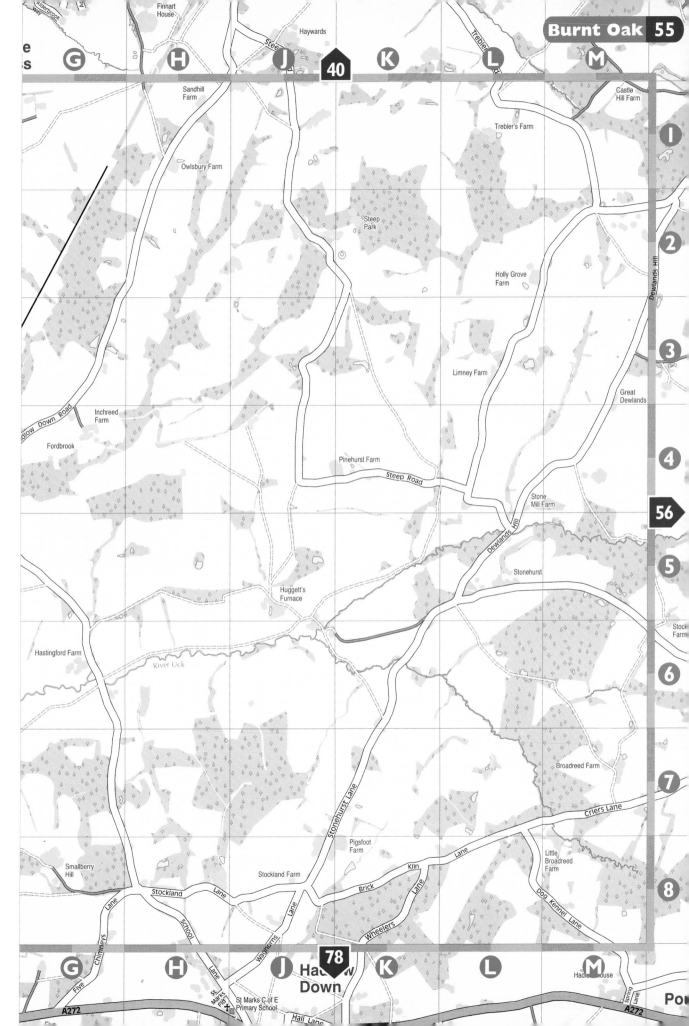

G    H    J    40    K    L    M

Finnart
House

Haywards

Sandhill
Farm

Alderbrook
Way

Owlsbury Farm

Castle
Hill Farm

Trebler's Farm

I

Steep
Park

Holly Grove
Farm

2

Dewlands Hill

3

dlow Down Road

Inchreed
Farm

Limney Farm

Great
Dewlands

Fordbrook

Pinehurst Farm

Steep Road

Stone
Mill Farm

4

56

Dewlands Hill

Stonehurst

5

Huggett's
Furnace

Stock
Farm

Hastingford Farm

River Uck

6

Broadreed Farm

7

Criers Lane

Stonehurst Lane

Pigsfoot
Farm

Little
Broadreed
Farm

Smallberry
Hill

Stockland Farm

Kiln
Lane

Lane

Dog Kennel Lane

8

Stockland      Lane

Brick      Lane

Chinneys
Lane

School
Lane

Wagtorns
Lane

Wheelers

Five

St Marks
Fld

G    H    J    78    K    L    M

Had
Down

Hadl
House

St Marks C of E
Primary School

Spring Lane

A272

Hall Lane

Po

A272

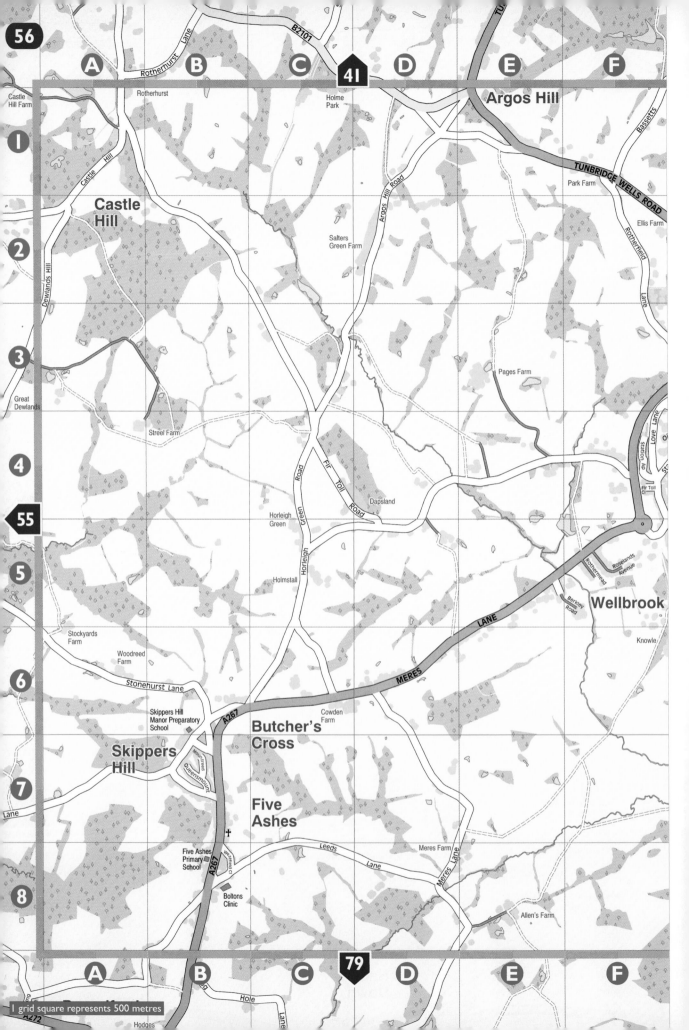

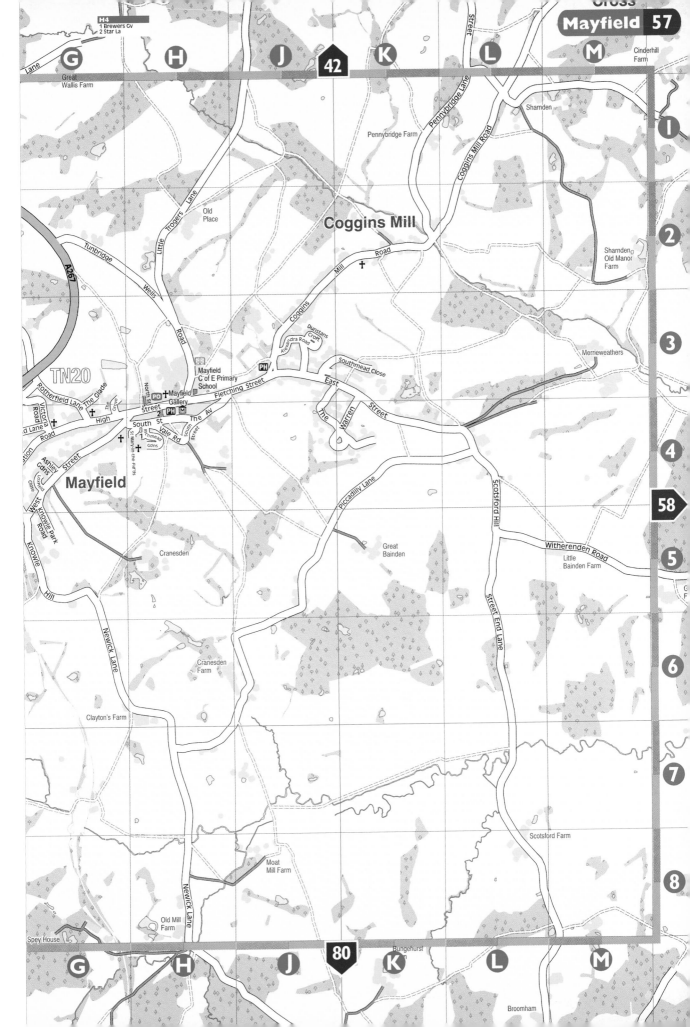

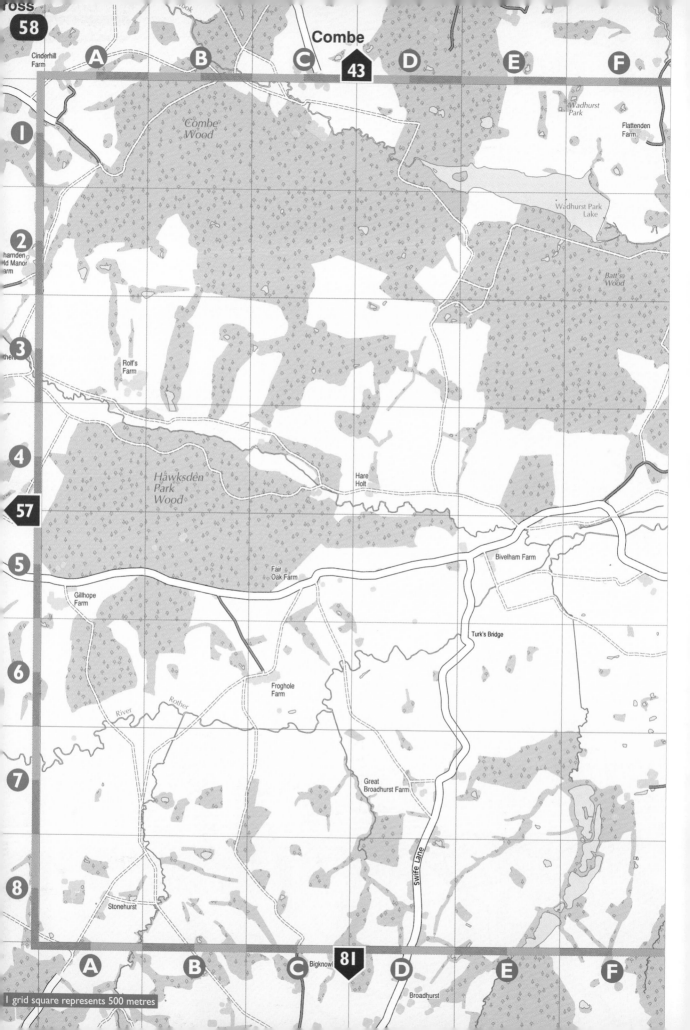

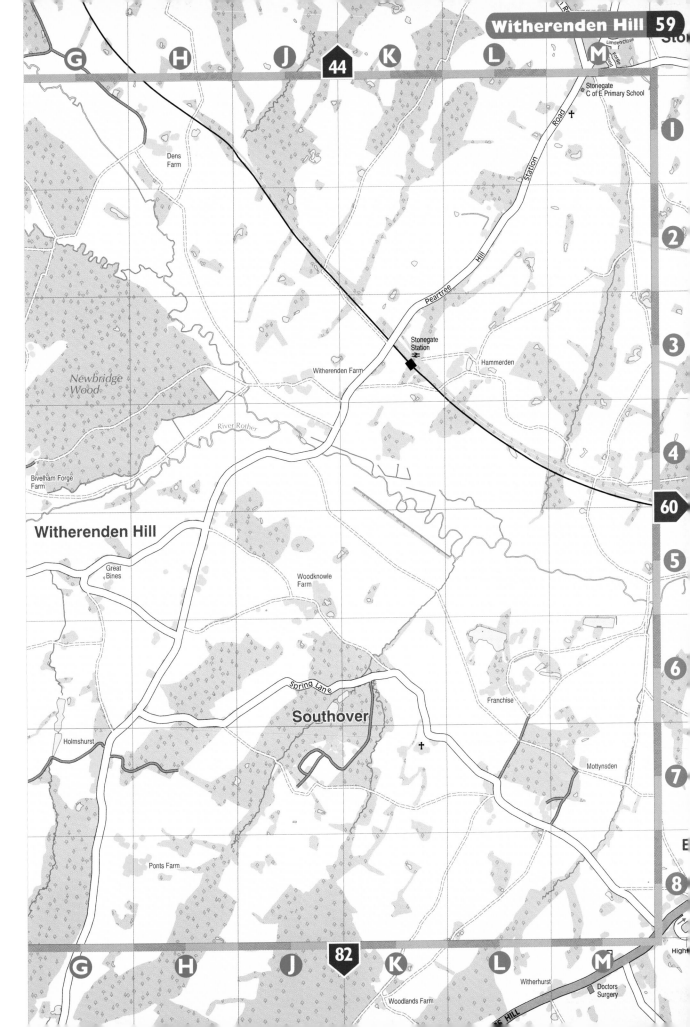

G   H   J   **44**   K   L   M

**I**

**2**

**3**

**4**

**60**

**5**

**6**

**7**

**8**

Sto

Limden Close

Forge Field

Stonegate
C of E Primary School

Station Road

Peartree Hill

Stonegate
Station

Hammerden

Dens
Farm

*Newbridge
Wood*

Witherenden Farm

*River Rother*

Bivelham Forge
Farm

**Witherenden Hill**

Great
Bines

Woodknowle
Farm

Holmshurst

*Spring Lane*

**Southover**

Franchise

Mottynsden

Ponts Farm

E

G   H   J   **82**   K   L   M

Witherhurst

Doctors
Surgery

High

Woodlands Farm

A   B   C   D   E   F

1

2

3

4

59

5

6

7

8

A   B   C   D   E   F

Cottenden

Bearhurst
Farm

sheepstreet  Lane

Fox Farm

Shoyswell
Manor

Shortridge Farm

Old Shoyswell
Manor

Battenhurst
Farm

Turzes
Farm

Shrub Lane

LC

Crowhurst
Bridge Farm

River   Rother

Shrubb
Farm

Park Wood

Court Farm

A265

Brooksmarle

March Farm

Greenfield
Road

TN19

Dudwell
St Mary

Ham Lane

Strand Meadow

Hornbeam

Beechwood Close

Rother
VW

Wealden

A265

Glebe House

Burwash

Rother Close

Borders

Hoppers
Croft Lane

Ham Lane

PO

Rectory Close

Garston
Park

HIGH   STREET

Burwash
School

Bell

Grandturzel

River Dudwell

Fairfield
Surgery

Highfield

mary School

nden Close

1 grid square represents 500 metres

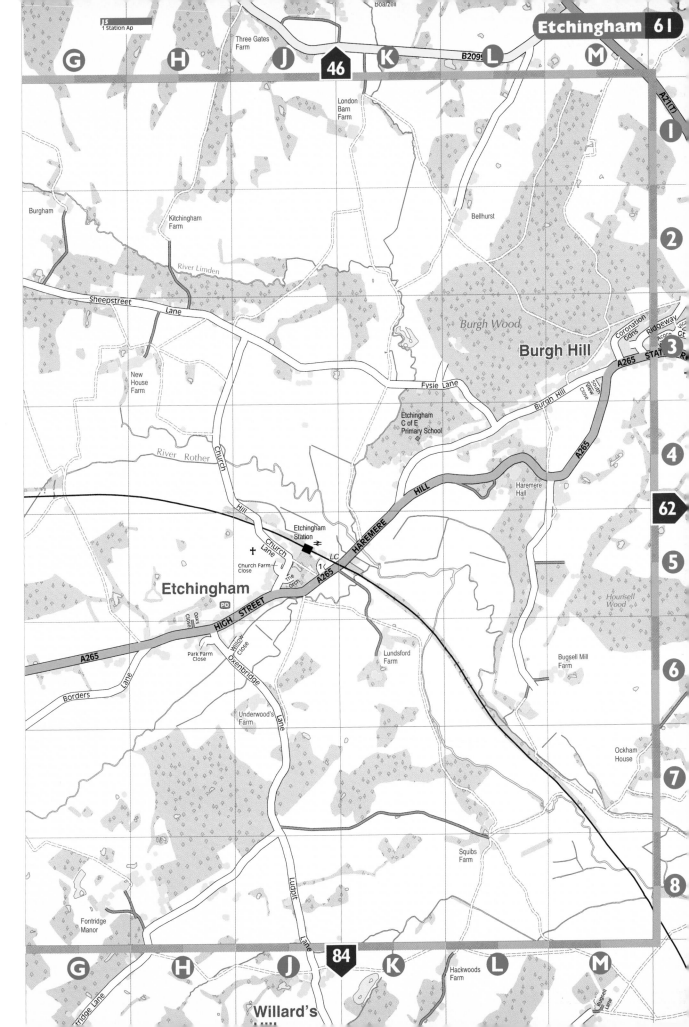

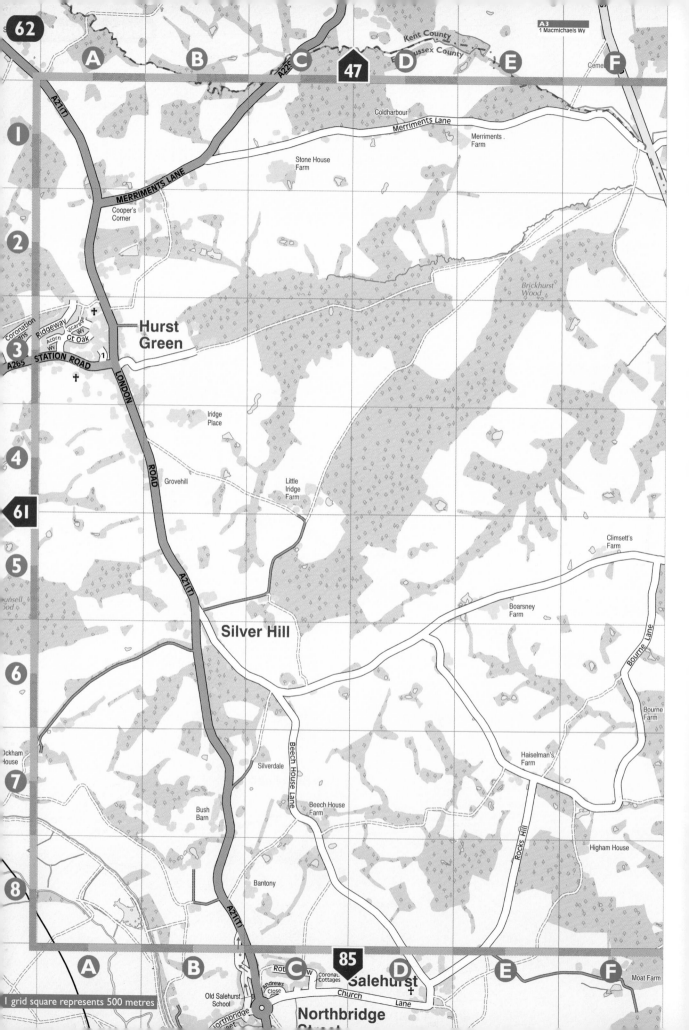

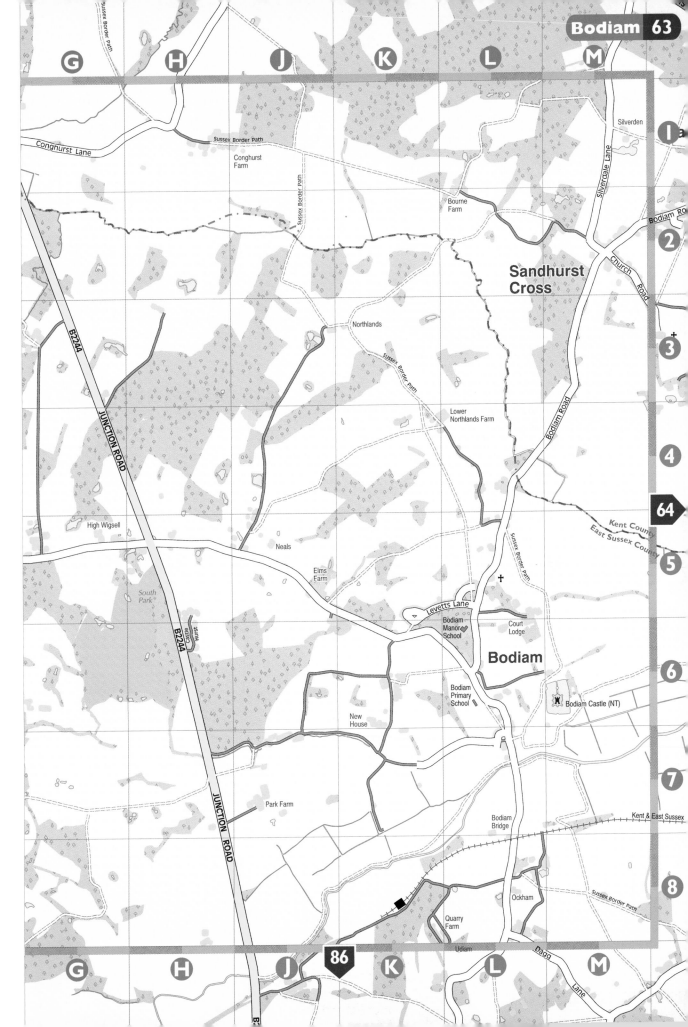

G  H  J  K  L  M

Silverden

I a

Conghurst Lane

Sussex Border Path

Conghurst Farm

Sussex Border Path

Bodiam Ro

2

Bourne Farm

Church Road

**Sandhurst Cross**

3

Northlands

Sussex Border Path

4

Lower Northlands Farm

Bodiam Road

64

Kent County

High Wigsell

East Sussex County

5

Neals

Sussex Border Path

Elms Farm

South Park

Levetts Lane

Bodiam Manor School

Court Lodge

B2244

Hurst

B2244

JUNCTION ROAD

**Bodiam**

6

Bodiam Primary School

Bodiam Castle (NT)

New House

7

Park Farm

Bodiam Bridge

Kent & East Sussex

Kent & East Sussex

8

Sussex Border Path

Ockham

Quarry Farm

JUNCTION ROAD

Udiam

Dagg Lane

G  H  86  J  K  L  M

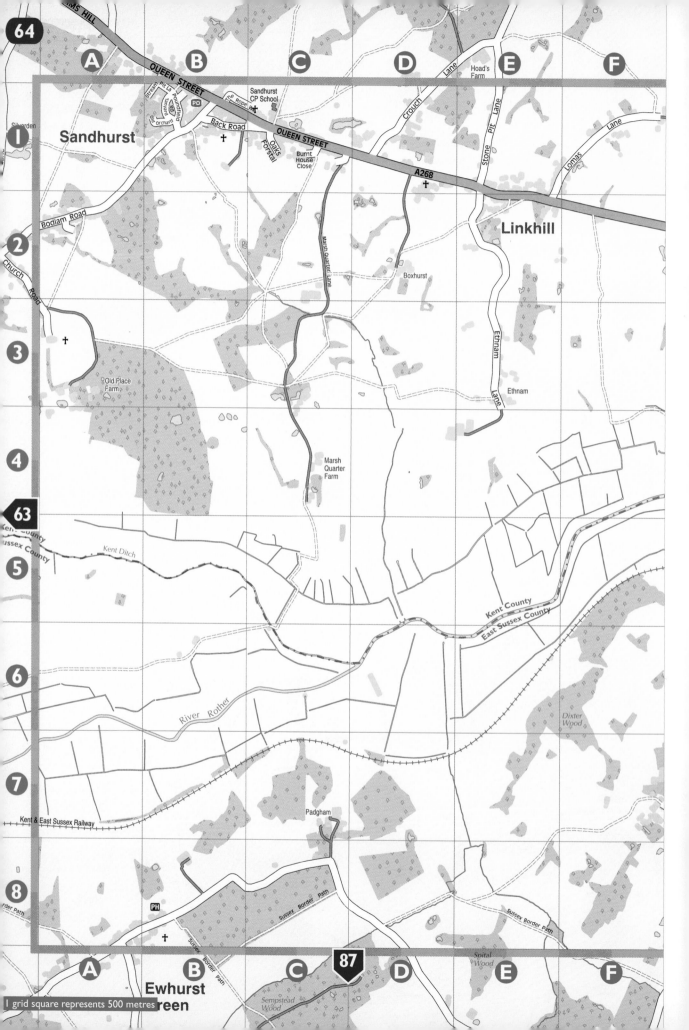

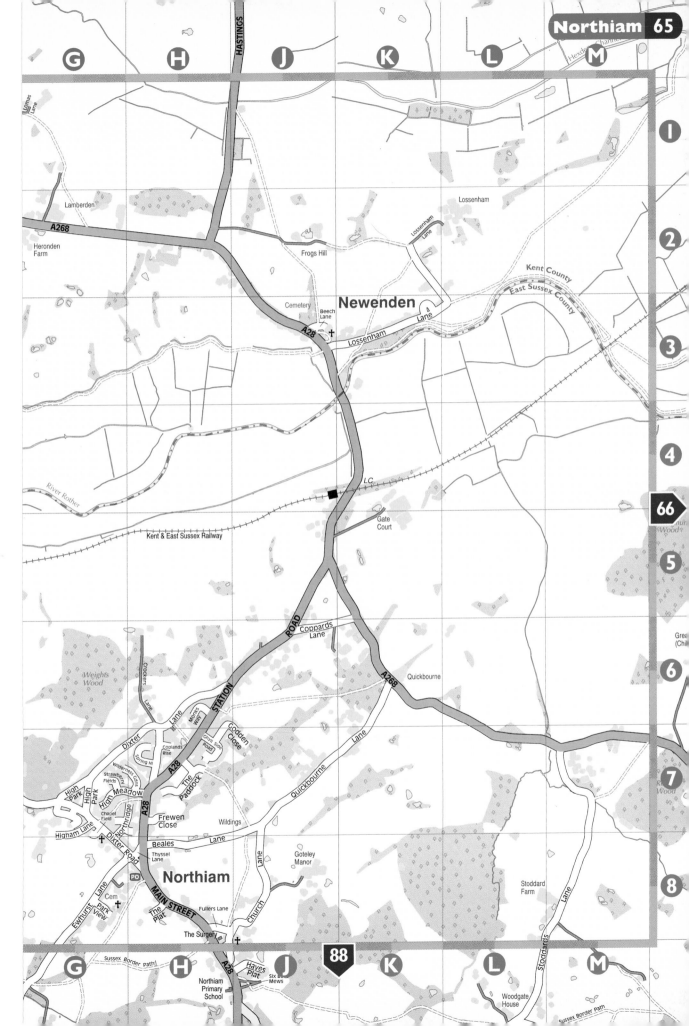

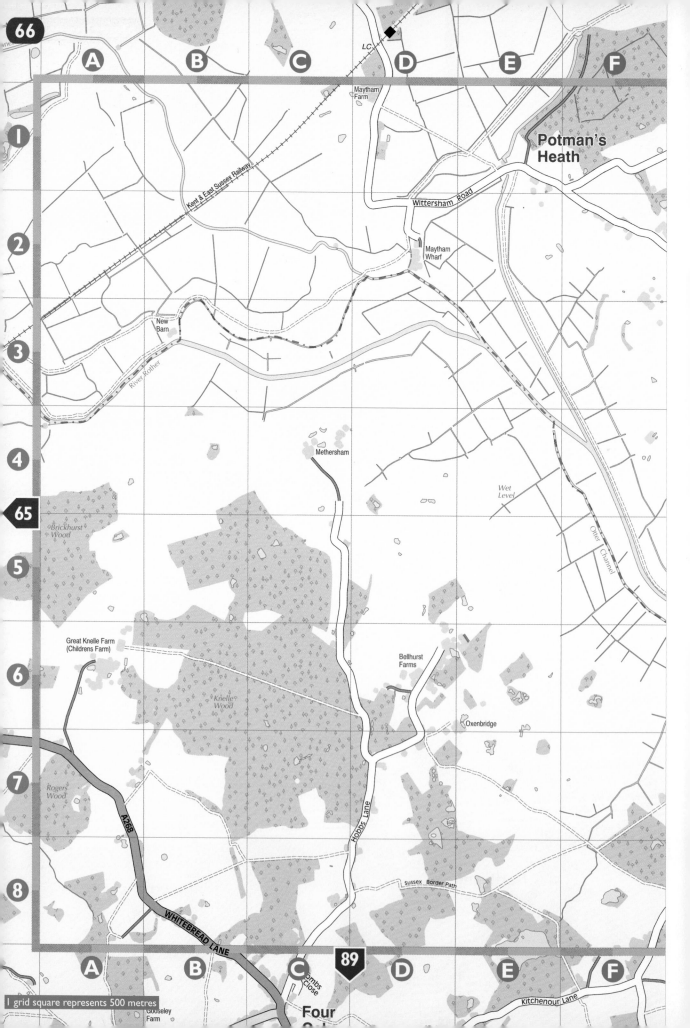

**Potman's Heath**

Maytham Farm

Wittersham Road

Maytham Wharf

Kent & East Sussex Railway

New Barn

River Rother

Methersham

Wet Level

Otter Channel

Brickhurst Wood

Great Knelle Farm (Childrens Farm)

Knelle Wood

Bellhurst Farms

Oxenbridge

Rogers Wood

A268

Hobbs Lane

Sussex Border Path

WHITEBREAD LANE

Combs Close

Four

Gooseley Farm

Kitchenour Lane

1 grid square represents 500 metres

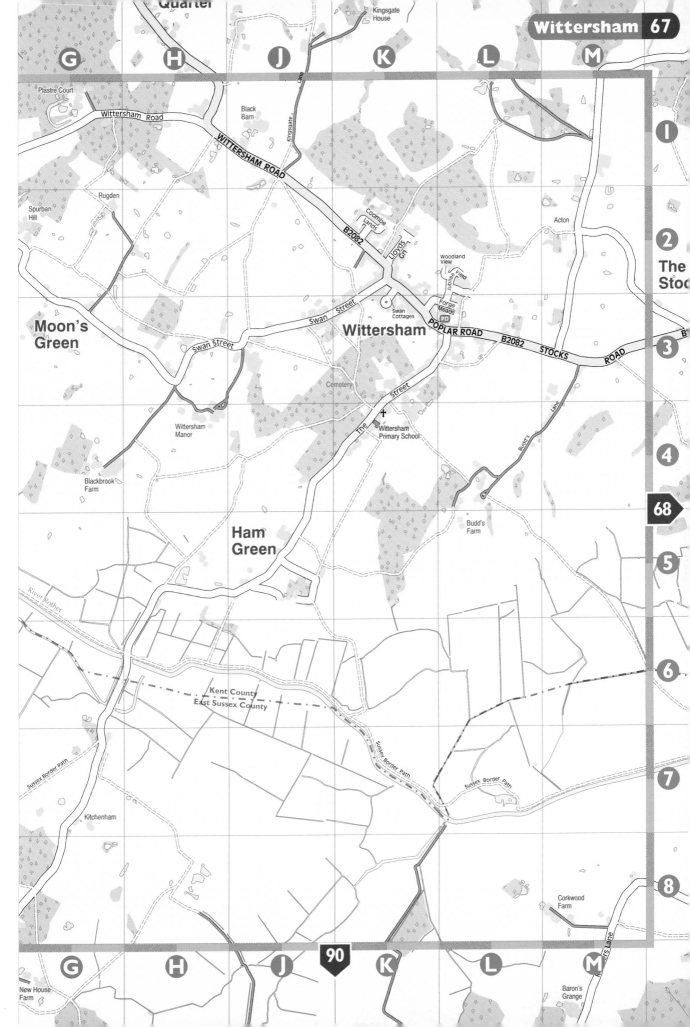

Quarter

Kingsgate House

G  H  J  K  L  M

Plastre Court

Wittersham Road

Black Barn

WITTERSHAM ROAD

I

Rugden

B2082

Coombe Lands

Acton

2

Spurban Hill

Lloyd's Ch

Woodland View

The Stoc

Jubilee Field

Moon's Green

Swan Street

Swan Cottages

Wittersham

Forge Meads

PO

POPLAR ROAD

B2082

STOCKS

ROAD

B

3

Cemetery

The Street

Budd's Lane

4

Wittersham Manor

✝

Wittersham Primary School

68

Blackbrook Farm

Ham Green

Budd's Farm

5

River Rother

6

Kitchenham

Kent County

East Sussex County

Sussex Border Path

7

Sussex Border Path

Sussex Border Path

Corkwood Farm

8

New House Farm

G  H  J  K  L  M

90

Baron's Grange

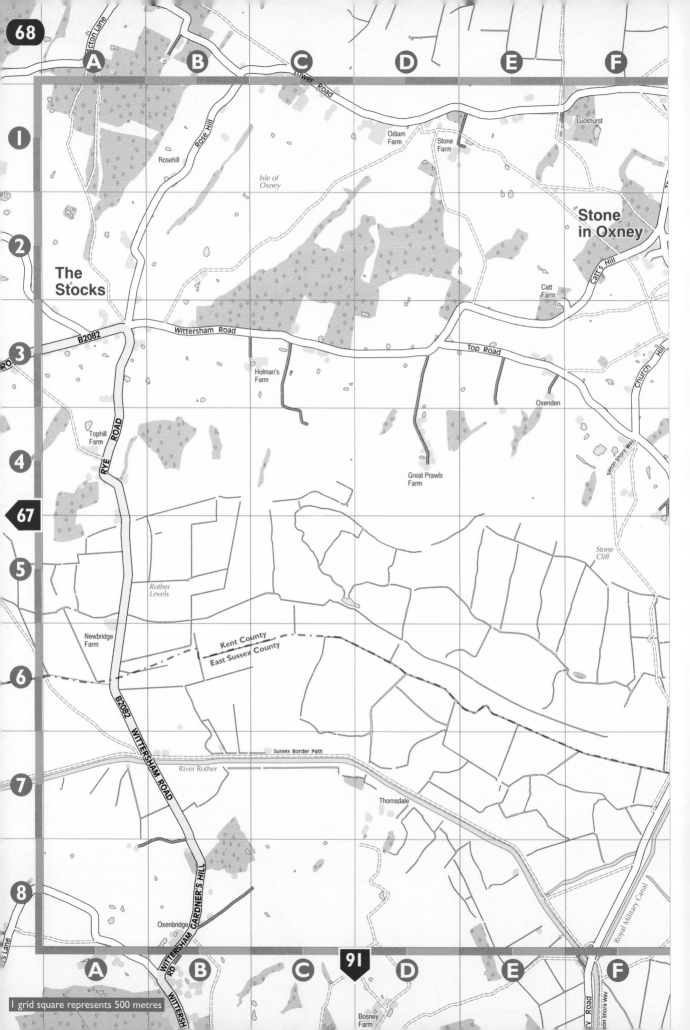

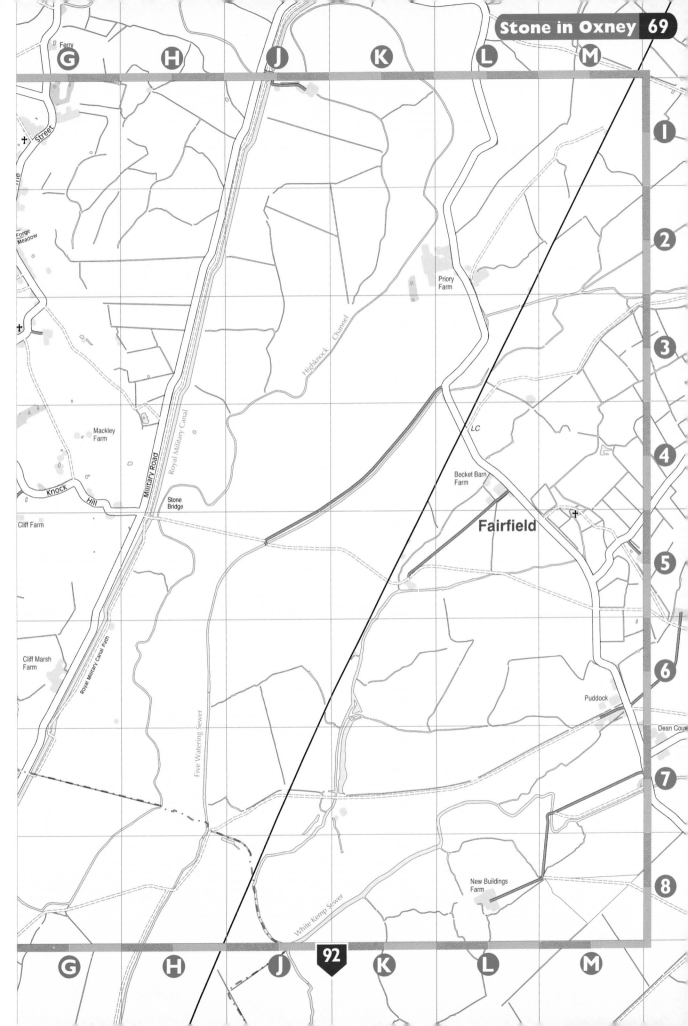

Ferry

Street

Forge
Meadow

Mackley
Farm

Knock

Hill

Military Road

Royal Military Canal

Highknock Channel

Priory
Farm

LC

Becket Barn
Farm

**Fairfield**

Stone
Bridge

Cliff Farm

Cliff Marsh
Farm

Royal Military Canal Path

Five Watering Sewer

Puddock

Dean Cou

New Buildings
Farm

White Kemp Sewer

G  H  J  K  L  M

1

2

3

4

5

6

7

8

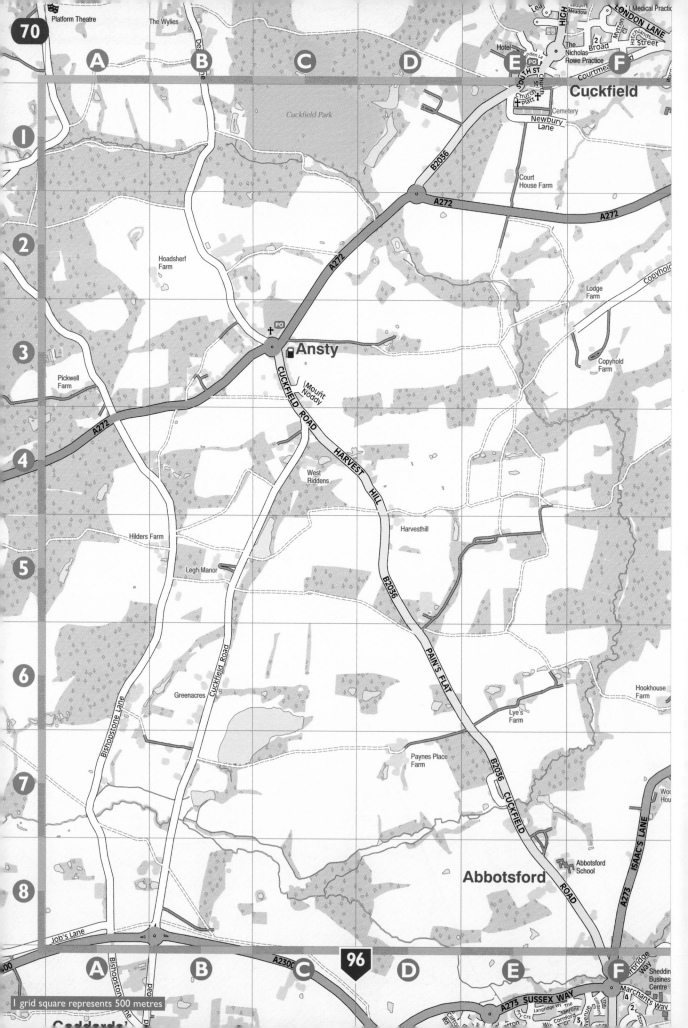

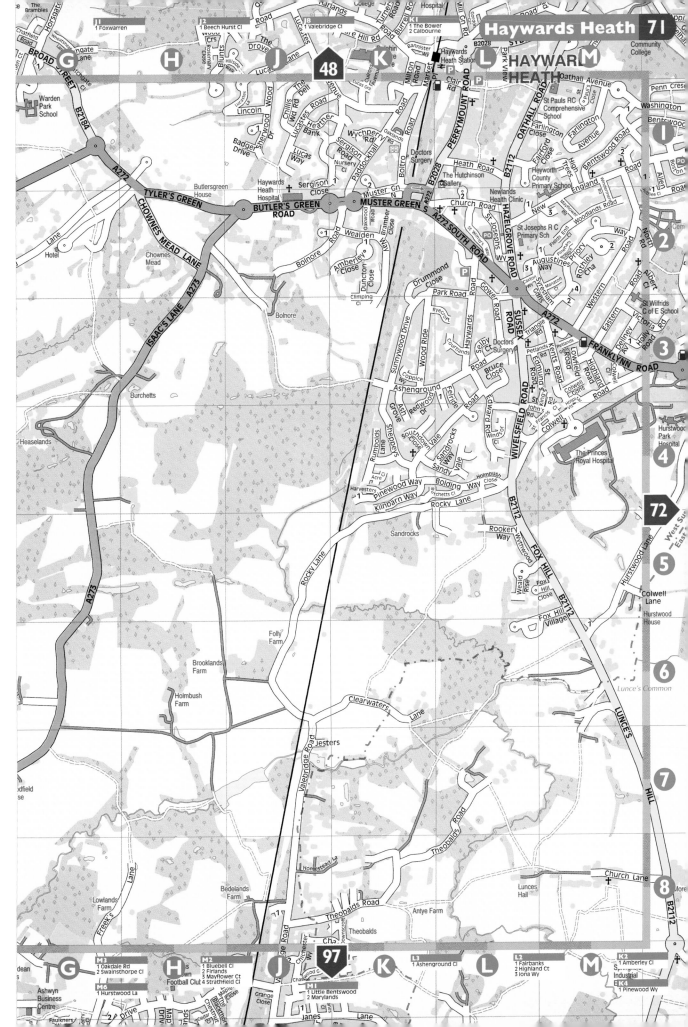

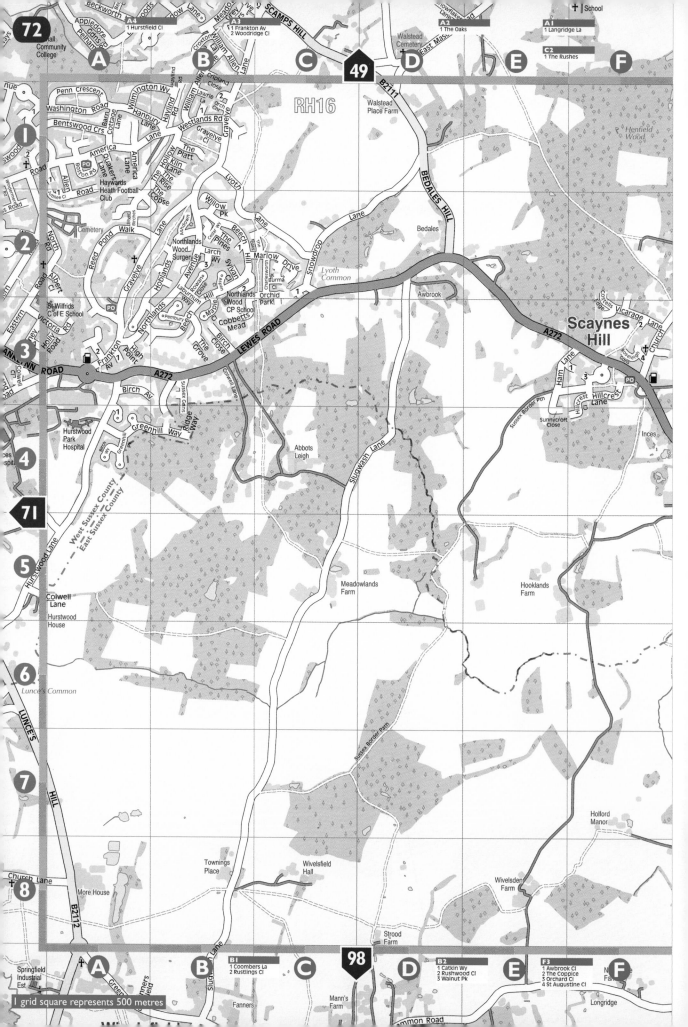

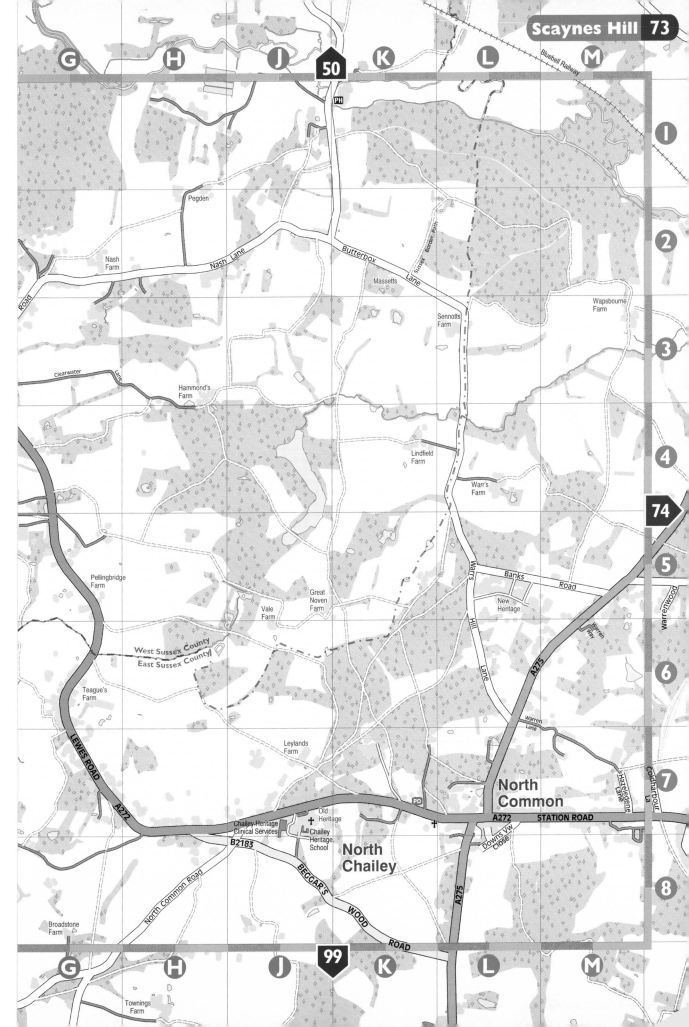

A · B · C **51** D · E · F

I
2
3
4

73

5
6
7
8

Ketche's Farm
Ketche's Lane

A275

Spring Farm
C8
1 Badens Cl

Sheffield Park Farm

Sheffield Park Garden (NT)

PH

Fletching C of E School

Sheffield Bridge

Parsonage Farm

A275

River Ouse

Mill Farm

Netherall Farm

Goldstrow

Lane End Common

Rotherfield Farmhouse

Warrenwood

Redgill Lane

**Fletching Common**

River Ouse

The Warren

Newick

Cricketfield

**Newick**

Cox's Farm

Jackies

Harmers La

WESTERN ROAD A272  HIGH ST THE GREEN

Goldbridge Farm

Coldharbour La

edene La

Painters Way
Leveller Rd
The Nursery
Crodden Road
Vernons Rd
Newick Dr
Oldaker Road
Powell Rd
Growers End
Rough The Rough
Newick Health Cen
High Close
Matches
The Green

GOLDBRIDGE ROAD A272

Bannisters Field

Allington Crs
The Ridings
Westpoint
Millfield Cl
Brooke Gdns
Allington Road
PO

Oxbottom Close

Newick School

Blind Lane

Gt Rough
Lower Station Road

Ketches

A · B **100** C · D · E · F

Oxb

Church Road

Chailey La

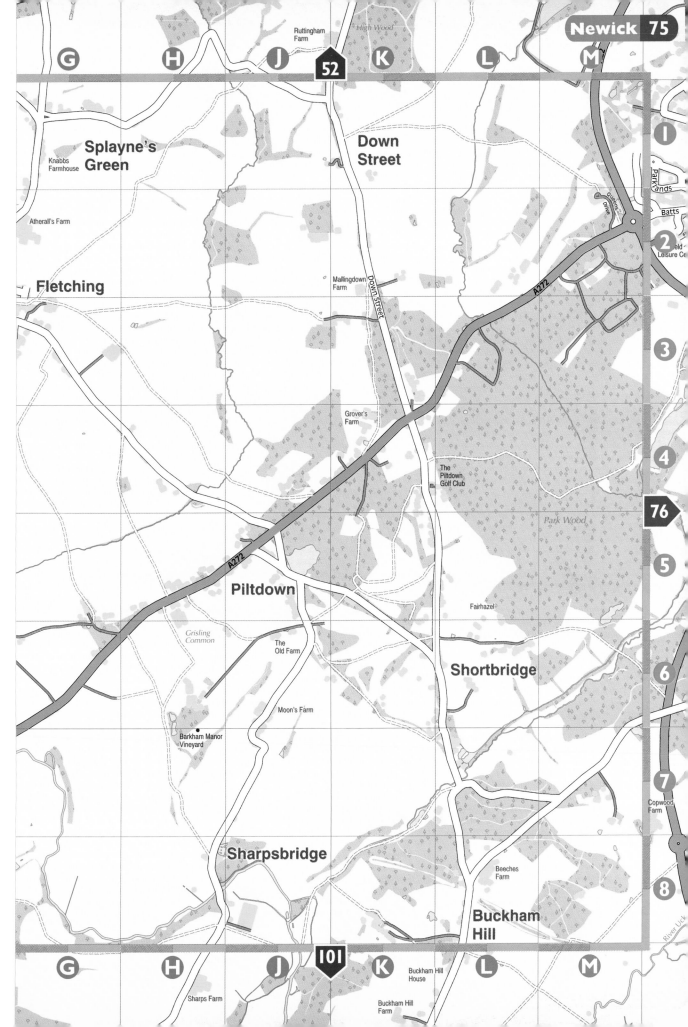

G H J K L M

52

Ruttingham Farm

High Wood

I

Parklands

Batts

Knabbs Farmhouse

Splayne's Green

Down Street

Queens Drive

2

...field Leisure Ce...

Atherall's Farm

Fletching

Mallingdown Farm

Down Street

A272

3

4

Grover's Farm

The Piltdown Golf Club

76

Park Wood

5

Piltdown

A272

Fairhazel

Grisling Common

The Old Farm

Shortbridge

6

Moon's Farm

Barkham Manor Vineyard

7

Copwood Farm

Sharpsbridge

Beeches Farm

8

River Uck

Buckham Hill

101

Buckham Hill House

Sharps Farm

Buckham Hill Farm

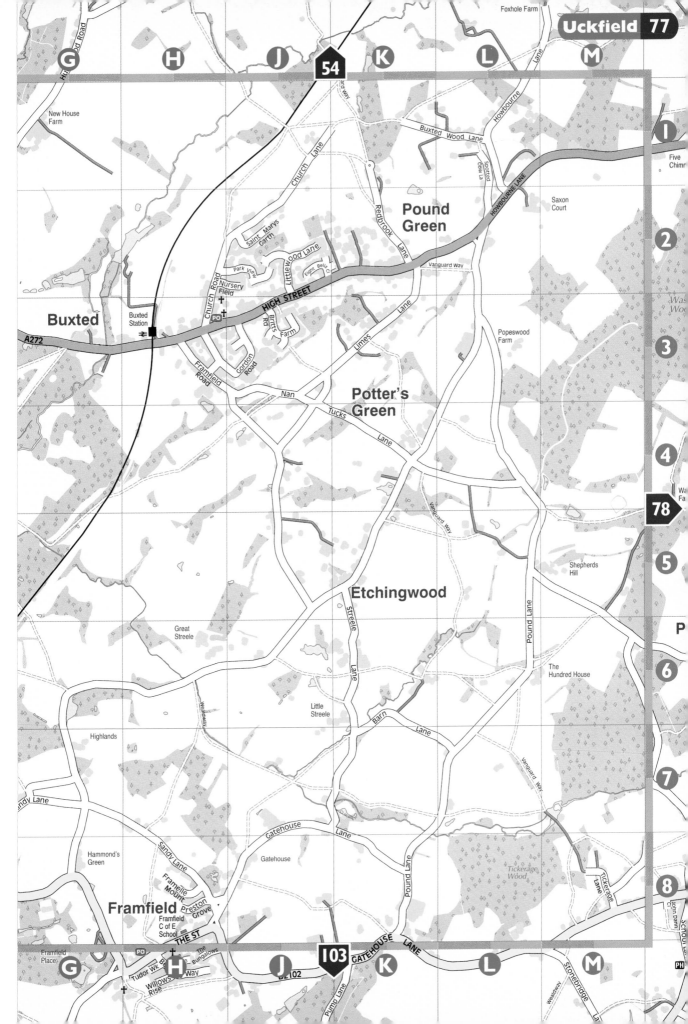

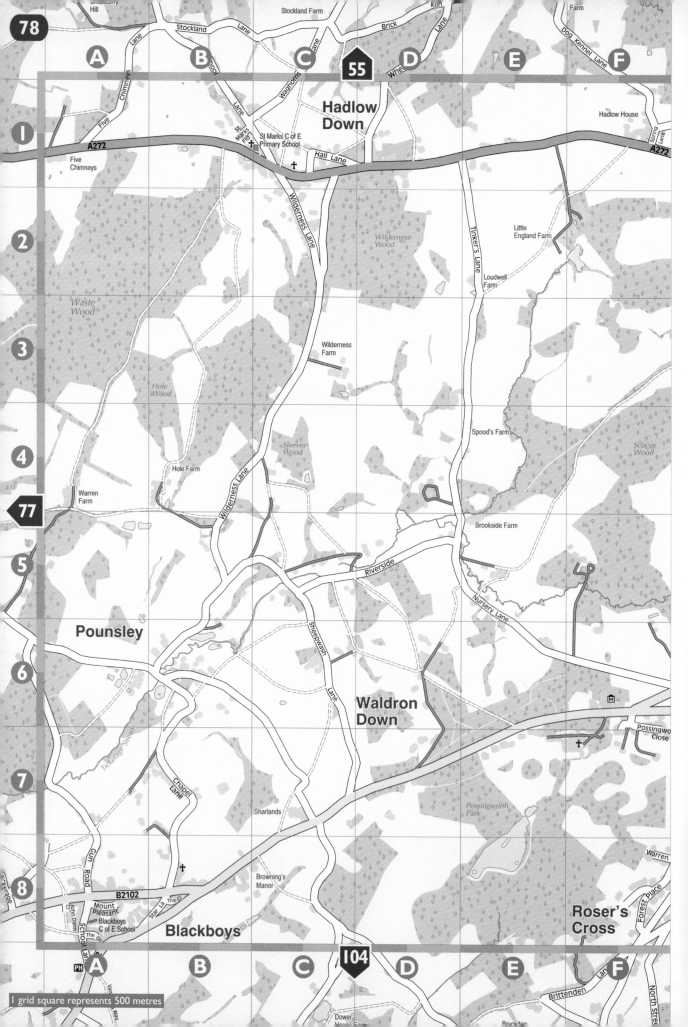

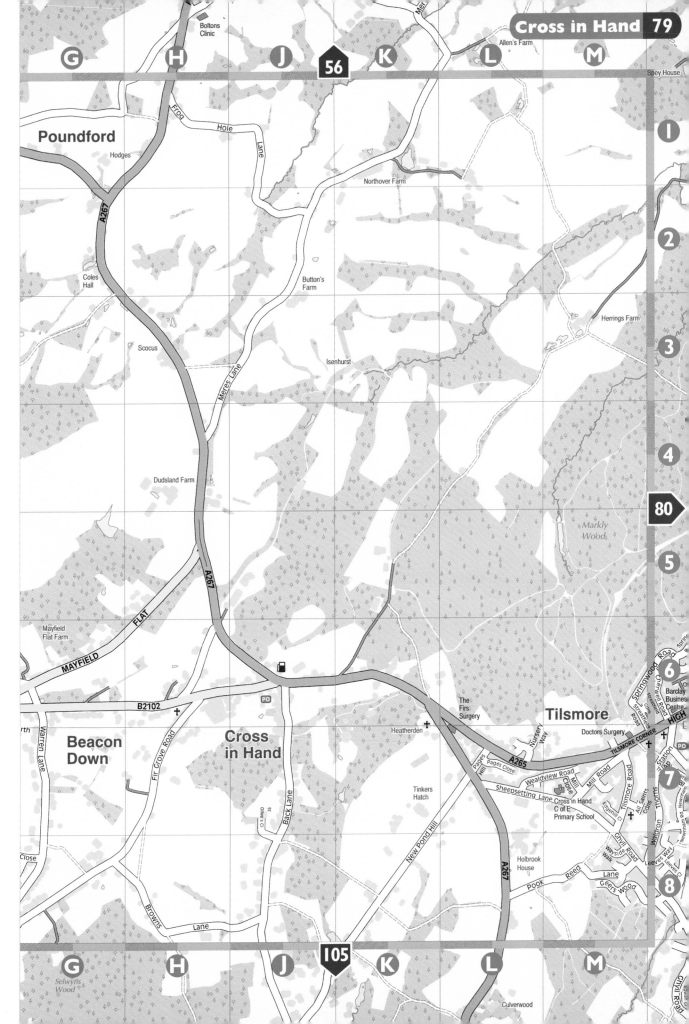

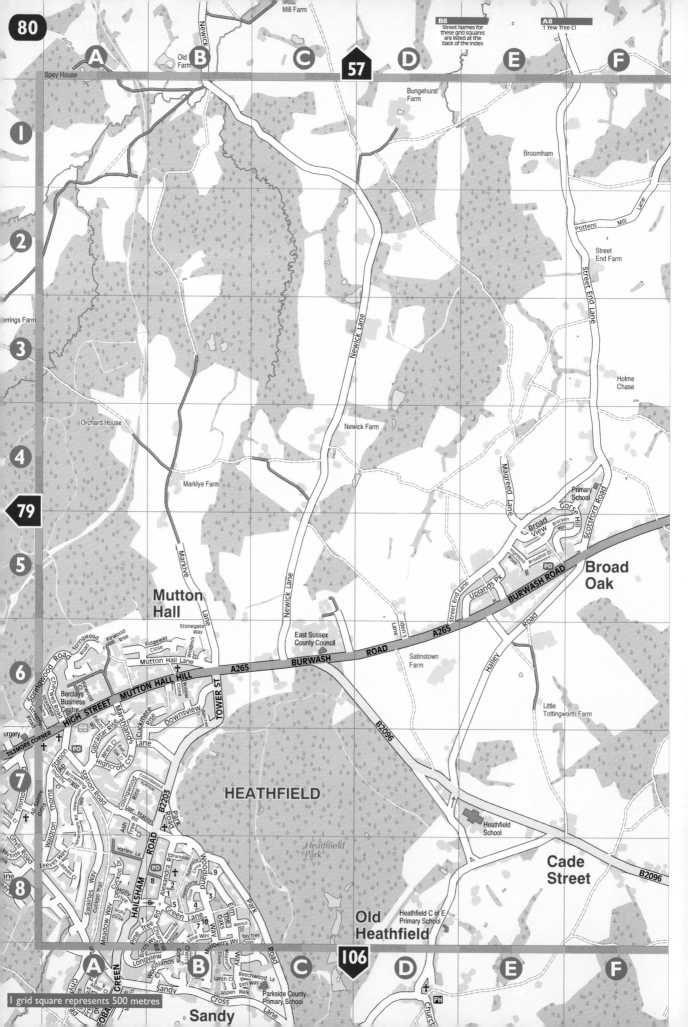

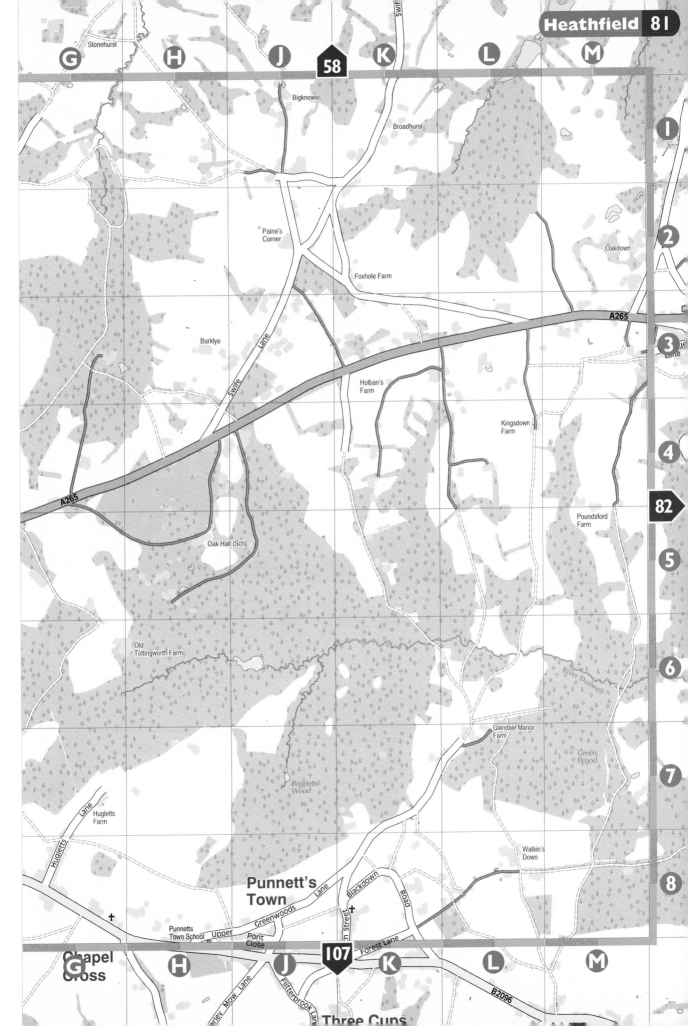

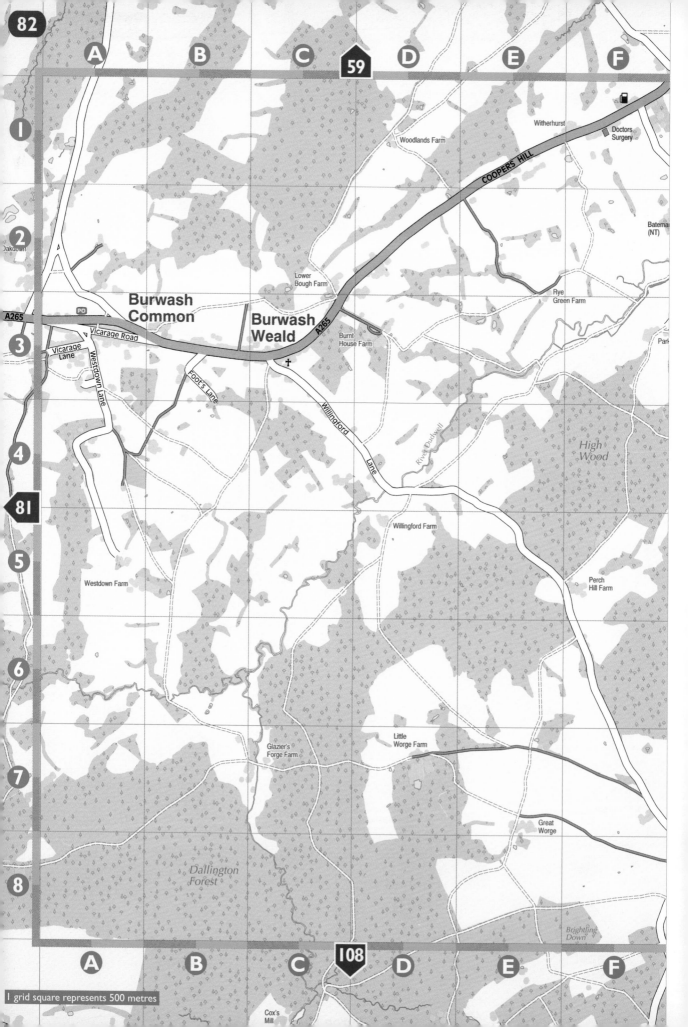

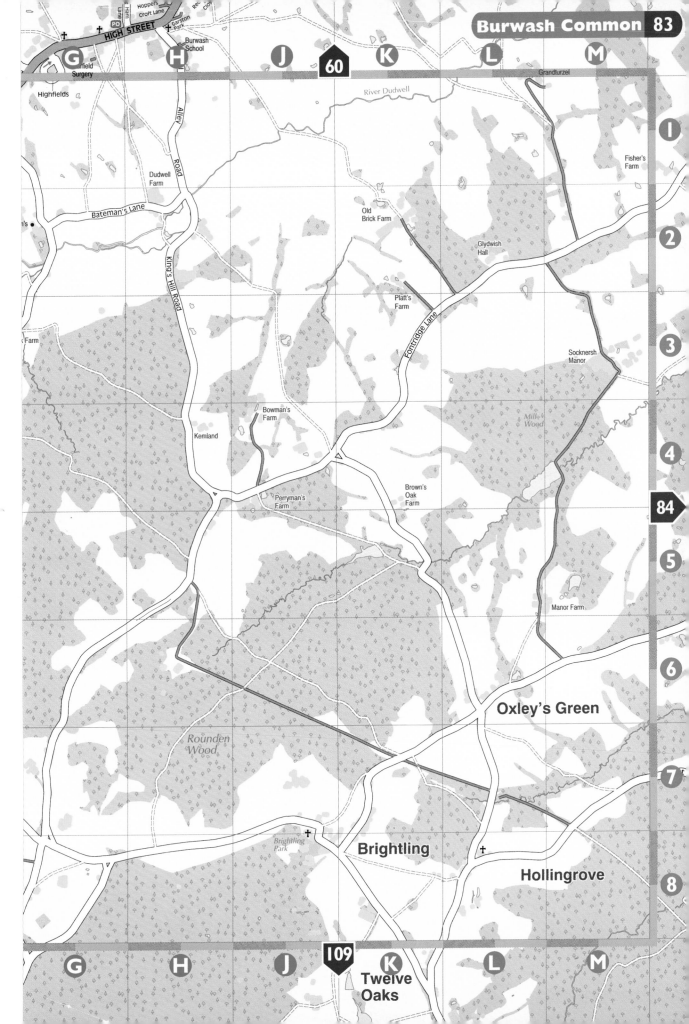

Grandturzel

River Dudwell

Fisher's
Farm

Highfields

Dudwell
Farm

Old
Brick Farm

Glydwish
Hall

Bateman's Lane

Alley Road

King's Hill Road

Platt's
Farm

Fontridge Lane

Socknersh
Manor

Bowman's
Farm

Kemland

Mill
Wood

Perryman's
Farm

Brown's
Oak
Farm

Manor Farm

Rounden
Wood

Oxley's Green

Brightling
Park

**Brightling**

**Hollingrove**

**Twelve
Oaks**

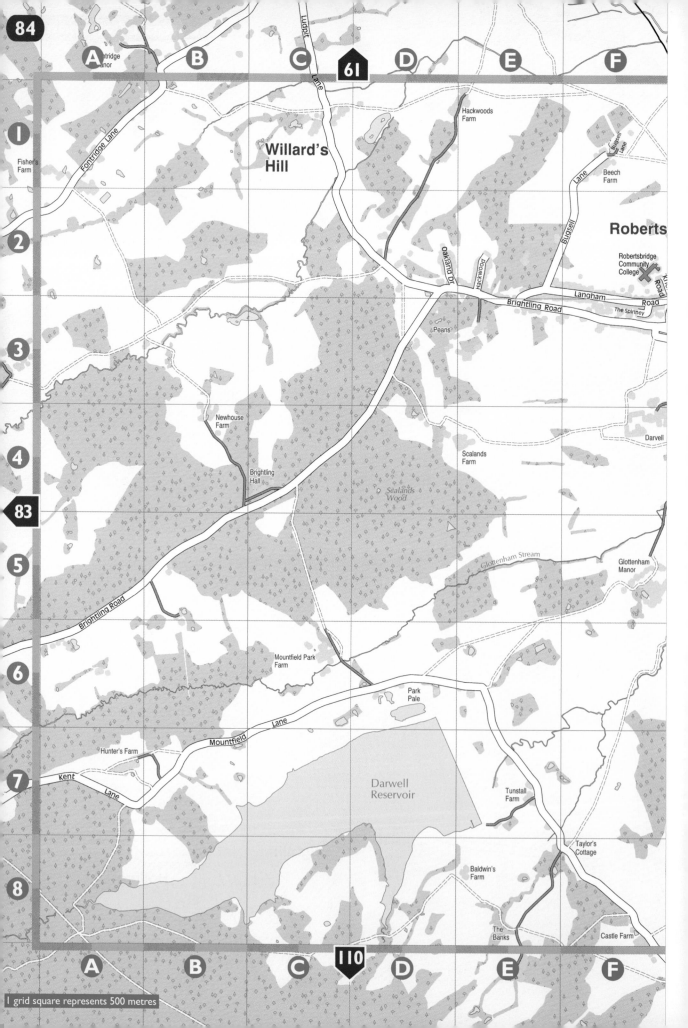

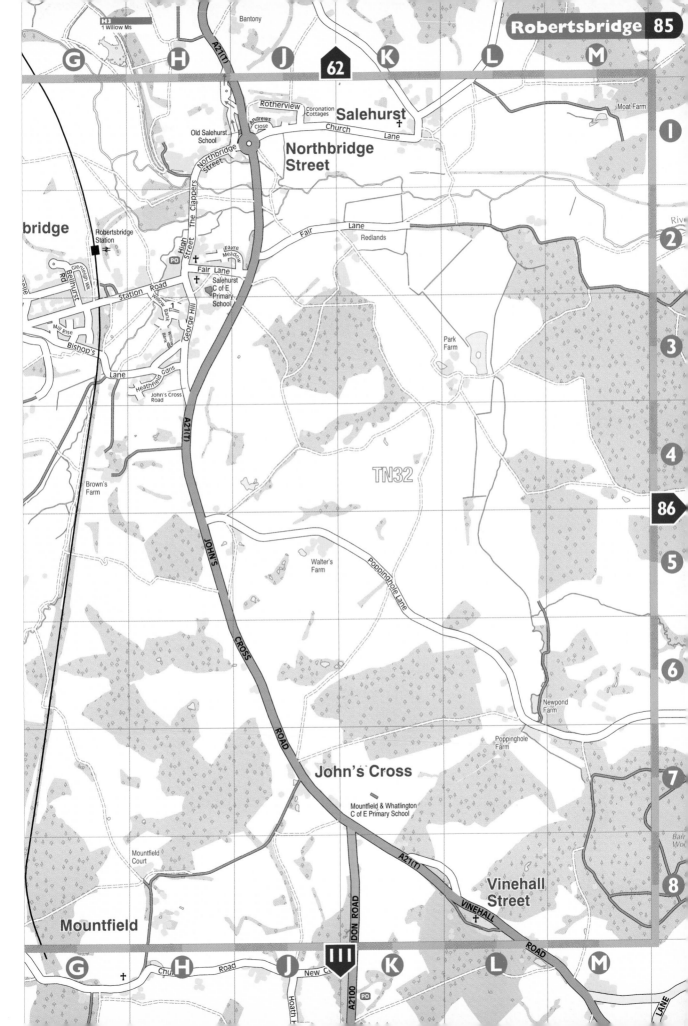

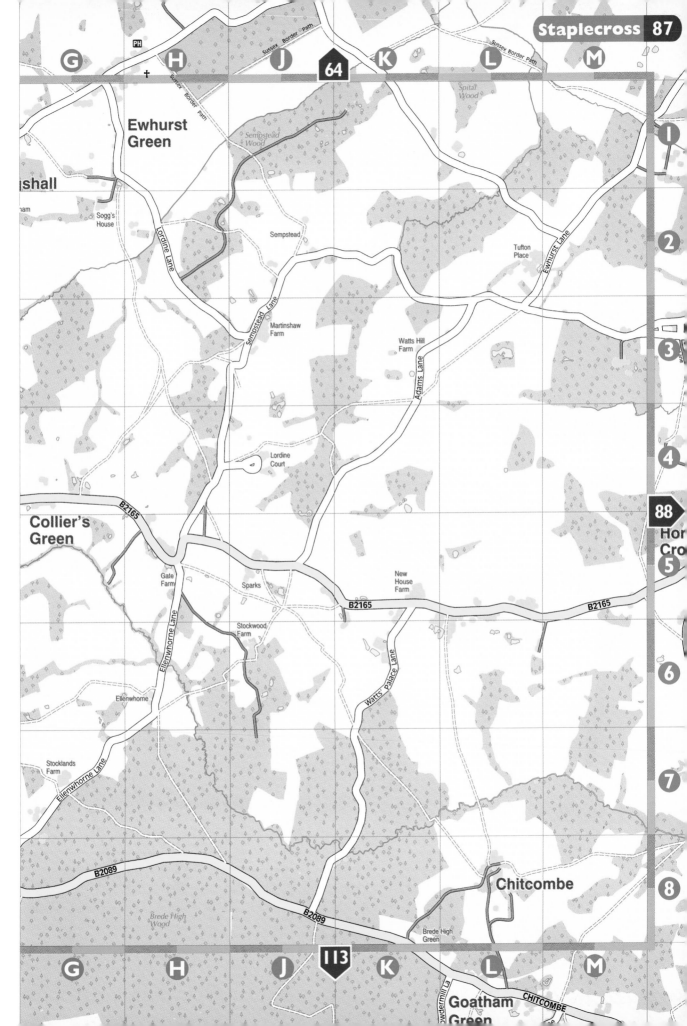

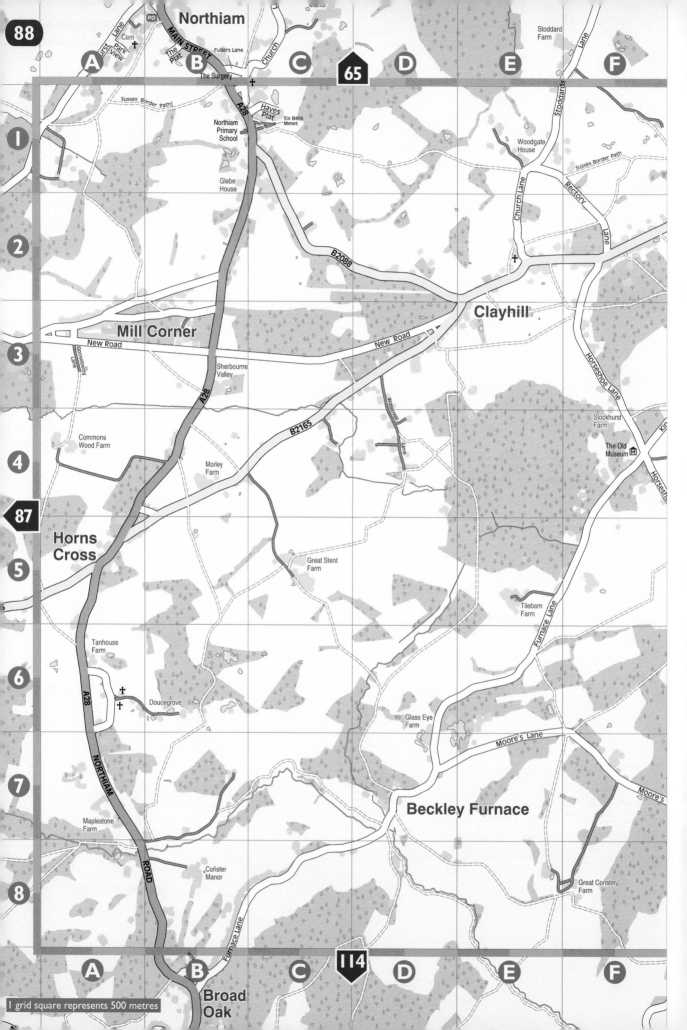

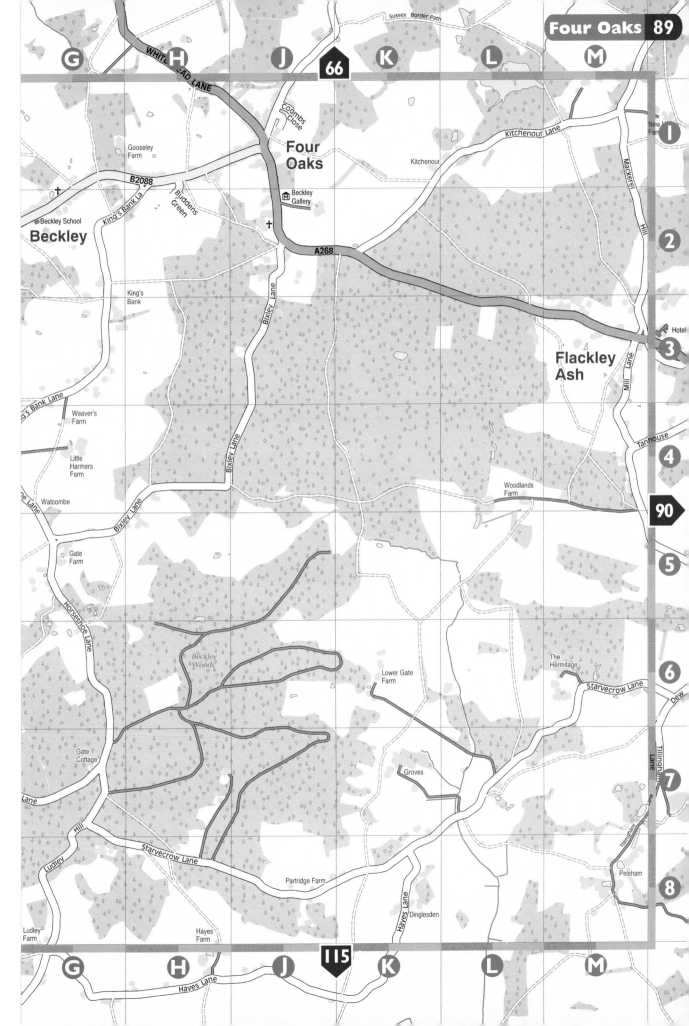

G H J 66 K L M

Sussex Border Path

WHITE HEAD LANE

Coombs Close

Gooseley Farm

New Farm 1

Kitchenour Lane

Kitchenour

Four Oaks

B2088

Buddens Green

Beckley Gallery

† Beckley School

Beckley

King's Bank La

Mackerel Hill

2

A268

Flackley Ash

Hotel 3

King's Bank

Bixley Lane

Mill Lane

Tanhouse

King's Bank Lane

Weaver's Farm

4

Little Harmers Farm

Bixley Lane

Woodlands Farm

90

ne Lane Watcombe

Bixley Lane

5

Gate Farm

Horseshoe Lane

Beckley Woods

Lower Gate Farm

The Hermitage

6

Starvecrow Lane

Dew Lane

Gate Cottage

Groves

Tillingham Lane

7

Lane

Hill

Starvecrow Lane

Pelsham

Ludley

Partridge Farm

Ludley Farm

Hayes Farm

Hayes Lane

Dinglesden

8

G H J 115 K L M

Hayes Lane

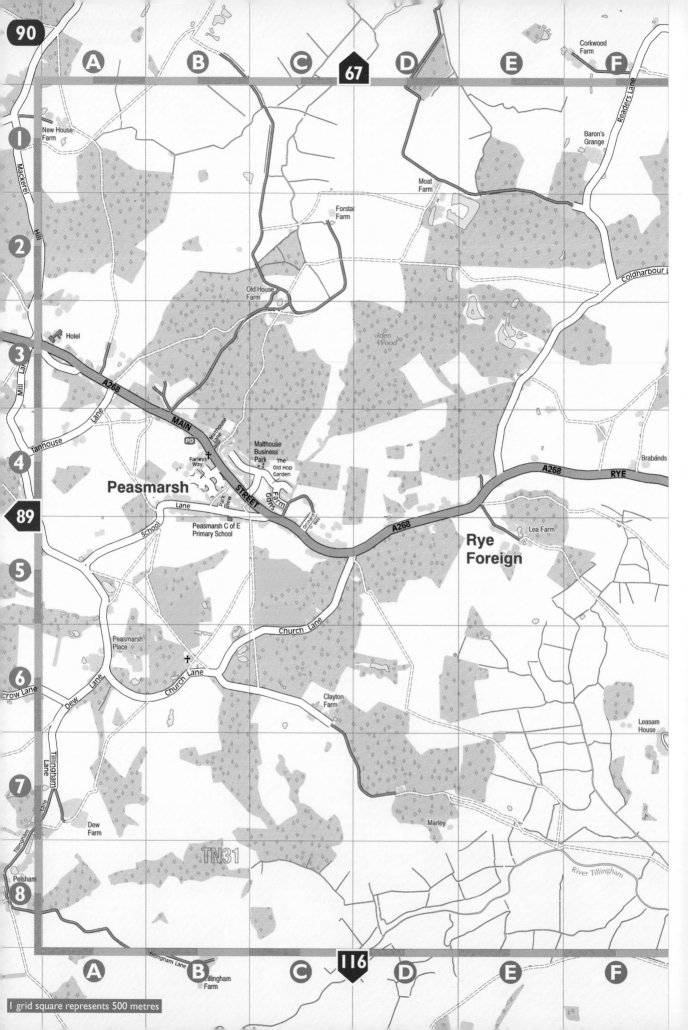

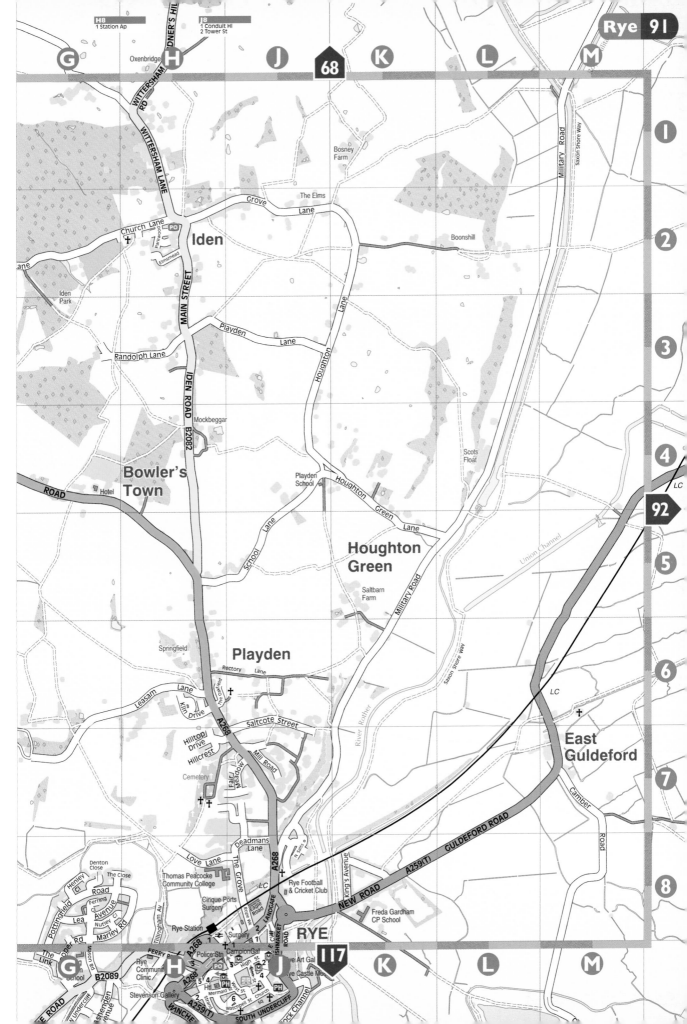

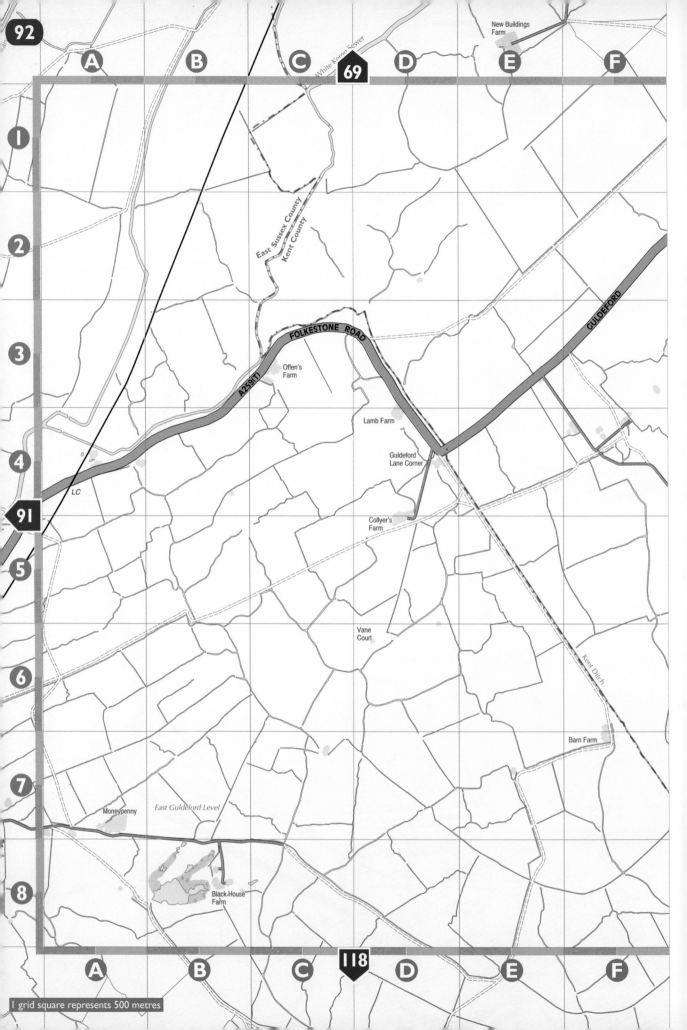

A  B  C  69  D  E  F

White Kemp Sewer

I

East Sussex County
Kent County

2

FOLKESTONE ROAD

GULDEFORD

3

A259(T)

Offen's
Farm

Lamb Farm

4

Guldeford
Lane Corner

LC

5

Collyer's
Farm

Vane
Court

Kent Ditch

6

Barn Farm

7

Moneypenny

East Guldeford Level

8

Black House
Farm

A  B  C  118  D  E  F

New Buildings
Farm

I grid square represents 500 metres

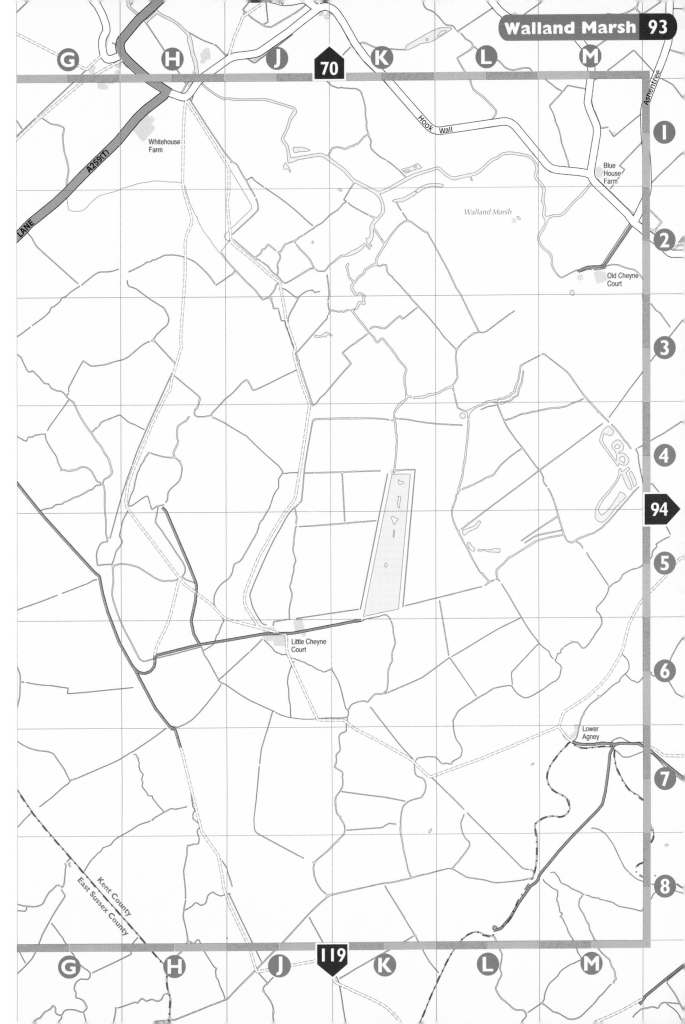

G    H    J    70    K    L    M

I

Whitehouse
Farm

Hook    Wall

Walland Marsh

Blue
House
Farm

2

Old Cheyne
Court

3

4

94

5

Little Cheyne
Court

6

Lower
Agney

7

Kent County
East Sussex County

8

G    H    J    119    K    L    M

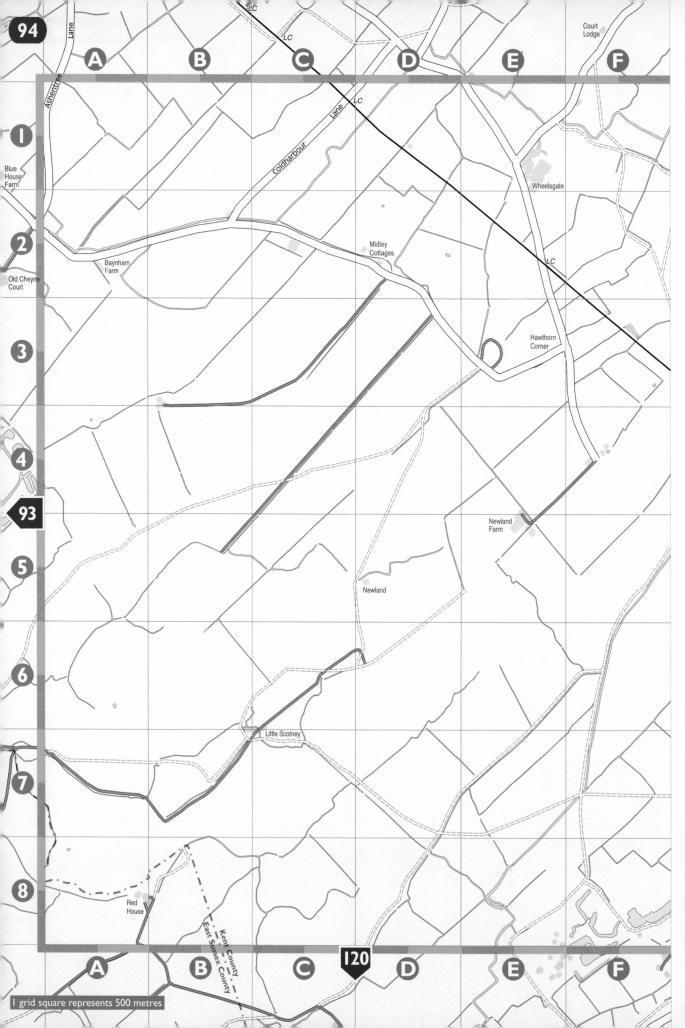

Court
Lodge

A   B   C   D   E   F

Ashentree Lane

LC

LC

Coldharbour Lane

LC

I

Blue
House
Farm

Wheelsgate

2

Old Cheyne
Court

Baynham
Farm

Midley
Cottages

LC

3

Hawthorn
Corner

4

Newland
Farm

5

Newland

6

Little Scotney

7

8

Red
House

Kent County
East Sussex County

A   B   C     D   E   F

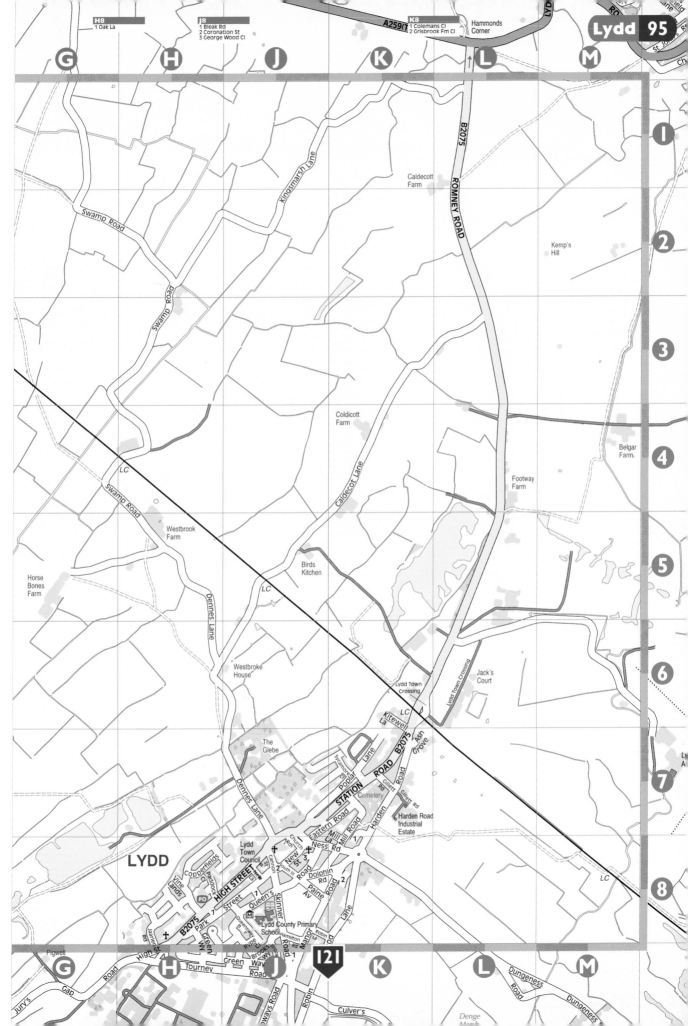

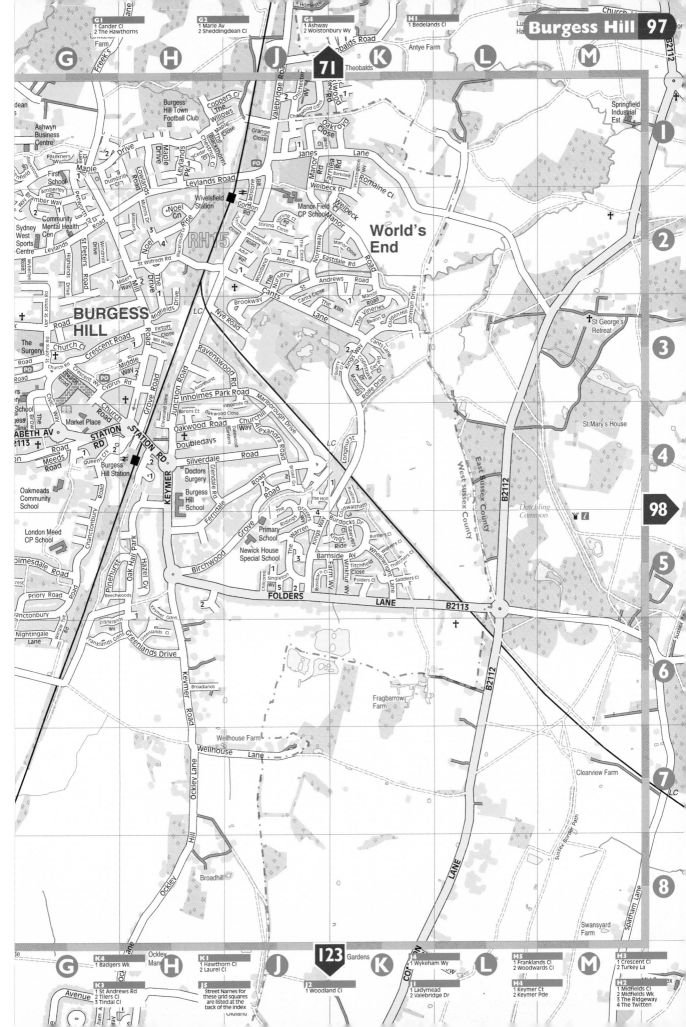

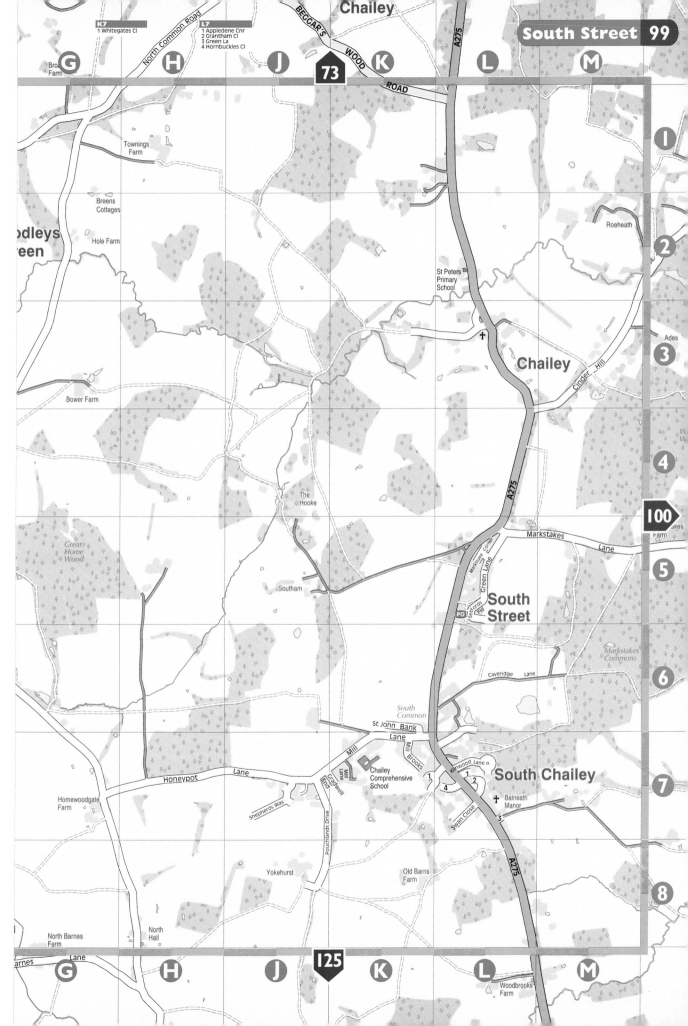

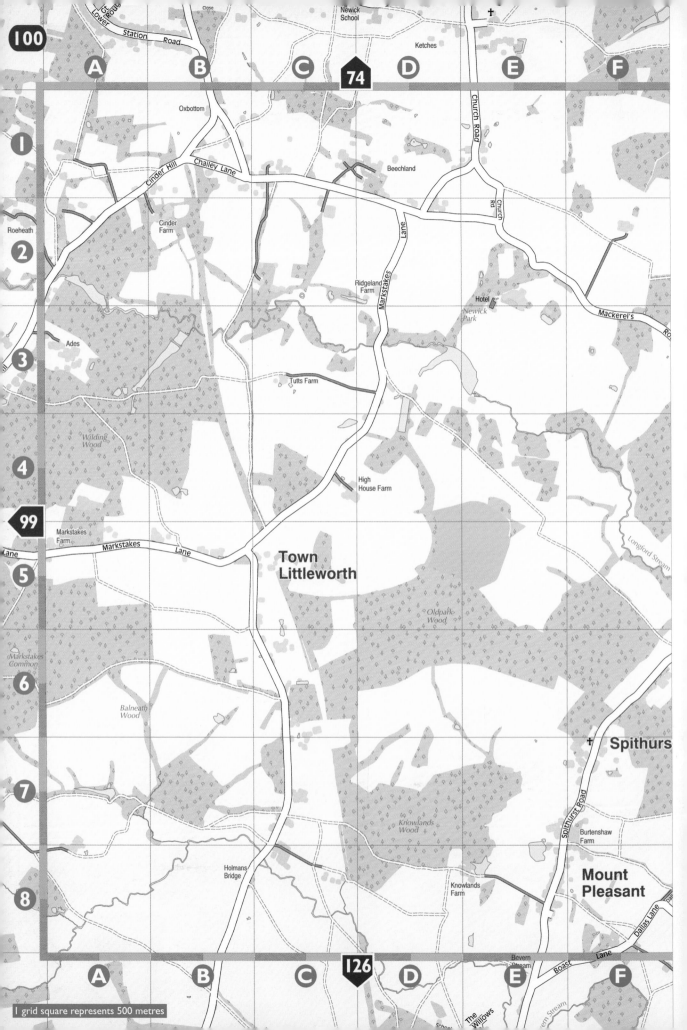

G H J **75** K L M

Beeches
Farm

Buckham
Hill

I

Buckham Hill
House

Owlsbury F

Sharps Farm

Buckham Hill
Farm

2

Broomlye

Little Buckham
Farm

Lodge
Wood

3

Vuggles
Farm

Constantia
Manor

Gipp's
Farm

4

River Uck

Gipp's
Wood

Sutton
Hall

New
House Farm

**102**

5

Worth
Farm

Beaks
Farm

Longford
Farm

†

River Ouse

6

Station Road

Tile Barn
Cl

**Isfield**

Horsted          Lane

7

PO

Lavender Line

t

Birches Farm

Lewes Road

8

6

Anchor Lane

Scufflings

Boathouse
Farm

**Rose
Hill**

Delves Farm

G H **127** J K L M

Banks
Farm

Lane

Batchelor's
Hall

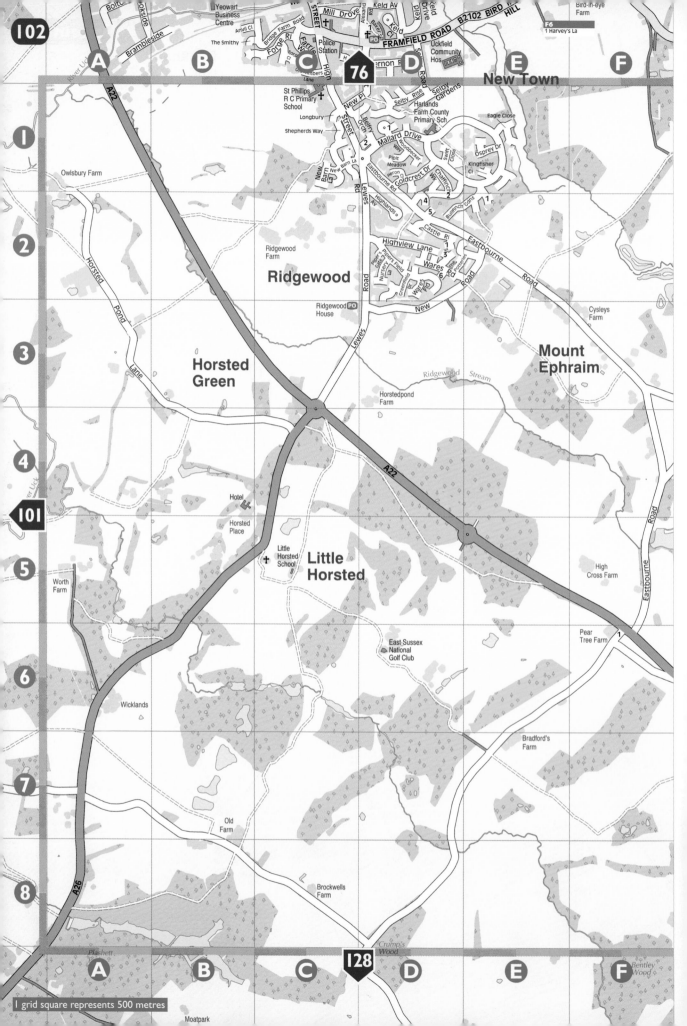

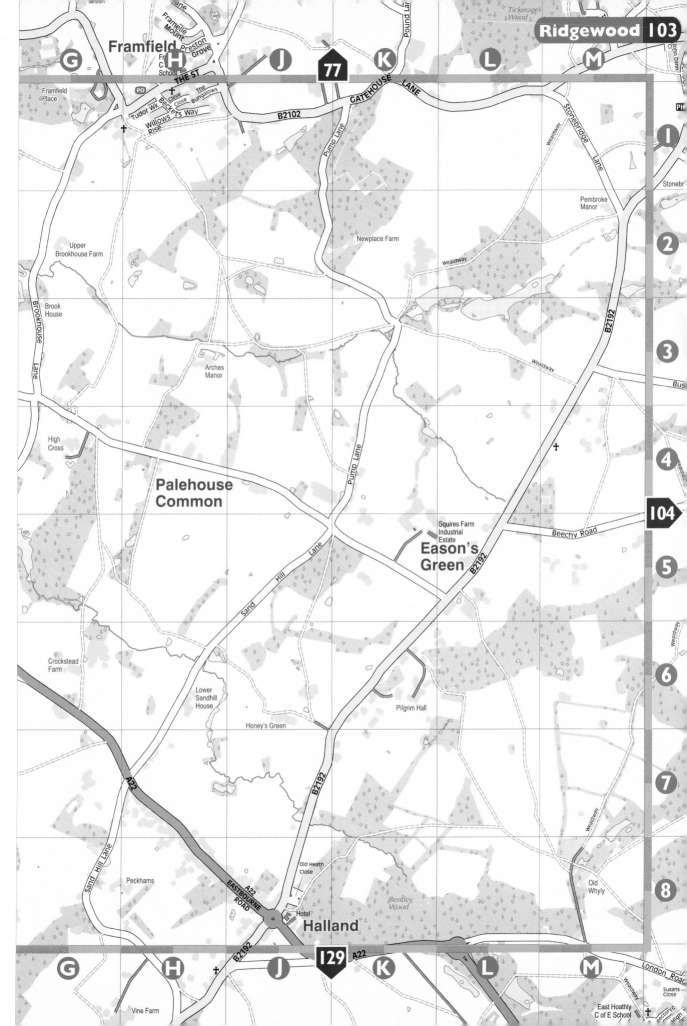

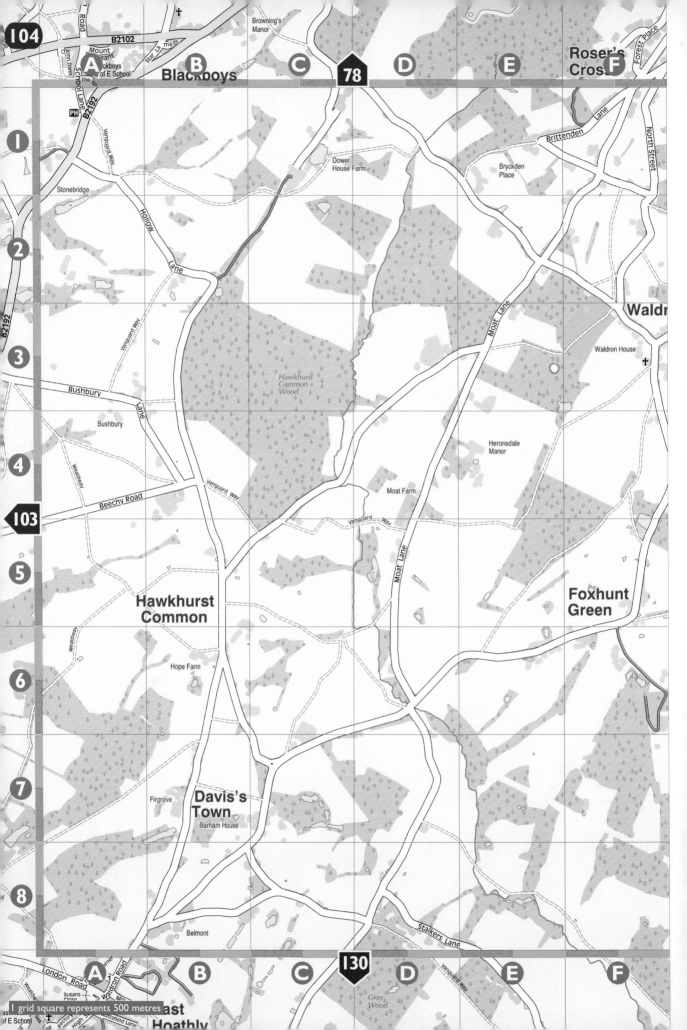

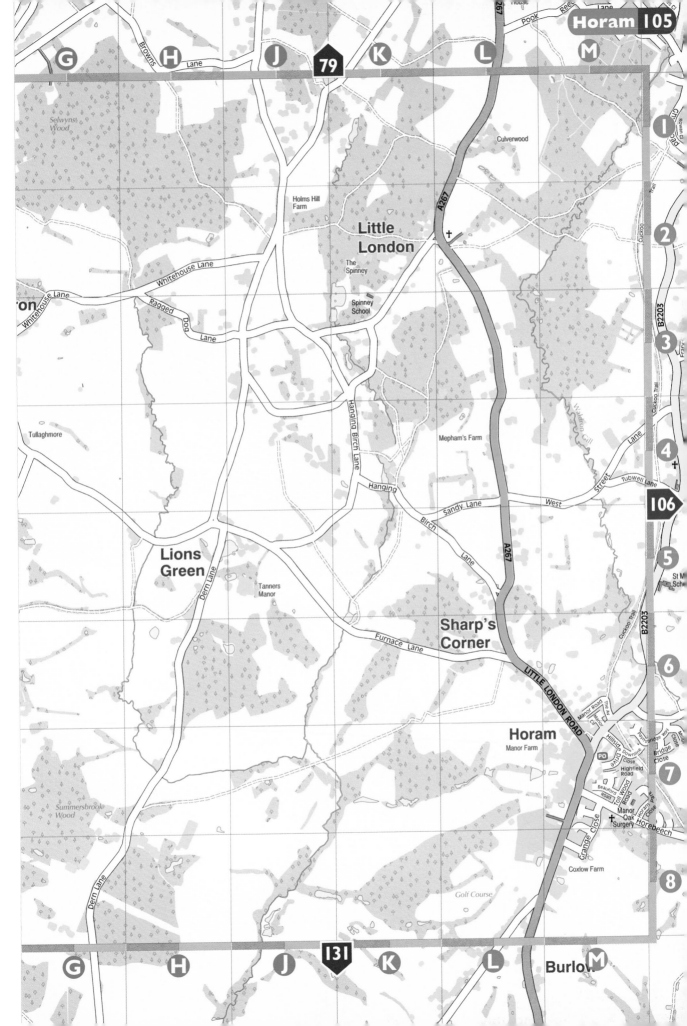

G    H    J    79    K    L    M

1

Selwyns
Wood

Culverwood

2

Holms Hill
Farm

Little
London

B2203

The
Spinney

3

Whitehouse Lane

Spinney
School

Whitehouse Lane

Ragged   Dog

Lane

Waldron Gill

Tullaghmore

Hanging Birch Lane

Mepham's Farm

Street

Tubwell Lane

4

Hanging

106

Sandy Lane

West

Cuckoo Trail

A267

Birch

5

Lions
Green

St M
Sche

Dern Lane

Tanners
Manor

Lane

Furnace Lane

Sharp's
Corner

6

B2203

Cuckoo Trail

LITTLE LONDON ROAD

Manor Road

The A

Bridge

Manor
Close

Close

Horam

Hillside   Downview

Tanyersidge Way

Manor Farm

PO

Close

7

Beauford

Col Wood

Highfield
Road

Road

Horam Pk

Summersbrook
Wood

Grange Close

Manor
Oak   Horebeech

Surgery

Close

Coxlow Farm

8

Golf Course

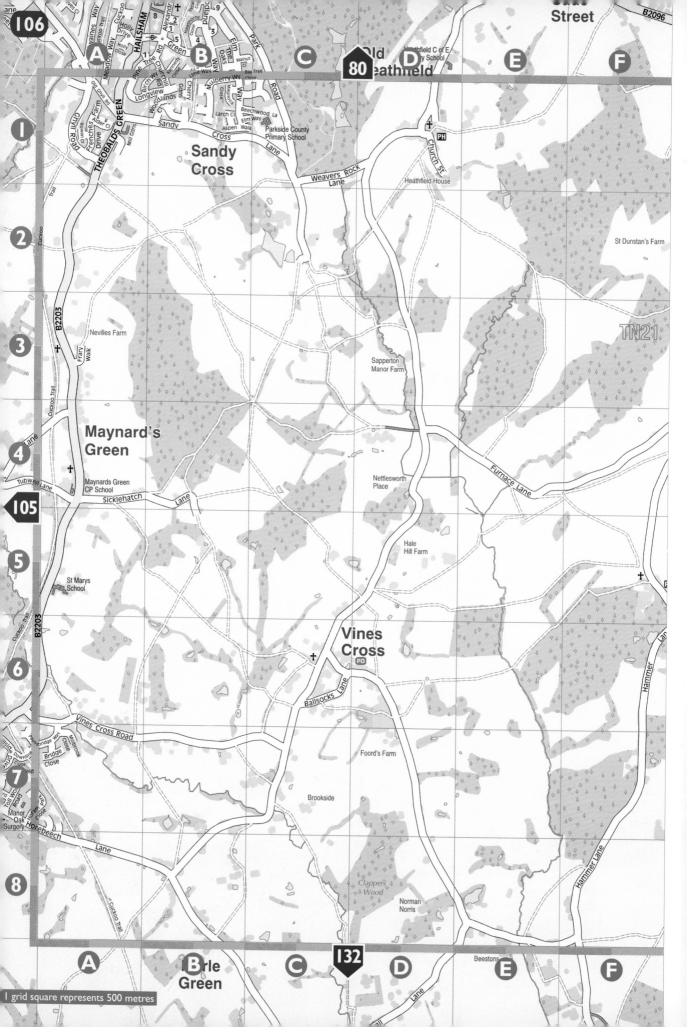

A  B  C  **80** D  E  F
Old
Heathfield

Street
B2096

**I**

Sandy
Cross

Heathfield House
St Dunstan's Farm

**2**
Cuckoo Trail

**3**
Nevilles Farm
B2203
Frary Walk

Sapperton
Manor Farm

TN21

**4**
Tubwell Lane
Maynard's
Green
Maynards Green
CP School
Nettlesworth
Place
Furnace Lane

Sicklehatch Lane
**105**

**5**
St Marys
School
Hale
Hill Farm

**6**
Cuckoo Trail
B2203
Vines
Cross
PO

Ballsocks Lane
Hammer Lane

Vines Cross Road
Bridge Close
Hillbrook Close
Foord's Farm

**7**
Toll Wood Road
Manor
Oak
Surgery
Horebeech
Lane
Brookside

**8**
Cuckoo Trail
Clappers
Wood
Norman
Norris

A  **B**rle C  **I32** D  E  F
Green
Beestons

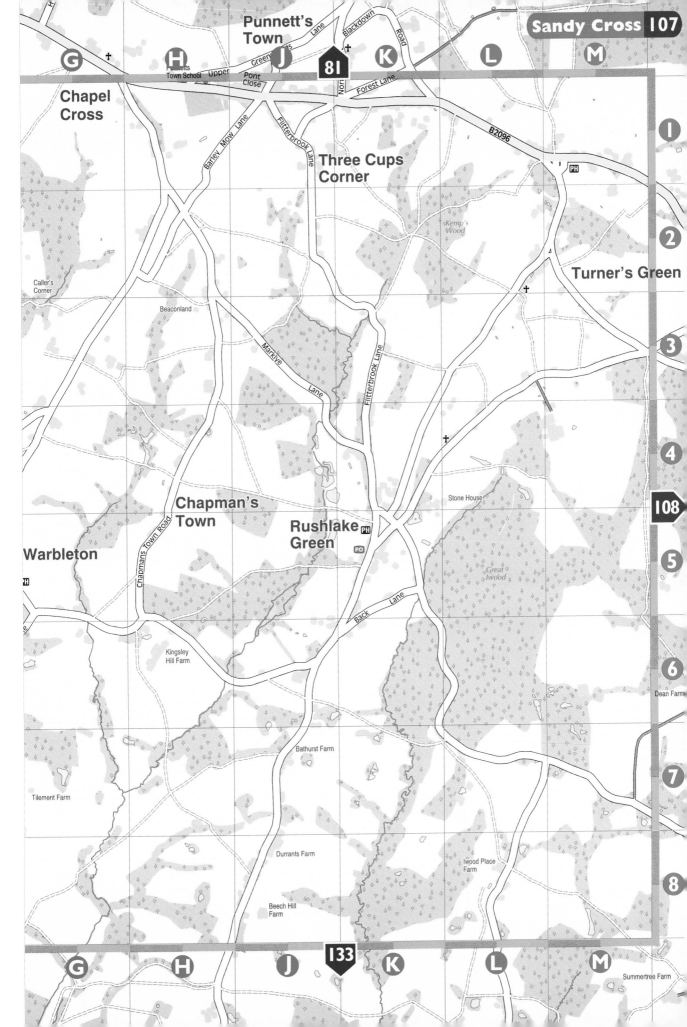

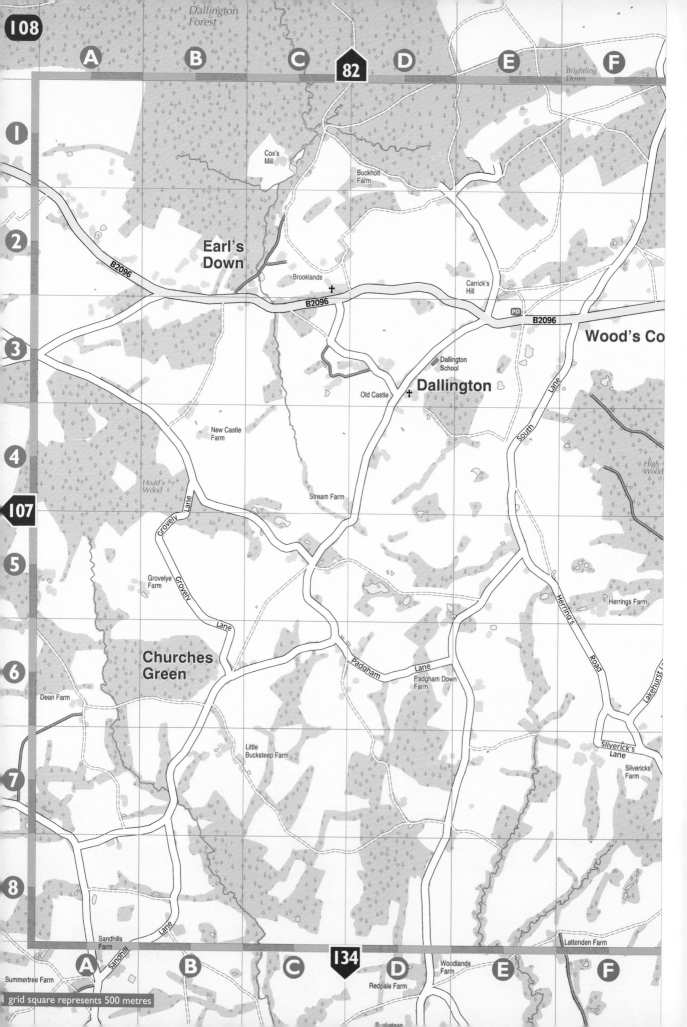

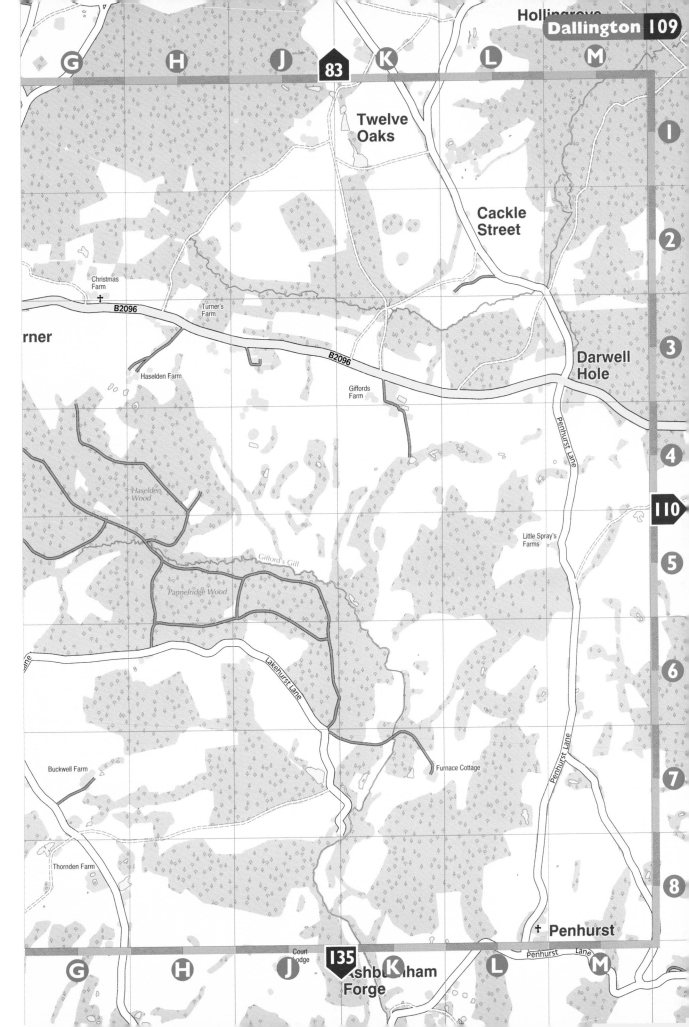

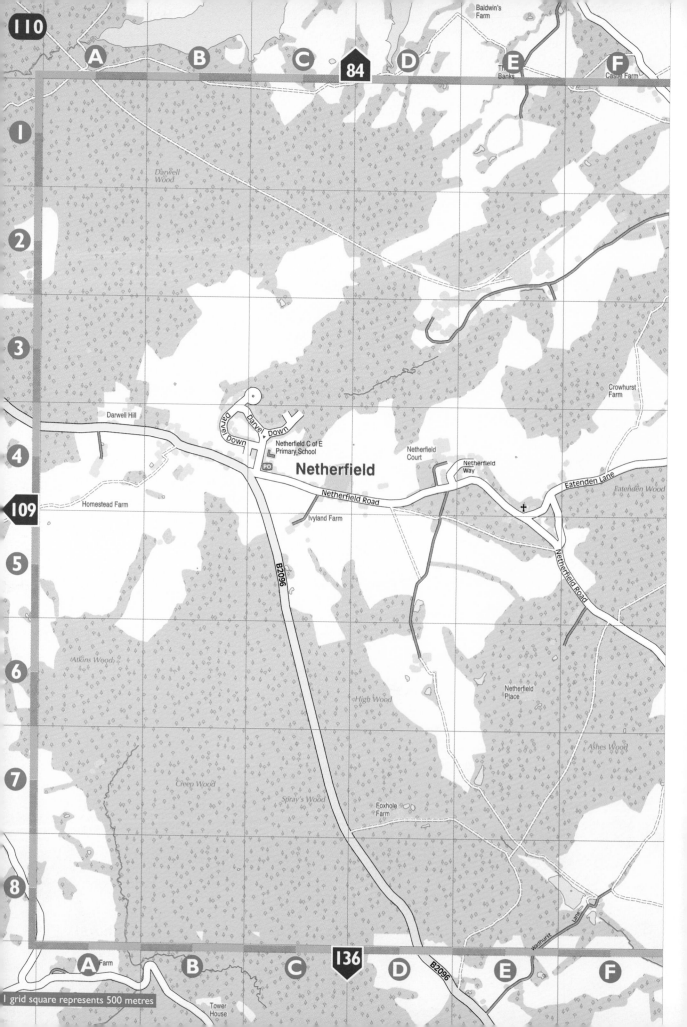

110

A    B    C    84    D    E    F

I

Darwell
Wood

2

3

Crowhurst
Farm

Darvell Hill    Darvel Down    Netherfield C of E    Netherfield
    Primary School    Court    Netherfield Way
4    Eatenden Lane    Eatenden Wood
109    Homestead Farm    PO
    Netherfield    †
    Netherfield Road
    Ivyland Farm
5    B2096    Netherfield Road

6    Atkins Wood    Netherfield
    Place
    High Wood
    Ashes Wood

7    Creep Wood    Spray's Wood
    Foxhole
    Farm

8    Wadhurst Lane

A    Farm    B    C    136    D    B2096    E    F

Tower
House

Baldwin's
Farm

Th.
Banks    Castle Farm

1 grid square represents 500 metres

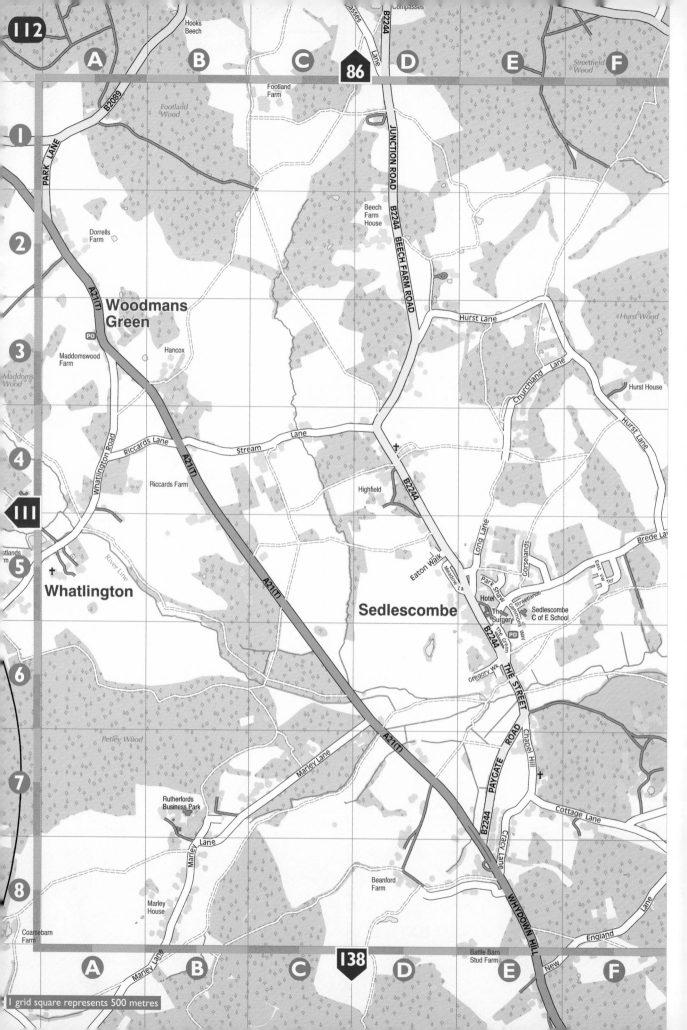

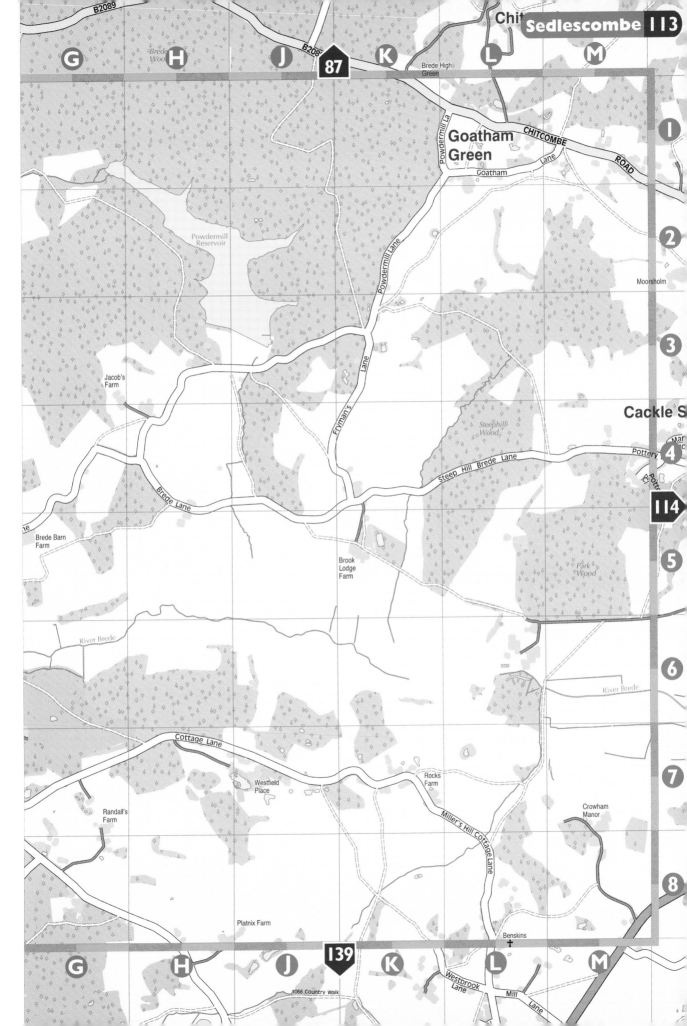

G H J K L M

B2089

B208

87

Chi⁺

Brede
Wood

Brede High
Green

**Goatham
Green**

CHITCOMBE ROAD

Powdermill La

Goatham Lane

Moorsholm

Powdermill
Reservoir

Powdermill Lane

Cackle S

Jacob's
Farm

Fryman's Lane

Steephill
Wood

Pottery

Man

Steep Hill Brede Lane

114

Brede Lane

Pott

Brede Barn
Farm

Brook
Lodge
Farm

Park
Wood

River Brede

River Brede

Cottage Lane

Westfield
Place

Rocks
Farm

Crowham
Manor

Randall's
Farm

Miller's Hill cottage Lane

Platnix Farm

Benskins

G H J K L M

139

1066 Country Walk

Westbrook
Lane

Mill
Lane

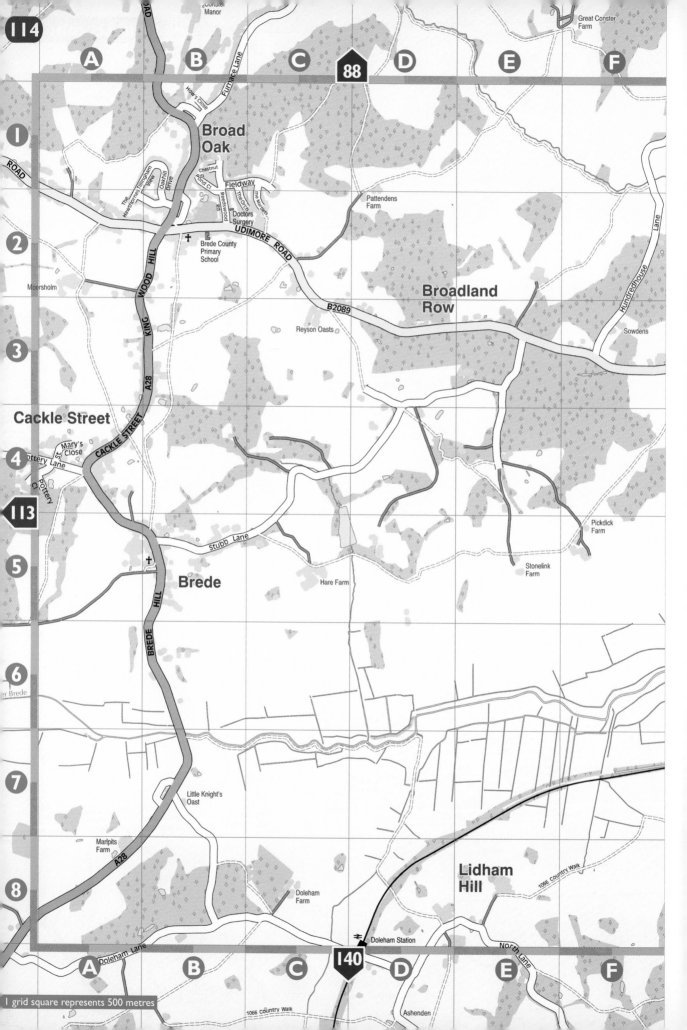

88

A    B    C    D    E    F

1

**Broad
Oak**

Furnace Lane

How's Close

Conster
Manor

Great Conster
Farm

ROAD

The Hawthornes
Tillingham
Oakhill
Drive

Chestnut
Bend Cl

Fieldway

The Martlets

Reedswood
Rd

The Orch

Doctors
Surgery

Pattendens
Farm

Hundredhouse
Lane

2

Moorsholm

Brede County
Primary
School

**UDIMORE ROAD**

B2089

**Broadland
Row**

Sowdens

3

KING    WOOD    HILL

A28

Reyson Oasts

**Cackle Street**

St Mary's
Close

CACKLE    STREET

4

Pottery
Lane

Pottery Cl

113

Pickdick
Farm

Stubb Lane

5

BREDE    HILL

**Brede**

Hare Farm

Stonelink
Farm

r Brede

6

7

Little Knight's
Oast

8

Marlpits
Farm

A28

Doleham
Farm

**Lidham
Hill**

1066 Country Walk

Doleham Station

140

North Lane

Ashenden

A    B    C    D    E    F

Doleham Lane

1066 Country Walk

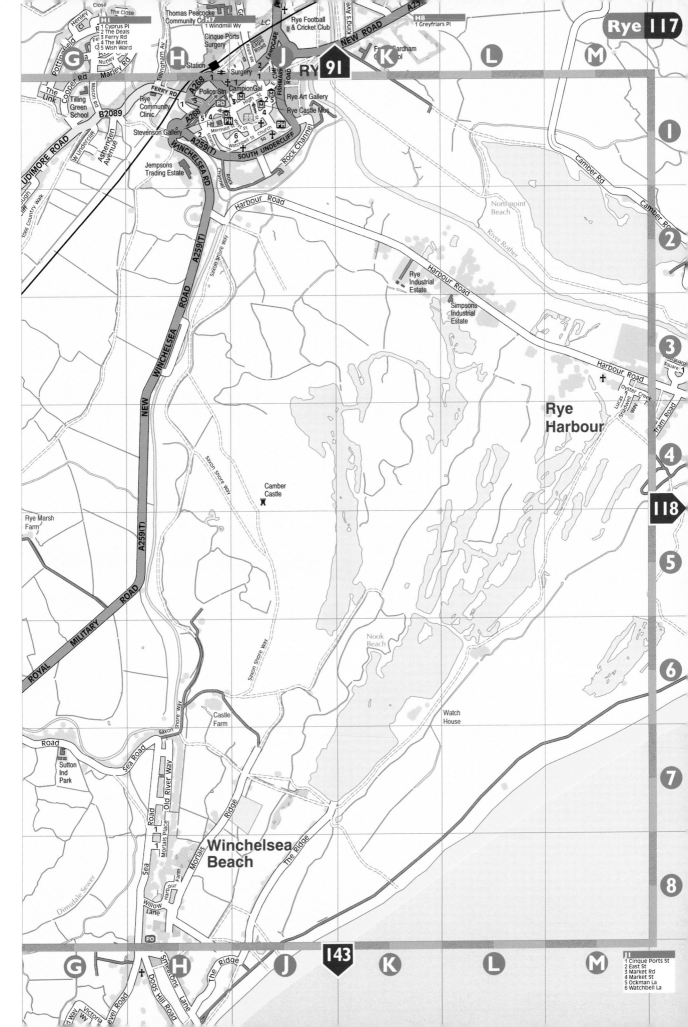

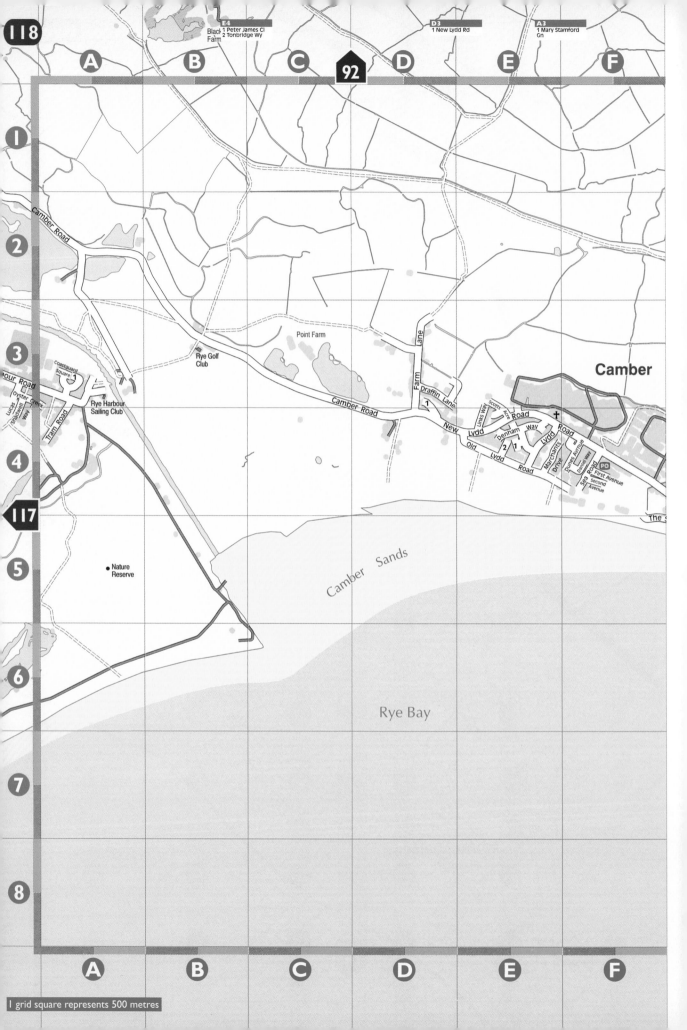

A B C **92** D E F

92

E4
1 Peter James Cl
2 Tonbridge Wy

D3
1 New Lydd Rd

A3
1 Mary Stamford
Gn

1

2

Camber Road

3

Coastguard
Square

Luca's

Oyster Creek

Shadwell

Way

our Road

Tram Road

Rye Harbour
Sailing Club

Rye Golf
Club

Point Farm

Camber Road

Farm Lane

Draffin Lane

New Lydd

Old Lydd Road

Links Way

Scores

Acre Road

Cobenham Way

Marchants Drive

Lydd Road

Dunes Avenue

Daniel Way

Sea Road

Road

First Avenue

Second Avenue

PO

**Camber**

4

117

5

• Nature
Reserve

Camber Sands

6

Rye Bay

7

8

The

A B C D E F

1 grid square represents 500 metres

G

H

J

93

K

L

M

I

2

3

4

120

5

6

7

8

1 Skinner Rd

East Sussex County

Broomhill Level

Yates Close

Delwood Road

Belwood Road

1 Suttons

Lydd Road

Broomhill Farm

**Jury's Gap**

Lydd Road

Neath Road

*Broomhill Sands*

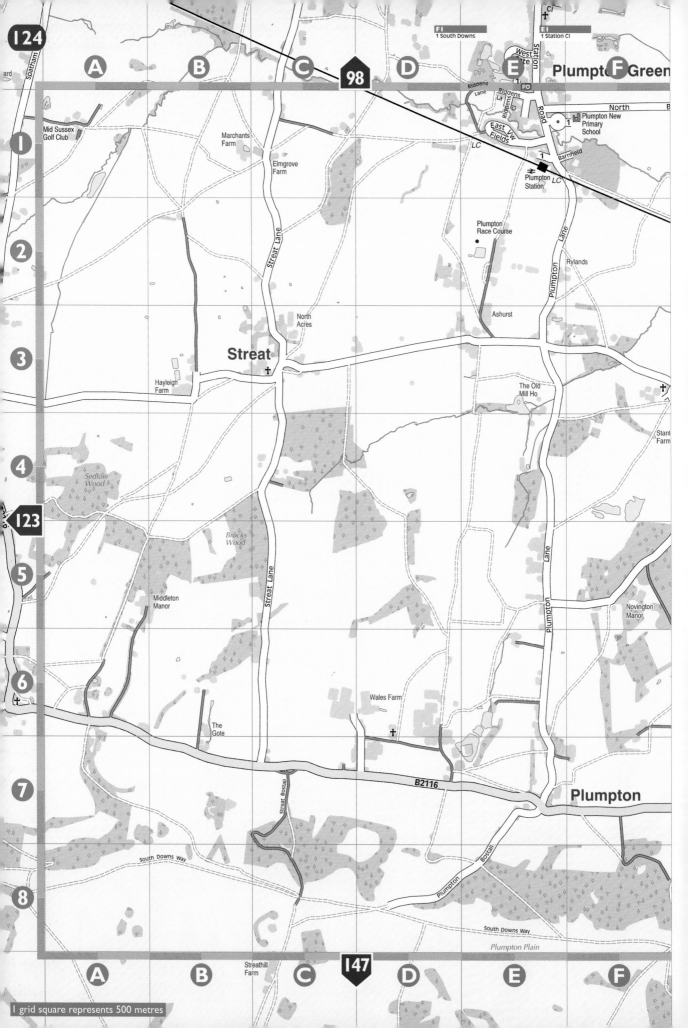

**A** **B** **C** 98 **D** **E** **F** Plumpton Green

**F1**
1 South Downs

**E1**
1 Station Cl

**1**

Cl

Station
West
Gate

Riddens
Lane

Riddens
La

PO

North

North

Plumpton
Road

1

Plumpton New
Primary
School

East
Fields

LC

1

Barnfield

LC

Mid Sussex
Golf Club

Marchants
Farm

Elmgrove
Farm

Plumpton
Station

**I**

Spatham

Street Lane

**2**

Plumpton
Race Course

Plumpton Lane

Rylands

North
Acres

Ashurst

**Streat**

**3**

Hayleigh
Farm

The Old
Mill Ho

Stant
Farm

**4**

Sedlow
Wood

Street Lane

**123**

A26

Brocks
Wood

Lane

**5**

Middleton
Manor

Novington
Manor

**6**

The
Gote

Wales Farm

**7**

Streat Bostall

B2116

**Plumpton**

Plumpton Bostall

South Downs Way

Streathill
Farm

**8**

South Downs Way

Plumpton Plain

**A** **B** 147 **C** **D** **E** **F**

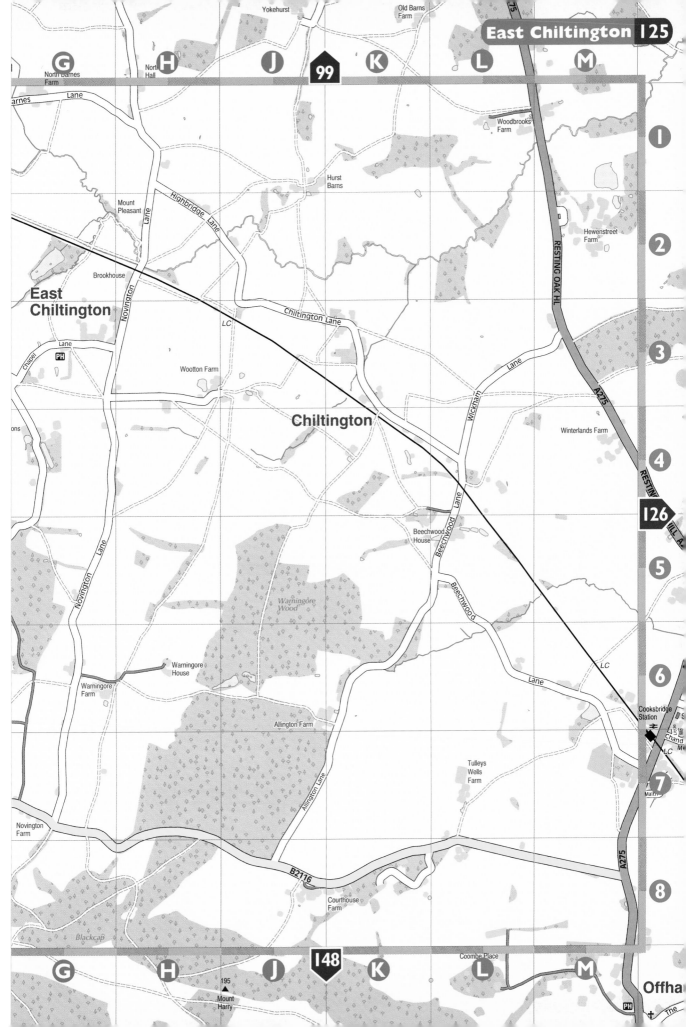

126

A  B  C  [100]  D  E  F

Mount
Pleasant

E2
1 Munster Gn
2 Oaktree
3 Weald Cl

1

Bridge

Knowlands
Farm

Bevern
Stream

Boast
Lane

Dallas Lane

Bevern Stream

2

renstreet
n

Sewell's
Farm

Gallybird
Hall

The
Willows

School
Fld

Deans Hl

Deans Meadow

Schools Fld

School

Grantham

Barcombe
Primary
School

Grange
Gdns

PO

Grange
Rd

7

3

2

High Street

Barcombe
Cross

Weald View

Monger's
Md

Barcombe Pk

Mills Road

Camoys
Court

A275

Handlye Farm

Deadmantree Hill

Bridgelands

The Grange

Crink Hill

Barcombe Rd

3

Curds Farm

Shelley's
Folly

✕
Mill
Lane

Church Road

4

125

Conyboro

Barcombe

Culver
Farm

5

Averys

✝

6

LC

Cooksbridge

Cowlease
Farm

Cooksbridge
Station

School

Little Chandler's Mead

Hamsey
Lane

North
End

Wellingham
House

7

A275

Malthouse Wy

LC

Whitfield Lane

Hamsey
House

Hamsey

Chalkham
Farm

8

A275

Offham

A  B  Ivors Lane  C  [149]  D  E  F

Hamseyplace
Farm

Drove

1 grid square represents 500 metres

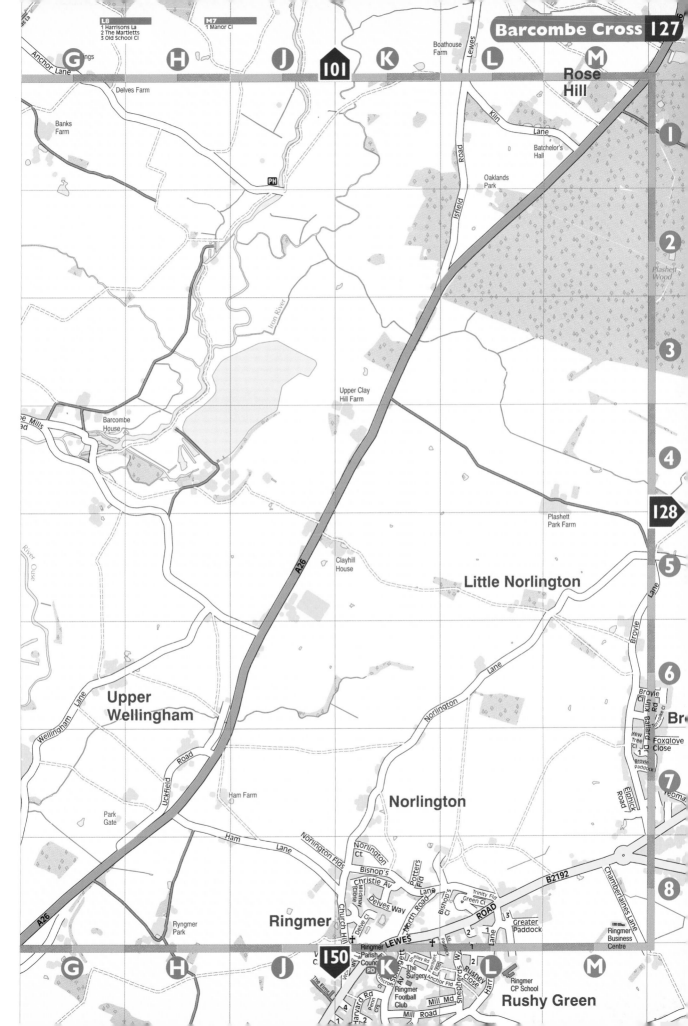

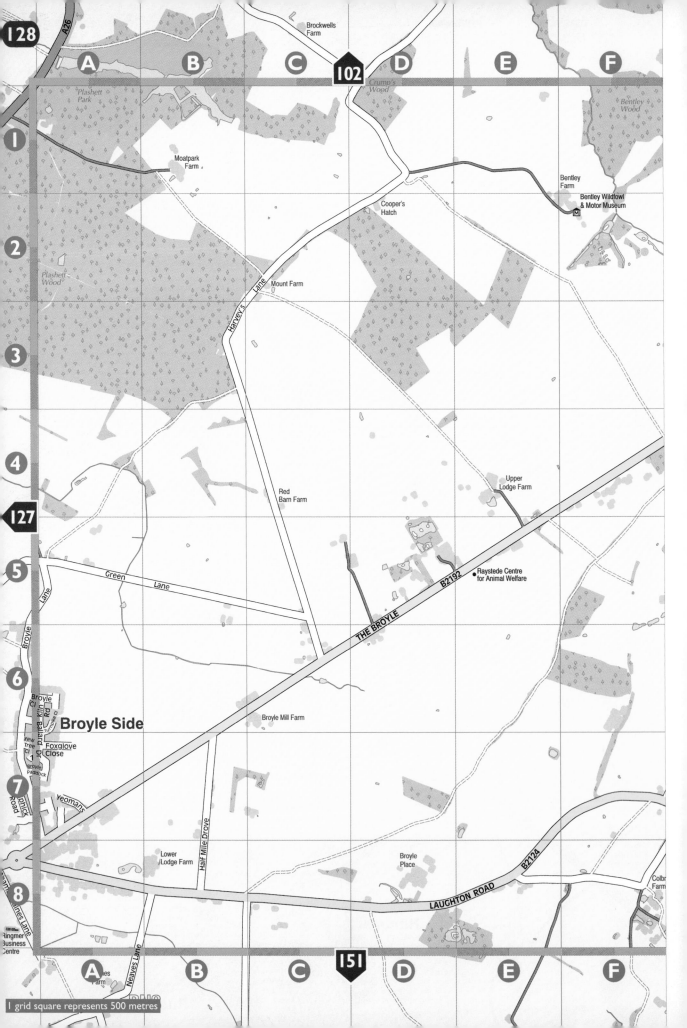

A26

A  B  C  102  D  E  F

Brockwells
Farm

Crump's
Wood

Bentley
Wood

Plashett
Park

1

Moatpark
Farm

Cooper's
Hatch

Bentley
Farm

Bentley Wildfowl
& Motor Museum
M

2

Plashett
Wood

Mount Farm

Harvey's Lane

3

4

Red
Barn Farm

Upper
Lodge Farm

5

Green      Lane

Raystede Centre
for Animal Welfare

B2192

THE BROYLE

Broyle Lane

6

Broyle
Cl
Kiln Rd
Ballard Dr
Turnpike Cl

Broyle Side

Broyle Mill Farm

Yew
Tree Dr
Foxglove
Close
1
Broyle
Paddock

7

Dinnick Road

Yeomans

Half Mile Drove

Lower
Lodge Farm

Broyle
Place

B2124

8

Ringmer
Business
Centre

Eames Lane

Neaves Lane

Laughton Road

Colbran
Farm

A  B  C  151  D  E  F

1 grid square represents 500 metres

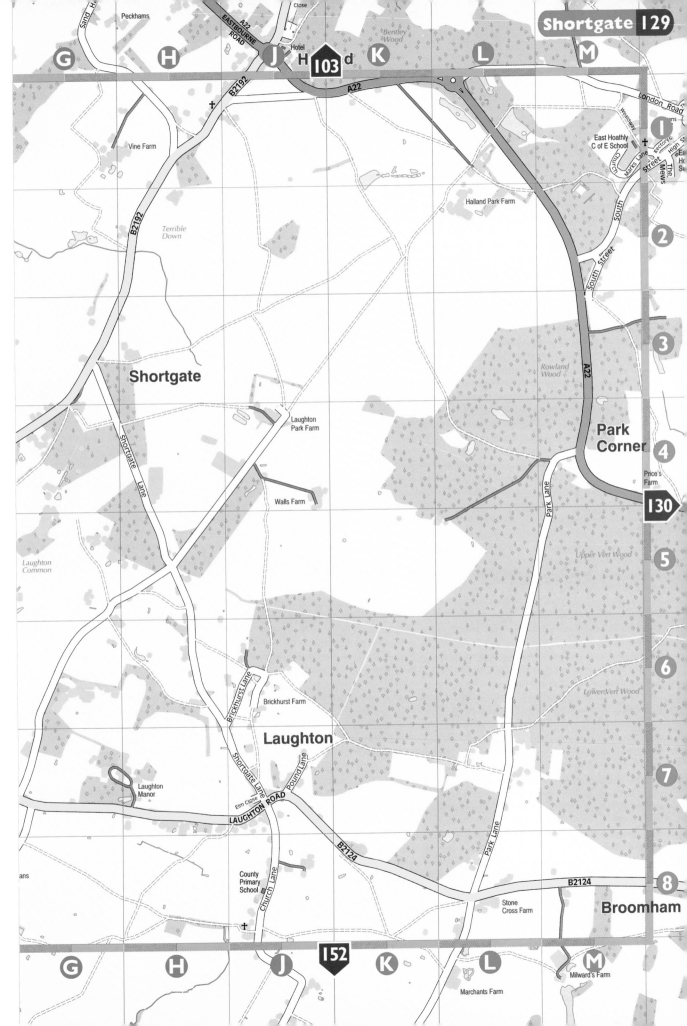

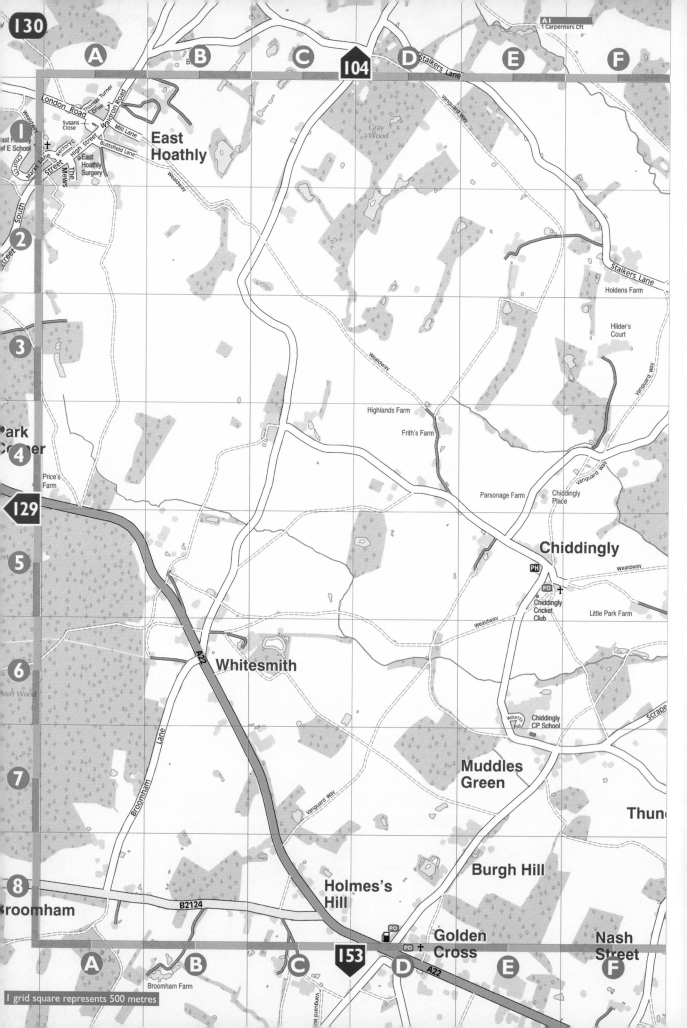

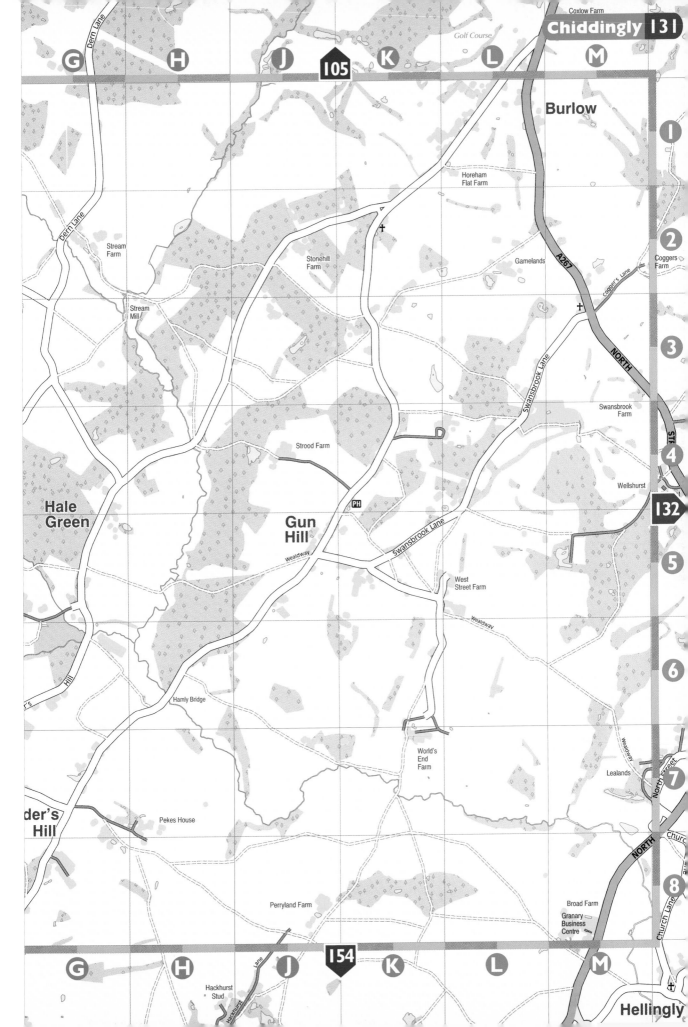

**G** **H** **J** **105** **K** **L** **M**

**Burlow**

**1**

Coxlow Farm

**2**
Coggers
Farm

Horeham
Flat Farm

Stream
Farm

Gamelands

Coggers Lane

A267

**3**

Stonehill
Farm

Dern Lane

†

NORTH

Stream
Mill

Swansbrook
Farm

Swansbrook Lane

**4**

STR

**132**

Strood Farm

Wellshurst

**5**

PH

**Hale
Green**

**Gun
Hill**

Swansbrook Lane

West
Street Farm

**6**

Wealdway

Wealdway

Hamly Bridge

Wealdway

North Street

Lealands

**7**

's
Hill

World's
End
Farm

NORTH

Church La

**8**

der's
Hill

Pekes House

Perryland Farm

Broad Farm

Granary
Business
Centre

Church Lane

**G** **H** **154** **J** **K** **L** **M**

Hackhurst
Stud

Hackhurst Lane

†

**Hellingly**

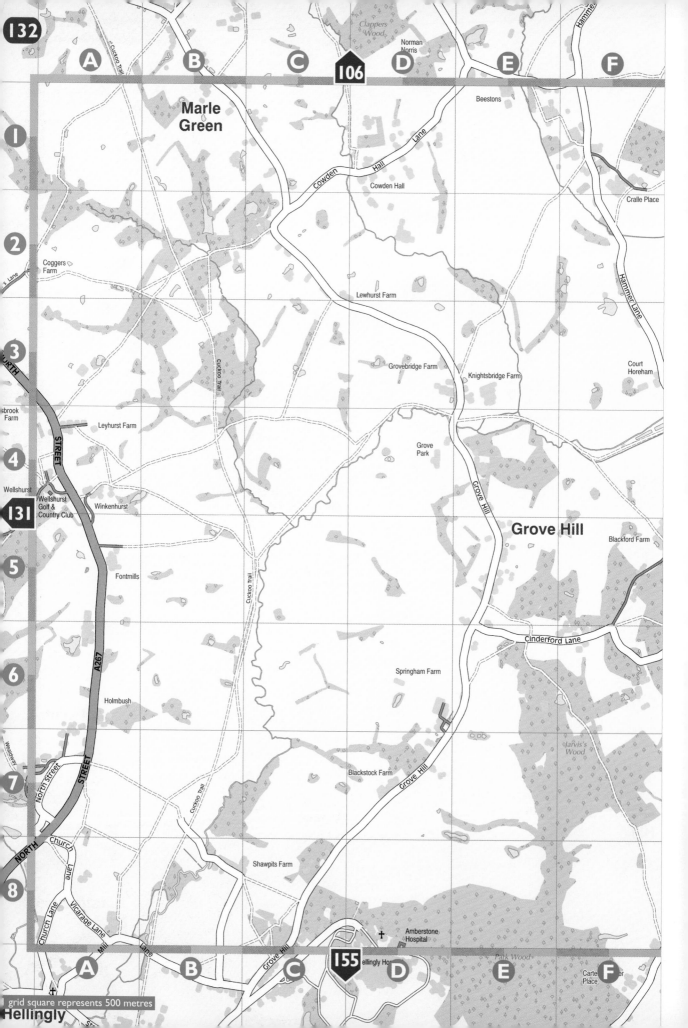

Ⓐ Ⓑ Ⓒ **106** Ⓓ Ⓔ Ⓕ

**1**

**2**

**3**

**4**

**131**

**5**

**6**

**7**

**8**

Ⓐ Ⓑ Ⓒ **155** Ⓓ Ⓔ Ⓕ

Marle Green

Clappers Wood

Norman Morris

Beestons

Cowden Hall Lane

Cowden Hall

Cralle Place

Coggers Farm

Hammer Lane

Lewhurst Farm

Grovebridge Farm

Knightsbridge Farm

Court Horeham

sbrook Farm

NORTH

Leyhurst Farm

STREET

Grove Park

Wellshurst

Wellshurst Golf & Country Club

Winkenhurst

Grove Hill

Grove Hill

Blackford Farm

Fontmills

Cuckoo Trail

A267

Cinderford Lane

Springham Farm

Holmbush

Jarvis's Wood

Westway

NORTH STREET

Cuckoo Trail

Blackstock Farm

Grove Hill

North Street

NORTH

Church Lane

Shawpits Farm

Amberstone Hospital

Park Wood

Church Lane

Vicarage Lane

Grove Hill

Hellingly Ho

Carter er Place

Mill Lane

grid square represents 500 metres

**Hellingly**

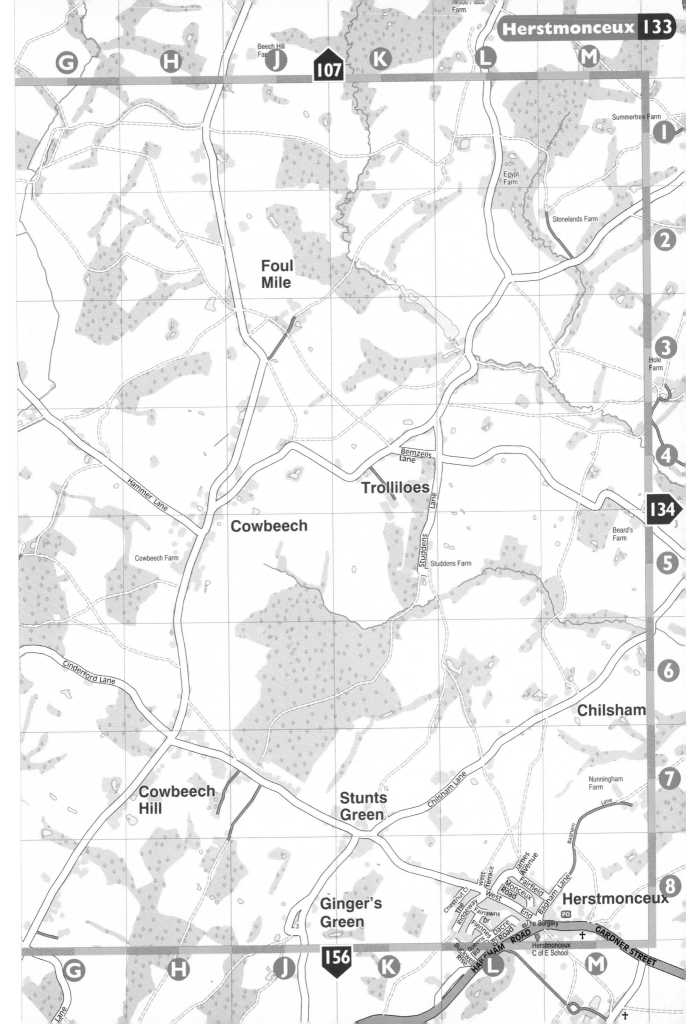

G  H  J  107  K  L  M

1

2

3

4

134

5

6

7

8

Beech Hill Farm

Summertree Farm

Egypt Farm

Stonelands Farm

Hole Farm

Furnace Brook

**Foul Mile**

Bemzells Lane

**Trolliloes**

Beard's Farm

Hammer Lane

Studdens Lane

**Cowbeech**

Studdens Farm

Cowbeech Farm

Cinderford Lane

**Chilsham**

Nunningham Farm

**Cowbeech Hill**

**Stunts Green**

Chilsham Lane

Bagham Lane

James Avenue

West Terrace

Fairfield

Monceux Road

West End

**Ginger's Green**

Chestnut Cl

The Ridgeway

Fairlawns Dr

Flennes Dacre

Queens Rd

Buckwell Rise

The Surgery

PO

**Herstmonceux**

Herstmonceux C of E School

G  H  J  156  K  L  M

HAILSHAM ROAD

GARDNER STREET

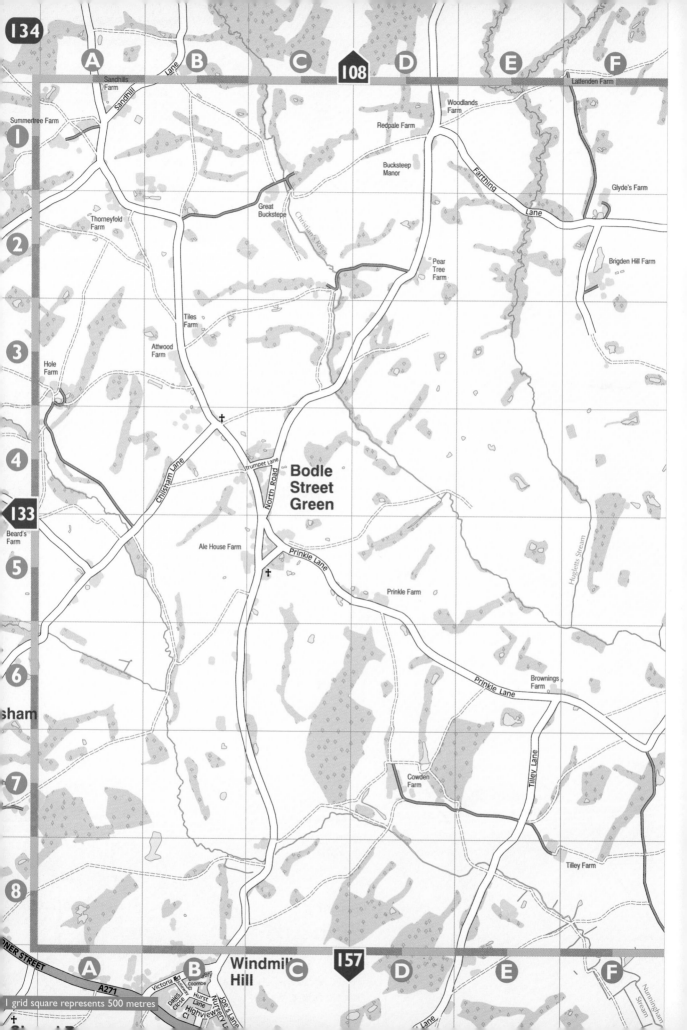

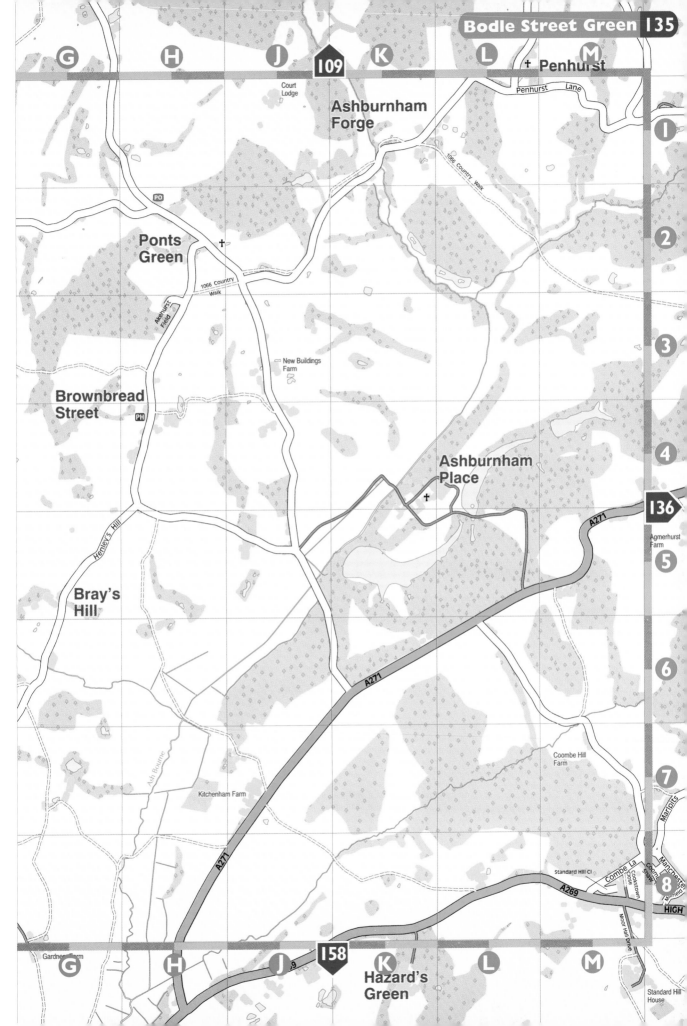

G H J **109** K L M † **Penhurst**

Penhurst Lane

Court
Lodge

**Ashburnham
Forge**

1066 Country Walk

I

PO

**Ponts
Green** †

1066 Country Walk

Akehurst Field

2

New Buildings
Farm

3

**Brownbread
Street**

PH

**Ashburnham
Place**

†

4

Henley's Hill

**136**

A271

Agmerhurst
Farm

5

**Bray's
Hill**

Ash Bourne

A271

6

Coombe Hill
Farm

Kitchenham Farm

7

A271

Marliots

Coomb Staple

Cookstown Close

Manchester

Mayfield

Standard Hill Cl

Combe La

A269

8

HIGH

Moot Hall Drive

G H J .9 **158** K **Hazard's
Green** L M

Gardner Farm

Standard Hill
House

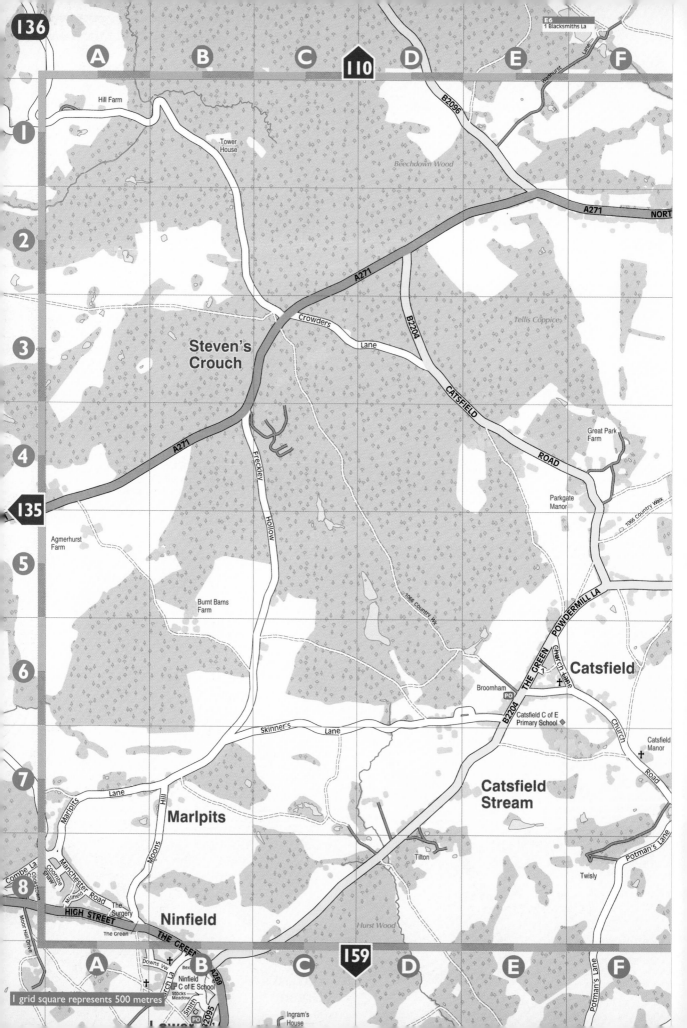

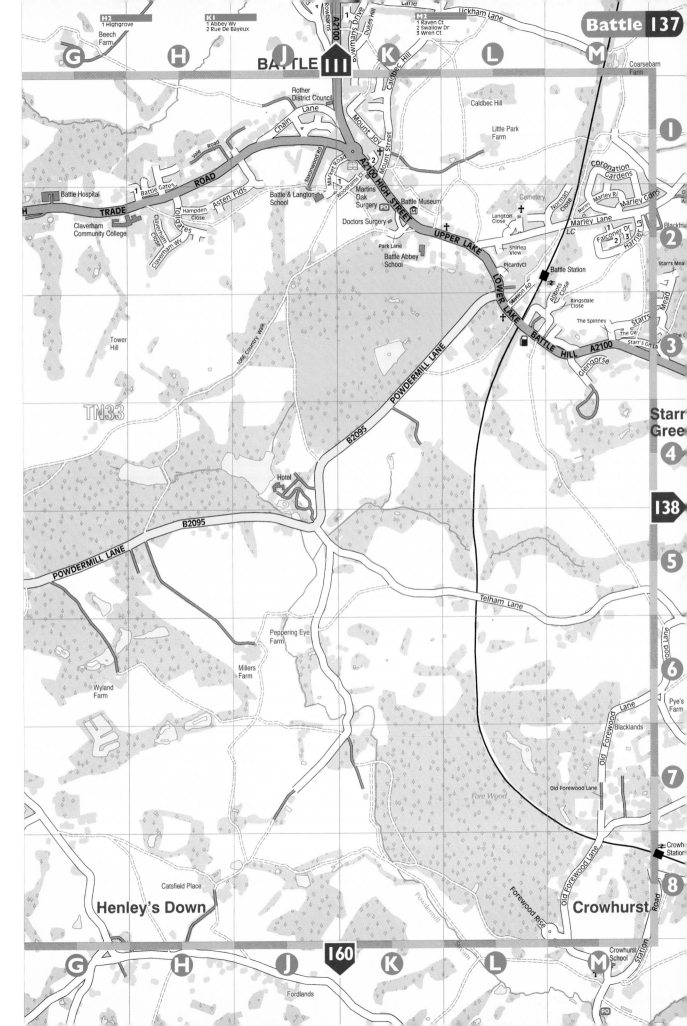

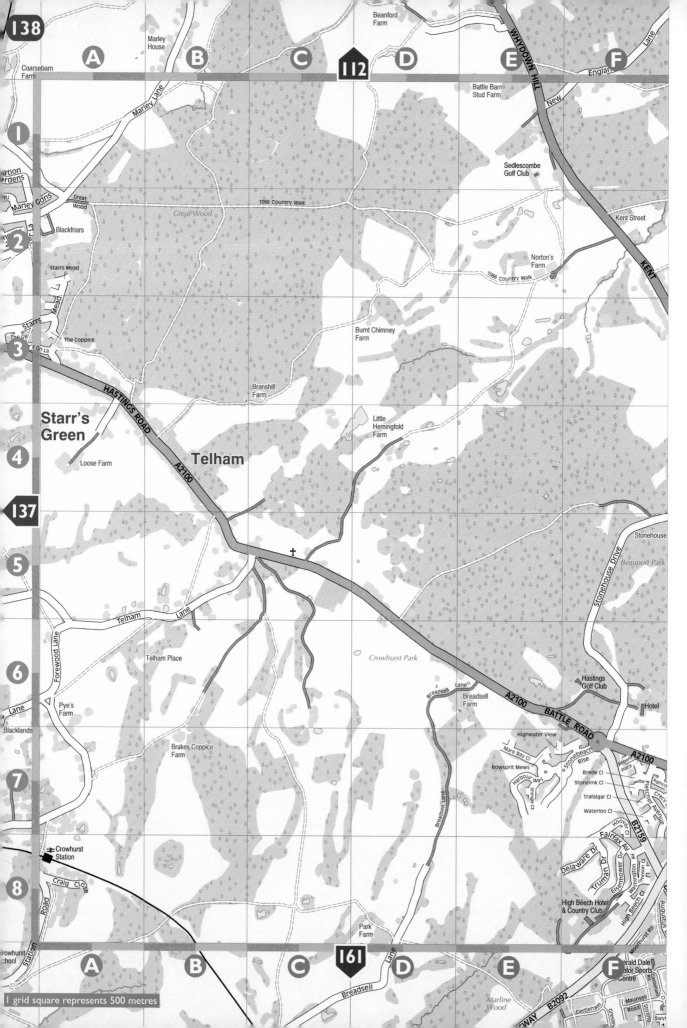

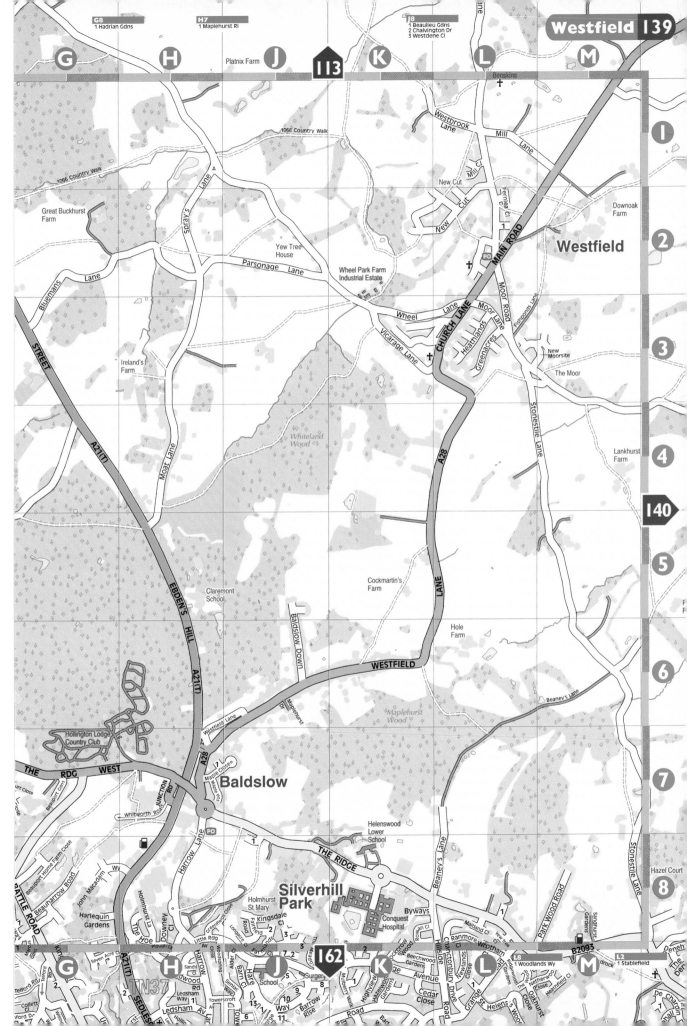

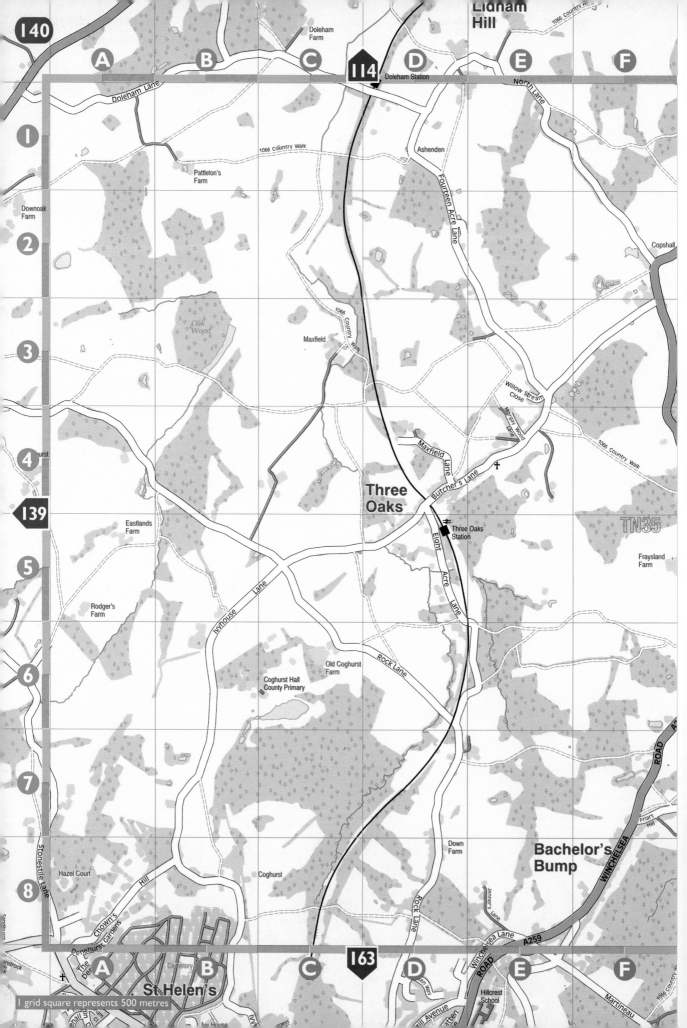

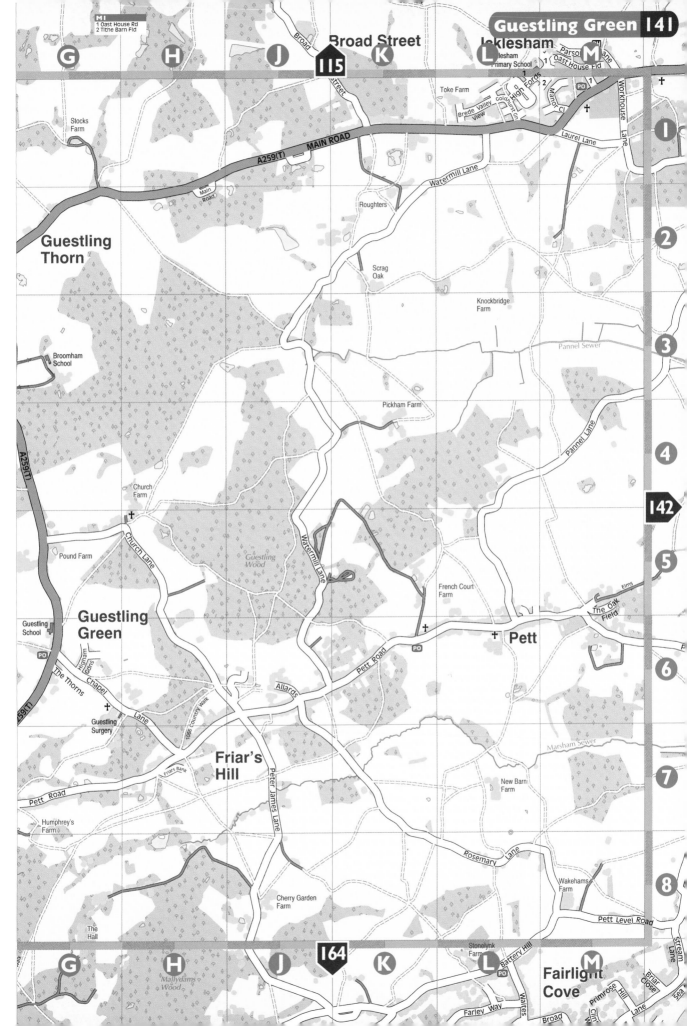

M1
1 Oast House Rd
2 Tithe Barn Fld

G   H   J   115   Broad Street   K   Icklesham   L   M

Broad Street

Icklesham Primary School

Parsonage Lane

Oast House Fld

Toke Farm

Brede Valley View

Goldhurst Cr

High St

Fords

Manor Cl

PO 7

Workhouse Lane

I

Stocks Farm

A259(T)   MAIN ROAD   MAIN ROAD

Main Road

Laurel Lane

Watermill Lane

2

Guestling Thorn

Roughters

Scrag Oak

Knockbridge Farm

Pannel Sewer

3

A259(T)

Broomham School

Pickham Farm

Pannel Lane

4

Church Farm

142

Pound Farm

Church Lane

Guestling Wood

Watermill Lane

French Court Farm

Elms

The Oak Field

5

Guestling School

Guestling Green

PO

Higham Gdns

The Thorns

Chapel Lane

1066 Country Walk

Allards

Pett Road

PO

Pett

6

A259(T)

Guestling Surgery

Friar's Bank

Friar's Hill

Peter James Lane

Marsham Sewer

New Barn Farm

7

Pett Road

Humphrey's Farm

Rosemary Lane

Wakehams Farm

8

Cherry Garden Farm

Pett Level Road

The Hall

G   H   J   164   K   Stonelynk Farm   L   Battery Hill   M

Mallydams Wood

Fairlight Cove

Farley Way

Waites

Broad

Primrose Hill

Stream Lane

Briar Close

Sea

PO

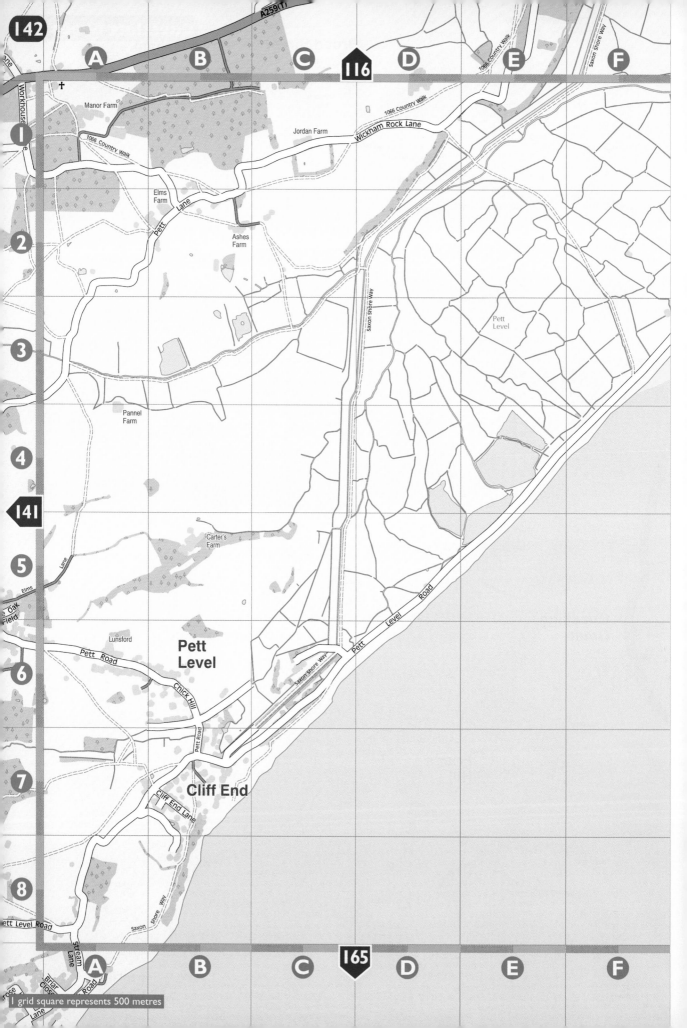

142

A B C 116 D E F

I

2

141

3

4

5

6

7

8

A B 165 C D E F

† Workhouse

Manor Farm

1066 Country Walk

Elms Farm

Pett Lane

Ashes Farm

Jordan Farm

Wickham Rock Lane

1066 Country Walk

Saxon Shore Way

Pett Level

Pannel Farm

Carter's Farm

Elms

The Oak Field

Lunsford

Pett Road

Pett Level

Chick Hill

Pett Road

Saxon Shore Way

Pett Level Road

Cliff End

Cliff End Lane

Saxon Shore Way

Stream Lane

Pett Level Road

Briar Close

Rose Lane

A259(T)

1 grid square represents 500 metres

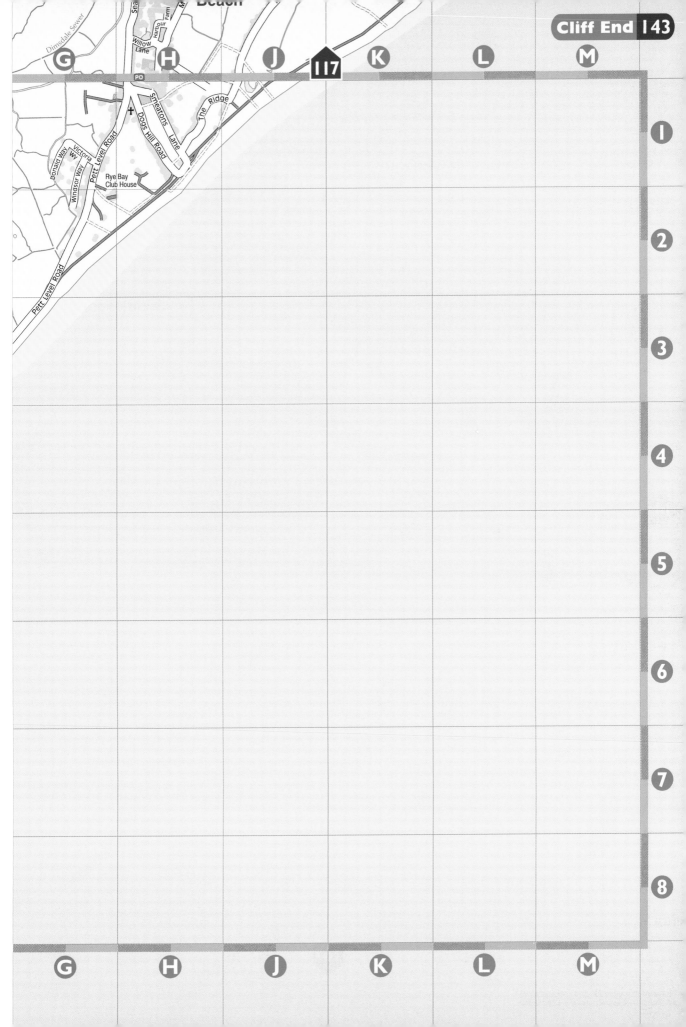

G H J 117 K L M

Dimsdale Sewer

Beach

Willow Lane

Harbour

Sea

Farm

The Ridge

Smeatons Lane

Dogs Hill Road

Pett Level Road

Donald Way

Victoria Way

Windsor Way

Pett Level Road

Rye Bay
Club House

PO

Pett Level Road

1
2
3
4
5
6
7
8

G H J K L M

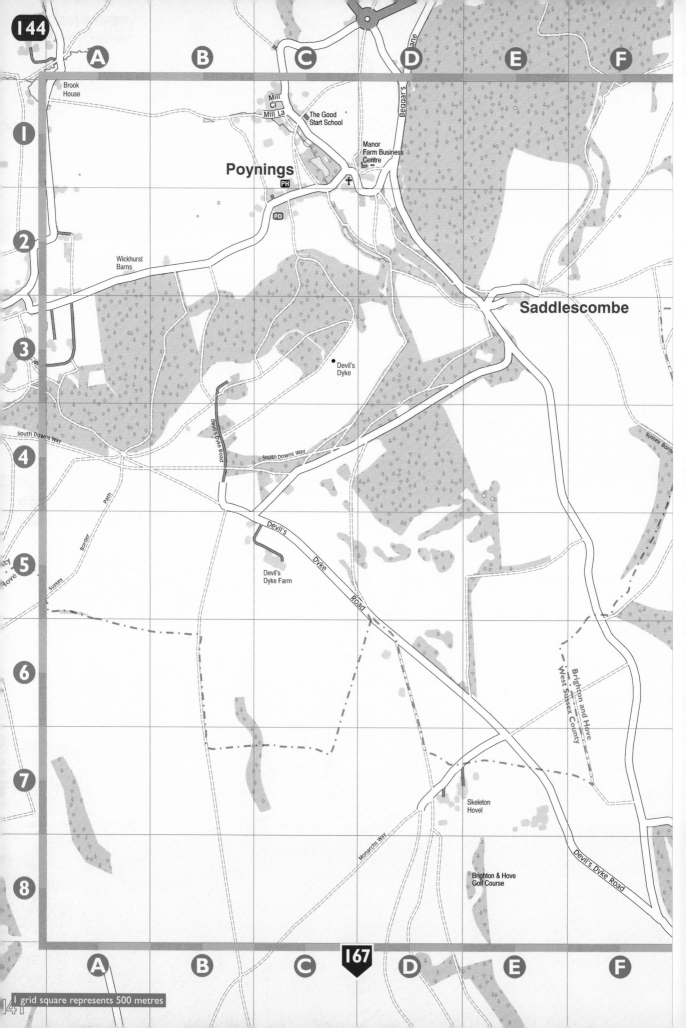

Ⓐ Ⓑ Ⓒ Ⓓ Ⓔ Ⓕ

Brook
House

Ⓘ

Mill
Cl
Mill La
The Good
Start School

Manor
Farm Business
Centre

**Poynings**

PH

PO

Ⓢ2

Wickhurst
Barns

**Saddlescombe**

Ⓢ3

Devil's
Dyke

Devil's Dyke Road

south Downs Way

Ⓢ4

South Downs Way

Border Path

Devil's

Ⓢ5

Sussex

Devil's
Dyke Farm

Dyke

Road

Ⓢ6

Brighton and Hove
West Sussex County

Ⓢ7

Skeleton
Hovel

Sussex Border

Monarchs Way

Devil's Dyke Road

Ⓢ8

Brighton & Hove
Golf Course

Ⓐ Ⓑ Ⓒ ▼167 Ⓓ Ⓔ Ⓕ

1 grid square represents 500 metres

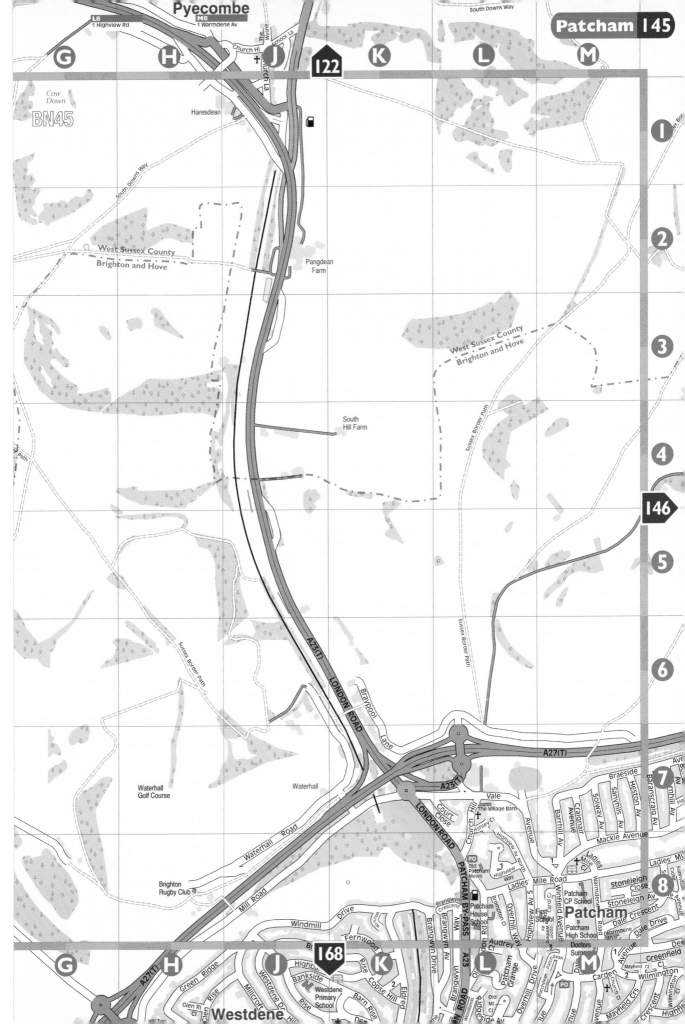

G H J 124 K L M

Plumpton

South Downs Way

Plumpton Plain

I

2

3

4

148

5

6

7

8

Streathill
Farm

Buckland
Bank

South Downs Way

South Downs Way

Stanmer
Down

St Mary's
Farm

East Sussex County
Brighton and Hove

Ridge Rd

Ridge Road

Balmer
Farm

Housedean
Farm

University
of Sussex

Ridge
Road

Falmer House Road

Park Street

Mill Street

Middle
Street

A27(T)

New
Barn

LEWES ROAD

Station S

Falmer
Station

South
St

Park St

East St

Falmer

B2123

G H J 170 K L M

University
of Brighton

versity
of Brighton

Egginton

Village Way

THE DR

Loose
Bottom

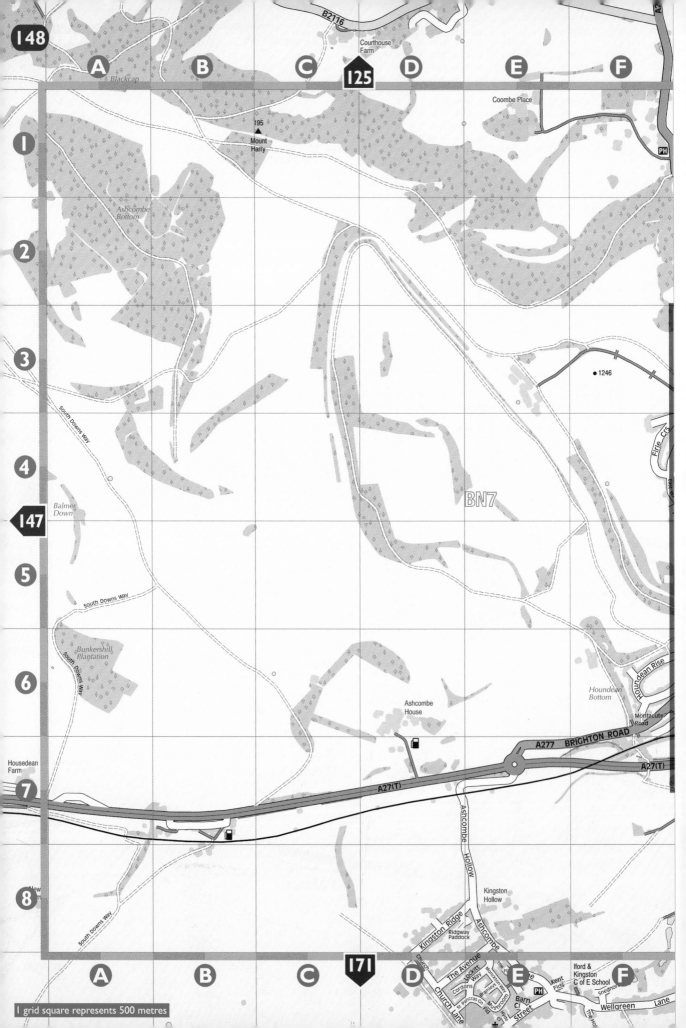

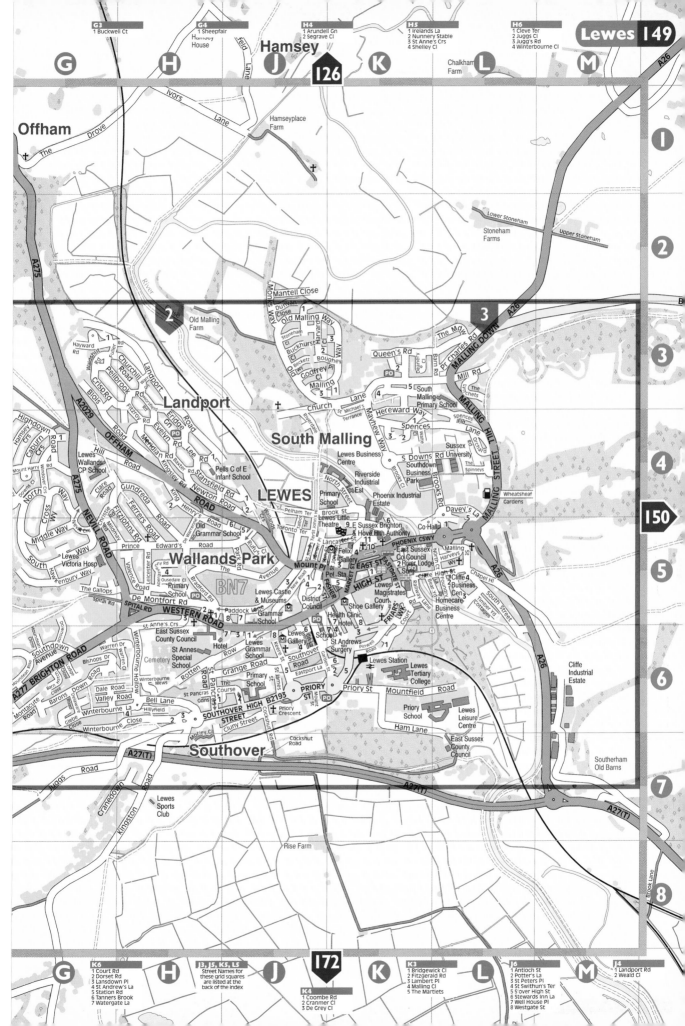

Hamsey

126

Offham

Landport

South Malling

LEWES

Wallands Park

Southover

150

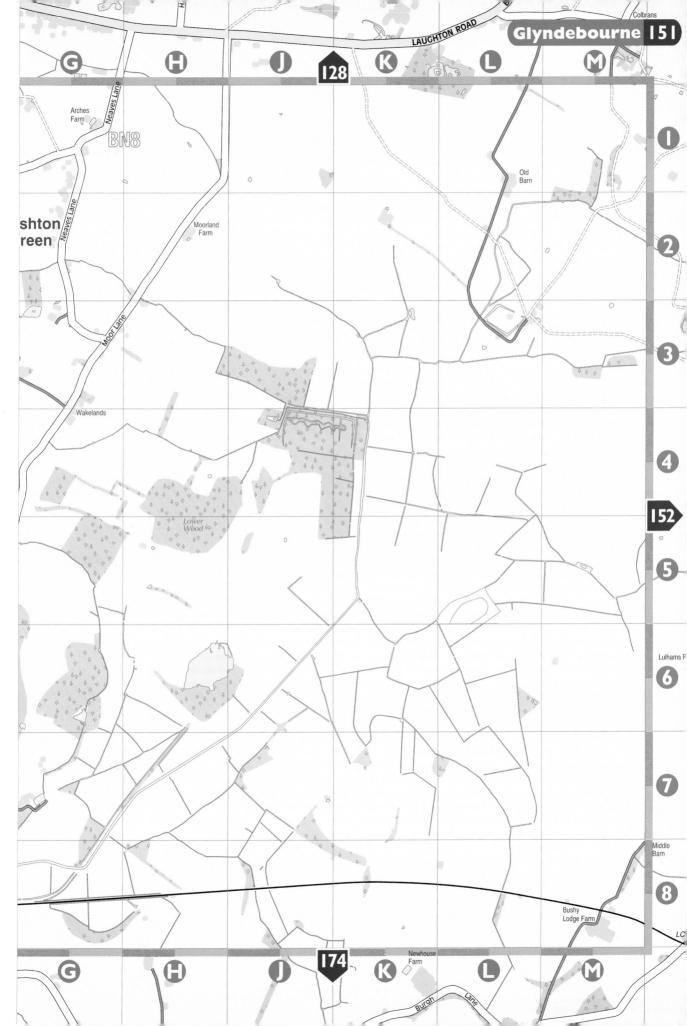

Colbrans

G    H    J    **128**    K    L    M

**I**

Arches
Farm

**BN8**

**2**

shton
reen

Moorland
Farm

Old
Barn

Neaves Lane

Neaves Lane

Moor Lane

**3**

Wakelands

**4**

Lower
Wood

**152**

**5**

Lulhams F

**6**

**7**

Middle
Barn

**8**

Bushy
Lodge Farm

LC

Newhouse
Farm

Burgh Lane

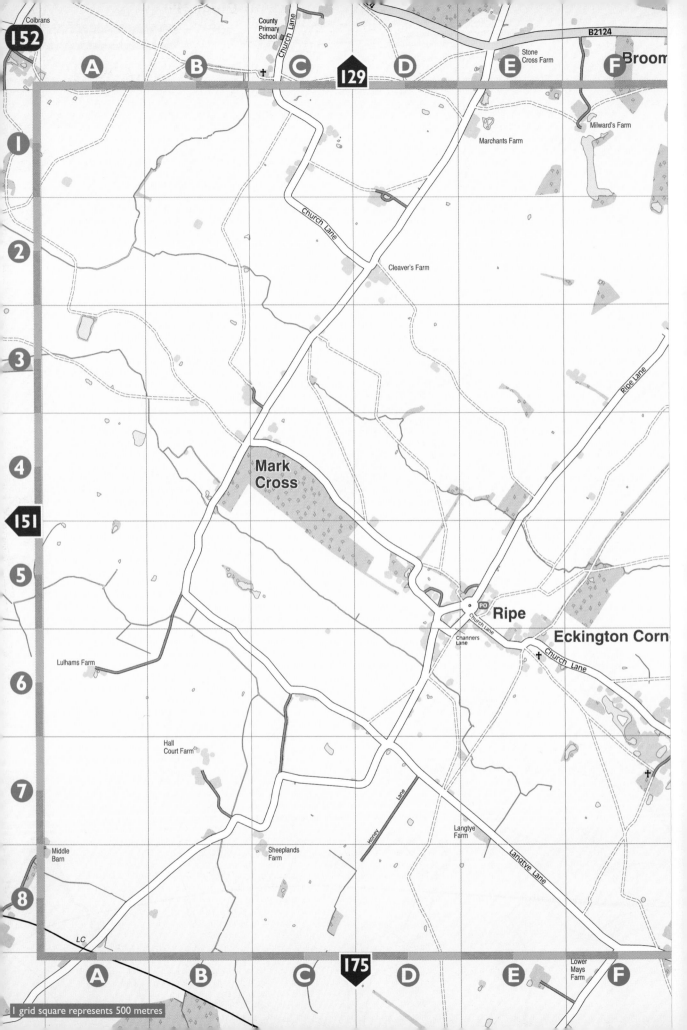

Colbrans

A B C 129 D E F Broom

County
Primary
School

Church Lane

Stone
Cross Farm

B2124

1

Milward's Farm

Church Lane

Marchants Farm

2

Cleaver's Farm

3

Ripe Lane

4

Mark
Cross

151

5

PO Ripe

Eckington Corn

Channers
Lane

Church Lane

Lulhams Farm

Church Lane

6

Hall
Court Farm

7

Honey Lane

Langtye
Farm

Langtye Lane

Middle
Barn

Sheeplands
Farm

8

LC

Lower
Mays
Farm

A B C 175 D E F

1 grid square represents 500 metres

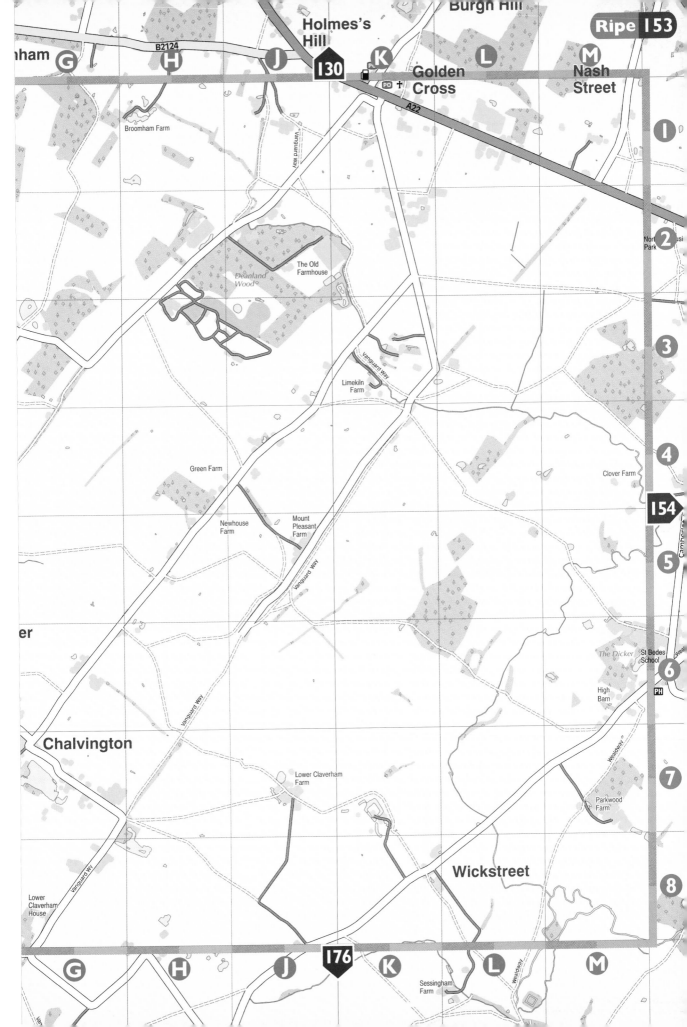

Burgh Hill

Holmes's Hill

Golden Cross

Nash Street

**G** **H** **J** **130** **K** **L** **M**

B2124

A22

Broomham Farm

North Busi Park

Deanland Wood

The Old Farmhouse

Vanguard Way

Vanguard Way

Limekiln Farm

Clover Farm

**154**

Green Farm

Newhouse Farm

Mount Pleasant Farm

Vanguard Way

The Dicker

St Bedes School

High Barn

Camberl

Weald

PH

Chalvington

Vanguard Way

Lower Claverham Farm

Wealdway

Parkwood Farm

Wickstreet

Lower Claverham House

Vanguard Wy

**G** **H** **J** **176** **K** **L** **M**

Sessingham Farm

Wealdway

**I**

**2**

**3**

**4**

**5**

**6**

**7**

**8**

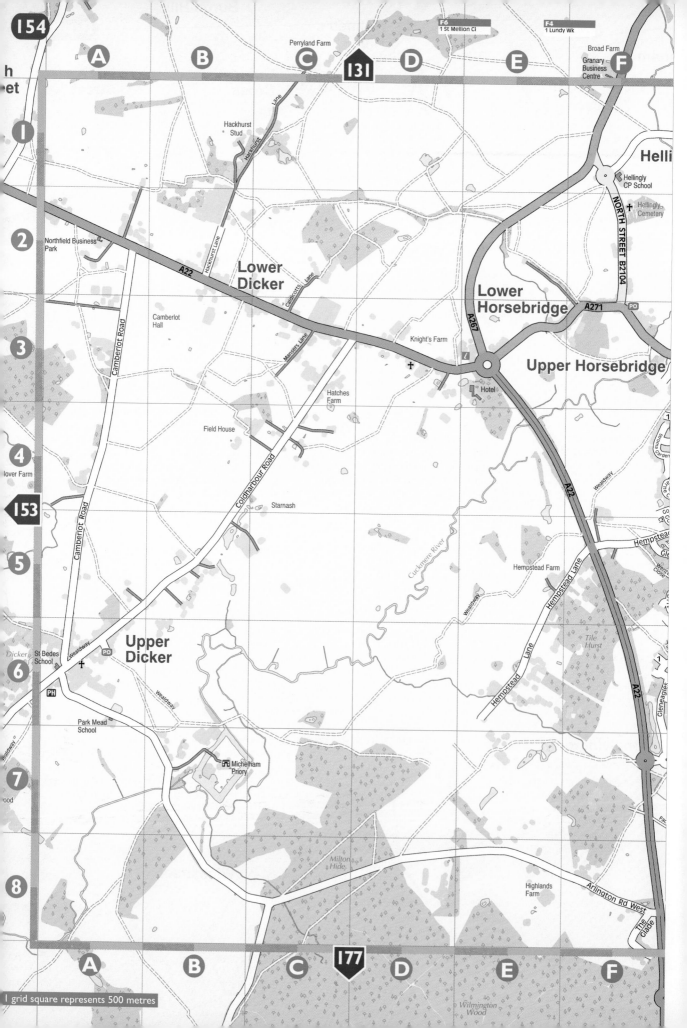

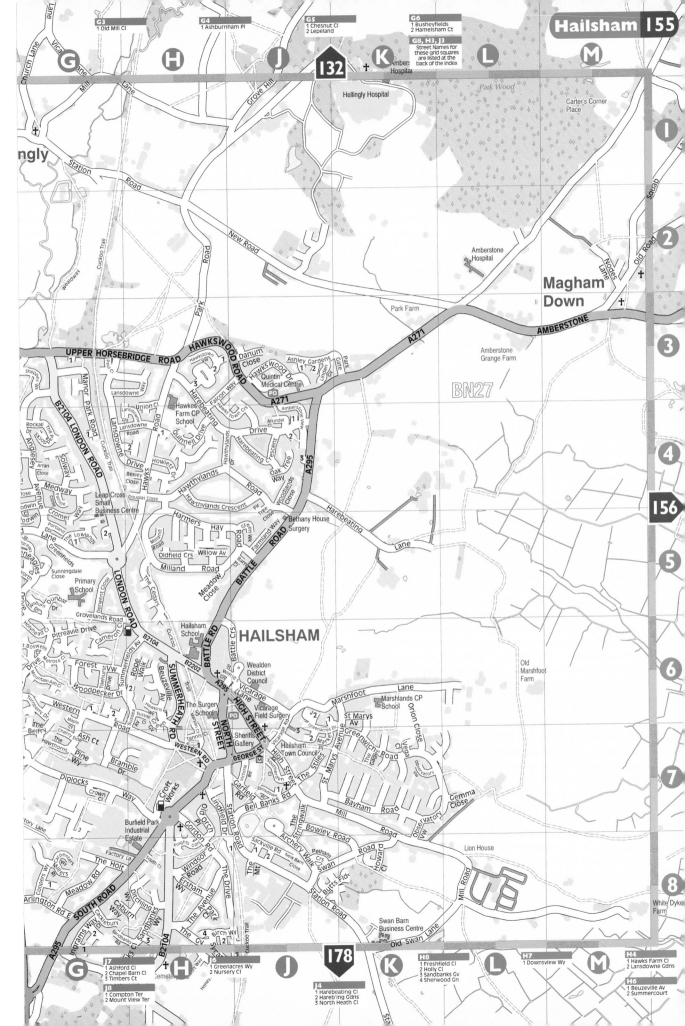

**132**

I

2

3

4

**156**

5

6

7

8

**Magham
Down**

BN27

**HAILSHAM**

**178**

G          H          J          K          L          M

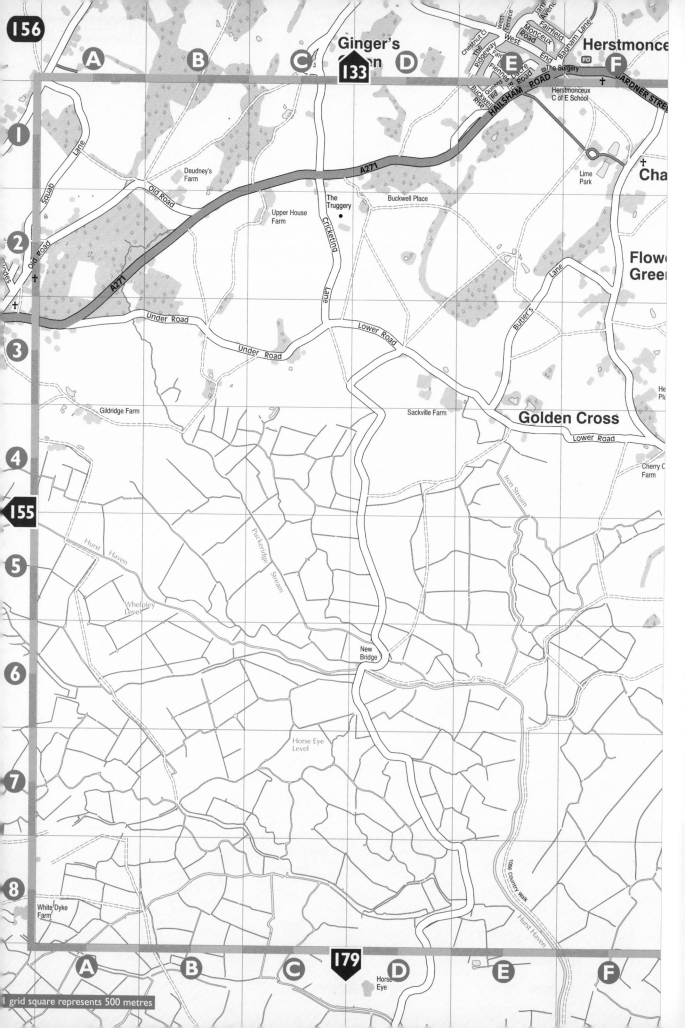

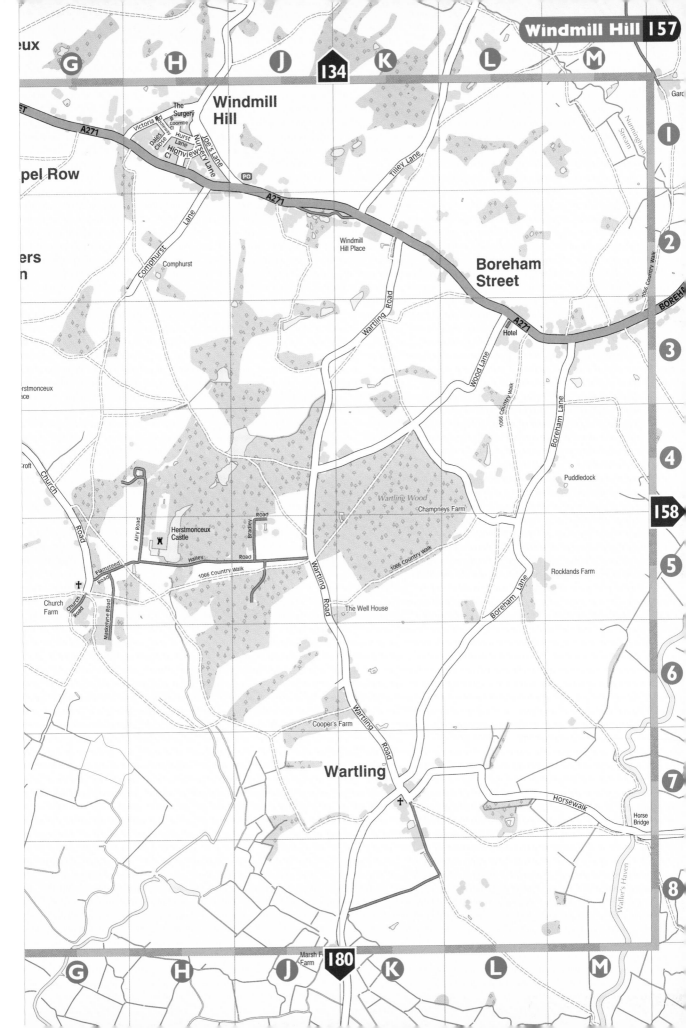

G H J **134** K L M

**I**

eux

Garc

Nunningham Stream

The Surgery

**Windmill Hill**

Victoria Rd

Coombe

Scaleway

Hurst

pel Row

Dales Close

A271

Highview

Cl

Joe's Lane

Nursery Lane

PO

A271

Comphurst Lane

Comphurst

ers n

Windmill Hill Place

Tilley Lane

**Boreham Street**

A271

Hotel

BOREHA

1066 Country Walk

**2**

**3**

Herstmonceux lace

Church Road

Croft

Airy Road

Wartling Road

Wood Lane

1066 country walk

Boreham Lane

Puddledock

**4**

**158**

Road

Herstmonceux Castle

Bradley

Wartling Wood

Champneys Farm

Rocklands Farm

**5**

Flamsteed Road

Halley

Road

1066 Country Walk

Wartling Road

The Well House

1066 Country Walk

Boreham Lane

Church Farm

Church Road

Maskelyne Road

**6**

Cooper's Farm

Wartling Road

**7**

**Wartling**

Horsewalk

Horse Bridge

**8**

Waller's Haven

G H J **180** K L M

Marsh F Farm

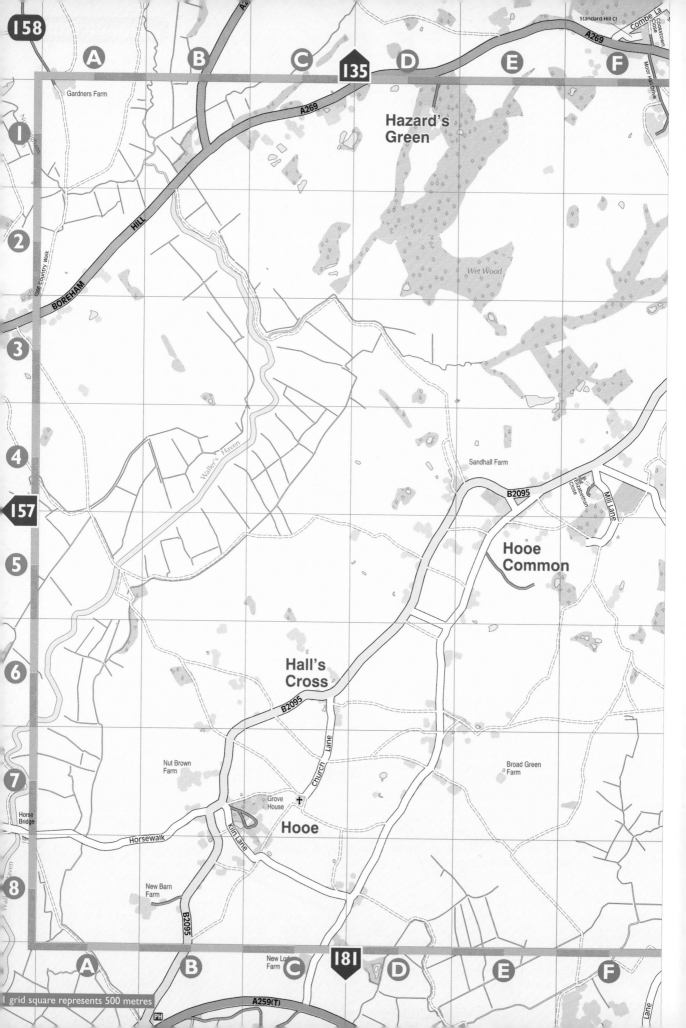

A    B    C    135    D    E    F

135

I

2

3

Gardners Farm

Hazard's
Green

BOREHAM    HILL

A269

A269

Standard Hill Cl
Cookstown
Close

Combe La

Moor Hall Drive

Rye Country Walk

Wet Wood

Waller's Haven

4

157

5

6

7

8

Sandhall Farm

B2095

Elizabethan
Close

Mill Lane

Hooe
Common

Hall's
Cross

B2095

Church Lane

Nut Brown
Farm

Broad Green
Farm

Grove
House

Hooe

Horse
Bridge

Horsewalk

Kiln Lane

Waller's Haven

New Barn
Farm

B2095

A    B    C    181    D    E    F

New Lodge
Farm

181

A259(T)

PH

1 grid square represents 500 metres

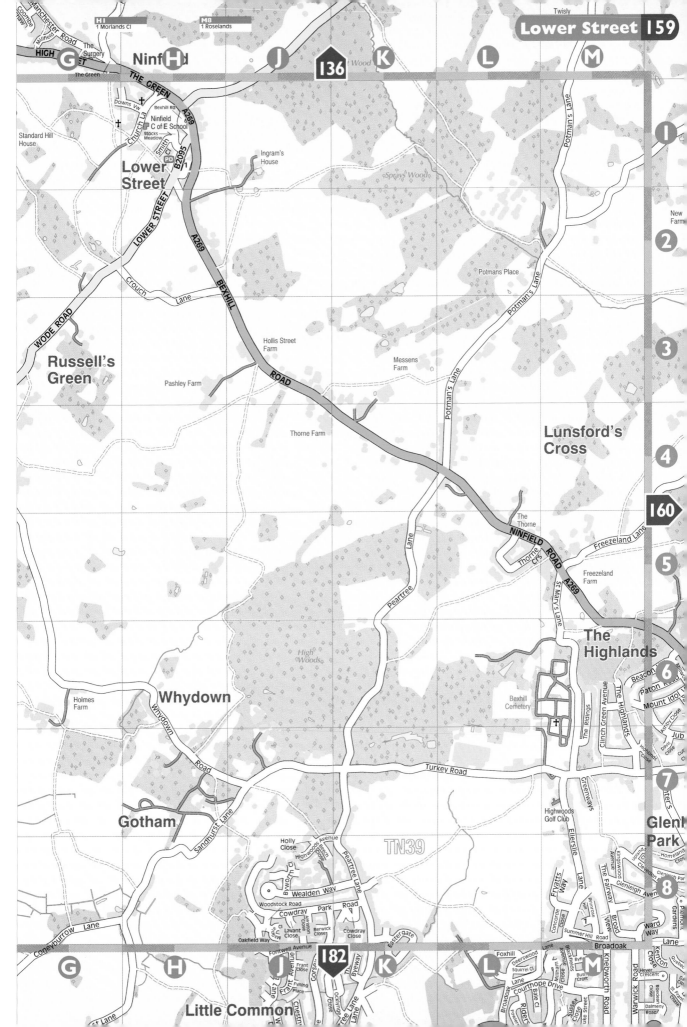

G  Ninf**H**d  J  **136**  K  L  M

HIGH St
The Surgery
The Green
THE GREEN
Downs Vw
Bexhill Rd
Ninfield C of E School
Church La
Stocks Meadow
Smith
PO
B2095
A269
Wood

Standard Hill House
**Lower Street**
LOWER STREET

Ingram's House

Sprays Wood

1

New Farm
2

Potmans Place

WODE ROAD
Crouch Lane
BEXHILL
A269

**Russell's Green**

Hollis Street Farm
ROAD
Messens Farm
Potman's Lane

3

Pashley Farm

Thorne Farm

**Lunsford's Cross**
4

160

Peartree Lane
NINFIELD ROAD
The Thorne
Thorne Crs
Freezeland Lane
5
Freezeland Farm
St Mary's Lane
A269

High Woods

**The Highlands**

Beacon
6
Paton Rd
Mount Idol
The Highlands

**Whydown**
Holmes Farm
Whydown Road

Bexhill Cemetery
The Ridings
Clinch Green Avenue

7

**Gotham**
Sandhurst Lane

Turkey Road
Highwoods Golf Club
Greenways
Ellerslie Lane

**Glenl Park**

Holly Close
Highwoods Avenue
TN39
Wealden Way
Woodstock Road
Cowdray Park Road
Peartree Lane
Eastergate

Fryatts Way
Glenleigh Aven
The Fairway
Broad View
Ward Way
8

Coneyburrow Lane
Oakfield Way
Fontwell Avenue
Lavant Close
Berwick Close
Cowdray Close
Concorde Close
Summer Hill Road
Broadoak
Foxhill
Deerswood

G  H  J  **182**  K  L  M

**Little Common**

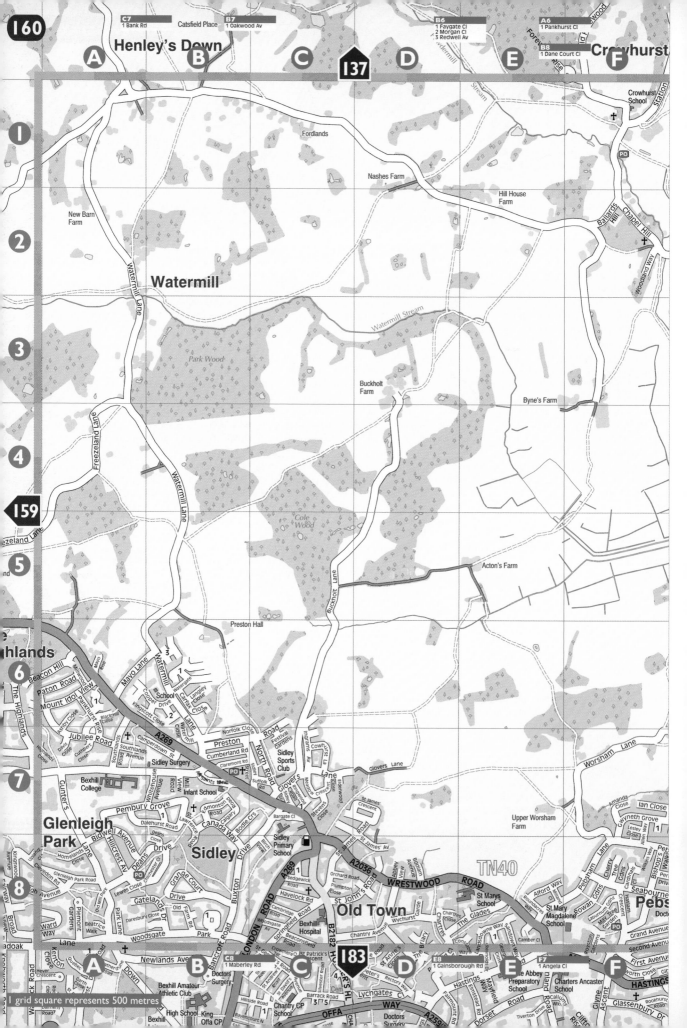

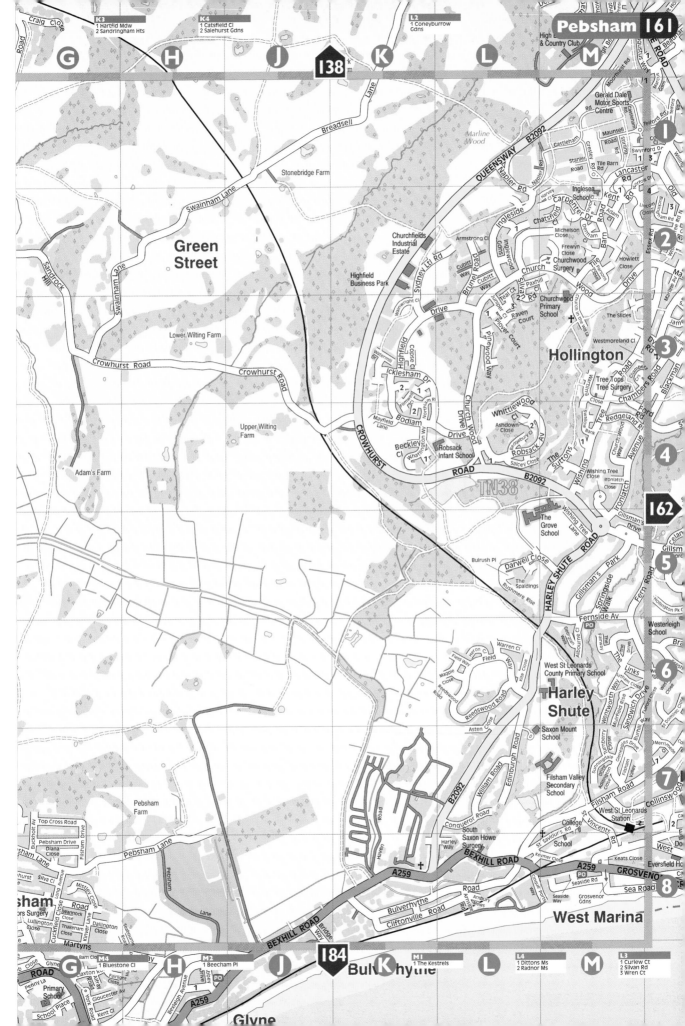

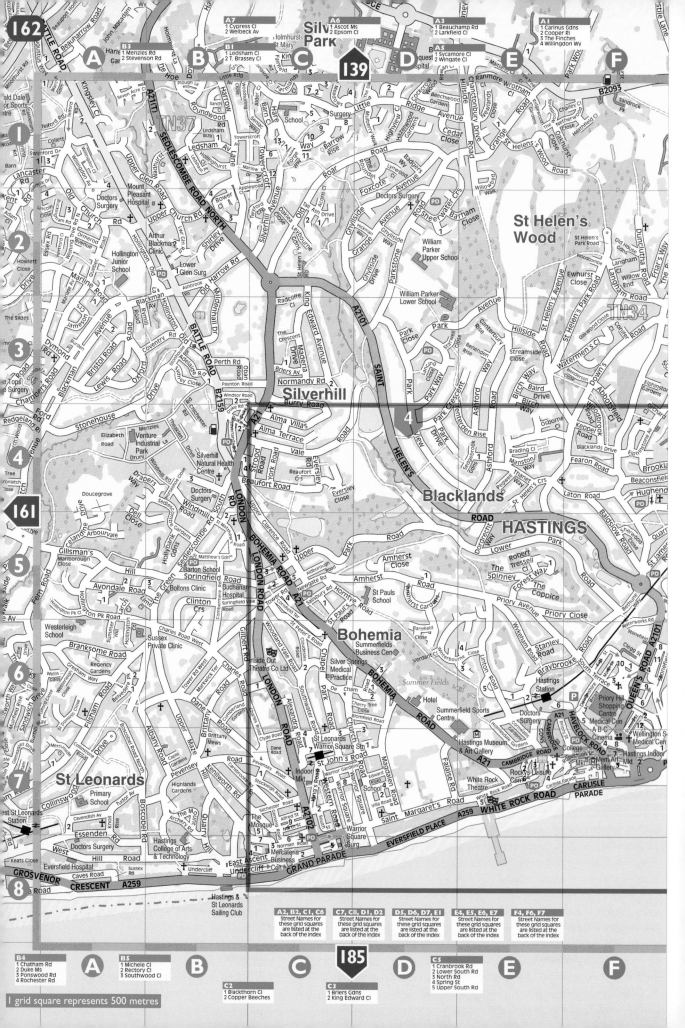

G1 1 Burwash Cl
G2 1 Amberstone Cl
G5 1 Becket Cl
2 Gladstone Rd
3 Saunders Cl
H2 1 Kenwood Cl
H3 1 Clement Hill Rd

164

St Helen's

THE RIDGE

Hillcrest School

North Seat

Ore

Clive Vale

Broomsgrove

Belmont

West Hill

Old Town

Hastings Castle

ELHAM PLACE - A259

The Fishermans Museum

Sea Life Centre

Rock-A-Nore Parade

Fairlight Place

A   B   C   **141**   D   E   F

The Hall

Country Walk

Cherry Garden Farm

     akehams Farm

ett Level Ro

Stonelynk Farm

Battery Hill

PO

**Fairlight Cove**

I

Lane

Mallydams Wood

Battery Hill

Hill Road

Farley Way

Broad Way

Primrose Hill

Cliff Way

Clinton Way

Waites

Knowle Road

Woodland Way

Lane

2

Fairlight Road

Coastguard

The Close

Lane

**Fairlight**

Warren Road

New Road

Meadow Way

Lower Waites

The Avenue

Rockmead Road

Commanders Walk

Shepherds Way

Corsethorn Way

Eyrsway

Blackthorn Way

Smugglers Way

Stock Dale

Bramble Way

Heather Way

3

Hastings County Park

Channel

Fire Hills

Saxon Shore Way

4

Fairlight Glen

Covehurst Bay

5

6

7

8

A   B   C   D   E   F

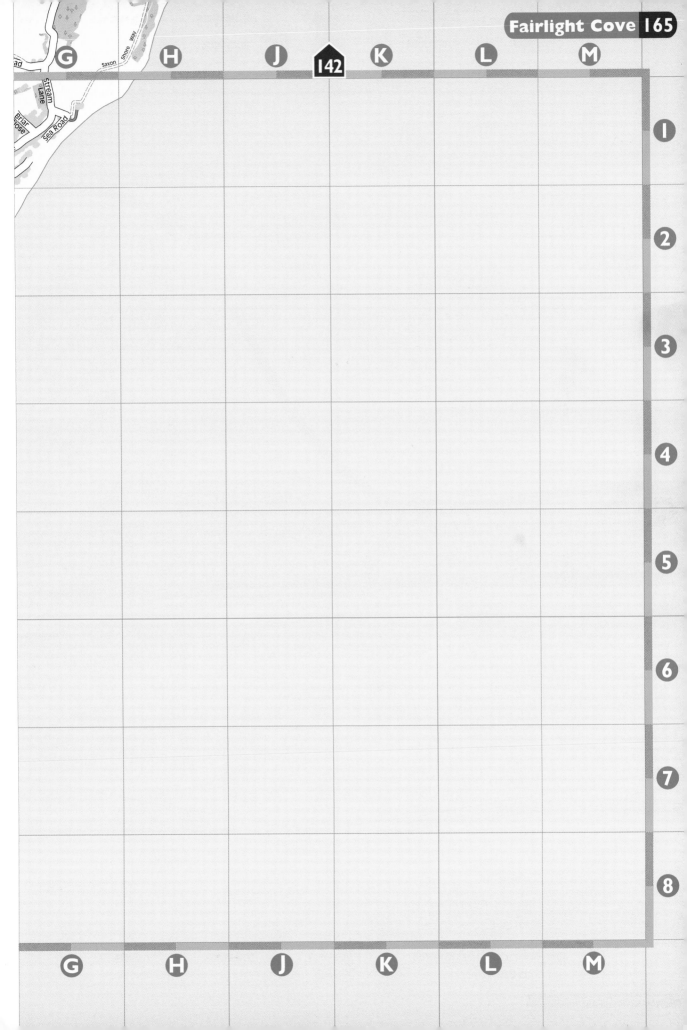

142

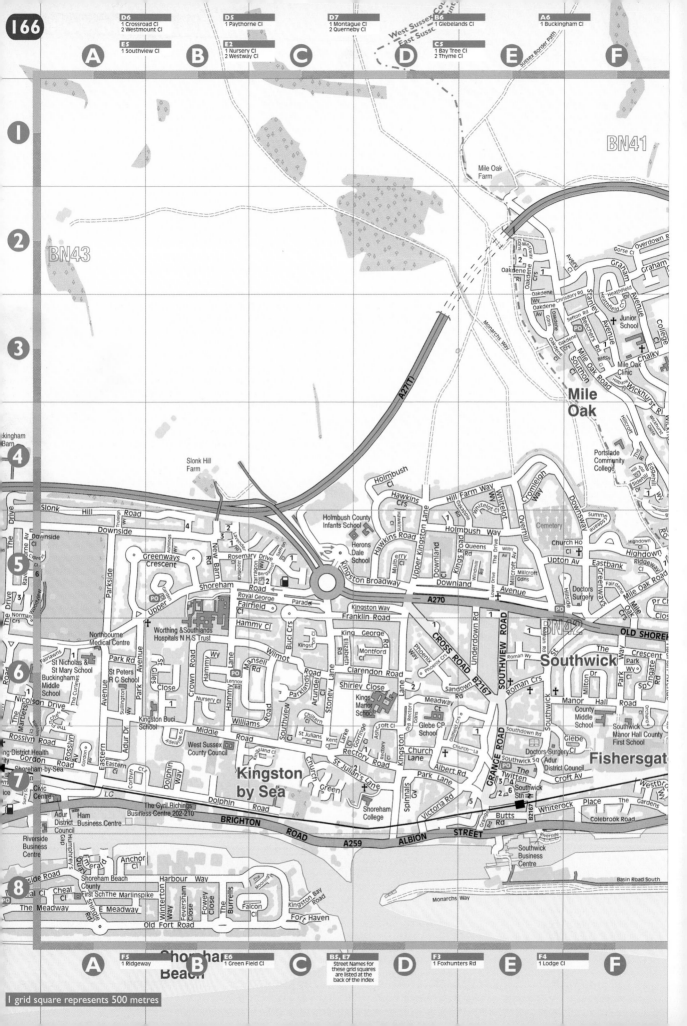

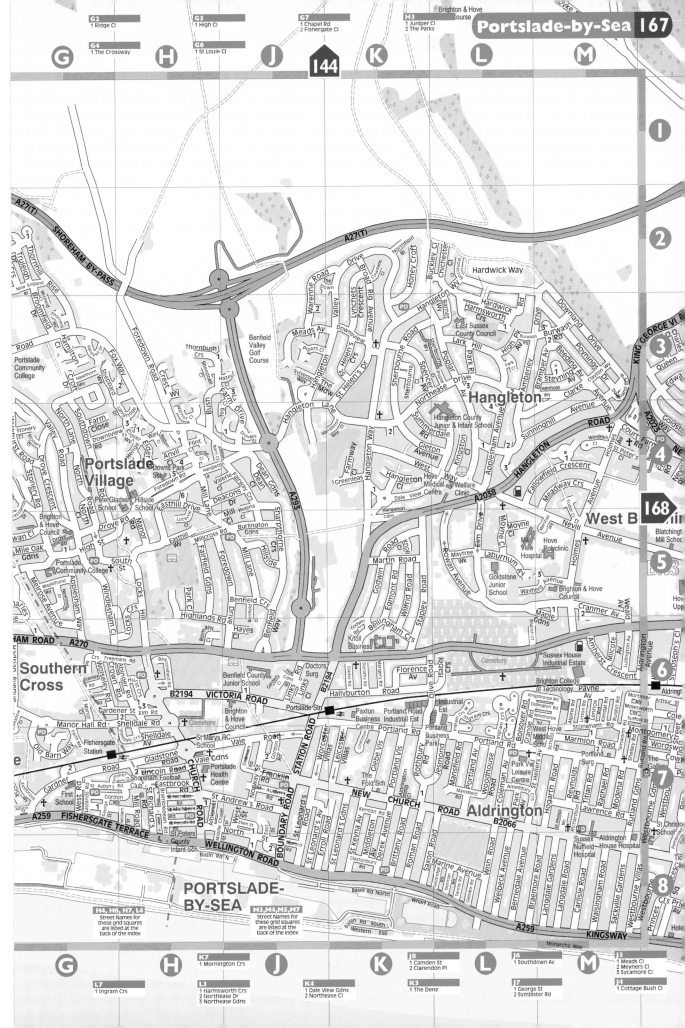

144

168

167

Brighton & Hove
Course

SHOREHAM BY-PASS

A27(T)

A27(T)

Benfield
Valley
Golf
Course

Thornbush
Crs

Portslade
Community
College

Portslade
Village

Hangleton

Hangleton County
Junior & Infant School

East Sussex
County Council

Hardwick Way

West B

Blatchingt
Mill Scho

Hove
Polyclinic

Brighton
& Hove
Council

Portslade
Community College

Goldstone
Junior
School

Brighton & Hove
Council

Sussex House
Industrial Estate

Bellingham
Knoll
Business Cen

Cemetery

SHAM ROAD

A270

Southern
Cross

Benfield County
Junior School

Doctors
Surg

B2194

B2194

VICTORIA ROAD

Hallyburton

Portslade Stn

Brighton
& Hove
Council

Fishersgate
Station

Paxton
Business
Centre

Portland Road Industrial Est

Industrial
Est

Portland
Business
Park

Brighton College
of Technology

Kingsthorpe Rd

West Hove
Middle
Sch/

Park View
Leisure
Centre

Portslade
Health Centre

Shoreham Football
Club

First
School

A259

FISHERGATE TERRACE

St Marys RC
School

St Peters
County
Infant Sch

WELLINGTON ROAD

STATION ROAD

NEW
CHURCH

ROAD

Aldrington

B2066

The
Fold Sch

Sussex Aldrington
Nuffield House Hospital
Hospital

A259

KINGSWAY

Monarchs Way

PORTSLADE-
BY-SEA

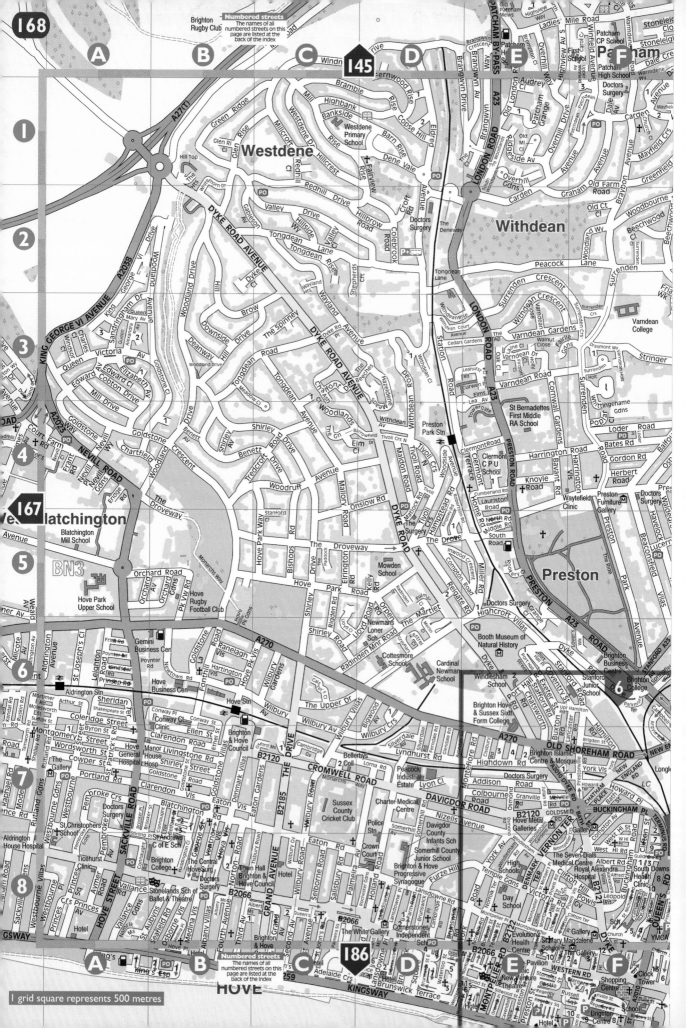

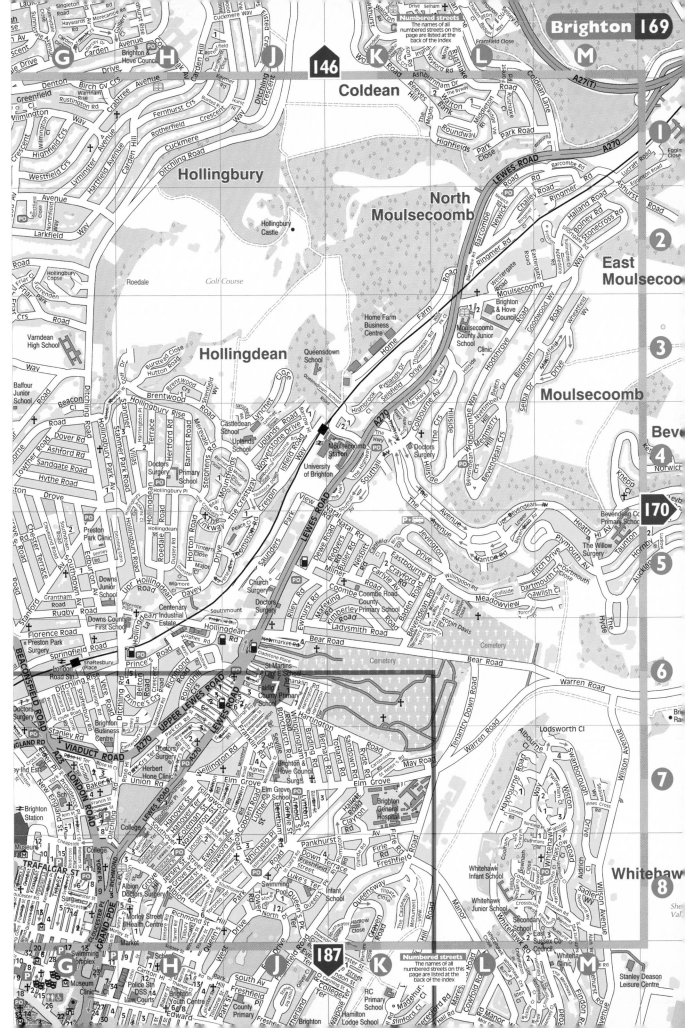

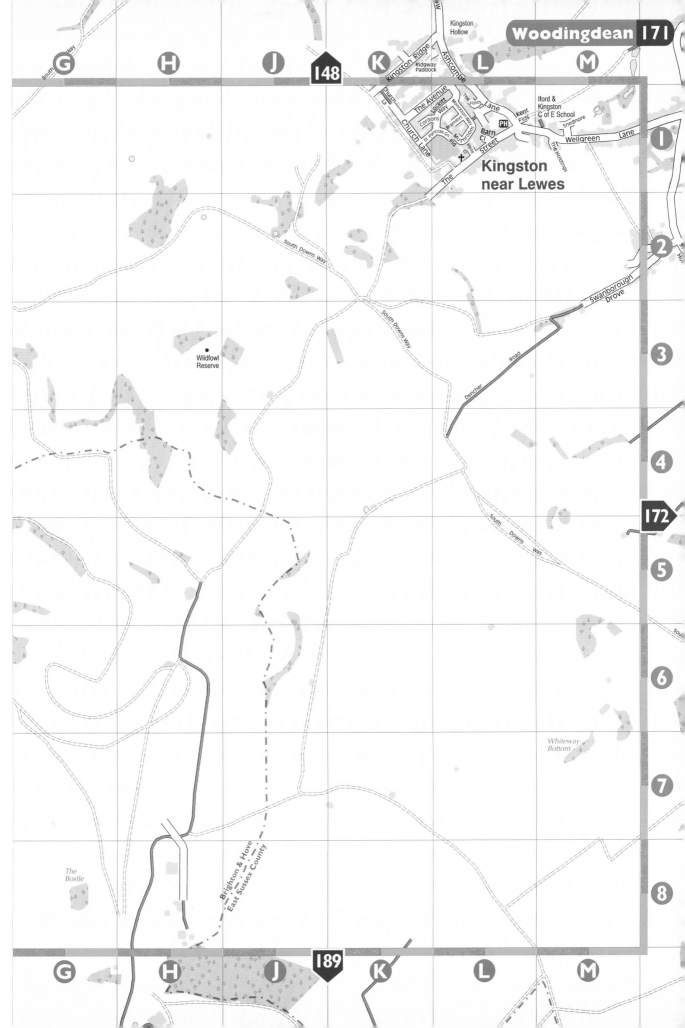

G

H

J

148

K

L

M

Kingston
Hollow

Kingston Ridge

Ridgway
Paddock

Ashcombe

Iford &
Kingston
C of E School

Snegnore

Wellgreen Lane

I

The Avenue

Kingston Ridge

Lockitt Way

Monceux Way

The Flints

Kent
Flds

PH

Church Lane

Cordons

St Pancras Gn

Bramleys

Fld

Mushroom

Barn
Cl

The Street

The Holdings

2

✝

**Kingston
near Lewes**

South Downs Way

Swanborough Drove

3

South Downs Way

Dencher

Road

4

172

South

Downs

Way

5

6

•
Wildfowl
Reserve

Whiteway
Bottom

7

*The
Bostle*

Brighton & Hove

East Sussex County

8

G

H

J

189

K

L

M

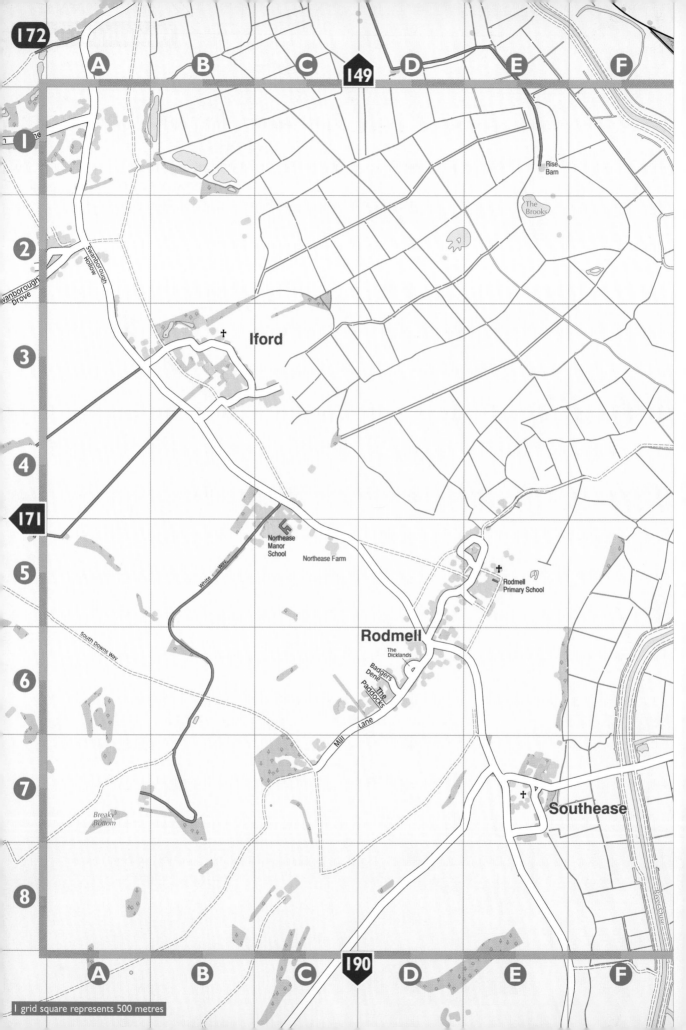

A    B    C    149    D    E    F

I

Rise
Barn

The
Brooks

2
Swanborough
Drove

Swanborough
Hollow

3    † Iford

4

171

Northease
Manor
School

Northease Farm

White    Way

5    † Rodmell
Primary School

South Downs Way

Rodmell

The Dicklands

6    Badgers
Dene    The Paddocks

Mill    Lane

7    Breaky
Bottom

† Southease

8

River Ouse

A    B    C    190    D    E    F

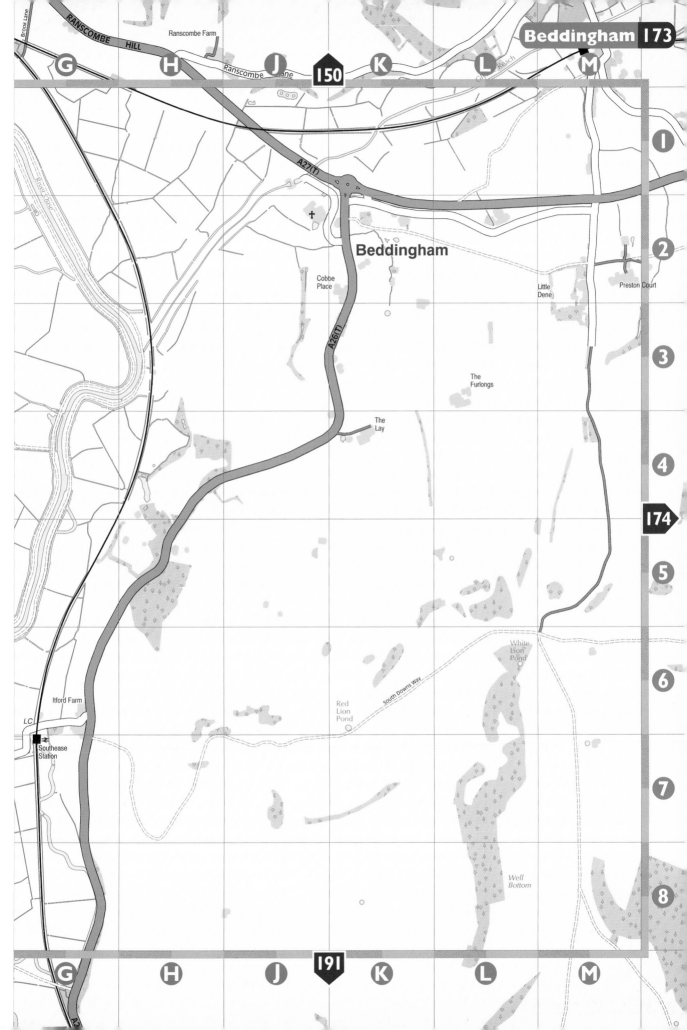

RANSCOMBE HILL

Ranscombe Farm

Ranscombe Lane

Brook Lane

River Ouse

A27(T)

**Beddingham**

Cobbe Place

A26(T)

The Furlongs

The Lay

Little Dene

Preston Court

Green Reach

White Lion Pond

Red Lion Pond

South Downs Way

Itford Farm

LC

Southease Station

Well Bottom

1   2   3   4   **174**   5   6   7   8

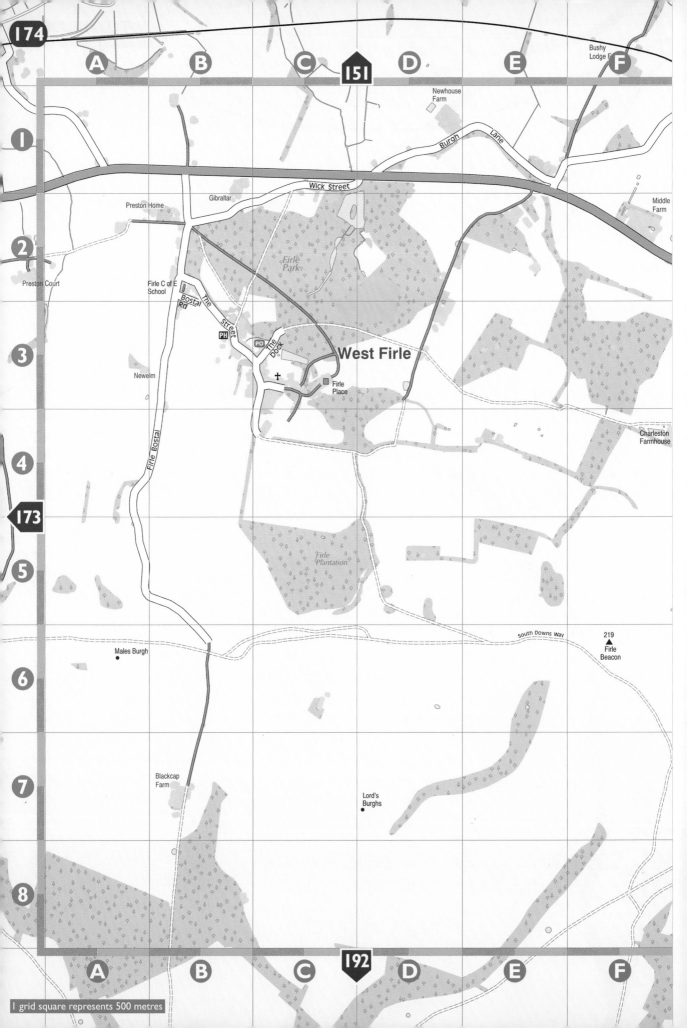

**A**  **B**  **C** 151 **D**  **E** Bushy Lodge F **F**

**1**

**2**

**3**

**4**

173

**5**

**6**

**7**

**8**

**A**  **B**  **C** 192 **D**  **E**  **F**

Newhouse Farm

Burgh Lane

Middle Farm

Wick Street

Preston Home

Gibraltar

Preston Court

Firle C of E School

Bostal Rd

The Street

Firle Park

PH

PO

The Dock

**West Firle**

Firle Place

Newelm

†

Firle Bostal

Charleston Farmhouse

Firle Plantation

South Downs Way

219 ▲ Firle Beacon

Males Burgh ●

Blackcap Farm

Lord's Burghs ●

I grid square represents 500 metres

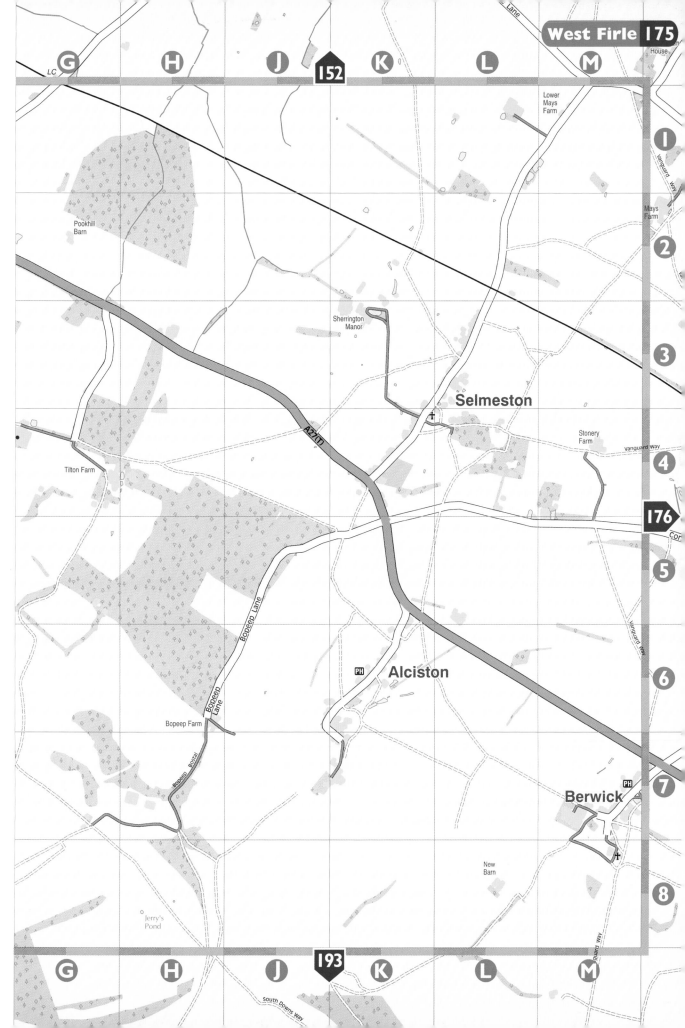

G    H    J  152    K    L    M

LC

House

Lane

Lower
Mays
Farm

1

Mays
Farm

Vanguard Way

2

3

Sherrington
Manor

**Selmeston**

Stonery
Farm

Vanguard Way

4

A27 (T)

176

cor

5

Tilton Farm

Bopeep Lane

Vanguard Way

6

PH

**Alciston**

Bopeep Lane

Bopeep Farm

Bopeep Bostal

PH

7

**Berwick**

New
Barn

8

Jerry's
Pond

south Downs Way

guard Way

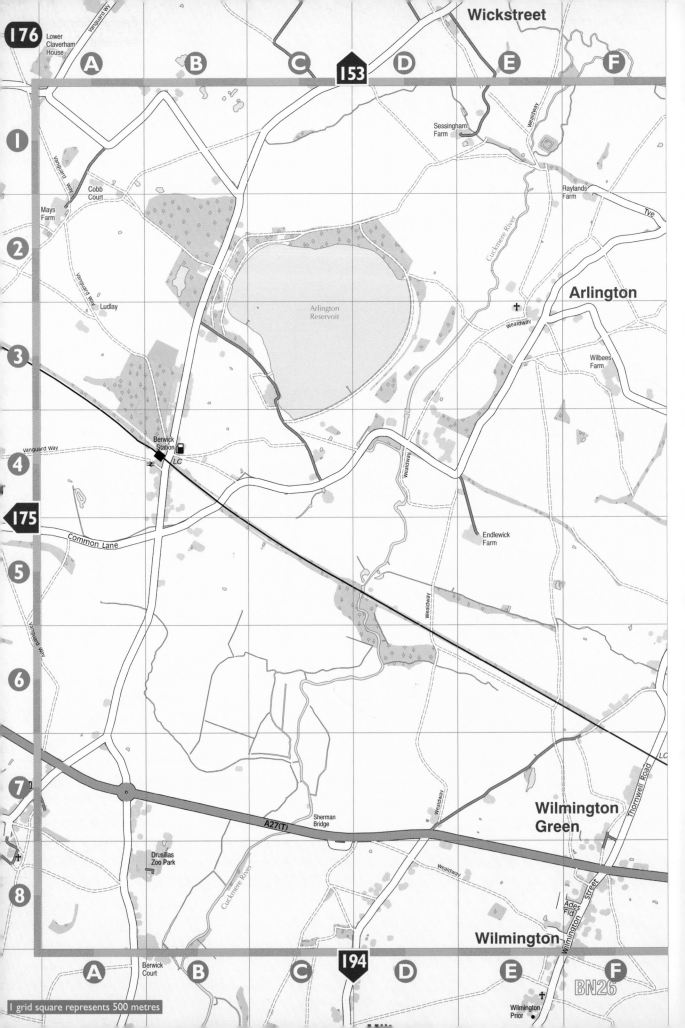

M8
1 Brown Jack Av
2 Diplock Cl
3 Grand Pde
4 Reynoldstown La

154

G  H  J  K  L  M

I

2

3

4

178

5

6

7

8

Highlands
Farm

The Glade

A295

A22

Woodside
Hall

Wilmington
Wood

Nate
Wood

Abbot's
Wood

● Nature Reserve

Caneheath

PH

Hill
Road

Bayley's
Lane

Post
Lane

Robin

Hayreed

Thornwell Road

Monkyn
Pyn

Wootton
Manor

Bay Tree Lane

POLEGATE BY-PASS

A22

A27(T)

Saverland
Palma
Honeycragg
Oakleaf Way
Green
Road

HAILSHAM ROAD

Brookside Av
St Leonards Ter
Albert Rd
Victoria Road
Brook street
Gosford Wy

Old Drive

A27(T)  LEWES ROAD

Hyperion Avenue
Sunstar Lane
Guisborough
Bahram Rd
Golden Miller
Lane

Manor Park
Medical Centre

Barons Way
Hilary Cl
Willow Dr
Wannock Road

Polegate Town
Council Office

Southfield

A22

G  H  J  K  L  M

195

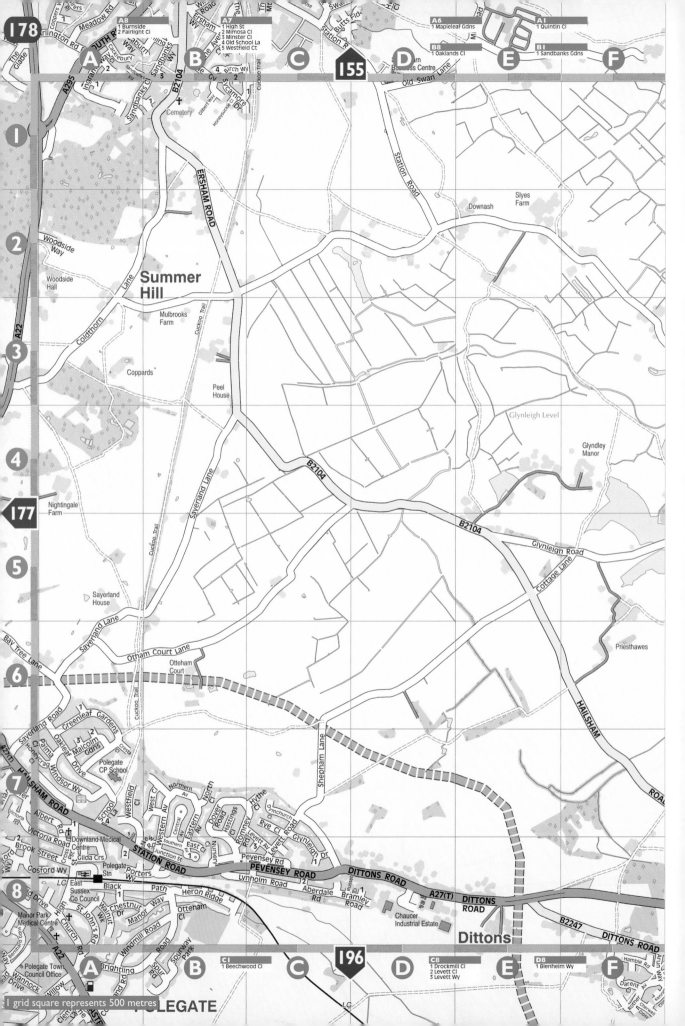

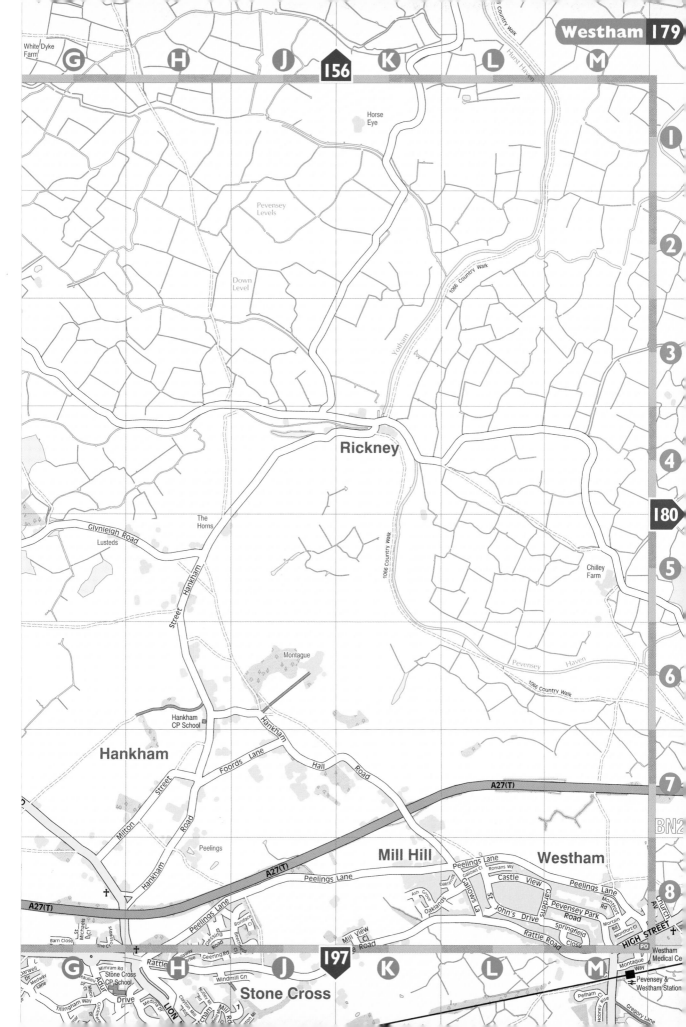

156

G H J K L M

Horse Eye

Pevensey Levels

Down Level

1066 Country Walk

Yotham

**Rickney**

The Horns

Glynleigh Road

Lusteds

1066 Country Walk

Chilley Farm

180

Hankham Street

Montague

Pevensey Haven

1066 Country Walk

Hankham CP School

**Hankham**

Foords Lane

Hankham

Hall Road

A27(T)

Milton Street

Hankham Road

Peelings

A27(T)

**Mill Hill**

Peelings Lane

Peelings Lane

Romans Wy

Callows Cl

Oakfields

Ash Grove

Oaklands

St John's Drive

Callows La

Castle View Gardens

Pevensey Park Road

Montfort Rd

**Westham**

Peelings Lane

Springfield Close

Mortain Rd

Montfort Rd

BN2

HIGH STREET

Church Av

PO

Westham Medical Ce

A27(T)

St Michaels Cl

Barn Close

The C

Mimram Rd

Rattle

Geering Rd

Windmill Gn

Beaulieu Dr

Medway Lane

Stone Cross CP School

Tillingham Way

Drive

LION

Merchant

Mill Rd

**Stone Cross**

197

Mill View Cl

Rattle Road

Glessing Road

Boniface Cl

Beechmill Cl

Mill View Cl

Pelham Cl

Montague Way

Pevensey & Westham Station

Gregory Lane

G H J K L M

I 1
2
3
4
5
6
7
8

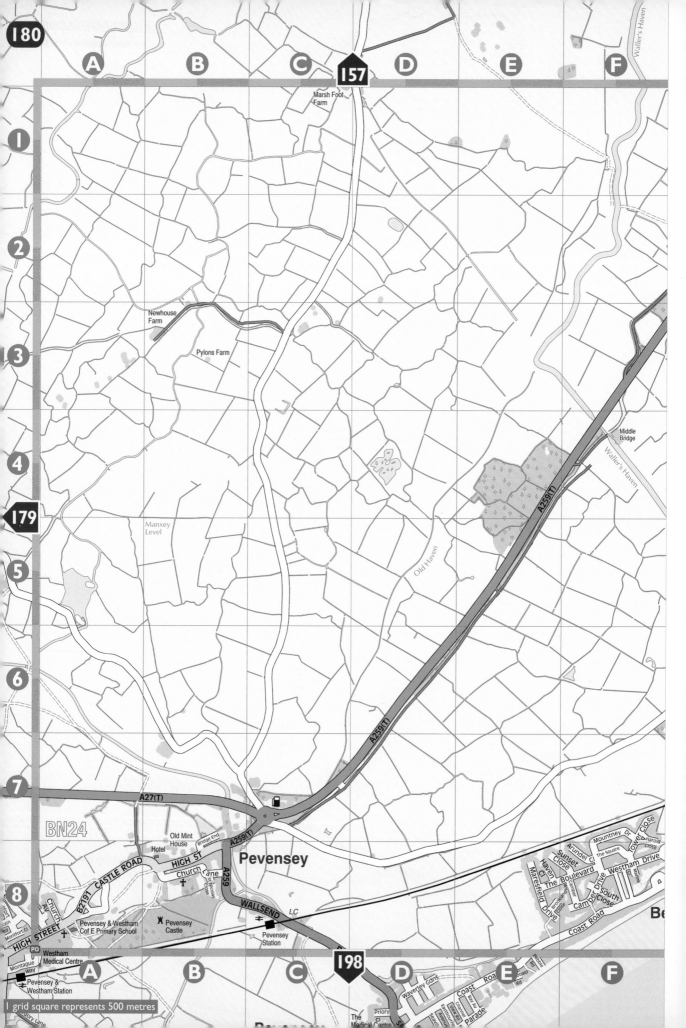

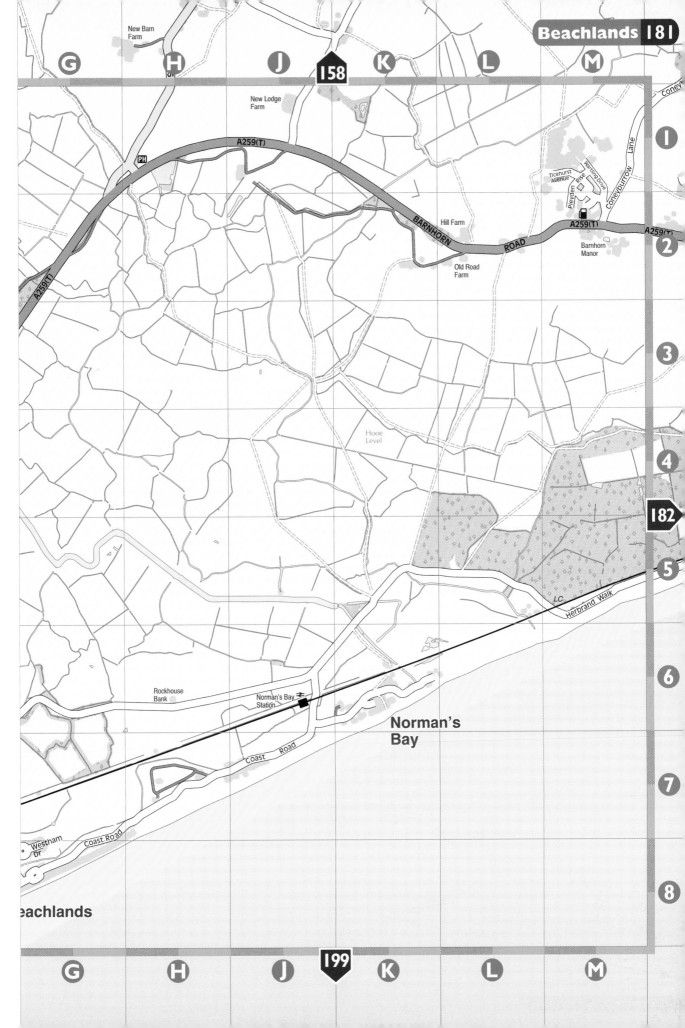

G      H      J      158      K      L      M

New Barn Farm

New Lodge Farm

A259(T)

PH

BARNHORN

Hill Farm

ROAD

A259(T)

A259(T)

Ticehurst Avenue

Pleyden Rise

Worting Drive

Coneyburrow Lane

Coney

Barnhorn Manor

Old Road Farm

I

2

3

Hooe Level

4

182

5

LC

Herbrand Walk

6

Rockhouse Bank

Norman's Bay Station

Norman's Bay

Coast Road

7

8

Westham Dr

Coast Road

eachlands

G      H      J      199      K      L      M

Pebsham

Doctors Surgery

Grand Avenue

Second Avenue

First Avenue

Rth Close

HASTINGS ROAD

Penny La

School Place

Primary School

A259(T)

AD

Brett Drive

Boxgrove Close

Megabowl

Mistler Close

Road

Silva Ci

Lullington Close

Gibb Close

Cuckfield Close

Khiver Lane

Dallington Close

Glyne Drive

Glyne Barn Close

Hurstwood Close

Claxton Road

York Road

Kent Ci

Gloucester Av.

Fairlight Close

Alfray Road

Martyns

Way

Bexleigh Avenue

Abbey Drive

A259

PO

1

Bexhill Road

BEXHILL ROAD

A259

Pebsham Lane

Seaborne

Road

161

Bulverhythe

Bulverhythe Road

Road

Sirtonville Road

Arnbury Mews

Arnbury Road

Road

Seaside Way

Grosvenor Gdns

Seaside Rd

PO

A259

GROSV

Sea Rd

Wes Marina

**Bulverhythe**

**Glyne Gap**

A 184

B

C

161

D

E

Wes Marina F

I

2

3

4

183

5

6

7

8

A B C D E F

A B C D E F

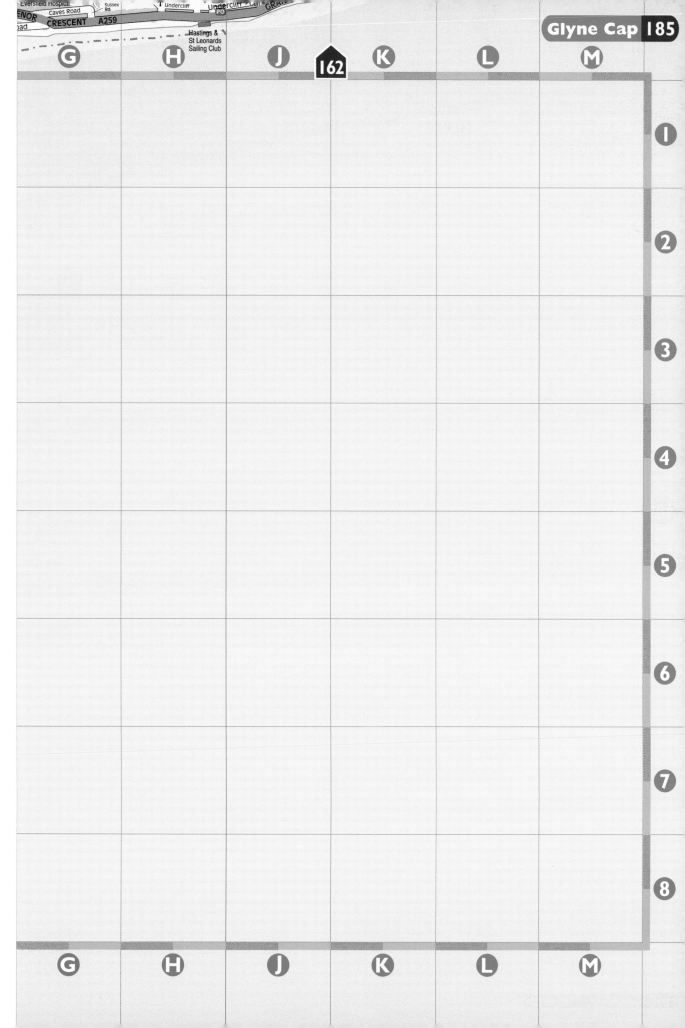

G H J 162 K L M

1
2
3
4
5
6
7
8

Eversfield Hospital
Caves Road
ENOR
CRESCENT A259
Sussex Rd
Undercliff
Undercliff
GRA
Hastings &
St Leonards
Sailing Club

Eversfield Hospital
Sussex
Undercliff
Undercliff
Cen
GRA
ad CRESCENT A259
Hastings &
St Leonards
Sailing Club

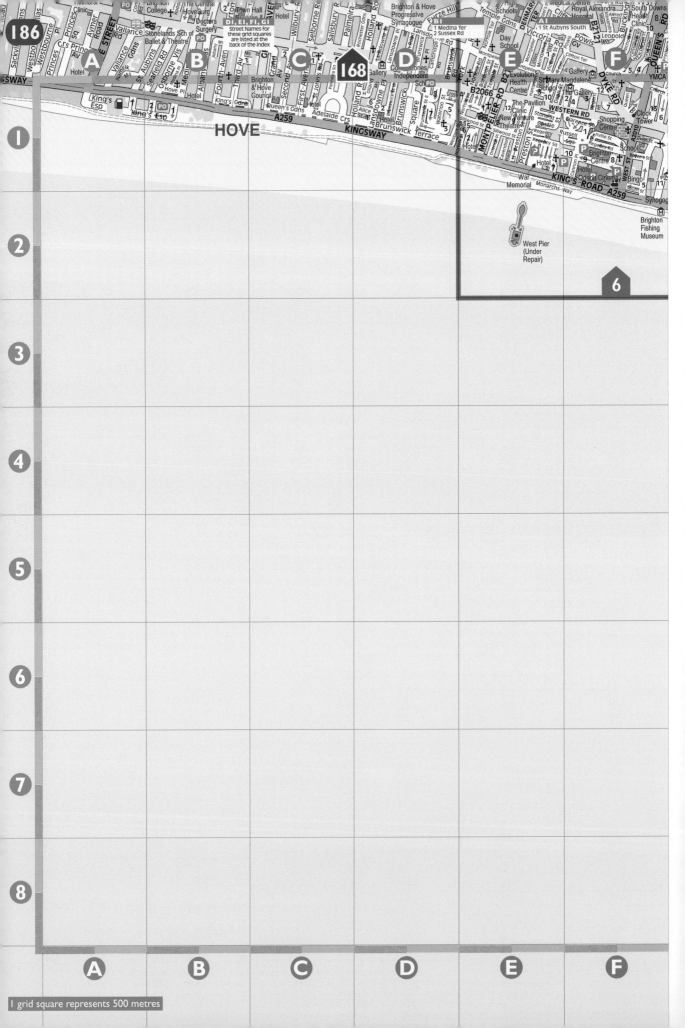

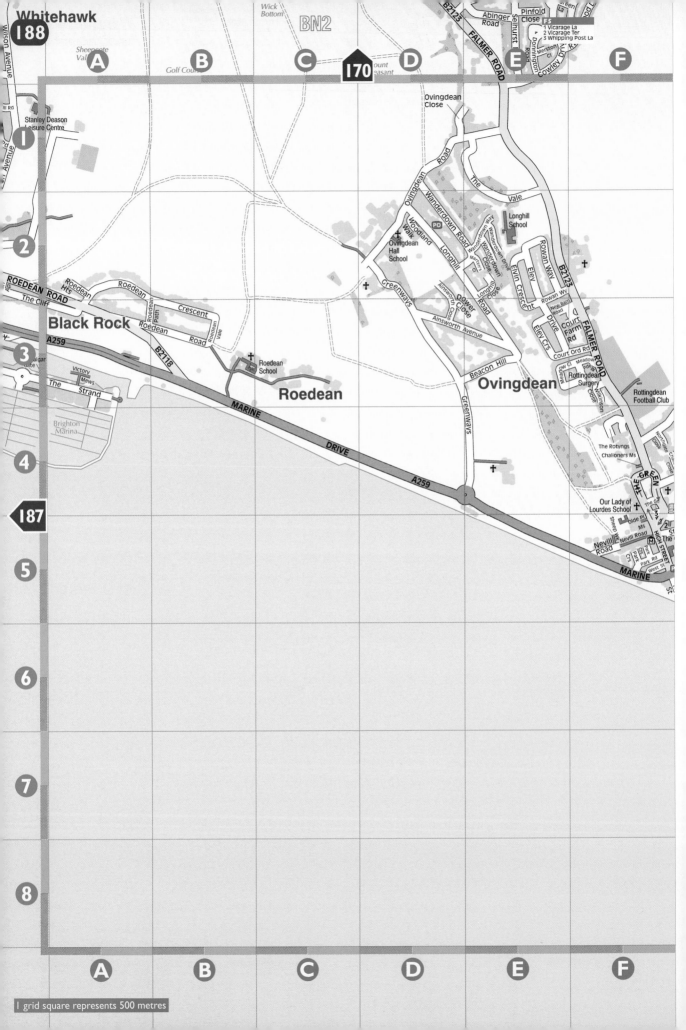

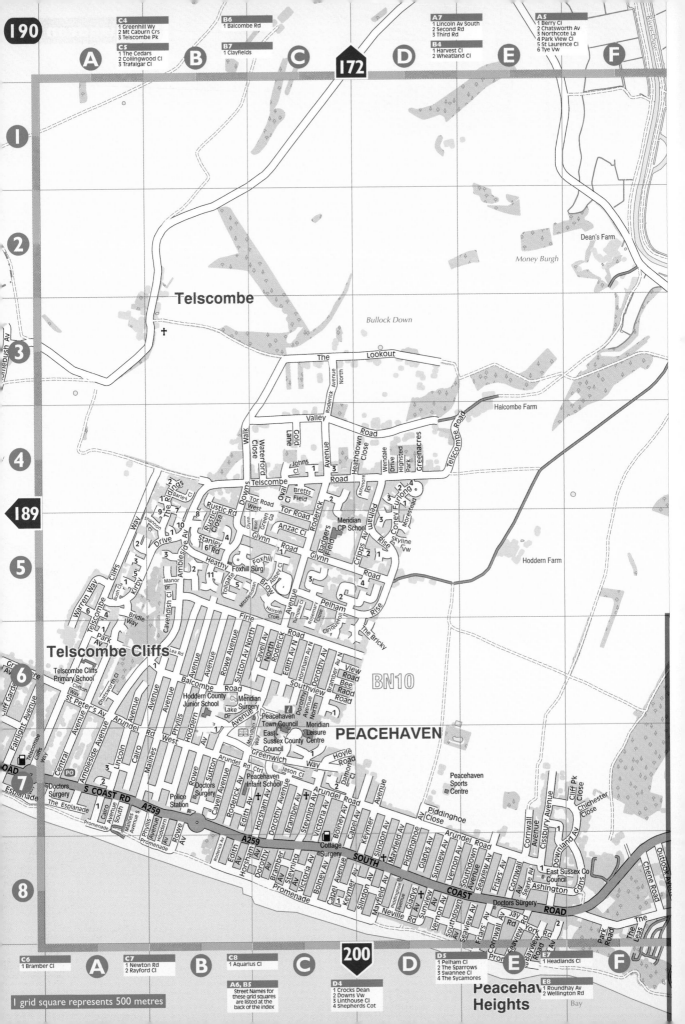

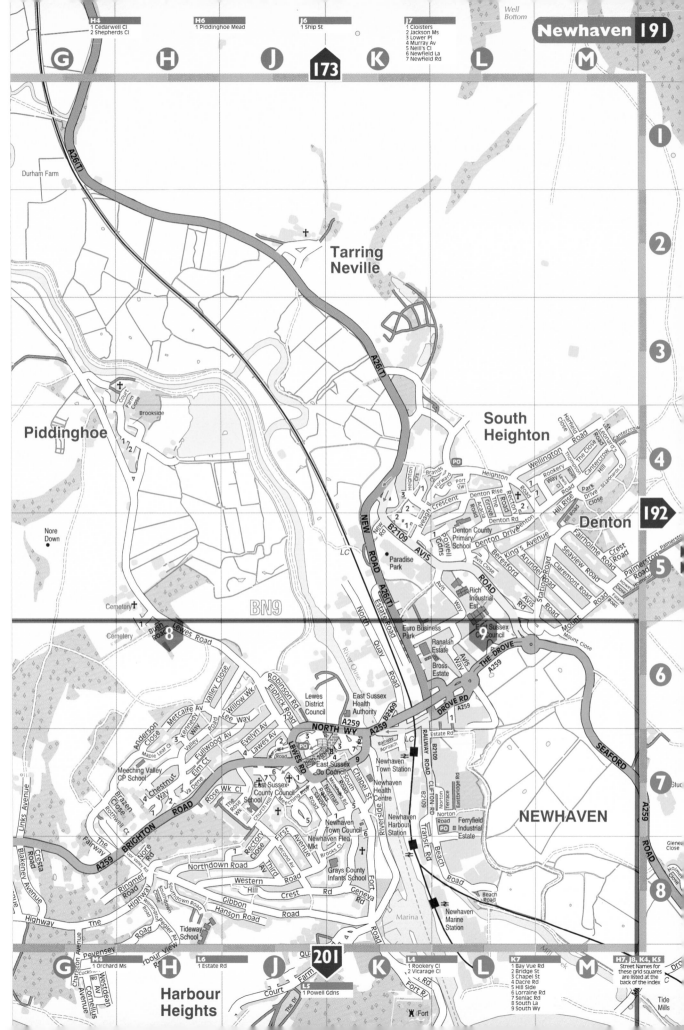

A  B  C  174  D  E  F

E8
1 Chartwell Cl

B8
1 Harbour View Cl
2 Norman Cl
3 Roman Cl

A8
1 Edward Cl
2 Seagrave Cl
3 Troon Cl

1

2

Five Lord's
Burgh

3

4

191

St Leonard's
Cantercrow
Hill

Crest Road
Palmerston Road

Poverty
Bottom

5
Mount
Pleasant
Palmerston Road
Helmdale Road

Bishopstone Road

Norton

6

SEAFORD

7
A259 ROAD

Stud Farm

Bishopstone

The
Lords
Duchess
Dr

Seaford
Golf
Club

Gleneagles
Close
Holmes
Close
Rosemount
Close
St Margaret's Rd
Elizabeth
Close
Hurdis
St Andrews
Freeland
Close
Windsor
Close
Viking Close
Hanover
Close
Antony
Close

Rookery
Hill

Whiteway
Close

Crown Hill

Royal
Road

Firle
Drive

Bowden
Rise

Lexden Road
North
Way

8

A  B  202  C  D  E  F

NEWHAVEN ROAD
A259

Marine Drive
Rochford Way
Rookery Way
Bishopstone Road

Clementine
Churchill Rd
Katherine
Drive
Avenue
Isabel
Way
Princess
Drive
Victor Close
Firle
Grange
The
Holt Way
Firle
Drive
St Peter
North Way
North Way
Lower Dr
Belgrave Crescent
Calvington

1 grid square represents 500 metres

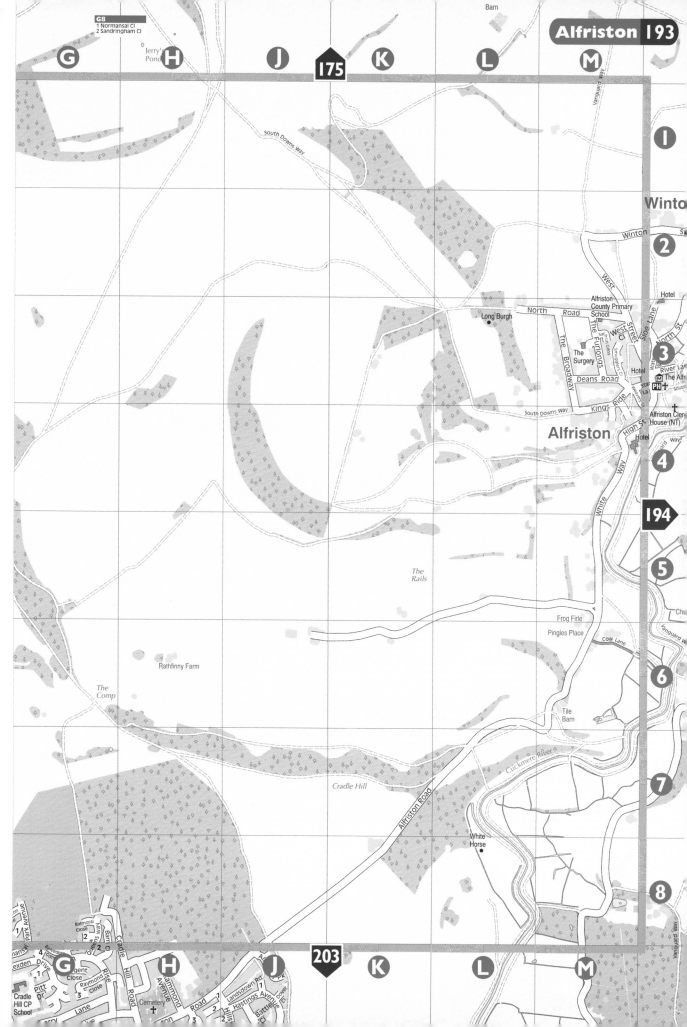

G8
1 Normansal Cl
2 Sandringham Cl

G

H

J

**175**

K

L

M

I

Jerry's Pond

South Downs Way

Winton

Winton

West Street

Sloe Lane

North St

Hotel

2

Long Burgh

North Road

Alfriston County Primary School

The Furlongs

The Broadway

The Surgery

West Cl

Saffron Gdns

Smugglers Cl

Hotel

River La

The Alfr

Star

Deans Road

Kings Ride

South Downs Way

**Alfriston**

High St

Weavers La

Alfriston Cler House (NT)

3

Hotel

4

White Way

**194**

5

The Rails

Ch

Frog Firle

Pingles Place

Cow Lane

Vanguard W

6

Rathfinny Farm

Tile Barn

The Comp

Cradle Hill

Cuckmere River

7

Alfriston Road

White Horse

8

Park Avenue

Balmoral Close

Cradle Hill Rise

Barn

Belvedere

Queens Mead

Regent Close

Raymond Close

Hammond Avenue

Cradle Hill CP School

Pitt Dr

Exden Drive

Lane

Cemetery

Hill Road

Landsdown Rd

Hastings Cl

Battle Cl

Dover

G

H

J

**203**

K

L

M

A B C **176** D E F

I

**Wilmington**

BN26

Winton

Berwick
Court

Wilmington
Prior

2 Winton Street

Milton
Court Farm

**Milton
Street**

Hunter's
Burgh

Hotel

South Downs Way

The Long Man
of Wilmington

West

Sloe Lane

North St

iston
unty Primary
ool

West St
Cl

River Lane

South Downs Way

3

Road

The Alfriston Gallery

Hotel

South Downs Way

Tenantry
Ground

Alfriston Clergy
House (NT)

High St

Hotel

Vanguard Way

4

Lullington
Court

5

South Downs Way

Winchester's
Pond

Church Farm

Vanguard Way

**Litlington**

Cow Lane

Fore
Down

Lullington Heath
Nature Reserve

6 PH

Clapham Lane

Clapham
House

7

8

A B C **204** D E F

Charlston
Bottom

I grid square represents 500 metres

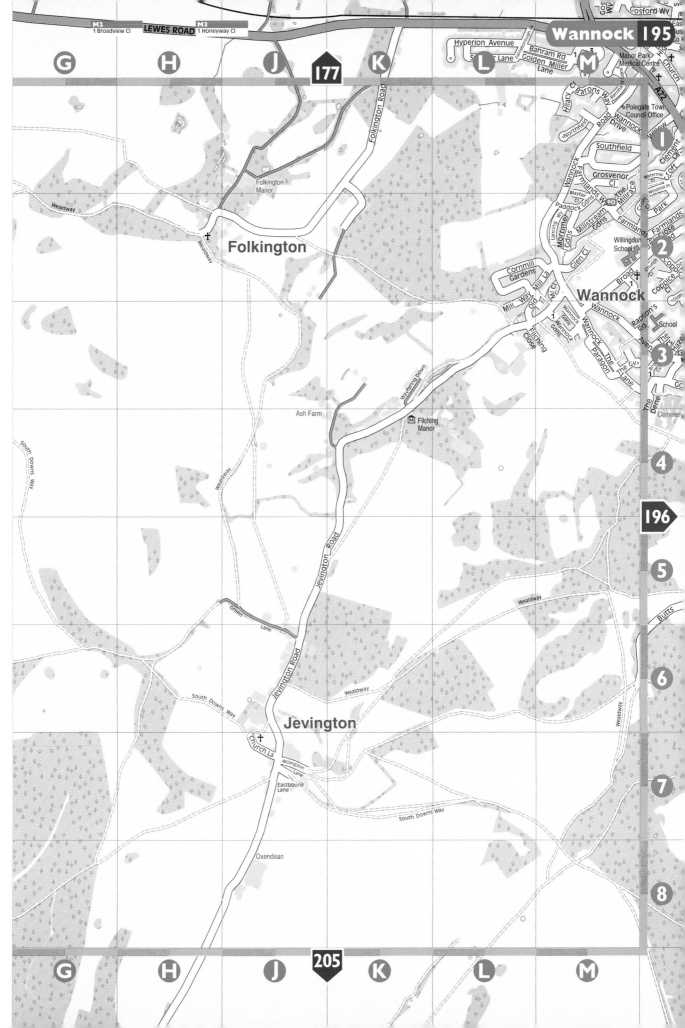

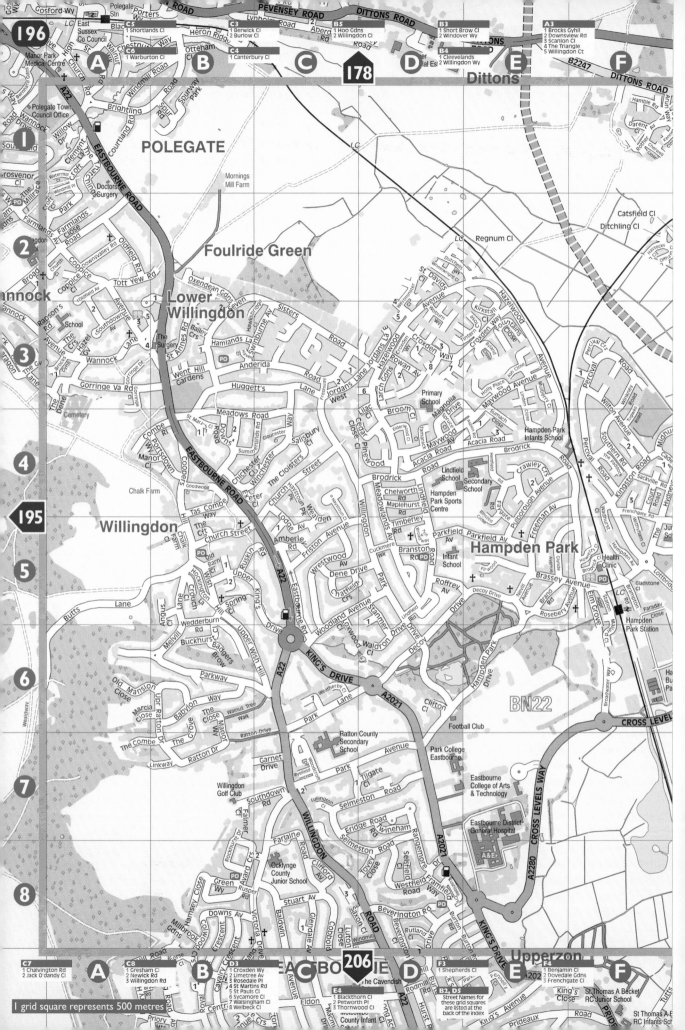

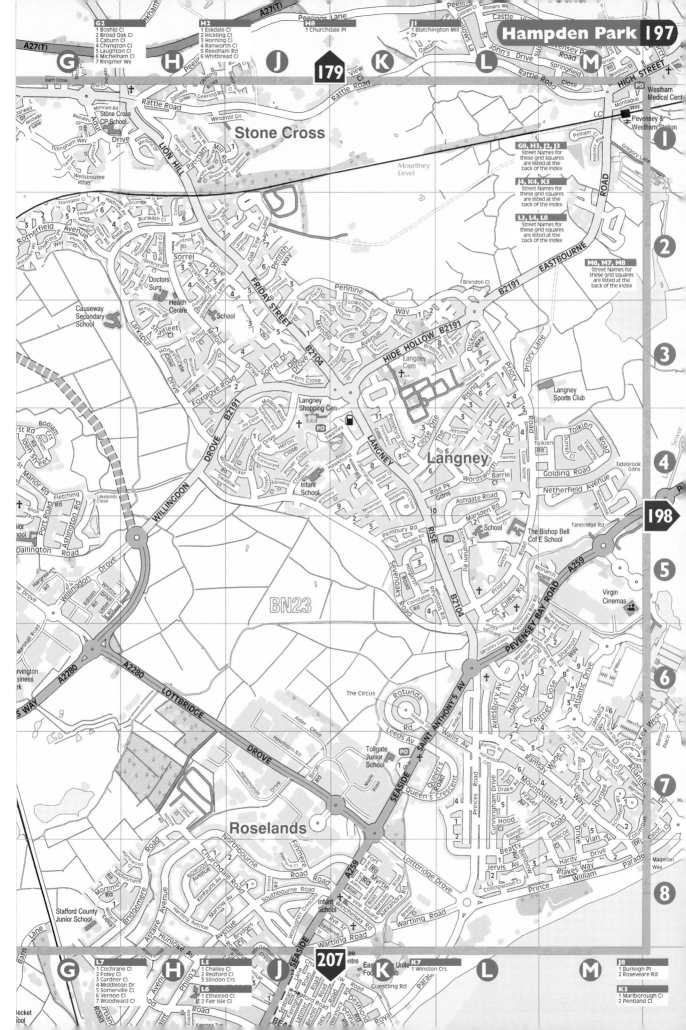

Peacehaven
Heights

Friars'
Bay

190

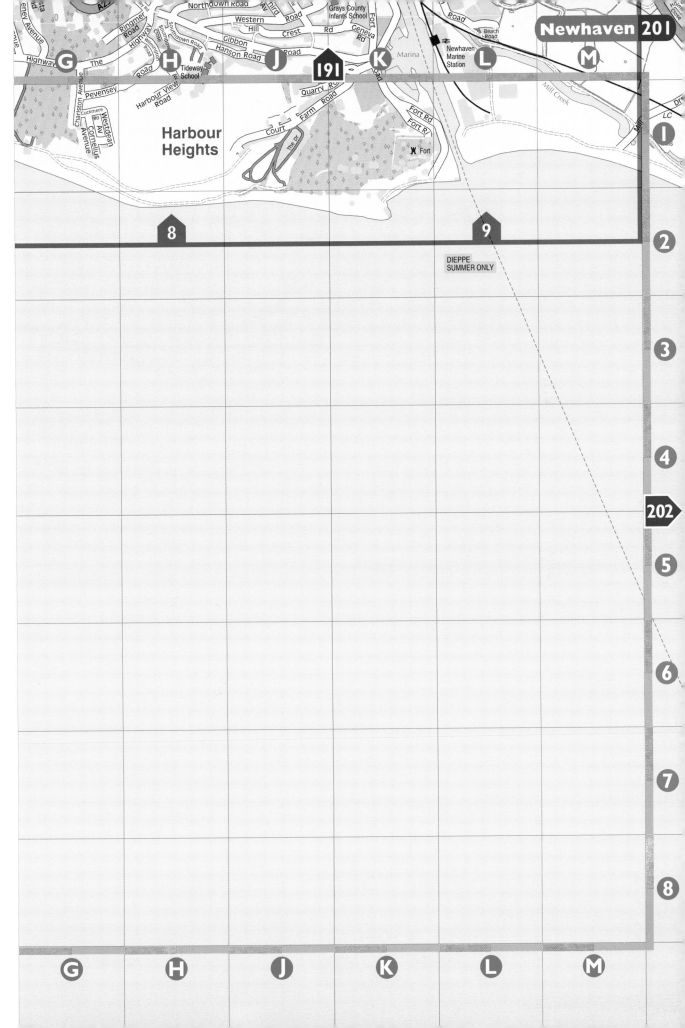

G  H  Tideway School  J  191  K  Marina  L  Newhaven Marine Station  M  I

Northdown Road
Western Hill  Crest  Rd
Gibbon Road
Hanson Road
Grays County Infants School
Geneva Rd
Quarry Rd
Fort Rd
Fort Rd
Fort Rd
Beach Road
Road
Mill Creek
LC
Ringmer Road
Highway
Soundown Road
Wilmington Close
Charlston Avenue
Pevensey
Cuckmere  Rd  Av
Westdean
Cornelius Avenue
Highway
The Road
Harbour View Road
Court
The Dr
Farm Road
Harbour Heights
✠ Fort
DIEPPE SUMMER ONLY

8  9  2

3

4

202

5

6

7

8

G  H  J  K  L  M

**193**

G

H

J

K

L

M

**G1**
1 Jubilee Gdns
2 Monarch Gdns
3 The Peverells
4 Sovereign Cl

**G2**
1 Benenden Cl
2 Hindover Crs
3 Lexden Ct
4 Roadean Cl
5 Sandore Cl

**G4**
1 Sunningdale Cl

Balmoral Close
Benvedere Gdns
New Barn Cl
Cradle Hill Road
Queens Cl
Park Avenue
Mansel Rd
Lexden Drive
Pitt Dr
Barn Close
Argent Close
Raymond Close
Cradle Hill CP School
Quarry Lane
Valley Drive
West Dean Rise
Vale Road
Vale Ct
Cemetery
Alfriston Road
Kammond Avenue
Landsdown Rd
Hastings Avenue
Alfriston Pk
Battle Rd
Hilside Av
Deal Av
Hythe Cl
Short Brow
Rough Brow
Etherton Road
Hindover Road
Bydown
Sandore Rd
Farm Close
Chyngton Gardens
Blue Haze Av
Bromley Rd
Eton Cl
Rigby Av
School
Preparatory School
**Sutton**
Pevensey Garden
Upr Chyngton Garden
The Shepway
Green Wall
Walner Road
Chyngton Av
Sartwood Road
Chyngton Lane North
Stirling Avenue
Millberg Road
Rye Close
Hythe Crs
Chinel Ports
Hilside
Hythe Crescent
Hythe Avenue
Bodiam Close
Dymchurch
Elgin Gardens
**BN25**
Dymock Farm
Downs Leisure Centre
**N ROAD**  **A259**
Downs Pk
Wellington Road
Hartfield Road
Downsview Road
Headland Avenue
Meadow Way
Arundel Rd
Stoke Cl
Chesterton Av
Chesterton Drive
Manor Cl
Manor Rd
Kingston Gdn
Kingston Av
Kingston Way
May Av
Perth close
Ash Drive
Badgers Copse
Willow Drive
Jubilee Way
Barcombe Avenue
Lindfield Avenue
**EASTBOURNE**      **ROAD**
**A259**
Daf Wall Dr
St Wilfred's
Seaford Head Community College
Sutton Links Rd
Links Rd
Green Wk
Cuckmere Road
Rodmell Rd
Field Row
Rother Road
Bracken Rd
Chyngton Pl
Fairways Road
Steyning Road
Hamsey Lane
Chyngton Lane
Chyngton Farm
Chyngton Road
Lullington
Chyngton Way
South-Way
**PH**
Exceat Bridge
**Exceat**
Vanguard Rd
**A2**
Cuckmere River
**204**
Foxhole
South
Southdown Rd
*Golf Course*
Vanguard Way
Hill Fort
South Hill
Vanguard Way
*Seaford Head*
Nature Reserve
*Cuckmere Haven*
Vanguard Way

I

2

3

4

5

6

7

8

G

H

J

K

L

M

**G3, H1, J3, J4**
Street Names for these grid squares are listed at the back of the index

**J2**
1 Bodiam Cl
2 Dymock Cl
3 Hythe Crs
4 Hythe Vw
5 Stonewood Cl

**J1**
1 Folkestone Cl
2 Winchelsea Cl

**H2**
1 Dulwich Cl

A B C **194** D E F

I

**2** Westdean

Exceat

Vanguard Way

Vanguard Way

A259

Charlston Bottom

Friston Forest

**3** South Downs Way

The Living World

River

**4** South Downs Way

Seven Sisters Country Park

**203**

Exceat New Barn

Foxhole

**5**

Gayles

South Downs Way

Fris

**6** Cliff End

Crowlink

**7** South Downs Way

Seven Sisters

south Downs Way

**8**

A B C D E F

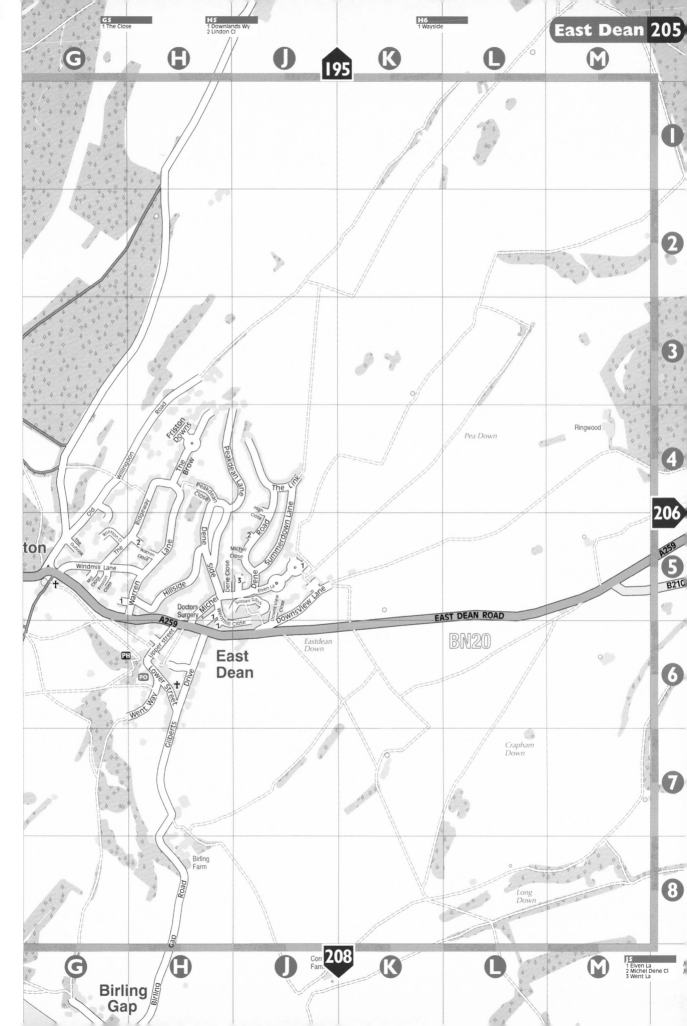

G H J K L M

195

1

2

3

4

206

A259

5

B210

6

7

8

G5
1 The Close

H5
1 Downlands Wy
2 Lindon Cl

H6
1 Wayside

Pea Down

Ringwood

Friston Downs

Road

Willingdon

The Brow

Peakdean Lane

The Link

Peakdean Close

High Close

Summerdown Lane

Old

Ridgeway

Royston Cl

The

Warren Close

Dene

Road

Dene

2

Michel Close

Mill Close

Warren

Hillside

Dene Side

Dene Close

3

Elven La

Friston Close

1

Michel

Sussex Gdns

Downs View Close

Downsview Lane

Doctors Surgery

Wenthill Close

Windmill Lane

A259

Upper Street

PH

PO

Lower Street

Drive

Gilberts

Went Way

Road

Birling Farm

Birling Gap

EAST DEAN ROAD

Eastdean Down

BN20

Crapham Down

Long Down

East Dean

G H J K L M

208

Corn... Farm

J5
1 Elven La
2 Michel Dene Cl
3 Went La

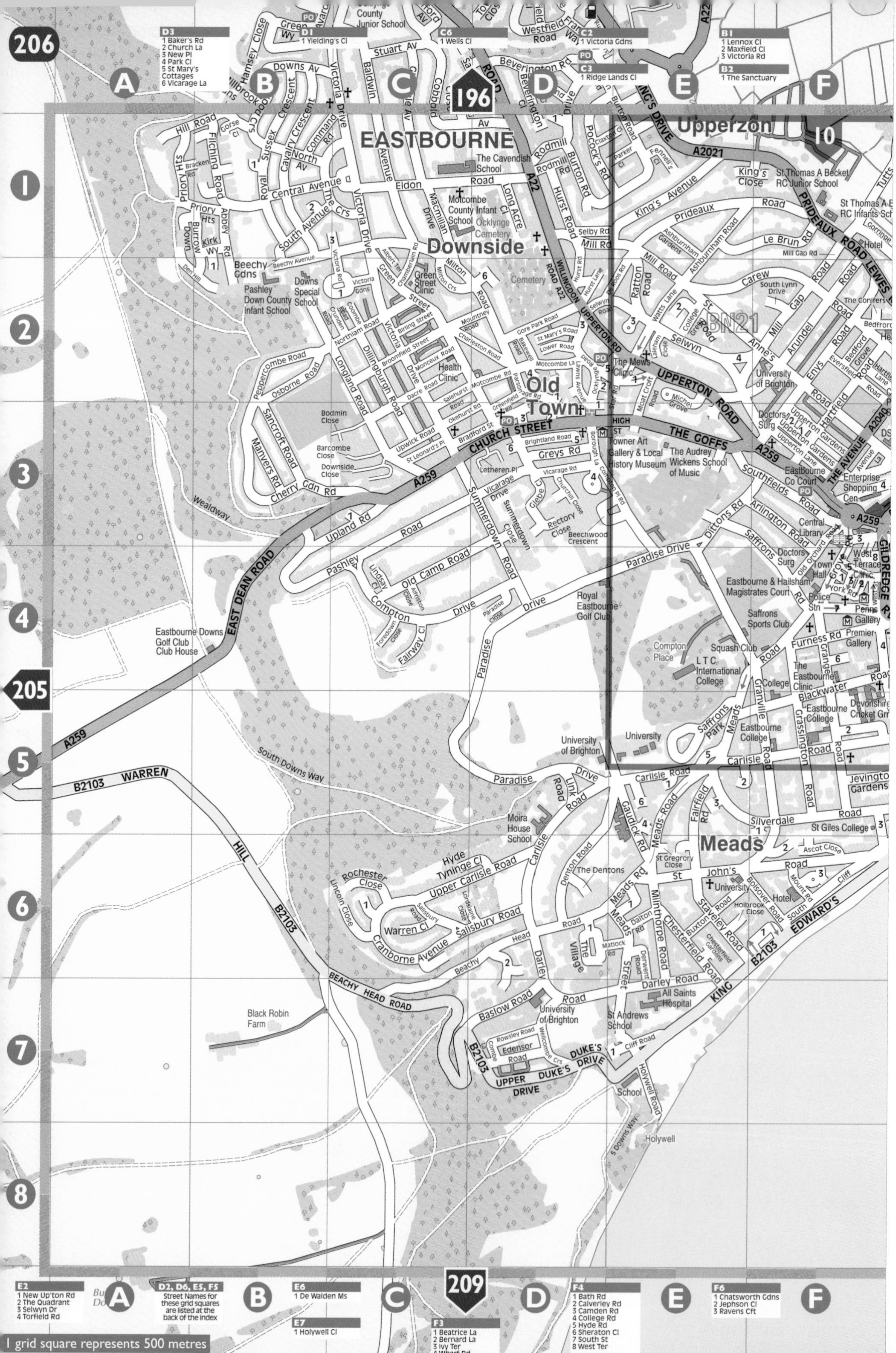


D3
1 Baker's Rd
2 Church La
3 New Pl
4 Park Cl
5 St Mary's Cottages
6 Vicarage La

D1
1 Yielding's Cl

C6
1 Wells Cl

C2
1 Victoria Gdns

C3
1 Ridge Lands Cl

B1
1 Lennox Cl
2 Maxfield Cl
3 Victoria Rd

B2
1 The Sanctuary

E2
1 New Up'ton Rd
2 The Quadrant
3 Selwyn Dr
4 Torfield Rd

D2, D6, E5, F5
Street Names for these grid squares are listed at the back of the index

E6
1 De Walden Ms

E7
1 Holywell Cl

F3
1 Beatrice La
2 Bernard La
3 Ivy Ter
4 Wharf Rd

F4
1 Bath Rd
2 Calverley Rd
3 Camden Rd
4 College Rd
5 Hyde Rd
6 Sheraton Cl
7 South St
8 West Ter

F6
1 Chatsworth Gdns
2 Jephson Cl
3 Ravens Cft

1 grid square represents 500 metres

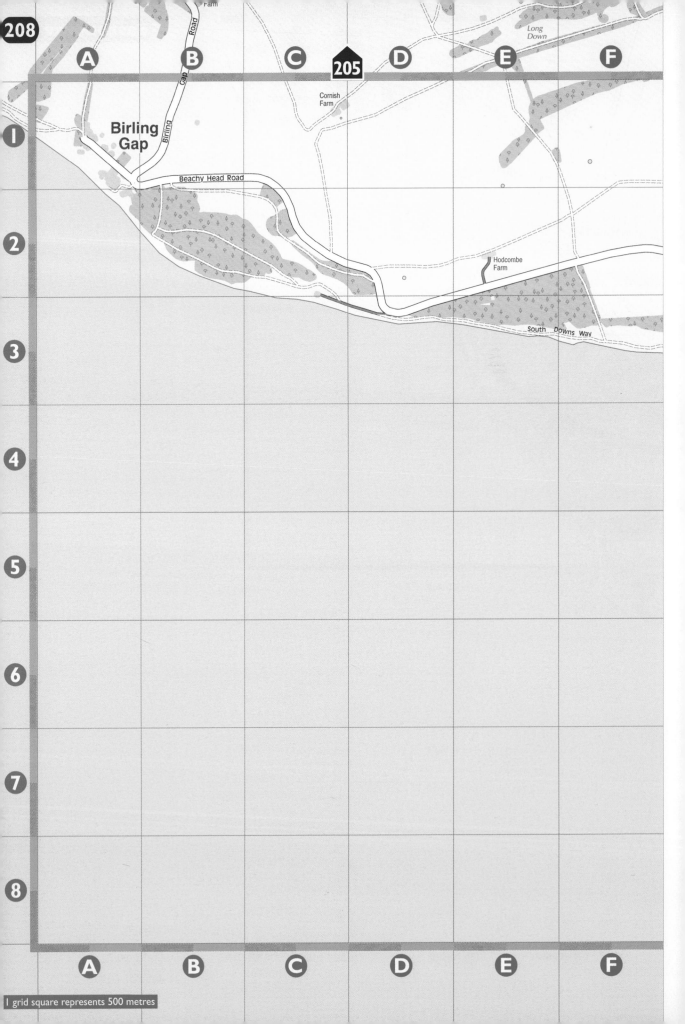

208

A    B    C    205    D    E    F

Birling Gap

Birling Gap Road

Birling

Cornish
Farm

Long
Down

Beachy Head Road

1

2

Hodcombe
Farm

South    Downs    Way

3

4

5

6

7

8

A    B    C    D    E    F

1 grid square represents 500 metres

G H J K L M

206

**I**

**2**

**3**

**4**

**5**

**6**

**7**

**8**

*Bullock
Down*

Beachy Head
Countryside Centre
(visitor centre)

Beachy Head Road

Cow
Gap

Beachy Head

Abbotsford .................... 70 E8
Alciston ...................... 175 K6
Alderbrook ................... 39 M7
Aldrington ................... 167 L7
Alfriston .................... 193 M4
Ansty ........................ 70 C3
Ardingly ..................... 34 B6
Argos Hill ................... 56 E1
Arlington .................... 176 F2
Ashburnham Forge ......... 135 K1
Ashburnham Place ......... 135 L4
Ashton Green ............... 150 F2
Ashurst ...................... 17 K4
Ashurst Wood ............... 14 E8
Bachelor's Bump ........... 140 E8
Baldslow ..................... 139 H7
Baldwins Hill ............... 13 J5
Balls Green .................. 27 G1
Barcombe .................... 126 E5
Barcombe Cross ........... 126 E2
Bardown ...................... 44 D7
Battle ........................ 111 J8
Beachlands ................. 180 F6
Beacon Down ............... 79 G7
Beckley ...................... 89 G2
Beckley Furnace ........... 88 D7
Beddingham ................. 173 K2
Bells Yew Green ........... 31 H1
Belmont ..................... 163 J5
Berner's Hill ............... 46 A4
Berwick ..................... 175 M7
Best Beech Hill ........... 43 J3
Bevendean .................. 170 A4
Bexhill ...................... 183 G2
Birchden ..................... 18 D8
Birchett's Green .......... 44 E3
Birchgrove .................. 36 A5
Birling Gap ................ 208 A1
Bishopstone ............... 192 C1
Blackboys ................... 78 B8
Blackham .................... 17 G2
Blacklands .................. 4 D2
Blackness ................... 40 A5
Black Rock ................. 188 A3
Blackwell ................... 13 L4
Boarshead .................. 28 B8
Bodiam ....................... 63 L6
Bodle Street Green ...... 134 C4
Bohemia ...................... 4 B5
Boreham Street .......... 157 L2
Bowler's Town ............ 91 H4
Bray's Hill ................ 135 G5
Brede ....................... 114 B5
Brightling .................. 83 K8
Brighton ..................... 6 E8
Broadland Row ............ 114 D2
Broad Oak .................. 80 F5
Broad Oak ................. 114 B1
Broad Street .............. 115 J8
Broadwater Down ......... 19 M6
Broomham .................. 129 M8
Broomsgrove ................ 5 K1
Brownbread Street ....... 135 G3
Broyle Side ............... 128 A6
Buckham Hill .............. 75 L8
Budlett's Common ....... 76 C3
Bulverhythe ............... 184 D1
Burgess Hill ............... 61 L3
Burgh Hill ................ 130 E8
Burlow ...................... 131 M1
Burnt Oak .................. 54 F3
Burrswood .................. 18 A6
Burwash ..................... 60 A8
Burwash Common ......... 82 A3
Burwash Weald ........... 82 C3
Butcher's Cross .......... 56 C6
Buxted ...................... 77 G3
Cackle Street .............. 52 E4
Cackle Street ............ 109 L2
Cackle Street ............ 113 M4
Cade Street ................ 80 E8
Camber .................... 118 F2
Camden Park ............... 20 C4
Canadia .................... 111 J8
Castle Hill ................. 56 A2
Catsfield .................. 136 F6
Catsfield Stream ........ 136 E7
Chailey ...................... 99 L3
Chalvington ............... 153 G7
Chapel Cross .............. 107 G1
Chapel Row ............... 156 F1
Chapman's Town ......... 107 H4
Charlwood ................... 23 L5
Chelwood Common ......... 36 D8
Chelwood Gate ............ 36 C5
Chiddingly ................ 130 E5
Chilsham .................. 133 M6
Chiltington ............... 125 J4
Chitcombe .................. 87 L8
Chuck Hatch ............... 26 C7
Churches Green .......... 108 B6
Cinder Hill ................ 35 G6
Clayhill .................... 88 E3
Clayton .................... 122 E6
Cliff End .................. 142 B7
Clive Vale ................ 163 K4
Cock Marling ............. 115 M4
Coggins Mill .............. 57 J2
Coldean .................... 169 K1
Coleman's Hatch .......... 25 L5

Collier's Green ........... 87 G5
Combe ....................... 43 J8
Cooden ..................... 182 D3
Cooksbridge .............. 126 A6
Cooper's Green ............ 76 D3
Cousley Wood .............. 32 C7
Cowbeech .................. 133 J5
Cowbeech Hill ............ 133 H7
Crawley Down ............. 12 A7
Cripp's Corner ............ 86 D7
Cross in Hand ............. 79 H7
Crowborough .............. 39 M5
Crowborough Warren ...... 39 J4
Crowhurst ................. 137 M8
Cuckfield ................... 70 F1
Dale Hill ................... 45 M4
Dallington ................ 108 D3
Danegate ................... 29 J6
Danehill .................... 51 G2
Darwell Hole ............. 109 M3
Davis's Town ............. 104 B7
Denny Bottom .............. 19 K3
Denton ..................... 191 M5
Ditchling ................. 123 K3
Dittons ................... 178 E8
Domewood ................... 12 B1
Down Park .................. 12 A5
Downside .................. 206 C1
Down Street ............... 75 K1
The Down ................... 32 F3
Duddleswell ................ 53 G2
Durgates .................... 43 L1
Earl's Down ............... 108 B2
Eason's Green ............ 103 K5
East Blatchington ....... 202 E2
Eastbourne ................ 10 C4
Eastbourne ............... 206 C1
East Chiltington ........ 125 G2
East Dean ................ 205 H6
East Grinstead ........... 13 L5
East Guldeford ........... 91 M7
East Hoathly ............ 130 B1
East Moulsecoomb ...... 169 M2
Eckington Corner ....... 152 E6
Eridge Green .............. 29 J2
Etchingham ................ 61 H5
Etchingwood ............... 77 K5
Ewhurst Green ............ 87 H1
Exceat .................... 203 M2
Fairfield ................... 69 L5
Fairlight ................. 164 C2
Fairlight Cove .......... 164 F1
Fairwarp ................... 53 H5
Falmer .................... 147 K8
Felbridge ................. 12 F2
Ferndale ................... 20 C1
Fishersgate .............. 166 F7
Five Ash Down ............ 76 E1
Five Ashes ................. 56 C7
Flackley Ash ............. 89 M3
Fletching .................. 75 G2
Fletching Common ....... 74 B6
Flimwell .................... 46 C3
Flowers Green ........... 156 F2
Folkington ............... 195 J2
Fordcombe .................. 18 A1
Ford's Green .............. 52 C3
Forest Row ................. 24 F5
Foul Mile ................. 133 J2
Foulride Green .......... 196 B2
Four Oaks .................. 89 J1
Foxhunt Green ........... 104 F5
Framfield ................... 77 G8
Frant ....................... 30 C3
Friar's Gate ............... 27 H7
Friar's Hill .............. 141 H7
Friston ................... 204 F5
Furnace Wood .............. 12 C3
Furner's Green ........... 51 J5
Gallypot Street ........... 26 B3
Gill's Green .............. 47 M1
Ginger's Green .......... 133 J8
Glenleigh Park .......... 160 A7
Glynde .................... 150 E7
Glyndebourne ............ 150 E4
Glyne Gap ................ 184 C1
Goatham Green .......... 113 L1
Goddards' Green .......... 96 A1
Godleys Green ............ 98 F2
Golden Cross ............. 130 D8
Golden Cross ............ 156 E4
Gotham .................... 159 G7
Green Street ............. 161 H2
Groombridge ............... 18 A7
Grove Hill ............... 132 E5
Guestling Green ......... 141 G6
Guestling Thorn ........ 141 G2
Gun Hill .................. 131 J5
Hadlow Down .............. 78 C1
Hailsham .................. 155 J6
Hale Green ............... 131 G5
Halland ................... 103 J8
Hall's Close ............. 158 C6
Ham Green .................. 67 J5
Hammerwood ................ 15 H3
Hampden Park ............ 196 E5
Hampers Green .......... 126 C8
Hangleton ............... 167 L4
Hankham .................. 179 G7
Harbour Heights .......... 8 C8
Harley Shute ............ 161 M6

Hartfield ................... 26 C2
Hassocks .................. 122 E2
Hastings ..................... 4 E5
Hawkenbury ................ 20 D4
Hawkhurst ................. 47 L5
Hawkhurst Common ...... 104 A5
Haywards Heath ........... 48 E8
Hazard's Green .......... 158 D1
Heathfield .................. 41 J4
Heathfield ................ 80 B7
Hellingly ................. 154 F1
Henley's Down .......... 137 G8
Herstmonceux ........... 133 M8
Heron's Ghyll ............ 53 K3
Highbrook .................. 34 E5
High Cross ................. 41 J7
Highgate ................... 24 F5
High Hurstwood .......... 53 M5
The Highlands .......... 159 M6
High Street .............. 47 K4
Hollingbury .............. 169 H1
Hollingdean .............. 169 H3
Hollingrove ................ 83 L8
Hollington ............... 161 M3
Holmes's Hill ........... 130 C8
Holtye ...................... 15 L3
Hooe ...................... 158 C7
Hooe Common ............ 158 E5
Hook Green ................ 32 D2
Horam ..................... 105 L7
Horney Common ........... 52 E6
Horns Cross ............... 88 A5
Horsted Green .......... 102 B3
Horsted Keynes .......... 50 C1
Houghton Green .......... 91 K5
Hove ...................... 186 B1
Hungershall Park ........ 19 L4
Hurst Green ................ 62 A3
Hurst Wickham ........... 96 C8
Icklesham ................ 115 L8
Iden ........................ 91 H2
Iford ...................... 172 B3
Isfield ................... 101 L6
Jarvis Brook .............. 40 D6
Jevington ................ 195 J6
John's Cross .............. 85 J7
Jumper's Town ............ 26 B7
Jury's Gap ............... 119 L5
Kemp Town ................ 187 K3
Keymer .................... 123 H2
Kingston by Sea ......... 166 B7
Kingston near Lewes .. 171 L1
Lamberhurst ............... 33 H1
Landport .................... 2 D3
Langney .................. 197 K4
Langton Green ............ 18 F2
Laughton ................. 129 J7
Lewes ....................... 3 K5
Lidham Hill .............. 114 E8
Lindfield .................. 49 H6
Linkhill .................... 64 E2
Lions Green .............. 105 H5
Litlington ............... 194 A6
Little Bayham ............ 31 M2
Little Common .......... 182 B1
Little Horsted .......... 102 C5
Little London ............ 105 K2
Little Norlington ....... 127 L5
Lower Cousley Wood ..... 32 E6
Lower Dicker ............ 154 B2
Lower Green ............... 19 J1
Lower Horsebridge ..... 154 E2
Lower Street ............ 159 H1
Lower Willingdon ....... 196 B3
Lunsford's Cross ....... 159 M4
Lydd ....................... 95 H8
Lye Green .................. 27 L5
Lyewood Common ......... 17 H7
Magham Down ............ 155 M2
Manor Park ................ 76 E5
Marden's Hill ............ 39 H1
Maresfield Park ......... 76 A1
Mark Cross ............... 42 A2
Mark Cross ............... 152 C4
Marle Green .............. 132 B1
Marlpits .................... 37 K8
Marlpits ................. 136 B7
Mayfield ................... 57 G4
Maynard's Green ......... 106 A4
Meads .................... 206 E6
Mile Oak ................. 166 F3
Mill Corner ................ 88 A3
Mill Hill ................ 179 K8
Milton Street ........... 194 D1
Moon's Green .............. 67 G3
The Moor .................. 47 M6
Mott's Mill ............... 28 A3
Moulsecoomb ............ 169 M3
Mount Ephraim .......... 102 E3
Mountfield ................ 85 G8
Mount Pleasant ......... 100 F8
Mount Pleasant ......... 192 A5
Muddles Green .......... 130 C7
Mutton Hall ............... 80 B5
Nash Street .............. 130 F8
Netherfield .............. 110 C4
Newbridge .................. 25 L8
Newenden ................... 65 K3
Newhaven .................... 8 F6
Newick ...................... 74 E6
New Town ................... 76 E8

Ninfield .................. 136 B8
Norlington ............... 127 K7
Norman's Bay ............ 181 K6
Northbridge Street ...... 85 J1
North Chailey ............ 73 K8
North Common ............ 73 L7
North End ................. 13 H2
Northiam ................... 65 H8
North Moulsecoomb ..... 169 K2
Norton ................... 192 C6
Nutley ..................... 52 C3
Offham .................... 149 G1
Old Heathfield .......... 80 D8
Old Town .................... 5 M6
Old Town ................. 160 C8
Old Town ................. 206 D2
Ore ....................... 163 J3
Ovingdean ................ 188 C3
Oxley's Green ............ 83 L6
Palehouse Common ..... 103 H4
Park Corner .............. 28 E1
Park Corner ............. 129 M4
Patcham .................. 145 M8
Peacehaven .............. 190 C7
Peacehaven Heights ... 200 E1
Peasmarsh ................. 90 A4
Pebsham .................. 160 F8
Pell Green ................. 32 B7
Penhurst ................. 109 M8
Pett ...................... 141 L6
Pett Level ............... 142 B6
Pevensey ................. 180 B8
Pevensey Bay ............ 181 C1
Piddinghoe .............. 191 G4
Piltdown ................... 75 J5
Playden ................... 91 J6
Plumpton ................. 124 F7
Plumpton Green .......... 98 E8
Polegate ................. 196 A1
Ponts Green ............. 135 H2
Portslade-by-Sea ...... 167 H8
Portslade Village ...... 167 G4
Potman's Heath .......... 66 E1
Potter's Green .......... 77 K3
Poundfield ................ 40 B4
Poundford ................. 79 G1
Poundgate ................. 39 G7
Pound Green .............. 77 K2
Pounsley ................... 78 A6
Poynings ................. 144 B1
Preston .................. 168 E5
Punnett's Town .......... 81 J8
Pyecombe ................ 122 B8
Quabrook ................... 25 J5
Ramslye .................... 19 K5
Rickney ................... 179 K4
Ridgewood ............... 102 C2
Ringles Cross ............ 76 C4
Ringmer .................. 127 J8
Ripe ...................... 152 E5
Robertsbridge ............ 84 F2
Rockrobin .................. 31 K7
Rocks Park ................ 76 A7
Rodmell .................. 172 D6
Roedean .................. 188 C3
Rose Hill ................ 101 M8
Roselands ................ 197 J7
Roser's Cross ............ 78 F8
Rotherfield ............... 41 G6
Rottingdean ............. 189 G4
Royal Tunbridge Wells . 19 M3
Rusher's Cross .......... 42 F8
Rushlake Green ......... 107 J5
Rushy Green .............. 150 E1
Russell's Green ......... 159 G3
Rusthall ................... 19 J2
Rye ........................ 91 J8
Rye Foreign .............. 90 E5
Rye Harbour ............. 117 M4
Saddlescombe ........... 144 E3
St Helen's ............... 163 G1
St Helen's Wood ........ 162 E2
St John's .................. 39 J2
St Leonards ............. 162 A7
Salehurst ................. 85 J1
Saltdean ................. 189 K4
Sandhurst ................ 64 A1
Sandhurst Cross ......... 63 L2
Sandy Cross ............. 106 B1
Scayne's Hill ............ 72 E3
Seacox Heath ............. 46 E4
Seaford .................. 202 D4
Sedlescombe ............. 112 D5
Selmeston ............... 175 L3
Selsfield Common ....... 22 B5
Sharpsbridge ............. 75 J8
Sharp's Corner ......... 105 L6
Sharpthorne .............. 23 G8
Sheffield Green ......... 51 H7
Shortbridge .............. 75 L6
Shortgate ............... 129 H5
Shover's Green .......... 44 C4
Sidley ................... 160 B8
Silver Hill ............... 62 B6
Silverhill ............... 162 C3
Silverhill Park ........ 139 J8
Skippers Hill ............ 56 A7
Sleeches Cross .......... 30 B4
Snagshall ................. 86 F1
South Chailey ............ 99 L7
Southease ............... 172 E7

Southern Cross ......... 167 G6
South Heighton ........ 191 L4
South Malling ............. 3 G3
Southover ................... 2 D9
Southover ................. 59 J6
South Street ............. 99 L5
Southwick ............... 166 E6
Sparrow's Green ........ 43 M1
Spithurst ............... 100 F7
Splayne's Green .......... 75 G1
Stanmer .................. 146 E6
Staplecross .............. 86 E5
Starr's Green ........... 138 A4
Steel Cross ............... 40 B3
Steven's Crouch ....... 136 B3
The Stocks ................ 68 A2
Stone Cross .............. 17 M4
Stone Cross .............. 39 M8
Stone Cross .............. 44 A3
Stone Cross ............. 197 J1
Stonecrouch .............. 33 L7
Stonegate ................. 45 G8
Stone in Oxney .......... 68 F2
Stonequarry .............. 14 A3
Strawberry Hill ......... 19 K6
Streat .................... 124 B3
Stunts Green ........... 133 K7
Summer Hill ............. 178 A2
Sunnyside ................. 13 L8
Sutton ................... 203 G2
Swaile's Green .......... 86 C7
Sweethaws ................. 39 J8
Tarring Neville ........ 191 K2
Teasley Mead ............ 17 J3
Telham ................... 138 B4
Telscombe ............... 190 B3
Telscombe Cliffs ...... 190 A6
Three Cups Corner ..... 107 J1
Three Leg Cross ......... 45 K3
Three Oaks .............. 140 D4
Thunder's Hill .......... 130 F7
Ticehurst ................. 45 L4
Tidebrook ................. 43 H6
Tilsmore .................. 79 M6
Tolhurst .................. 44 F4
Tompset's Bank .......... 24 F6
Town Littleworth ...... 100 C5
Town Row .................. 41 J5
Trolliloes ............... 133 K4
Turner's Green ........... 31 L8
Turner's Green .......... 107 M2
Turners Hill .............. 22 A2
Twelve Oaks ............ 109 K1
Uckfield ................... 76 D7
Udimore .................. 115 K4
Union Street .............. 46 B3
Upper Dicker ............ 154 A6
Upper Hartfield ......... 26 B4
Upper Horsebridge .... 154 E3
Upperton .................. 10 B3
Upper Wellingham ...... 127 G6
Vinehall Street .......... 85 L8
Vines Cross ............. 106 C6
Wadhurst .................. 44 A2
Waldron .................. 104 F3
Waldron Down ............ 78 D6
Wallands Park ............. 2 C5
Wallcrouch ............... 44 F5
Wannock .................. 195 M2
Warbleton ............... 107 G5
Wartling ................. 157 J7
Watermill ............... 160 B2
Wellbrook ................. 56 F5
West Blatchington ..... 167 M5
Westdean ................ 204 B2
Westdene ................ 168 B1
Westfield ............... 139 M2
West Firle ............... 174 C3
Westham .................. 179 L8
West Hill ................... 5 K4
West Hoathly ............. 22 E8
West Marina ............ 161 M8
Westmeston .............. 123 L6
Whatlington ............. 112 A5
Whitehawk ............... 169 M8
Whitehill ................. 39 L6
Whitesmith ............. 130 B6
Whydown ................. 159 H6
Wickstreet ............... 153 L8
Willard's Hill ............ 84 C1
Willingdon ............... 196 A5
Wilmington .............. 176 E8
Wilmington Green ....... 176 E7
Winchelsea .............. 116 D7
Winchelsea Beach ...... 117 H8
Windmill Hill .......... 157 H1
Winton ................... 194 A2
Withdean ................ 168 E2
Witherenden Hill ........ 59 G5
Withyham .................. 27 G3
Wittersham ............... 67 K3
Wivelsfield .............. 98 A1
Woodingdean ............ 170 C7
Woodmans Green ........ 112 A3
Wood's Corner .......... 108 F3
Wood's Green ............ 31 M6
World's End .............. 97 K2
Wych Cross ............... 36 E2

## USING THE STREET INDEX

Street names are listed alphabetically. Each street name is followed by its postal town or area locality, the Postcode District, the page number, and the reference to the square in which the name is found.

Abbey Wy *BAT* TN33 ................. **137** K1 **1**

Some entries are followed by a number in a blue box. This number indicates the location of the street within the referenced grid square. The full street name is listed at the side of the map page.

# GENERAL ABBREVIATIONS

| | | | | |
|---|---|---|---|---|
| ACC ...ACCESS | CTYD ...COURTYARD | HLS ...HILLS | MWY ...MOTORWAY | SE ...SOUTH EAST |
| ALY ...ALLEY | CUTT ...CUTTINGS | HO ...HOUSE | N ...NORTH | SER ...SERVICE AREA |
| AP ...APPROACH | CV ...COVE | HOL ...HOLLOW | NE ...NORTH EAST | SH ...SHORE |
| AR ...ARCADE | CYN ...CANYON | HOSP ...HOSPITAL | NW ...NORTH WEST | SHOP ...SHOPPING |
| ASS ...ASSOCIATION | DEPT ...DEPARTMENT | HRB ...HARBOUR | O/P ...OVERPASS | SKWY ...SKYWAY |
| AV ...AVENUE | DL ...DALE | HTH ...HEATH | OFF ...OFFICE | SMT ...SUMMIT |
| BCH ...BEACH | DM ...DAM | HTS ...HEIGHTS | ORCH ...ORCHARD | SOC ...SOCIETY |
| BLDS ...BUILDINGS | DR ...DRIVE | HVN ...HAVEN | OV ...OVAL | SP ...SPUR |
| BND ...BEND | DRO ...DROVE | HWY ...HIGHWAY | PAL ...PALACE | SPR ...SPRING |
| BNK ...BANK | DRY ...DRIVEWAY | IMP ...IMPERIAL | PAS ...PASSAGE | SQ ...SQUARE |
| BR ...BRIDGE | DWGS ...DWELLINGS | IN ...INLET | PAV ...PAVILION | ST ...STREET |
| BRK ...BROOK | E ...EAST | IND EST ...INDUSTRIAL ESTATE | PDE ...PARADE | STN ...STATION |
| BTM ...BOTTOM | EMB ...EMBANKMENT | INF ...INFIRMARY | PH ...PUBLIC HOUSE | STR ...STREAM |
| BUS ...BUSINESS | EMBY ...EMBASSY | INFO ...INFORMATION | PK ...PARK | STRD ...STRAND |
| BVD ...BOULEVARD | ESP ...ESPLANADE | INT ...INTERCHANGE | PKWY ...PARKWAY | SW ...SOUTH WEST |
| BY ...BYPASS | EST ...ESTATE | IS ...ISLAND | PL ...PLACE | TDG ...TRADING |
| CATH ...CATHEDRAL | EX ...EXCHANGE | JCT ...JUNCTION | PLN ...PLAIN | TER ...TERRACE |
| CEM ...CEMETERY | EXPY ...EXPRESSWAY | JTY ...JETTY | PLNS ...PLAINS | THWY ...THROUGHWAY |
| CEN ...CENTRE | EXT ...EXTENSION | KG ...KING | PLZ ...PLAZA | TNL ...TUNNEL |
| CFT ...CROFT | F/O ...FLYOVER | KNL ...KNOLL | POL ...POLICE STATION | TOLL ...TOLLWAY |
| CH ...CHURCH | FC ...FOOTBALL CLUB | L ...LAKE | PR ...PRINCE | TPK ...TURNPIKE |
| CHA ...CHASE | FK ...FORK | LA ...LANE | PREC ...PRECINCT | TR ...TRACK |
| CHYD ...CHURCHYARD | FLD ...FIELD | LDG ...LODGE | PREP ...PREPARATORY | TRL ...TRAIL |
| CIR ...CIRCLE | FLDS ...FIELDS | LGT ...LIGHT | PRIM ...PRIMARY | TWR ...TOWER |
| CIRC ...CIRCUS | FLS ...FALLS | LK ...LOCK | PROM ...PROMENADE | U/P ...UNDERPASS |
| CL ...CLOSE | FLS ...FLATS | LKS ...LAKES | PRS ...PRINCESS | UNI ...UNIVERSITY |
| CLFS ...CLIFFS | FM ...FARM | LNDG ...LANDING | PRT ...PORT | UPR ...UPPER |
| CMP ...CAMP | FT ...FORT | LTL ...LITTLE | PT ...POINT | V ...VALE |
| CNR ...CORNER | FWY ...FREEWAY | LWR ...LOWER | PTH ...PATH | VA ...VALLEY |
| CO ...COUNTY | FY ...FERRY | MAG ...MAGISTRATE | PZ ...PIAZZA | VIAD ...VIADUCT |
| COLL ...COLLEGE | GA ...GATE | MAN ...MANSIONS | QD ...QUADRANT | VIL ...VILLA |
| COM ...COMMON | GAL ...GALLERY | MD ...MEAD | QU ...QUEEN | VIS ...VISTA |
| COMM ...COMMISSION | GDN ...GARDEN | MDW ...MEADOWS | QY ...QUAY | VLG ...VILLAGE |
| CON ...CONVENT | GDNS ...GARDENS | MEM ...MEMORIAL | R ...RIVER | VLS ...VILLAS |
| COT ...COTTAGE | GLD ...GLADE | MKT ...MARKET | RBT ...ROUNDABOUT | VW ...VIEW |
| COTS ...COTTAGES | GLN ...GLEN | MKTS ...MARKETS | RD ...ROAD | W ...WEST |
| CP ...CAPE | GN ...GREEN | ML ...MALL | RDG ...RIDGE | WD ...WOOD |
| CPS ...COPSE | GND ...GROUND | ML ...MILL | REP ...REPUBLIC | WHF ...WHARF |
| CR ...CREEK | GRA ...GRANGE | MNR ...MANOR | RES ...RESERVOIR | WK ...WALK |
| CREM ...CREMATORIUM | GRG ...GARAGE | MS ...MEWS | RFC ...RUGBY FOOTBALL CLUB | WKS ...WALKS |
| CRS ...CRESCENT | GT ...GREAT | MSN ...MISSION | RI ...RISE | WLS ...WELLS |
| CSWY ...CAUSEWAY | GTWY ...GATEWAY | MT ...MOUNT | RM ...RAMP | WY ...WAY |
| CT ...COURT | GV ...GROVE | MTN ...MOUNTAIN | RW ...ROW | YD ...YARD |
| CTRL ...CENTRAL | HGR ...HIGHER | MTS ...MOUNTAINS | S ...SOUTH | YHA ...YOUTH HOSTEL |
| CTS ...COURTS | HL ...HILL | MUS ...MUSEUM | SCH ...SCHOOL | |

# POSTCODE TOWNS AND AREA ABBREVIATIONS

| | | | | |
|---|---|---|---|---|
| BAT ...Battle | EAST ...Eastbourne | HFD ...Henfield | LYDD ...Lydd | RBTBR ...Robertsbridge |
| BEX ...Bexhill | EDEN ...Edenbridge | HOVE ...Hove | MAYF ...Mayfield | RHAS ...Rural Hastings |
| BEXW ...Bexhill west | EDN/EASTW ...East Dean/Eastbourne west | HPPT/KEY ...Hurstpierpoint/Keymer | NEWHV ...Newhaven | RHWH ...Rural Haywards Heath |
| BRI ...Brighton | EGRIN ...East Grinstead | HRTF ...Hartfield | NROM ...New Romney | RING/NEW ...Ringmer/Newick |
| BUR/ETCH ...Burwash/Etchingham | FROW ...Forest Row | HTHF ...Heathfield | PEAHV ...Peacehaven | ROTT ...Rottingdean |
| BURH ...Burgess Hill | HAIL ...Hailsham | HWH ...Haywards Heath | PEV ...Pevensey | RRTW ...Rural Royal Tunbridge Wells |
| CRAWE ...Crawley east | HAS ...Hastings | LEW ...Lewes | POLE ...Polegate | RTW ...Royal Tunbridge Wells |
| CRBK ...Cranbrook | HAWK ...Hawkhurst | LGNY ...Langney | POY/PYE ...Poynings/Pyecombe | |
| CROW ...Crowborough | | LW/ROSE ...Lower Willingdon/Roselands | PTSD ...Portslade | |

## Index - streets

## 106 - Ast

1066 Country Wk BAT TN33 ..... 138 C2
  HAIL BN27 ..... 156 E8
  RHAS TN350 ..... 140 C3
  RHAS TN35 ..... 163 J6
  WSEA TN36 ..... 115 K8

### A

Abberton Fld HPPT/KEY BN6 ..... 122 B1
Abbey Cl PEAHV BN10 ..... 190 C5
Abbey Dr STLEO TN38 ..... 184 B1
Abbey Rd EDN/EASTW BN20 ..... 206 B1
  ROTT BN2 ..... 7 L8
Abbey Vw BEX TN40 ..... 160 D8
Abbey Wy BAT TN33 ..... 137 K1
Abbotsbury Cl ROTT BN2 ..... 189 H5
Abbots Cl BAT TN33 ..... 137 M3
  HPPT/KEY BN6 ..... 122 E2
Abbotsfield Cl HAS TN34 ..... 162 F3
Aberdale Rd POLE BN26 ..... 178 C8
Aberdeen Rd ROTT BN2 ..... 7 H1
Abergavenny Rd LEW BN7 ..... 2 C6
Abinger Pl LEW BN7 ..... 2 F5
Abinger Rd PTSD BN41 ..... 167 H6
  ROTT BN2 ..... 170 E8
Acacia Av HOVE BN3 ..... 167 M5
Acacia Rd LW/ROSE BN22 ..... 196 C5
  NEWHV BN9 ..... 191 L4
Acer Av RTWE/PEM TN2 ..... 20 C6
Acorn Cl EGRIN RH19 ..... 13 L6
  SLVH TN37 ..... 162 C2
The Acorns HPPT/KEY BN6 ..... 96 D2
  WADH TN5 ..... 44 F8
Acorn Wy BUR/ETCH TN19 ..... 62 A3
Acre Cl HWH RH16 ..... 71 K4
Acres Ri WADH TN5 ..... 45 L5
Adam Cl CROW TN6 ..... 40 A8
  STLEO TN38 ..... 161 M2
Adams Cl BRI BN1 ..... 169 H4
Adams La RYE TN31 ..... 87 K3
Adastra Av HPPT/KEY BN6 ..... 123 G2
Addingham Rd LW/ROSE BN22.... 11 J3
Addington Cl STLEO TN38 ..... 161 M7
Addison Rd HOVE BN3 ..... 6 A3
Adelaide Cl SEAF BN25 ..... 202 E1
Adelaide Crs HOVE BN3 ..... 186 C1
Adelaide Rd STLEO TN38 ..... 162 B3
Adelaide Sq SHOR BN43 ..... 166 B7
Ades Fld POLE BN26 ..... 176 F8
Admiral's Bridge La
  EGRIN RH19 ..... 23 J4
Adur Dr PEV BN24 ..... 197 G1
  SHOR BN43 ..... 166 A7
Adur Rd BURH RH15 ..... 97 J2
Agincourt Cl STLEO TN38 ..... 138 F7
Agnes St ROTT BN2 ..... 7 J2
Ainsworth Av ROTT BN2 ..... 188 D3
Ainsworth Cl ROTT BN2 ..... 188 D2
Airy Rd HAIL BN27 ..... 157 H5
Akehurst Fld BAT TN33 ..... 135 H3
Alan Wy ROTT BN2 ..... 169 M8

Albany Hl RTWE/PEM TN2 ..... 20 C1
Albany Ms HOVE BN3 ..... 168 B8
Albany Rd BEX TN40 ..... 183 J3
  SEAF BN25 ..... 202 C3
  STLEO TN38 ..... 162 B6
Albany Vls HOVE BN3 ..... 186 B1
Albert Cl HWH RH16 ..... 72 A2
Albert Dr BURH RH15 ..... 96 E4
Albert Ms HOVE BN3 ..... 168 B8
Albert Rd BEX TN40 ..... 183 J3
  BRI BN1 ..... 6 C4
  HAS TN34 ..... 5 H7
  POLE BN26 ..... 177 M7
  STHW BN42 ..... 167 G2
  UCK TN22 ..... 76 D8
Albert Ter EAST BN21 ..... 206 C1
Albion Cl BURH RH15 ..... 96 F4
Albion Hl ROTT BN2 ..... 7 H5
Albion Rd LW/ROSE BN22 ..... 11 G3
  RTW TN1 ..... 20 B1
Albion St LEW BN7 ..... 3 G5
  PTSD BN41 ..... 166 D8
  PTSD BN41 ..... 167 H7
  ROTT BN2 ..... 7 G4
  STHW BN42 ..... 167 G7
Albourne Cl ROTT BN2 ..... 169 L7
  STLEO TN38 ..... 161 M6
Aldborough Rd SLVH TN37 ..... 4 B4
Alderbrook Cl CROW TN6 ..... 40 A8
Alderbrook Wy CROW TN6 ..... 40 A8
Alder Cl CRAWE RH10 ..... 12 B6
  HTHF TN21 ..... 106 A1
  SLVH TN37 ..... 162 C1
Alders Av EGRIN RH19 ..... 13 K3
Alders View Dr EGRIN RH19 ..... 13 L2
Aldervale Cottages CROW TN6.... 40 A7
Aldrich Cl ROTT BN2 ..... 169 M8
Aldrington Av HOVE BN3 ..... 168 A6
Aldrington Cl HOVE BN3 ..... 167 K7
Alexander Dr BEXW TN39 ..... 182 E2
Alexandra Cl SEAF BN25 ..... 202 E1
Alexandra Rd BURH RH15 ..... 97 J4
  HTHF TN21 ..... 80 B8
  LW/ROSE BN22 ..... 197 K8
  MAYF TN20 ..... 57 J7
  SLVH TN37 ..... 4 A6
  UCK TN22 ..... 76 D8
Alexandra Vls BRI BN1 ..... 6 C4
Alford Wy BEX TN40 ..... 160 E8
Alfray Rd BEX TN40 ..... 184 A1
Alfred Rd BRI BN1 ..... 6 C4
  LGNY BN23 ..... 197 M6
  RHAS TN35 ..... 163 J3
Alfred St STLEO TN38 ..... 4 A8
Alfriston Rd SEAF BN25 ..... 159 J8
  EDN/EASTW BN20 ..... 206 C4
  ROTT BN2 ..... 169 M8
Alfriston Pk SEAF BN25 ..... 203 J1
Alfriston Rd SEAF BN25 ..... 203 H1
Alice Bright La CROW TN6 ..... 39 M7
Alice St HOVE BN3 ..... 186 D1
Allan Cl SBGH/RUST TN4 ..... 19 J2
Allards RHAS TN35 ..... 141 J6

Allen Rd HWH RH16 ..... 72 A1
Alien's Cl EGRIN RH19 ..... 14 D8
Allen Wy BEX TN40 ..... 160 F8
Allfrey Rd LW/ROSE BN22 ..... 197 K8
Allfreys La CROW TN6 ..... 39 K8
Allington Crs RING/NEW BN8 ..... 74 C7
Allington La LEW BN7 ..... 125 J7
Allington Rd RING/NEW BN8 ..... 74 C8
All Saints Gdns HTHF TN21 ..... 79 M7
All Saints La BEXW TN39 ..... 160 B7
All Saints' St HAS TN34 ..... 5 L6
Allwood Crs RHWH RH17 ..... 98 C2
Alma Rd HWH RH16 ..... 49 H6
Alma Ter SLVH TN37 ..... 4 A1
Alma Vls SLVH TN37 ..... 4 A1
Alpine Rd HAS TN34 ..... 5 K5
  HOVE BN3 ..... 167 M6
Alverstone Cl LGNY BN23 ..... 197 H2
Amanda Cl BEX TN40 ..... 160 F7
Amberley Cl BURH RH15 ..... 97 G2
  HWH RH16 ..... 71 K2
Amberley Dr HOVE BN3 ..... 167 L3
Amberley Rd LW/ROSE BN22 ..... 196 F5
Amberstone HAIL BN27 ..... 155 L3
Amberstone Cl HAS TN34 ..... 163 G2
Amberstone Vw HAIL BN27 ..... 155 J4
Ambleside Av PEAHV BN10 ..... 190 A7
Ambleside Rd RBTBR TN32 ..... 85 J1
America La HWH RH16 ..... 72 A1
Amesbury Crs HOVE BN3 ..... 167 L7
Amherst Cl SLVH TN37 ..... 4 C3
Amherst Crs HOVE BN3 ..... 167 M6
Amherst Gdns HAS TN34 ..... 4 D4
Amherst Rd BEX TN40 ..... 183 J2
  SBGH/RUST TN4 ..... 20 A1
  SLVH TN37 ..... 4 B4
Amhurst Rd PEAHV BN10 ..... 189 M7
Anchor Cl SHOR BN43 ..... 166 A8
Anchor Fld RING/NEW BN8 ..... 150 D1
Anchor La RING/NEW BN8 ..... 101 G8
Anderida Rd LW/ROSE BN22 ..... 196 B3
Anderson Cl NEWHV BN9 ..... 8 C3
Andrews Cl RBTBR TN32 ..... 85 J1
  RTWE/PEM TN2 ..... 20 D1
Angela Cl BEX TN40 ..... 160 F7
Anglesey Av HAIL BN27 ..... 155 G4
Angus Cl EDN/EASTW BN20 ..... 196 B6
Ann Cl HPPT/KEY BN6 ..... 123 G1
Annington Rd LW/ROSE BN22.... 11 H2
Ann St BRI BN1 ..... 6 E3
  HAS TN34 ..... 5 M1
Anson Cl LGNY BN23 ..... 197 L7
Ansty Cl ROTT BN2 ..... 187 L1
Antioch St LEW BN7 ..... 2 E7
Antony Cl SEAF BN25 ..... 192 B8
Antrona Cl BEXW TN39 ..... 182 C3
Anvil Cl PTSD BN41 ..... 167 H4
  UCK TN22 ..... 76 C7
Anvil Ct SLVH TN37 ..... 162 C1
Anzac Cl PEAHV BN10 ..... 190 C5
Appledene Cnr
  RING/NEW BN8 ..... 99 L7
Appledore Cl LGNY BN23 ..... 197 K4
Appledore Gdns HWH RH16 ..... 48 F8

Appledore Rd ROTT BN2 ..... 169 M2
Applesham Av HOVE BN3 ..... 167 L4
Applesham Wy PTSD BN41 ..... 167 G5
Applewood Cl SLVH TN37 ..... 162 B2
The Approach BRI BN1 ..... 168 E3
Apsley St SBGH/RUST TN4 ..... 19 K2
Aquarius Cl PEAHV BN10 ..... 190 C8
Aquila Pk SEAF BN25 ..... 203 G3
Arbourvale STLEO TN38 ..... 162 A5
Archery Rd STLEO TN38 ..... 162 B7
Archery Wk HAIL BN27 ..... 155 J8
Ardingly Rd HWH RH16 ..... 49 J4
  ROTT BN2 ..... 189 K6
Ardingly St ROTT BN2 ..... 7 G7
Ardings Cl RHWH RH17 ..... 34 B7
Argent Cl SEAF BN25 ..... 203 G1
Argos Hill Rd MAYF TN20 ..... 56 D2
Argyle Rd BRI BN1 ..... 6 D2
Arlington Crs BRI BN1 ..... 169 L1
Arlington Gdns ROTT BN2 ..... 189 K4
Arlington Rd EAST BN21 ..... 10 C6
Arlington Rd East HAIL BN27 ..... 154 F8
Arlington Rd West HAIL BN27 ..... 154 F8
Armstrong Cl STLEO TN38 ..... 161 L2
Arnbury Ms STLEO TN38 ..... 161 L8
Arnold St ROTT BN2 ..... 7 K3
Arnside Rd STLEO TN38 ..... 161 L8
Arran Cl HAIL BN27 ..... 155 G4
Arthur Rd BEXW TN39 ..... 183 H2
Arthur St HOVE BN3 ..... 168 A6
Arundel Cl HAIL BN27 ..... 155 J4
  PEV BN24 ..... 180 F8
  SHOR BN43 ..... 166 C6
Arundel Dr East ROTT BN2 ..... 189 J5
Arundel Dr West ROTT BN2 ..... 189 H5
Arundel Gn SEAF BN25 ..... 203 G3
Arundel Pl ROTT BN2 ..... 187 L2
Arundel Rd EAST BN21 ..... 10 B4
  NEWHV BN9 ..... 191 L5
  PEAHV BN10 ..... 190 C7
  ROTT BN2 ..... 187 L3
  RTW TN1 ..... 20 B4
  SEAF BN25 ..... 203 G3
Arundel Road Central
  PEAHV BN10 ..... 190 B7
Arundel Rd West PEAHV BN10 .. 190 A6
Arundel St ROTT BN2 ..... 187 L3
Arundel Ter ROTT BN2 ..... 187 L3
Arun Wy PEV BN24 ..... 196 F1
Ascham Pl EDN/EASTW BN20 ... 206 E5
Ascot Cl EDN/EASTW BN20 ..... 206 F6
Ascot Ms STLEO TN38 ..... 162 A6
Ashbrook Rd SLVH TN37 ..... 162 B2
Ashburnham Cl BRI BN1 ..... 169 L1
Ashburnham Dr BRI BN1 ..... 146 D8
Ashburnham Gdns EAST BN21 ... 10 A2
Ashburnham Pl HAIL BN27 ..... 155 J4
Ashburnham Rd EAST BN21 ..... 10 B3
  RHAS TN35 ..... 163 J5
Ashby Cl BEXW TN39 ..... 160 A7
Ash Cl CRAWE RH10 ..... 12 C5
  HOVE BN3 ..... 168 C3
  LW/ROSE BN22 ..... 196 E3

  RTWE/PEM TN2 ..... 20 D6
Ashcombe Dr BEXW TN39 ..... 182 D3
Ashcombe Hollow LEW BN7 ..... 148 D7
Ashcombe La LEW BN7 ..... 148 E8
Ash Ct HAIL BN27 ..... 155 G8
Ashcroft Cl RING/NEW BN8 ..... 150 D1
  SHOR BN43 ..... 166 D1
Ashdown Av ROTT BN2 ..... 189 H5
Ashdown Cha UCK TN22 ..... 52 C1
Ashdown Cl FROW RH18 ..... 25 G4
  HWH RH16 ..... 72 B2
  SBGH/RUST TN4 ..... 19 M2
  STLEO TN38 ..... 161 M4
Ashdown Pl HTHF TN21 ..... 80 B8
Ashdown Rd BEX TN40 ..... 183 L2
  FROW RH18 ..... 24 F4
  ROTT BN2 ..... 169 H6
Ashdown Vw EGRIN RH19 ..... 13 L7
Ashenden Av RYE TN31 ..... 117 J2
Ash Dr SEAF BN25 ..... 203 J3
Ashenden Av RYE TN31 ..... 117 J2
Ashenground Cl HWH RH16 ..... 71 L3
Ashenground Rd HWH RH16 ..... 71 K3
Ashentree La LYDD TN29 ..... 94 A1
Asher Reeds RRTW TN3 ..... 19 G2
Ashford Cl HAIL BN27 ..... 155 J7
Ashford Rd BRI BN1 ..... 169 G4
  EAST BN21 ..... 10 C5
  HAS TN34 ..... 4 E2
Ashford Sq EAST BN21 ..... 10 C5
Ashford Wy HAS TN34 ..... 4 E1
Ashgate Rd LGNY BN23 ..... 197 L4
  LYDD TN29 ..... 95 K7
  PEV BN24 ..... 179 K8
Ashington Gdns PEAHV BN10 ... 190 B8
Ashington Rd LW/ROSE BN22 .... 197 G5
Ashleigh Gdns CROW TN6 ..... 39 L2
Ashley Cl BRI BN1 ..... 145 L7
Ashley Gdns HAIL BN27 ..... 155 J3
  MAYF TN20 ..... 57 G4
  SBGH/RUST TN4 ..... 19 J1
Ashley Park Cl SBGH/RUST TN4 .. 19 J1
Ashley Rd CROW TN6 ..... 41 K5
Ashlings Wy HOVE BN3 ..... 167 L4
  SHOR BN43 ..... 166 B5
Ashmore Cl PEAHV BN10 ..... 190 C4
Ashton Ri ROTT BN2 ..... 7 G5
Ashtonville Cl
  RING/NEW BN8 ..... 150 E1
Ash Tree Cl HTHF TN21 ..... 80 A7
Ashurst Av ROTT BN2 ..... 189 L6
Ashurst Rd ROTT BN2 ..... 189 L6
  RRTW TN3 ..... 18 B4
  SEAF BN25 ..... 202 F4
Ashway BURH RH15 ..... 97 G4
Aspen Cl HWH RH16 ..... 72 B2
Aspen Rd LW/ROSE BN22 ..... 196 E4
Aspen Wk BEXW TN39 ..... 182 C2
Astaire Av LW/ROSE BN22 ..... 11 G3
Asten Cl STLEO TN38 ..... 161 L2
Asten Flds BAT TN33 ..... 137 H2

Athelstan Cl LGNY BN23 197 M6
Athelstan Rd RHAS TN35 163 K4
Atlantic Dr LGNY BN23 197 M7
Atlingworth St ROTT BN2 7 H8
Attree Dr ROTT BN2 7 J5
Auckland Dr ROTT BN2 169 M5
Audrey Cl BRI BN1 168 E1
SEAF BN25 202 D1
Augustines Wy HWH RH16 71 L2
Augustus Wy STLEO TN38 138 F8
Austen Cl EGRIN RH19 13 H5
Austen Wy RHAS TN35 163 K1
Avard Crs EDN/EASTW BN20 196 B8
Avards Cl HAWK TN18 47 L6
Avenue La EAST BN21 10 D5
The Avenue EAST BN21 10 D5
HAIL BN27 155 H8
HTHF TN21 80 B8
HTHF TN21 105 M6
LEW BN7 2 D5
LEW BN7 171 K1
MAYF TN20 57 H4
RHAS TN35 164 F2
ROTT BN2 169 K4
Avery Cl PTSD BN41 166 F2
Aviary Wy CRAWE RH10 12 C5
Aviemore Rd CROW TN6 39 K4
Avis Cl NEWHV BN9 191 L5
Avis Rd NEWHV BN9 191 K5
Avis Wy NEWHV BN9 9 J1
Avondale Rd HOVE BN3 168 D7
LW/ROSE BN22 11 H3
SEAF BN25 202 F3
STLEO TN38 162 A5
Avonhurst BURH RH15 97 H3
Avon St RTW TN1 20 C1
Awbrook Cl RHWH RH17 72 F3
Aylesbury Av LGNY BN23 197 L6
Aymer Rd HOVE BN3 168 A8
Ayscue Cl LGNY BN23 197 M7


## B


Babylon Wy EDN/EASTW BN20 196 B6
Back La HTHF TN21 79 J7
HTHF TN21 107 K6
UCK TN22 53 H4
WSEA TN36 116 E7
Back Rd HAWK TN18 64 B1
Backwoods Cl HWH RH16 49 H8
Backwoods La HWH RH16 49 G8
Baden Rd ROTT BN2 169 K6
Badens Cl RING/NEW BN8 74 C8
Badger Cl PTSD BN41 167 H4
Badger Dr RHWH RH17 71 J1
Badgers Brow
EDN/EASTW BN20 196 B6
Badgers Cl CROW TN6 39 L3
Badgers Copse SEAF BN25 203 J3
Badgers Dene LEW BN7 172 D6
Badgers Fld PEAHV BN10 190 C5
Badgers Holt RTWE/PEM TN2 20 E1
Badgers Mt BEXW TN39 182 E1
Badgers Wk BURH RH15 97 K4
Badgers Wy EGRIN RH19 13 L3
HAS TN34 162 D1
Badger Wy BRI BN1 146 E8
Badlesmere Rd
LW/ROSE BN22 197 G8
Bagham La HAIL BN27 133 M8
Bahram Rd POLE BN26 177 L8
Bailey Crs LW/ROSE BN22 196 B3
Baillie Av LW/ROSE BN22 11 J1
Bainbridge Cl SEAF BN25 202 F4
Bainden Cl CROW TN6 41 K5
Baird Dr HAS TN34 162 E3
Baker's Rd EAST BN21 206 D3
Baker St BRI BN1 6 F3
NEWHV BN9 9 J4
UCK TN22 76 D8
Bakewell Rd EAST BN21 206 D2
Balaclava La WADH TN5 31 M7
Balcombe La RHWH RH17 35 L4
Balcombe Rd HWH RH16 48 D6
PEAHV BN10 190 B6
Baldock Rd WADH TN5 43 K2
Baldslow Down SLVH TN37 139 J5
Baldslow Rd HAS TN34 5 G2
Baldwin Av EAST BN21 196 C8
Bale Cl BEXW TN39 182 E1
Balfour Gdns FROW RH18 24 E6
Balfour Rd BRI BN1 168 F4
Ballard Dr RING/NEW BN8 127 M6
Ballards Hl BAT TN33 160 F2
Ballsocks La HTHF TN21 106 C6
Balmoral Cl SEAF BN25 193 G8
Balsdean Rd ROTT BN2 170 D5
Bamford Cl ROTT BN2 170 A4
Bampfield St PTSD BN41 167 H6
Bancroft Rd BEXW TN39 183 H1
Bank Rd BEXW TN39 160 C7
Banks Castle LEW BN7 2 F6
Bankside BRI BN1 168 C1
HPPT/KEY BN6 122 F1
WADH TN5 43 L1
Banks Rd RING/NEW BN8 73 L5
Banner Farm Rd
RTWE/PEM TN2 20 B4
Bannings V ROTT BN2 189 K6
Bannisters Fld RING/NEW BN8 74 F7
Bannister Wy HWH RH16 48 D8
Baranscraig Av BRI BN1 146 A7
Barcombe Av SEAF BN25 203 J3
Barcombe Cl SEAF BN25 203 J3
Barcombe Mills Rd
RING/NEW BN8 126 F4
Barcombe Rd BRI BN1 169 L2
Barden Rd LW/ROSE BN22 11 J3
Bardown Rd WADH TN5 44 E8
Bargate Cl BEXW TN39 160 C7
Barham Cl HAS TN34 162 D2
Barkdale BURH RH15 97 K1
Barley Cl PEAHV BN10 190 B4
Barley Dr BURH RH15 96 C2
Barley La RHAS TN35 163 J5
Barley Mow La HTHF TN21 107 H1
Barming Cl LGNY BN23 197 K4
Barnard Ga HWH RH16 48 E7
Barn Cl HAIL BN27 155 J5
LEW BN7 171 L1
PEV BN24 179 G8
SEAF BN25 193 G8
SLVH TN37 162 C1
Barn Cottage La HWH RH16 72 A1
Barnes Rd PTSD BN41 167 H6
Barnett Rd BRI BN1 169 H4
Barnett Wy UCK TN22 76 D7
Barnet Wy HOVE BN3 167 L3
Barnfield CROW TN6 40 A4
LEW BN7 124 E1
RTWE/PEM TN2 19 M7
Barnfield Cl HAS TN34 4 D4
Barnfield Gdns
HPPT/KEY BN6 123 L3
Barn Field Gdns ROTT BN2 7 K5
The Barnhams BEXW TN39 182 E3
Barn Hatch Cl LEW BN7 2 A8
Barnhorn Cl BEXW TN39 182 C2
Barnhorn Rd BAT TN33 181 K2
BEXW TN39 182 A2
Barn La UCK TN22 77 K6
Barnmead HWH RH16 48 D7
Barn Ri BRI BN1 168 D1
SEAF BN25 203 G1
Barn Rd LEW BN7 3 J2
Barnside Av BURH RH15 97 J5
Barons Cl SEAF BN25 202 C1
Barons Ct BURH RH15 97 H4
Barons Down Rd LEW BN7 2 A8
Barons Wy POLE BN26 195 M1
Barrack Rd BEX TN40 183 J1
Barrack Sq WSEA TN36 116 F7
Barrhill Av BRI BN1 145 M7
Barrie Cl LGNY BN23 197 L4
Barrington Cl HWH RH16 49 G6
Barrington Wd HWH RH16 48 F6
Barrow Cl BRI BN1 169 J4
Barrowfield Cl HOVE BN3 168 C3
Barrowfield Dr HOVE BN3 168 C4
Barrow Hl BRI BN1 169 J4
Barrow La RRTW TN3 18 F5
Barrow Ri SLVH TN37 162 C1
Barry Wk ROTT BN2 7 K5
Bartholomews BRI BN1 6 E7
Bartley Mill Cl PEV BN24 197 H1
Bartley Mill Rd RRTW TN3 31 L2
Barton Crs EGRIN RH19 14 A6
Basin Rd South PTSD BN41 166 F8
Baslow Rd EDN/EASTW BN20 206 D7
Bassetts La CROW TN6 42 E3
MAYF TN20 56 F1
Batchelor Wy UCK TN22 76 A7
Bateman's La BUR/ETCH TN19 83 G2
Batemans Rd ROTT BN2 170 E7
Bates Rd BRI BN1 168 F4
Bathford Cl LGNY BN23 197 K4
Bath Rd EAST BN21 10 D7
Bath St BRI BN1 6 C3
Battery Hl RHAS TN35 164 B2
Battle Cl SEAF BN25 203 J1
Battle Crs HAIL BN27 155 J6
SLVH TN37 162 B2
Battle Gates BAT TN33 137 H2
Battle Hl BAT TN33 137 L3
Battle Rd BAT TN33 138 E6
HAIL BN27 155 H6
SLVH TN37 138 F8
Batts Bridge Rd UCK TN22 76 A2
Bavant Rd BRI BN1 168 E4
Baxter Rd LEW BN7 2 D3
Baxters La RHWH RH17 36 C8
Baxter St ROTT BN2 7 K3
Bay Av PEV BN24 198 E1
Bayencourt North BEXW TN39 183 H1
Bayhall Rd RTWE/PEM TN2 20 D3
Bayham Rd HAIL BN27 155 K7
LW/ROSE BN22 11 J4
RTWE/PEM TN2 20 A6
Bayhams Fld EGRIN RH19 22 F8
Bayley's La POLE BN26 177 G3
Baylis Crs BURH RH15 96 E2
Bay Pond Rd EAST BN21 206 D2
Bay Rd PEV BN24 198 D2
Bay Tree Cl HTHF TN21 80 B8
SHOR BN43 166 C5
Bay Tree La POLE BN26 177 M6
Bayview Rd PEAHV BN10 200 E1
Bay Vue Rd NEWHV BN9 8 F4
Baywood Gdns ROTT BN2 170 C5
Bazehill Rd ROTT BN2 189 G3
Beach Cl SEAF BN25 202 D3
The Beachings PEV BN24 198 C2
Beach Rd LW/ROSE BN22 11 K2
NEWHV BN9 9 J5
Beachy Head Rd
EDN/EASTW BN20 206 B6
EDN/EASTW BN20 208 B1
Beacon Cl BRI BN1 169 G4
CROW TN6 39 L4
SEAF BN25 202 D1
Beacon Dr SEAF BN25 202 D1
Beacon Gdns CROW TN6 39 L3
Beacon Hl BEXW TN39 159 M8
ROTT BN2 188 E3
Beacon Hurst HPPT/KEY BN6 123 H3
Beacon La RBTBR TN32 86 E6
Beacon Rd CROW TN6 39 J6
HPPT/KEY BN6 123 K5
RHAS TN35 163 L2
SEAF BN25 202 D2
Beacon Rd West CROW TN6 39 K4
Beaconsfield Rd BEX TN40 160 C8
BRI BN1 6 E2
BRI BN1 169 G6
HAS TN34 5 H2
PTSD BN41 167 H6
RHWH RH17 36 D6
Beaconsfield Vls BRI BN1 168 F5
The Beacon EGRIN RH19 22 E7
Beal Crs BRI BN1 169 H4
Beales La RYE TN31 65 H8
Beale St BURH RH15 96 E5
Beamsley Rd LW/ROSE BN22 11 J3
Beaney's La HAS TN34 139 L8
RHAS TN35 139 M6
Bear Rd ROTT BN2 169 J6
Bear Yd LEW BN7 3 H6
Beatrice La EAST BN21 10 C5
Beatrice Wk BEXW TN39 160 A8
Beatty Av BRI BN1 146 D7
Beatty Rd LGNY BN23 197 L8
Beauchamp Rd STLEO TN38 162 A3
STLEO TN38 162 A2
Beauford Rd HTHF TN21 105 M7
Beaufort Crs SLVH TN37 4 A2
Beaufort Rd SLVH TN37 4 A2
Beaufort Ter ROTT BN2 7 J4
Beauharrow Rd SLVH TN37 139 G8
Beaulieu Dr PEV BN24 197 G1
Beaulieu Gdns SLVH TN37 139 J8
Beaulieu Rd BEXW TN39 182 C4
Beau Nash Wy
RTWE/PEM TN2 20 B5
Beauport Gdns SLVH TN37 139 G7
Beauport Home Farm Cl
SLVH TN37 139 G8
Beaver Cl CROW TN6 40 A5
Beckenham Cl HAIL BN27 155 H3
Becket Cl HAS TN34 5 J4
Beckets Wy UCK TN22 103 H1
Beckett Wy EGRIN RH19 13 M6
LEW BN7 2 F2
Beckley Cl ROTT BN2 187 L1
STLEO TN38 161 K4
Beckworth Cl HWH RH16 49 G8
Beckworth La HWH RH16 49 G8
Bedales Hl HWH RH16 72 D1
Bedelands Cl BURH RH15 97 H1
Bedford Av BEX TN40 183 K2
Bedford Ct UCK TN22 76 C6
Bedford Gv EAST BN21 10 D4
Bedford Pl BRI BN1 6 A6
Bedford Rd RHAS TN35 163 J4
Bedford Sq BRI BN1 6 A7
Bedford St ROTT BN2 7 J8
Bedfordwell Rd EAST BN21 10 D3
LW/ROSE BN22 10 F3
Bedgebury Cl STLEO TN38 161 L4
Beecham Pl STLEO TN38 161 M2
Beech Cl BAT TN33 111 H7
BEXW TN39 159 J8
PTSD BN41 166 F3
Beechers Rd PTSD BN41 166 F3
Beeches Cl HTHF TN21 80 B6
UCK TN22 76 D6
Beeches Farm Rd CROW TN6 40 A5
Beeches La EGRIN RH19 23 M2
Beeches Rd CROW TN6 40 B4
The Beeches BRI BN1 168 D3
Beech Farm Rd BAT TN33 112 D2
Beechfield Cl PEV BN24 179 J8
Beech Flds EGRIN RH19 13 M3
Beech Gdns CRAWE RH10 12 A7
Beech Green La HRTF TN7 16 F6
Beech Gv ROTT BN2 169 L3
Beech Hl HWH RH16 72 B3
Beech Holme CRAWE RH10 12 A6
Beech House La RBTBR TN32 62 C7
Beech Hurst Cl HWH RH16 71 J2
Beeching Cl BEXW TN39 183 H2
Beeching Rd BEXW TN39 183 H2
Beeching Wy EGRIN RH19 13 L5
Beech La HAWK TN18 65 J3
Beech St RTW TN1 20 B1
Beechwood Av BRI BN1 168 F2
Beechwood Cl BRI BN1 168 F2
BUR/ETCH TN19 60 B7
HAIL BN27 178 C1
Beechwood Crs
EDN/EASTW BN20 206 D3
Beechwood Gdns HAS TN34 162 D1
Beechwood La HTHF TN21 106 B1
LEW BN7 125 L5
Beechwood Ms RTWE/PEM TN2 20 E2
Beechwoods BURH RH15 97 G5
Beechy Av EDN/EASTW BN20 206 B2
Beechy Gdns
EDN/EASTW BN20 206 B2
Beechy Rd UCK TN22 103 M5
Beeding Av HOVE BN3 167 M3
Bee Rd PEAHV BN10 190 C6
Beggar's La POY/PYE BN45 144 D1
Beggar's Wood Rd
RING/NEW BN8 73 J8
Belfast St HOVE BN3 168 B8
Belfry Orch UCK TN22 102 D1
The Belfry HAIL BN27 155 G6
Belgrave Crs SEAF BN25 202 F1
Belgrave Pl ROTT BN2 7 L9
Belgrave Rd RTW TN1 20 A2
SEAF BN25 202 D2
Belgrave St ROTT BN2 7 G4
Bell Alley Rd BUR/ETCH TN19 60 B8
Bell Banks Rd HAIL BN27 155 J7
Belle Hl BEX TN40 183 J1
Bellevue Gdns ROTT BN2 7 K7
Belle Vue Rd LW/ROSE BN22 11 J1
Bell Hammer EGRIN RH19 13 L6
Bellhurst Rd RBTBR TN32 85 G3
Bellingham Cl SLVH TN37 162 B2
Bellingham Crs HOVE BN3 167 K6
Bell La LEW BN7 2 C8
UCK TN22 52 A2
UCK TN22 76 C8
Bell Wk UCK TN22 76 C8
Belmont BRI BN1 6 A1
Belmont Cl HPPT/KEY BN6 122 E1
Belmont La HPPT/KEY BN6 122 C2
Belmont Rd RHAS TN35 5 M4
UCK TN22 76 C7
Belmont St BRI BN1 6 F3
Belmore Rd LW/ROSE BN22 11 G4
Belton Rd ROTT BN2 7 G1
Beltring Rd LW/ROSE BN22 11 H4
Beltring Ter LW/ROSE BN22 11 H3
Belvedere Gdns CROW TN6 40 A5
SEAF BN25 203 G1
Belvedere Pk STLEO TN38 162 A6
Bembridge Rd LGNY BN23 197 H3
Bembridge St ROTT BN2 7 K1
Bembrook Rd HAS TN34 5 L4
Bemzells La HAIL BN27 133 K4
Benbow Av LGNY BN23 197 L8
Benchfield Cl EGRIN RH19 14 A6
Benenden Cl SEAF BN25 203 G2
Benenden Ri HAS TN34 162 E3
Benett Av HOVE BN3 168 B4
Benett Dr HOVE BN3 168 B4
Benfield Cl PTSD BN41 167 J6
Benfield Crs PTSD BN41 167 J5
Benfield Wy PTSD BN41 167 J6
Bengairn Av BRI BN1 146 A7
Benhall Mill Rd RTWE/PEM TN2 20 C6
Benjamin Cl LW/ROSE BN22 196 F4
Bennett Rd ROTT BN2 187 L2
Bentham Rd ROTT BN2 7 J3
Bentswood Crs HWH RH16 72 A1
Bentswood Rd HWH RH16 71 M1
Berberis Ct SHOR BN43 166 B5
Beresford Rd NEWHV BN9 191 L5
ROTT BN2 7 M7
Bergamot Crs SHOR BN43 166 C5
Beristede Cl EDN/EASTW BN20 10 B9
EDN/EASTW BN20 206 E5
Berkeley Rd RTW TN1 20 A4
Berkley Rd MAYF TN20 56 F5
Berlin Rd RHAS TN35 163 J4
Bermuda Pl LGNY BN23 198 A7
Bernard La EAST BN21 10 C5
Bernard Pl ROTT BN2 7 K2
Bernard Rd ROTT BN2 7 K2
Berriedale Gdns POLE BN26 195 M1
Berriedale Av HOVE BN3 167 L8
Berry Cl BURH RH15 97 G1
PEAHV BN10 190 A5
Berry La RHWH RH17 34 C7
Berwick Cl BEXW TN39 159 J8
LW/ROSE BN22 196 C3
SEAF BN25 202 D2
Berwick Rd ROTT BN2 189 K3
Betchley Cl EGRIN RH19 13 L3
Bethune Rd BEX TN40 183 L3
Bethune Wy HAS TN34 5 H4
Beulah Rd RTW TN1 20 C2
Beuzeville Av HAIL BN27 155 H6
Bevendean Av ROTT BN2 189 K5
Bevendean Crs ROTT BN2 169 L4
Bevendean Rd ROTT BN2 169 K6
Beverington Cl EAST BN21 196 D8
Beverington Rd EAST BN21 196 D8
Bewl Bridge Cl WADH TN5 46 B3
Bewlbridge La RRTW TN3 33 J5
Bexhill Rd BAT TN33 159 H1
LW/ROSE BN22 11 K2
ROTT BN2 170 D5
STLEO TN38 184 B1
Bexleigh Av STLEO TN38 184 B1
Bexley Cl HAIL BN27 155 H4
Bicton Gdns BEXW TN39 182 E2
Biddenden Cl LGNY BN23 197 K4
Bidwell Av BEXW TN39 160 A8
Bigwood Av HOVE BN3 168 D7
Billingham La RYE TN31 115 J3
Binsted Cl LW/ROSE BN22 196 E4
Birch Av HWH RH16 72 A3
Birch Cl CRAWE RH10 12 C6
HWH RH16 72 B3
UCK TN22 76 E6
Birchen La HWH RH16 48 E6
Birches Cl CROW TN6 39 M2
Birchetts Av RRTW TN3 18 E3
Birchetts Green La WADH TN5 44 E3
Birch Grove Crs BRI BN1 169 G1
Birchgrove La RHWH RH17 35 M5
Birchgrove Rd RHWH RH17 50 D1
Birchington Cl BEXW TN39 182 D2
Birch Rd LGNY BN23 197 J7
Birch Vw BEXW TN39 160 C8
Birch Wy HAIL BN27 155 H8
HAS TN34 162 E3
HTHF TN21 106 A1
HWH RH16 72 A4
Birchwood Grove Rd
BURH RH15 97 H5
Birdham Rd ROTT BN2 169 L3
Bird In Eye Hl UCK TN22 76 E8
Bird in Hand St RRTW TN3 18 C6
Bird La WADH TN5 43 H2
Birk Dl BEXW TN39 182 D2
Birling Cl ROTT BN2 169 K5
SEAF BN25 202 D2
Birling Dr RTWE/PEM TN2 20 A6
Birling Gap Rd
EDN/EASTW BN20 208 B1
Birling Park Av RTWE/PEM TN2 20 B6
Birling Rd RTWE/PEM TN2 20 B6
Birling St EDN/EASTW BN20 206 C2
Bishop's Cl RING/NEW BN8 127 L8
SEAF BN25 202 C2
Bishop's Down SBGH/RUST TN4 19 L3
Bishop's Down Park Rd
SBGH/RUST TN4 19 L2
Bishop's Down Rd
SBGH/RUST TN4 19 L3
Bishops Dr LEW BN7 2 B7
Bishop's La RBTBR TN32 85 G3
RING/NEW BN8 127 K8
Bishops Rd HOVE BN3 168 C5
Bishopstone Dr ROTT BN2 189 H4
Bishopstone La HPPT/KEY BN6 96 A1
RHWH RH17 70 A7
Bishopstone Rd SEAF BN25 192 C8
Bishop's Wk BEX TN40 160 F8
Bixley La RYE TN31 89 G5
Blackdon Hl CROW TN6 29 J8
Blackdown Rd HTHF TN21 81 K8
Blackfields Av BEXW TN39 182 F1
Black Hl HWH RH16 49 G7
Blackhouse La BURH RH15 97 H2
Blacklands Crs FROW RH18 24 F4
Blacklands Dr HAS TN34 5 G1
Black Lion St BRI BN1 6 E8
Blackman Av STLEO TN38 162 A3
Blackman St BRI BN1 6 E4
Blackmill Cl BEXW TN39 160 A6
Blackness Rd CROW TN6 39 M5
Black Pth POLE BN26 178 A8
Blacksmiths Copse
HAIL BN27 155 G8
Blacksmiths La BAT TN33 136 E6
WADH TN5 44 A1
Blackstone Wy BURH RH15 97 G1
Blackthorn Cl BRI BN1 168 D3
LW/ROSE BN22 196 E4
PTSD BN41 167 H4
SLVH TN37 162 C2
Blackthorns HWH RH16 49 G7
Blackthorns Cl HWH RH16 49 G7
The Blackthorns BURH RH15 97 H1
Blackthorn Wy RHAS TN35 164 F2
Blackwater Rd
EDN/EASTW BN20 10 C9
Blackwell Farm Rd EGRIN RH19 13 M3
Blackwell Hollow EGRIN RH19 13 M4
Blackwell Rd EGRIN RH19 13 M4
Blakeney Av PEAHV BN10 8 A5
Blaker St ROTT BN2 7 G7
Blakes Wy LGNY BN23 197 M8
Blatchington Cl SEAF BN25 202 F2
Blatchington Hl SEAF BN25 202 E2
Blatchington Mill Dr
PEV BN24 197 J1
Blatchington Rd HOVE BN3 168 B7
RTW TN1 20 A5
SEAF BN25 202 E3
Bleak Rd LYDD TN29 95 J8
Blenheim Cl EGRIN RH19 14 A3
Blenheim Flds FROW RH18 24 E3
Blenheim Pl BRI BN1 6 F5
Blenheim Wy POLE BN26 178 D8
WADH TN5 46 C3
Bletchinglye La CROW TN6 41 L5
Blind La RING/NEW BN8 74 E8
Blois Rd LEW BN7 2 B2
Blomfield Rd SLVH TN37 4 B6
Bloomsbury Pl ROTT BN2 7 K9
Bloomsbury St ROTT BN2 7 K8
Blount Av EGRIN RH19 13 J5
Bluebell Cl EGRIN RH19 13 H5
HWH RH16 71 M2
Blue Haze Av SEAF BN25 203 H2
Bluemans La BAT TN33 139 G3
Bluestone Cl STLEO TN38 161 M4
Blunts Wood Crs RHWH RH17 48 B8
Blunts Wood Rd RHWH RH17 48 B8
The Blytons EGRIN RH19 13 H5
Boarders La WADH TN5 45 J3
Boast La RING/NEW BN8 126 E1
Bocking Cl WADH TN5 43 L2
Boddingtons La
HPPT/KEY BN6 123 K3
Bodiam Av BEX TN40 160 D8
ROTT BN2 170 B5
Bodiam Cl ROTT BN2 170 B4
SEAF BN25 203 J2
Bodiam Crs LW/ROSE BN22 197 G4
Bodiam Dr STLEO TN38 161 K4
Bodiam Rd HAWK TN18 63 M4
Bodle Crs BEXW TN39 160 B7
Bohemia Rd SLVH TN37 4 A4
STLEO TN38 162 B5
Bolding Wy HWH RH16 71 K4
Bolebrooke Rd BEX TN40 183 K3
Bolney Av PEAHV BN10 190 C8
Bolney Rd ROTT BN2 169 M2
Bolnore Rd HWH RH16 71 J2
Bolsover Rd EDN/EASTW BN20 206 E6
HOVE BN3 167 L7
Bolton Cl UCK TN22 76 A8
Bolton Rd EAST BN21 10 F7
Boltro Rd HWH RH16 71 K1
Bonchurch Rd ROTT BN2 7 K1
Bond St BRI BN1 6 E6
Bonfire La RHWH RH17 50 C2
Boniface Cl PEV BN24 179 J8
Bonny Wood Rd
HPPT/KEY BN6 122 E3
Booker Cl CROW TN6 40 A5
Bopeep Bostal POLE BN26 175 H7
Bopeep La POLE BN26 175 H6
Bordehill La HWH RH16 48 D2
Border Ct EGRIN RH19 13 M2
Borders La BUR/ETCH TN19 61 G6
Boreham Hl HAIL BN27 158 A3
Boreham La HAIL BN27 157 L5
Borough La EDN/EASTW BN20 206 D3
Borough St BRI BN1 6 A6
Borrowdale Cl LGNY BN23 197 J2
Borrow King Cl ROTT BN2 169 K5
Boscawen Cl LGNY BN23 197 M7
Boscobel Rd STLEO TN38 162 A7
Boscobel Rd North
STLEO TN38 162 A6
Boship Cl LGNY BN23 197 G2
Bostal Rd RING/NEW BN8 174 B2
Boston Cl LGNY BN23 197 M7
Boston Rd HWH RH16 72 A1
Boston St BRI BN1 6 E2
Bough Beeches BURH RH15 97 J5
Boughey Pl LEW BN7 2 F1
The Boulevard PEV BN24 180 E8
Boundary & Station Roads
PTSD BN41 167 J8
Boundary Rd ROTT BN2 187 L3
RTWE/PEM TN2 20 D5
The Boundary RRTW TN3 19 H3
SEAF BN25 202 E4
Bourg-de-peage Av
EGRIN RH19 14 A5
Bourne La RBTBR TN32 62 F6
Bourne St LW/ROSE BN22 11 G5
The Bourne HAS TN34 5 L5
HPPT/KEY BN6 96 E8
Bowden Ri SEAF BN25 192 E8
Bowen Rd SBGH/RUST TN4 19 H1
Bower Cl SLVH TN37 162 B2
Bowers Pl CRAWE RH10 12 B6
The Bower HWH RH16 71 K1
Bowley Rd HAIL BN27 155 J7
Bowmans Dr BAT TN33 111 K8
Bowood Av LW/ROSE BN22 197 H8
Bowrey Pl BEX TN40 183 J1
Bowring Wy ROTT BN2 7 M8
Bowsprit Ms STLEO TN38 138 E7
Boxes La RHWH RH17 50 C2
Boxgrove Cl BEX TN40 183 M2
Box La EGRIN RH19 14 E8
Box's La RHWH RH17 36 C8

Boyce's St *BRI* BN1 .......... 6 D7
Boyne Pk *SBGH/RUST* TN4 ... 19 M2
Boyne Rd *RHAS* TN35 ......... 163 J5
Brackenbury Cl *PTSD* BN41 .. 167 H4
Bracken Cl *CROW* TN6 ......... 40 C5
  *RTWE/PEM* TN2 ............ 20 E1
Brackendale *RHAS* TN35 ...... 163 K4
Brackenhill *HRTF* TN7 ......... 26 A5
Bracken Rd *EDN/EASTW* BN20 .. 206 A1
  *RTWE/PEM* TN2 ............ 20 E1
  *SEAF* BN25 ................ 203 G4
Bracken Wy *HTHF* TN21 ........ 80 E5
Brackerne Cl *HOVE* BN3 ....... 182 C4
Brading Cl *HAS* TN34 ......... 4 F1
  *LGNY* BN23 ............... 197 H2
Brading Rd *ROTT* BN2 ........... 7 K2
Bradley Rd *HAIL* BN27 ........ 157 J5
  *RRTW* TN3 ................ 17 K1
Braemore Rd *HOVE* BN3 ....... 167 L8
Braeside Av *BRI* BN1 ......... 145 M7
Bramber Av *HOVE* BN3 ........ 167 M3
  *PEAHV* BN10 .............. 190 C7
Bramber Av North
  *PEAHV* BN10 .............. 190 C6
Bramber Cl *HWH* RH16 ......... 71 K3
  *PEAHV* BN10 .............. 190 C6
  *SEAF* BN25 ............... 202 F4
Bramber La *SEAF* BN25 ........ 202 F4
Bramber Rd *SEAF* BN25 ....... 202 F4
Bramber Wy *BURH* RH15 ....... 97 G2
Bramble Cl *LGNY* BN23 ....... 197 H3
Bramble Cft *CROW* TN6 ....... 40 A4
Brambledean Rd *PTSD* BN41 .. 167 H7
Bramble Dr *HAIL* BN27 ....... 155 G2
Bramble Gdns *BURH* RH15 .... 96 D2
Bramble Ri *BRI* BN1 ......... 168 C1
Brambles *HPPT/KEY* BN6 ..... 122 F1
Brambleside *UCK* TN22 ........ 76 A8
The Brambles *RHWH* RH17 ..... 48 A8
Brambletye La *FROW* RH18 .... 24 D3
Brambletyne Av *ROTT* BN2 ... 189 K5
Bramble Wy *RHAS* TN35 ....... 164 F2
Bramley Rd *POLE* BN26 ....... 178 C8
Bramleys *LEW* BN7 ........... 171 L1
Brampton Av *BEXW* TN39 ...... 182 F2
Brampton Rd *LW/ROSE* BN22 .. 196 F5
Brands Cl *NEWHV* BN9 ........ 191 K4
Brangwyn Av *BRI* BN1 ........ 145 L8
Brangwyn Crs *BRI* BN1 ....... 145 L8
Brangwyn Dr *BRI* BN1 ........ 145 K8
Brangwyn Wy *BRI* BN1 ........ 168 L1
Branksome Rd *STLEO* TN38 ... 162 A6
Branston Rd *LW/ROSE* BN22 .. 196 D5
Brassey Av *LW/ROSE* BN22 ... 196 C5
Brassey Rd *BEX* TN40 ........ 183 K3
Brasslands Dr *PTSD* BN41 .... 166 F5
Braybon Av *BRI* BN1 ......... 168 F2
Braybrooke Cl *HAS* TN34 ..... 4 F6
Braybrooke Rd *HAS* TN34 ..... 5 G5
Braybrooke Ter *HAS* TN34 .... 4 E6
Braypool La *BRI* BN1 ........ 145 K4
Brazen Cl *NEWHV* BN9 .......... 8 B4
Breadsell La *BAT* TN33 ...... 138 D7
  *BAT* TN33 ................ 161 J1
Bread St *BRI* BN1 ............. 6 E6
Brede Cl *LW/ROSE* BN22 ...... 197 K8
  *ROTT* BN2 ................. 7 J8
  *STLEO* TN38 .............. 138 F7
Brede Hl *RYE* TN31 .......... 114 B6
Brede La *BAT* TN33 .......... 112 F5
Brede Valley Vw *WSEA* TN36 .. 141 J8
Brendon Cl *LGNY* BN23 ...... 197 L2
  *RTWE/PEM* TN2 ............ 20 D1
Brendon Rd *HAS* TN34 ....... 163 H3
Brentwood Cl *BRI* BN1 ....... 169 H3
Brentwood Crs *BRI* BN1 ...... 169 H3
Brentwood Rd *BRI* BN1 ....... 169 H3
Bretland Rd *SBGH/RUST* TN4 .. 19 K2
Brett Dr *BEX* TN40 .......... 183 M1
Bretton *BURH* RH15 .......... 96 F4
Bretts Fld *PEAHV* BN10 ...... 190 C4
Brewers Gv *MAYF* TN20 ....... 57 H4
Brewer St *ROTT* BN2 ............ 7 L2
  *RRTW* TN3 ................ 33 L1
Briar Cl *RHAS* TN35 ......... 165 G1
  *ROTT* BN2 ................ 170 D6
Briarcroft Rd *ROTT* BN2 ..... 170 D7
Briar Pl *LGNY* BN23 ......... 197 H3
Brickhurst La *RING/NEW* BN8 . 129 J6
Bricklands *CRAWE* RH10 ....... 12 B7
Brickyard Cl *CRAWE* RH10 ..... 12 B6
  *CROW* TN6 ................ 41 M2
The Bricky *PEAHV* BN10 ...... 190 D6
Bridge Cl *BURH* RH15 ........ 96 F2
  *HTHF* TN21 ............... 106 A7
Bridge End *PEV* BN24 ........ 180 B8
Bridge Farm Rd *UCK* TN22 .... 76 C8
Bridgelands *RING/NEW* BN8 .. 126 D2
Bridgemere Rd
  *LW/ROSE* BN22 ........... 197 H8
Bridge Rd *HWH* RH16 ......... 48 F7
Bridgersmill *HWH* RH16 ...... 48 D7
Bridger Wy *CROW* TN6 ........ 39 M5
Bridge St *NEWHV* BN9 .......... 9 G3
Bridge Wy *STLEO* TN38 ...... 161 J8
Bridgewick Cl *LEW* BN7 ........ 3 G2
Bridle Wy *PEAHV* BN10 ....... 190 A5
Briers Av *SLVH* TN37 ........ 162 C3
Briers Gdns *SLVH* TN37 ..... 162 C3
Brigden St *BRI* BN1 ........... 6 C2
Brightland Rd
  *EDN/EASTW* BN20 ......... 206 D3
Brightling Av *RHAS* TN35 .... 163 M5
Brightling Rd *POLE* BN26 .... 196 A1
  *RBTBR* TN32 .............. 84 A6
Brighton Pl *BRI* BN1 .......... 6 E7
Brighton Rd *HPPT/KEY* BN6 .. 122 D4
  *LEW* BN7 ................. 148 E7
  *NEWHV* BN9 ................. 8 C4
Brills La *BRI* BN1 ............ 6 E8
Brincliffe *CROW* TN6 ......... 44 A1
Brinkers La *WADH* TN5 ........ 44 A4
Bristol Gdns *ROTT* BN2 ...... 187 L2
Bristol Ga *ROTT* BN2 .......... 7 M8

Bristol Ms *ROTT* BN2 ........ 187 L2
Bristol Pl *ROTT* BN2 ........ 187 L2
Bristol Rd *ROTT* BN2 .......... 7 J8
  *STLEO* TN38 .............. 162 A3
Bristol St *ROTT* BN2 ........ 187 L2
Brittany Ms *STLEO* TN38 ..... 162 B7
Brittany Rd *HOVE* BN3 ....... 167 K8
  *STLEO* TN38 .............. 162 B7
Britten Cl *LGNY* BN23 ....... 197 K3
Brittenden La *HTHF* TN21 .... 104 F1
Britts Farm Rd *UCK* TN22 .... 77 J3
Broadcroft *RTWE/PEM* TN2 .... 19 M6
Broadfield *EGRIN* RH19 ...... 22 E7
Broadfields *ROTT* BN2 ....... 169 L3
Broadfields Rd *ROTT* BN2 .... 169 L3
Broad Gn *ROTT* BN2 .......... 170 E8
Broad Green Av *BURH* RH15 ... 97 J4
Broad Gv *CROW* TN6 .......... 20 A5
Broadhill *HTHF* TN21 ......... 80 E5
Broadlands *BURH* RH15 ....... 97 H6
  *RHAS* TN35 ............... 163 K2
Broad La *RRTW* TN3 ........... 18 A3
Broad Oak Cl *LW/ROSE* BN22 .. 197 G2
  *RTWE/PEM* TN2 ............ 19 M5
Broadoak La *BEXW* TN39 ...... 182 E1
Broad Rig Av *HOVE* BN3 ...... 167 K2
Broad Rd *EDN/EASTW* BN20 ... 195 M2
Broadstone Pk *FROW* RH18 .... 25 G4
Broad St *RHWH* RH17 ......... 48 A8
  *ROTT* BN2 .................. 6 F8
  *SEAF* BN25 ............... 202 E3
  *WSEA* TN36 ............... 115 J8
Broad Vw *BEXW* TN39 ........ 159 M8
  *HTHF* TN21 ............... 80 E5
Broadview Cl
  *EDN/EASTW* BN20 ......... 195 M2
The Broadwalk *BEXW* TN39 ... 182 B2
Broadwater Down
  *RTWE/PEM* TN2 ............ 19 M6
Broadwater La *RTWE/PEM* TN2 . 19 M5
Broadwater Ri *RTWE/PEM* TN2 . 19 M5
Broadwater Wy
  *LW/ROSE* BN22 ........... 196 F6
Broad Wy *RHAS* TN35 ........ 164 F1
The Broadway *CROW* TN6 ..... 39 M4
  *HWH* RH16 ................ 71 K1
  *LW/ROSE* BN22 ........... 196 D5
  *POLE* BN26 ............... 193 M3
  *RHAS* TN35 ............... 163 K2
  *HTHF* TN21 ............... 33 H1
Brockley Rd *BEXW* TN39 ..... 183 G3
Brocks Gyhll
  *EDN/EASTW* BN20 ......... 196 A3
Brodie Pl *EAST* BN21 ........ 206 D2
Brodrick Cl *LW/ROSE* BN22 .. 196 F5
Brodrick Rd *LW/ROSE* BN22 .. 196 D4
Bromley Cl *HPPT/KEY* BN6 ... 123 J2
  *LGNY* BN23 ............... 197 J4
  *SEAF* BN25 ............... 203 H2
Brompton Cl *BRI* BN1 ........ 145 L8
The Brontes *EGRIN* RH19 ..... 13 K5
Brook Av *HPPT/KEY* BN6 ..... 122 F3
  *EGRIN* RH19 .............. 14 B5
Brooke Gdns *RING/NEW* BN8 .. 74 D8
Brooker Pl *HOVE* BN3 ....... 168 A7
Brooker St *HOVE* BN3 ....... 168 A7
Brookfield Rd *BEX* TN40 .... 183 L2
Brookhouse Bottom
  *RHWH* RH17 ............... 51 J3
Brookhouse La *UCK* TN22 .... 103 J3
Brookland Cl *HAS* TN34 ....... 5 L2
  *PEV* BN24 ................ 180 E8
Brooklands Av *CROW* TN6 .... 39 M7
Brooklands Wy *EGRIN* RH19 .. 13 K6
Brook La *HWH* RH16 .......... 48 F6
  *RING/NEW* BN8 ........... 150 A8
Brooklyn Rd *SEAF* BN25 ..... 202 E3
Brookmead Cl *LW/ROSE* BN22 . 197 H1
Brooks Cl *LEW* BN7 ........... 3 H4
  *NEWHV* BN9 ................. 8 F5
Brookside *NEWHV* BN9 ....... 191 H4
  *UCK* TN22 ................ 76 A8
Brookside Av *POLE* BN26 .... 177 M7
Brooks Rd *LEW* BN7 ........... 3 J4
The Brooks *BURH* RH15 ...... 96 E1
Brook St *HAS* TN34 ........... 5 H5
  *LEW* BN7 ................... 2 F5
  *POLE* BN26 ............... 177 M8
Brooks Wy *LYDD* TN29 ....... 121 J1
Brookway *BURH* RH15 ......... 97 J3
  *HWH* RH16 ................ 49 G6
Broomans La *LEW* BN7 ......... 3 G6
Broom Cl *LW/ROSE* BN22 ..... 196 D4
Broomfield Av *PEAHV* BN10 .. 189 M7
Broomfield Dr *PTSD* BN41 ... 167 G2
Broomfield St
  *EDN/EASTW* BN20 ......... 206 C2
Broomgrove Rd *HAS* TN34 ..... 5 L2
Broomham La *RING/NEW* BN8 .. 130 A7
Broom La *RRTW* TN3 ......... 18 F5
Broom Pk *RRTW* TN3 ......... 18 E3
Browning Rd *HTHF* TN21 ..... 80 A7
The Brownings *EGRIN* RH19 .. 13 J5
Brown Jack Av *POLE* BN26 ... 177 M8
Brownleaf Rd *ROTT* BN2 ..... 170 E8
Browns Cl *UCK* TN22 ......... 76 D6
Browns La *HTHF* TN21 ....... 79 H8
  *UCK* TN22 ................ 76 D5
Browns Wd *EGRIN* RH19 ...... 13 L2
The Brow *BURH* RH15 ........ 97 G4
  *EDN/EASTW* BN20 ......... 205 H4
  *ROTT* BN2 ................ 170 D6
Broyle Cl *RING/NEW* BN8 .... 127 M6
Broyle Paddock
  *RING/NEW* BN8 ........... 127 M7
The Broyle *RING/NEW* BN8 ... 128 D6
Bruce Cl *HWH* RH16 .......... 71 L3
Brunel Rd *STLEO* TN38 ...... 161 J4
Brunswick Ms *HOVE* BN3 ..... 186 D1
Brunswick Pl *HOVE* BN3 ..... 168 D8
Brunswick Rd *HOVE* BN3 ..... 168 D8

Brunswick Sq *HOVE* BN3 ..... 186 D1
Brunswick St East *HOVE* BN3 . 186 D1
Brunswick St West
  *HOVE* BN3 ............... 186 D1
Brunswick Ter *HOVE* BN3 .... 186 D1
Brushes La *HWH* RH16 ....... 49 H6
Bryants Fld *CROW* TN6 ...... 39 L3
Brydges La *LW/ROSE* BN22 ... 197 J8
Buci Crs *SHOR* BN43 ........ 166 C6
Buckholt Av *EGRIN* RH19 .... 13 H3
Buckholt La *BEXW* TN39 ..... 160 C5
Buckhurst Cl
  *EDN/EASTW* BN20 ......... 196 B6
  *EGRIN* RH19 .............. 13 J3
  *LEW* BN7 .................. 2 F1
Buckhurst La *CROW* TN6 ..... 42 F2
Buckhurst Rd *BEX* TN40 ..... 183 J2
  *PEAHV* BN10 .............. 189 M7
Buckhurst Wy *EGRIN* RH19 ... 13 J3
Buckingham Cl *SEAF* BN25 ... 202 E2
  *SHOR* BN43 .............. 166 A6
Buckingham Pl *BRI* BN1 ....... 6 C3
Buckingham Rd *BRI* BN1 ....... 6 D4
  *RTW* TN1 ................. 20 B4
  *STLEO* TN38 .............. 162 A2
Buckingham St *BRI* BN1 ....... 6 D4
Buckland Rd *SEAF* BN25 ..... 202 F1
Buckle By-pass *SEAF* BN25 .. 202 C1
Buckle Cl *SEAF* BN25 ....... 202 C2
Buckle Dr *SEAF* BN25 ....... 202 C2
Buckle Ri *SEAF* BN25 ....... 202 C2
Bucklers Cl *RTWE/PEM* TN2 .. 20 C5
Buckler St *PTSD* BN41 ...... 167 H6
Buckley Cl *HOVE* BN3 ....... 167 L2
Buckthorn Cl *SEAF* BN25 .... 203 J3
Buckwell Ct *LEW* BN7 ......... 2 B1
Buckwell Ri *HAIL* BN27 ..... 156 E1
Buddens Gn *RYE* TN31 ....... 89 H2
Budd's La *TENT* TN30 ....... 67 L4
Bugsell La *RBTBR* TN32 ..... 84 F1
Bulbeck Cl *BURH* RH15 ...... 96 E5
Buller Cl *CROW* TN6 ......... 40 A5
Buller Rd *ROTT* BN2 ........ 169 K5
Bullfinch Gdns *UCK* TN22 ... 102 D2
Bull La *LEW* BN7 ............. 2 F7
Bulrush Pl *STLEO* TN38 ..... 161 L5
Bulverhythe Rd *STLEO* TN38 . 161 K8
The Bungalows *UCK* TN22 .... 103 H1
Burchetts Cl *HWH* RH16 ..... 71 K4
Burden Pl *STLEO* TN38 ...... 162 A3
Burdett Rd *CROW* TN6 ....... 40 C5
  *SBGH/RUST* TN4 .......... 19 H2
Burdocks Dr *BURH* RH15 .... 97 J5
Burfield Rd *LW/ROSE* BN22 .. 11 H5
Burgh Cl *RING/NEW* BN8 ..... 174 D1
Burghurst Rd *BUR/ETCH* TN19 . 61 L4
Burgh La *RING/NEW* BN8 ..... 174 D1
Burhill Wy *STLEO* TN38 ..... 161 M7
Burleigh Cl *CRAWE* RH10 .... 12 B6
Burleigh La *CRAWE* RH10 .... 12 C7
Burleigh Pl *RTWE/PEM* TN2 .. 197 J8
Burleigh Wy *CRAWE* RH10 .... 12 B6
Burlington Gdns *PTSD* BN41 . 167 J8
Burlington Pl *EAST* BN21 ... 10 F8
Burlington Rd *EAST* BN21 ... 11 G7
Burlington St *ROTT* BN2 ...... 7 J9
Burlow Cl *LW/ROSE* BN22 ... 196 C3
  *ROTT* BN2 ............... 187 L1
Burma Cl *HWH* RH16 ......... 72 C2
Burners Cl *BURH* RH15 ...... 97 K5
Burnham Ct *ROTT* BN2 ...... 170 F7
Burnside *POLE* BN26 ........ 178 A8
Burns Wy *EGRIN* RH19 ....... 13 J5
Burnthouse Bostall
  *HPPT/KEY* BN6 ........... 123 J7
Burnt House Cl *HAWK* TN18 .. 64 C1
Burnt House La *RRTW* TN3 ... 18 F1
Burnt Lodge La *WADH* TN5 ... 45 H5
Burnt Oak Rd *UCK* TN22 ..... 54 B5
Burrell Rd *HWH* RH16 ....... 48 D8
Burrells La *UCK* TN22 ...... 53 G7
The Burrells *SHOR* BN43 .... 166 B8
Burrow Down
  *EDN/EASTW* BN20 ......... 206 A1
Burry Rd *SLVH* TN37 ........ 162 C3
Burstead Cl *BRI* BN1 ....... 169 H3
Burston Gdns *EGRIN* RH19 ... 13 K2
Burstowhill La *RHWH* RH17 .. 34 D8
Burton Rd *EAST* BN21 ....... 10 A1
Burton Vls *HOVE* BN3 ....... 168 D6
Burwash Cl *HAS* TN34 ....... 163 G1
  *LGNY* BN23 .............. 197 H2
Burwash Rd *HOVE* BN3 ...... 167 L3
  *HTHF* TN21 ............... 80 C6
Bushbury La *UCK* TN22 ..... 104 A3
Bush Cl *PEAHV* BN10 ........ 190 A5
  *ROTT* BN2 ............... 170 D5
Busheyfields *HAIL* BN27 .... 155 G6
Bush Farm Dr *PTSD* BN41 ... 167 H4
Bush Rd *NEWHV* BN9 .......... 8 C1
Bushy Cft *BEXW* TN39 ....... 182 F1
Bushy Gill *RRTW* TN3 ....... 19 G3
Butcherfield La *HRTF* TN7 ... 26 A7
Butcher's La *RHAS* TN35 .... 140 A4
Bute St *ROTT* BN2 ........... 7 L6
Butler's Green Rd *HWH* RH16 . 71 J2
Butler's La *HAIL* BN27 ..... 156 E3
Butlers Wy *RING/NEW* BN8 .. 150 D1
Butterbox La *RHWH* RH17 .... 73 K2
Buttercup Wk *BRI* BN1 ...... 146 B8
Butterfield *EGRIN* RH19 .... 13 H3
Buttermere Wy *LGNY* BN23 .. 197 J2
Butts Cl *EDN/EASTW* BN20 .. 196 A5
Butts La *EDN/EASTW* BN20 .. 196 A5
Butts Rd *STHW* BN42 ....... 166 E7
Buxshalls Hl *HWH* RH16 ..... 49 J5
Buxted Ri *BRI* BN1 ......... 169 H1
Buxted Wood La *UCK* TN22 ... 77 K1
Buxton Dr *BEXW* TN39 ...... 160 B8
Buxton Rd *BRI* BN1 ........... 6 B2
Bydown *SEAF* BN25 ......... 203 G2
The Byeways *SEAF* BN25 .... 202 F2
The Byeway *BEXW* TN39 ..... 182 D1

  *HAS* TN34 ................ 162 F2
Byfields Cft *BEXW* TN39 .... 182 F1
Byland Cl *LW/ROSE* BN22 ... 196 E3
Byng Rd *SBGH/RUST* TN4 ..... 19 L1
Byron Gv *EGRIN* RH19 ....... 13 J6
Byron St *HOVE* BN3 ......... 168 A7
By Sunte *HWH* RH16 ......... 48 F6
Byways *HAS* TN34 ........... 139 K8
The Byway *BRI* BN1 ......... 169 L1
Byworth Cl *BEXW* TN39 ..... 160 C5
  *ROTT* BN2 ............... 169 M8

## C

Cabbage Stalk La
  *SBGH/RUST* TN4 .......... 19 L4
Cabot Cl *LGNY* BN23 ........ 198 A8
Caburn Cl *LW/ROSE* BN22 ... 197 G2
Caburn Crs *LEW* BN7 .......... 2 A3
Caburn Rd *HOVE* BN3 ......... 6 B2
Caburn Wy *HAIL* BN27 ...... 155 G8
Cacklebury Cl *HAIL* BN27 ... 155 G8
Cackle St *RYE* TN31 ........ 114 A4
  *UCK* TN22 ................ 52 E5
Cadborough Cliff *RYE* TN31 . 116 F2
Cade St *LW/ROSE* BN22 ..... 196 F4
Cairngorm Cl *LGNY* BN23 ... 197 K3
Cairo Av *PEAHV* BN10 ...... 190 A7
Cairo Av South *PEAHV* BN10 . 190 A7
Caister's Cl *HOVE* BN3 ..... 168 C6
Calbourne Rd *HWH* RH16 .... 71 K1
Caldbec Hl *BAT* TN33 ....... 137 K1
Caldecot La *LYDD* TN29 ..... 95 K4
Caldicotts La *HAIL* BN27 ... 154 A5
Caledonian Rd *ROTT* BN2 ..... 7 H1
Calgary Rd *BEXW* TN39 ..... 160 B7
Callums Wk *ROTT* BN2 ...... 183 L1
Calverley Ct *RTWE/PEM* TN2 . 20 C3
Calverley Pk *RTWE/PEM* TN2 . 20 B3
Calverley Park Crs
  *RTWE/PEM* TN2 ........... 20 B3
Calverley Park Gdns *RTW* TN1 . 20 B3
  *RTW* TN1 ................. 20 B2
  *RTWE/PEM* TN2 ........... 20 B2
Calverley St *RTW* TN1 ...... 20 B2
Calvert Cl *UCK* TN22 ......... 76 A7
Calvert Rd *HAS* TN34 ......... 5 K2
  *UCK* TN22 ................ 76 A7
Camber Cl *BEX* TN40 ....... 160 E8
Camber Dr *PEV* BN24 ....... 180 F8
Camberlot Rd *HAIL* BN27 ... 154 A5
Camber Rd *RYE* TN31 ....... 117 M2
Camber Wy *PEV* BN24 ....... 180 F8
Cambridge Gdns *HAS* TN34 .... 4 F7
  *RTWE/PEM* TN2 ........... 20 B4
Cambridge Gv *HOVE* BN3 .... 168 C7
Cambridge Rd *BEXW* TN39 ... 160 C8
  *HAS* TN34 ................. 4 F7
  *HOVE* BN3 ............... 168 D8
  *LW/ROSE* BN22 ........... 11 H4
Cambridge St
  *RTWE/PEM* TN2 ........... 20 C3
Cambridge Wy *UCK* TN22 .... 76 C5
Camden Hl *RTWE/PEM* TN2 ... 20 B3
Camden Pk *RTWE/PEM* TN2 ... 20 C4
  *RTWE/PEM* TN2 ........... 20 D4
Camden Rd *PTSD* BN41 ...... 167 J8
  *RTW* TN1 ................. 20 D7
Camden St *PTSD* BN41 ...... 167 J8
Camelford St *ROTT* BN2 ...... 7 G8
Cameron Cl *HAIL* BN27 ..... 155 G6
Campbell Cl *UCK* TN22 ...... 76 C5
Campbell Crs *EGRIN* RH19 .. 13 H5
Campbell Rd *BRI* BN1 ........ 6 D1
Camperdown St *BEXW* TN39 .. 160 A7
Canada Cl *PEAHV* BN10 ..... 190 B5
Canada Wy *BEXW* TN39 ...... 160 B7
Canadia Rd *BAT* TN33 ...... 111 K6
Canfield Cl *ROTT* BN2 ...... 169 K5
Canfield Rd *ROTT* BN2 ...... 169 K5
Canning St *ROTT* BN2 ......... 7 K6
Cannon Pl *BRI* BN1 .......... 6 C7
Cannon St *LYDD* TN29 ....... 95 J8
Cansiron La *EDEN* TN8 ...... 15 L4
  *FROW* RH18 .............. 24 F5
Cantelupe Rd *BEX* TN40 .... 183 K3
  *EGRIN* RH19 .............. 13 M7
Canterbury Cl
  *LW/ROSE* BN22 ........... 196 C4
Canterbury Dr *ROTT* BN2 ..... 7 C2
Canterbury Rd *HAS* TN34 .... 162 E3
Cantercrow Hl *NEWHV* BN9 .. 191 M4
Cants Cl *BURH* RH15 ........ 97 J3
Cants La *BURH* RH15 ........ 97 J2
Canute Cl *LGNY* BN23 ...... 197 M6
Canute Rd *RHAS* TN35 ...... 163 K3
Capel Av *PEAHV* BN10 ...... 190 C8
Capenors *BURH* RH15 ....... 96 F5
Caple Gdns *STLEO* TN38 .... 162 B7
Carden Av *BRI* BN1 ......... 168 F1
Carden Cl *BRI* BN1 ......... 146 A8
Carden Crs *BRI* BN1 ....... 146 A8
Carden Hl *BRI* BN1 ......... 169 H1
Card Hl *FROW* RH18 ......... 24 F5
Cardiff Rd *STLEO* TN38 ...... 4 A7
Cardinals Cl *BEX* TN40 .... 160 E8
Carew Rd *EAST* BN21 ........ 10 B3
Carey Down *PEAHV* BN10 ... 190 B5
Carfax Cl *BEXW* TN39 ...... 160 B6
Carinus Gdns *STLEO* TN38 .. 162 A1
Carisbrooke Cl *LGNY* BN23 . 197 H2
Carisbrooke Rd *ROTT* BN2 .... 7 L2
  *STLEO* TN38 ............. 162 B7
Carlisle Pde *HAS* TN34 ...... 4 F7
Carlisle Rd *EAST* BN21 ..... 10 F7
  *EDN/EASTW* BN20 ......... 10 C9
  *HOVE* BN3 ............... 168 D8
Carlton Cl *SEAF* BN25 ..... 202 C2
Carlton Crs *RTWE/PEM* TN2 .. 20 C2
Carlton Hl *ROTT* BN2 ......... 7 G6
Carlton Pl *ROTT* BN2 ......... 7 H6
Carlton Rd *LW/ROSE* BN22 .. 11 J2
  *RTWE/PEM* TN2 ........... 20 C2
  *SEAF* BN25 .............. 202 C1

Carlton Ter *HOVE* BN3 ...... 167 K5
Carlyle Av *ROTT* BN2 ....... 169 K5
Carlyle St *ROTT* BN2 ......... 7 K3
Carmel Cl *BEXW* TN39 ...... 182 D3
Carol Cl *BRI* BN1 .......... 145 M8
Caroline Cl *SEAF* BN25 .... 202 D1
Carpenter Dr *STLEO* TN38 .. 161 M2
Carpenters Cft
  *RING/NEW* BN8 ........... 130 A1
Carpenters Wy *HAIL* BN27 .. 155 G8
Castle Ditch La *LEW* BN7 .... 2 F6
Castledown Av *HAS* TN34 ..... 5 J6
Castle Dr *PEV* BN24 ....... 198 C2
Castlefields *HRTF* TN7 ..... 26 D2
Castle Gdns *HAS* TN34 ....... 5 H7
Castle Ga *LEW* BN7 ........... 2 F6
Castle Hl *MAYF* TN20 ....... 56 A1
Castle Hill Pas *HAS* TN34 ... 5 H6
Castle Hill Rd *HAS* TN34 .... 5 H7
Castle Hurst *RBTBR* TN32 ... 63 H6
Castle Ri *UCK* TN22 ....... 102 D2
Castle Rd *PEV* BN24 ....... 180 A8
  *SBGH/RUST* TN4 .......... 19 J3
Castleross Rd *PEV* BN24 ... 198 C2
Castle Sq *BRI* BN1 .......... 6 E7
Castle St *BRI* BN1 .......... 6 B6
  *HAS* TN34 ................. 5 H7
  *RTW* TN1 ................. 20 A4
  *WSEA* TN36 .............. 116 F7
Castle View Gdns *PEV* BN24 . 179 M8
Castle Wk *WADH* TN5 ........ 45 J2
Castle Wy *UCK* TN22 ....... 102 D2
Catherine Pl *RTW* TN1 ...... 20 B3
Catherine V *ROTT* BN2 ..... 170 C4
Catkin Wy *HWH* RH16 ....... 72 B2
Catsfield Cl *POLE* BN26 .... 196 F2
  *STLEO* TN38 ............. 161 K4
Catsfield Rd *BAT* TN33 .... 136 D3
Cat St *HRTF* TN7 ........... 25 M5
Catt's Hl *CROW* TN6 ........ 41 K5
  *TENT* TN30 ............... 68 F2
The Causeway *ROTT* BN2 ..... 7 M5
  *SEAF* BN25 .............. 202 D1
Cavalier Wy *EGRIN* RH19 ... 13 M7
Cavalry Crs *EDN/EASTW* BN20 . 206 A1
Cavell Av *PEAHV* BN10 ..... 190 B7
Cavell Av North *PEAHV* BN10 . 190 B7
Cavendish Av *LW/ROSE* BN22 . 11 G4
  *STLEO* TN38 ............. 162 A7
Cavendish Cl *PEAHV* BN10 .. 190 B6
Cavendish Dr *RTWE/PEM* TN2 . 20 B4
Cavendish Pl *BRI* BN1 ........ 6 A7
  *EAST* BN21 ............... 10 F5
Cavendish St *ROTT* BN2 ...... 7 G7
Caveridge La *RING/NEW* BN8 . 99 L6
Caves Rd *STLEO* TN38 ...... 162 A8
Caxton Wy *HWH* RH16 ....... 71 L2
Cedar Cl *BURH* RH15 ........ 97 H1
  *HAS* TN34 ............... 162 D1
  *LW/ROSE* BN22 ........... 196 C4
Cedars Cl *UCK* TN22 ........ 76 C6
Cedars Gdns *BRI* BN1 ...... 168 D3
The Cedars *HAIL* BN27 ..... 155 H5
  *HWH* RH16 ................ 48 D7
  *PEAHV* BN10 ............. 190 C5
  *UCK* TN22 ................ 76 C6
Cedar Wy *HWH* RH16 ......... 72 B2
Cedarwell Cl *NEWHV* BN9 ... 191 H4
Celandine Dr *STLEO* TN38 .. 162 A5
Central Av *EDN/EASTW* BN20 . 206 B1
  *PEAHV* BN10 ............. 190 A7
  *POLE* BN26 .............. 178 B7
Centurion Ri *HAS* TN34 .... 163 G8
Centurion Rd *BRI* BN1 ....... 6 D5
Ceylon Pl *LW/ROSE* BN22 ... 11 G8
Ceylon Wk *BEXW* TN39 ...... 182 E3
Chadborn Cl *ROTT* BN2 ....... 7 M8
Chaffinch Cl *BURH* RH15 ... 96 D2
Chaffinch Rd *LGNY* BN23 ... 197 J4
Chaffinch Wk *UCK* TN22 .... 102 D1
Chafford La *RRTW* TN3 ...... 18 A1
Chailey Av *ROTT* BN2 ...... 189 G5
Chailey Cl *HAS* TN34 ...... 162 E1
  *LGNY* BN23 .............. 197 L5
Chailey Crs *ROTT* BN2 ..... 189 L5
Chailey La *RING/NEW* BN8 .. 100 B1
Chailey Rd *BRI* BN1 ....... 169 L2
Chain La *BAT* TN33 ......... 137 J1
Chalfont Dr *HOVE* BN3 ..... 168 C3
Chalkers La *HPPT/KEY* BN6 . 96 B6
Chalket La *RTWE/PEM* TN2 .. 21 J1
Chalk Farm Cl
  *EDN/EASTW* BN20 ......... 196 B5
Chalkland Ri *ROTT* BN2 .... 170 B6
Chalky Rd *PTSD* BN41 ...... 166 F3
Challoners *RHWH* RH17 ...... 50 C2
Challoners Cl *ROTT* BN2 ... 188 F4
Challoners Ms *ROTT* BN2 ... 188 F4
Challow Cl *HPPT/KEY* BN6 .. 122 E2
Chaloner Cl *HWH* RH16 ..... 49 H7
Chaloner Rd *HWH* RH16 ..... 49 H7
Chalvington Cl *BRI* BN1 ... 146 E8
  *SEAF* BN25 .............. 192 F8
Chalvington Dr *SLVH* TN37 . 139 J8
Chalvington Rd *EAST* BN21 . 196 C7
Chamberlaines La
  *RING/NEW* BN8 ........... 127 M8
Chamberlain Rd *EAST* BN21 . 206 C2
Chambers Crs *STLEO* TN38 .. 161 M3
Chambers Rd *STLEO* TN38 .. 161 M4
Chancellors Pk *HPPT/KEY* BN6 . 122 F2
Chanctonbury Dr *HAS* TN34 . 139 L8
Chanctonbury Rd *BURH* RH15 . 96 F5
  *HOVE* BN3 ................ 168 A1
Chandler Rd *BEXW* TN39 .... 183 G1
Chandler's Md *RING/NEW* BN8 . 126 B4
Chandos Rd *RTW* TN1 ....... 20 C1
Channel Vw East *BEX* TN40 . 183 J3
Channel View Rd
  *LW/ROSE* BN22 ........... 11 K1
  *PEV* BN24 ............... 198 C1
  *ROTT* BN2 ............... 170 B6
Channel Vw West *RHAS* TN35 . 164 E3
Channers La *RING/NEW* BN8 . 152 D6
Chant La *CROW* TN6 ......... 41 H5
Chantlers Cl *EGRIN* RH19 .. 13 J4
Chantlers Md *EDEN* TN8 ...... 8 G1

Chantry Av BEX TN40 160 C8
Chantry La BEX TN40 183 J1
Chapel Barn Cl HAIL BN27 155 J7 2
Chapel Cl BURH RH15 96 F1
SEAF BN25 202 E2
Chapel Fld RYE TN31 65 G7
Chapel Gn CROW TN6 39 M4 1
Chapel Hl BAT TN33 112 E6
BAT TN33 160 F2
LEW BN7 3 J6
Chapel La EGRIN RH19 14 D8
FROW RH18 24 F5
LEW BN7 125 G3
RHAS TN35 141 G6
RHWH RH17 50 C1
UCK TN22 78 B7
Chapel Ms HOVE BN3 186 D1 3
Chapel Park Rd SLVH TN37 4 B5
Chapel Pl PTSD BN41 167 H7
Chapel Rd LEW BN7 98 E7
PTSD BN41 167 G7 1
Chapel Rw EGRIN RH19 22 E7
Chapel St NEWHV BN9 9 G3
ROTT BN2 7 G7
Chapel Ter ROTT BN2 7 L8
Chapman's La EGRIN RH19 13 K5 2
Chapmans Town Rd
HTHF TN21 107 H5
Charity Farm Wy CROW TN6 40 A3
Charles Av BURH RH15 96 E4
Charles Cl HOVE BN3 168 A3
SEAF BN25 202 D1 2
Charles Rd STLEO TN38 4 A7
Charles Rd West STLEO TN38 162 B6
Charles St ROTT BN2 6 F8
Charleston Rd EAST BN21 206 C2
Charlesworth Pk HWH RH16 72 C2
Charlotte St ROTT BN2 7 H8
Charlston Av NEWHV BN9 8 B7
The Charltons BRI BN1 146 D8 1
Charlton's Wy
SBGH/RUST TN4 19 L5 1
Charlwood Gdns BURH RH15 97 J1
Charlwood Rd BURH RH15 97 J1
Charlwoods Business Centre
EGRIN RH19 13 K4 1
Charlwoods Pl EGRIN RH19 13 L3 2
Charlwoods Rd EGRIN RH19 13 K4
Chartfield HOVE BN3 168 A4
Chartres BEX TN40 160 D8
Chartres Cl BEX TN40 160 D8
Chartwell Cl SEAF BN25 192 E8 1
Chatfield Crs LW/ROSE BN22 196 C5
Chatfield Rd RHWH RH17 48 A8
Chatham Pl BRI BN1 6 C3
SEAF BN25 202 E4 1
Chatham Rd SLVH TN37 162 B4 1
Chatsfield Cl STLEO TN38 161 L2
Chatsworth Av PEAHV BN10 190 A5 2
Chatsworth Cl PEAHV BN10 190 A6
Chatsworth Gdns
EDN/EASTW BN20 206 F6 1
Chatsworth Pk PEAHV BN10 190 B5 3
Chatsworth Rd BRI BN1 6 B1
Chaucer Av EGRIN RH19 13 J6
Chawbrook Rd LW/ROSE BN22 11 G3
Cheal Cl SHOR BN43 166 A8
Cheapside BRI BN1 6 E4
Cheeleys RHWH RH17 50 C1
Chelgates BEXW TN39 182 C4
Chelsea Cl BEX TN40 183 K2
Chelston Av HOVE BN3 167 K7
Cheltenham Pl BRI BN1 6 F5
Chelwood Cl BRI BN1 146 C8
Chelwood Gate Rd UCK TN22 36 F8
Chelworth Rd LW/ROSE BN22 196 D4
Chene Rd PEAHV BN10 190 F8
Chenies Cl RTWE/PEM TN2 20 A6
Chepbourne Rd BEX TN40 183 H2
Chequer Gra FROW RH18 24 E5
Chequer Rd EGRIN RH19 13 M5 1
Chequers Cl CROW TN6 40 A4 1
Chequers Wy CROW TN6 40 A4
Cherington Cl
HPPT/KEY BN6 122 B1 1
Cherry Cl BURH RH15 96 E3
Cherry Garden Rd
EDN/EASTW BN20 206 B3
Cherry Gdns HTHF TN21 106 B1
Cherry Side HAIL BN27 155 G7
Cherry Tree Cl SLVH TN37 4 B6
Cherry Tree Gdns BEX TN40 160 F8
Cherry Tree Rd RTWE/PEM TN2 19 L5
Cherwell Cl POLE BN26 196 F1
Cherwell Rd HTHF TN21 80 A6
Chesham Pl ROTT BN2 7 M9
Chesham Rd ROTT BN2 7 M9
Chesham St ROTT BN2 7 M9
Chesnut Cl HAIL BN27 155 G5 1
Chester Av RTWE/PEM TN2 20 D4
Chesterfield Cl CRAWE RH10 12 C2
Chesterfield Gdns
EDN/EASTW BN20 206 E6
Chesterfield Rd
EDN/EASTW BN20 206 E6
Chester Ter BRI BN1 169 G5
Chesterton Av SEAF BN25 203 H3
Chesterton Cl EGRIN RH19 13 M7
Chesterton Dr SEAF BN25 203 H3
Chestnut Cl BURH RH15 97 H1
EGRIN RH19 14 A5
HAIL BN27 133 L8
RYE TN31 114 B1
Chestnut Dr POLE BN26 178 A8
Chestnuts Cl HWH RH16 49 G7
The Chestnuts HAWK TN18 47 L6
HWH RH16 48 F7
Chestnut Wk BEXW TN39 182 C1
Chestnut Wy NEWHV BN9 8 C4
Cheviot Cl LGNY BN23 197 J3
The Cheviots HAS TN34 163 H2
Chichester Cl BEXW TN39 160 B8
HOVE BN3 167 L2
LW/ROSE BN22 196 B4
PEAHV BN10 190 F7
Chichester Dr East ROTT BN2 189 J6
Chichester Dr West ROTT BN2 189 H5
Chichester Pl ROTT BN2 7 M9
Chichester Rd SEAF BN25 202 E3
Chichester Ter ROTT BN2 7 M9
Chichester Wy BURH RH15 97 J1
Chick Hl RHAS TN35 142 B6
Chiddingly Cl ROTT BN2 187 M1
Chieveley Dr RTWE/PEM TN2 20 C5
Chilcomb BURH RH15 97 J5
Chilham Cl LGNY BN23 197 K4 1
Chillies La UCK TN22 54 A5
Chilling St EGRIN RH19 35 H6
Chillis Wood Rd HWH RH16 71 J1
Chilsham La HAIL BN27 133 K7
Chilston Cl SBGH/RUST TN4 20 A1
Chilston Rd SBGH/RUST TN4 20 A1
Chiltern Cl LGNY BN23 197 K3
SHOR BN43 166 C6
Chiltern Dr HAS TN34 163 H3
Chiltington Cl BURH RH15 96 F1 1
ROTT BN2 189 J4
Chiltington La LEW BN7 125 J3
Chiltington Wy ROTT BN2 189 J4
Chiswick Pl EAST BN21 10 F8
Chitcombe Rd RYE TN31 113 L1
Chorley Av ROTT BN2 189 H4
Chownes Mead La RHWH RH17 71 H2
Chown's Hl HAS TN34 140 A8
Chrisdory Rd PTSD BN41 166 E3
Christie Av RING/NEW BN8 127 K8
Christie Rd LEW BN7 2 B5
Christies EGRIN RH19 13 K6 1
Christopher Rd EGRIN RH19 13 L5
Church Av HWH RH16 48 E8
PEV BN24 180 A8
Church Cl BRI BN1 168 F1
BURH RH15 97 G3
EDN/EASTW BN20 196 A2
Churchdale Pl
LW/ROSE BN22 197 H8 1
Churchdale Rd LW/ROSE BN22 197 H8
Church Farm Cl
BUR/ETCH TN19 61 J5
Churchfields UCK TN22 52 C1
Church Gn SHOR BN43 166 C7
Church Hl BRI BN1 145 L8
BUR/ETCH TN19 61 H4
NEWHV BN9 8 E5
POY/PYE BN45 122 C8
RING/NEW BN8 127 K8
TENT TN30 68 F3
Church Hill Av BEXW TN39 182 C2
Church House Cl STHW BN42 166 E5
Churchill Av RHAS TN35 163 K1
Churchill Cl EDN/EASTW BN20 206 D3
Churchill Rd HTHF TN21 80 B8
LEW BN7 2 C2
SEAF BN25 202 D1
Churchill Wy BURH RH15 97 J4
Church In the Wood La
STLEO TN38 161 M3
Churchland La BAT TN33 112 E3
Church La BAT TN33 136 E6
BAT TN33 158 C7
BAT TN33 159 H1
BUR/ETCH TN19 61 J5
EAST BN21 206 D3 2
EGRIN RH19 13 M5
HAIL BN27 132 A8
HAIL BN27 155 G1
HPPT/KEY BN6 123 J3
HWH RH16 71 M8
LEW BN7 2 F3
LEW BN7 171 K1
PEV BN24 180 B8
POLE BN26 195 J7
POY/PYE BN45 122 C8
RBTBR TN32 85 J1
RHAS TN35 139 L3
RHAS TN35 141 H5
RHWH RH17 35 J8
RHWH RH17 51 G3
RING/NEW BN8 129 J8
RING/NEW BN8 152 E6
RRTW TN3 30 B2
RYE TN31 65 J8
RYE TN31 88 E2
RYE TN31 90 B6
RYE TN31 91 H2
SEAF BN25 202 E4 2
STHW BN42 166 D7
UCK TN22 77 J1
Church Marks La
RING/NEW BN8 129 M1
Church Md HPPT/KEY BN6 123 G3
Church Pl ROTT BN2 187 L2
Church Platt RHWH RH17 70 E1
Church Rd BAT TN33 136 F6
BURH RH15 97 G4
CRBK TN17 33 M4
CROW TN6 39 L4
EGRIN RH19 22 E8
HAIL BN27 157 G5
HAWK TN18 63 M2
HOVE BN3 168 B8
HWH RH16 71 L2
LEW BN7 2 F5
LYDD TN29 95 J7
POLE BN26 178 A8
PTSD BN41 167 H7
RBTBR TN32 111 H1
RHWH RH17 72 F3
RING/NEW BN8 100 E2
RING/NEW BN8 126 E4
SBGH/RUST TN4 19 M3
SLVH TN37 4 B6
UCK TN22 77 H3
Churchsettle La WADH TN5 44 C7
Church Sq RYE TN31 117 J1
Church St BEX TN40 183 K1
BRI BN1 6 C5
CROW TN6 41 G6
EDEN TN8 16 B1
EDN/EASTW BN20 196 B5
EDN/EASTW BN20 206 D3
HRTF TN7 26 D2
HTHF TN21 106 D1
LW/ROSE BN22 196 C4
PTSD BN41 167 H7 1
RHAS TN35 163 J3
SEAF BN25 202 E3
UCK TN22 76 C6
Church Vale Rd BEX TN40 183 J1
Church Wood Dr STLEO TN38 161 L2
Church Wood Wy STLEO TN38 161 M4
Chyngton Av SEAF BN25 203 H2
Chyngton Cl LGNY BN23 197 G2 4
Chyngton Gdns SEAF BN25 203 H2
Chyngton La SEAF BN25 203 J3
Chyngton La North SEAF BN25 203 J3
Chyngton Pl SEAF BN25 203 H4
Chyngton Rd SEAF BN25 203 G4
Chyngton Wy SEAF BN25 203 J4
Cinderford La HAIL BN27 132 E6
Cinder Hl EGRIN RH19 35 H5
RING/NEW BN8 99 M3
RING/NEW BN8 100 B1
Cinquefoil PEAHV BN10 190 C6
Cinque Ports St RYE TN31 117 J1 1
Cinque Ports Wy SEAF BN25 203 J2
STLEO TN38 161 L8
Circus St ROTT BN2 6 F6
The Circus LGNY BN23 197 K6
Cissbury Av PEAHV BN10 190 E8
Cissbury Crs ROTT BN2 189 L5
Cissbury Rd BURH RH15 96 E2
HOVE BN3 6 A2
Civic Ap UCK TN22 76 C7
Civic Wy BURH RH15 97 G3
Clackhams La CROW TN6 40 D7
Clair Rd HWH RH16 71 L1
Clanricarde Gdns RTW TN1 20 A3 1
Clanricarde Rd
SBGH/RUST TN4 19 M3 1
Clapham La POLE BN26 194 A6
Claphatch La WADH TN5 45 G1
The Clappers RBTBR TN32 85 H2
Claremont HAS TN34 4 F7
Claremont Gdns RTW TN1 20 B4
Claremont Ri UCK TN22 76 C5
Claremont Rd BEXW TN39 160 B7
NEWHV BN9 191 M5
RTW TN1 20 B4
SEAF BN25 202 D3
Clarence Dr EGRIN RH19 13 M7
Clarence Rd LW/ROSE BN22 11 G3
RTW TN1 20 A3 2
SLVH TN37 4 A3
Clarence Rw RTW TN1 20 A2 2
Clarence Sq BRI BN1 6 C6
Clarendon Cl SLVH TN37 162 B2 3
Clarendon Gdns
RTWE/PEM TN2 20 A5 2
Clarendon Pl PTSD BN41 167 J8 2
Clarendon Rd HOVE BN3 168 B7
SHOR BN43 166 C6
Clarendon Ter ROTT BN2 7 M9 1
Clarendon Vls HOVE BN3 168 A7
Clarendon Wy RTWE/PEM TN2 19 M5
Clare Rd LEW BN7 2 B4
Clarke Av HOVE BN3 167 M3
Claverham Cl BAT TN33 137 H2
Claverham Wy BAT TN33 137 H2
Clavering Wk BEXW TN39 182 B4
Claxton Cl EAST BN21 206 D1
Claxton Rd BEX TN40 184 A1
Clayfields PEAHV BN10 190 B7 1
Clay Hill Rd RRTW TN3 32 D1
Clays Cl EGRIN RH19 13 L6 1
Clayton Av HPPT/KEY BN6 122 E3
Clayton Dr BURH RH15 96 F5
Clayton Hl POY/PYE BN45 122 D7
Clayton Mill Rd PEV BN24 197 H1
Clayton Rd HPPT/KEY BN6 123 J4
ROTT BN2 7 L3
Clayton's La RRTW TN3 17 L4
Clayton Wy HOVE BN3 167 M3
Clearwater La RHWH RH17 73 G3
Clearwaters La BURH RH15 71 K6
Cleeve Av RTWE/PEM TN2 20 D4
Cleevelands LW/ROSE BN22 196 B4 1
Clegg St HAS TN34 5 H5
Clement Hill Rd HAS TN34 163 H3 1
Clementine Av SEAF BN25 202 D1
Clement La POLE BN26 196 A1
Clerks Acre HPPT/KEY BN6 123 G2 1
Clermont Rd BRI BN1 168 D4
Clermont Ter BRI BN1 168 E4
Cleve Cl UCK TN22 103 H1
Clevedon Rd BEXW TN39 159 M8
Cleveland RTWE/PEM TN2 20 D1
Cleveland Cl LGNY BN23 197 J3 1
Cleveland Gdns BURH RH15 97 H4
Cleveland Rd BRI BN1 169 G5
Cleve Ter LEW BN7 2 E8
Cliff Ap ROTT BN2 187 M2
Cliff Av PEAHV BN10 200 E1
Cliff Cl SEAF BN25 202 F5
Cliffe High St LEW BN7 3 H6
Cliff End La RHAS TN35 142 B7
Cliff Gdns PEAHV BN10 189 M6
SEAF BN25 202 F5
Clifford Av EAST BN21 196 C8
Clifford Rd BEX TN40 183 J2
Cliff Park Cl PEAHV BN10 190 F7
Cliff Rd EDN/EASTW BN20 206 E7
ROTT BN2 187 M3
SEAF BN25 202 F5
The Cliff ROTT BN2 187 M2
Cliff Wy RHAS TN35 164 F1
Clifton Cl LW/ROSE BN22 196 D6
Clifton Hl BRI BN1 6 B4
Clifton Pl BRI BN1 6 B5
RTW TN1 20 B4 2
Clifton Ri BEX TN40 183 M1
Clifton Rd BRI BN1 6 C4
BURH RH15 96 D1
NEWHV BN9 9 H4
RHAS TN35 163 J3
Clifton St BRI BN1 6 D4
Clifton Ter BRI BN1 6 C5
Cliftonville Rd STLEO TN38 161 K8
Clifton Wy PEAHV BN10 190 A6
Climping Cl HWH RH16 71 K3
Clinch Green Av BEXW TN39 159 M7
Clinton Crs STLEO TN38 162 B5
Clinton La SEAF BN25 202 E3
Clinton Pl SEAF BN25 202 E3
Clinton Wy RHAS TN35 164 F1
Clive Av RHAS TN35 163 J4
Clock House La UCK TN22 52 C2
Cloisters NEWHV BN9 8 F3
The Cloisters BAT TN33 111 K8 1
LW/ROSE BN22 196 C4
SLVH TN37 4 C7
Close Eight LGNY BN23 197 L3 1
Close Eighteen LGNY BN23 197 L4 1
Close Eleven LGNY BN23 197 L3 2
Close Fifteen LGNY BN23 197 L4 2
Close Five LGNY BN23 197 L3 3
Close Four LGNY BN23 197 L4 3
Close Fourteen LGNY BN23 197 L3 4
Close Nine LGNY BN23 197 L4
Close One LGNY BN23 197 K4
Close Seven LGNY BN23 197 L3 5
Close Seventeen LGNY BN23 197 L4
Close Six LGNY BN23 197 L3 6
Close Sixteen LGNY BN23 197 L4
Close Ten LGNY BN23 197 L4 4
The Close BRI BN1 168 D1
BURH RH15 97 J2
CROW TN6 39 L3
EDN/EASTW BN20 196 B6
EDN/EASTW BN20 205 G5 1
EGRIN RH19 13 K6
HPPT/KEY BN6 122 F2
NEWHV BN9 191 M4
RHAS TN35 164 C2
RHWH RH17 34 B7
RRTW TN3 18 C8 1
RYE TN31 91 G8
SEAF BN25 202 F4
UCK TN22 78 B8
Close Three LGNY BN23 197 K4 5
Close Twelve LGNY BN23 197 L4 5
Close Twenty LGNY BN23 197 L4
Close Twentyfive
LGNY BN23 197 K4 6
Close Twentyfour
LGNY BN23 197 L4 6
Close Two LGNY BN23 197 K4 7
Cloudesley Rd SLVH TN37 4 A5
Cloverlea HAS TN34 162 E1 1
Clovers End BRI BN1 146 B7
Clover Wy PTSD BN41 167 H4
Cluny St LEW BN7 2 E8
Clyde Rd BRI BN1 6 E1
STLEO TN38 4 A7
Coach & Horses La RHWH RH17 36 C8
Coach La RHWH RH17 36 C8
Coastguard La RHAS TN35 164 B2
Coastguard Sq RYE TN31 118 A3
Coast Rd PEV BN24 198 E1
Cobald Rd PEV BN24 198 E1
Cobbetts Md HWH RH16 72 B3
Cobbett's Ride
RTWE/PEM TN2 19 M5 1
Cobbold Av EAST BN21 196 C8
Cob Cl CRAWE RH10 12 C6
Cobden Rd ROTT BN2 7 J3
Cobdown La UCK TN22 76 C2
Cob La RHWH RH17 34 B5
Cobton Dr HOVE BN3 168 A3
Cochrane Cl LGNY BN23 197 L7 1
Cockcrow Wd HAS TN34 162 D1
Cockmount La WADH TN5 31 L8
Cockshut Rd LEW BN7 2 E9
Cogger's La HTHF TN21 131 M3
Coggins Mill Rd MAYF TN20 57 J3
Coghurst Rd RHAS TN35 163 J2
Colbourne Av ROTT BN2 169 K4
Colbourne Rd HOVE BN3 6 A3
Colchester V FROW RH18 24 E4
Colchins BURH RH15 96 F5 1
Coldean La BRI BN1 146 C6
Coldharbour Cl CROW TN6 40 A5 1
Coldharbour La LYDD TN29 94 C1
RING/NEW BN8 74 A7
RYE TN31 90 F2
Coldharbour Rd HAIL BN27 154 B4
Coldthorn La HAIL BN27 178 A3
Coldwaltham La BURH RH15 97 K5
Colebrooke Rd BEXW TN39 183 G3
Colebrook Rd BRI BN1 168 D2
STHW BN42 166 F7
Coleman Av HOVE BN3 167 L7
Colemans Cl LYDD TN29 95 K8 1
Colemans Hatch Rd
FROW RH18 37 H1
Coleman St ROTT BN2 7 H3
Coleridge St HOVE BN3 168 A6
Colgate Cl ROTT BN2 169 M8
College Cl EGRIN RH19 13 M5 2
PTSD BN41 166 F3
College Dr RTWE/PEM TN2 20 D2
College Gdns ROTT BN2 7 K8
College Gn EAST BN21 10 B3
College La EGRIN RH19 13 M5
HPPT/KEY BN6 122 C1
College Pl HPPT/KEY BN6 96 C8
ROTT BN2 7 K8
College Rd BEX TN40 183 L2
EAST BN21 10 D8
HWH RH16 48 E8
ROTT BN2 7 K8
SEAF BN25 202 E4
College St ROTT BN2 7 K8
College Ter ROTT BN2 7 K6
Collier Cl LW/ROSE BN22 197 H7
Collier Rd HAS TN34 5 K5
PEV BN24 198 D2
Collingford La RHWH RH17 51 H2
Collington Av BEXW TN39 182 F3
Collington Cl
EDN/EASTW BN20 206 E5 3
Collington Gv BEXW TN39 182 E2
Collington La East BEXW TN39 182 E2
Collington La West
BEXW TN39 182 D3
Collington Park Crs
BEXW TN39 182 F2
Collington Ri BEXW TN39 182 E2
Collingwood Av HTHF TN21 80 A7
Collingwood Cl EGRIN RH19 13 M7 1
LGNY BN23 197 L8
PEAHV BN10 190 C5 2
Collingwood Ri HTHF TN21 80 A7
Collinstone Rd STLEO TN38 162 A7
Collinswood Dr STLEO TN38 162 A7
Colmer Ct BURH RH15 96 E3
Colmer Pl BURH RH15 96 E3 1
Colonnade Rd LW/ROSE BN22 11 H6
Coltstocks Rd
EDN/EASTW BN20 206 D6 1
Columbus Dr LGNY BN23 197 M8
Colwell Cl HWH RH16 71 M3
Colwell Gdns HWH RH16 71 M3
Colwell La HWH RH16 72 B3
RHWH RH17 71 M5
Colwell Rd HWH RH16 71 M4
Colwood Crs
EDN/EASTW BN20 196 B8
Combe End CROW TN6 39 M6
Combe La BAT TN33 135 M8
EDN/EASTW BN20 206 D7
Combe Ri EDN/EASTW BN20 196 A4
Combermere Rd STLEO TN38 162 B5
The Combe EDN/EASTW BN20 196 A7
Commanders Wk RHAS TN35 164 E2
Command Rd
EDN/EASTW BN20 206 B1
Commercial Rd BURH RH15 96 F3 1
EAST BN21 10 E5
RTW TN1 20 B1
Common La HPPT/KEY BN6 123 K1
POLE BN26 176 A5
Common Vw SBGH/RUST TN4 19 J3
Common Wood Ri CROW TN6 39 M2
Compasses La RBTBR TN32 86 C8
Comphurst La HAIL BN27 157 H2
Compton Av BRI BN1 6 C4
Compton Cl BEX TN40 183 L1 1
Compton Dr EDN/EASTW BN20 206 C4
Compton Place Rd
EDN/EASTW BN20 206 D3
Compton Rd BRI BN1 168 D5
HWH RH16 49 H6
Compton St EAST BN21 10 F9
EDN/EASTW BN20 207 G5
Compton Ter HAIL BN27 155 J8 1
The Compts PEAHV BN10 190 B5 4
Concord Cl RTWE/PEM TN2 20 C2 2
Concorde Cl BEXW TN39 159 M8
Condor Wy BURH RH15 96 E3
Conduit Hl RYE TN31 91 J8 1
Coneyburrow Gdns
STLEO TN38 161 L2 1
Coneyburrow La BEXW TN39 181 M2
Coneyburrow Rd
RTWE/PEM TN2 20 E1
Coney Furlong PEAHV BN10 190 D5
Conghurst La HAWK TN18 63 G1
Conifer Cl HAS TN34 162 F3
The Conifers EAST BN21 10 D3
Coniston Av SBGH/RUST TN4 19 L2
Coniston Rd LGNY BN23 197 J2 3
Connaught Rd EAST BN21 10 E7
HOVE BN3 168 A8
SEAF BN25 202 C3
Connaught Ter HOVE BN3 168 B7
Connaught Wy SBGH/RUST TN4 19 M1
Connell Dr ROTT BN2 170 E7
Conqueror Rd STLEO TN38 161 M7
Consort Wy BURH RH15 96 E4
Constable Rd LGNY BN23 197 K5
Constable Wy BEX TN40 160 D8
Conway Pl HOVE BN3 168 B6
Conway St HOVE BN3 168 B6
Cooden Cl BEXW TN39 182 C3
Cooden Dr BEXW TN39 182 D4
Cooden Sea Rd BEXW TN39 182 B4
Cook Av LGNY BN23 197 L8 1
Cookham Dene BEX TN40 183 J2 1
Cooksbridge Rd ROTT BN2 169 L8
Cookstown Cl BAT TN33 135 M8
Coolham Dr ROTT BN2 169 L8
Coombe Cl HAIL BN27 157 H1
Coombe Hill Rd EGRIN RH19 13 J8
Coombe Lands TENT TN30 67 K2
Coombe La WADH TN5 43 J7
Coombe Ri ROTT BN2 189 K3
Coombe Rd EDN/EASTW BN20 206 C2
LEW BN7 3 H3
ROTT BN2 169 K5
Coombers La HWH RH16 72 B1 1
Coombe Shaw BAT TN33 136 A8
Coombe V ROTT BN2 189 K3
Coombs Cl RYE TN31 89 J1
Cooper Dr BEXW TN39 160 A6
Cooper Ri STLEO TN38 162 A1 2
Cooper Rd RYE TN31 117 G1
Coopers Cl BURH RH15 97 H1
Coopers Hl EDN/EASTW BN20 196 B4
Coopers La CROW TN6 39 K2
Coopers Wy HAIL BN27 155 G8
Coopers Wd CROW TN6 39 K2
Copestake Dr BURH RH15 97 K3
Coplands Ri RYE TN31 65 H7
Coppards Cl RHWH RH17 98 C2 1
Coppards La RYE TN31 65 J6
Copper Beeches SLVH TN37 162 C2 2
Copperfields LYDD TN29 95 H8
Coppice Av EDN/EASTW BN20 196 A2
Coppice Cl EDN/EASTW BN20 196 A2
The Coppice BAT TN33 138 A3
CRAWE RH10 12 B6
HAS TN34 4 F4
RHWH RH17 72 F3 2
Coppice Vw HTHF TN21 80 B8 3
Coppice Wy HWH RH16 71 K3
Copse Cl CRAWE RH10 12 B6 1
EGRIN RH19 13 M3
STLEO TN38 161 K3
Copse Hl BRI BN1 168 D1
Copse Rd BEXW TN39 182 E2
The Copse HWH RH16 72 B1
Copthall Av HAWK TN18 47 M5
Copthorne Rd CRAWE RH10 12 B2
EGRIN RH19 12 E2
Copwood Av UCK TN22 76 B7
Copyhold La HWH RH16 48 D4
RHWH RH17 70 F2
Copyhold Rd EGRIN RH19 13 K6
Corbyn Crs SHOR BN43 166 A7

Cordons *LEW* BN7 ... 171 K1
Cormorant Cl *LGNY* BN23 ... 197 J4
Cornelius Av *NEWHV* BN9 ... 8 B7
Cornfield Cl *SEAF* BN25 ... 202 E5
Cornfield Rd *EAST* BN21 ... 10 E8
  *SEAF* BN25 ... 202 F3
Cornfield Ter *EAST* BN21 ... 10 E8
  *SLVH* TN37 ... 4 A4
Cornford Cl *BURH* RH15 ... 96 E1
  *CROW* TN6 ... 40 A5
  *PTSD* BN41 ... 167 H4
Cornford La *RTWE/PEM* TN2 ... 20 E2
Cornish Cl *LGNY* BN23 ... 197 H2
Cornmill Gdns *POLE* BN26 ... 195 L2
Cornwall Av *PEAHV* BN10 ... 190 E8
  *PEAHV* BN10 ... 200 E1
Cornwall Gdns *BRI* BN1 ... 168 E3
  *EGRIN* RH19 ... 13 M6
Cornwallis Gdns *HAS* TN34 ... 4 F7
Cornwallis St *HAS* TN34 ... 5 G6
Cornwallis Ter *HAS* TN34 ... 4 F6
Cornwall Rd *BEXW* TN39 ... 183 H3
Coronation Cottages
  *RBTBR* TN32 ... 85 J1
Coronation Gdns *BAT* TN33 ... 137 M1
  *BUR/ETCH* TN19 ... 61 M3
Coronation Rd *EGRIN* RH19 ... 13 L7
  *ROTT* BN2 ... 7 J2
Coronation St *LYDD* TN29 ... 95 J8
Corseley Rd *RRTW* TN3 ... 28 A3
Corsica Cl *SEAF* BN25 ... 202 F5
Corsica Rd *SEAF* BN25 ... 202 F5
Costells Edge *RHWH* RH17 ... 72 F2
Cotchford Hl *HRTF* TN7 ... 26 D5
Cotchford La *HRTF* TN7 ... 26 B5
Cotswold Cl *HAS* TN34 ... 163 H2
  *LGNY* BN23 ... 197 J2
The Cotswolds *STHW* BN42 ... 166 E7
Cottage Bush Cl *PTSD* BN41 ... 167 J4
Cottage Cl *NEWHV* BN9 ... 191 K5
Cottage La *BAT* TN33 ... 112 E7
  *PEV* BN24 ... 178 E5
Coulstock Rd *HPPT/KEY* BN6 ... 96 C2
County Oak Av *BRI* BN1 ... 146 B8
The Course *LEW* BN7 ... 2 D8
Court Cl *BRI* BN1 ... 145 L7
  *EGRIN* RH19 ... 13 M5
Court Crs *EGRIN* RH19 ... 14 A5
Court Farm Cl *NEWHV* BN9 ... 191 H5
Court Farm Rd *HOVE* BN3 ... 167 M4
  *NEWHV* BN9 ... 8 E7
  *ROTT* BN2 ... 188 E3
Courthope Av *WADH* TN5 ... 43 M2
Courthope Dr *BEXW* TN39 ... 182 E1
Courthouse St *HAS* TN34 ... 5 K6
Courtland Rd *POLE* BN26 ... 196 A1
Courtlands *HWH* RH16 ... 71 L3
  *UCK* TN22 ... 52 D4
Courtlands Pl *CROW* TN6 ... 39 L5
Courtlands Rd *LW/ROSE* BN22 ... 10 F1
Court Meadow *CROW* TN6 ... 41 H6
Court Ord Rd *ROTT* BN2 ... 188 E3
Court Rd *LEW* BN7 ... 3 H7
  *LW/ROSE* BN22 ... 196 F4
  *SBGH/RUST* TN4 ... 19 L2
The Courtyard *EGRIN* RH19 ... 14 B5
Cousley Wood Rd *WADH* TN5 ... 32 A8
Coventry St *BRI* BN1 ... 168 C6
Coverdale Av *BEXW* TN39 ... 182 C3
The Covers *SEAF* BN25 ... 202 F4
The Covert *BEXW* TN39 ... 182 C4
Cowden Cl *HAWK* TN18 ... 47 L6
Cowden Hall La *HTHF* TN21 ... 132 C1
Cowden La *HAWK* TN18 ... 47 L7
Cowden Ms *EDEN* TN8 ... 16 A1
Cowden Rd *ROTT* BN2 ... 189 K6
Cowdens Cl *HOVE* BN3 ... 167 K2
Cowdray Av *BEXW* TN39 ... 159 K8
Cowdray Park Rd *BEXW* TN39 ... 159 L9
Cowfold Rd *ROTT* BN2 ... 187 L1
Cowhurst La *BEXW* TN39 ... 160 C7
Cow La *POLE* BN26 ... 193 M6
Cowley Dr *ROTT* BN2 ... 170 E8
Cowper St *HOVE* BN3 ... 168 A7
Cox Gv *BURH* RH15 ... 96 F1
Crabtree Av *BRI* BN1 ... 169 G1
Cradle Hill Rd *SEAF* BN25 ... 193 G8
Craig Cl *BAT* TN33 ... 138 A8
Craignair Av *BRI* BN1 ... 145 M7
Cranborne Av
  *EDN/EASTW* BN20 ... 206 C6
Cranbrook Rd *HAWK* TN18 ... 47 M2
  *SLVH* TN37 ... 4 B4
Cranedown *LEW* BN7 ... 149 G7
Cranfield Rd *BEX* TN40 ... 183 J1
Cranleigh Av *ROTT* BN2 ... 189 H5
Cranleigh Cl *BEXW* TN39 ... 183 G2
Cranmer Av *HOVE* BN3 ... 167 K6
Cranmer Cl *LEW* BN7 ... 3 H3
Cranston Av *BEXW* TN39 ... 182 F2
Cranston Cl *BEXW* TN39 ... 182 F2
Cranston Ri *BEXW* TN39 ... 182 F2
Cranston Rd *EGRIN* RH19 ... 13 M4
Cranwell Rd *SBGH/RUST* TN4 ... 19 J2
Craven Rd *ROTT* BN2 ... 7 L6
Crawfurd Wy *EGRIN* RH19 ... 13 M3
Crawley Crs *LW/ROSE* BN22 ... 196 E4
Crawley Down Rd *EGRIN* RH19 ... 12 E3
Crawley Rd *BRI* BN1 ... 146 D8
Crayford Rd *ROTT* BN2 ... 169 K5
Crazy La *BAT* TN33 ... 112 E7
Crecy Cl *SLVH* TN37 ... 138 F7
Crescent Dr North *ROTT* BN2 ... 170 E6
Crescent Dr South *ROTT* BN2 ... 170 E8
Crescent Pl *ROTT* BN2 ... 7 K9
Crescent Rd *BURH* RH15 ... 97 H3
  *EGRIN* RH19 ... 13 K5
  *ROTT* BN2 ... 7 C1
The Crescent
  *DN/EASTW* BN20 ... 196 A3
  *EDN/EASTW* BN20 ... 206 B1
  *HPPT/KEY* BN6 ... 123 H3
  *ROTT* BN2 ... 169 L4

  *SLVH* TN37 ... 162 C3
  *STHW* BN42 ... 166 F6
Crescent Wy *BURH* RH15 ... 97 G3
Crespin Wy *BRI* BN1 ... 169 J5
Cresta Cl *POLE* BN26 ... 178 A7
Cresta Rd *NEWHV* BN9 ... 8 A5
Crest Rd *NEWHV* BN9 ... 191 M5
Crest Wy *PTSD* BN41 ... 167 H3
Cricket Ct *EGRIN* RH19 ... 13 L3
Cricketers Fld *RBTBR* TN32 ... 86 E5
Cricketfield Rd *SEAF* BN25 ... 202 F4
Cricketing La *HAIL* BN27 ... 156 C2
Criers La *MAYF* TN20 ... 55 M7
Crink Hl *RING/NEW* BN8 ... 126 F3
Cripland Cl *HWH* RH16 ... 49 H8
Cripps Av *PEAHV* BN10 ... 190 D5
Crisp Rd *LEW* BN7 ... 2 B8
Crockers La *RYE* TN31 ... 91 M8
Crocks Dean *PEAHV* BN10 ... 190 D4
Croft Av *STHW* BN42 ... 166 E2
Croft Cl *POLE* BN26 ... 195 M2
Croft Ct *SEAF* BN25 ... 202 E5
Croft Dr *PTSD* BN41 ... 167 G3
Croft La *SEAF* BN25 ... 202 E5
Crofton Park Av *BEXW* TN39 ... 182 E1
Croft Rd *BRI* BN1 ... 168 D2
  *CROW* TN6 ... 39 M5
  *HAS* TN34 ... 5 K4
The Croft *EDN/EASTW* BN20 ... 196 B5
  *HAS* TN34 ... 5 K5
  *HPPT/KEY* BN6 ... 122 F1
Croft Works *HAIL* BN27 ... 155 H7
Croham Rd *CROW* TN6 ... 39 M3
Cromer Wy *HAIL* BN27 ... 155 G4
Cromleigh Wy *STHW* BN42 ... 166 E5
Cromwell Pl *EGRIN* RH19 ... 13 M7
Cromwell Rd *BURH* RH15 ... 96 F3
  *HOVE* BN3 ... 168 C7
  *RTWE/PEM* TN2 ... 20 C3
Cromwell St *ROTT* BN2 ... 7 K3
Crooked La *SEAF* BN25 ... 202 F4
Crossbush Rd *ROTT* BN2 ... 169 L8
Cross Lane Gdns *WADH* TN5 ... 45 K5
Cross Levels Wy *EAST* BN21 ... 196 E8
Cross Rd *STHW* BN42 ... 166 D6
Crossroad Cl *STHW* BN42 ... 166 D6
Cross St *BRI* BN1 ... 6 E2
  *HOVE* BN3 ... 186 D1
  *POLE* BN26 ... 178 A8
  *SLVH* TN37 ... 4 B8
Cross Wy *LEW* BN7 ... 2 A5
Crossways Av *EGRIN* RH19 ... 13 J5
The Crossways *BRI* BN1 ... 166 H1
  *PTSD* BN41 ... 167 G4
  *SBGH/RUST* TN4 ... 19 K4
Crouch Cl *EDN/EASTW* BN20 ... 196 B5
Crouch La *BAT* TN33 ... 159 H2
  *HAWK* TN18 ... 64 D1
  *SEAF* BN25 ... 202 E4
Crowborough Hl *CROW* TN6 ... 40 C6
Crowborough Rd *RHAS* TN35 ... 163 K2
  *ROTT* BN2 ... 189 K6
  *UCK* TN22 ... 37 M8
Crowders La *BAT* TN33 ... 136 C3
Crowhurst Cl *LGNY* BN23 ... 197 G2
Crowhurst Rd *BAT* TN33 ... 161 G3
  *STLEO* TN38 ... 161 K4
Crowmere Av *BEX* TN40 ... 183 J1
Crowmere Ter *BEX* TN40 ... 183 J1
Crown Cl *HAIL* BN27 ... 155 G7
  *UCK* TN22 ... 76 C6
Crown Hl *SEAF* BN25 ... 192 E8
Crown La *HAS* TN34 ... 5 L6
Crown Rd *PTSD* BN41 ... 167 G6
  *SHOR* BN43 ... 166 B6
Crown St *BRI* BN1 ... 6 C6
Croxden Wy *LW/ROSE* BN22 ... 196 D3
Croxton La *HWH* RH16 ... 49 H8
Crunden Rd *EDN/EASTW* BN20 ... 206 B2
Cubitt Wy *STLEO* TN38 ... 161 L2
Cuckfield Cl *BEX* TN40 ... 161 G8
Cuckfield Rd *BURH* RH15 ... 70 F7
  *HPPT/KEY* BN6 ... 96 A4
  *RHWH* RH17 ... 70 B6
Cuckmere Dr *PEV* BN24 ... 197 G1
Cuckmere Ri *HTHF* TN21 ... 80 A7
Cuckmere Rd *NEWHV* BN9 ... 8 B7
  *SEAF* BN25 ... 203 H4
Cuckmere Wk *LW/ROSE* BN22 ... 196 D5
Cuckmere Wy *BRI* BN1 ... 146 B8
  *BRI* BN1 ... 169 H1
Cuckoo Dr *HTHF* TN21 ... 80 A8
Cuckoo Trail *HAIL* BN27 ... 155 H6
  *HTHF* TN21 ... 80 A8
  *HTHF* TN21 ... 105 K3
  *POLE* BN26 ... 178 A6
Culpepper *BURH* RH15 ... 96 F2
Culpepper Cl *ROTT* BN2 ... 169 K4
Culross Av *HWH* RH16 ... 71 L2
Culver Cl *LGNY* BN23 ... 197 H2
Culverden Down
  *SBGH/RUST* TN4 ... 19 M1
Culverden Pk *SBGH/RUST* TN4 ... 19 M1
Culverden Sq *SBGH/RUST* TN4 ... 20 A1
Culverden St *RTW* TN1 ... 20 A2
Culver's La *LYDD* TN29 ... 121 K1
Cumberland Dr *BRI* BN1 ... 168 E4
Cumberland Gdns *STLEO* TN38 ... 162 B6
Cumberland Rd *BEXW* TN39 ... 160 B7
  *BRI* BN1 ... 168 E4
Cumberland Yd *RTW* TN1 ... 20 A4
Cunningham Dr *LGNY* BN23 ... 197 L7
Curlew Ct *STLEO* TN38 ... 161 L3
The Curlews *SHOR* BN43 ... 166 A6
Curwen Pl *BRI* BN1 ... 168 E3
Cuthbert Cl *BEXW* TN39 ... 160 A7
Cuthbert Rd *ROTT* BN2 ... 7 K6
Cuttinglye La *CRAWE* RH10 ... 12 C1
Cuttinglye Rd *CRAWE* RH10 ... 12 B4
Cypress Cl *STLEO* TN38 ... 162 A7
Cypress Gv *RTWE/PEM* TN2 ... 20 C6
Cyprus Pl *RYE* TN31 ... 117 H1
Cyprus Rd *BURH* RH15 ... 97 G3

## D

Dacre Rd *EDN/EASTW* BN20 ... 206 C2
  *HAIL* BN27 ... 133 L8
Dagg La *RBTBR* TN32 ... 86 E1
The Dakins *EGRIN* RH19 ... 13 L6
Dale Av *BRI* BN1 ... 168 F1
  *HPPT/KEY* BN6 ... 122 F3
Dale Crs *BRI* BN1 ... 145 M8
Dale Dr *BRI* BN1 ... 145 M8
Dale Hl *POY/PYE* BN45 ... 122 A8
Dalehurst Rd *BEXW* TN39 ... 160 A7
Dales Cl *HAIL* BN27 ... 157 H1
Dale St *RTW* TN1 ... 20 B2
Dale Vw *HOVE* BN3 ... 167 K4
Dale View Gdns *HOVE* BN3 ... 167 K4
Dalewood Gdns *BURH* RH15 ... 97 J4
Dallas La *RING/NEW* BN8 ... 100 F8
Dallaway Dr *PEV* BN24 ... 197 H1
Dallaway Gdns *EGRIN* RH19 ... 13 L5
Dallington Cl *BEX* TN40 ... 161 G8
Dallington Rd *HOVE* BN3 ... 167 L6
  *LW/ROSE* BN22 ... 196 F5
Dalmeny Rd *EDN/EASTW* BN20 ... 183 G1
Dalton Rd *EDN/EASTW* BN20 ... 206 E6
Damian Wy *HPPT/KEY* BN6 ... 123 H2
Damon Cl *PEAHV* BN10 ... 190 C7
Damon Rd *PEAHV* BN10 ... 202 D4
Dane Court Cl *BEXW* TN39 ... 160 B8
Danehill La *RHWH* RH17 ... 50 E1
Dane Rd *SEAF* BN25 ... 202 D4
  *STLEO* TN38 ... 162 B6
Daniel Wy *RYE* TN31 ... 118 F4
Danum Cl *HAIL* BN27 ... 155 J3
Danworth La *HPPT/KEY* BN6 ... 96 E5
Darby's La *WADH* TN5 ... 44 A4
Darcey Dr *BRI* BN1 ... 146 A8
Darent Cl *POLE* BN26 ... 196 F1
Daresbury Cl *BEXW* TN39 ... 160 A8
Darley Rd *EDN/EASTW* BN20 ... 206 D6
Dartmouth Cl *LGNY* BN23 ... 197 G2
Dartmouth Crs *ROTT* BN2 ... 169 L5
Darvel Down *BAT* TN33 ... 110 B4
Darwall Dr *SEAF* BN25 ... 203 G3
Darwell Cl *STLEO* TN38 ... 161 L5
Darwell Dr *POLE* BN26 ... 196 F1
Davey Dr *BRI* BN1 ... 169 H5
Davey's La *LEW* BN7 ... 3 J4
Davigdor Rd *HOVE* BN3 ... 168 D7
Davis Cl *BEXW* TN39 ... 160 A7
Dawlish Cl *ROTT* BN2 ... 169 L5
Dawson Ter *ROTT* BN2 ... 7 K5
Daynes Wy *BURH* RH15 ... 96 E5
Deacons Dr *PTSD* BN41 ... 167 H4
Deadmans La *RYE* TN31 ... 91 J8
Deadmantree Hl
  *RING/NEW* BN8 ... 126 B3
Deal Av *SEAF* BN25 ... 203 J1
The Deals *RYE* TN31 ... 117 H1
Dean Cl *PTSD* BN41 ... 167 J4
Dean Court Rd *ROTT* BN2 ... 189 G4
Deanery Cl *LEW* BN7 ... 3 H2
Dean Gdns *PTSD* BN41 ... 167 J4
Dean Rd *SEAF* BN25 ... 202 F4
Deans Cl *BEXW* TN39 ... 160 B7
  *ROTT* BN2 ... 170 E6
Dean St *BEXW* TN39 ... 160 A8
Deans Meadow
  *RING/NEW* BN8 ... 126 E1
Deans Rd *POLE* BN26 ... 193 M3
Dean St *BRI* BN1 ... 6 B6
Deanway *HOVE* BN3 ... 168 B3
Dean Wood Cl *LGNY* BN23 ... 197 G2
De Cham Av *SLVH* TN37 ... 4 A6
De Cham Rd *SLVH* TN37 ... 4 B6
De Chardin Dr *HAS* TN34 ... 163 G1
De Courcel Rd *ROTT* BN2 ... 187 L3
Decoy Dr *LW/ROSE* BN22 ... 196 D6
Deepdene *WADH* TN5 ... 31 M8
Deepdene Gdns *HAS* TN34 ... 163 H3
Deerswood La *BEXW* TN39 ... 182 E1
The Deeside *BRI* BN1 ... 146 A7
De Grey Cl *LEW* BN7 ... 3 H3
Delaware Dr *STLEO* TN38 ... 138 F8
Dell Cl *STLEO* TN38 ... 162 A4
Dell Dr *RTWE/PEM* TN2 ... 20 D2
Dellney Av *HWH* RH16 ... 71 M3
The Dell *EGRIN* RH19 ... 14 B5
  *HWH* RH16 ... 71 J1
Delmonden Rd *HAWK* TN18 ... 47 J6
Delves Av *RTWE/PEM* TN2 ... 20 C5
Delves Cl *RING/NEW* BN8 ... 127 K8
Delves Wy *RING/NEW* BN8 ... 127 K8
De Moleyns Cl *BEX* TN40 ... 183 K2
De Montfort Rd *LEW* BN7 ... 2 C6
  *ROTT* BN2 ... 7 J2
Dencher Rd *LEW* BN7 ... 171 L3
Dene Cl *EDN/EASTW* BN20 ... 205 H5
Dene Dr *LW/ROSE* BN22 ... 196 C5
Dene Pth *UCK* TN22 ... 76 D5
Deneside *EDN/EASTW* BN20 ... 205 H5
Dene Side *EDN/EASTW* BN20 ... 205 H5
The Dene *EDN/EASTW* BN20 ... 196 A4
  *HAS* TN34 ... 163 G1
Dene V *BRI* BN1 ... 168 D1
The Deneway *BRI* BN1 ... 168 D2
Dengemarsh Rd *LYDD* TN29 ... 121 J3
Denham Cl *STLEO* TN38 ... 161 M2
Denham Rd *BURH* RH15 ... 96 D2
Denham Wy *RYE* TN31 ... 118 E4
Den Hl *EDN/EASTW* BN20 ... 206 A2
Denman's Cl *HWH* RH16 ... 49 G7
Denman's La *HWH* RH16 ... 49 G7
Denmark Pl *HAS* TN34 ... 5 G7
Denmark Rd *PTSD* BN41 ... 167 J7
Denmark Ter *BRI* BN1 ... 6 B4

Denmark Vls *HOVE* BN3 ... 168 B7
Dennes La *LYDD* TN29 ... 95 H5
Dennis Hobden Cl *ROTT* BN2 ... 169 L5
Denton Cl *RYE* TN31 ... 91 G8
Denton Dr *BRI* BN1 ... 169 G1
  *NEWHV* BN9 ... 191 L5
Denton Ri *NEWHV* BN9 ... 191 L4
Denton Rd *EDN/EASTW* BN20 ... 206 D6
  *NEWHV* BN9 ... 191 L5
The Dentons
  *EDN/EASTW* BN20 ... 206 D6
Derek Av *HOVE* BN3 ... 167 K8
Dern La *HTHF* TN21 ... 131 K2
De Roos Rd *EAST* BN21 ... 206 D2
Derwent Cl *HAIL* BN27 ... 155 G5
Derwent Dr *SBGH/RUST* TN4 ... 19 L1
Derwent Rd *EDN/EASTW* BN20 ... 206 E6
Desmond Rd *LW/ROSE* BN22 ... 11 L2
Desmond Wy *ROTT* BN2 ... 169 M8
Devil's Dyke Rd *HOVE* BN3 ... 144 F8
  *POY/PYE* BN45 ... 144 A5
  *PTSD* BN41 ... 144 C5
Devonshire Cl
  *RTWE/PEM* TN2 ... 19 M6
Devonshire Pl *EAST* BN21 ... 10 F7
  *ROTT* BN2 ... 7 G8
Devonshire Rd *BEX* TN40 ... 183 J3
  *HAS* TN34 ... 5 G6
De Walden Ms
  *EDN/EASTW* BN20 ... 206 E6
De Warrenne Rd *LEW* BN7 ... 2 D5
Dewe Rd *ROTT* BN2 ... 169 J5
Dewhurst La *WADH* TN5 ... 31 H6
Dewlands Hl *MAYF* TN20 ... 55 L5
Dew La *RYE* TN31 ... 90 A8
The Dewpond *PEAHV* BN10 ... 190 B5
Dexter Dr *EGRIN* RH19 ... 13 L6
Diana Cl *BEX* TN40 ... 161 G8
Dickens Cl *EGRIN* RH19 ... 13 J5
Dickens Wy *LGNY* BN23 ... 197 L3
Dillingburgh Rd
  *EDN/EASTW* BN20 ... 206 C2
Diplock Cl *POLE* BN26 ... 177 M8
Diplocks Wy *HAIL* BN27 ... 155 G7
Dirty La *EGRIN* RH19 ... 14 E8
Ditchling Bostall
  *HPPT/KEY* BN6 ... 123 K7
Ditchling Cl *POLE* BN26 ... 196 F2
Ditchling Crs *BRI* BN1 ... 169 J1
Ditchling Dr *RHAS* TN35 ... 163 L2
Ditchling Gdns *BRI* BN1 ... 169 G5
Ditchling Ri *BRI* BN1 ... 6 E1
Ditchling Rd *BRI* BN1 ... 146 C6
  *ROTT* BN2 ... 169 J2
Ditchling Wy *HAIL* BN27 ... 155 H8
Dittons Ms *STLEO* TN38 ... 161 L4
Dittons Rd *EAST* BN21 ... 10 B6
  *POLE* BN26 ... 178 C8
Dixter La *RYE* TN31 ... 65 G7
Dixter Rd *RYE* TN31 ... 65 G7
The Dock *RING/NEW* BN8 ... 174 C3
Dodshill *CROW* TN6 ... 40 A5
Dog Kennel La *UCK* TN22 ... 55 L8
Dogs Hill Rd *WSEA* TN36 ... 143 H1
Doleham La *RHAS* TN35 ... 140 A1
Dolphin Rd *LYDD* TN29 ... 95 J8
  *SHOR* BN43 ... 166 B7
Dolphin Wy *SHOR* BN43 ... 166 B7
Donald Hall Rd *ROTT* BN2 ... 7 M7
Donald Wy *WSEA* TN36 ... 143 G1
Donkey Ms *HOVE* BN3 ... 186 D1
Donnington Rd *ROTT* BN2 ... 170 E8
Dordrecht Wy *HAS* TN34 ... 4 E3
Dormans Park Rd *EGRIN* RH19 ... 13 K3
Dornden Dr *RRTW* TN3 ... 19 C2
Dorothy Av *PEAHV* BN10 ... 190 C6
Dorothy Av North
  *PEAHV* BN10 ... 190 C6
Dorothy Rd *HOVE* BN3 ... 167 K6
Dorset Av *EDN/EASTW* BN20 ... 206 D2
Dorset Gdns *EGRIN* RH19 ... 13 J3
  *ROTT* BN2 ... 7 G7
Dorset Pl *HAS* TN34 ... 4 F7
  *ROTT* BN2 ... 7 G7
Dorset Rd *BEX* TN40 ... 183 K2
  *LEW* BN7 ... 2 D4
  *RTWE/PEM* TN2 ... 20 D4
Dorset Rd South *BEX* TN40 ... 183 K2
Dorset St *ROTT* BN2 ... 7 G7
Doubledays *BURH* RH15 ... 97 H4
Doucegrove *STLEO* TN38 ... 162 A4
Douglas Cl *HAIL* BN27 ... 155 H4
Douglas Rd *CROW* TN6 ... 41 K5
Dove Ct *UCK* TN22 ... 76 C5
Dovedale Gdns
  *LW/ROSE* BN22 ... 196 F4
Dover Cl *SEAF* BN25 ... 203 J1
Dover Rd *BRI* BN1 ... 169 G4
  *POLE* BN26 ... 178 B7
Dower Cl *ROTT* BN2 ... 188 D3
Downash Cl *ROTT* BN2 ... 169 L8
Down Av *RRTW* TN3 ... 33 G3
Downey Cl *SLVH* TN37 ... 139 H8
Downland Av *PEAHV* BN10 ... 190 C6
  *STHW* BN42 ... 166 D5
Downland Cl *ROTT* BN2 ... 170 B6
  *STHW* BN42 ... 166 D5
Downland Copse *UCK* TN22 ... 76 C6
Downland Crs *HOVE* BN3 ... 167 M3
Downland Dr *HOVE* BN3 ... 167 M3
Downland Rd *ROTT* BN2 ... 170 B6
Downlands Av *BEXW* TN39 ... 183 G2
Downlands Cl *BEXW* TN39 ... 183 G2
Downlands Wy
  *EDN/EASTW* BN20 ... 205 H5
Down La *RRTW* TN3 ... 30 C6
Downline Cl *HTHF* TN21 ... 105 M7
Down Rd *BEXW* TN39 ... 168 J5
Downs Av *EDN/EASTW* BN20 ... 196 B8
Downs Cl *LEW* BN7 ... 2 A4
Downscroft *BURH* RH15 ... 97 K1
Downside *BRI* BN1 ... 168 D1
  *HOVE* BN3 ... 168 B3
  *LEW* BN7 ... 2 A7
  *SHOR* BN43 ... 166 A5
Downs Rd *BURH* RH15 ... 96 E2
  *HAS* TN34 ... 162 F3
  *LW/ROSE* BN22 ... 196 B4

  *SEAF* BN25 ... 203 G3
Downsvalley Rd
  *EDN/EASTW* BN20 ... 196 A2
Downs Valley Rd *ROTT* BN2 ... 170 E6
Downs Vw *BAT* TN33 ... 159 G3
Downsview *HOVE* BN3 ... 167 K3
  *HTHF* TN21 ... 80 B3
Downs Vw *PEAHV* BN10 ... 190 D4
Downsview Av *ROTT* BN2 ... 170 C5
Downs View Cl
  *EDN/EASTW* BN20 ... 205 J6
  *RING/NEW* BN8 ... 73 L8
Downsview Crs *UCK* TN22 ... 76 D6
Downsview Dr *RHWH* RH17 ... 98 C2
Downs View La
  *EDN/EASTW* BN20 ... 205 J6
Downsview Rd
  *EDN/EASTW* BN20 ... 196 A3
Down View Rd
  *HPPT/KEY* BN6 ... 122 F3
Downsview Rd *PTSD* BN41 ... 167 G4
  *SEAF* BN25 ... 203 G3
Downsview Wy *HAIL* BN27 ... 155 H7
Downs Wk *PEAHV* BN10 ... 190 B4
Downsway *ROTT* BN2 ... 170 D6
  *STHW* BN42 ... 166 F4
Down Ter *ROTT* BN2 ... 7 K4
The Down *HOVE* BN3 ... 167 J2
Draffin La *RYE* TN31 ... 118 D3
Drake Av *LGNY* BN23 ... 197 L7
Drapers Wy *STLEO* TN38 ... 162 A4
Draxmont Wy *BRI* BN1 ... 168 F3
Drayton Ri *BEXW* TN39 ... 182 D2
The Drive *RHWH* RH15 ... 42 H2
  *CROW* TN6 ... 39 K4
  *HAIL* BN27 ... 155 H8
  *HOVE* BN3 ... 168 C7
  *NEWHV* BN9 ... 8 E8
  *RTWE/PEM* TN2 ... 20 A5
  *STHW* BN42 ... 166 E5
  *STLEO* TN38 ... 161 M6
  *UCK* TN22 ... 53 G8
  *UCK* TN22 ... 76 A1
  *UCK* TN22 ... 76 C5
Drockmill Cl *POLE* BN26 ... 178 C3
Drove Av *ROTT* BN2 ... 170 D4
Drove Crs *PTSD* BN41 ... 167 G4
Drove Rd *NEWHV* BN9 ... 9 J2
  *PTSD* BN41 ... 167 G5
  *ROTT* BN2 ... 170 C5
Drovers Cl *PTSD* BN41 ... 167 J4
Drovers Wy *BURH* RH15 ... 97 J3
The Drove *BRI* BN1 ... 168 D5
  *BRI* BN1 ... 170 C1
  *NEWHV* BN9 ... 9 K1
  *RING/NEW* BN8 ... 149 G1
The Droveway *HOVE* BN3 ... 168 C5
  *RHWH* RH17 ... 48 C8
Drummond Cl *HWH* RH16 ... 71 K2
Duchess Dr *SEAF* BN25 ... 192 E8
Dudley Rd *BRI* BN1 ... 169 H5
  *LW/ROSE* BN22 ... 11 G5
  *RTW* TN1 ... 20 A2
Dudwell Rd *ROTT* BN2 ... 170 E7
Duke Ms *SLVH* TN37 ... 162 B4
Duke Rd *SLVH* TN37 ... 162 B4
Dukes Cl *SEAF* BN25 ... 202 D1
Duke's Dr *EDN/EASTW* BN20 ... 206 D7
Dukes Hl *BAT* TN33 ... 111 K8
Duke's Mound *ROTT* BN2 ... 7 L9
Dukes Rd *HWH* RH16 ... 49 H6
  *RTW* TN1 ... 20 C1
Duke St *BEXW* TN39 ... 182 F1
  *BRI* BN1 ... 6 D7
  *SLVH* TN37 ... 162 B4
Duke Ter *SLVH* TN37 ... 162 B4
Dulwich Cl *SEAF* BN25 ... 203 H2
Dumbrells Court Rd
  *HPPT/KEY* BN6 ... 123 K2
Dumbrills Cl *BURH* RH15 ... 97 G5
Dumb Woman's La *RYE* TN31 ... 116 D3
Dunbar Dr *HAIL* BN27 ... 155 G5
Dunclutha Rd *HAS* TN34 ... 162 F2
Duncton Cl *HWH* RH16 ... 71 K2
Dundale Rd *RRTW* TN3 ... 21 L5
Dunes Av *RYE* TN31 ... 118 F4
Dungeness Rd *LYDD* TN29 ... 121 M1
Dunning's Rd *EGRIN* RH19 ... 13 L7
  *EGRIN* RH19 ... 13 L8
Dunstall Av *BURH* RH15 ... 96 E2
Dunstall Farm Rd *BURH* RH15 ... 96 F2
Dunstan Gv *SBGH/RUST* TN4 ... 20 B1
Dunstans Cft *MAYF* TN20 ... 57 J3
Dunster Cl *BRI* BN1 ... 169 H5
Dunvan Cl *LEW* BN7 ... 2 F1
Durham Cl *ROTT* BN2 ... 170 A5
Durkins Rd *EGRIN* RH19 ... 13 K3
Durrell Cl *LGNY* BN23 ... 197 M4
Dursley Rd *LW/ROSE* BN22 ... 10 F4
Dutchells Wy *LW/ROSE* BN22 ... 196 D2
Dyall Cl *BURH* RH15 ... 96 E1
Dyke Cl *HOVE* BN3 ... 168 B2
Dyke Rd *BRI* BN1 ... 6 B5
  *HOVE* BN3 ... 6 B2
  *HOVE* BN3 ... 168 E6
Dyke Road Av *HOVE* BN3 ... 168 B2
Dyke Road Dr *BRI* BN1 ... 168 E6
Dyke Road Pl *HOVE* BN3 ... 168 B2
Dymchurch Cl *POLE* BN26 ... 178 C7
  *SEAF* BN25 ... 203 H1
Dymock Cl *SEAF* BN25 ... 203 J2
The Dymock's
  *HPPT/KEY* BN6 ... 123 K3
Dymond Rd *STLEO* TN38 ... 162 A3

## E

Eagle Cl *UCK* TN22 ... 102 E1
Eagle Rd *RYE* TN31 ... 91 J8
Earls Cl *SEAF* BN25 ... 202 C1
Earls Gdn *LEW* BN7 ... 3 G5
Earl's Rd *SBGH/RUST* TN4 ... 19 M2
Earl St *HAS* TN34 ... 5 G5
East Albany Rd *SEAF* BN25 ... 202 F2
East Ascent *STLEO* TN38 ... 162 B8

Eastbank *STHW* BN42 ....... 166 F5
East Beach St *HAS* TN34 ....... 5 K7
East Beeches Rd *CROW* TN6 ..... 40 A4
Eastbourne Av *PEV* BN24 ...... 198 C5
Eastbourne La *POLE* BN26 ..... 195 J7
Eastbourne Rd
  *EDN/EASTW* BN20 ....... 196 B4
  *LGNY* BN23 ....... 197 M2
  *LW/ROSE* BN22 ...... 196 C5
  *PEV* BN24 ....... 198 B3
  *POLE* BN26 ....... 196 A1
  *RING/NEW* BN8 ....... 103 J8
  *ROTT* BN2 ....... 169 K5
  *SEAF* BN25 ....... 203 J3
  *UCK* TN22 ....... 102 F5
Eastbridge Rd *NEWHV* BN9 ...... 9 J4
Eastbrook Rd *PTSD* BN41 ...... 167 H7
Eastbrook Wy *STHW* BN42 ...... 167 C7
East Cliff *RYE* TN31 ....... 117 J1
East CI *POLE* BN26 ....... 178 B8
Eastdale Rd *BURH* RH15 ....... 97 J2
East Dean Ri *SEAF* BN25 ...... 203 G1
East Dean Rd
  *EDN/EASTW* BN20 ....... 205 K6
East Dr *ROTT* BN2 ....... 7 J6
East End La *HPPT/KEY* BN6 ..... 123 K3
Eastergate *BEXW* TN39 ...... 182 D1
Eastergate Rd *ROTT* BN2 ...... 169 L2
Eastern Av *POLE* BN26 ...... 178 B8
  *SHOR* BN43 ....... 166 A4
Eastern CI *SHOR* BN43 ...... 166 A4
Eastern PI *ROTT* BN2 ....... 187 L2
Eastern Rd *HWH* RH16 ....... 49 H7
  *HWH* RH16 ....... 71 M3
  *LYDD* TN29 ....... 95 J3
  *ROTT* BN2 ....... 7 K7
  *ROTT* BN2 ....... 187 L2
Eastern Ter *ROTT* BN2 ....... 7 L9
Eastern Terrace Ms *ROTT* BN2 ..... 7 J4
East Gdns *HPPT/KEY* BN6 ...... 123 K3
Eastgate *LEW* BN7 ....... 3 G5
Eastgate Whf *LEW* BN7 ....... 3 H5
Easthill Dr *PTSD* BN41 ...... 167 H5
Easthill Wy *PTSD* BN41 ...... 167 H5
Eastlands CI *SBGH/RUST* TN4 ..... 19 L6
Eastlands Rd *SBGH/RUST* TN4 .... 19 L6
East Mascalls La *HWH* RH16 ..... 49 K8
East Meadway *SHOR* BN43 ..... 166 A8
East Pde *HAS* TN34 ....... 5 K7
Eastport La *LEW* BN7 ....... 2 F8
East St *BRI* BN1 ....... 6 E7
  *CRAWE* RH10 ....... 22 B2
  *HAS* TN34 ....... 5 K7
  *LEW* BN7 ....... 3 G5
  *MAYF* TN20 ....... 57 J3
  *PTSD* BN41 ....... 167 J8
  *RYE* TN31 ....... 117 J2
  *SEAF* BN25 ....... 202 E3
East View Flds *LEW* BN7 ...... 124 E1
East View Ter *BAT* TN33 ...... 112 F5
Eastway *BEXW* TN39 ...... 182 C2
East Wy *LEW* BN7 ....... 148 F4
East Wick *HWH* RH16 ....... 49 J7
Eastwick CI *BRI* BN1 ....... 146 E8
Eastwood Rd *BEXW* TN39 ..... 183 G2
Eatenden La *BAT* TN33 ...... 110 F4
Eaton Gdns *HOVE* BN3 ...... 168 C7
Eaton Gv *HOVE* BN3 ....... 168 C7
Eaton PI *ROTT* BN2 ....... 7 M9
Eaton Rd *HOVE* BN3 ....... 168 C8
Eaton Vis *HOVE* BN3 ....... 168 B7
Eaton Wk *BAT* TN33 ....... 112 D5
Ebden's HI *BAT* TN33 ....... 139 H5
Ebenezer Rd *HAS* TN34 ....... 5 M5
Ecmod Rd *LW/ROSE* BN22 ..... 197 J8
Edburton Av *BRI* BN1 ....... 169 C5
Edenbridge Rd *EDEN* TN8 ..... 16 D4
  *HRTF* TN7 ....... 16 D4
Eden Dr *BEXW* TN39 ...... 182 E2
Eden Rd *RTW* TN1 ....... 20 A4
Edensor Rd *EDN/EASTW* BN20 ... 206 D7
Eden V *EGRIN* RH19 ....... 13 L2
Edgar Rd *RHAS* TN35 ...... 163 J4
Edgehill CI *HTHF* TN21 ...... 79 M7
Edgehill Wy *PTSD* BN41 ..... 166 F4
Edinburgh Rd *BEX* TN40 ...... 183 J1
  *ROTT* BN2 ....... 7 H1
  *SEAF* BN25 ....... 202 D3
  *STLEO* TN38 ....... 161 L7
Edinburgh Wy *EGRIN* RH19 ..... 13 M7
Edith Av *PEAHV* BN10 ...... 190 B7
Edith Av North *PEAHV* BN10 ... 190 C6
Edith Rd *RHAS* TN35 ...... 163 K3
Edmond CI *LGNY* BN23 ...... 197 L6
Edmonton Rd *BEXW* TN39 ..... 160 B7
Edmund Rd *RHAS* TN35 ...... 163 J4
Edward Av *HOVE* BN3 ...... 168 A3
  *ROTT* BN2 ....... 189 K3
Edward CI *HOVE* BN3 ...... 168 A3
  *SEAF* BN25 ....... 192 A8
Edward Rd *HWH* RH16 ...... 71 L3
  *SLVH* TN37 ....... 4 C7
Edward St *LEW* BN7 ....... 3 G5
  *ROTT* BN2 ....... 7 G7
  *SBGH/RUST* TN4 ....... 19 H2
Edward Ter *STLEO* TN38 ..... 162 A2
Edwin Rd *RHAS* TN35 ...... 163 J4
Effingham CI *BRI* BN1 ...... 189 J4
Effingham Dr *BEXW* TN39 ..... 182 D3
Egerton Rd *BEXW* TN39 ..... 183 H3
Egginton CI *BRI* BN1 ...... 170 A1
Egginton Rd *ROTT* BN2 ...... 169 M2
Egles Gv *UCK* TN22 ....... 76 B6
Egmont Rd *HOVE* BN3 ...... 167 K5
Egremont PI *HAS* TN34 ...... 5 L2
  *ROTT* BN2 ....... 7 H7
Eight Acre La *RHAS* TN35 ..... 140 D5
Eight Bells *UCK* TN22 ...... 77 J2
Eileen Av *ROTT* BN2 ...... 189 H5
Eisenhower Dr *STLEO* TN38 .... 138 F8
Elder CI *PTSD* BN41 ...... 167 H4
Elder PI *BRI* BN1 ....... 6 E2
Elderwood CI *BEXW* TN39 ..... 160 C7
  *LW/ROSE* BN22 ...... 196 D4
Eldon Rd *EAST* BN21 ...... 206 C1
Eldred Av *BRI* BN1 ...... 168 D1
Eleanor CI *LEW* BN7 ....... 2 D4
  *SEAF* BN25 ....... 202 D1

Eley Crs *ROTT* BN2 ....... 188 E3
Eley Dr *ROTT* BN2 ....... 188 E2
Elford St *HAS* TN34 ....... 5 H5
Elgar Wy *LGNY* BN23 ...... 197 L3
Elgin Gdns *SEAF* BN25 ...... 203 J2
Elim Court Gdns *CROW* TN6 ..... 39 L2
Elizabethan CI *BAT* TN33 ..... 158 F4
Elizabeth Av *HOVE* BN3 ..... 168 A3
Elizabeth CI *HOVE* BN3 ...... 168 A3
  *SEAF* BN25 ....... 192 A8
Elizabeth Crs *EGRIN* RH19 ..... 13 M3
Elizabeth Rd *SHOR* BN43 ..... 166 C6
Ellenslea Rd *SLVH* TN37 ...... 4 B7
Ellen St *HOVE* BN3 ...... 168 B7
  *PTSD* BN41 ....... 167 J7
Ellenwhorne La *RBTBR* TN32 ... 87 G7
Ellerslie La *BEXW* TN39 ..... 159 M7
Elliots Wy *HTHF* TN21 ...... 80 A6
Ellison CI *CROW* TN6 ...... 39 L2
Ellis Wy *UCK* TN22 ....... 76 A7
Elm CI *HOVE* BN3 ....... 168 C4
  *RING/NEW* BN8 ....... 129 J7
  *SEAF* BN25 ....... 203 J3
Elm Ct *NEWHV* BN9 ....... 8 D3
Elm Dr *EGRIN* RH19 ....... 14 A5
  *HOVE* BN3 ....... 167 L5
Elm Gv *LW/ROSE* BN22 ...... 196 F5
  *ROTT* BN2 ....... 7 J3
Elmore Rd *ROTT* BN2 ...... 7 G5
Elm PI *PTSD* BN41 ...... 167 H6
Elms Av *EAST* BN21 ...... 11 G7
Elmsdown PI *HAIL* BN27 ...... 155 J7
Elms La *RHAS* TN35 ...... 141 M5
Elms Lea Av *BRI* BN1 ...... 168 E3
Elmsmead *RYE* TN31 ....... 91 H2
Elm Rd *EAST* BN21 ...... 11 G7
Elmstead Rd *BEX* TN40 ...... 183 L1
The Elms *RING/NEW* BN8 ..... 150 C1
Elm Wy *HTHF* TN21 ....... 80 B8
  *HTHF* TN21 ....... 106 B1
Elmwood CI *LGNY* BN23 ...... 197 J2
Elmwood Gdns *LGNY* BN23 .... 197 J2
Elphick PI *CROW* TN6 ...... 39 M3
Elphick Rd *NEWHV* BN9 ...... 8 C2
  *RING/NEW* BN8 ....... 127 M7
Elphick's PI *RTWE/PEM* TN2 .... 20 B6
Elphinstone Av *HAS* TN34 ..... 5 H1
Elphinstone Gdns *HAS* TN34 ... 162 F3
Elphinstone Rd *HAS* TN34 ..... 5 H2
Elrington Rd *HOVE* BN3 ...... 168 C5
Elsted Crs *BRI* BN1 ...... 146 C8
Elsted Rd *BEXW* TN39 ...... 182 C4
Elven La *EDN/EASTW* BN20 .... 205 J5
Elvin Crs *ROTT* BN2 ...... 188 C2
Elwood CI *BURH* RH15 ...... 96 F5
Emerald Quay *SHOR* BN43 ..... 166 A8
Emmanuel Rd *HAS* TN34 ...... 5 K3
Endwell Rd *BEX* TN40 ...... 183 J3
Engalee *EGRIN* RH19 ...... 13 J4
English CI *HOVE* BN3 ...... 167 L6
Enys Rd *EAST* BN21 ...... 10 C5
Epsom CI *STLEO* TN38 ...... 162 A6
Erica CI *LGNY* BN23 ...... 197 H4
Eridge CI *BEXW* TN39 ...... 182 F2
Eridge Dr *CROW* TN6 ...... 39 M3
Eridge Gdns *CROW* TN6 ...... 40 A3
Eridge Gn *LEW* BN7 ....... 2 C3
Eridge La *CROW* TN6 ...... 41 H4
Eridge Rd *CROW* TN6 ...... 28 D8
  *CROW* TN6 ....... 40 C2
  *EAST* BN21 ....... 196 C2
  *HOVE* BN3 ....... 168 A4
  *RRTW* TN3 ....... 18 D8
  *SBGH/RUST* TN4 ....... 19 M4
Erin Wy *BURH* RH15 ...... 96 E3
Erroll Rd *HOVE* BN3 ...... 167 J8
Ersham Rd *HAIL* BN27 ...... 178 B1
  *HAIL* BN27 ....... 155 H8
Erskine Park Rd
  *SBGH/RUST* TN4 ....... 19 H2
Esher CI *SEAF* BN25 ...... 202 F2
Eshton Rd *LW/ROSE* BN22 ..... 11 J2
Eskbank Av *BRI* BN1 ....... 146 A7
Eskdale CI *LGNY* BN23 ...... 197 H2
Esplanade *SEAF* BN25 ...... 202 F5
Esplanade Ms *SEAF* BN25 ..... 202 E4
The Esplanade *PEAHV* BN10 .... 189 M7
Essenden Rd *STLEO* TN38 ..... 162 A8
Essex CI *RTWE/PEM* TN2 ...... 19 M6
Essex Rd *STLEO* TN38 ...... 162 A2
Essex St *ROTT* BN2 ...... 7 H7
Estate Rd *NEWHV* BN9 ...... 9 H3
Estcots Dr *EGRIN* RH19 ...... 14 B5
Etchingham Rd *LGNY* BN23 .... 197 L5
Ethelred CI *LGNY* BN23 ...... 197 L6
Ethel St *HOVE* BN3 ...... 168 B7
Etherton Wy *SEAF* BN25 ..... 203 G2
Ethnam La *HAWK* TN18 ...... 64 E3
Eton CI *SEAF* BN25 ...... 203 G2
Evelyn Av *NEWHV* BN9 ...... 8 E3
Evelyn Rd *LEW* BN7 ....... 2 C3
Evelyn Ter *ROTT* BN2 ...... 7 K6
Eversfield PI *SLVH* TN37 ...... 4 C7
Eversfield Rd *EAST* BN21 ..... 10 D4
Eversley CI *SLVH* TN37 ...... 4 B2
Eversley Crs *SLVH* TN37 ...... 4 B2
Eversley Rd *BEX* TN40 ...... 183 J3
  *SLVH* TN37 ....... 4 B2
Ewart St *ROTT* BN2 ...... 7 H4
Ewhurst CI *HAS* TN34 ...... 162 F2
Ewhurst La *RYE* TN31 ...... 87 M2
Exceat CI *ROTT* BN2 ...... 169 L8
Exeat CI *LGNY* BN23 ...... 197 G2
Exeter La *LW/ROSE* BN22 ..... 196 B4
Exeter St *BRI* BN1 ....... 6 B1
Exmouth PI *HAS* TN34 ...... 5 K7

## F

Factory La *HAIL* BN27 ...... 155 G8
Fairbanks *HWH* RH16 ...... 71 L2
Fairbridge Wy *BURH* RH15 ..... 96 F1
Faircrouch La *WADH* TN5 ...... 43 H1
Fairdene *STHW* BN42 ...... 166 F5
Fairfax Av *STLEO* TN38 ...... 138 F7

Fairfield *HAIL* BN27 ...... 133 L8
Fairfield Av *RTWE/PEM* TN2 ..... 20 C1
Fairfield Cha *BEXW* TN39 ..... 182 F2
Fairfield CI *BURH* RH15 ...... 96 F2
  *RHWH* RH17 ....... 34 A6
  *SHOR* BN43 ....... 166 B5
Fairfield Crs *HPPT/KEY* BN6 .... 96 M6
Fairfield Gdns *PTSD* BN41 ..... 167 H5
Fairfield Rd *BURH* RH15 ...... 96 F3
  *EDN/EASTW* BN20 ....... 206 E5
  *EGRIN* RH19 ....... 13 M6
  *SLVH* TN37 ....... 139 J7
Fairfield Wy *HWH* RH16 ...... 48 D6
Fairford CI *HWH* RH16 ...... 71 L1
Fairglen Rd *WADH* TN5 ...... 43 H3
Fairholme Rd *NEWHV* BN9 ..... 191 M5
Fairisle CI *HAIL* BN27 ...... 155 G4
Fair Isle CI *LGNY* BN23 ...... 197 L6
Fairlawn Crs *EGRIN* RH19 ..... 13 H4
Fairlawn Dr *EGRIN* RH19 ...... 13 H4
Fairlawns *SHOR* BN43 ...... 166 A6
Fairlawns Dr *HAIL* BN27 ...... 133 L8
Fairlea CI *BURH* RH15 ...... 96 F2
Fairlie Gdns *BRI* BN1 ...... 168 E3
Fairlight CI *PEAHV* BN10 ..... 189 M7
  *RHAS* TN35 ....... 163 K3
Fairlight CI *BEX* TN40 ...... 184 A1
  *POLE* BN26 ....... 178 A8
Fairlight Fld *RING/NEW* BN8 .... 150 D1
Fairlight Gdns *RHAS* TN35 ..... 164 F2
Fairlight PI *ROTT* BN2 ...... 7 J1
Fairlight Rd *LW/ROSE* BN22 .... 11 K2
  *RHAS* TN35 ....... 163 K3
Fair Meadow *RYE* TN31 ...... 91 J7
Fairmile Rd *RTWE/PEM* TN2 .... 20 E1
Fairmount Rd *BEX* TN40 ...... 183 M2
Fair Oak CI *HTHF* TN21 ...... 80 A7
Fairstone CI *RHAS* TN35 ...... 163 L2
Fairview Av *ROTT* BN2 ...... 189 L5
Fairview La *CROW* TN6 ...... 39 L2
Fairview Ri *BRI* BN1 ...... 168 D1
Fairway *EDN/EASTW* BN20 ..... 206 C4
Fairway Crs *PTSD* BN41 ...... 167 J4
Fairways CI *SEAF* BN25 ...... 203 J4
Fairways Rd *SEAF* BN25 ...... 203 H4
The Fairway *BEXW* TN39 ..... 159 M8
  *NEWHV* BN9 ....... 191 L5
  *STLEO* TN38 ....... 161 M6
Falaise Rd *HAS* TN34 ...... 4 D7
  *NEWHV* BN9 ....... 191 M5
Falconbury Dr *BEXW* TN39 .... 182 D3
Falcon CI *SHOR* BN43 ...... 166 C8
Falconer Dr *BAT* TN33 ...... 137 M2
Falcon Wy *HAIL* BN27 ...... 155 H4
Fallowfield CI *HOVE* BN3 ..... 167 M4
Fallowfield Crs *HOVE* BN3 ..... 167 L4
Falmer Av *ROTT* BN2 ...... 189 H4
Falmer CI *EDN/EASTW* BN20 ... 196 B7
Falmer Gdns *ROTT* BN2 ...... 170 D6
Falmer House Rd *BRI* BN1 ..... 147 J7
Falmer Rd *ROTT* BN2 ...... 170 D4
Falmouth CI *LGNY* BN23 ...... 197 M6
Faraday Av *EGRIN* RH19 ...... 13 M6
Farlaine Rd *EAST* BN21 ...... 196 C8
Farley Bank *HAS* TN34 ...... 5 L2
Farleys Wy *RYE* TN31 ...... 90 B4
Farley Wy *RHAS* TN35 ...... 164 F1
Farlington Av *HWH* RH16 ..... 71 M1
Farlington CI *HWH* RH16 ...... 71 L1
Farm CI *EGRIN* RH19 ...... 14 B6
  *HPPT/KEY* BN6 ....... 122 F2
  *PTSD* BN41 ....... 167 G4
  *SEAF* BN25 ....... 203 H1
Farmcombe CI *RTW* TN1 ...... 20 B4
Farmcombe La *RTW* TN1 ...... 20 B4
Farmcombe Rd *RTW* TN1 ...... 20 B4
Farm Gdns *RYE* TN31 ...... 90 C4
Farm HI *ROTT* BN2 ...... 170 C6
Farmlands Av *POLE* BN26 ..... 195 M2
Farmlands CI *POLE* BN26 ..... 196 A2
  *SLVH* TN37 ....... 162 C1
Farmlands Wy *POLE* BN26 .... 195 M1
Farmland Wy *HAIL* BN27 ...... 155 J5
Farm La *HPPT/KEY* BN6 ...... 123 L3
  *RYE* TN31 ....... 118 D3
Farm Ms *HOVE* BN3 ...... 168 D8
Farm Rd *HOVE* BN3 ...... 168 D8
Farm Wy *BURH* RH15 ...... 97 J3
  *STHW* BN42 ....... 167 G7
Farmway CI *HOVE* BN3 ...... 167 M4
Farncombe CI *RHWH* RH17 ..... 98 D1
Farncombe Rd *LEW* BN7 ...... 2 F5
Farne CI *HAIL* BN27 ...... 155 H4
Farnham Av *HPPT/KEY* BN6 .... 123 C1
Farnham Crs *HPPT/KEY* BN6 ... 123 C1
Farnham La *RRTW* TN3 ...... 19 G2
Farnham PI *RRTW* TN3 ...... 19 G3
Farningham Rd *CROW* TN6 .... 40 C7
Farnlea Rd *BURH* RH15 ...... 97 K1
Farriers Wy *UCK* TN22 ...... 76 C3
Farthing HI *WADH* TN5 ...... 45 L5
Farthing La *HAIL* BN27 ...... 134 E1
The Farthings *CROW* TN6 ..... 40 A3
Fastnet CI *LGNY* BN23 ...... 197 L6
Faulkners Wy *BURH* RH15 ..... 97 G1
Faversham Rd *LGNY* BN23 .... 197 K4
Faygate CI *BEXW* TN39 ...... 160 B6
Faygate Rd *LW/ROSE* BN22 ... 196 E4
Fayre Meadow *RBTBR* TN32 .... 85 J2
Fearon Rd *HAS* TN34 ...... 5 G2
Felbridge CI *BEXW* TN39 ...... 182 E2
Felbridge Ct *EGRIN* RH19 ..... 13 G3
Felbridge Rd *EGRIN* RH19 ..... 12 D3
Felcot Rd *CRAWE* RH10 ...... 12 C3
Fellows Rd *HAS* TN34 ...... 163 G3
Felride *HWH* RH16 ...... 71 L3
Fennell's *EAST* BN21 ...... 10 A1
Ferguson Rd *LYDD* TN29 ...... 120 C4
Fermandy La *CRAWE* RH10 .... 12 A5
Fermor Rd *CROW* TN6 ...... 39 M7
Fermor Wy *CROW* TN6 ...... 39 M6
Fern CI *LGNY* BN23 ...... 197 J3
Ferndale *RTWE/PEM* TN2 ...... 20 C2
Ferndale CI *RTWE/PEM* TN2 .... 20 C2
  *RTWE/PEM* TN2 ....... 20 C2
Ferndale Rd *BURH* RH15 ..... 97 H5

HOVE BN3 ...... 168 D7
Fernhill CI *CRAWE* RH10 ...... 12 B5
Fernhurst CI *BRI* BN1 ...... 146 C8
Fernhurst Crs *BRI* BN1 ...... 168 H1
Fernlea CI *RHAS* TN35 ...... 139 L2
Fernside Av *STLEO* TN38 ..... 161 M5
Fern Rd *STLEO* TN38 ...... 161 M5
Ferrers Rd *LEW* BN7 ...... 2 C4
Ferring CI *RYE* TN31 ...... 91 G8
Ferry HI *WSEA* TN36 ...... 116 E6
Ferry Rd *RYE* TN31 ...... 117 H3
Festival Gdns *BEXW* TN39 ..... 160 C7
Feversham CI *SHOR* BN43 ..... 166 B8
Field CI *BURH* RH15 ...... 96 F2
  *SEAF* BN25 ....... 203 H4
Field End *UCK* TN22 ...... 76 A2
Fielden La *CROW* TN6 ...... 39 L6
Fielden Rd *CROW* TN6 ...... 39 L6
Fields End CI *HWH* RH16 ...... 71 M2
Fieldway *HPPT/KEY* BN6 ...... 123 K3
  *HWH* RH16 ....... 48 F6
  *RYE* TN31 ....... 114 B1
Field Wy *STLEO* TN38 ...... 161 L6
Fiennes Rd *HAIL* BN27 ...... 133 L8
Figg La *CROW* TN6 ...... 39 M6
Filching CI *POLE* BN26 ...... 195 L3
Filching Rd *EDN/EASTW* BN20 ... 206 B1
Filder CI *LW/ROSE* BN22 ...... 197 G8
Filsham Dr *BEX* TN40 ...... 161 G8
Filsham Rd *STLEO* TN38 ...... 161 M7
Filsham Va *STLEO* TN38 ...... 161 M7
Finches Gdns *HWH* RH16 ...... 49 G5
Finches La *HWH* RH16 ...... 49 G6
Finches Park Rd *HWH* RH16 .... 49 G6
The Finches *BEX* TN40 ...... 183 M2
  *SHOR* BN43 ....... 166 A7
  *STLEO* TN38 ....... 162 A1
Findon Av *ROTT* BN2 ...... 189 L5
Findon CI *BEXW* TN39 ...... 182 E3
  *HOVE* BN3 ....... 167 M3
  *SEAF* BN25 ....... 203 J3
Findon Rd *ROTT* BN2 ...... 187 M1
Finistere Av *LGNY* BN23 ...... 197 M6
Finmere CI *LW/ROSE* BN22 .... 197 J8
Finmere Rd *LW/ROSE* BN22 ... 197 J8
Finsbury Rd *ROTT* BN2 ...... 7 H4
Fir CI *ROTT* BN2 ...... 170 F7
Fircroft CI *BRI* BN1 ...... 168 C3
Fir Grove Rd *HTHF* TN21 ...... 79 H7
Firlands *HWH* RH16 ...... 71 M2
Firle Bostal *RING/NEW* BN8 ..... 174 B6
Firle CI *RHAS* TN35 ...... 163 L2
  *SEAF* BN25 ....... 202 E1
Firle Crs *LEW* BN7 ...... 148 F4
Firle Dr *SEAF* BN25 ...... 202 E1
Firle Gra *SEAF* BN25 ...... 202 E1
Firle Rd *BEXW* TN39 ...... 182 D2
  *LW/ROSE* BN22 ....... 11 G3
  *PEAHV* BN10 ....... 190 B5
  *ROTT* BN2 ....... 7 M3
  *SEAF* BN25 ....... 202 E1
First Av *BEX* TN40 ...... 183 M1
  *HOVE* BN3 ....... 186 C1
  *NEWHV* BN9 ....... 8 E5
  *RYE* TN31 ....... 118 F4
First St *RRTW* TN3 ...... 18 F3
Firtoft CI *BURH* RH15 ...... 97 H3
Fir Toll CI *MAYF* TN20 ...... 56 F4
Fir Toll Rd *MAYF* TN20 ...... 56 C4
Fir Tree CI *BEXW* TN39 ...... 182 C1
  *HAIL* BN27 ....... 155 J4
Firtree Rd *HAS* TN34 ...... 5 K1
Fir Tree Rd *SBGH/RUST* TN4 .... 19 M4
Fir Tree Wy *HPPT/KEY* BN6 .... 123 G2
Firwood CI *HTHF* TN21 ...... 80 A6
  *LW/ROSE* BN22 ....... 196 E5
Firwood Ri *HTHF* TN21 ...... 80 A6
Fisher CI *LGNY* BN23 ...... 197 M7
Fishergate CI *PTSD* BN41 ..... 167 G7
Fishersgate Ter *PTSD* BN41 .... 167 G7
Fisher St *LEW* BN7 ...... 2 F6
Fishmarket Rd *RYE* TN31 ..... 117 J1
Fishponds La *RHAS* TN35 ..... 139 L3
Fitch Dr *ROTT* BN2 ...... 169 L5
Fitzgerald Av *SEAF* BN25 ..... 202 F4
Fitzgerald CI
  *EDN/EASTW* BN20 ....... 206 F5
Fitzgerald Pk *SEAF* BN25 ..... 202 F4
Fitzgerald Rd *LEW* BN7 ...... 3 H2
Fitzherbert Dr *ROTT* BN2 ..... 169 K6
Fitzjohns Rd *LEW* BN7 ...... 2 B4
Fitzmaurice Av *LW/ROSE* BN22 ... 11 H1
Fitzroy Rd *LEW* BN7 ...... 2 C2
Five Chimneys La *UCK* TN22 .... 78 A1
Flamsteed Rd *HAIL* BN27 ..... 157 G5
Fleming CI *LGNY* BN23 ...... 197 M4
Fletcher Av *STLEO* TN38 ..... 138 F7
Fletching CI *ROTT* BN2 ...... 169 M8
Fletching Rd *LW/ROSE* BN22 ... 197 G4
Fletching St *MAYF* TN20 ...... 57 H3
Flimwell CI *LGNY* BN23 ...... 197 J2
  *ROTT* BN2 ....... 187 L1
  *STLEO* TN38 ....... 161 K4
  *WADH* TN5 ....... 46 D2
Flint CI *PTSD* BN41 ...... 167 H4
  *SEAF* BN25 ....... 192 E8
The Flints *LEW* BN7 ...... 171 L1
Flitterbrook La *HTHF* TN21 .... 107 K4
Florance La *RRTW* TN3 ...... 18 D3
Florence Av *HOVE* BN3 ...... 167 K6
Florence PI *BRI* BN1 ...... 169 G6
Florence Rd *BRI* BN1 ...... 169 G6
Folders CI *BURH* RH15 ...... 97 K5
Folders La *BURH* RH15 ...... 97 K5
Foley CI *LGNY* BN23 ...... 197 L7
Folkestone Rd *RYE* TN31 ..... 92 C3
Folkington Gdns *SLVH* TN37 ... 162 C1
Folkington Rd *POLE* BN26 ..... 195 L3
Folly Fld *NEWHV* BN9 ...... 9 G3
Fonthill Rd *HOVE* BN3 ...... 168 B6
Fontridge La *BUR/ETCH* TN19 ... 83 K3
Fontwell Av *BEXW* TN39 ...... 182 C1
Foords La *PEV* BN24 ...... 179 H7
Foot's La *BUR/ETCH* TN19 ..... 82 B3
Fordbrook HI *CROW* TN6 ...... 54 E4

Fordcombe Rd *RRTW* TN3 ...... 18 D3
Ford Rd *STLEO* TN38 ...... 161 M4
Foredown CI
  *EDN/EASTW* BN20 ....... 206 C4
  *HWH* RH16 ....... 167 H4
Foredown Dr *PTSD* BN41 ...... 167 H5
Foredown Rd *PTSD* BN41 ..... 167 H3
Forest CI *CRAWE* RH10 ...... 12 B6
Forest Dene *CROW* TN6 ...... 40 D5
Forest La *HTHF* TN21 ...... 107 K1
Forest Pk *CROW* TN6 ...... 39 K4
Forest Ri *CROW* TN6 ...... 40 D5
Forest Rd *BRI* BN1 ...... 169 L1
  *FROW* RH18 ....... 25 H5
  *RTWE/PEM* TN2 ....... 20 C5
Forest Vw *HAIL* BN27 ...... 155 C6
  *UCK* TN22 ....... 52 C3
Forest View Rd *EGRIN* RH19 ... 13 L8
Forest Wy *EGRIN* RH19 ...... 24 B1
  *HAS* TN34 ....... 4 F4
  *HRTF* TN7 ....... 17 J8
  *RTWE/PEM* TN2 ....... 20 C5
Forewood La *BAT* TN33 ...... 138 A6
Forewood Ri *BAT* TN33 ...... 137 L8
Forge CI *PTSD* BN41 ...... 167 H4
  *UCK* TN22 ....... 76 C8
Forge Fld *WADH* TN5 ...... 44 F8
Forge La *RBTBR* TN32 ...... 86 E5
Forge Meadow *TENT* TN30 ..... 69 G2
Forge Meads *TENT* TN30 ...... 67 L3
Forge Ri *UCK* TN22 ...... 76 C8
Forge Rd *RRTW* TN3 ...... 28 B3
Forge Wy *BURH* RH15 ...... 96 F2
  *SLVH* TN37 ....... 162 C1
Forstall *RRTW* TN3 ...... 19 G2
Fort Hvn *SHOR* BN43 ...... 166 C8
Fort La *LW/ROSE* BN22 ...... 197 K8
Fort Ri *NEWHV* BN9 ...... 9 H7
Fort Rd *LW/ROSE* BN22 ...... 197 K8
  *NEWHV* BN9 ....... 9 H7
Forward CI *NEWHV* BN9 ...... 191 L4
Foster CI *SEAF* BN25 ...... 202 E2
Foundry La *LEW* BN7 ...... 3 J6
Foundry St *BRI* BN1 ...... 6 E5
Fountains CI *BRI* BN1 ...... 169 H4
  *LW/ROSE* BN22 ....... 196 E3
Founthill Av *ROTT* BN2 ...... 189 H5
Founthill Rd *ROTT* BN2 ...... 189 H5
Fourteen Acre La *RHAS* TN35 ... 140 D1
Fourth Av *BEX* TN40 ...... 186 B1
Fowey CI *SHOR* BN43 ...... 166 B8
Fowlers CI *BEXW* TN39 ...... 182 E1
Fowly La *UCK* TN22 ...... 54 C7
Fox CI *BURH* RH15 ...... 96 F5
Foxcote *SLVH* TN37 ...... 162 D2
Foxdown Rd *ROTT* BN2 ...... 170 F7
Foxglove CI *BURH* RH15 ...... 96 F5
  *RING/NEW* BN8 ....... 128 A7
Foxglove Rd *LGNY* BN23 ...... 197 H3
Foxhill *BEXW* TN39 ...... 182 E1
Fox HI *HWH* RH16 ...... 71 L5
Foxhill *PEAHV* BN10 ...... 190 C5
Fox Hill CI *HWH* RH16 ...... 71 L5
Fox Hill Village *HWH* RH16 .... 71 M6
Foxhole La *WADH* TN5 ...... 44 B3
Foxhunters Rd *PTSD* BN41 ..... 166 F5
Foxwarren *HWH* RH16 ...... 71 J1
Fox Wy *PTSD* BN41 ...... 167 G3
Framelle Mt *UCK* TN22 ...... 77 H8
Framfield CI *BRI* BN1 ...... 146 E8
Framfield Rd *UCK* TN22 ...... 76 D8
  *UCK* TN22 ....... 77 H3
Framfield Wy *EAST* BN21 ..... 196 D8
Frampton CI *HWH* RH16 ...... 49 H6
Francis St *BRI* BN1 ...... 6 F3
Frankfield Ri *RTWE/PEM* TN2 .... 19 M5
Franklands CI *BURH* RH15 ..... 97 H5
Franklands Gdns *BURH* RH15 ... 97 G6
Franklin Rd *PTSD* BN41 ...... 167 J7
  *ROTT* BN2 ....... 7 J2
  *SHOR* BN43 ....... 166 C6
Franklin St *ROTT* BN2 ...... 7 J2
Franklynn Rd *HWH* RH16 ...... 71 M3
Frankton Av *HWH* RH16 ...... 72 A3
Frant Av *BEXW* TN39 ...... 182 C1
Frant CI *BEXW* TN39 ...... 182 C1
Frant Rd *HOVE* BN3 ...... 168 A4
  *RTWE/PEM* TN2 ....... 20 A7
Frary Wk *HTHF* TN21 ...... 106 A3
Fraser Av *LGNY* BN23 ...... 197 L7
Freckley Hollow *BAT* TN33 ..... 136 B4
Frederick PI *BRI* BN1 ...... 6 E4
Frederick Rd *RHAS* TN35 ...... 163 J3
Frederick St *BRI* BN1 ...... 6 D5
Free Heath Rd *RRTW* TN3 ..... 32 C3
Freehold Ter *ROTT* BN2 ...... 169 H6
Freek's La *BURH* RH15 ...... 71 G8
Freeland CI *SEAF* BN25 ...... 192 B8
Freeman Av *LW/ROSE* BN22 ... 196 E5
Freemans Rd *PTSD* BN41 ..... 167 G6
Freezeland La *BEXW* TN39 .... 159 M5
Fremlin CI *SBGH/RUST* TN4 ..... 19 H2
Frenches Farm Dr *HTHF* TN21 ... 106 A1
French Gdns *HWH* RH16 ...... 48 F8
Frenchgate CI
  *LW/ROSE* BN22 ....... 196 F4
Frenchgate Rd
  *LW/ROSE* BN22 ....... 196 F4
Freshfield Bank *FROW* RH18 .... 24 E4
Freshfield CI *HAIL* BN27 ...... 155 H8
Freshfield La *RHWH* RH17 ..... 50 C6
Freshfield PI *ROTT* BN2 ...... 7 J6
Freshfield Rd *ROTT* BN2 ...... 7 J7
Freshfield St *ROTT* BN2 ...... 7 K4
Freshfield Wy *ROTT* BN2 ...... 7 J7
Freshford CI *LGNY* BN23 ...... 197 K4
Freshwater Av *HAS* TN34 ..... 4 F1
Freshway *LW/ROSE* BN22 ..... 196 C3
Frewen CI *RYE* TN31 ...... 65 H7
Frewyn CI *STLEO* TN38 ...... 161 M2
Friar CI *BRI* BN1 ...... 169 G2
Friar Crs *BRI* BN1 ...... 168 F3
Friar Rd *BRI* BN1 ...... 169 G2
Friars' Av *PEAHV* BN10 ...... 190 E8
  *PEAHV* BN10 ....... 200 E1
Friars Bank *RHAS* TN35 ...... 141 H7

Friars CI HPPT/KEY BN6 ...... 122 E2
Friars HI RHAS TN35 ...... 140 F7
Friars Oak Rd HPPT/KEY BN6 .. 122 E1
Friars Wk WSEA TN36 ...... 116 F7
Friars' Wk LEW BN7 ........ 3 H6
Friar's Wy HAS TN34 ...... 162 F1
Friar Wk BRI BN1 ...... 168 F2
Friday St LGNY BN23 ...... 197 M3
Friezland Rd SBGH/RUST TN4 .. 19 K5
Frimley CI ROTT BN2 ...... 170 E2
Friston Av LW/ROSE BN22 .. 196 C5
Friston CI EDN/EASTW BN20 .. 205 C5
  ROTT BN2 ...... 169 M2
  SEAF BN25 ...... 202 C2
Friston Downs
  EDN/EASTW BN20 ...... 205 H4
Frith Pk EGRIN RH19 ...... 13 L5
Frith Rd HOVE BN3 ...... 168 A6
Frobisher La MAYF TN20 .... 79 H1
Frog Hole La MAYF TN20 .... 79 F1
Frog La RTW TN1 ...... 20 A4
Fryatts Wy BEXW TN39 ...... 159 M8
Fryman's La RYE TN31 ...... 113 K4
Fulford St STLEO TN38 ...... 162 A6
Fuller CI WADH TN5 ...... 43 L1
Fuller Rd LEW BN7 ...... 2 B1
Fullers La RYE TN31 ...... 65 H8
Fullwood Av NEWHV BN9 .... 8 D5
Fulmar CI HOVE BN3 ...... 168 D5
Fulmar Dr EGRIN RH19 ...... 14 A3
The Furlongs POLE BN26 .. 193 M3
Furnace Av RRTW TN3 ...... 32 F3
Furnace La HTHF TN21 ...... 105 K6
  HTHF TN21 ...... 106 E4
  RRTW TN3 ...... 32 D2
  RYE TN31 ...... 114 B1
Furnace Rd CRAWE RH10 .... 12 C3
Furnace Wy UCK TN22 ...... 76 E2
Furness Rd EDN/EASTW BN20.. 10 C8
Furzefield Rd EGRIN RH19 .... 13 K2
Furze HI HOVE BN3 ...... 168 D8
Furze La EGRIN RH19 ...... 13 H3
Fyning PI BEXW TN39 ...... 182 C1
Fyrsway RHAS TN35 ...... 164 E3
Fysie La BUR/ETCH TN19 .... 61 K3

## G

Gableson Av BRI BN1 ...... 168 B2
Gage CI CRAWE RH10 ...... 12 C5
Gage Rdg FROW RH18 ...... 24 E5
The Gages HAIL BN27 ...... 155 K7
Gainsborough Crs
  LGNY BN23 ...... 197 K5
Gainsborough La POLE BN26 .. 177 L8
Gainsborough Rd BEX TN40 .. 160 E8
Galley Hill Vw BEX TN40 ...... 183 L2
Galliers CI BRI BN1 ...... 146 B8
Gallipot HI HRTF TN7 ...... 26 C3
The Gallops LEW BN7 ...... 2 B6
Galloways Rd LYDD TN29 .. 121 J3
Gallows CI PEV BN24 ...... 179 L8
Gallows La PEV BN24 ...... 179 L8
Galveston CI LGNY BN23 .. 197 M7
Gammons Wy BAT TN33 .... 112 E5
Gander CI BURH RH15 ...... 97 G1
Gander Gn HWH RH16 ...... 48 F7
Gander HI HWH RH16 ...... 48 F7
Garden CI BEX TN40 ...... 183 K2
  EGRIN RH19 ...... 13 M7
  PTSD BN41 ...... 167 J6
  SHOR BN43 ...... 166 B5
Gardener Dr PTSD BN41 ...... 167 G7
Garden House La EGRIN RH19.. 13 L7
Garden Rd RTW TN1 ...... 20 B2
The Gardens PTSD BN41 ...... 167 J6
  STHW BN42 ...... 166 F7
Garden St LEW BN7 ...... 2 F7
  RTW TN1 ...... 20 B2
Garden Wood Rd EGRIN RH19.. 13 J5
Gardner CI LGNY BN23 ...... 197 L7
Gardner La CRAWE RH10 .... 12 A6
Gardner Rd PTSD BN41 ...... 167 G7
Gardner's HI RYE TN31 ...... 68 B8
Gardner St BRI BN1 ...... 6 E6
  HAIL BN27 ...... 133 M8
Garfield Rd HAIL BN27 ...... 155 H7
Garland Rd EGRIN RH19 .... 13 K5
Garnet Dr EDN/EASTW BN20 .. 196 C2
Garston Pk BUR/ETCH TN19 .. 60 B8
Garth CI BEXW TN39 ...... 183 G1
Gatehouse CI BEXW TN39 .. 182 C4
Gatehouse La BURH RH15 .... 96 C2
  HPPT/KEY BN6 ...... 96 B1
  UCK TN22 ...... 77 J8
  UCK TN22 ...... 103 K1
Gatelands Dr BEXW TN39 .. 160 A8
Gatesmead HWH RH16 ...... 48 E6
The Gattons BURH RH15 .... 96 E3
Gaudick CI EDN/EASTW BN20 .. 206 E5
Gaudick Rd EDN/EASTW BN20 .. 206 E5
Geering Rd PEV BN24 ...... 197 H1
Geers Wd HTHF TN21 ...... 79 M8
Gemma CI HAIL BN27 ...... 155 L7
Geneva Rd NEWHV BN9 .... 9 G6
Gensing Rd STLEO TN38 .... 4 A8
George HI RBTBR TN32 .... 85 H3
George St HAIL BN27 ...... 155 J7
  HAS TN34 ...... 5 J7
  HOVE BN3 ...... 168 B8
  PTSD BN41 ...... 167 J7
  PTSD BN41 ...... 167 G7
  ROTT BN2 ...... 7 G7
  WADH TN5 ...... 43 M1
George Wood CI LYDD TN29 .. 95 J8
Georgian CI BEX TN40 ...... 160 E8
  BEX TN40 ...... 183 L1
Georgian Wk STLEO TN38 .. 161 M6
Gerald CI BURH RH15 ...... 97 K5
Gerald Rd SEAF BN25 ...... 202 F5
Gerard St BRI BN1 ...... 6 E1
German St WSEA TN36 ...... 116 E7
Ghyll Rd CROW TN6 ...... 39 K2
  HTHF TN21 ...... 79 M8
Ghyllside ROTT BN2 ...... 169 L5

Ghyllside Av SLVH TN37 ...... 162 C2
Ghyllside Dr HAS TN34 ...... 162 D2
Ghyll Side Rd RYE TN31 ...... 65 H7
Ghyllside Wy HAS TN34 ...... 162 D2
Gibb St LEW BN7 ...... 183 M1
Gibbets RRTW TN3 ...... 18 F3
Gibbon Rd NEWHV BN9 ...... 8 D6
Gibraltar Ri HTHF TN21 ...... 80 A7
Giffards CI EGRIN RH19 ...... 13 M5
Gilbert Rd LW/ROSE BN22 .. 11 H3
  STLEO TN38 ...... 162 B6
Gilberts Dr EDN/EASTW BN20 .. 205 H7
Gilbert Wy HAIL BN27 ...... 178 B1
Gilda Crs POLE BN26 ...... 178 A8
  SEAF BN25 ...... 202 F3
Gilham La FROW RH18 ...... 24 C4
Gillett Rd LYDD TN29 ...... 95 K7
Gillham Wood Rd BEXW TN39 .. 182 D3
The Gilligans BURH RH15 .... 96 F1
Gillridge Gn CROW TN6 ...... 39 M2
Gillsman's Dr STLEO TN38 .. 161 M5
Gillsman's HI STLEO TN38 .. 162 A5
Gillsman's Pk STLEO TN38 .. 161 M5
Gingerbread La HAWK TN18 .. 46 F3
Gipps Cross La RRTW TN3 .. 18 F3
Githa Rd RHAS TN35 ...... 163 J4
The Glades BEX TN40 ...... 160 E6
  EGRIN RH19 ...... 14 B5
The Glade HAIL BN27 ...... 154 F8
  MAYF TN20 ...... 57 G4
  UCK TN22 ...... 76 D7
Gladstone CI LW/ROSE BN22 .. 196 F5
Gladstone PI ROTT BN2 ...... 169 J6
Gladstone Rd BURH RH15 .... 97 J1
  CROW TN6 ...... 39 M6
  HAS TN34 ...... 5 K4
  PTSD BN41 ...... 167 H7
  SBGH/RUST TN4 ...... 19 H2
Gladys Av PEAHV BN10 ...... 190 D8
Gladys Rd HOVE BN3 ...... 167 K6
Glassenbury Dr BEX TN40 .. 183 M1
Glastonbury Rd HOVE BN3 .. 167 K8
Gleave CI BURH RH15 ...... 14 A4
Glebe CI BEXW TN59 ...... 182 D2
  EDN/EASTW BN20 ...... 206 D3
  LEW BN7 ...... 2 B3
  STHW BN42 ...... 166 F7
Glebe Dr SEAF BN25 ...... 202 E3
Glebelands CRAWE RH10 .... 12 A6
Glebelands CI SHOR BN43 .. 166 B6
The Glebelands CROW TN6 .. 39 M4
The Glebe EGRIN RH19 ...... 13 G2
  HAS TN34 ...... 5 L3
  HWH RH16 ...... 49 G6
Glebe Vls HOVE BN3 ...... 167 K7
Glen CI POLE BN26 ...... 195 M2
Glendale Av EAST BN21 ...... 196 C8
Glendale Rd BURH RH15 .... 97 H4
  HOVE BN3 ...... 168 D7
Glendor Rd HOVE BN3 ...... 167 L8
Glendyne CI EGRIN RH19 .... 14 A6
Glendyne Wy EGRIN RH19 .. 14 A6
Gleneagles CI BEX TN40 .... 183 L1
  SEAF BN25 ...... 192 A8
Gleneagles Dr HAIL BN27 .. 154 F6
  STLEO TN38 ...... 161 M7
Glenfalls Av BRI BN1 ...... 146 A7
Glengorse BAT TN33 ...... 137 M3
Glenleigh Av BEXW TN39 .. 159 M8
Glenleigh Park Rd BEXW TN39 .. 160 A8
Glenleigh Wk RBTBR TN32 .. 85 G2
Glenmore Pk RTWE/PEM TN2 .. 19 M6
Glenmore Rd CROW TN6 .... 39 J3
Glenmore Rd East CROW TN6.. 39 K3
Glen Ri BRI BN1 ...... 168 B1
Glen Rise CI BRI BN1 ...... 168 B1
The Glen UCK TN22 ...... 76 D5
Glenthorn Rd BEXW TN39 .. 183 G2
Glenview CI RHAS TN35 ...... 163 K5
Glen Vue EGRIN RH19 ...... 13 L5
Glessing Rd PEV BN24 ...... 197 H1
Gleton Av HOVE BN3 ...... 167 K4
Gloucester Av BEXW TN39 .. 184 A1
Gloucester CI LW/ROSE BN22 .. 196 C4
Gloucester Pas BRI BN1 ...... 6 F5
Gloucester PI ROTT BN2 ...... 6 F5
Gloucester Rd BRI BN1 ...... 6 E5
  BURH RH15 ...... 96 F3
  WADH TN5 ...... 31 M3
Gloucester St BRI BN1 ...... 6 F5
Glovers La BEX TN40 ...... 160 C7
  BEXW TN39 ...... 160 C7
Glynde Av LW/ROSE BN22 .. 196 C5
  ROTT BN2 ...... 189 J4
Glyndebourne Av ROTT BN2 .. 189 G5
Glyndebourne Gdns
  SLVH TN37 ...... 162 C1
Glynde CI NEWHV BN9 ...... 191 K4
Glynde Rd ROTT BN2 ...... 7 L4
Glyne Ascent BEX TN40 .... 183 M1
Glyne Barn CI BEX TN40 .... 184 A1
Glyne Dr BEX TN40 ...... 184 A1
Glynleigh Dr POLE BN26 .... 178 C8
Glynleigh Rd PEV BN24 .... 178 E5
Glynn Ri PEAHV BN10 ...... 190 B5
Glynn Rd PEAHV BN10 ...... 190 B5
Goatham La RYE TN31 ...... 113 L1
Godden CI RYE TN31 ...... 65 H6
Godden Rd RING/NEW BN8 .. 74 C7
Godfrey CI LEW BN7 ...... 2 F7
Godwin Rd HOVE BN3 ...... 167 K6
  RHAS TN35 ...... 163 J1
The Goffs EAST BN21 ...... 10 A5
Goldbridge Rd RING/NEW BN8 .. 74 D7
Goldcrest Dr UCK TN22 ...... 102 D1
Golden HI BURH RH15 ...... 97 K5
Golden Miller La POLE BN26 .. 177 L8
Goldhurst Gn WSEA TN36 .. 141 L1
Golding Rd LGNY BN23 ...... 197 M4
Gold La PEAHV BN10 ...... 190 C4
Goldsmid Rd HOVE BN3 .... 6 B3
Goldsmith CI LGNY BN23 .. 197 L3
Goldsmiths Av CROW TN6 .. 39 K3
Goldstone CI HOVE BN3 ...... 168 B3
Goldstone Crs HOVE BN3 .. 168 A4
Goldstone La HOVE BN3 .... 168 B6
Goldstone Rd HOVE BN3 .... 168 A7

Goldstone St HOVE BN3 ...... 168 B7
Goldstone Vls HOVE BN3 .... 168 B7
Goldstone Wy HOVE BN3 .... 168 A4
Golf Dr BRI BN1 ...... 169 H3
Goods Station Rd RTW TN1 .. 20 A4
Goodtrees La EDEN TN8 .... 16 B4
Goodwin CI HAIL BN27 ...... 154 F4
Goodwins CI EGRIN RH19 .. 13 K3
The Goodwins
  RTWE/PEM TN2 ...... 19 M5
Goodwood CI
  EDN/EASTW BN20 ...... 196 B4
Goodwood Wy ROTT BN2 .. 169 L3
Gooseberry La RYE TN31 .... 88 A3
Gordon Av SHOR BN43 ...... 166 A7
Gordon CI HWH RH16 ...... 48 C8
Gordon Rd BRI BN1 ...... 168 F4
  BURH RH15 ...... 97 J2
  CROW TN6 ...... 39 M4
  HAIL BN27 ...... 155 H7
  HAS TN34 ...... 5 J5
  HWH RH16 ...... 48 C8
  PTSD BN41 ...... 167 G7
  UCK TN22 ...... 77 J3
Gore Park Av EAST BN21 .. 206 D2
Gore Park Rd EAST BN21 .. 206 D2
Gorham Av ROTT BN2 ...... 189 G4
Gorham CI ROTT BN2 ...... 189 G4
Gorham Wy PEAHV BN10 .. 189 L6
Gorringe CI EDN/EASTW BN20.. 196 A3
  SHOR BN43 ...... 166 D7
Gorringe Dr EDN/EASTW BN20 .. 196 A3
Gorringe Rd EAST BN21 .... 10 D2
Gorringe Valley Rd
  EDN/EASTW BN20 ...... 196 A3
Gorse CI EDN/EASTW BN20 .. 206 B1
  PTSD BN41 ...... 166 F2
Gorse Dr SEAF BN25 ...... 192 F8
Gorse Rd RTWE/PEM TN2 .. 20 E1
Gorselands BAT TN33 ...... 112 E5
The Gorses BEXW TN39 .... 182 C4
Gorsethorn Wy RHAS TN35 .. 164 C2
The Gorseway BEXW TN39 .. 182 C1
Gosford Wy POLE BN26 .... 177 M8
Gote La RING/NEW BN8 ...... 150 D2
Goudhurst CI LGNY BN23 .. 197 K5
Gower Rd HWH RH16 ...... 71 L2
Gowers CI RHWH RH17 ...... 34 B6
Gradwell End RING/NEW BN8 .. 99 J7
Graffham CI ROTT BN2 ...... 189 J5
Grafton St ROTT BN2 ...... 7 H8
Graham Av BRI BN1 ...... 168 D2
  PTSD BN41 ...... 166 F2
Graham Crs PTSD BN41 .... 166 F2
Grampian CI LGNY BN23 .. 197 J3
  RTWE/PEM TN2 ...... 20 D1
Grand Av BEX TN40 ...... 160 F8
  HOVE BN3 ...... 168 C8
  HPPT/KEY BN6 ...... 122 F2
  SEAF BN25 ...... 202 C1
Grand Crs ROTT BN2 ...... 189 G5
Grand Junction Rd BRI BN1 .. 6 E8
Grand Pde EAST BN21 ...... 10 F8
  POLE BN26 ...... 177 M8
  ROTT BN2 ...... 6 F5
  STLEO TN38 ...... 4 A9
Grand Parade Ms ROTT BN2.. 6 F6
Grange Av SLVH TN37 ...... 162 C2
Grange CI BRI BN1 ...... 168 E5
  BURH RH15 ...... 97 J1
  CROW TN6 ...... 39 K5
  HTHF TN21 ...... 105 M8
Grange Court Dr BEXW TN39 .. 160 B8
Grange La CRAWE RH10 .... 12 B7
Grange Gdns SBGH/RUST TN4 .. 19 K2
Grange Rd CRAWE RH10 .... 12 A7
  EAST BN21 ...... 10 D8
  HAS TN34 ...... 162 E1
  HOVE BN3 ...... 167 L7
  LEW BN7 ...... 2 E1
  RING/NEW BN8 ...... 126 D2
  SBGH/RUST TN4 ...... 19 K2
  UCK TN22 ...... 76 C7
The Grange RING/NEW BN8 .. 126 D2
Grangeways BRI BN1 ...... 168 E1
Granston Wy CRAWE RH10 .. 12 C6
Grantham Bank
  RING/NEW BN8 ...... 126 E2
Grantham CI RING/NEW BN8 .. 99 L7
Grantham Rd BRI BN1 ...... 169 G5
Grant St ROTT BN2 ...... 7 H3
Granville Rd EDN/EASTW BN20.. 10 C9
  HOVE BN3 ...... 6 A3
  RTW TN1 ...... 20 B1
Grasmere CI LGNY BN23 .. 197 H2
Grassington Rd
  EDN/EASTW BN20 ...... 10 C9
Grassmere Av PEAHV BN10 .. 189 M6
Gravelye CI HWH RH16 ...... 72 B1
Gravelye La HWH RH16 ...... 72 B1
Gravett Ct BURH RH15 ...... 96 F4
Graycoats Dr CROW TN6 .... 39 M4
Graystone La RHAS TN35 .. 163 J3
Grazebrook CI BEXW TN39 .. 182 C3
Great Cliffe Rd LGNY BN23.. 197 L5
Great College St ROTT BN2 .. 7 K8
Great Courtlands RRTW TN3 .. 19 C3
Greater Paddock
  RING/NEW BN8 ...... 127 L8
Great Footway RRTW TN3 .. 18 F2
Great Oak BUR/ETCH TN19 .. 62 A3
Great Rough RING/NEW BN8 .. 74 A8
Great Wd BAT TN33 ...... 138 A2
Grecian Rd RTW TN1 ...... 20 B4
Greenacres PEAHV BN10 .. 190 D4
  RHAS TN35 ...... 139 L3
Greenacres Dr HAIL BN27 .. 155 J6
  RING/NEW BN8 ...... 150 C2
Greenacres Wy HAIL BN27 .. 155 J6
Greenbank Av ROTT BN2 .. 189 J5
Green CI RING/NEW BN8 ...... 127 L8
  STHW BN42 ...... 166 E7

Greenfield Dr UCK TN22 ...... 102 D2
Greenfield Rd BUR/ETCH TN19.. 60 C7
  EAST BN21 ...... 206 D3
Greenfields HAIL BN27 ...... 155 G5
Greenfields CI SLVH TN37 .. 139 H8
Green Ga PEAHV BN10 ...... 190 C5
Green Gv HAIL BN27 ...... 155 H6
Green Hedges Av EGRIN RH19 .. 13 K4
Green Hedges CI EGRIN RH19 .. 13 K4
Greenhill Pk HWH RH16 .... 72 A4
Greenhill Wy HWH RH16 .... 72 A4
  PEAHV BN10 ...... 190 C4
Greenlands CI BURH RH15 .. 97 H6
Greenlands Dr BURH RH15 .. 97 H6
Green La BEXW TN39 ...... 182 D1
  CROW TN6 ...... 40 B3
  HTHF TN21 ...... 80 B8
  LEW BN7 ...... 2 F7
  POLE BN26 ...... 195 J3
  RING/NEW BN8 ...... 99 L7
  RING/NEW BN8 ...... 99 L7
  RING/NEW BN8 ...... 128 A5
  ROTT BN2 ...... 170 E8
  SEAF BN25 ...... 202 E4
Greenleaf Gdns POLE BN26 .. 178 A7
Greenleas HOVE BN3 ...... 167 K4
Green Mdw HWH RH16 ...... 49 H6
Green Park Cnr RHWH RH17 .. 98 A2
Green Rdg BRI BN1 ...... 168 B1
Green Rd RHWH RH17 ...... 98 A1
Green Sq WADH TN5 ...... 43 M1
Greenstede Av EGRIN RH19 .. 13 M3
Green St EDN/EASTW BN20 .. 206 C2
The Green BAT TN33 ...... 112 E6
  BAT TN33 ...... 136 A8
  HOVE BN3 ...... 168 C4
  RING/NEW BN8 ...... 74 D7
  ROTT BN2 ...... 188 F4
  RRTW TN3 ...... 18 E5
  STLEO TN38 ...... 162 B5
  UCK TN22 ...... 78 A8
Green Wk HAIL BN27 ...... 155 J5
  SEAF BN25 ...... 203 H4
Green Wy EDN/EASTW BN20.. 196 A3
  LYDD TN29 ...... 95 H8
  LYDD TN29 ...... 121 J1
Greenways BEXW TN39 .... 159 M7
  HWH RH16 ...... 48 F8
  ROTT BN2 ...... 188 D2
  STHW BN42 ...... 166 E7
Greenways Crs SHOR BN43 .. 166 A5
Greenwell CI SEAF BN25 .. 203 H2
Greenwich Rd HAIL BN27 .. 155 H7
Greenwich Wy PEAHV BN10 .. 190 B7
Gregory La PEV BN24 ...... 197 M1
Gregory Wk BAT TN33 ...... 112 E6
Grenada CI BEXW TN39 .... 182 D2
Grenville Dr PEV BN24 ...... 198 C2
Grenville St BRI BN1 ...... 6 C6
Gresham CI EAST BN21 .... 196 C8
Gresham Wy STLEO TN38 .. 162 A6
Greville Rd RHAS TN35 ...... 163 J3
Grey Alders HWH RH16 .... 49 H8
Greyfriars HOVE BN3 ...... 168 D6
Greyfriars Ct LEW BN7 ...... 3 H6
Greyfriars PI WSEA TN36 .. 117 H8
Greys Rd EDN/EASTW BN20 .. 206 D3
Grinstead La EGRIN RH19 .. 23 J6
Grisbrook Farm CI LYDD TN29 .. 95 K8
Gromenfield RRTW TN3 .... 18 C7
Groombridge HI RRTW TN3 .. 18 C6
Groombridge Rd RRTW TN3.. 18 C7
Grosvenor Br SBGH/RUST TN4 .. 20 B1
Grosvenor CI POLE BN26 .. 195 M1
Grosvenor Crs STLEO TN38 .. 161 M8
Grosvenor Gdns STLEO TN38.. 161 M8
Grosvenor Pk RTW TN1 .... 20 A1
Grosvenor Rd EGRIN RH19 .. 13 K5
  SEAF BN25 ...... 202 F2
Grosvenor St ROTT BN2 .... 7 G7
Grove Av RTW TN1 ...... 20 A4
Grove HI HAIL BN27 ...... 132 C4
  HAIL BN27 ...... 155 J1
  ROTT BN2 ...... 7 G5
Grove Hill Gdns RTW TN1 .. 20 B4
Grove Hill Rd RTW TN1 ...... 20 A3
Grovelands CI BURH RH15 .. 96 F5
Grovelands Rd HAIL BN27 .. 155 G5
Grove La RYE TN31 ...... 91 J2
Grovely La HTHF TN21 ...... 108 B5
Grove Rd BURH RH15 ...... 97 H4
  EAST BN21 ...... 10 D7
  RHAS TN35 ...... 163 K2
  SEAF BN25 ...... 202 F3
Grove St ROTT BN2 ...... 7 H4
The Grove BAT TN33 ...... 137 M3
  BEXW TN39 ...... 182 C4
  CROW TN6 ...... 39 L5
  EDN/EASTW BN20 ...... 195 M3
  EDN/EASTW BN20 ...... 196 C3
  HAIL BN27 ...... 155 G5
  HWH RH16 ...... 72 B3
  MAYF TN20 ...... 57 G4
  NEWHV BN9 ...... 191 L4
  RYE TN31 ...... 91 J3
Growers End RING/NEW BN8 .. 74 D7
Guardswell PI SEAF BN25 .. 202 E3
Guestling Rd LW/ROSE BN22 .. 11 L2
Guildford Rd BRI BN1 ...... 6 D4
  RTW TN1 ...... 20 B3
Guildford La RYE TN31 ...... 92 F3
Guildford St BRI BN1 ...... 6 D4
Guldeford Rd RYE TN31 .... 91 L8
Gundreda Rd LEW BN7 ...... 2 C4
Gun Rd UCK TN22 ...... 78 A7
Gunter's La BEXW TN39 .... 160 A7
Gurth Rd RHAS TN35 ...... 163 J5
Gwyneth Gv BEX TN40 ...... 160 F7
Gwynne Gdns EGRIN RH19 .. 13 J4

## H

Hackenden CI EGRIN RH19 .. 13 L3
Hackenden La EGRIN RH19 .. 13 L3
Hackhurst La HAIL BN27 .. 154 B1

Hackwood RBTBR TN32 ...... 84 E3
Haddington CI HOVE BN3 .. 168 A5
Haddington St HOVE BN3 .. 168 B7
Hadlow Av LGNY BN23 ...... 197 G2
Hadlow CI ROTT BN2 ...... 7 L5
Hadlow Down Rd CROW TN6 .. 54 F4
Hadrian Av STHW BN42 .... 166 F4
Hadrian Gdns STLEO TN38 .. 139 G8
Haig Av BRI BN1 ...... 146 D8
Hailsham Av ROTT BN2 ...... 189 K3
Hailsham Rd HAIL BN27 .... 156 E1
  HTHF TN21 ...... 80 A8
  POLE BN26 ...... 177 M7
  POLE BN26 ...... 178 F6
Hairpin Cft PEAHV BN10 .. 190 C5
Half Mile Dro RING/NEW BN8 .. 128 E5
Halland CI LW/ROSE BN22 .. 196 D5
Halland Rd ROTT BN2 ...... 169 M2
Hallett Rd ROTT BN2 ...... 7 L3
Halley Rd HAIL BN27 ...... 157 H5
  HTHF TN21 ...... 80 E6
Hall La UCK TN22 ...... 78 C1
Hall's Hole Rd RTWE/PEM TN2.. 20 E3
Hallsland CRAWE RH10 ...... 12 C6
Hallyburton Rd HOVE BN3 .. 167 K6
Halsford La EGRIN RH19 .... 13 H4
Halsford Park Rd EGRIN RH19.. 13 J4
Halton Crs HAS TN34 ...... 5 M2
Halton PI HAS TN34 ...... 5 M2
Halton Rd LW/ROSE BN22 .. 11 J4
Halton Ter HAS TN34 ...... 5 M2
Hamble Rd POLE BN26 ...... 196 F1
Hambleton CI LGNY BN23 .. 197 J3
Hambrook BURH RH15 ...... 97 J5
Hamelsham Ct HAIL BN27 .. 155 G6
Hamilton CI PTSD BN41 .... 167 G3
Hamilton Gdns RHAS TN35 .. 163 K3
Hamilton Rd BRI BN1 ...... 6 C1
  LYDD TN29 ...... 95 J3
Hamilton Ter BEXW TN39 .. 183 G2
Hamlands La LW/ROSE BN22.. 196 B3
Ham La BUR/ETCH TN19 .... 60 A7
  LEW BN7 ...... 3 G1
  RHWH RH17 ...... 72 C3
  RING/NEW BN8 ...... 127 H8
Hammer La HTHF TN21 ...... 106 F6
Hammerwood Rd EGRIN RH19.. 14 C8
Hammingden La EGRIN RH19.. 34 E3
  RHWH RH17 ...... 34 E7
Hammonds Gdns BURH RH15.. 96 F5
Hammonds Rdg BURH RH15.. 96 E5
Hammy CI SHOR BN43 ...... 166 B6
Hammy La SHOR BN43 ...... 166 B6
Hammy Wy SHOR BN43 .... 166 B6
Hampden Av LW/ROSE BN22.. 196 F5
Hampden CI BAT TN33 ...... 137 H2
Hampden Park Dr
  LW/ROSE BN22 ...... 196 E6
Hampden Rd ROTT BN2 .... 7 J3
Hampton PI BRI BN1 ...... 6 A5
Hampton St BRI BN1 ...... 6 B6
Hampton Wy EGRIN RH19 .. 13 M7
Hamsey CI EDN/EASTW BN20 .. 196 B8
  ROTT BN2 ...... 187 M1
Hamsey La RING/NEW BN8 .. 126 A7
  SEAF BN25 ...... 203 J1
Hamsey Rd EGRIN RH19 .... 13 J5
  ROTT BN2 ...... 189 K6
Hamsland RHWH RH17 ...... 50 C2
Hanbury La HWH RH16 ...... 72 A1
Hanging Birch La HTHF TN21 .. 105 K3
Hangleton CI HOVE BN3 .... 167 K5
Hangleton Gdns HOVE BN3 .. 167 K5
Hangleton La HOVE BN3 .... 167 K4
  PTSD BN41 ...... 167 H4
Hangleton Manor CI
  HOVE BN3 ...... 167 J3
Hangleton Rd HOVE BN3 .. 167 L4
Hangleton Valley Dr
  HOVE BN3 ...... 167 J3
Hangleton Wy HOVE BN3 .. 167 K4
Hankham Hall Rd PEV BN24 .. 179 J6
Hankham Rd PEV BN24 .... 179 H5
Hankham St PEV BN24 ...... 179 H5
Hanlye La RHWH RH17 ...... 48 K6
Hannington PI HPPT/KEY BN6.. 96 K4
Hanover CI BEX TN40 ...... 183 J1
  SEAF BN25 ...... 192 B8
Hanover Crs ROTT BN2 ...... 7 G3
Hanover Ms ROTT BN2 ...... 7 H3
Hanover Rd LW/ROSE BN22.. 11 J4
  RTW TN1 ...... 20 A2
Hanover St ROTT BN2 ...... 7 H3
Hanover Ter ROTT BN2 ...... 7 H3
Hanson Rd NEWHV BN9 .... 8 E6
Harbour Farm WSEA TN36 .. 117 J2
Harbour Rd RYE TN31 ...... 91 H8
Harbour View CI SEAF BN25 .. 192 B8
Harbour View Rd NEWHV BN9 .. 8 C7
Harbour Wy SHOR BN43 .. 166 B8
  STLEO TN38 ...... 138 E7
Harcourt CI UCK TN22 ...... 76 C8
Harcourt Rd UCK TN22 ...... 76 C8
Harden Rd LYDD TN29 ...... 95 K7
Harding Av LW/ROSE BN22 .. 197 H6
Hardwicke Rd HAS TN34 .... 5 M2
Hardwick Rd EAST BN21 .. 10 E8
  HOVE BN3 ...... 167 L3
Hardwick Wy HOVE BN3 .. 167 L2
Hardy Dr LGNY BN23 ...... 197 M8
Harebeating CI HAIL BN27 .. 155 J4
Harebeating Crs HAIL BN27 .. 155 J3
Harebeating Dr HAIL BN27 .. 155 H3
Harebeating Gdns HAIL BN27 .. 155 J4
Harebell CI LGNY BN23 ...... 197 J3
Harebell Dr PTSD BN41 .... 167 G3
Harecombe Rd CROW TN6 .. 39 L6
Harecombe Ri CROW TN6.. 39 L6
Haremere HI BUR/ETCH TN19.. 61 K5
Harescroft RTWE/PEM TN2 .. 19 M7
Hare Wy SLVH TN37 ...... 162 C1
Harewood CI BEXW TN39 .. 182 F3
Harfield CI NEWHV BN9 .... 191 M4
Hargate CI RTWE/PEM TN2 .. 19 M7
Harison Rd SEAF BN25 ...... 203 G2
Harkness Dr HAS TN34 .... 163 H1

Harlands Cl *RHWH* RH17 .......... 48 C8
Harlands Rd *HWH* RH16 .......... 48 C8
Harlequin Gdns *SLVH* TN37 ........ 139 G8
Harlequin La *CROW* TN6 .......... 39 L6
Harlequin Pl *CROW* TN6 .......... 39 L6
Harley La *HTHF* TN21 .......... 80 A8
Harley Shute Rd *STLEO* TN38 ...... 161 L7
Harley Wy *STLEO* TN38 .......... 161 L8
Harmans Md *EGRIN* RH19 .......... 14 A5
Harmers Hay Rd *HAIL* BN27 ........ 155 H5
Harmers Hl *RING/NEW* BN8 ......... 74 C7
Harmony St *SBGH/RUST* TN4 ....... 19 K2
Harold Cl *PEV* BN24 .......... 180 F7
Harold Dr *LGNY* BN23 .......... 197 L6
Harold Hl *HAS* TN34 .......... 5 G7
Harold Rd *NEWHV* BN9 .......... 8 E3
*RHAS* TN35 .......... 163 K4
Harpers Rd *NEWHV* BN9 .......... 8 E3
Harrier La *BAT* TN33 .......... 137 M2
Harrington Pl *BRI* BN1 .......... 169 H4
Harrington Rd *BRI* BN1 .......... 168 E4
Harrington Vls *BRI* BN1 .......... 168 F4
Harris Ct *EAST* BN21 .......... 10 F6
Harrisons La *RING/NEW* BN8 ...... 127 L8
*RING/NEW* BN8 .......... 150 L1
Harrow Cl *SEAF* BN25 .......... 203 G1
Harrow La *SLVH* TN37 .......... 139 H8
*SLVH* TN37 .......... 162 B1
Hart Cl *UCK* TN22 .......... 76 A7
Hartfield Av *BRI* BN1 .......... 169 G2
Hartfield La *EAST* BN21 .......... 10 D4
Hartfield Meadow
*STLEO* TN38 .......... 161 K3
Hartfield Rd *BEXW* TN39 .......... 182 D4
*EAST* BN21 .......... 10 D4
*EDEN* TN8 .......... 16 D3
*FROW* RH18 .......... 25 G4
*ROTT* BN2 .......... 189 K5
*SEAF* BN25 .......... 203 G3
Hartington Pl *EAST* BN21 ......... 10 F7
*ROTT* BN2 .......... 7 K1
Hartington Rd *ROTT* BN2 .......... 7 K1
Hartington Ter *ROTT* BN2 .......... 7 K1
Hartington Vls *HOVE* BN3 ......... 168 B6
Harvard Cl *LEW* BN7 .......... 2 F1
Harvard Rd *RING/NEW* BN8 ........ 150 D1
Harvest Cl *HWH* RH16 .......... 49 H7
*PEAHV* BN10 .......... 190 B4
Harvesters *HWH* RH16 .......... 71 K4
Harvest Hl *EGRIN* RH19 .......... 13 L6
*RHWH* RH17 .......... 70 C4
Harvest Wy *SLVH* TN37 .......... 162 C1
Harvey Cl *STLEO* TN38 .......... 161 M2
Harvey's La *RING/NEW* BN8 ....... 128 B3
*UCK* TN22 .......... 102 F6
Harveys Wy *LEW* BN7 .......... 3 J5
Harwarden Cl *CRAWE* RH10 ....... 12 C6
Harwood Cl *LGNY* BN23 .......... 197 L7
Harwoods Cl *EGRIN* RH19 ......... 13 M7
Harwood's La *EGRIN* RH19 ........ 13 M6
*EGRIN* RH19 .......... 13 M8
Haslam Crs *BEX* TN40 .......... 160 F8
Hassocks Cl *LW/ROSE* BN22 ...... 196 F2
Hassocks La *HPPT/KEY* BN6 ...... 122 B1
Hastings Av *SEAF* BN25 .......... 203 J1
Hastings Cl *POLE* BN26 .......... 178 B7
Hastings Rd *BAT* TN33 .......... 138 A3
*BEX* TN40 .......... 183 K1
*HAWK* TN18 .......... 47 M7
*ROTT* BN2 .......... 7 J1
*STPH/PW* TN12 .......... 21 M1
Hatch End *FROW* RH18 .......... 24 F4
Hatchgate Cl *RHWH* RH17 ......... 48 A8
Hatchgate La *RHWH* RH17 ......... 48 A8
Hatherley Rd *SLVH* TN37 .......... 4 A7
Havelock Rd *BEXW* TN39 .......... 160 C8
*BRI* BN1 .......... 168 F5
*HAS* TN34 .......... 5 G6
*LW/ROSE* BN22 .......... 11 G3
Haven Brow *SEAF* BN25 .......... 203 G3
Haven Cl *LW/ROSE* BN22 ......... 196 B3
*PEV* BN24 .......... 180 C4
Haven Gdns *CRAWE* RH10 ........ 12 A5
Haven Rd *STLEO* TN38 .......... 161 K8
Hawkenbury Cl
*RTWE/PEM* TN2 .......... 20 D4
Hawkenbury Md
*RTWE/PEM* TN2 .......... 20 D5
Hawkenbury Rd
*RTWE/PEM* TN2 .......... 20 E5
Hawkenbury Wy *LEW* BN7 ........ 2 A6
Hawkhurst Cl *LGNY* BN23 ......... 197 J4
Hawkhurst Rd *BRI* BN1 .......... 146 D8
*BUR/ETCH* TN19 .......... 46 E4
Hawkhurst Wy *BEXW* TN39 ....... 182 A5
Hawkins Cl *SHOR* BN43 .......... 166 D5
Hawkins Rd *SHOR* BN43 .......... 166 D5
Hawkins Wy *HAIL* BN27 .......... 155 H6
Hawksbridge Cl
*LW/ROSE* BN22 .......... 196 B3
Hawks Farm Cl *HAIL* BN27 ....... 155 H4
Hawks Rd *HAIL* BN27 .......... 155 H4
Hawkstown Cl *HAIL* BN27 ......... 155 H3
Hawkstown Crs *HAIL* BN27 ....... 155 H3
Hawkstown Gdns *HAIL* BN27 ..... 155 H3
Hawkstown Vw *HAIL* BN27 ....... 155 J3
Hawkswood Dr *HAIL* BN27 ....... 155 J3
Hawkswood Rd *HAIL* BN27 ....... 155 H3
Hawmead *CRAWE* RH10 .......... 12 C6
Hawth Cl *SEAF* BN25 .......... 202 C2
Hawth Crs *SEAF* BN25 .......... 202 C2
Hawth Gv *SEAF* BN25 .......... 202 C1
Hawth Hl *SEAF* BN25 .......... 202 B1
Hawthorn Av *BEXW* TN39 ........ 182 D3
Hawthorn Cl *BURH* RH15 ......... 97 K1
*ROTT* BN2 .......... 189 J4
Hawthorne Cl *HTHF* TN21 ........ 80 B8
The Hawthornes *RYE* TN31 ....... 114 A2
Hawthorn Ri *NEWHV* BN9 ........ 8 C4
Hawthorn Rd *RHAS* TN35 ......... 163 K4
The Hawthorns *BURH* RH15 ...... 97 K1
*HAIL* BN27 .......... 155 G7
Hawth Ri *SEAF* BN25 .......... 202 C1

Hawth Wy *SEAF* BN25 .......... 202 D2
Hawthylands Crs *HAIL* BN27 ..... 155 H4
Hawthylands Dr *HAIL* BN27 ...... 155 H4
Hawthylands Rd *HAIL* BN27 ...... 155 H4
Haybourne Rd *ROTT* BN2 ......... 169 L7
Hayes Cl *ROTT* BN2 .......... 169 J1
Hayes Cl *PTSD* BN41 .......... 167 J6
*RING/NEW* BN8 .......... 150 D1
Hayes Plat *WSEA* TN36 .......... 115 H1
Hayland Rd *HWH* RH16 .......... 72 B1
Haystoun Cl *HAWK* TN18 ........ 47 M5
Haystoun Pk *LW/ROSE* BN22 ..... 196 C4
Hayward La *LEW* BN7 .......... 2 B1
Haywards Rd *BRI* BN1 .......... 146 A8
*HWH* RH16 .......... 71 L3
Hazelbank *RRTW* TN3 .......... 18 F3
Hazel Cl *CRAWE* RH10 .......... 12 C6
*NEWHV* BN9 .......... 8 C4
*PTSD* BN41 .......... 167 H3
Hazeldene *SEAF* BN25 .......... 203 G3
Hazeldene Meads *BRI* BN1 ....... 168 D4
Hazeledene La *RING/NEW* BN8 ... 73 H7
Hazel Gv *BURH* RH15 .......... 97 H5
*EDN/EASTW* BN20 .......... 196 A3
Hazelgrove Rd *HWH* RH16 ........ 71 L2
Hazel Wy *CRAWE* RH10 .......... 12 B6
Hazelwood Av *LW/ROSE* BN22 .... 196 D3
Hazelwood Cl *BEXW* TN39 ....... 182 B3
Hazelwood Gdns *HAS* TN34 ...... 162 D1
Headland Av *SEAF* BN25 ......... 203 G3
Headlands Cl *PEAHV* BN10 ....... 190 E7
Heansill La *HAWK* TN18 .......... 47 L6
Heathcote Dr *EGRIN* RH19 ....... 13 H4
Heathdown Cl *PEAHV* BN10 ..... 190 D4
Heather Bank *HWH* RH16 ......... 71 J1
Heather Cl *LGNY* BN23 .......... 197 H5
Heatherdune Rd *BEXW* TN39 .... 183 G1
Heather Wy *RHAS* TN35 .......... 164 F2
Heathfield Av *ROTT* BN2 ......... 189 K4
Heathfield Cl *HAS* TN34 ......... 162 F1
Heathfield Crs *PTSD* BN41 ...... 166 F5
Heathfield Dr *PTSD* BN41 ........ 166 F5
Heathfield Gdns *RBTBR* TN32 .... 85 H3
Heathfield Rd *SEAF* BN25 ....... 202 F3
Heath Hill Av *ROTT* BN2 ......... 169 M5
Heathlands *RHAS* TN35 .......... 139 L3
Heath Rd *HWH* RH16 .......... 71 L1
Heathy Brow *PEAHV* BN10 ....... 190 B5
Heavegate Rd *CROW* TN6 ......... 39 L4
Heighton Cl *BEXW* TN39 ......... 182 D3
Heighton Crs *NEWHV* BN9 ....... 191 K4
Heighton Rd *NEWHV* BN9 ........ 191 K4
The Heights *BRI* BN1 .......... 168 B1
*RHAS* TN35 .......... 163 L2
Helena Cl *PTSD* BN41 .......... 167 J5
Helena Rd *ROTT* BN2 .......... 170 D5
Hellingly Cl *ROTT* BN2 .......... 187 L1
Hempstead Gdns *UCK* TN22 ..... 76 D7
Hempstead La *HAIL* BN27 ........ 154 E6
*UCK* TN22 .......... 76 E6
Hempstead Ri *UCK* TN22 ........ 76 C7
Hempstead Rd *ROTT* BN2 ........ 189 K4
*UCK* TN22 .......... 76 C7
Henderson Cl *HAS* TN34 ......... 162 F3
Hendon St *ROTT* BN2 .......... 7 L6
Henfield Cl *ROTT* BN2 .......... 187 M2
Henfield Rd *LW/ROSE* BN22 ..... 196 C4
Henfield Wy *HOVE* BN3 .......... 167 M3
Henge Wy *PTSD* BN41 .......... 167 H4
Hengist Cl *LGNY* BN23 .......... 197 M6
Henley Dr *RTWE/PEM* TN2 ....... 20 A6
*RYE* TN31 .......... 91 G8
Henley Rd *ROTT* BN2 .......... 187 M2
Henley's Hl *BAT* TN33 .......... 135 G5
Henry Burt Wy *BURH* RH15 ...... 96 E5
Herbert Rd *BRI* BN1 .......... 168 F4
Herbrand Wk *PEV* BN24 ......... 181 M5
Hereford St *ROTT* BN2 .......... 7 H7
Hereward Rd *LGNY* BN23 ........ 197 M5
Hereward Wy *LEW* BN7 .......... 3 H2
Hermitage La *EGRIN* RH19 ....... 13 K3
Hermitage Rd *EGRIN* RH19 ...... 13 K3
Herne Down *CROW* TN6 .......... 39 M7
Herne Rd *CROW* TN6 .......... 39 M6
Heron Cl *LGNY* BN23 .......... 197 J4
*STLEO* TN38 .......... 161 L6
*UCK* TN22 .......... 102 D1
Heron Pl *EGRIN* RH19 .......... 13 M6
Heron Rdg *POLE* BN26 .......... 178 B8
Herons Cl *CRAWE* RH10 .......... 12 A1
Heronsdale Rd *ROTT* BN2 ........ 170 F6
Herons Lea *CRAWE* RH10 ......... 12 A1
Herontye Dr *EGRIN* RH19 ........ 13 M6
Herring's Rd *HTHF* TN21 ......... 108 E5
Hertford Cl *STLEO* TN38 ......... 162 A2
Hertford Rd *BRI* BN1 .......... 169 H4
Heston Av *BRI* BN1 .......... 145 M7
Hever Cl *LGNY* BN23 .......... 197 K4
Hever Crs *BEXW* TN39 .......... 182 F1
Heyworth Cl *ROTT* BN2 .......... 170 F6
Hickling Cl *LGNY* BN23 .......... 197 H2
Hickman's Cl *HWH* RH16 ......... 49 H6
Hickman's La *HWH* RH16 ........ 49 G6
Hickman Wy *SLVH* TN37 ......... 162 D2
Hide Hollow *LGNY* BN23 ......... 197 K3
Higham Gdns *RHAS* TN35 ........ 141 G6
Higham La *RYE* TN31 .......... 65 G8
Highbank *BRI* BN1 .......... 168 C1
High Bank *RHAS* TN35 .......... 163 J4
High Bank Cl *RHAS* TN35 ........ 163 J4
High Beech *STLEO* TN38 ......... 138 F8
High Beech La *HWH* RH16 ....... 48 F6
High Branches *BEXW* TN39 ...... 182 E2
Highbridge La *LEW* BN7 .......... 125 H2
Highbrook Cl *ROTT* BN2 ......... 169 K4
High Broom La *CROW* TN6 ....... 39 L7
High Broom Rd *CROW* TN6 ...... 39 L7
High Cl *EDN/EASTW* BN20 ....... 205 J4
*PTSD* BN41 .......... 167 G5
Highcliff *HTHF* TN21 .......... 80 A7
Highcroft Rd *EGRIN* RH19 ....... 23 G8
Highcroft Vls *BRI* BN1 .......... 168 E3
High Cross Flds *CROW* TN6 ...... 39 M3
Highdown *STHW* BN42 .......... 166 F5
Highdown Cl *STHW* BN42 ........ 166 F5
Highdown Rd *HOVE* BN3 ......... 6 A2
*LEW* BN7 .......... 2 A3

Highfield Crs *BRI* BN1 .......... 169 G1
Highfield Dr *HPPT/KEY* BN6 ...... 122 B1
*STLEO* TN38 .......... 161 K3
Highfield Rd *EGRIN* RH19 ........ 13 K3
*HTHF* TN21 .......... 80 E5
*HTHF* TN21 .......... 105 M7
Highfields *BRI* BN1 .......... 169 L1
*BUR/ETCH* TN19 .......... 83 C1
*FROW* RH18 .......... 24 F4
High Fords *WSEA* TN36 .......... 116 E3
High Fords Cl *WSEA* TN36 ....... 115 L8
Highgate Hl *HAWK* TN18 ......... 47 M5
Highgate Rd *FROW* RH18 ........ 24 F5
Highgrove *BAT* TN33 .......... 137 H2
*RTWE/PEM* TN2 .......... 20 A6
High Hurst Cl *RING/NEW* BN8 ... 74 D7
Highland Ct *HWH* RH16 .......... 71 L2
Highland Rd *HWH* RH16 ......... 71 M3
Highlands Av *UCK* TN22 ......... 102 D2
Highlands Cl *BEXW* TN39 ....... 159 M7
*CROW* TN6 .......... 39 L3
*HPPT/KEY* BN6 .......... 123 G3
Highlands Dr *BURH* RH15 ....... 97 G2
Highlands Gdns *STLEO* TN38 .... 162 B7
Highlands Rd *PTSD* BN41 ........ 167 H5
*SEAF* BN25 .......... 202 F3
The Highlands *BEXW* TN39 ...... 159 M6
Highlea Cl *SLVH* TN37 .......... 162 C1
High Meadow *RYE* TN31 ......... 65 G7
High Pk *RYE* TN31 .......... 65 G7
High Park Av *HOVE* BN3 ......... 167 L3
High Point *HWH* RH16 .......... 72 A3
High Rocks La *RRTW* TN3 ....... 19 J5
Highsted Pk *PEAHV* BN10 ....... 190 D4
High St *BAT* TN33 .......... 137 K1
*BAT* TN33 .......... 136 A8
*BUR/ETCH* TN19 .......... 60 A8
*BUR/ETCH* TN19 .......... 61 H6
*CROW* TN6 .......... 39 M3
*CROW* TN6 .......... 41 H6
*EAST* BN21 .......... 10 A5
*EDEN* TN8 .......... 16 A1
*EGRIN* RH19 .......... 13 M6
*HAIL* BN27 .......... 155 J7
*HAS* TN34 .......... 5 L5
*HAWK* TN18 .......... 47 K4
*HPPT/KEY* BN6 .......... 122 A1
*HPPT/KEY* BN6 .......... 123 K3
*HRTF* TN7 .......... 26 D2
*HTHF* TN21 .......... 80 A7
*HWH* RH16 .......... 49 H6
*LEW* BN7 .......... 2 D7
*LYDD* TN29 .......... 95 H8
*LYDD* TN29 .......... 121 H1
*MAYF* TN20 .......... 57 G4
*NEWHV* BN9 .......... 8 F3
*PEV* BN24 .......... 180 B8
*POLE* BN26 .......... 178 A7
*POLE* BN26 .......... 193 M4
*PTSD* BN41 .......... 167 G5
*RBTBR* TN32 .......... 85 H2
*RHWH* RH17 .......... 34 B6
*RING/NEW* BN8 .......... 74 D7
*RING/NEW* BN8 .......... 126 D2
*RING/NEW* BN8 .......... 130 A1
*ROTT* BN2 .......... 7 G7
*ROTT* BN2 .......... 188 F5
*RRTW* TN3 .......... 30 C2
*RRTW* TN3 .......... 33 G2
*RTW* TN1 .......... 20 A4
*RYE* TN31 .......... 117 J1
*SEAF* BN25 .......... 202 E4
*UCK* TN22 .......... 52 C2
*UCK* TN22 .......... 76 C8
*UCK* TN22 .......... 76 B2
*UCK* TN22 .......... 77 J3
*WADH* TN5 .......... 43 L1
*WADH* TN5 .......... 44 D5
*WADH* TN5 .......... 46 D3
*WSEA* TN36 .......... 116 E7
High Trees *HWH* RH16 .......... 71 M1
Highview Av North *BRI* BN1 ..... 145 L8
Highview Av South *BRI* BN1 ..... 168 E1
Highview Cl *HAIL* BN27 ......... 157 H1
*HAS* TN34 .......... 162 D1
Highview La *UCK* TN22 ......... 102 D2
Highview Rd *BRI* BN1 .......... 145 L8
*PEAHV* BN10 .......... 189 L7
Highview Wy *BRI* BN1 .......... 145 L8
Highwater Vw *BAT* TN33 ........ 138 E7
Highway Cl *ROTT* BN2 .......... 169 K4
Highways *PTSD* BN41 .......... 167 H4
The Highway *PEAHV* BN10 ...... 190 F8
*ROTT* BN2 .......... 169 K3
High Weald Landscape Trail
*CROW* TN6 .......... 27 H3
*EGRIN* RH19 .......... 13 K7
*EGRIN* RH19 .......... 15 J3
*EGRIN* RH19 .......... 34 D1
*HRTF* TN7 .......... 27 H2
*RHWH* RH17 .......... 48 B5
High Weald Wk *RRTW* TN3 ...... 18 C7
*RTWE/PEM* TN2 .......... 20 E6
*SBGH/RUST* TN4 .......... 19 M4
High Wickham *RHAS* TN35 ...... 5 M4
Highwoods Av *BEXW* TN39 ...... 159 J8
High Woods La *RTWE/PEM* TN2 ... 20 F4
Hiham Gn *WSEA* TN36 .......... 116 E7
Hilary Cl *POLE* BN26 .......... 195 M1
Hilbert Cl *RTW* TN1 .......... 20 C1
Hilders Farm Cl *CROW* TN6 ...... 40 A8
Hilgrove Rd *ROTT* BN2 .......... 189 K3
Hillary Cl *EGRIN* RH19 .......... 14 A4
Hillbank Cl *PTSD* BN41 .......... 166 F3
Hillborough Cl *BEXW* TN39 ...... 182 D2
Hill Brow *HOVE* BN3 .......... 168 B2
Hillbrow Rd *BRI* BN1 .......... 168 B2
Hillbury Gdns *WADH* TN5 ....... 45 K5
Hill Cl *CROW* TN6 .......... 39 L5
Hillcrest *BRI* BN1 .......... 168 C1
*RYE* TN31 .......... 91 H7
Hillcrest Av *BEXW* TN39 ........ 160 A8
Hillcrest Cl *RHWH* RH17 ........ 72 F3
Hillcrest La *RHWH* RH17 ........ 72 F3
Hill Crest Rd *NEWHV* BN9 ....... 8 E6
Hillcroft *PTSD* BN41 .......... 166 F4
Hill Dr *HOVE* BN3 .......... 168 B3

Hill Farm Wy *STHW* BN42 ....... 166 D4
Hill House Cl *CRAWE* RH10 ...... 22 A2
Hill Md *UCK* TN22 .......... 52 C2
Hill Ri *NEWHV* BN9 .......... 191 M5
*SEAF* BN25 .......... 202 C1
Hill Rd *EDN/EASTW* BN20 ....... 206 A1
*LEW* BN7 .......... 2 B3
*NEWHV* BN9 .......... 191 M5
*RHAS* TN35 .......... 164 C2
*ROTT* BN2 .......... 189 H5
Hill Side *EDN/EASTW* BN20 ..... 205 H5
Hillside *CRAWE* RH10 .......... 12 B6
*EDN/EASTW* BN20 .......... 205 H5
*PTSD* BN41 .......... 167 J5
*ROTT* BN2 .......... 169 K4
*STHW* BN42 .......... 166 F5
Hillside Av *SEAF* BN25 ......... 203 H1
Hillside Cl *EGRIN* RH19 ......... 13 L3
Hillside Dr *HTHF* TN21 .......... 105 M7
Hillside Rd *BEX* TN40 .......... 183 H1
*HAS* TN34 .......... 139 L8
*HAS* TN34 .......... 162 E3
Hillside Wk *RHWH* RH17 ........ 48 C8
Hillside Wy *BRI* BN1 .......... 168 C2
Hill St *HAS* TN34 .......... 5 K6
*RTW* TN1 .......... 20 B1
Hill Top *BRI* BN1 .......... 168 B1
Hill Top Cl *PTSD* BN41 .......... 166 F4
Hilltop Dr *RYE* TN31 .......... 91 H7
Hilltop Rd *EGRIN* RH19 .......... 22 E8
Hillview Rd *ROTT* BN2 .......... 170 A6
Hill View Rd *SBGH/RUST* TN4 .... 19 J2
Hillyfield *LEW* BN7 .......... 2 C8
Hillyglen Cl *HAS* TN34 .......... 4 E5
Hindover Crs *SEAF* BN25 ........ 203 G2
Hindover Rd *SEAF* BN25 ........ 203 G2
Hinton Cl *BRI* BN1 .......... 169 J4
Hither Chantlers *RRTW* TN3 ..... 19 G3
Hoad La *ROTT* BN2 .......... 49 J2
Hoadleys La *CROW* TN6 ......... 39 K1
Hoad Rd *LW/ROSE* BN22 ........ 11 H4
Hoad's Wood Rd *HAS* TN34 ..... 162 F3
Hoath Hl *RBTBR* TN32 .......... 111 J1
Hobbs La *RYE* TN31 .......... 66 D8
Hobdens La *RHWH* RH17 ........ 34 A7
Hoblands *HWH* RH16 .......... 72 B2
Hobney Ri *PEV* BN24 .......... 197 M1
Hockington La
*EDN/EASTW* BN20 .......... 196 B5
Hodcombe Cl *LGNY* BN23 ....... 197 H2
Hoddern Av *PEAHV* BN10 ....... 190 B7
Hodshrove Rd *ROTT* BN2 ........ 169 L3
The Hoe *SLVH* TN37 .......... 139 H8
Hogarth Rd *HOVE* BN3 .......... 167 M7
*LGNY* BN23 .......... 197 K5
Hoghole La *RRTW* TN3 .......... 32 E4
Hogtrough La *WSEA* TN36 ...... 116 E7
Hogthrob Cl *EDN/EASTW* BN20 ... 206 E6
The Holdings *LEW* BN7 .......... 171 M1
Hole Farm Cl *HAS* TN34 ........ 4 E1
Holland Av *BEXW* TN39 ......... 182 C2
Holland Ms *HOVE* BN3 .......... 186 D1
Holland Rd *HOVE* BN3 .......... 168 D8
Hollands St *ROTT* BN2 .......... 7 H5
Hollands Wy *EGRIN* RH19 ....... 14 A2
Hollier's Hl *BEX* TN40 .......... 183 J1
Hollin Cl *SBGH/RUST* TN4 ....... 19 M2
Hollingbury Copse *BRI* BN1 ..... 169 G3
Hollingbury Crs *BRI* BN1 ....... 169 G3
Hollingbury Park Av *BRI* BN1 ... 169 G4
Hollingbury Pl *BRI* BN1 ......... 169 H3
Hollingbury Ri *BRI* BN1 ......... 169 H3
Hollingbury Ri West *BRI* BN1 .... 169 H3
Hollingbury Ter *BRI* BN1 ....... 169 G4
Hollingdean La *BRI* BN1 ........ 169 H4
Hollingdean Rd *ROTT* BN2 ...... 169 H5
Hollingdean St *BRI* BN1 ........ 169 H5
Hollingdean Ter *BRI* BN1 ....... 169 H4
Hollinghurst Rd *SLVH* TN37 ..... 162 B1
Hollington Ct *STLEO* TN38 ...... 162 A6
Hollington Old La *STLEO* TN38 ... 162 A5
Hollington Park Cl *STLEO* TN38 ... 162 A5
Hollington Park Rd
*STLEO* TN38 .......... 162 A5
Hollow La *UCK* TN22 .......... 104 A5
The Hollow *EGRIN* RH19 ........ 22 F8
*HWH* RH16 .......... 72 B1
Hollybank Gdns *STLEO* TN38 .... 162 B5
Holly Cl *BEXW* TN39 .......... 159 J8
*BRI* BN1 .......... 169 J8
*HAIL* BN27 .......... 155 H8
*HTHF* TN21 .......... 80 A8
Holly Ct *CROW* TN6 .......... 39 L4
Hollydene Rd *WADH* TN5 ....... 31 M8
Holly Dr *HTHF* TN21 .......... 80 A8
Holly Pl *LW/ROSE* BN22 ......... 196 E3
Holly Rd *HWH* RH16 .......... 71 M3
Hollyshaw Cl *RTWE/PEM* TN2 ... 20 C4
Holmans *RHWH* RH17 .......... 34 A6
Holmbush Cl *HWH* RH16 ........ 71 L4
*SHOR* BN43 .......... 166 D4
Holmbush Wy *STHW* BN42 ...... 166 D5
Holmdale Rd *NEWHV* BN9 ....... 191 M5
Holmes Cl *HOVE* BN3 .......... 167 M4
Holmes Cl *SEAF* BN25 .......... 192 A8
Holmesdale Cl *WADH* TN5 ....... 43 L1
Holmesdale Gdns *HAS* TN34 .... 4 E6
Holmesdale Rd *BEXW* TN39 ..... 183 G2
*BURH* RH15 .......... 96 F5
Holmewood Rdg *RRTW* TN3 ..... 18 F3
Holmhurst Cl
*SBGH/RUST* TN4 .......... 19 M2
Holmhurst La *SLVH* TN37 ....... 139 H8
Holm Oak Cl *BEXW* TN39 ....... 182 E3
Holters Wy *SEAF* BN25 ......... 202 F1
Holton Hl *ROTT* BN2 .......... 170 E7
The Holt *BURH* RH15 .......... 97 J4
*HAIL* BN27 .......... 155 G8
*SEAF* BN25 .......... 202 F1
Holtview Rd *ROTT* BN2 .......... 170 B6
Holtye Av *EGRIN* RH19 .......... 13 M3
Holtye Rd *EGRIN* RH19 ......... 13 M4
*EGRIN* RH19 .......... 14 E3
Holyhead Cl *HAIL* BN27 ........ 155 C5

Holywell Cl
*EDN/EASTW* BN20 .......... 206 E7
Holywell Rd *EDN/EASTW* BN20 ... 206 E7
Homebush Av *ROTT* BN2 ......... 189 M3
*ROTT* BN2 .......... 189 K5
Home Farm Rd *BRI* BN1 ......... 169 K3
Homefield Cl *SEAF* BN25 ........ 202 F2
Homefield Rd *SEAF* BN25 ....... 202 F2
Homelands *BEXW* TN39 ......... 160 A8
Home Platt *EGRIN* RH19 ......... 23 G8
Home Rd *BRI* BN1 .......... 168 E4
Homestall Rd *EGRIN* RH19 ...... 14 E6
The Homestead *RRTW* TN3 ...... 18 C7
Homewood Cl *LW/ROSE* BN22 ... 197 H8
Homewood Rd *RRTW* TN3 ....... 18 F3
Honeycrag Cl *POLE* BN26 ....... 177 M7
Honey Cft *HOVE* BN3 .......... 167 K2
Honey La *RING/NEW* BN8 ....... 152 D7
Honeypot La *RING/NEW* BN8 .... 99 H7
Honeysuckle Cl *HAIL* BN27 ..... 178 B1
*LGNY* BN23 .......... 197 H3
*SLVH* TN37 .......... 162 D1
Honeyway Cl *POLE* BN26 ....... 195 M3
Hood Cl *LGNY* BN23 .......... 197 L7
Hoo Gdns *EDN/EASTW* BN20 .... 196 B5
Hook Hl *WADH* TN5 .......... 33 G8
Hook La *EGRIN* RH19 .......... 34 C4
*RHWH* RH17 .......... 34 C4
Hookswood Cl *CROW* TN6 ....... 40 A3
Hook Wall *LYDD* TN29 .......... 93 K1
Hoopers Cl *LEW* BN7 .......... 2 F1
Hoover Cl *STLEO* TN38 .......... 138 F7
Hopfield Gdns *UCK* TN22 ....... 76 E6
Hop Gdn *UCK* TN22 .......... 53 J4
Hopgarden Cl *HAS* TN34 ........ 4 E5
Hophurst Cl *CRAWE* RH10 ...... 12 B6
Hophurst Dr *CRAWE* RH10 ...... 12 D4
Hophurst Hl *CRAWE* RH10 ...... 12 D4
Hophurst La *CRAWE* RH10 ...... 12 B5
Hoppers Croft La
*BUR/ETCH* TN19 .......... 60 B8
Horam Park Cl *HTHF* TN21 ...... 105 M7
Horebeech La *HTHF* TN21 ....... 105 M7
Horleigh Green Rd *MAYF* TN20 ... 56 C5
Horley Pl *ROTT* BN2 .......... 169 L8
Hornbeam *BUR/ETCH* TN19 ..... 60 B7
Hornbuckles Cl
*RING/NEW* BN8 .......... 99 L7
Hornby Rd *ROTT* BN2 .......... 169 M5
Horning Cl *LGNY* BN23 ......... 197 H2
Hornshurst Rd *CROW* TN6 ...... 41 H6
Horns Rd *HAWK* TN18 .......... 47 M5
Horntye Rd *SLVH* TN37 .......... 4 B4
Horse Br *BAT* TN33 .......... 157 M7
Horsegrove Av *WADH* TN5 ...... 45 M5
Horsegrove La *CROW* TN6 ...... 41 H6
Horseshoe Cl *STLEO* TN38 ...... 162 B4
Horseshoe La *RYE* TN31 ......... 88 F3
Horsewalk *HAIL* BN27 .......... 157 M7
Horsfield Rd *LEW* BN7 .......... 2 C1
Horsgate La *RHWH* RH17 ........ 48 A8
Horsham Av *PEAHV* BN10 ....... 190 B8
Horsham Av North
*PEAHV* BN10 .......... 190 C6
Horsham Cl *ROTT* BN2 .......... 169 M8
Horsted La *EGRIN* RH19 ......... 35 H2
*RHWH* RH17 .......... 48 A8
*UCK* TN22 .......... 101 L7
Horsted Pond La *UCK* TN22 ..... 102 A2
Horsye Rd *LW/ROSE* BN22 ...... 197 H7
Horton Rd *BRI* BN1 .......... 169 H5
Hoskins Pl *EGRIN* RH19 ......... 13 M2
Hosmers Fld *CROW* TN6 ......... 41 K5
Hospital Vls *HWH* RH16 ......... 71 M4
Houghton Green La *RYE* TN31 ... 91 K4
Houghton La *RYE* TN31 ......... 91 H7
Houndean Cl *LEW* BN7 .......... 2 L1
Houndean Ri *LEW* BN7 .......... 148 F6
Hova Vls *HOVE* BN3 .......... 168 B8
Hove Park Gdns *HOVE* BN3 ..... 168 B6
Hove Park Rd *HOVE* BN3 ........ 168 C5
Hove Park Vls *HOVE* BN3 ....... 168 B6
Hove Park Wy *HOVE* BN3 ....... 168 C5
Hove Pl *HOVE* BN3 .......... 186 B1
Hove St *HOVE* BN3 .......... 168 A8
Howard Av *BURH* RH15 ......... 96 E2
Howard Cl *HAIL* BN27 .......... 155 K8
Howard Pl *BRI* BN1 .......... 6 C3
Howard Rd *ROTT* BN2 .......... 7 J3
Howards Crs *BEXW* TN39 ....... 182 C2
Howard Sq *EAST* BN21 .......... 10 F8
Howard Ter *BRI* BN1 .......... 6 C3
Howbourne La *UCK* TN22 ....... 77 L1
Howey Cl *NEWHV* BN9 .......... 191 M5
Howlett Cl *STLEO* TN38 ......... 161 M4
Howlett Dr *HAIL* BN27 .......... 155 H4
Howletts Cl *LW/ROSE* BN22 ..... 196 C4
How's Cl *RYE* TN31 .......... 114 B1
Hoyle Rd *PEAHV* BN10 .......... 190 A7
Hudson Cl *LGNY* BN23 .......... 198 A7
Huggett's La *LW/ROSE* BN22 ..... 196 B3
Hughenden Pl *HAS* TN34 ........ 5 H2
Hughenden Rd *HAS* TN34 ........ 5 H2
Hughes Rd *ROTT* BN2 .......... 169 H6
Hughes Wy *UCK* TN22 .......... 76 C6
Hugletts La *HTHF* TN21 ......... 81 G8
Humboldt Ct *RTWE/PEM* TN2 ... 20 D1
Humphrey's Gap *SHOR* BN43 ... 166 A8
Hundred Acre La
*HPPT/KEY* BN6 .......... 98 B5
Hundredhouse La *RYE* TN31 ..... 114 F3
Hungershall Pk
*SBGH/RUST* TN4 .......... 19 L4
Hunloke Av *LW/ROSE* BN22 ..... 197 H8
Hunston Cl *ROTT* BN2 .......... 170 F7
Hunters Wy *RTWE/PEM* TN2 .... 20 B6
*UCK* TN22 .......... 76 B6
Hunting Cl *BEX* TN40 .......... 183 J1
Huntingdon Wy *BURH* RH15 ..... 97 K1
Huntley Mill Rd *WADH* TN5 ...... 45 K3
Hurdis Rd *SEAF* BN25 .......... 192 A8
Hurrell Rd *HAS* TN34 .......... 5 L1
Hurst Crs *PTSD* BN41 .......... 167 H6
Hurst Farm Rd *EGRIN* RH19 ..... 13 L6
Hurstfield Cl *HWH* RH16 ........ 72 A4
Hurst Hl *BRI* BN1 .......... 169 J1
Hurst La *BAT* TN33 .......... 112 C9

EAST BN21 206 D2
HAIL BN27 157 H1
Hurst Rd EAST BN21 206 D1
HPPT/KEY BN6 122 D2
Hurstwood Cl BEX TN40 184 B1
Hurstwood La HWH RH16 71 M6 [2]
RHWH RH17 35 K5
SBGH/RUST TN4 19 L3
Hurstwood Rd UCK TN22 54 A8
Hurtis Hl CROW TN6 39 L7
Hutton Rd BRI BN1 169 H5
Hyde Cl LEW BN7 171 L1
Hyde Gdns EAST BN21 10 E7
Hydehurst Cl CROW TN6 39 M5
Hyde Rd EAST BN21 10 D7
The Hyde ROTT BN2 169 M5
Hyde Tynings Cl
EDN/EASTW BN20 206 C6
The Hydneye LW/ROSE BN22 196 F5
Hydney St LW/ROSE BN22 11 J2
Hylden Cl ROTT BN2 170 B6 [2]
Hyperion Av POLE BN26 177 L8
Hythe Av STLEO TN38 184 B1 [2]
Hythe Cl POLE BN26 178 C7
SEAF BN25 203 J1
Hythe Crs SEAF BN25 203 J2 [2]
Hythe Rd BRI BN1 169 G4
Hythe Vw SEAF BN25 203 J2 [2]

## I

Ian Cl BEX TN40 160 F7
Icklesham Dr STLEO TN38 161 K3
Iden Cl ROTT BN2 187 L1
Iden Hurst HPPT/KEY BN6 96 A7
Iden Rd RYE TN31 91 H3
Iden's La HTHF TN21 80 D6
Iden St LW/ROSE BN22 197 C4
Ifield Cl ROTT BN2 189 L4
Ifield Mill Cl PEV BN24 197 H1
Iford Cl NEWHV BN9 191 K4 [2]
Imberhorne Dr EGRIN RH19 13 H3
Ingham Dr BRI BN1 146 D8
Ingleside STLEO TN38 161 L2
Ingleside Dr CROW TN6 39 L4
Inglewood Gdns STLEO TN38 161 L2
Ingram Crs HOVE BN3 167 L1
Ingram Crs East HOVE BN3 167 L1
Ingram Crs West HOVE BN3 167 L1
Ingrams Av BEXW TN39 160 C7
Ingrams Wy HAIL BN27 178 A1
Inholmes Cl BURH RH15 97 H4
Inholmes Park Rd BURH RH15 97 H3
Inkpen La FROW RH18 24 F5
Innham's Wd CROW TN6 39 K2
Innings Dr PEV BN24 198 C2
Innovation Rd HPPT/KEY BN6 96 D4
Inverness Rd ROTT BN2 7 J1 [2]
Invicta Rd LYDD TN29 121 C4
Inwood Crs BRI BN1 168 D5
Iona Wy HWH RH16 71 L2 [2]
Irelands La LEW BN7 2 D6 [2]
Ironlatch Av STLEO TN38 161 M5
Ironlatch Cl STLEO TN38 161 M4
Ironstones RRTW TN3 19 H3 [2]
Ironstone Wy UCK TN22 76 E7 [2]
Isaac's La BURH RH15 70 F8
Isabel Cl SEAF BN25 202 E1
Isabel Crs HOVE BN3 167 H4
Isfield Rd BRI BN1 169 J4
UCK TN22 127 L2
Islingford Pl ROTT BN2 7 H4
Islingford Rd ROTT BN2 7 H3
Islingword St ROTT BN2 7 H4
Iveagh Crs NEWHV BN9 191 K5
Ivor Rd ROTT BN2 170 C5
Ivors La RING/NEW BN8 149 H1
Ivory Pl ROTT BN2 7 C5
Ivy Dene La EGRIN RH19 14 D8
Ivyhouse La HAS TN34 163 H1
RHAS TN35 140 B6
Ivy Pl HOVE BN3 186 D1 [2]
Ivy Ter EAST BN21 10 D6

## J

Jaarlen Rd LYDD TN29 95 H8
The Jackdaws UCK TN22 102 E2 [2]
Jackies La RING/NEW BN8 74 B7
Jack O'dandy Cl EAST BN21 196 C7 [2]
Jackson St ROTT BN2 7 H3
Jacobs Acre BEX TN40 183 J1 [2]
Jamaica Wy LGNY BN23 197 M6
James Av HAIL BN27 133 L8
Jameson Crs STLEO TN38 162 A3
Jameson Rd BEX TN40 183 K3
Jane Murray Wy BURH RH15 96 E5
HPPT/KEY BN6 96 C4
Janes Cl BURH RH15 97 J1
Janes La BURH RH15 97 J1
Japonica Cl SHOR BN43 166 B5
Jardine Cl CROW TN6 39 M4
Jarvisbrook Cl BEXW TN39 159 M8
BEXW TN39 182 D3
Jason Cl PEAHV BN10 190 D7
Jay Cl LGNY BN23 197 J4
Jay Rd PEAHV BN10 190 E8
The Jays BURH RH15 96 F2
UCK TN22 102 D2 [2]
Jefferies RHWH RH17 50 C2
Jefferies Wy CROW TN6 39 M2
Jellicoe Cl LGNY BN23 197 L5
Jenner's La RHAS TN35 140 E8
Jephson Cl
EDN/EASTW BN20 206 F6 [2]
Jerome Cl LGNY BN23 197 L4
Jersey St ROTT BN2 7 C4
Jervis Av LGNY BN23 197 L8
Jesmond Rd HOVE BN3 167 L7
Jesters BURH RH15 71 J7
Jevington Cl BEXW TN39 182 D4
Jevington Dr ROTT BN2 169 K5

SEAF BN25 202 C2
Jevington Gdns
EDN/EASTW BN20 206 F5
Jevington Rd POLE BN26 195 J6
Jew St BRI BN1 6 E6
Job's La HPPT/KEY BN6 70 A8
Joe's La HAIL BN27 157 H1
John Dann Cl UCK TN22 78 A8
John Macadam Wy SLVH TN37 139 G8
Johns Cl PEAHV BN10 190 C4
John's Cross Rd RBTBR TN32 85 H3
Johnson Cl STLEO TN38 138 F8
Johnson Dr BURH RH15 97 K3
John St ROTT BN2 7 G6
SBGH/RUST TN4 20 A1
Jonas Dr WADH TN5 43 L1
Jonas La WADH TN5 43 L1
Jordans La East
LW/ROSE BN22 196 D3
Jordans La West
LW/ROSE BN22 196 C3
The Jordans EGRIN RH19 13 L6
Jubilee Cl HWH RH16 72 A2
Jubilee Fld TENT TN30 67 L2
Jubilee Rd SEAF BN25 203 G1 [2]
Jubilee Rd BEXW TN39 160 A7
BURH RH15 96 E4
PTSD BN41 167 G6
Jubilee St BRI BN1 6 E5
Judge's Ter EGRIN RH19 13 L6 [2]
Juggs Cl LEW BN7 2 C8
Juggs Rd LEW BN7 2 C8
LEW BN7 2 D8
LEW BN7 149 G7
Julian Rd HOVE BN3 6 B3
Junction Cl BURH RH15 97 J2
Junction Rd BRI BN1 6 D4 [2]
BURH RH15 97 H4
EAST BN21 10 E6
RBTBR TN32 63 C4
RBTBR TN32 112 D1
SLVH TN37 139 H7
Junction St POLE BN26 178 B8
Juniper Cl PTSD BN41 167 H5 [2]
SEAF BN25 203 J3
STLEO TN38 161 L3
Jury's Gap Rd LYDD TN29 120 E2
LYDD TN29 121 G1

## K

Kammond Av SEAF BN25 203 H1
Katherine Wy SEAF BN25 202 D1
Keats Cl STLEO TN38 161 M8
Keats Pl EGRIN RH19 13 K5 [2]
Kedale Rd SEAF BN25 202 E2
Keere St LEW BN7 2 E7
Keld Av UCK TN22 76 D8
Keld Cl UCK TN22 76 D8
Keld Dr UCK TN22 76 D8
Kelly Rd HOVE BN3 168 D5
Kemps Farm Rd CROW TN6 40 B5 [2]
Kemp St BRI BN1 6 E5
Kemp Town Pl ROTT BN2 7 M9 [2]
Kendal Pk SBGH/RUST TN4 19 L1
Kendal Rd HOVE BN3 167 M6
Kenilworth Cl ROTT BN2 170 A4
Kenilworth Rd STLEO TN38 162 B7
Kenmure Av BRI BN1 146 A7
Kennedy Av EGRIN RH19 13 K3
Kennedy Cl HTHF TN21 80 B8
Kennedy Rd BEX TN40 183 L2
Kennedy Wy NEWHV BN9 8 D3
Kennel La BEXW TN39 182 C2
Kennett Cl POLE BN26 196 F1
Kensington Gdns BRI BN1 6 E5
Kensington Pl BRI BN1 6 E5
Kensington St BRI BN1 6 E5
Kent Cl BEX TN40 184 A1
SHOR BN43 166 C7
WSEA TN36 116 E7
Kent Flds LEW BN7 171 L1
Kentish Gdns RTWE/PEM TN2 19 L6
Kent La RBTBR TN32 84 A7
Kenton Cl BEXW TN39 183 G1
Kenton Rd HOVE BN3 167 K7
Kent Rd STLEO TN38 161 M2
Kent's La HPPT/KEY BN6 98 C7
Kents Rd HWH RH16 71 H3
Kent St BAT TN33 138 F2
Kenwards BRI BN1 146 D7
Kenwood Cl HAS TN34 163 H2 [2]
Keppel Rd HAS TN34 5 C1
Kerrara Ter LW/ROSE BN22 11 H2
Kestrel Cl BEX TN40 183 L2
HOVE BN3 168 D6
The Kestrels STLEO TN38 161 M1 [2]
Ketche's La RHWH RH17 50 K7
UCK TN22 51 G8
Kevin Gdns ROTT BN2 170 E6
Kewhurst Av BEXW TN39 182 C3
Kew St BRI BN1 6 D5
Keymer Av PEAHV BN10 190 D8
Keymer Cl LGNY BN23 197 L5
STLEO TN38 161 L8
Keymer Ct BURH RH15 97 H4 [2]
Keymer Gdns BURH RH15 97 H5
Keymer Pde BURH RH15 97 H4 [2]
Keymer Pk HPPT/KEY BN6 123 H3
Keymer Rd BRI BN1 146 B8
BURH RH15 97 H6
HPPT/KEY BN6 122 F3 [2]
Keysford La HWH RH16 49 L3
Key West LGNY BN23 197 M7
Kidbrook HWH RH16 49 J8 [2]
Kidd's Hl HRTF TN7 37 M1
Kildare St HAS TN34 163 H2
Kilda St LW/ROSE BN22 11 H3
Kilnbarn Wy HWH RH16 71 K4
Kiln Cl UCK TN22 102 D2 [2]
Kiln Dr RYE TN31 91 H6
Kiln La BAT TN33 158 B7
BURH RH15 72 B1
UCK TN22 127 L1
Kiln Rd CRAWE RH10 12 B7
RING/NEW BN8 128 A6

The Kiln BURH RH15 97 J3
Kilnwood La RING/NEW BN8 99 L7
Kilpatrick Cl LGNY BN23 197 K3
Kimberley Rd ROTT BN2 169 K6
SEAF BN25 202 C2
Kindersley Cl EGRIN RH19 14 B3 [2]
Kinfauns Av LW/ROSE BN22 197 H8
King Edward Av SLVH TN37 162 C2
King Edward Cl SLVH TN37 162 C3 [2]
King Edward's Pde
EDN/EASTW BN20 206 E7
Kingfisher Cl UCK TN22 102 E1
Kingfisher Dr LGNY BN23 197 J4
Kingfisher Ri EGRIN RH19 13 M6
King George Av EGRIN RH19 13 J3
King George V Hl RTW TN1 20 C1
King George Vi Av HOVE BN3 167 J8
King George Vi Dr HOVE BN3 168 A3
King Henry's Rd LEW BN7 2 C1
King Offa Wy BEX TN40 183 J1
King Pl BRI BN1 6 D6
King's Av EAST BN21 10 A2
NEWHV BN9 191 L5
RYE TN31 91 K8
King's Bank La RYE TN31 88 F4
Kingsbury Rd BRI BN1 6 F2
Kings Cha CROW TN6 39 K3
Kings Cl BEX TN40 183 J2
EAST BN21 10 C1
PEAHV BN10 190 B5 [2]
Kings Copse EGRIN RH19 13 M6 [2]
Kingscott Cl BEXW TN39 160 A6
Kingsdale Cl BAT TN33 137 M3
SLVH TN37 139 J8
King's Dr EAST BN21 196 C6
King's Esp HOVE BN3 186 A1
King's Gdns HOVE BN3 186 B1
Kingsgate La TENT TN30 67 J1
King's Hill Rd BUR/ETCH TN19 83 H2
Kingsland Cl SHOR BN43 166 C7
Kingsley Cl SLVH TN37 162 A1
Kingsley Rd BRI BN1 168 D5
LEW BN7 2 C2
Kingsmarsh La LYDD TN29 95 J2
Kingsmead SEAF BN25 202 D1
Kingsmead Cl SEAF BN25 202 E2 [2]
King's Mead La SEAF BN25 202 D2
Kingsmead Wk SEAF BN25 202 E2
Kingsmead Wy SEAF BN25 202 E2
Kingsmere Wy LGNY BN23 197 L6
Kings Ms HOVE BN3 168 B8 [2]
Kings Ride BURH RH15 97 K5
POLE BN26 193 M4
SEAF BN25 202 D2
King's Rd BRI BN1 6 A7
HWH RH16 71 M4
SLVH TN37 4 B8
STHW BN42 166 D5
Kingsthorpe Rd HOVE BN3 167 L6
Kingston Av SEAF BN25 203 H3
Kingston Bay Rd SHOR BN43 166 C8
Kingston Broadway
SHOR BN43 166 C5
Kingston Cl BRI BN1 146 E8
HOVE BN3 167 L4
SEAF BN25 203 H3
SHOR BN43 166 C6
Kingston Gn SEAF BN25 203 H3
Kingston La SHOR BN43 166 D7
Kingston Rdg LEW BN7 148 D3
Kingston Rd LEW BN7 149 H7
LW/ROSE BN22 196 F4
Kingston Wy SEAF BN25 203 H4
SHOR BN43 166 C5
King St BRI BN1 6 E6 [2]
Kings Wy BURH RH15 97 J5
Kingsway HOVE BN3 167 M8
SEAF BN25 202 D2
Kingswood Av BEXW TN39 159 M8
Kingswood Rd RTWE/PEM TN2 20 C3
Kingswood St ROTT BN2 6 F7
King Wood Hl RYE TN31 114 B3
Kinver La BEX TN40 161 G8
Kipling Av ROTT BN2 170 E6
Kipling Wy EGRIN RH19 13 J5
Kirby Dr PEAHV BN10 190 A5
Kirdford Cl BURH RH15 97 J5 [2]
Kirkdale Rd RTW TN1 20 B2
Kirkstall Cl LW/ROSE BN22 196 E3
Kirk Wy EDN/EASTW BN20 206 B1
Kitchenour La RYE TN31 89 L1
Kite Cl STLEO TN38 161 L6
Kitewell La LYDD TN29 95 K6
Knebworth Rd BEXW TN39 182 F1
Knelle Rd RBTBR TN32 84 F2
Knepp Cl ROTT BN2 169 M4
Knightsbridge Cl
SBGH/RUST TN4 19 M1
Knights Gdn HAIL BN27 155 H8
Knights Meadow UCK TN22 76 E6 [2]
Knock Hl TENT TN30 69 G4
Knole Cl BEX TN40 183 K3
ROTT BN2 189 G5
Knoll Cl HOVE BN3 167 K7
Knoll Ri STLEO TN38 162 A7
Knoll Rd LW/ROSE BN22 197 G4
Knowle Av RHAS TN35 164 E1 [2]
Knowle Cl CROW TN6 40 C6
RRTW TN3 18 E3
Knowle Hl MAYF TN20 57 G5
Knowle Pk CROW TN6 39 K4
Knowle Park Rd MAYF TN20 57 G4
Knowle Rd RHAS TN35 164 E1
Knoyle Rd BRI BN1 168 E4
Kymer Gdns HPPT/KEY BN6 123 G3

## L

Laburnum Av HOVE BN3 167 L5
Laburnum Gdns BEX TN40 160 F8
Laburnum Wy HWH RH16 72 B2
Lacys Hl RING/NEW BN8 150 E6
Ladies Mile RRTW TN3 27 K2

Ladies Mile Cl BRI BN1 145 M8
Ladies' Mile Rd BRI BN1 145 L8
Ladycross Cl SEAF BN25 203 J3 [2]
Ladymead BURH RH15 97 J1 [2]
Ladysmith Rd ROTT BN2 169 K6
Laine Cl BRI BN1 168 E3
Lake House Cl BEXW TN39 182 D2
Lakehurst La BAT TN33 108 F6
Lakelands Cl LW/ROSE BN22 197 G4
Lakelands Dr BEXW TN39 182 D2
Lake Rd SBGH/RUST TN4 19 L2
Lake St CROW TN6 42 A5
MAYF TN20 42 C6
Lake View Rd CRAWE RH10 12 B3
EGRIN RH19 13 M1
Laleham Cl EAST BN21 10 A4
SLVH TN37 162 C1 [2]
Lambert Pl LEW BN7 2 C6
Lambert Rd LGNY BN23 197 L3 [2]
Lambourn Cl EGRIN RH19 13 L3 [2]
Lambourne Cl BRI BN1 169 J4
Lambourne Rd BRI BN1 169 J4
Lambourn Wy RTWE/PEM TN2 20 D5
Lampington Rw RRTW TN3 18 E3 [2]
Lancaster Dr EGRIN RH19 14 A3
Lancaster Rd BRI BN1 6 C2
STLEO TN38 161 M1
Lancaster St LEW BN7 3 C5 [2]
Lancing Cl HAS TN34 162 D3
Lancing Wy POLE BN26 195 M2
Landgate RYE TN31 91 J8
Landport Rd LEW BN7 2 E4
Landsdown Wy BEX TN40 189 L1 [2]
Landsdown Rd SEAF BN25 203 H1 [2]
Landseer Rd HOVE BN3 168 A6
The Lane RRTW TN3 18 C1
Langdale Cl LGNY BN23 197 J2
Langdale Gdns HOVE BN3 167 M8
Langdale Rd HOVE BN3 167 M8
Langham Cl HAS TN34 162 F2
RING/NEW BN8 150 D1 [2]
Langham Rd HAS TN34 162 F2
RBTBR TN32 84 F2
Langholm Rd RRTW TN3 18 F3
Langley Cl BEXW TN39 160 B6
Langley Crs ROTT BN2 170 D5
Langney Gn LGNY BN23 197 J3
Langney Ri LGNY BN23 197 K4
Langney Rd EAST BN21 11 G6
Langridge Dr EGRIN RH19 13 L6 [2]
PTSD BN41 167 H4
Langridge La HWH RH16 72 A1 [2]
Langridge Wy BURH RH15 96 E1
Langton Cl BAT TN33 137 L2
Langton Rd RRTW TN3 18 F3
Langtye La RING/NEW BN8 152 E8
Lansdowne Crs HAIL BN27 155 G4
Lansdowne Dr HAIL BN27 155 G4
Lansdowne Gdns HAIL BN27 155 H4 [2]
Lansdowne Ms HOVE BN3 168 D8 [2]
Lansdowne Pl HOVE BN3 186 D1
HOVE BN3 186 D1
Lansdowne Rd HOVE BN3 168 D8
HOVE BN3 168 D8
RTW TN1 20 C2 [2]
Lansdowne Sq HOVE BN3 186 D1 [2]
RTW TN1 20 B2 [2]
Lansdowne St HOVE BN3 168 D8
Lansdowne Wy HAIL BN27 155 G3
Lansdown Pl LEW BN7 3 C7
Lapierre Rd NEWHV BN9 8 D3
Lapwing Cl LGNY BN23 197 J4
Larch Cl HTHF TN21 106 B1
ROTT BN2 170 F7
STLEO TN38 162 A5
Larches Wy CRAWE RH10 12 C6
Larch Gdns LW/ROSE BN22 196 D3
Larch Wy HWH RH16 72 B2
Larke Cl SHOR BN43 166 C7
Larkfield Cl STLEO TN38 162 A3 [2]
Larkfield Wy BRI BN1 169 G2
Larkhill BEX TN40 183 J2
Lark Hl HOVE BN3 167 L3
Larkspur Dr LGNY BN23 197 H3
Larnach Cl UCK TN22 76 D6
Lascelles Ter EAST BN21 10 F9
Lashbrooks Rd UCK TN22 76 B7
Latimer Rd LW/ROSE BN22 11 K2
Laton Rd HAS TN34 5 C2
Laughton Cl LW/ROSE BN22 197 G2 [2]
Laughton Rd RING/NEW BN8 128 D3
RING/NEW BN8 129 J7
ROTT BN2 170 F6
Laundry La RHWH RH17 36 D6
Laurel Cl BURH RH15 97 K1 [2]
Laurel Dene EGRIN RH19 13 M5
Laurel La WSEA TN36 141 M1
The Laurels UCK TN22 76 E6 [2]
Lauriston Rd BRI BN1 168 E6
Lavant Cl BEXW TN39 159 J8
Lavender Cl LGNY BN23 197 H3 [2]
Lavender Gdns WADH TN5 45 L5 [2]
Lavender Hl SHOR BN43 166 B5
Lavender St ROTT BN2 7 H8
Lawes Av NEWHV BN9 8 E3
Lawns Av EAST BN21 206 D2
The Lawn STLEO TN38 4 A8
Lawrence Cl LGNY BN23 197 K5 [2]
Lawrence Rd HOVE BN3 167 M7
Lawrie La HWH RH16 71 K4
Laylands Rd PTSD BN41 167 G2
Lea Av RYE TN31 91 G8
Leaf Hall Rd LW/ROSE BN22 11 H5
Leaf Rd EAST BN21 10 F5
Leahurst Court Rd BRI BN1 168 E3
Lealands Cl RRTW TN3 18 C7
Lealands Dr UCK TN22 76 C6
Lea Rd PEAHV BN10 190 B6
Leasam La RYE TN31 91 H6
Leasingham Gdns
BEXW TN39 183 C1 [2]
The Leas PEAHV BN10 200 F1
WADH TN5 32 A8
Ledsham Av SLVH TN37 162 B1
Ledsham Cl SLVH TN37 162 B1 [2]

Ledsham Pk SLVH TN37 162 B1
Ledsham Wy SLVH TN37 162 B1
Leeds Av LGNY BN23 197 K6
Leeds Cl RHAS TN35 163 K3
Leeds La MAYF TN20 56 C8
Lee Rd LEW BN7 2 D3
Leeves Cl HTHF TN21 80 A8
Leeves Wy HTHF TN21 79 M8
Leeward Quay LGNY BN23 197 M6 [2]
Lee Wy NEWHV BN9 8 E2
Leggs' La RRTW TN3 18 E1
Legsheath La EGRIN RH19 23 M7
Leicester Dr RTWE/PEM TN2 19 M6 [2]
Leicester Rd LEW BN7 2 C6
Leicester St ROTT BN2 7 H7
Leicester Vls HOVE BN3 167 K7
Leighton Rd HOVE BN3 168 A6
RHWH RH17 50 C1
Leneda Dr RTWE/PEM TN2 19 L6
Lenham Av ROTT BN2 189 H5
Lenham Rd East ROTT BN2 189 H5
Lenham Rd West ROTT BN2 189 H5
Lennox Cl EDN/EASTW BN20 206 B1 [2]
Lennox Rd HOVE BN3 167 M6
SHOR BN43 166 B6
Lennox St ROTT BN2 7 H6
Leopold Rd BEXW TN39 183 H2
BRI BN1 6 C5
Lepeland HAIL BN27 155 C3 [2]
Lesley Cl BEX TN40 160 F7
Leslie St LW/ROSE BN22 11 H3
Leveller Rd RING/NEW BN8 74 A7
Levett Av POLE BN26 178 C8 [2]
Levett Cl POLE BN26 178 C8
Levett Rd POLE BN26 178 C8
Levetts La RBTBR TN32 63 K3
Levett Wy POLE BN26 178 C8 [2]
Lewes Cl BEXW TN39 160 A8
ROTT BN2 189 L5
Lewes Crs ROTT BN2 187 L2
Lewes Rd BRI BN1 147 G8
EAST BN21 10 D3
EGRIN RH19 13 M6
FROW RH18 24 F3
HPPT/KEY BN6 123 L4
HWH RH16 49 H7
HWH RH16 72 B3
NEWHV BN9 8 F3
POLE BN26 177 M8
RHWH RH17 36 C5
RHWH RH17 50 C2
RHWH RH17 51 C3
RING/NEW BN8 150 D1
ROTT BN2 7 H2
ROTT BN2 169 J5
UCK TN22 101 L8
Lewes St ROTT BN2 7 G4
Lewis Cl NEWHV BN9 191 M4
Lewis Rd STLEO TN38 162 A3
Lewry Cl NEWHV BN9 8 C3
Lexden Ct SEAF BN25 203 C2 [2]
Lexden Dr SEAF BN25 202 F1
Lexden Rd SEAF BN25 192 F8
SEAF BN25 202 F1
Leybourne Cl ROTT BN2 170 A3 [2]
Leybourne Gdns SLVH TN37 162 C2
Leybourne Rd ROTT BN2 170 A4
Leyland Rd PEV BN24 198 C2
Leylands Pk BURH RH15 97 H1
Leylands Rd BURH RH15 97 G2
Library Wy UCK TN22 76 C7
Lilac Cl LW/ROSE BN22 196 D4
Lillywhite Cl BURH RH15 96 F1
Limden Cl WADH TN5 44 B3
Lime Cl RRTW TN3 30 B3
STLEO TN38 162 A5
UCK TN22 76 D6
Lime Hill Rd RTW TN1 20 A2 [2]
Limekiln Ct CROW TN6 40 B3
Limes Gv HAWK TN18 47 M1
Limes La UCK TN22 77 K3
The Limes EGRIN RH19 13 L4
Limetree Av LW/ROSE BN22 196 D3 [2]
Lime Tree Av UCK TN22 76 D7
Lime Wy HTHF TN21 106 B1
Limney Rd ROTT BN2 169 L7
Linchmere Av ROTT BN2 189 J5
Lincoln Av PEAHV BN10 190 A7
Lincoln Av South
PEAHV BN10 190 A7 [2]
Lincoln Cl EDN/EASTW BN20 206 C6
STLEO TN38 161 M2
Lincoln Cottages ROTT BN2 7 H4 [2]
Lincoln Rd PTSD BN41 167 H1
Lincoln St ROTT BN2 7 H4
Lincoln Wy CROW TN6 40 A6
Lincoln Wd PEAHV BN10 71 J1
Linden Av EGRIN RH19 13 J4
Linden Cha UCK TN22 76 C7
Linden Cl LW/ROSE BN22 196 E3
RTWE/PEM TN2 76 C7 [2]
Linden Ct UCK TN22 76 C7 [2]
Linden Gdns RTWE/PEM TN2 19 M5
Linden Gv HAIL BN27 155 J3
HWH RH16 49 C8
Linden Park Rd RTWE/PEM TN2 19 M5
Linden Rd BEX TN40 183 J3
Lindfield Av SEAF BN25 203 J4
Lindfield Cl ROTT BN2 189 H4
Lindfield Dr HAIL BN27 155 H7
Lindfield Rd LW/ROSE BN22 196 D5
RHWH RH17 34 C8
Lindon Cl EDN/EASTW BN20 205 H5 [2]
Lindsay Cl EDN/EASTW BN20 206 C5
Lingfield Rd EGRIN RH19 13 K3 [2]
Link Rd EDN/EASTW BN20 206 D5
Links Av NEWHV BN9 8 A4
Links Cl CROW TN6 39 K5
PTSD BN41 167 J6
SEAF BN25 203 C3
Links Dr BEX TN40 183 L2
Links Rd PTSD BN41 167 J6
SEAF BN25 203 C4
The Links STLEO TN38 161 M6
Links Wy RYE TN31 118 C4
The Link EDN/EASTW BN20 205 J4
RYE TN31 117 C1
Linkway EDN/EASTW BN20 196 A3

The Linkway BRI BN1 169 H5
Linley Cl BEX TN40 183 K2
Linley Dr HAS TN34 163 G3
Linnet Cl LGNY BN23 197 J4
Linnet Gn UCK TN22 102 D1 1
Linthouse Cl PEAHV BN10 190 D4 3
Linton Crs HAS TN34 4 E6
Linton Rd HAS TN34 4 E4
HOVE BN3 167 M6
Lionel Rd BEX TN40 183 L3
Lion Hl PEV BN24 197 H1
Lion La CRAWE RH10 22 A2
LW/ROSE BN22 11 H6
Lions Pl SEAF BN25 202 F4
Lion St RYE TN31 117 J1
Liphook Cl BRI BN1 169 J5 1
Lismore Rd EAST BN21 10 F7
Lister Av EGRIN RH19 13 L8
Little Bentswood HWH RH16 71 M1 1
Little Black Hl HWH RH16 49 H7
Little Common Rd BEXW TN39 182 D2
Little Copse Rd HPPT/KEY BN6 122 E1
Little Crs ROTT BN2 189 H5
Little East St LEW BN7 3 G5
Little Footway RRTW TN3 18 F3
Little King St EGRIN RH19 13 L5 1
Little London Rd HTHF TN21 105 L6
Little Mallett RRTW TN3 18 F3 3
Little Md RING/NEW BN8 126 A7
Little Mount Sion RTW TN1 20 A4 5
Little Paddock CROW TN6 39 L5
RING/NEW BN8 127 L8
Little Pk WADH TN5 43 L1
Little Preston St BRI BN1 6 B7
Little Ridge Av SLVH TN37 139 H8
Little Sunnyside CROW TN6 39 M5 1
Little Trogers La MAYF TN20 57 H2
Little Twitten BEXW TN39 182 C3
Littlewood La UCK TN22 77 J2
Littleworth Cl ROTT BN2 170 F7
Livingstone Rd BURH RH15 96 F3
HOVE BN3 168 B7
Livingstone St ROTT BN2 7 L6 1
Lloyd Cl HOVE BN3 168 C6
Lloyd Rd HOVE BN3 168 C6
Lloyds Gn TENT TN30 67 K2
Lockitt Wy LEW BN7 171 L1
Locks Crs PTSD BN41 167 H6
Locks Hl PTSD BN41 167 H5
Lockwood Cl ROTT BN2 170 E7
Lockwood Crs ROTT BN2 170 E7
Loder Pl BRI BN1 168 F4
Loder Rd BRI BN1 168 F4
Lodge Av LW/ROSE BN22 196 C4
Lodge Cl EGRIN RH19 13 J5
LEW BN7 2 B7
PTSD BN41 166 F4 1
Lodge Hill La HPPT/KEY BN6 123 J2
Lodgelands RHWH RH17 34 B8
Lodge La HPPT/KEY BN6 123 G3
Lodge Rd RHAS TN35 163 J5 1
Lodsworth Cl ROTT BN2 169 M7
Lomas La HAWK TN18 64 F1
Lomond Av BRI BN1 146 A7
London Rd BAT TN33 111 J4
BEXW TN39 183 H1
BRI BN1 6 F2
BRI BN1 145 K6
BRI BN1 168 E3
BUR/ETCH TN19 62 A3
BURH RH15 96 F3 2
CROW TN6 39 L2
EGRIN RH19 13 L5
FROW RH18 24 E2
HAIL BN27 155 H6
HPPT/KEY BN6 122 E1
RBTBR TN32 62 B8
RBTBR TN32 111 K1
RHWH RH17 51 G2
RING/NEW BN8 129 M1
SBGH/RUST TN4 20 A3
STLEO TN38 4 A4
STLEO TN38 162 B4
UCK TN22 76 B2
WADH TN5 46 D3
London Ter BRI BN1 6 F2
Long Acre CRAWE RH10 12 A6
Long Acre Cl EAST BN21 206 D1
Longacre Cl SLVH TN37 139 J8
Long Av BEX TN40 161 G8
Longbury UCK TN22 102 C1
Longhill Cl ROTT BN2 188 E2
Longhill Rd ROTT BN2 188 D2
Longhurst BURH RH15 97 K4
Longland Rd
EDN/EASTW BN20 206 C2
Long La BAT TN33 112 E5
Long Meads RRTW TN3 19 H3
Long Park Cnr HPPT/KEY BN6 123 K4
Longridge Av ROTT BN2 189 J6
Long Slip RRTW TN3 19 G3
Longstone Rd EAST BN21 10 F6
Longview HTHF TN21 106 A1
Lonsdale Gdns RTW TN1 20 A3 3
The Lookout PEAHV BN10 190 C3
Lordine La RBTBR TN32 87 H2
Lordslaine Cl
EDN/EASTW BN20 206 C6
Lords La RHAS TN35 163 K3
The Lords SEAF BN25 192 E8
Lordswell La CROW TN6 39 L6
Lorna Rd HOVE BN3 168 D7
Lorne Rd BRI BN1 6 F1
Lorraine Rd NEWHV BN9 9 G4
Lossenham La HAWK TN18 65 K2
Lottbridge Dro LW/ROSE BN22 196 F5
LW/ROSE BN22 197 H6
Love La MAYF TN20 56 F4
RYE TN31 91 H8
Lover's Wk BRI BN1 168 F6
Lowdells Cl EGRIN RH19 13 J2
Lowdells Dr EGRIN RH19 13 K2
Lowdells La EGRIN RH19 13 J3
Lower Bevendean Av
ROTT BN2 169 L5
Lower Chalvington Pl
ROTT BN2 187 L1 2
Lower Church Rd BURH RH15 96 F3
Lower Dene EGRIN RH19 14 A5
Lower Dr SEAF BN25 202 F1
STHW BN42 166 E5
Lower Glen Rd SLVH TN37 162 B2
Lower Green Rd RRTW TN3 19 J1
SBGH/RUST TN4 19 J2
Lower Hazelhurst WADH TN5 45 H3
Lower High St WADH TN5 44 A3
Lower Lake BAT TN33 137 L2
Lower Market St HOVE BN3 186 D1 2
Lower Mere EGRIN RH19 13 M6
Lower Park Rd HAS TN34 4 E3
Lower Pl NEWHV BN9 8 F3
Lower Platts WADH TN5 45 L5
Lower Rd EAST BN21 206 D2
HAIL BN27 156 D3
Lower Rock Gdns ROTT BN2 7 H8
Lower Saxonbury CROW TN6 39 M4 3
Lower South Rd STLEO TN38 4 A4
Lower Station Rd
RING/NEW BN8 74 A8
Lower Stoneham
RING/NEW BN8 149 L2
Lower St BAT TN33 159 H2
EDN/EASTW BN20 205 H6
Lower Waites La RHAS TN35 164 F2
Lowfield Rd HWH RH16 71 M3
Lowlands Rd BURH RH15 97 H1
The Lowlands HAIL BN27 155 G5
Lowther Cl LGNY BN23 197 K3
Lowther Rd BRI BN1 169 G4
Loxfield Cl MAYF TN20 57 G4
Loxwood Cl BEXW TN39 182 C1
LW/ROSE BN22 196 C5
Lucas RHWH RH17 50 D1
Lucas Cl EGRIN RH19 13 M5 4
Lucas Gra HWH RH16 71 K1
Lucas Shadwell Wy RYE TN31 117 M4
Lucastes Av HWH RH16 48 C8
Lucastes La RHWH RH17 48 C8
RHWH RH17 71 J1
Lucastes Rd HWH RH16 71 J1
Lucas Wy HWH RH16 71 J1
Lucerne Cl PTSD BN41 167 H5
Lucerne Rd BRI BN1 168 F5
Lucinda Wy SEAF BN25 202 F1
Lucraft Rd ROTT BN2 169 M1
Ludley Hl RYE TN31 89 G8
Ludlow Ri ROTT BN2 170 A5
Ludpit La BUR/ETCH TN19 61 J8
Lulham Cl PEAHV BN10 190 B5 2
Lullington Av HOVE BN3 167 M6
Lullington Cl BEX TN40 161 G8
EAST BN21 196 C7
SEAF BN25 203 H4
Lullington Gdns SLVH TN37 162 C1 2
Lunce's Hl RHWH RH17 71 M6
Lundy Wk HAIL BN27 154 F4 1
Lurgashall BURH RH15 97 J5 4
Lushington La EAST BN21 10 E7
Lushington Rd EAST BN21 10 E7
Lustrells Cl ROTT BN2 189 H4
Lustrells Crs ROTT BN2 189 H4
Lustrells V ROTT BN2 189 H4
Luther St ROTT BN2 7 J3
Luton Cl EAST BN21 196 C8
Luxford Dr CROW TN6 40 A6
Luxford La CROW TN6 40 A6
Luxford Rd CROW TN6 40 A7
HWH RH16 49 H7
Luxford's La EGRIN RH19 14 B8
EGRIN RH19 24 B1
Lychgates Cl BEX TN40 183 K1
Lydd Cl LGNY BN23 197 K4 3
Lydd Rd RYE TN31 118 E4
Lydd Town Crossing LYDD TN29 95 K6
Lymden La WADH TN5 45 G7
Lyminster Av BRI BN1 169 G1
Lynchet Cl BRI BN1 169 J4
Lynchet Down BRI BN1 169 J4
Lynchets Crs HOVE BN3 167 K3
The Lynchets LEW BN7 3 J2
Lynchet Wk BRI BN1 169 J4
Lyndhurst Av HAS TN34 163 G2
Lyndhurst Farm Cl EGRIN RH19 12 D2
Lyndhurst Rd HOVE BN3 168 D7
Lynholm Rd POLE BN26 178 B8
Lynton Cl HPPT/KEY BN6 122 B1
Lynton Park Av EGRIN RH19 14 A4
Lynton St ROTT BN2 7 K3
Lynwood RRTW TN3 18 C8
Lynwood Cl HAS TN34 162 D1
Lynwood Rd ROTT BN2 189 J6
Lyon Cl HOVE BN3 168 D7
Lyoth La HWH RH16 72 B1
Lytham Cl STLEO TN38 161 M6


## M


Maberley Rd BEX TN40 160 C8 1
Mackerel Hl RYE TN31 89 M1
Mackerel's Rocks
RING/NEW BN8 100 F3
Mackie Av BRI BN1 145 M8
HPPT/KEY BN6 123 G1
Macmichaels Wy
BUR/ETCH TN19 62 A3 1
Macmillan Dr EAST BN21 206 C1
Madehurst Cl ROTT BN2 7 M7
Madeira Dr ROTT BN2 7 G8
Madeira Pk RTW TN1 20 B4 5
Madeira Pl ROTT BN2 7 G8
Maderia Dr SLVH TN37 162 C3
Mafeking Rd ROTT BN2 169 J6
Magdalen Cl LGNY BN23 197 J3 5
Magdalen Rd BEX TN40 183 K2
SLVH TN37 4 C7
Magellan Wy LGNY BN23 198 A8
Magnolia Cl HTHF TN21 106 B1
Magnolia Dr LW/ROSE BN22 196 D4
Magpie Cl BEXW TN39 159 J8
STLEO TN38 161 L6
Magpie Rd LGNY BN23 197 J3
Magreed La HTHF TN21 80 E4
Main Rd RHAS TN35 139 L2
RHAS TN35 141 H2
Mainstone Rd HOVE BN3 167 M7 1
Main St RYE TN31 65 H8
RYE TN31 90 B4
RYE TN31 91 H3
Maitland Cl HAS TN34 139 L8
Major Cl BRI BN1 169 H5
Major York's Rd
SBGH/RUST TN4 19 M3
Malcolm Gdns POLE BN26 178 A7
Maldon Rd BRI BN1 168 D4
Malines Av PEAHV BN10 190 B7
Malines Av South PEAHV BN10 190 A7
Mallard Cl LW/ROSE BN22 196 F5
Mallard Dr UCK TN22 102 D1
Mallard Pl EGRIN RH19 13 M6
Mallett Cl SEAF BN25 202 E4 3
Malling Cl LEW BN7 3 G2
Malling Down LEW BN7 3 J2
Malling Hl LEW BN7 3 J2
Malling St LEW BN7 3 J5
Mallory Rd HOVE BN3 168 C4
Malthouse La HPPT/KEY BN6 96 C6
HPPT/KEY BN6 96 C3
ROTT BN2 7 G4 2
RYE TN31 90 B4
Malthouse Wy RING/NEW BN8 126 A7
The Maltings BURH RH15 96 D2
Malvern St HOVE BN3 168 B7 2
Malvern Wy HAS TN34 163 H3
Manaton Cl HWH RH16 71 M2
Manchester Rd BAT TN33 136 A8
Manchester St ROTT BN2 6 F8
Manifold Rd LW/ROSE BN22 11 G4
Manning Cl EGRIN RH19 13 K4
Mann St HAS TN34 5 G6
Manor Av HPPT/KEY BN6 123 G1
Manor Cl BURH RH15 97 K2
EDN/EASTW BN20 196 A4
HTHF TN21 105 M6
RING/NEW BN8 127 M7 1
ROTT BN2 187 L1
SBGH/RUST TN4 19 L2
SEAF BN25 203 H3
STHW BN42 167 G6
UCK TN22 76 C6
WSEA TN36 141 M1
Manor Dr PEAHV BN10 190 B5
Manor End UCK TN22 76 C6
Manor Gdns ROTT BN2 187 L1
Manor Gn ROTT BN2 187 L1
Manor Hall Rd STHW BN42 166 E6
Manor Hl ROTT BN2 169 L8
Manor Paddock ROTT BN2 187 L2
Manor Pk SBGH/RUST TN4 19 L3
Manor Park Rd HAIL BN27 155 G3
Manor Pl ROTT BN2 187 L2
Manor Rd BEX TN40 183 K2
BURH RH15 97 J2
BURH RH15 97 K3
EGRIN RH19 13 J4
HAS TN34 5 J3
HTHF TN21 105 M6
LW/ROSE BN22 197 G4
LYDD TN29 121 J1
PTSD BN41 167 H5
ROTT BN2 187 L2
SBGH/RUST TN4 19 J2
SEAF BN25 203 H3
Manor Rd North SEAF BN25 203 H3
Manor Wy CROW TN6 39 L6
EDN/EASTW BN20 196 B6
POLE BN26 178 A8
ROTT BN2 187 L1
UCK TN22 76 C6
Mansell Cl BEXW TN39 182 C2
Mansell Rd SHOR BN43 166 B6
Mansers La HAIL BN27 154 C3
Mansfield Rd HOVE BN3 167 L7
Mansion Cl BURH RH15 97 K3
Manston Wy HAS TN34 4 E2
Mantell Cl LEW BN7 149 J2
Manton Rd ROTT BN2 169 L5
Manvers Rd EDN/EASTW BN20 206 B3
Maple Av BEXW TN39 182 C3
Maple Cl BEXW TN39 182 C3
BURH RH15 97 H1
HWH RH16 72 B3
ROTT BN2 170 E7
UCK TN22 76 A2 1
Maple Ct HAIL BN27 155 G6
Maple Dr BURH RH15 96 F2
EGRIN RH19 14 A5
Maple Gdns HOVE BN3 167 L5
Maple Hts SLVH TN37 139 H7
Maplehurst Cl SLVH TN37 139 H7
Maplehurst Dr SLVH TN37 139 J6
Maplehurst Ri SLVH TN37 139 H7 1
Maplehurst Rd LW/ROSE BN22 196 D4
PTSD BN41 167 G5
Maple Leaf Cl NEWHV BN9 8 C3
Mapleleaf Gdns POLE BN26 178 A6 1
Maple Wk BEXW TN39 182 C3
Marbles Rd RING/NEW BN8 74 D7
Marchants Cl HPPT/KEY BN6 96 A8
Marchants Dr RYE TN31 118 E4
Marchants Rd HPPT/KEY BN6 96 A8
Marchants Wy BURH RH15 96 F1
Marcia Cl EDN/EASTW BN20 196 A6
Marcus Gdns STLEO TN38 162 A1
Marden's Hl CROW TN6 27 H8
Mare Bay Cl STLEO TN38 138 E7
Maresfield Dr PEV BN24 180 E8
Maresfield Rd ROTT BN2 187 L1
Margaret St ROTT BN2 7 G8
Margery Rd HOVE BN3 167 K6
Marina BEX TN40 183 J3
STLEO TN38 162 A8
Marina Court Av BEX TN40 183 J3
Marina Wk LGNY BN23 197 L6
Marina Wy ROTT BN2 187 L3
Marine Av HOVE BN3 167 K8
Marine Cl PEV BN24 180 F8
ROTT BN2 189 H5
Marine Crs SEAF BN25 202 E4
Marine Dr ROTT BN2 187 M3
SEAF BN25 192 A8
Marine Gdns ROTT BN2 7 H8
Marine Pde HAS TN34 5 J7
LW/ROSE BN22 11 H7
ROTT BN2 7 G8
SEAF BN25 202 B2
Marine Parade Rd
LW/ROSE BN22 11 H6
Marine Rd LW/ROSE BN22 11 H6
PEV BN24 198 D1
Marine Sq ROTT BN2 7 K9
Marine Terrace Ms ROTT BN2 7 J8
Marine Vw ROTT BN2 7 H6
Marjoram Pl SHOR BN43 166 B5 2
Mark Cl SEAF BN25 203 J4 2
Market La LEW BN7 3 G6
Market Pl HAIL BN27 155 J7
HWH RH16 71 K1
Market Rd BAT TN33 137 J1
RYE TN31 117 J1 3
Market St BRI BN1 6 E7
LEW BN7 3 G6
RTWE/PEM TN2 20 A4 6
RYE TN31 117 J1 4
STLEO TN38 4 A9
Markland Wy UCK TN22 76 A7
Mark La EAST BN21 10 E7
Marklye La HTHF TN21 80 B5
HTHF TN21 107 J3
Markstakes Cnr RING/NEW BN8 99 L5
Markstakes La RING/NEW BN8 99 L5
Markwick Ter STLEO TN38 162 B6
Marlborough Cl LGNY BN23 197 K3 1
SBGH/RUST TN4 19 L2
STLEO TN38 162 A5
Marlborough Dr BURH RH15 97 J3
Marlborough Ms BRI BN1 6 C6 1
Marlborough Pl BRI BN1 6 F6 2
Marlborough St BRI BN1 6 C6
Marle Av BURH RH15 97 G2 1
Marley Cl BAT TN33 137 M2
Marley Gdns BAT TN33 137 M2
Marley La BAT TN33 137 M2
Marley Ri BAT TN33 137 M2
Marley Rd RYE TN31 91 G8
Marline Av STLEO TN38 162 A3
Marline Rd STLEO TN38 162 A2
The Marlinspike SHOR BN43 166 A8
Marlow Av LW/ROSE BN22 197 H8
Marlow Dr HWH RH16 72 B2
SLVH TN37 162 B1
Marlow Rd ROTT BN2 187 M2
Marlpit Cl EGRIN RH19 13 L3
Marlpit Rd EGRIN RH19 23 G8
Marlpits La BAT TN33 136 A7
The Marlpit WADH TN5 43 L1
Marmion Rd HOVE BN3 167 M7
Marsden Rd LGNY BN23 197 L5
Marshall La NEWHV BN9 8 F3
Marshalls Rw BRI BN1 6 F3
Marshall Wy HOVE BN3 167 M5
Marshfoot La HAIL BN27 155 J6
Marshlands La HTHF TN21 80 A6
Marsh Quarter La HAWK TN18 64 C2
Martello Rd LW/ROSE BN22 197 K8
SEAF BN25 202 E4
Martha Gunn Rd ROTT BN2 169 K5
Martineau La RHAS TN35 163 M1
Martingale Cl SLVH TN37 162 C1 3
Martin Rd HOVE BN3 167 K5
The Martins CRAWE RH10 12 C6
PEAHV BN10 190 B5 3
Martlets BEX TN40 183 L1 3
The Martlets CROW TN6 39 M5
LEW BN7 3 H2 2
RYE TN31 114 C2
The Martlet HOVE BN3 168 D6
The Martletts
RING/NEW BN8 127 L8 2
Martyn's Cl ROTT BN2 188 E2
Martyns Pl EGRIN RH19 14 A6
Martyns Wy BEX TN40 184 A1
Maryan Ct HAIL BN27 155 H6
Maryland Rd RTWE/PEM TN2 20 D5
Marylands HWH RH16 71 M1 2
Mary Stamford Gn
RYE TN31 118 A3 1
Maskelyne Rd HAIL BN27 157 G6
Mason Cl EGRIN RH19 13 L4
Mason Rd RYE TN31 117 G1
SEAF BN25 202 F2
Matlock Rd BRI BN1 168 D5
EDN/EASTW BN20 206 D6
Maurice Rd SEAF BN25 202 F5
Maxfield Cl
EDN/EASTW BN20 206 B1 2
Maxfield La RHAS TN35 140 D4
May Av SEAF BN25 203 H3
Mayfair Cl POLE BN26 195 M2
Mayfield Av PEAHV BN10 190 D8
Mayfield Cl BRI BN1 168 F1
Mayfield Crs BRI BN1 168 F1
Mayfield Flat HTHF TN21 79 G6
Mayfield La STLEO TN38 161 K4
WADH TN5 43 J2
Mayfield Pk WADH TN5 43 K1
Mayfield Pl LW/ROSE BN22 10 E3
Mayfield Rd CROW TN6 42 A4
SBGH/RUST TN4 19 M2
Mayfield Wy BEX TN40 183 L1
Mayflower Ct HWH RH16 71 M2 3
Mayflower Rd HWH RH16 71 M2
Mayhew Wy LEW BN7 3 G3
Mayhouse Rd BURH RH15 96 F5 3
Mayne Waye HAS TN34 163 G2
Mayo La BEXW TN39 160 A6
Mayo Ri BEXW TN39 160 A6
Mayo Rd ROTT BN2 169 H6
Maypole Cottages UCK TN22 54 B6
Maypole Rd EGRIN RH19 13 K4
EGRIN RH19 14 E8
May Rd ROTT BN2 7 M2
May Tree Gdns BEX TN40 160 F8
Maytree Wk HOVE BN3 167 L5
Maywood Av LW/ROSE BN22 196 D4
Mcindoe Rd EGRIN RH19 13 K3
Mciver Cl EGRIN RH19 12 F2
Mcwilliam Rd ROTT BN2 170 C5
Meadow Cl HAIL BN27 155 H5
HOVE BN3 168 B3
PTSD BN41 167 H4 5
ROTT BN2 188 E3
STHW BN42 167 G6
STLEO TN38 162 A2 3
Meadow Crs BEXW TN39 160 C7
Meadowcroft Cl EGRIN RH19 13 J4
Meadow Dr HWH RH16 49 H8
Meadow Hill Rd RTW TN1 20 B3 6
Meadowlands Av
LW/ROSE BN22 196 D4
Meadow La BAT TN33 112 D5
BURH RH15 96 F5
HWH RH16 49 H8
Meadow Pde ROTT BN2 188 F3
Meadow Rd HAIL BN27 155 G8
RRTW TN3 18 B7
SBGH/RUST TN4 19 J2
Meadows HPPT/KEY BN6 122 E1
Meadows Rd LW/ROSE BN22 196 B4
The Meadows HOVE BN3 167 J3
LEW BN7 3 J1
SLVH TN37 139 J8
Meadow Vw CROW TN6 41 G7
Meadowview ROTT BN2 169 L5
Meadow Wy HTHF TN21 106 A1
RHAS TN35 164 E2
SEAF BN25 203 G3
Meads Av BEXW TN39 182 C2
HOVE BN3 167 J3
Meads Brow
EDN/EASTW BN20 206 D6 2
Meads Cl HOVE BN3 167 J3 1
Meads Rd BEXW TN39 182 C2
EDN/EASTW BN20 206 E6
SEAF BN25 202 F3
Meads St EDN/EASTW BN20 206 E6
The Meads BRI BN1 169 K1
EGRIN RH19 13 L7
RTWE/PEM TN2 20 C4
The Mead BEXW TN39 182 D2
Meadway Ct STHW BN42 166 D6
Meadway Crs HOVE BN3 167 M4
The Meadway ROTT BN2 187 M1
Mealla Cl LEW BN7 2 F1
Medina Dr PEV BN24 197 H1
Medina Pl HOVE BN3 186 B1
Medina Ter HOVE BN3 186 B1 1
Medina Vls HOVE BN3 186 B1
Medmerry Hl ROTT BN2 169 L4
Medway CRAWE RH10 22 A1
CROW TN6 40 C5
HAIL BN27 155 G4
Medway Dr EGRIN RH19 13 K8
FROW RH18 25 G4
Medway La PEV BN24 197 G1
Medway Rd RTW TN1 20 B1
Meeching Ri NEWHV BN9 8 F4
Meeching Rd NEWHV BN9 9 G4 1
Meeds Rd BURH RH15 97 G4
Meeting House La BRI BN1 6 E7 3
Melbourne Rd LW/ROSE BN22 11 G5
Melbourne St ROTT BN2 7 J1
Melfort Rd CROW TN6 39 K5
Melrose Av PTSD BN41 167 G5
Melrose Cl BRI BN1 169 J4
HAIL BN27 155 G6
Melville Rd HOVE BN3 6 B3
Melvill La EDN/EASTW BN20 196 B6
Mendip Av LGNY BN23 197 J3
Mendip Gdns HAS TN34 163 H3
Menzies Rd SLVH TN37 162 B3 1
Meon Cl PEV BN24 197 G1
Mercatoria STLEO TN38 4 A9
Mercers RRTW TN3 19 G3
Mercer St RTW TN1 20 B1 2
Mercread Rd SEAF BN25 202 F3
Meres La MAYF TN20 56 D6
MAYF TN20 79 H3
Merevale BRI BN1 169 H4
Meridian Rd LEW BN7 2 C3
Meridian Wy EGRIN RH19 13 M3
Merlin Cl HOVE BN3 168 D6
Merlin Wy EGRIN RH19 14 A3
Mermaid St RYE TN31 117 H1
Merrimede Cl STLEO TN38 162 A7
Merriments La BUR/ETCH TN19 62 A2
Merston Cl ROTT BN2 170 E8
Metcalfe Av NEWHV BN9 8 C3
Mews Ct EGRIN RH19 13 M8
The Mews RING/NEW BN8 130 A1
Meyners Cl HOVE BN3 167 J3 2
Michael Flds FROW RH18 24 E4
Michelbourne Cl BURH RH15 96 E5 1
Michel Cl EDN/EASTW BN20 205 H5
Michel Dene Cl
EDN/EASTW BN20 205 J5 2
Michel Dene Rd
EDN/EASTW BN20 205 H5
Michele Cl STLEO TN38 162 B5 1
Michel Gv EAST BN21 10 A4
Michelham Cl LGNY BN23 197 G2 1
Michelham Rd UCK TN22 76 E5
Michelson Cl STLEO TN38 161 M2
Middle Dr UCK TN22 53 G8
Middle Furlong SEAF BN25 202 F3
Middleham Cl RING/NEW BN8 150 C2
Middleham Wy LGNY BN23 197 J2 1
Middle Rd BRI BN1 168 E5
RHAS TN35 163 K3
RRTW TN3 31 G1
SHOR BN43 166 B7
Middlesex Rd BEX TN40 183 K3
Middle St BRI BN1 6 D8
BRI BN1 147 J8
HAS TN34 5 G6
PTSD BN41 167 H8
Middleton Av HOVE BN3 167 K8
Middleton Dr LGNY BN23 197 L7 4
Middleton Ri BRI BN1 169 L1
Middle Wy BURH RH15 97 H3
Middleway HAIL BN27 157 H1
Middle Wy LEW BN7 2 A5
Midfields Cl BURH RH15 97 H2 1
Midfields Dr BURH RH15 97 H3
Midfields Wk BURH RH15 97 H2 2
Midhurst Ri BRI BN1 146 B8
Midhurst Rd LW/ROSE BN22 196 F4
Midhurst Wk HOVE BN3 167 M3 2
Midway Rd ROTT BN2 170 C6

The Midway SBGH/RUST TN4 ...... 19 K4
Mighell St ROTT BN2 ........ 7 G6
Milcote Av HOVE BN3 ...... 167 M6
Mildenhall Dr SLVH TN37 ...... 162 B2
Mildmay Cl RING/NEW BN8 ...... 127 K8
Mildmay Rd LEW BN7 ......... 2 B5
Mile Oak Crs STHW BN42 ...... 166 F5
Mile Oak Gdns PTSD BN41 ...... 167 G5
Mile Oak Rd PTSD BN41 ...... 166 F3
Milfoil Dr LGNY BN23 ...... 197 J3
Military Rd RYE TN31 ...... 91 K5
Milland Cl BEX TN40 ...... 160 E8
Milland Rd HAIL BN27 ...... 155 H5
Millbank BURH RH15 ...... 97 H2
Millberg Rd SEAF BN25 ...... 203 H2
Millbrook Cl HTHF TN21 ...... 106 A7
Millbrook Gdns
  EDN/EASTW BN20 ...... 196 B8
Millbrook Rd CROW TN6 ...... 40 A4
Mill Brooks RING/NEW BN8 ...... 99 K7
Mill Cl EDN/EASTW BN20 ...... 205 C3
  EGRIN RH19 ...... 13 L7
  HTHF TN21 ...... 79 M7
  POLE BN26 ...... 195 M2
  POY/PYE BN45 ...... 144 C1
  PTSD BN41 ...... 167 J5
  RBTBR TN32 ...... 86 E4
  RHAS TN35 ...... 139 L1
  RHAS TN35 ...... 163 L2
Mill Crs CROW TN6 ...... 39 M3
Millcroft BRI BN1 ...... 168 C1
Millcroft Av STHW BN42 ...... 166 E5
Millcroft Gdns STHW BN42 ...... 166 E5
Millcross Rd PTSD BN41 ...... 167 H5
Milldown Rd SEAF BN25 ...... 202 F2
Mill Dr CROW TN6 ...... 39 M4
  HOVE BN3 ...... 168 A3
  SEAF BN25 ...... 203 C3
Mill Dro UCK TN22 ...... 76 C8
Miller Rd BRI BN1 ...... 169 H3
Miller's Hill Cottage La
  RHAS TN35 ...... 113 K7
Millers Ri HAIL BN27 ...... 155 H5
Miller's Rd BRI BN1 ...... 168 E5
Millers Wy BURH RH15 ...... 97 G2
Millfield BAT TN33 ...... 136 A4
Millfield Cl RING/NEW BN8 ...... 74 C7
  SEAF BN25 ...... 203 G2
Millfield Cottages ROTT BN2 ...... 7 L9
Millfield Ri BEX TN40 ...... 183 J2
Mill Gap Rd EAST BN21 ...... 10 C4
Mill Gdns HTHF TN21 ...... 106 A1
  RING/NEW BN8 ...... 150 D1
Mill Green Rd HWH RH16 ...... 48 E8
Millham Cl BEXW TN39 ...... 182 F1
Mill Hill Cl HWH RH16 ...... 48 E7
Mill La BAT TN33 ...... 158 F4
  CROW TN6 ...... 39 J4
  EGRIN RH19 ...... 12 D1
  HAIL BN27 ...... 155 G1
  HPPT/KEY BN6 ...... 96 A3
  LEW BN7 ...... 172 C7
  LYDD TN29 ...... 95 J7
  POY/PYE BN45 ...... 144 C1
  PTSD BN41 ...... 167 H4
  RHAS TN35 ...... 139 L1
  RHAS TN35 ...... 163 L1
  RING/NEW BN8 ...... 99 K7
  RING/NEW BN8 ...... 126 D4
  RING/NEW BN8 ...... 130 A1
  RYE TN31 ...... 89 M3
  UCK TN22 ...... 76 C8
Mill Md RING/NEW BN8 ...... 150 D1
Mill Race HPPT/KEY BN6 ...... 96 E6
The Millrace POLE BN26 ...... 195 M2
Mill Ri BRI BN1 ...... 168 C1
  RBTBR TN32 ...... 85 C3
Mill Rd BRI BN1 ...... 145 J4
  BURH RH15 ...... 97 H2
  EAST BN21 ...... 206 D1
  HAIL BN27 ...... 155 J7
  HTHF TN21 ...... 79 M7
  LEW BN7 ...... 3 J2
  LYDD TN29 ...... 95 K8
  PTSD BN41 ...... 167 H7
  RING/NEW BN8 ...... 150 D1
  RYE TN31 ...... 91 J7
  WSEA TN36 ...... 116 E6
Millstream Cl RRTW TN3 ...... 17 K4
Millstream Gdns POLE BN26 ...... 195 M2
Mill Stream Meadow
  HWH RH16 ...... 48 D7
Mill St BRI BN1 ...... 147 J7
Mill Vw RING/NEW BN8 ...... 150 C2
Mill View Rd BEXW TN39 ...... 160 B7
Millward Rd PEV BN24 ...... 198 C3
Mill Wy EGRIN RH19 ...... 13 L7
  POLE BN26 ...... 195 L4
Mill Wd BURH RH15 ...... 97 H3
Millwood EGRIN RH19 ...... 22 E1
Millwood Cl UCK TN22 ...... 76 D2
Millwood La UCK TN22 ...... 76 C2
Millwood Rd BEXW TN39 ...... 160 A4
Millyard Crs ROTT BN2 ...... 170 D7
Milner Rd ROTT BN2 ...... 169 J5
Milnthorpe Rd
  EDN/EASTW BN20 ...... 206 E6
  HOVE BN3 ...... 167 L6
Milton Crs EAST BN21 ...... 206 C2
  EGRIN RH19 ...... 13 L5
Milton Dr STHW BN42 ...... 166 F6
Milton Rd EAST BN21 ...... 206 C2
  HWH RH16 ...... 71 K1
  ROTT BN2 ...... 7 H3
Milton St EAST BN21 ...... 179 G8
Milward Crs HAS TN34 ...... 5 J5
Milward Rd HAS TN34 ...... 5 J5
Mimosa Cl POLE BN26 ...... 178 A7
Mimram Rd PEV BN24 ...... 197 G1
Mindleheim Av EGRIN RH19 ...... 14 B4
The Minnels HPPT/KEY BN6 ...... 122 F3
Minsted Sq BEXW TN39 ...... 182 C4
Minster Cl POLE BN26 ...... 178 A7
The Mint RYE TN31 ...... 117 H1
Mistley Cl BEX TN40 ...... 161 G8
Mistley Cl BEX TN40 ...... 161 G8
Mitchelldean PEAHV BN10 ...... 190 B5

Mitten Rd BEX TN40 ...... 183 J2
Moat Croft Rd EAST BN21 ...... 10 A5
Moat Farm RTWE/PEM TN2 ...... 20 A7
Moat La BAT TN33 ...... 139 H4
  HTHF TN21 ...... 104 D5
Moat Rd EGRIN RH19 ...... 13 L5
Mocatta Wy BURH RH15 ...... 96 D1
Modena Rd HOVE BN3 ...... 167 M7
Molesworth St HOVE BN3 ...... 167 M6
Molyneux Park Rd
  SBGH/RUST TN4 ...... 19 M4
Monarch Gdns LGNY BN23 ...... 197 L6
  SEAF BN25 ...... 203 G1
Monarchs Wy HOVE BN3 ...... 168 C7
  PTSD BN41 ...... 144 D8
  STHW BN42 ...... 166 E3
Mona Rd LW/ROSE BN22 ...... 11 G1
Monceux Rd
  EDN/EASTW BN20 ...... 206 C2
  HAIL BN27 ...... 133 L8
Monckton Wy LEW BN7 ...... 171 L1
Monger's Md RING/NEW BN8 ...... 126 C2
Monk Cl BRI BN1 ...... 146 E8
Monks La WADH TN5 ...... 32 B7
Monks' Wk HWH RH16 ...... 116 E8
Monks Wy LEW BN7 ...... 2 E1
  RYE TN31 ...... 91 J5
Monmouth St HOVE BN3 ...... 168 B7
Monson Rd RTW TN1 ...... 20 B2
Monson Wy RTW TN1 ...... 20 B2
Montacute Gdns
  RTWE/PEM TN2 ...... 19 M4
Montacute Rd LEW BN7 ...... 2 A8
  RTWE/PEM TN2 ...... 20 A5
Montacute Wy UCK TN22 ...... 76 D1
Montague Cl SHOR BN43 ...... 166 D7
Montague Pl ROTT BN2 ...... 7 J8
Montague St ROTT BN2 ...... 7 J8
Montague Wy PEV BN24 ...... 197 M5
Montargis Wy CROW TN6 ...... 39 M5
Montefiore Rd HOVE BN3 ...... 6 A3
Monteith Cl RRTW TN3 ...... 19 G3
Monterey Gdns BEXW TN39 ...... 182 D3
Montes Hl HWH RH16 ...... 49 M6
Monteswood La RHWH RH17 ...... 50 B6
Montford Cl SHOR BN43 ...... 166 D6
Montfort Rd PEV BN24 ...... 179 M8
Montfort Pl PEV BN24 ...... 179 M8
Montgomery Rd RHAS TN35 ...... 163 K1
Montgomery St HOVE BN3 ...... 167 M7
Montpelier Crs BRI BN1 ...... 6 B4
Montpelier Pl BRI BN1 ...... 6 A5
Montpelier Rd BRI BN1 ...... 6 A6
Montpelier St BRI BN1 ...... 6 B5
Montpelier Ter BRI BN1 ...... 6 B5
Montpelier Vls BRI BN1 ...... 6 B5
Montreal Rd ROTT BN2 ...... 7 H5
Monument Vw ROTT BN2 ...... 7 M5
Moons Hl BAT TN33 ...... 136 B8
Moore's La RYE TN31 ...... 88 E7
Moor Hall Dr BAT TN33 ...... 135 M8
Moor Hl HAWK TN18 ...... 47 M6
The Moorings EGRIN RH19 ...... 13 G3
  SHOR BN43 ...... 166 C4
Moor La RHAS TN35 ...... 139 L3
  RING/NEW BN8 ...... 151 G3
Moor Pl EGRIN RH19 ...... 13 K4
Moor Rd RHAS TN35 ...... 139 L2
The Moor HAWK TN18 ...... 47 M6
Morecambe Rd BRI BN1 ...... 146 A8
Morestead PEAHV BN10 ...... 190 D5
Morgan Cl BEXW TN39 ...... 160 B6
Morgay Wood La RHAS TN35 ...... 140 E4
Morlais Pl WSEA TN36 ...... 117 H8
Morlais Rdg WSEA TN36 ...... 117 H8
Morland Dr RRTW TN3 ...... 19 J5
Morlands Cl BAT TN33 ...... 159 H1
Morley Cl LEW BN7 ...... 2 D9
Morley St ROTT BN2 ...... 6 F5
Morningside Cl SEAF BN25 ...... 203 H2
Mornington Crs BEXW TN39 ...... 167 K7
Morris Rd LEW BN7 ...... 3 J6
Mortain Rd PEV BN24 ...... 179 M8
Mortimer Gdns POLE BN26 ...... 195 M2
Mortimer Rd HOVE BN3 ...... 167 M6
  LW/ROSE BN22 ...... 197 G8
Morton Rd EGRIN RH19 ...... 13 L7
Moscow Rd RHAS TN35 ...... 163 J3
Motcombe La EAST BN21 ...... 206 D2
Motcombe Rd EAST BN21 ...... 206 D2
Motte Fld HRTF TN7 ...... 26 E2
Mottins Hl CROW TN6 ...... 40 D6
Moulsecoomb Wy ROTT BN2 ...... 169 L3
Mountain Ash Cl HAIL BN27 ...... 155 C6
Mountbatten Cl RHAS TN35 ...... 163 K1
Mountbatten Dr LGNY BN23 ...... 197 L7
Mount Caburn Crs
  PEAHV BN10 ...... 190 C4
Mount Cl NEWHV BN9 ...... 9 L1
Mount Dr ROTT BN2 ...... 189 K4
Mount Edgcumbe Rd
  SBGH/RUST TN4 ...... 20 A5
Mount Ephraim RTW TN1 ...... 20 A2
Mount Ephraim Rd RTW TN1 ...... 20 A2
Mountfield Gdns
  RTWE/PEM TN2 ...... 20 B3
Mountfield La RBTBR TN32 ...... 84 B7
Mountfield Rd LEW BN7 ...... 3 G8
  RTWE/PEM TN2 ...... 20 B3
Mountfields BRI BN1 ...... 169 J4
Mount Idol Vw BEXW TN39 ...... 159 M6
Mount Joy BAT TN33 ...... 137 K1
Mount La CRAWE TN40 ...... 22 A2
Mountney Dr PEV BN24 ...... 180 F8
Mountney Rd EAST BN21 ...... 206 C2
Mount Noddy RHWH RH17 ...... 70 C3
Mount Pl EGRIN RH19 ...... 2 F6
Mount Pleasant CROW TN6 ...... 40 C7
  ROTT BN2 ...... 7 H7
  UCK TN22 ...... 78 A8
  WADH TN5 ...... 43 L1
Mount Pleasant Av
  RTWE/PEM TN2 ...... 20 B3
Mount Pleasant Rd HAS TN34 ...... 5 J4
  RTW TN1 ...... 20 A3
Mountreed MAYF TN20 ...... 56 B7
Mount Rd EDN/EASTW BN20 ...... 206 F6
  NEWHV BN9 ...... 9 L1

RHAS TN35 ...... 163 J4
Mount Sion RTW TN1 ...... 20 A4
Mount St BAT TN33 ...... 137 K1
  LEW BN7 ...... 2 F8
The Mount HAIL BN27 ...... 155 J8
  UCK TN22 ...... 76 C6
Mount View Ter HAIL BN27 ...... 155 J8
Mount Zion Pl BRI BN1 ...... 6 D5
Moy Av LW/ROSE BN22 ...... 11 G2
Moyne Cl ROTT BN2 ...... 167 L5
Muirfield Ri STLEO TN38 ...... 161 M7
Mulberry La BEXW TN39 ...... 182 C2
  BRI BN1 ...... 168 F5
  LW/ROSE BN22 ...... 196 E3
  SHOR BN43 ...... 166 D5
Mulberry Wk SLVH TN37 ...... 162 D1
Mulberry Wy HTHF TN21 ...... 106 B1
Munnion Rd RHWH RH17 ...... 34 B7
Munster Dr BURH RH15 ...... 97 H2
Munster Gn RING/NEW BN8 ...... 126 E2
Murray Av NEWHV BN9 ...... 8 E3
Musgrave Av EGRIN RH19 ...... 13 L7
Mushroom Fld LEW BN7 ...... 171 L1
Muster Gn North HWH RH16 ...... 71 K2
Muster Gn South HWH RH16 ...... 71 K2
Mutton Hall Hl HTHF TN21 ...... 80 A6
Mutton Hall La HTHF TN21 ...... 80 A6
Myrtle Rd CROW TN6 ...... 39 M5
  LW/ROSE BN22 ...... 197 K8

# N

Namrik Ms HOVE BN3 ...... 168 A8
Nanson Rd BRI BN1 ...... 146 D8
Nan Tucks La UCK TN22 ...... 77 J3
Napier Rd RTWE/PEM TN2 ...... 20 D4
  STLEO TN38 ...... 161 L1
Nash La RHWH RH17 ...... 73 H2
Natal Rd ROTT BN2 ...... 169 K5
Neale Cl EGRIN RH19 ...... 13 H3
Neath Rd LYDD TN29 ...... 119 M5
Neaves La RING/NEW BN8 ...... 151 G2
Neill's Cl NEWHV BN9 ...... 8 F4
Neills Rd RRTW TN3 ...... 32 E4
Nellington Rd RRTW TN3 ...... 19 H2
Nelson Dr LGNY BN23 ...... 197 L8
Nelson Rd HAS TN34 ...... 5 J4
  RTWE/PEM TN2 ...... 20 D4
Nesbitt Rd ROTT BN2 ...... 169 K5
Ness Rd LYDD TN29 ...... 95 J8
Netherfield Av LGNY BN23 ...... 197 M4
Netherfield Gn ROTT BN2 ...... 170 F6
Netherfield Hl BAT TN33 ...... 111 H7
Netherfield Rd BAT TN33 ...... 110 C3
Netherfield Wy BAT TN33 ...... 110 E4
Nether La UCK TN22 ...... 52 C3
Netherwood Cl HAS TN34 ...... 162 E1
Nevill Av HOVE BN3 ...... 167 M5
  LW/ROSE BN22 ...... 196 E5
Nevill Cl HOVE BN3 ...... 168 A4
Nevill Crs LEW BN7 ...... 2 B4
Neville Rd LW/ROSE BN22 ...... 11 G3
Nevill Gdns HOVE BN3 ...... 168 A4
Nevill Ga RTWE/PEM TN2 ...... 20 B5
Nevill Pk SBGH/RUST TN4 ...... 19 L3
Nevill Pl HOVE BN3 ...... 168 A4
Nevill Rdg SBGH/RUST TN4 ...... 19 L3
Nevill Rd CROW TN6 ...... 39 M3
  HOVE BN3 ...... 168 A4
  LEW BN7 ...... 2 C6
  ROTT BN2 ...... 188 F5
  UCK TN22 ...... 76 D5
Nevill St RTWE/PEM TN2 ...... 20 A4
Nevill Ter RTWE/PEM TN2 ...... 19 M4
Nevill Wy HOVE BN3 ...... 168 A4
Newark Pl ROTT BN2 ...... 7 G4
New Barn Cl HAIL BN27 ...... 155 J8
  PTSD BN41 ...... 167 H4
  SHOR BN43 ...... 166 B5
New Barn La UCK TN22 ...... 102 C1
New Barn Rd ROTT BN2 ...... 188 E3
  SHOR BN43 ...... 166 B5
Newbury La RHWH RH17 ...... 70 E1
  WADH TN5 ...... 32 C6
New Church Rd HOVE BN3 ...... 167 K7
Newcomen Rd SBGH/RUST TN4 ...... 20 A1
New Cut RBTBR TN32 ...... 111 J1
  RHAS TN35 ...... 139 L2
New Dorset St BRI BN1 ...... 6 D5
Newells Cl ROTT BN2 ...... 170 E5
New England La BAT TN33 ...... 138 E1
New England Ri PTSD BN41 ...... 167 G2
New England Rd BRI BN1 ...... 6 D2
  HWH RH16 ...... 71 L2
New England St BRI BN1 ...... 6 E2
Newfield La NEWHV BN9 ...... 8 E3
Newfield Rd NEWHV BN9 ...... 8 D5
Newgate Rd SLVH TN37 ...... 4 A4
Newhaven Rd SEAF BN25 ...... 202 A1
Newhaven St ROTT BN2 ...... 7 G4
Newick Cl EAST BN21 ...... 205 J4
Newick Dr RING/NEW BN8 ...... 74 D4
Newick Hl RING/NEW BN8 ...... 74 D4
Newick La MAYF TN20 ...... 57 G6
Newick Rd BRI BN1 ...... 169 L2
  EDN/EASTW BN20 ...... 196 C8
Newlands Av BEXW TN39 ...... 183 G1
Newlands Cl HAS TN34 ...... 162 E1
  HPPT/KEY BN6 ...... 123 G3
Newlands Crs EGRIN RH19 ...... 13 K4
Newlands Rd ROTT BN2 ...... 189 G5
New La LYDD TN29 ...... 95 J8
New Lydd Rd RYE TN31 ...... 118 D3
Newmans Wy RHAS TN35 ...... 163 K2
Newmarket Rd ROTT BN2 ...... 169 J6
New Moorsite RHAS TN35 ...... 139 M3
Newnham Rd HTHF TN21 ...... 80 A7
Newnham Wy HTHF TN21 ...... 80 A7
New Park Av BEX TN40 ...... 183 J2
New Pl EAST BN21 ...... 206 D3
  UCK TN22 ...... 102 C1
New Pond Hl HTHF TN21 ...... 79 K8

  HWH RH16 ...... 72 A2
  PEV BN24 ...... 198 A2
  POLE BN26 ...... 193 L3
  PTSD BN41 ...... 167 G4
  RING/NEW BN8 ...... 127 K8
  STLEO TN38 ...... 4 A4
North Rw UCK TN22 ...... 76 C6
North Salts RYE TN31 ...... 91 J3
North St BRI BN1 ...... 6 D6
  CRAWE RH10 ...... 22 A2
  CROW TN6 ...... 41 H6
  EAST BN21 ...... 10 F6
  HAIL BN27 ...... 131 M8
  HAIL BN27 ...... 154 F2
  HAIL BN27 ...... 155 H6
  HTHF TN21 ...... 104 F1
  HTHF TN21 ...... 107 K1
  LEW BN7 ...... 3 G5
  MAYF TN20 ...... 57 H3
  POLE BN26 ...... 194 A3
  PTSD BN41 ...... 167 H7
  RTWE/PEM TN2 ...... 20 C3
  STLEO TN38 ...... 4 A4
  WSEA TN36 ...... 116 E6
North Ter HAS TN34 ...... 5 M2
North Trade Rd BAT TN33 ...... 136 F2
Northway BURH RH15 ...... 97 J2
North Wy LEW BN7 ...... 2 A4
  NEWHV BN9 ...... 9 G3
  SEAF BN25 ...... 192 F8
  SEAF BN25 ...... 202 F1
Northwood Av ROTT BN2 ...... 189 L6
Norton Cl HOVE BN3 ...... 168 B8
Norton Dr ROTT BN2 ...... 170 D5
Norton Rd HOVE BN3 ...... 168 B8
  NEWHV BN9 ...... 9 J4
Norton Ter NEWHV BN9 ...... 9 J4
Norway Rd LW/ROSE BN22 ...... 197 K8
Norway St PTSD BN41 ...... 167 J7
Norwich Cl ROTT BN2 ...... 170 A4
Norwich Dr ROTT BN2 ...... 170 A4
Nottidge Rd SBGH/RUST TN4 ...... 19 K5
Novington La LEW BN7 ...... 125 G3
Nunnery Stable LEW BN7 ...... 2 D6
Nursery Cl HAIL BN27 ...... 155 J6
  HWH RH16 ...... 71 K1
  POLE BN26 ...... 178 B8
  PTSD BN41 ...... 166 E2
  SHOR BN43 ...... 166 B6
  WADH TN5 ...... 46 B3
Nursery Fld UCK TN22 ...... 77 M2
Nursery La HAIL BN27 ...... 157 H1
  UCK TN22 ...... 52 C2
  UCK TN22 ...... 76 B1
  UCK TN22 ...... 78 E5
  UCK TN22 ...... 102 D2
The Nursery BURH RH15 ...... 97 J2
Nursery Wy HTHF TN21 ...... 79 L7
Nuthatch Rd LGNY BN23 ...... 197 J3
Nuthurst Cl ROTT BN2 ...... 169 M8
Nuthurst Pl ROTT BN2 ...... 187 M1
Nutley Av ROTT BN2 ...... 189 K6
Nutley Cl HOVE BN3 ...... 167 M3
  RYE TN31 ...... 91 G4
Nutley Mill Rd PEV BN24 ...... 197 H1
Nye Cl CROW TN6 ...... 39 M5
Nye La HPPT/KEY BN6 ...... 123 K6
Nye Rd BURH RH15 ...... 97 H3
Nyetimber Hl ROTT BN2 ...... 169 L4

# O

Oakapple Rd STHW BN42 ...... 166 D4
Oak Bank HWH RH16 ...... 48 F7
Oak Cl BRI BN1 ...... 168 E3
Oak Cft EGRIN RH19 ...... 14 A6
Oakdale Av PTSD BN41 ...... 166 E3
Oakdene Cl PTSD BN41 ...... 166 E3
Oakdene Crs PTSD BN41 ...... 166 E3
Oakdene Gdns PTSD BN41 ...... 166 E3
Oakdene Ri PTSD BN41 ...... 166 E3
Oakdene Wy PTSD BN41 ...... 166 E3
Oakenfield BURH RH15 ...... 96 F1
Oakfield Court Rd
  RTWE/PEM TN2 ...... 20 C3
Oakfield Rd RHAS TN35 ...... 163 J3
The Oak Fld RHAS TN35 ...... 141 M5
The Oakfield RYE TN31 ...... 91 H6
Oakfield Wy BEXW TN39 ...... 159 J8
  EGRIN RH19 ...... 13 M3
Oak Hall Pk BURH RH15 ...... 97 H5
Oakhill Cl HAS TN34 ...... 162 E1
Oakhurst Cl HAS TN34 ...... 162 E1
Oakhurst Dr CROW TN6 ...... 40 A3
Oakhurst Gdns EGRIN RH19 ...... 13 L4
Oakhurst La HWH RH16 ...... 48 D7
Oakhurst Rd BAT TN33 ...... 111 L6
Oakland Dr RBTBR TN32 ...... 84 D2
Oaklands PEV BN24 ...... 179 K8
  RHWH RH17 ...... 34 B6
Oaklands Av ROTT BN2 ...... 189 L5
Oaklands Cl POLE BN26 ...... 178 B8
Oaklands Rd HAWK TN18 ...... 47 M5
  HWH RH16 ...... 71 K1
  RRTW TN3 ...... 18 B3
Oaklands Wy HAIL BN27 ...... 155 H5
Oak La LYDD TN29 ...... 95 H8
Oaklea Cl SLVH TN37 ...... 162 C2
Oakleaf Dr POLE BN26 ...... 178 A7
Oaklea Wy UCK TN22 ...... 76 D1
Oakleigh Dr HTHF TN21 ...... 80 B8
Oakleigh Rd BEXW TN39 ...... 182 C2
Oakley Cl EGRIN RH19 ...... 14 B7
Oakmead Rd BURH RH15 ...... 96 F5
Oakmede Wy RING/NEW BN8 ...... 150 C1
Oakroyd Cl BURH RH15 ...... 97 J1
Oaks Cl BUR/ETCH TN19 ...... 61 H5
Oaks Forstal HAWK TN18 ...... 64 C4
The Oaks BURH RH15 ...... 96 C2
  EGRIN RH19 ...... 14 A4
  HTHF TN21 ...... 80 B8
  HWH RH16 ...... 72 A5

HWH RH16 ... 72 A2 ⓵
SLVH TN37 ... 162 D1
Oaktree RING/NEW BN8 ... 126 E2 ⓶
Oak Tree Ct UCK TN22 ... 76 D6
Oak Tree La LGNY BN23 ... 197 J2
Oak Tree Wy HAIL BN27 ... 155 J4
Oakwood Av BEXW TN39 ... 160 B7 ⓵
Oakwood Cl BURH RH15 ... 97 H4
HAS TN34 ... 162 F3
Oakwood Dr UCK TN22 ... 76 E6
Oakwood Rd UCK TN22 ... 52 C1
Oakwood Rd BURH RH15 ... 97 H4
HWH RH16 ... 71 K2
Oasthouse Cl HAS TN34 ... 162 D1 ⓵
Oast House Dr RYE TN31 ... 116 F2
Oast House Fld WSEA TN36 ... 115 M8
Oast House Vw WSEA TN36 ... 141 M1 ⓵
Oathall Av HWH RH16 ... 48 F8
Oathall Rd HWH RH16 ... 71 L1
Oban Rd SLVH TN37 ... 162 B3
Observatory Vw HAIL BN27 ... 155 K8
Ochiltree Cl HAS TN34 ... 163 G2
Ochiltree Rd HAS TN34 ... 163 G2
Ockenden Wy HPPT/KEY BN6 ... 122 E3
Ockley Hl HPPT/KEY BN6 ... 97 H8
Ockley La BURH RH15 ... 97 H7
HPPT/KEY BN6 ... 123 C2
Ockley Vw HPPT/KEY BN6 ... 123 C2
Ocklynge Cl BEXW TN39 ... 182 D1
Ocklynge Rd EAST BN21 ... 206 D2
Ockman La RYE TN31 ... 117 J1 ⓵
Offa Rd RHAS TN35 ... 163 K3
Offham Cl LW/ROSE BN22 ... 196 F2
SEAF BN25 ... 202 F1 ⓵
Offham Rd LEW BN7 ... 2 C3
Okehurst Rd EAST BN21 ... 206 C3
Oldaker Rd RING/NEW BN8 ... 74 A1
Old Barn Cl EDN/EASTW BN20 ... 196 B5
Old Barn Wy STHW BN42 ... 167 G2
Old Boat Wk BRI BN1 ... 146 B7
Old Camp Rd
EDN/EASTW BN20 ... 206 C4
Old Church Rd STEO TN38 ... 162 A2
Old Court Cl BRI BN1 ... 168 F2
Old Dr POLE BN26 ... 177 M8
Old Dro LGNY BN23 ... 197 J3
Olde Place Ms ROTT BN2 ... 188 F5
Old Farm Rd BEXW TN39 ... 160 B8
BRI BN1 ... 168 F1
Oldfield Av EDN/EASTW BN20 ... 196 A3
Oldfield Crs HAIL BN27 ... 155 H5
STHW BN42 ... 166 D7
Oldfield Rd EDN/EASTW BN20 ... 196 A2
Old Forest La CROW TN6 ... 40 E6
Old Forewood La BAT TN33 ... 137 M7
Old Forge La UCK TN22 ... 52 F6
Old Fort Rd SHOR BN43 ... 166 A8
Old Gardens Cl RTWE/PEM TN2 ... 20 B6
Old Ghyll Rd HTHF TN21 ... 106 A1
Old Harrow Rd SLVH TN37 ... 162 B2
Old Heath Cl RING/NEW BN8 ... 103 J8
The Old Hop Gdn RYE TN31 ... 90 C4
Old House Gdns HAS TN34 ... 162 F1
Old House La RRTW TN3 ... 18 D1
Oldlands Av HPPT/KEY BN6 ... 123 C4
Oldlands Hl UCK TN22 ... 53 J4
Old La CROW TN6 ... 39 K3
CROW TN6 ... 40 B3
MAYF TN20 ... 56 F4
Old London Rd BRI BN1 ... 168 E1
HAS TN34 ... 5 M3
RHAS TN35 ... 163 K2 ⓵
Old Lydd Rd RYE TN31 ... 118 E4
Old Malling Wy LEW BN7 ... 2 F1
Old Manor Cl BEX TN40 ... 183 K2
Old Mansion Cl
EDN/EASTW BN20 ... 196 A4
Old Mill Cl BRI BN1 ... 168 E1
HAIL BN27 ... 155 G3 ⓵
Old Mill La POLE BN26 ... 195 L3
Old Mill Pk BEXW TN39 ... 160 A8
Old Motcombe Ms
EAST BN21 ... 206 D2 ⓵
Old Orch HAWK TN18 ... 64 B1
Old Orchard Pl HAIL BN27 ... 155 H7
Old Orchard Rd EAST BN21 ... 10 C7
Old Parish La ROTT BN2 ... 170 D6
Old Park Cl RHWH RH17 ... 48 B1 ⓵
Old Patcham Ms BRI BN1 ... 145 L8
Old Rectory Gdns STHW BN42 ... 166 D5 ⓵
Old River Wy WSEA TN36 ... 117 H1
Old Rd EGRIN RH19 ... 13 M6
HAIL BN27 ... 155 M2
Old Roar Rd SLVH TN37 ... 162 C2
Old Station Cl CRAWE TN10 ... 12 B7
Old Station Rd WADH TN5 ... 31 H1
Old Top Rd RHAS TN35 ... 163 K2
Old Wardsdown WADH TN5 ... 46 B3
Old Wickham La HWH RH16 ... 48 D7
Old Willingdon Rd
EDN/EASTW BN20 ... 205 G5
Old Wish Rd EAST BN21 ... 10 D9
Oliver Cl CROW TN6 ... 40 A5
ROTT BN2 ... 7 K6
Olive Rd HOVE BN3 ... 167 L6
Olives Meadow UCK TN22 ... 76 D7
Onslow Rd HOVE BN3 ... 168 A5
Orchard Av HOVE BN3 ... 168 A5
Orchard Cl HAS TN34 ... 162 D3
HWH RH16 ... 48 D6
RHWH RH17 ... 72 F3 ⓵
STHW BN42 ... 166 F6
Orchard Cnr HWH RH16 ... 72 B1
Orchard Gdns HOVE BN3 ... 168 B5
Orchard La HPPT/KEY BN6 ... 122 F2
HPPT/KEY BN6 ... 123 C1
Orchard Ms NEWHV BN9 ... 191 M4 ⓵
Orchard Ri RRTW TN3 ... 18 B1

Orchard Rd BEX TN40 ... 160 C8
BURH RH15 ... 96 E3
HOVE BN3 ... 168 A5
LEW BN7 ... 3 J3
The Orchard BUR/ETCH TN19 ... 61 J5
HWH RH16 ... 114 B2
UCK TN22 ... 52 C2
Orchard Wy BURH RH15 ... 96 F3 ⓵
EGRIN RH19 ... 13 L5
HWH RH16 ... 48 D6
RYE TN31 ... 90 C5
Orchid Cl LGNY BN23 ... 197 H3
Orchid Pk HWH RH16 ... 72 C3
Orchid Vw BRI BN1 ... 146 C8
Oriental Pl BRI BN1 ... 6 A7
Orion Cl HAIL BN27 ... 155 K6
Ormerod Av STLEO TN38 ... 162 A2
Orpen Rd HOVE BN3 ... 168 D5
Osborn Cl BEXW TN39 ... 182 C5
Osborne Cl HAS TN34 ... 4 F1
Osborne Rd BRI BN1 ... 168 F4
CROW TN6 ... 40 C5 ⓵
EDN/EASTW BN20 ... 206 B2
Osborne Vls HOVE BN3 ... 186 B1
Osmers Hl WADH TN5 ... 31 M7
Osmond Rd HOVE BN3 ... 6 A3
Osprey Dr UCK TN22 ... 102 E1
Otham Court La RING/NEW BN26 ... 178 A6
Otham Rd LW/ROSE BN22 ... 197 G4
Ottenham Cl POLE BN26 ... 178 B8
Oulton Cl LGNY BN23 ... 197 H3
Ousedale Cl LEW BN7 ... 2 D6 ⓵
Outlook Av PEAHV BN10 ... 190 F8
The Outlook EDN/EASTW BN20... 205 G5
Oval Cl PEAHV BN10 ... 190 C4
Overdown Ri PTSD BN41 ... 166 F2
Overhill STHW BN42 ... 166 E5
Overhill Dr BRI BN1 ... 168 E1
Overhill Gdns BRI BN1 ... 168 E1
Overhill Wy BRI BN1 ... 145 L8
Over St BRI BN1 ... 6 E5
Overton Shaw EGRIN RH19 ... 13 L3
Ovingdean Cl ROTT BN2 ... 188 D1
Ovingdean Rd ROTT BN2 ... 188 D1
Owen Cl BURH RH15 ... 96 F5
Oxbottom Cl RING/NEW BN8 ... 74 B8
Oxenbridge La BUR/ETCH TN19 ... 61 H6
Oxendean Gdns
LW/ROSE BN22 ... 196 B2
Oxford Ct BRI BN1 ... 6 F3 ⓵
Oxford Ms HOVE BN3 ... 168 C7
Oxford Pl BRI BN1 ... 6 F3
Oxford Rd LW/ROSE BN22 ... 11 H4
STLEO TN38 ... 162 A3
Oxford St BRI BN1 ... 6 F3 ⓵
Ox Lea RRTW TN3 ... 19 G3
Oyster Creek RYE TN31 ... 117 M3

# P

Packham Wy BURH RH15 ... 96 F2 ⓵
Paddock Cl LYDD TN29 ... 95 H8
RRTW TN3 ... 18 B1
Paddock Gdns EGRIN RH19 ... 13 L7
POLE BN26 ... 195 M2
Paddockhall Rd HWH RH16 ... 71 K1
Paddock La LEW BN7 ... 2 E6
Paddock Rd LEW BN7 ... 2 E6
The Paddocks HAIL BN27 ... 155 G4
LEW BN7 ... 98 E8 ⓵
LEW BN7 ... 172 D6
The Paddock HOVE BN3 ... 168 C5
LW/ROSE BN22 ... 196 F4
RYE TN31 ... 65 H7
UCK TN22 ... 76 A2
Padgham La HTHF TN21 ... 108 C6
Pages Av BEXW TN39 ... 182 F3
Pages Cl HTHF TN21 ... 79 L7
Pages Hl HTHF TN21 ... 79 L7
Pages La BEXW TN39 ... 182 E3
The Pagets RING/NEW BN8 ... 74 D7
Pagham La HTHF TN21 ... 108 C6
Paine Av LYDD TN29 ... 95 J8
Pain's Flat RHWH RH17 ... 70 D6
Palace Pl BRI BN1 ... 6 F7
Palesgate Rd CROW TN6 ... 40 E6
Palliser Cl LGNY BN23 ... 197 L8 ⓵
Palma Cl POLE BN26 ... 178 A7
Palmeira Av HOVE BN3 ... 168 C8
Palmeira Sq HOVE BN3 ... 186 C1
Palmerston Rd NEWHV BN9 ... 191 M5
Pangdean La HPPT/KEY BN6 ... 96 C2
Pangdene Cl BURH RH15 ... 96 E5
Pankhurst Av ROTT BN2 ... 7 K4
Pankhurst Ri BEXW TN39 ... 160 A6
Pannel La RHAS TN35 ... 141 M4
Pannell Cl EGRIN RH19 ... 13 K5
Pannett BURH RH15 ... 96 E2 ⓵
The Pantiles RTWE/PEM TN2 ... 20 A4 ⓶
Paradise Cl EDN/EASTW BN20 ... 206 D4
Paradise Dr EDN/EASTW BN20 ... 206 D5
The Paragon
EDN/EASTW BN20 ... 195 M3
Parham Cl ROTT BN2 ... 7 L6
Park Av BEXW TN39 ... 183 H3
EAST BN21 ... 196 C7
HAS TN34 ... 162 D3
HOVE BN3 ... 167 L7
HPPT/KEY BN6 ... 123 G4
PEAHV BN10 ... 190 A6
SHOR BN43 ... 166 A6
Park Cl BRI BN1 ... 169 L1
BURH RH15 ... 96 F3
EDN/EASTW BN20 ... 206 D3 ⓵
HAIL BN27 ... 155 J3
HAS TN34 ... 162 D3
HOVE BN3 ... 167 L3
RHAS TN35 ... 163 H5
SBGH/RUST TN4 ... 19 L4
Park Crs CROW TN6 ... 39 M3 ⓵
FROW RH18 ... 25 G4
HAS TN34 ... 4 A5
PTSD BN41 ... 167 G6

ROTT BN2 ... 188 F5
Park Crescent Pl ROTT BN2 ... 7 H2 ⓵
Park Crescent Rd ROTT BN2 ... 7 G2
Park Crescent Ter ROTT BN2 ... 7 G2
Park Cft POLE BN26 ... 196 A2
Park Dr HAS TN34 ... 4 D1
Park Drive Cl NEWHV BN9 ... 191 M4
Parker Rd HAS TN34 ... 5 J1
Park Farm Cl BUR/ETCH TN19 ... 61 H6
Parkfield Av LW/ROSE BN22 ... 196 D5
Park Ga HAIL BN27 ... 155 K3
Park Hl ROTT BN2 ... 7 H6
Parkhurst Rd BEXW TN39 ... 183 J5
Parklands SHOR BN43 ... 166 C6
UCK TN22 ... 76 A1
Parklands Rd HPPT/KEY BN6 ... 122 F3
BEXW TN39 ... 160 A8
EAST BN21 ... 196 C6
HWH RH16 ... 49 K4
RBTBR TN32 ... 112 A1
RING/NEW BN8 ... 129 L8
STHW BN42 ... 166 D7
Parkmore Ter BRI BN1 ... 6 D1
Park Ri HOVE BN3 ... 167 L3
Park Rd BEXW TN39 ... 183 H3
BRI BN1 ... 169 L1
BURH RH15 ... 96 F3
CROW TN6 ... 39 M3
EGRIN RH19 ... 13 K5
FROW RH18 ... 25 G4
HAIL BN27 ... 155 H3
HTHF TN21 ... 80 B8
HWH RH16 ... 71 K2
LEW BN7 ... 2 F5
PEAHV BN10 ... 200 F1
ROTT BN2 ... 188 F5
SBGH/RUST TN4 ... 20 B1
SEAF BN25 ... 202 D3
SHOR BN43 ... 166 A6
Park Road Ter ROTT BN2 ... 7 H6
Park Shaw BAT TN33 ... 112 E5
Parkside EGRIN RH19 ... 13 J5
HPPT/KEY BN6 ... 123 C3
HTHF TN21 ... 80 B8
SHOR BN43 ... 166 A5
Parkside Rd SEAF BN25 ... 202 F2
The Parks PTSD BN41 ... 167 H3 ⓵
Parkstone Rd HAS TN34 ... 162 D2
Park St BRI BN1 ... 147 J8
LYDD TN29 ... 95 H8
ROTT BN2 ... 7 H7
RTWE/PEM TN2 ... 20 C3 ⓵
The Park CROW TN6 ... 39 M4
ROTT BN2 ... 189 C5
Park Vw HAS TN34 ... 162 D3
HWH RH16 ... 48 E8
RYE TN31 ... 65 G8
RYE TN31 ... 90 B4
UCK TN22 ... 77 J2
Park View Cl PEAHV BN10 ... 190 A5 ⓵
Park View Ri PEAHV BN10 ... 190 A6 ⓵
Park View Rd HOVE BN3 ... 168 B5
Parkview Rd UCK TN22 ... 76 D5
Parkway EDN/EASTW BN20 ... 196 B6
Park Wy HAS TN34 ... 162 D3
STHW BN42 ... 166 F6
Park Way Cl STHW BN42 ... 166 F6
Parkwood Rd HAS TN34 ... 91 H2
Park Wood Rd HAS TN34 ... 139 M8
Parrock La HRTF TN7 ... 25 K4
Parry Cl LGNY BN23 ... 197 J3
Parsonage Cl SBGH/RUST TN4 ... 19 H1 ⓵
Parsonage La RHAS TN35 ... 139 J2
WSEA TN36 ... 115 M8
Parsonage Rd EAST BN21 ... 206 D2
SBGH/RUST TN4 ... 19 H1
Parsons Cl STLEO TN38 ... 161 M2
Partridges La WADH TN5 ... 42 E1
Pashley Rd EDN/EASTW BN20 ... 206 B4
Paston Pl ROTT BN2 ... 7 L9
Pasture Hill Rd HWH RH16 ... 48 D8
Patcham By-pass BRI BN1 ... 145 L8
BRI BN1 ... 168 E1
Patcham Gra BRI BN1 ... 168 E1
Patcham Mill Rd PEV BN24 ... 197 H1
Patchdean BRI BN1 ... 168 F1
Paton Rd BEXW TN39 ... 159 M6
Paul Cl HAIL BN27 ... 155 G3
Pavilion Buildings BRI BN1 ... 6 E7
Pavilion Cl HPPT/KEY BN6 ... 122 C1
Pavilion Pde ROTT BN2 ... 6 F6
Pavilion St ROTT BN2 ... 6 F7 ⓵
Pavilion Wy EGRIN RH19 ... 13 L6
Paxhill Cl STLEO TN38 ... 161 L2
Paygate Rd BAT TN33 ... 112 E7
Payne Av HOVE BN3 ... 167 M6
Paynesbridge Wy HTHF TN21 ... 105 M7
Paynters Wy RING/NEW BN8 ... 74 C7
Payton Rd SLVH TN37 ... 162 B3
Paythorne Cl STHW BN42 ... 166 D5 ⓵
Payton Dr BURH RH15 ... 96 F4
Peace Cl BRI BN1 ... 169 J5
Peacock La BRI BN1 ... 168 E2
Peakdean Cl
EDN/EASTW BN20 ... 205 H4
Peakdean La
EDN/EASTW BN20 ... 205 H4
Pearse Pl RRTW TN3 ... 33 G1
Peartree Cl BURH RH15 ... 96 E3
Peartree Fld WSEA TN36 ... 115 M8 ⓵
Peartree Hl WADH TN5 ... 59 K3
Peartree La BEXW TN39 ... 182 D1
Pebble Rd PEV BN24 ... 198 E1
Pebsham Dr BEX TN40 ... 161 G8
Pebsham La BEX TN40 ... 160 F8
Peckham Cl LEW BN7 ... 2 F2 ⓵
Peelings La PEV BN24 ... 179 H8
Peel Rd ROTT BN2 ... 187 M2
Pegasus Wy EGRIN RH19 ... 14 A3
Pegler Av NEWHV BN9 ... 8 C5
Pegwell Cl HAS TN34 ... 4 E2
Pelham Cl PEAHV BN10 ... 190 D5 ⓵
PEV BN24 ... 197 M1
Pelham Crs HAIL BN27 ... 155 J8
HAS TN34 ... 5 H7
Pelham Pl HAS TN34 ... 5 J7
Pelham Ri PEAHV BN10 ... 190 C5

Pelham Rd HWH RH16 ... 49 G8
SEAF BN25 ... 202 E4
Pelham Sq BRI BN1 ... 6 F4 ⓵
Pelham St BRI BN1 ... 6 F4
HAS TN34 ... 5 H7
Pelham Ter LEW BN7 ... 2 F5
Pelham Yd SEAF BN25 ... 202 E4 ⓵
Pellbrook Rd LEW BN7 ... 2 B2
Pell Cl WADH TN5 ... 32 A8
Pellings Farm Cl CROW TN6 ... 40 B4
Pellings Ri CROW TN6 ... 40 B3
Pelwood Rd RYE TN31 ... 119 G4
Pembroke Av HOVE BN3 ... 168 A8
Pembroke Cl HAIL BN27 ... 155 J3 ⓵
Pembroke Crs HOVE BN3 ... 168 A7
Pembroke Gdns HOVE BN3 ... 168 A8
Pembury Cl HWH RH16 ... 72 B3
Pembury Gv BEXW TN39 ... 160 A7
Pembury La LGNY BN23 ... 197 K5
RTWE/PEM TN2 ... 20 C2
Pendean BURH RH15 ... 97 J5 ⓵
Penhale Rd LW/ROSE BN22 ... 11 L2
Penhurst Dr BEX TN40 ... 160 F8
Penhurst La RHAS TN35 ... 135 L1
Penhurst Pl ROTT BN2 ... 169 M8 ⓵
Penland Cl HWH RH16 ... 48 D7
Penland Rd BEX TN40 ... 183 L1
HWH RH16 ... 48 D8
Penn Crs HWH RH16 ... 72 A1
RING/NEW BN8 ... 150 D1
Pennine Ri HAS TN34 ... 163 H2
Pennine Wy LGNY BN23 ... 197 K2
Pennybridge La MAYF TN20 ... 57 K1
Penny La BEX TN40 ... 184 A1
Penrith Wy LGNY BN23 ... 197 J2
Pensford Dr LGNY BN23 ... 197 K4
Pentland Cl LGNY BN23 ... 197 K3 ⓵
SLVH TN37 ... 162 C1 ⓵
Peppercombe Rd
EDN/EASTW BN20 ... 206 B2
Pepper Dr BURH RH15 ... 96 F5 ⓵
BURH RH15 ... 96 E4 ⓵
Percival Crs LW/ROSE BN22 ... 196 F3
Percival Rd LW/ROSE BN22 ... 196 F3
Percival Ter ROTT BN2 ... 7 M9
Percy Rd RHAS TN35 ... 163 J3
Perry Av EGRIN RH19 ... 13 L3
Perryfields BURH RH15 ... 96 E2
Perry Hl ROTT BN2 ... 189 J4
Perryman's La RHWH RH17 ... 51 K3
Perrymount Rd HWH RH16 ... 71 L1
Perth Cl SEAF BN25 ... 203 J3
Perth Cl SLVH TN37 ... 162 B3
Peter James Cl RYE TN31 ... 118 E4 ⓵
Peter James La RHAS TN35 ... 141 J7
Petlands Gdns HWH RH16 ... 71 M3
Petlands Rd HWH RH16 ... 71 L3
Pett Cl ROTT BN2 ... 169 M8 ⓵
Pett La WSEA TN36 ... 142 B2
Pett Level Rd RHAS TN35 ... 141 M8
WSEA TN36 ... 143 G3
Pett Rd RHAS TN35 ... 141 G7
Petworth Dr BURH RH15 ... 97 G2
Petworth Pl LW/ROSE BN22 ... 196 F3
Petworth Rd BRI BN1 ... 146 B8
Pevensey Bay Rd LGNY BN23 ... 197 L6
Pevensey Cl SEAF BN25 ... 203 H2
Pevensey Park Rd PEV BN24 ... 179 M8
Pevensey Rd EAST BN21 ... 11 G6
NEWHV BN9 ... 8 B7
POLE BN26 ... 178 B8
ROTT BN2 ... 7 J1
STLEO TN38 ... 162 B3
The Peverells SEAF BN25 ... 203 J4 ⓵
Peyton Cl LGNY BN23 ... 197 M7
Phoenix Cswy LEW BN7 ... 3 H5
Phoenix Crs STHW BN42 ... 166 D6
Phoenix La EGRIN RH19 ... 14 E8
Phoenix Pl LEW BN7 ... 3 G3
ROTT BN2 ... 7 G4 ⓵
Phoenix Ri ROTT BN2 ... 7 G4
Phoenix Wy STHW BN42 ... 166 D6
Phyllis Av PEAHV BN10 ... 190 A6
Picardy Cl BAT TN33 ... 137 L2
Piccadilly La MAYF TN20 ... 57 K5
Pickers Gn HWH RH16 ... 49 G6
Picketts La UCK TN22 ... 52 D7
Pickforde La WADH TN5 ... 45 L5
Picton St ROTT BN2 ... 7 J2
Piddinghoe Av PEAHV BN10 ... 190 D8
Piddinghoe Cl PEAHV BN10 ... 190 D7
Pilmer Rd CROW TN6 ... 39 M2
Pilot Rd HAS TN34 ... 163 G2
Piltdown Cl BEXW TN39 ... 183 H2
HAS TN34 ... 4 F3
Piltdown Ri UCK TN22 ... 76 D6
Piltdown Rd ROTT BN2 ... 169 M8
Piltdown Wy LW/ROSE BN22 ... 197 G2
Pinders Rd RHAS TN35 ... 163 K4
Pine Av HAS TN34 ... 163 H5
Pine Gv CROW TN6 ... 39 L4
EGRIN RH19 ... 13 H3
Pineham Copse HWH RH16 ... 71 M2
Pinehurst BURH RH15 ... 97 G5
The Pines HWH RH16 ... 72 B2
Pine Tree Cl HPPT/KEY BN6 ... 122 B1
Pine Tree Rd HTHF TN21 ... 106 A1
Pine Wk UCK TN22 ... 76 D6
Pine Wy HAIL BN27 ... 155 C7
Pine Way Cl EGRIN RH19 ... 13 L7
Pinewood Cha CROW TN6 ... 39 K3
Pinewood Cl LW/ROSE BN22 ... 196 D4
SEAF BN25 ... 202 F2 ⓵
Pinewood
RTWE/PEM TN2 ... 20 D1 ⓵
Pinewoods BEXW TN39 ... 182 E2
Pinewood Wy HWH RH16 ... 71 K4 ⓵
STLEO TN38 ... 161 L3
Pinfold Cl ROTT BN2 ... 170 D8
Pinton Hl WADH TN5 ... 45 H3
Pinwell Rd LEW BN7 ... 3 G3
Pipers Cl BEX TN40 ... 183 J1 ⓵
HOVE BN3 ... 167 J3
WADH TN5 ... 44 A3
Pipers Fld UCK TN22 ... 102 D2
Piper's Ga UCK TN22 ... 102 D3
Pipit Meadow UCK TN22 ... 102 D1
Pitreavie Dr HAIL BN27 ... 155 G6

Pit Rd HPPT/KEY BN6 ... 122 A1
Pitt Dr SEAF BN25 ... 203 G1
Pitt Gdns ROTT BN2 ... 170 D6
Place La SEAF BN25 ... 202 E3
Plainfields Av BRI BN1 ... 146 A7
The Plat RYE TN31 ... 65 H8
The Platt HWH RH16 ... 72 B1
Plaw Hatch La EGRIN RH19 ... 35 L1
Playden Cl BRI BN1 ... 187 L2
Playden Gdns HAS TN34 ... 163 H2
Playden La RYE TN31 ... 91 H3
Pleasant View Rd CROW TN6 ... 39 L2
Plemont Gdns BEXW TN39 ... 160 A8
Pleyden Ri BEXW TN39 ... 181 M2
Plough La SLVH TN37 ... 162 B1
Plover Cl LGNY BN23 ... 197 J4
Plover Ct STLEO TN38 ... 161 L3
Plummerden La HWH RH16 ... 49 L4
Plumpton Bostall LEW BN7 ... 124 D8
Plumpton Cl BEX TN40 ... 160 C8
LW/ROSE BN22 ... 197 G2
Plumpton La LEW BN7 ... 124 E6
Plumpton Rd ROTT BN2 ... 7 L4
Plymouth Av ROTT BN2 ... 169 M5
Plymouth Cl LGNY BN23 ... 197 M6 ⓵
Plymmon Rd HAS TN34 ... 5 J3
Pocock's Rd EAST BN21 ... 206 D1
Polegate By-pass POLE BN26 ... 177 M7
Polesden Rd RTWE/PEM TN2 ... 20 D4 ⓵
Pollington Pl CROW TN6 ... 39 M4 ⓵
Pomper La HPPT/KEY BN6 ... 96 A5
Pond Cl RYE TN31 ... 114 B1
Pondcroft Rd HWH RH16 ... 49 H7
Ponswood Rd STLEO TN38 ... 162 B4 ⓵
Pont Cl HTHF TN21 ... 81 J8
Pook Reed La HTHF TN21 ... 79 L8
Pool Va BRI BN1 ... 6 E8
Poona Rd RTWE/PEM TN2 ... 20 B4
Poplar Av HOVE BN3 ... 167 L3
Poplar Cl BRI BN1 ... 168 F4
HOVE BN3 ... 167 L3
Poplar La LYDD TN29 ... 95 K7
Poplar Rd TENT TN30 ... 67 K2
The Poplars HPPT/KEY BN6 ... 123 G3 ⓵
Poppinghole La RBTBR TN32 ... 85 K5
Popps La BEXW TN39 ... 182 C3
Porters Wy POLE BN26 ... 178 A8
Portfield Av BRI BN1 ... 146 A8
Portfield Cl BEX TN40 ... 183 K1
Port Hall Av BRI BN1 ... 168 E6 ⓵
Port Hall Ms BRI BN1 ... 6 A1
Port Hall Pl BRI BN1 ... 168 E6
Port Hall Rd BRI BN1 ... 6 B1
Port Hall St BRI BN1 ... 168 E6
Portland Av HOVE BN3 ... 167 L7
Portland Cl HAIL BN27 ... 155 G5
Portland Pl HAS TN34 ... 5 K9
ROTT BN2 ... 7 K9
Portland Rd BURH RH15 ... 96 F3 ⓵
EGRIN RH19 ... 13 L6
HOVE BN3 ... 6 A5
The Portlands LGNY BN23 ... 197 M7
Portland St BRI BN1 ... 6 D6
Portland Vls HOVE BN3 ... 167 K5
Port Rd LW/ROSE BN22 ... 197 G5
Portsdown Wy
EDN/EASTW BN20 ... 196 B4
Portsmouth La HWH RH16 ... 48 F7
Portsmouth Wd HWH RH16 ... 48 F6 ⓵
Portsmouth Wood Cl
HWH RH16 ... 48 F6
Port Vw NEWHV BN9 ... 191 L4
Possingworth Cl HTHF TN21 ... 78 F6
Post Horn La FROW RH18 ... 25 C5
Post Office Rd HAWK TN18 ... 47 M4 ⓶
Potato La RING/NEW BN8 ... 150 L1
Potman's La BEXW TN39 ... 159 L4
Pottens Mill La MAYF TN20 ... 80 F2
The Potteries UCK TN22 ... 102 D2
Potters Fld RING/NEW BN8 ... 127 K8
Potters La BURH RH15 ... 96 F5
Pottery Cl RYE TN31 ... 113 M4
Pottery La RYE TN31 ... 113 M4
Pottingfield Rd RYE TN31 ... 91 G8
Pound Cl LGNY BN23 ... 197 M8 ⓵
Poundfield Rd CROW TN6 ... 40 B4
HAWK TN18 ... 64 B1
Pound La RING/NEW BN8 ... 129 J7
UCK TN22 ... 77 K8
The Pound BURH RH15 ... 96 F2
Poveys Cl BURH RH15 ... 96 D3
Powdermill La BAT TN33 ... 136 E6
RYE TN31 ... 113 K3
Powell Gdns NEWHV BN9 ... 191 L5 ⓵
Powell Rd RING/NEW BN8 ... 74 A1
Powis Gv BRI BN1 ... 6 B5
Powis Rd BRI BN1 ... 6 B5
Powis Sq BRI BN1 ... 6 B4
Powis Vls BRI BN1 ... 6 C5 ⓵
Poynings Cl SEAF BN25 ... 203 J4 ⓵
Poynings Dr HOVE BN3 ... 167 M3
Poynter Rd HOVE BN3 ... 168 A6
Pratt's Folly La CROW TN6 ... 39 L5 ⓵
Precincts Castle LEW BN7 ... 2 F6
Preemans La UCK TN22 ... 53 L4
Preston Dro BRI BN1 ... 168 F4
Preston Gv UCK TN22 ... 77 H8
Preston Park Av BRI BN1 ... 168 F5
Preston Rd BEXW TN39 ... 160 B7
BRI BN1 ... 168 E5
Preston St BRI BN1 ... 6 A7
Prestonville Rd BRI BN1 ... 6 C3
Price Wy RHWH RH17 ... 34 B7
Prideaux Rd EAST BN21 ... 10 A3
Primrose Cl BURH RH15 ... 96 D2
LGNY BN23 ... 197 H3
Primrose Hl BEXW TN39 ... 159 M8
RHAS TN35 ... 141 K2
Primrose La FROW RH18 ... 25 C5
Prince Albert St BRI BN1 ... 6 E7 ⓵
Prince Charles Cl STHW BN42 ... 166 F5
Prince Charles Rd LEW BN7 ... 3 C2
Prince Edward's Rd LEW BN7 ... 2 C5
Prince Regent's Cl ROTT BN2 ... 187 L2
Princes Av HOVE BN3 ... 168 A8

Princes CI *SEAF* BN25 .............. 202 E2
  *UCK* TN22 .......................... 76 A7
Princes Crs *HOVE* BN3 ............ 168 A8
  *ROTT* BN2 ............................ 7 G1
Prince's PI *BRI* BN1 ................ 6 E7
Princes Rd *LGNY* BN23 .......... 197 L7
  *ROTT* BN2 ........................ 169 H6
  *SLVH* TN37 .......................... 4 C3
Princess Dr *SEAF* BN25 .......... 202 D1
Princes Sq *HOVE* BN3 ............ 168 A8
Prince's St *BRI* BN2 ................ 6 F7
  *RTWE/PEM* TN2 .................. 20 C3
Prince's Ter *ROTT* BN2 .......... 187 L2
Prince William Pde *LGNY* BN23 .. 197 L8
Prinkle La *HAIL* BN27 ............ 134 C5
Prinsep Rd *HOVE* BN3 ............ 168 A6
Priory Av *HAS* TN34 .............. 4 A4
  *PEV* BN24 .......................... 198 D1
Priory Crs *LEW* BN7 .............. 2 F8
Priory Hts *EDN/EASTW* BN20 .. 206 A4
Priory La *LGNY* BN23 ............ 197 L3
Priory Orch *LGNY* BN23 ........ 197 L3
Priory Rd *BURH* RH15 ............ 97 G5
  *FROW* RH18 ........................ 24 A8
  *HAS* TN34 ............................ 5 J6
  *HPPT/KEY* BN6 .................. 122 E1
  *LGNY* BN23 ...................... 197 L3
Priory St *HAS* TN34 .............. 4 F6
  *LEW* BN7 .............................. 2 F8
Priory Wy *HWH* RH16 ............ 71 M2
Promenade *PEAHV* BN10 ........ 190 A8
The Promenade *PEV* BN24 .... 198 D2
Prospect Gdns *EAST* BN21 .... 206 D2
Prospect PI *HAS* TN34 ............ 5 J6
Prospect Rd *HTHF* TN21 ........ 80 B8
  *RTWE/PEM* TN2 .................. 20 B3
Providence PI *BRI* BN1 .......... 6 E5
Prowting Md *BEXW* TN39 ...... 182 C2
Pudding Cake La *UCK* TN22 .... 76 C7
Pulborough Av *LW/ROSE* BN22.. 196 E2
Pulborough CI *ROTT* BN2 ...... 169 M7
Pump La *UCK* TN22 .............. 103 K4
Purbeck CI *LGNY* BN23 .......... 197 J3
Pyecombe St *POY/PYE* BN45 .. 122 A8

## Q

The Quadrant *EAST* BN21 ...... 10 B1
  *HPPT/KEY* BN6 .................. 123 G2
Quakers La *HWH* RH16 .......... 72 A1
Quantock CI *LGNY* BN23 ........ 197 K3
  *RTWE/PEM* TN2 .................. 20 D1
Quantock Gdns *HAS* TN34 .... 163 H3
Quarry Bank Rd *BRI* BN1 ...... 169 H4
Quarry CI *BURH* RH15 ............ 97 K3
Quarry Crs *HAS* TN34 ............ 5 J3
Quarry HI *RHWH* RH17 .......... 48 C7
  *STLEO* TN38 ...................... 162 B7
Quarry La *SEAF* BN25 ............ 203 C1
Quarry Ri *EGRIN* RH19 .......... 14 A3
Quarry Rd *HAS* TN34 ............ 5 H5
  *NEWHV* BN9 ........................ 8 F7
  *RTW* TN1 ............................ 20 B1
Quebec CI *BEXW* TN39 .......... 183 C1
  *LGNY* BN23 ...................... 197 M7
Quebec Rd *STLEO* TN38 ........ 162 A2
Quebec St *ROTT* BN2 ............ 7 H5
Queen Alexandra Av
  *HOVE* BN3 ........................ 168 A3
Queen Anne's CI *LEW* BN7 .... 2 E5
Queen Caroline CI *HOVE* BN3 .. 168 A3
Queen Elizabeth Av *BURH* RH15.. 96 F4
Queen Mary Av *HOVE* BN3 .... 168 A3
Queens Ap *UCK* TN22 ............ 76 D5
Queensbury Ms *BRI* BN1 ........ 6 B7
Queen's Colonnade Gdns
  *LW/ROSE* BN22 .................. 11 H6
Queens Cottages *WADH* TN5 .. 43 L1
Queens Crs *BURH* RH15 .......... 97 G4
  *LGNY* BN23 ...................... 197 K7
Queensdown School Rd
  *BRI* BN1 ............................ 169 J3
Queens Dr *HPPT/KEY* BN6 .... 122 F2
  *UCK* TN22 .......................... 75 M2
Queen's Gdns *BRI* BN1 .......... 6 E5
  *HOVE* BN3 ........................ 186 C1
Queensmount *MAYF* TN20 .... 56 B7
Queens Park Gdns *SEAF* BN25 .. 202 C2
Queen's Park Ri *ROTT* BN2 .... 7 K5
Queen's Park Rd *ROTT* BN2 .... 7 H6
Queen's Park Ter *ROTT* BN2 .... 7 J4
Queen's PI *BRI* BN1 .............. 6 F3
  *HOVE* BN3 ........................ 168 C8
Queen Sq *BRI* BN1 ................ 6 D6
Queen's Rd *BRI* BN1 .............. 6 E4
  *CROW* TN6 ........................ 39 M6
  *EGRIN* RH19 ...................... 13 L6
  *HAIL* BN27 ........................ 156 C1
  *HAS* TN34 ............................ 5 G7
  *HWH* RH16 ........................ 48 E8
  *LEW* BN7 .............................. 3 H2
  *LGNY* BN23 ........................ 197 K7
  *LYDD* TN29 ........................ 95 J8
  *STHW* BN42 ...................... 166 E5
Queen St *HAWK* TN18 .......... 64 C1
Queensway *EGRIN* RH19 ........ 13 L6
  *LYDD* TN29 ........................ 95 J8
  *ROTT* BN2 ............................ 7 L5
  *SEAF* BN25 ........................ 203 G1
  *STLEO* TN38 ...................... 161 L4
Queen Victoria Av *HOVE* BN3 .. 168 A3
Querneby CI *SHOR* BN43 ...... 166 D7
Quickbourne La *RYE* TN31 .... 65 J7
Quinnell Dr *HAIL* BN27 .......... 155 H4
Quintin CI *HAIL* BN27 ............ 178 A1

## R

Radcliffe CI *SLVH* TN37 .......... 162 C3
Radinden Dr *HOVE* BN3 .......... 168 D5
Radinden Manor Rd
  *HOVE* BN3 ........................ 168 D5
Radnor Ms *STLEO* TN38 ........ 161 L4

Ragged Dog La *HTHF* TN21 .... 105 H3
Railway Ap *EGRIN* RH19 ........ 13 K5
  *NEWHV* BN9 ........................ 9 H3
Railway La *LEW* BN7 .............. 3 H6
Railway Rd *NEWHV* BN9 ........ 9 H3
Railway St *BRI* BN1 ................ 6 D4
Raleigh CI *LGNY* BN23 ............ 197 L7
Ramsay Wy *LGNY* BN23 ........ 197 L7
Ramslye Rd *SBGH/RUST* TN4 .. 19 K5
Randolph La *RYE* TN31 .......... 91 J3
Ranelagh Vls *HOVE* BN3 ........ 168 B6
Rangemore Dr *EAST* BN21 .... 196 D7
Ranmore CI *HAS* TN34 .......... 139 L8
Rannoch Rd *CROW* TN6 ........ 39 K4
Rannoch Rd West *CROW* TN6 .. 39 K4
Ranscombe HI *RING/NEW* BN8 .. 150 A8
Ranscombe La *RING/NEW* BN8.. 150 B8
Raphael Rd *HOVE* BN3 .......... 167 M7
Rapson's Rd
  *EDN/EASTW* BN20 .............. 195 M3
Rastrick CI *BURH* RH15 .......... 96 F5
Rattle La *PEV* BN24 .............. 197 K1
Ratton Dr *EDN/EASTW* BN20 .. 196 B7
Ratton Rd *EAST* BN21 ............ 10 A3
Raven CI *BAT* TN33 .............. 137 M2
  *STLEO* TN38 ...................... 161 L3
Ravens CI *BEXW* TN39 .......... 182 C5
Ravens Cft
  *EDN/EASTW* BN20 .............. 206 F6
Ravenswood Dr *ROTT* BN2 .... 170 F8
Ravenswood Rd *BURH* RH15 .. 97 H3
Ravine CI *HAS* TN34 .............. 163 H3
Rayford CI *PEAHV* BN10 ........ 190 C7
Raymond CI *SEAF* BN25 ........ 203 G1
Readers La *RYE* TN31 ............ 90 F1
Reading Rd *ROTT* BN2 .......... 187 M2
Rectory CI *BUR/ETCH* TN19 .... 60 B8
  *EDN/EASTW* BN20 .............. 206 D3
  *NEWHV* BN9 ........................ 8 E5
  *RING/NEW* BN8 .................. 130 A1
  *SHOR* BN43 ...................... 166 D7
  *STLEO* TN38 ...................... 162 B5
Rectory Fld *HRTF* TN7 .......... 26 E2
Rectory La *RYE* TN31 ............ 88 F1
  *RYE* TN31 ............................ 91 H6
  *WSEA* TN36 ...................... 116 E8
  *SHOR* BN43 ...................... 166 C7
Rectory Rd *NEWHV* BN9 ........ 191 L4
  *SHOR* BN43 ...................... 166 C7
Rectory Wy *BEX* TN40 .......... 183 K1
Redbridge La *CROW* TN6 ........ 54 D1
Redbrook La *UCK* TN22 .......... 77 K2
Redcross St *BRI* BN1 .............. 6 F4
Redford CI *BURH* RH15 .......... 97 L5
Redgarth Ct *EGRIN* RH19 ...... 13 H3
Redgeland Ri *STLEO* TN38 .... 161 M4
Redgill La *RING/NEW* BN8 .... 74 B5
Redhill CI *BRI* BN1 ................ 168 C1
Redhill Dr *BRI* BN1 ................ 168 C1
Red Lake Ter *RHAS* TN35 ...... 163 K2
Red Oak *HAWK* TN18 ............ 47 L6
Redoubt Rd *LW/ROSE* BN22 .. 11 J3
Redvers Rd *ROTT* BN2 .......... 169 K5
Redwell Av *BEXW* TN39 ........ 160 B6
Redwood Dr *HWH* RH16 ........ 71 K4
Reedham Rd *LGNY* BN23 ...... 197 H2
Reed Pond Wk *HWH* RH16 .... 72 A2
Reedswood Rd *RYE* TN31 ...... 114 B2
  *STLEO* TN38 ...................... 161 L6
Reeves HI *BRI* BN1 ................ 169 K1
Reeves Ter *WADH* TN5 .......... 45 L5
Regal Dr *EGRIN* RH19 ............ 13 M6
Regency CI *UCK* TN22 ............ 76 C7
Regency Gdns *STLEO* TN38 .... 162 A6
Regency Ms *BRI* BN1 .............. 6 B6
Regency Rd *BRI* BN1 .............. 6 C7
Regency Sq *BRI* BN1 .............. 6 B7
Regent HI *BRI* BN1 ................ 6 C6
Regent PI *STLEO* TN38 .......... 138 F7
Regent Rw *BRI* BN1 .............. 6 C6
Regents CI *SEAF* BN25 .......... 202 E1
Regent St *BRI* BN1 ................ 6 E6
Reginald Rd *BEXW* TN39 ...... 183 H2
Regnum CI *LW/ROSE* BN22 .... 196 E2
Reigate Rd *BRI* BN1 .............. 168 D5
Resting Oak HI *RING/NEW* BN8.. 125 M2
Reynolds Dr *BEX* TN40 .......... 183 L1
Reynolds Rd *HOVE* BN3 ........ 167 M7
  *LGNY* BN23 ...................... 197 K5
Reynoldstown La
  *POLE* BN26 ........................ 177 M8
Riccards La *BAT* TN33 .......... 112 A4
Rices HI *EGRIN* RH19 ............ 13 L5
Richardson Rd *HOVE* BN3 ...... 167 M7
Richborough CI *HAS* TN34 .... 162 D2
Richington Wy *SEAF* BN25 .... 203 H1
Richland CI *RHAS* TN35 ........ 163 K2
Richmead Gdns *MAYF* TN20 .. 57 H4
Richmond CI *BEXW* TN39 ...... 182 F3
Richmond CI *BEXW* TN39 ...... 183 G3
Richmond Gv *BEXW* TN39 .... 183 G4
Richmond Pde *ROTT* BN2 ...... 6 F5
Richmond PI *ROTT* BN2 .......... 6 F5
Richmond Rd *BEXW* TN39 .... 182 F3
  *SEAF* BN25 ........................ 202 D5
Richmond St *HAS* TN34 ........ 163 J4
  *ROTT* BN2 ............................ 7 H5
Richmond Ter *SEAF* BN25 .... 202 E5
Richmond Wy *EGRIN* RH19 .... 13 M6
Riddens CI *LEW* BN7 ............ 124 E1
Riddens La *LEW* BN7 .............. 98 E8
  *LEW* BN7 .......................... 124 E1
Riders Bolt *BEXW* TN39 ........ 182 E1
Ridge Bolt *BRI* BN1 .............. 168 F5
Ridge CI *PTSD* BN41 ............ 167 G2
Ridge Lands CI
  *EDN/EASTW* BN20 .............. 206 C3
Ridge Rd *BRI* BN1 ................ 147 J6
Ridgeside Av *BRI* BN1 .......... 168 E1
The Ridge *HAS* TN34 ............ 163 H2
  *SLVH* TN37 ........................ 139 J8
  *WSEA* TN36 ...................... 143 H1
Ridge Vw *BRI* BN1 ................ 169 L1
Ridgeway *BUR/ETCH* TN19 .... 61 M3
  *EGRIN* RH19 ...................... 13 L7
Ridge Wy *HWH* RH16 ............ 72 B1

Ridgeway *PTSD* BN41 ............ 166 F5
Ridgeway CI *HTHF* TN21 ........ 80 A6
  *STHW* BN42 ...................... 166 F5
Ridgeway Gdns *ROTT* BN2 .... 170 E7
The Ridgeway *BURH* RH15 .... 97 H2
  *EDN/EASTW* BN20 .............. 205 G5
  *HAIL* BN27 ........................ 133 L4
  *SEAF* BN25 ........................ 202 F2
The Ridge West *SLVH* TN37 .. 139 G7
Ridgewood Av *ROTT* BN2 ...... 189 C6
Ridgewood CI *UCK* TN22 ...... 102 D2
Ridgewood Gdns *BEX* TN40 .. 183 M2
  *HAS* TN34 ........................ 162 E1
Ridgway CI *ROTT* BN2 .......... 170 D6
Rigden Rd *HOVE* BN3 ............ 168 C6
Riley Rd *ROTT* BN2 ................ 169 J5
Rill Wk *EGRIN* RH19 .............. 14 B5
Ringmer CI *BRI* BN1 .............. 169 L2
Ringmer Rd *BRI* BN1 ............ 169 M2
  *NEWHV* BN9 ........................ 8 C6
  *SEAF* BN25 ........................ 202 E4
Ringmer Wy *LGNY* BN23 ...... 197 G2
Ringwood CI *LW/ROSE* BN22.. 11 G3
Ringwood Rd *BEXW* TN39 .... 160 C2
  *LW/ROSE* BN22 .................. 10 E1
Ripe La *RING/NEW* BN8 ........ 152 F3
Riseden Rd *WADH* TN5 .......... 43 J6
Rise Park Gdns *LGNY* BN23 .. 197 K4
The Rise *EGRIN* RH19 ............ 13 M6
  *HWH* RH16 ........................ 72 B1
  *PTSD* BN41 ........................ 166 F4
The Rising *LGNY* BN23 .......... 197 L4
Riverdale *LEW* BN7 .............. 2 F3
River La *POLE* BN26 .............. 194 A3
Riverside *FROW* RH18 .......... 24 E3
  *NEWHV* BN9 ........................ 9 H6
  *PTSD* BN41 ...................... 166 E8
  *UCK* TN22 .......................... 78 D5
Riverside Gdns *CROW* TN6 .... 40 C6
River's Rd *HWH* RH16 ............ 48 D3
River Wy *UCK* TN22 .............. 78 D5
Rixons CI *RHWH* RH17 .......... 50 C1
Rixons Orch *RHWH* RH17 ...... 50 C1
Roadean CI *SEAF* BN25 ........ 203 G2
Robert's HI *WSEA* TN36 ........ 116 E7
Robertson Pas *HAS* TN34 ...... 4 F7
Robertson Rd *BRI* BN1 .......... 168 D4
Robertsons HI *HAS* TN34 ...... 5 M2
Robertson St *HAS* TN34 ........ 4 F7
Robertson Ter *HAS* TN34 ...... 5 G7
Robert St *BRI* BN1 ................ 6 E5
Robert Tressell CI *HAS* TN34 .. 4 E4
Robian CI *UCK* TN22 ............ 76 A7
Robin CI *EGRIN* RH19 ............ 13 L4
  *LGNY* BN23 ........................ 197 J4
Robin Davis CI *ROTT* BN2 ...... 169 L6
Robin Dene *ROTT* BN2 .......... 187 L2
Robin HI *BEXW* TN39 .......... 182 D2
Robin Hood La *LYDD* TN29 .... 121 J1
Robin La *LYDD* TN29 .............. 95 J8
Robin Post La *POLE* BN26 ...... 177 H5
Robin Rd *HPPT/KEY* BN6 ........ 96 D4
Robinson Rd *NEWHV* BN9 ...... 8 F7
Roborough CI *LW/ROSE* BN22.. 10 F4
Robsack Av *STLEO* TN38 ...... 161 L4
Rochester CI
  *EDN/EASTW* BN20 .............. 206 C6
Rochester Gdns *HOVE* BN3 .. 168 D8
Rochester Rd *SLVH* TN37 ...... 162 B4
Rochester St *ROTT* BN2 ........ 7 L6
Rochester Wy *CROW* TN6 ...... 40 C5
Rochford Wy *SEAF* BN25 ...... 203 G8
Rochmans Wy *CROW* TN6 .... 40 A6
Rockall Av *LGNY* BN23 .......... 197 M6
Rockall Dr *HAIL* BN27 .......... 155 C4
Rock-a-nore Pde *HAS* TN34 .. 5 M6
  *RHAS* TN35 ...................... 163 J6
Rock-a-nore Rd *HAS* TN34 .... 5 L7
Rock Channel *RYE* TN31 ........ 117 J1
Rock CI *RHAS* TN35 .............. 163 K2
Rock Gv *ROTT* BN2 ................ 7 M9
Rockhurst Dr
  *EDN/EASTW* BN20 .............. 196 B8
Rockington Wy *CROW* TN6 .... 40 B6
Rocklands La *RHAS* TN35 ...... 163 J5
Rocka La *RHAS* TN35 ............ 140 D6
Rockmead Rd *RHAS* TN35 .... 164 F2
Rock PI *ROTT* BN2 .................. 7 H8
Rocks La *UCK* TN22 .............. 53 M7
Rocks Park Rd *UCK* TN22 ...... 76 B7
The Rocks *EGRIN* RH19 .......... 14 C8
Rock St *ROTT* BN2 ................ 187 L2
Rock Villa Rd *RTW* TN1 ........ 20 A2
Rocky La *HWH* RH16 ............ 71 J5
Roderick Av *PEAHV* BN10 .... 190 C5
Roderick Av North
  *PEAHV* BN10 .................... 190 C4
Rodmell Av *ROTT* BN2 .......... 189 K5
Rodmell Rd *RTWE/PEM* TN2 .. 20 A5
  *SEAF* BN25 ........................ 203 H4
Rodmill Dr *EAST* BN21 .......... 206 D1
Rodmill Rd *EAST* BN21 .......... 206 D1
Rodney CI *LGNY* BN23 .......... 197 M7
Rodwell CROW* TN6 ................ 40 C5
Roebuck St *HAS* TN34 ............ 5 L6
Roedale Rd *BRI* BN1 .............. 169 H5
Roedean CI *BEXW* TN39 ........ 183 G1
Roedean Crs *ROTT* BN2 ........ 188 A2
Roedean Hts *ROTT* BN2 ........ 188 A2
Roedean Pth *ROTT* BN2 ........ 188 B3
Roedean Rd *ROTT* BN2 .......... 187 M2
  *RTWE/PEM* TN2 .................. 20 A5
Roedean V *ROTT* BN2 .......... 188 B3
Roffrey Av *LW/ROSE* BN22 .... 196 D5
Rolfe Dr *BURH* RH15 .............. 97 K1
Romaine CI *BURH* RH15 ........ 97 K1
Roman CI *SEAF* BN25 .......... 192 B8
Roman Crs *STHW* BN42 ........ 166 E6

Roman Rd *HOVE* BN3 ............ 167 K8
  *STHW* BN42 ...................... 166 E6
Romans Av *PEV* BN24 .......... 179 L8
Roman Wy *STHW* BN42 ........ 166 E6
  *UCK* TN22 .......................... 76 E7
Romany CI *PTSD* BN41 .......... 167 H6
Romney CI *SEAF* BN25 .......... 203 J3
Romney Rd *LYDD* TN29 ........ 95 L1
  *POLE* BN26 ........................ 178 B8
  *ROTT* BN2 ........................ 189 G5
Romney St *LW/ROSE* BN22 .... 11 K1
Romsey CI *BRI* BN1 .............. 169 H4
Rookery CI *BRI* BN1 .............. 168 E5
  *NEWHV* BN9 ...................... 191 L4
Rookery La *WSEA* TN36 ........ 116 F3
Rookery Wy *HWH* RH16 .......... 71 L5
  *NEWHV* BN9 ...................... 191 M4
  *SEAF* BN25 ........................ 202 B1
Rookhurst Rd *BEX* TN40 ........ 183 M1
Rookley CI *RTWE/PEM* TN2 .... 20 D2
Rookwood CI *UCK* TN22 ........ 76 E6
Rope Wk *HAIL* BN27 ............ 155 H6
  *RYE* TN31 .......................... 91 J8
The Rope Wk *HAWK* TN18 .... 64 B1
Rosebarn CI *BURH* RH15 ........ 97 J5
Rosebery Av *LW/ROSE* BN22 .. 196 E5
  *ROTT* BN2 ........................ 170 C6
Rosedale PI *LW/ROSE* BN22 .. 196 D3
Rosedene CI *ROTT* BN2 ........ 170 E8
Rose HI *ROTT* BN2 ................ 7 G2
  *TENT* TN30 ........................ 68 B1
Rose Hill CI *BRI* BN1 .............. 6 F2
Rose Hill Ter *BRI* BN1 ............ 6 F2
Rosehill Wk *RTW* TN1 ............ 20 A3
Roselands *BEXW* TN39 .......... 159 M8
  *MAYF* TN20 ........................ 56 F5
Roselands CI *LW/ROSE* BN22 .. 11 J1
Roseleigh Gdns *RHWH* RH17 .. 72 F3
  *RHWH* RH17 ...................... 48 B8
Rosemary Av *PEAHV* BN10 .... 190 C6
Rosemary Dr *SHOR* BN43 .... 166 B5
Rosemary La *RHAS* TN35 ...... 141 L3
  *WADH* TN5 ........................ 46 A1
Rosemount CI *SEAF* BN25 .... 192 A8
Rosetti Rd *PEV* BN24 ............ 198 C2
Roseveare Rd
  *LW/ROSE* BN22 .................. 197 J8
Rose Wk *SEAF* BN25 .......... 202 F2
Rose Walk CI *NEWHV* BN9 .... 8 D4
The Rose Wk *NEWHV* BN9 .... 8 E5
Rossdale *RTWE/PEM* TN2 .... 20 C1
Rosslyn Av *SHOR* BN43 ........ 166 A4
Rothbury Rd *HOVE* BN3 ........ 167 K7
Rother Av *POLE* BN26 .......... 196 F5
Rother CI *BUR/ETCH* TN19 .... 60 B8
  *CROW* TN6 ........................ 40 A7
Rotherfield Av *BEX* TN40 ...... 183 K2
  *LW/ROSE* BN22 .................. 197 G2
Rotherfield CI *BRI* BN1 .......... 146 B8
Rotherfield Crs *BRI* BN1 ........ 169 H1
Rotherfield Rd *MAYF* TN20 .... 56 F2
Rotherhill CI *CROW* TN6 ........ 40 C6
Rotherhurst La *CROW* TN6 .... 41 G8
Rothermead *MAYF* TN20 ...... 56 F5
Rother Rd *SEAF* BN25 .......... 203 G4
Rother Vw *BUR/ETCH* TN19 .. 60 B7
Rotherview *RBTBR* TN32 ........ 85 J1
Rothley Cha *HWH* RH16 ........ 71 M2
Rothwell Ct *NEWHV* BN9 ........ 8 B4
Rotunda Rd *LGNY* BN23 ........ 197 K6
The Rotyngs *ROTT* BN2 ........ 188 F4
Rough Brow *SEAF* BN25 ........ 203 G4
Rough Fld *EGRIN* RH19 .......... 13 K2
The Rough *RING/NEW* BN8 .... 74 C7
Roundacres Wy *BEX* TN40 .... 160 E8
The Roundel *SLVH* TN37 ...... 162 D1
Roundhay Av *PEAHV* BN10 .. 190 E8
Roundhill Crs *ROTT* BN2 .......... 7 J1
Round Hill Rd *BRI* BN1 ............ 7 G1
Roundhill Rd *RTWE/PEM* TN2 .. 20 D5
Roundway *BRI* BN1 ................ 169 L1
Roundwood La *HWH* RH16 .... 48 B7
Roundwood Rd *SLVH* TN37 .. 162 B1
Rowan Av *HOVE* BN3 ............ 167 L5
  *LW/ROSE* BN22 .................. 196 D5
Rowan CI *HAS* TN34 .............. 139 K8
  *HTHF* TN21 ...................... 106 A1
  *HWH* RH16 ........................ 72 B2
  *PTSD* BN41 ...................... 166 F5
Rowan Gdns *BEX* TN40 ........ 160 F8
Rowan Tree Rd
  *RTWE/PEM* TN2 .................. 19 L5
Rowan Wy *ROTT* BN2 .......... 188 E3
Rowbarns *BAT* TN33 ............ 111 J8
Rowe Av *PEAHV* BN10 .......... 190 B6
Rowlatt La *EGRIN* RH19 ........ 12 E3
Rowsley Rd *EDN/EASTW* BN20.. 206 D7
Royal Cha *SBGH/RUST* TN4 .. 19 M2
Royal Crs *ROTT* BN2 .............. 7 J8
Royal Crescent Ms *ROTT* BN2 .. 7 J8
Royal Dr *SEAF* BN25 ............ 192 E8
Royal George Pde *SHOR* BN43 .. 166 B5
Royal George Rd *BURH* RH15 .. 96 E3
Royal Military Canal Pth
  *TENT* TN30 ........................ 69 G6
Royal Military Rd *WSEA* TN36 .. 117 G6
Royal Oak La *UCK* TN22 ........ 54 B5
Royal Pde *LW/ROSE* BN22 .... 11 K3
Royal Sovereign Vw
  *LGNY* BN23 ...................... 197 M8
Royal Sussex Crs
  *EDN/EASTW* BN20 .............. 206 B1
Royles CI *ROTT* BN2 .............. 189 G4
Royston CI *EDN/EASTW* BN20.. 205 G5
Royston Gdns *BEX* TN40 ...... 183 M3
Rudyard CI *ROTT* BN2 .......... 170 E6
Rudyard Rd *ROTT* BN2 .......... 170 E6
Rue De Bayeux *BAT* TN33 .... 137 K1
Rufus CI *LEW* BN7 .................. 2 E5
Rugby CI *SEAF* BN25 ............ 203 J2
Rugby PI *ROTT* BN2 .............. 187 L2
Rugby Rd *BRI* BN1 ................ 169 G5
Rumbolds La *HWH* RH16 ...... 71 K4
Rusbridge La *LEW* BN7 .......... 3 J6

The Rushes *HWH* RH16 .......... 72 C2
Rushetts *RRTW* TN3 .............. 18 F2
Rushey CI *RING/NEW* BN8 .... 150 E1
Rushlake CI *BRI* BN1 .............. 169 L1
Rushlake Crs *EAST* BN21 ...... 196 D8
Rushlake Rd *BRI* BN1 ............ 146 E8
Rushlye CI *RRTW* TN3 ............ 30 F1
Rushmere Ri *STLEO* TN38 .... 161 L3
Rushwood CI *HWH* RH16 ...... 72 B2
Ruskin Rd *EDN/EASTW* BN20.. 196 B5
  *HOVE* BN3 ........................ 167 M6
Rusper Rd *BRI* BN1 .............. 146 E8
  *EDN/EASTW* BN20 .............. 196 B8
Ruspers *BURH* RH15 .............. 97 K4
Russell CI *BRI* BN1 .................. 6 C7
Russell PI *BRI* BN1 .................. 6 C7
Russell Rd *BRI* BN1 ................ 6 C7
Russell Sq *BRI* BN1 ................ 6 C7
Russell St *HAS* TN34 .............. 5 H7
Russet CI *POLE* BN26 ............ 178 C8
Rusthall Gra *SBGH/RUST* TN4.. 19 K2
Rusthall High St
  *SBGH/RUST* TN4 ................ 19 L3
Rusthall Pk *SBGH/RUST* TN4 .. 19 K2
Rusthall Rd *SBGH/RUST* TN4 .. 19 K3
Rustic CI *PEAHV* BN10 .......... 190 B5
Rustic Rd *PEAHV* BN10 ........ 190 B4
Rustington Rd *BRI* BN1 .......... 169 G1
Rustlings CI *HWH* RH16 ........ 72 B1
Rustwick *SBGH/RUST* TN4 .... 19 K2
Rutland CI *EAST* BN21 .......... 196 D8
Rutland Gdns *HOVE* BN3 ...... 167 M7
Rutland Rd *HOVE* BN3 .......... 168 A7
Rydal CI *SBGH/RUST* TN4 ...... 19 L1
Rydal Dr *SBGH/RUST* TN4 .... 19 L1
Rydal Wy *LGNY* BN23 .......... 197 G2
Ryde Rd *ROTT* BN2 ................ 7 L2
Ryders *RRTW* TN3 ................ 19 L3
Rye CI *POLE* BN26 ................ 178 C7
  *ROTT* BN2 ........................ 189 L4
  *SEAF* BN25 ........................ 203 J2
Ryecroft *HWH* RH16 .............. 71 K3
Ryefield CI *EAST* BN21 .......... 196 C7
Ryelands Dr *ROTT* BN2 .......... 169 K3
Rye Rd *RHAS* TN35 .............. 163 K2
  *RYE* TN31 .......................... 90 F4
  *TENT* TN30 ........................ 68 A4
Rye St *LW/ROSE* BN22 .......... 197 J8
Rylstone Rd *LW/ROSE* BN22 .. 11 J4
Rymill Rd *STLEO* TN38 .......... 162 A3
Rype CI *LYDD* TN29 .............. 121 J1
Ryst Wood Rd *FROW* RH18 .... 25 H4

## S

Sackville CI *EGRIN* RH19 ........ 13 J3
  *LEW* BN7 .............................. 2 E5
Sackville Gdns *HOVE* BN3 .... 167 M8
Sackville La *EGRIN* RH19 ...... 13 H3
Sackville Rd *BEXW* TN39 ...... 183 K5
  *HAIL* BN27 ........................ 155 J8
  *HOVE* BN3 ........................ 168 A8
  *LW/ROSE* BN22 .................. 196 F4
Saddlers CI *BURH* RH15 ........ 97 K5
Sadlers Wy *RING/NEW* BN8 .. 150 D2
Sadler Wy *ROTT* BN2 ............ 169 M8
Saffron CI *SHOR* BN43 .......... 166 C5
Saffron Gdns *POLE* BN26 ...... 193 M3
Saffrons Pk *EDN/EASTW* BN20 .. 10 B9
Saffrons Rd *EAST* BN21 ........ 10 C6
The Saffrons *BURH* RH15 ...... 96 E1
St Agnes Rd *EGRIN* RH19 ...... 13 L4
St Andrews CI *HAIL* BN27 ...... 155 G5
St Andrew's Dr *SEAF* BN25 .. 192 A8
St Andrew's La *LEW* BN7 ........ 2 F6
St Andrew's Rd *BEX* TN40 .... 183 L1
  *BRI* BN1 ............................ 169 G5
  *BURH* RH15 ........................ 97 K3
  *PTSD* BN41 ........................ 167 H7
St Andrew's Sq *HAS* TN34 .... 5 H6
St Anne's Crs *LEW* BN7 ........ 2 C7
St Anne's Rd *EAST* BN21 ...... 10 D5
  *LW/ROSE* BN22 .................. 196 B3
St Anthony's Av *LGNY* BN23 .. 197 K7
St Aubyns *HOVE* BN3 ............ 168 A8
St Aubyn's Crs *PTSD* BN41 .... 167 H7
St Aubyn's Md *PTSD* BN41 .... 189 C5
St Aubyn's Rd *LW/ROSE* BN22.. 11 H5
  *PTSD* BN41 ...................... 167 G7
St Aubyns South *HOVE* BN3 .. 186 A1
St Augustine CI *RHWH* RH17 .. 72 F3
St Augustine's CI
  *BEXW* TN39 ...................... 182 F3
St Barnabas' CI *RTW* TN1 ...... 20 B1
St Boswells CI *HAIL* BN27 .... 154 F6
St Catherine's CI *SLVH* TN37 .. 4 C6
St Crispians *SEAF* BN25 ........ 202 D3
St Cuthmans CI *ROTT* BN2 .... 169 L8
St David's Av *BEX* TN40 ........ 183 J1
St Davids CI *LW/ROSE* BN22 .. 196 D2
St Edmund's Rd *HWH* RH16 .. 71 M3
St Edward's CI *EGRIN* RH19 .. 13 J5
St Francis Cha *BEXW* TN39 .. 183 G1
St Francis CI *HWH* RH16 ........ 71 L4
St George's La *HPPT/KEY* BN6 .. 122 D1
St George's Ms *BRI* BN1 .......... 6 F5
St George's Pk *RTWE/PEM* TN2 .. 19 M6
St George's PI *BRI* BN1 .......... 6 F4
  *HPPT/KEY* BN6 .................. 122 D1
St George's Rd *BEXW* TN39 .. 183 J1
  *HAS* TN34 ............................ 5 K3
  *LW/ROSE* BN22 .................. 11 K2
  *ROTT* BN2 ............................ 7 M9
St George's Ter *ROTT* BN2 ...... 7 J8
St Giles CI *SHOR* BN43 .......... 166 B6
  *WSEA* TN36 ...................... 116 F7
St Gregory CI
  *EDN/EASTW* BN20 .............. 206 E6
St Helen's Av *HAS* TN34 ........ 162 E3
St Helen's Crs *HAS* TN34 ........ 4 F1
  *HOVE* BN3 ........................ 167 K3
St Helen's Down *HAS* TN34 .. 163 G3
St Helen's Dr *HOVE* BN3 ...... 167 K3
St Helen's Park Rd *HAS* TN34 .. 4 F2
St Helen's Rd *ROTT* BN2 ........ 7 L2

SLVH TN37 ............... 162 D3
St Helens's Wood Rd
  HAS TN34 ............... 162 E1
St Heliers Av HOVE BN3 ...... 167 L1
Saint Hill Rd EGRIN RH19 ..... 13 L6 🗖
St James' Av BEX TN40 ....... 160 D8
St James' Crs BEX TN40 ...... 160 D7
St James's Pk RTW TN1 ....... 20 C1
  RTWE/PEM TN2 ........... 20 C1
St James's Rd BEX TN40 ...... 160 C8
  LW/ROSE BN22 ........... 11 J4
  RTW TN1 ............... 20 C2
Stjames' Rd RTW TN1 ........ 20 C2
St James's Av ROTT BN2 ...... 7 H8
St James's Rd EGRIN RH19 .... 13 K5
  HAS TN34 ............... 5 J5
St James's St ROTT BN2 ...... 6 F7 🗖
St James's Street Ms ROTT BN2 . 7 G7
St James St LEW BN7 ........ 2 F7
St John Bank RING/NEW BN8 ... 99 K6
St John's Av BURH RH15 ...... 96 F3
St John's Cl CROW TN6 ....... 39 L3
  EGRIN RH19 ............. 13 L4
St John's Dr PEV BN24 ....... 179 L8
St John's Hl LEW BN7 ........ 2 F5
St John's Pl HOVE BN3 ....... 168 C8 🗖
  ROTT BN2 ............... 7 G6
St John's Rd BEX TN40 ....... 160 C8
  BURH RH15 .............. 97 G3
  CROW TN6 ............... 39 J1
  EDN/EASTW BN20 ......... 206 E6
  EGRIN RH19 ............. 13 L4
  HOVE BN3 .............. 186 C1
  HWH RH16 .............. 71 J3
  POLE BN26 ............. 178 A8
  SEAF BN25 ............. 202 E6
  SLVH TN37 .............. 4 B7
St John's Ter LEW BN7 ....... 2 F5
St John St LEW BN7 ......... 3 G5
St Joseph's Cl HOVE BN3 ...... 168 A6
St Josephs Wy HWH RH16 ..... 71 L2
St Julians Cl SHOR BN43 ...... 166 C7
St Julian's La SHOR BN43 ..... 166 C7
St Keyna Av HOVE BN3 ....... 167 K8
St Laurence Cl PEAHV BN10 .... 190 A5 🗖
St Lawrence Wy
  HPPT/KEY BN6 ........... 96 A7
St Leonards's Av HOVE BN3 .... 167 J8
St Leonards Cl NEWHV BN9 .... 191 M4
St Leonards's Gdns HOVE BN3 .. 167 K8
St Leonard's Pl
  EDN/EASTW BN20 ......... 206 C3
St Leonard's Rd EAST BN21 .... 10 D5
  HOVE BN3 .............. 167 J8
  NEWHV BN9 ............. 191 M4
  ROTT BN2 ............... 7 J1 🗖
St Leonards Ter POLE BN26 .... 177 M7
St Louie Cl STHW BN42 ...... 167 G6 🗖
St Luke's Rd ROTT BN2 ....... 7 K4
St Luke's Ter ROTT BN2 ...... 7 J4
St Margaret's Pl BRI BN1 ..... 6 B7
St Margaret's Ri EGRIN RH19 ... 192 A8
St Margaret's Rd EGRIN RH19 . 13 M3 🗖
  SLVH TN37 .............. 4 C8
St Margaret's Ter SLVH TN37 .. 4 C8
St Marks Cl BEXW TN39 ...... 182 D2
St Marks Fld UCK TN22 ...... 78 B1
St Mark's Rd RTWE/PEM TN2 .. 19 M7
St Mark's St ROTT BN2 ...... 187 L2
St Martins Cl NEWHV BN9 .... 191 K5 🗖
St Martin's La LEW BN7 ...... 2 F7
St Martin's Pl ROTT BN2 ..... 7 H2
St Martins Rd
  LW/ROSE BN22 .......... 196 D3 🗖
St Martin's St ROTT BN2 ..... 7 H1
St Mary-in-the-fields
  MAYF TN20 ............. 57 H4
St Mary Magdalene St
  ROTT BN2 .............. 7 H1
St Marys Av HAIL BN27 ...... 155 L9
St Mary's Cl LW/ROSE BN22 ... 196 A4
  RYE TN31 .............. 114 A4
  WADH TN5 .............. 45 K5
St Mary's Cottages
  EDN/EASTW BN20 ......... 206 D3 🗖
Saint Marys Garth UCK TN22 .. 77 J2
St Mary's La BEXW TN39 ..... 159 M5
  WADH TN5 .............. 45 K5
St Mary's Pl ROTT BN2 ...... 7 H8
St Mary's Rd EAST BN21 ..... 206 D2
  HAS TN34 .............. 5 J3
St Mary's Rd West BURH RH15 . 96 F2
St Mary's Sq ROTT BN2 ...... 7 M9
St Mary's Ter HAS TN34 ..... 5 J4
St Matthew's Gdns
  STLEO TN38 ............ 162 B5
St Matthew's Rd STLEO TN38 . 162 B5
St Mellion Cl HAIL BN27 ..... 154 F6 🗖
St Michaels Cl CROW TN6 .... 40 B6
  PEV BN24 .............. 179 G8
St Michael's Pl BRI BN1 ..... 6 B5
  HAS TN34 .............. 5 H4
St Michaels Rd EGRIN RH19 ... 13 L4
  PTSD BN41 ............. 167 H7
St Michael's Ter LEW BN7 .... 3 G2
St Nicholas La LEW BN7 ..... 3 G5
St Nicholas Rd BRI BN1 ..... 6 D5
  PTSD BN41 ............. 167 H7
St Nicolas Cl PEV BN24 ..... 180 B8
St Olive's Cl HTHF TN21 .... 79 J7
St Pancras Gdns LEW BN7 .... 2 D8
St Pancras Gn LEW BN7 ..... 171 K1
St Pancras Rd LEW BN7 ..... 2 D7
St Patrick's Crs BEX TN40 ... 183 J1
St Patrick's Rd HOVE BN3 ... 168 A7
St Paul's Cl HWH RH16 ..... 71 M1
  LW/ROSE BN22 ......... 196 D3 🗖
St Paul's Pl SLVH TN37 ..... 4 C6
St Paul's Rd SLVH TN37 ..... 4 B4
St Paul's St ROTT BN2 ..... 7 H1
  SBGH/RUST TN4 ........ 19 J2
St Peters Av PEAHV BN10 .... 190 A6
St Peter's Cl HOVE BN3 ..... 167 M4
  SEAF BN25 ............ 202 E1
St Peter's Crs BEX TN40 .... 183 K1
St Peter's Pl BRI BN1 ...... 6 F4
  LEW BN7 .............. 2 E6

St Peters Rd BURH RH15 ...... 97 G2
  PTSD BN41 ............. 167 H7
  SEAF BN25 ............. 202 E1
  SLVH TN37 ............. 4 A1
St Peter's St BRI BN1 ...... 6 F3
  RTWE/PEM TN2 ......... 20 C3 🗖
St Philip's Av LW/ROSE BN22 . 11 G2
St Philips Ms HOVE BN3 .... 167 M7
St Richards Rd CROW TN6 ... 40 A7
  PTSD BN41 ............. 167 H7
St Saviour's Rd STLEO TN38 . 161 L8
St Stephens Ct RTW TN1 .... 20 B1 🗖
St Swithun's Cl EGRIN RH19 . 13 M5 🗖
St Swithun's La LEW BN7 ... 2 F7
St Swithun's Ter LEW BN7 .. 2 F7 🗖
St Thomas's Rd HAS TN34 .. 5 K3
St Thomas's St WSEA TN36 . 116 F7
St Vincents Pl
  EDN/EASTW BN20 ...... 206 E5 🗖
St Vincents Rd STLEO TN38 . 161 M7
St Wilfred's Pl SEAF BN25 .. 203 H4
St Wilfreds Rd BURH RH15 .. 97 H2
St Wilfrid's Gn HAIL BN27 .. 155 H6
St Wilfrid's Wy HWH RH16 . 71 L2
Salcey Cl STLEO TN38 ..... 161 L4
Salehurst Gdns STLEO TN38 . 161 K4 🗖
Salehurst Rd EAST BN21 .... 206 C3
Salisbury Cl LW/ROSE BN22 . 196 C4
Salisbury Rd BEXW TN39 ... 183 H1
  EDN/EASTW BN20 ....... 206 C6
  HOVE BN3 ............. 168 C8
  RRTW TN3 ............. 18 F3
  SEAF BN25 ............ 202 E5
  SLVH TN37 ............ 4 B4
Saltcote St RYE TN31 ...... 91 J6
Saltdean Cl BEXW TN39 ... 182 E5
Saltdean Dr ROTT BN2 .... 189 H5
Saltdean Park Rd ROTT BN2 . 189 J5
Saltdean V ROTT BN2 ..... 189 K3
Saltdean Wy BEXW TN39 .. 182 D3
Saltwood Rd SEAF BN25 ... 203 J2
Salvador Cl LGNY BN23 .... 197 M7
Salvington Crs BEXW TN39 . 182 F2
Sancroft Rd EDN/EASTW BN20 . 206 B3
The Sanctuary
  EDN/EASTW BN20 ...... 206 B2 🗖
Sandbanks Cl HAIL BN27 ... 178 A1
Sandbanks Gdns HAIL BN27 . 178 B1 🗖
Sandbanks Gv HAIL BN27 .. 155 H8 🗖
Sandbanks Rd HAIL BN27 .. 155 G8
Sandbanks Wy HAIL BN27 . 155 H8
Sandgate Cl SEAF BN25 ... 203 J1
Sandore Cl BRI BN1 ...... 169 G4
Sandore Cl SEAF BN25 .... 203 G2
Sandore Rd SEAF BN25 ... 203 G2
Sandown Cl LGNY BN23 ... 197 H2
Sandown Pk RTWE/PEM TN2 . 20 C1
Sandown Rd RHAS TN35 ... 163 J3 🗖
  ROTT BN2 ............. 7 L2
  STHW BN42 ........... 166 D6
Sandown Wy BEX TN40 ... 160 B8
Sandridge CROW TN6 .... 39 M5 🗖
Sandridge La HWH RH16 . 48 F5
Sandringham Cl HOVE BN3 . 168 A3 🗖
  SEAF BN25 ........... 193 G8 🗖
Sandringham Dr HOVE BN3 . 168 A3
Sandringham Hts
  STLEO TN38 .......... 161 K3 🗖
Sand Rd RRTW TN3 ...... 33 G2
Sandrock Hl BAT TN33 ... 161 G2
Sandrock Pk HAS TN34 .. 162 F1
Sandrock Wy HWH RH16 . 71 H2
Sandwich Dr STLEO TN38 . 161 M7
Sandwich St LW/ROSE BN22 . 197 J8
Sandy Cl SLVH TN37 .... 162 B1
Sandy Cross La HTHF TN21 . 106 B1
Sandy La CRAWE RH10 ... 12 A6
  EGRIN RH19 .......... 13 L5
  EGRIN RH19 .......... 22 E8
  HRTF TN7 ............ 25 K8
  HTHF TN21 ........... 105 L5
  RHWH RH17 .......... 36 C6
  UCK TN22 ............ 76 F7
Sandy V HWH RH16 .... 71 K4
San Feliu Ct EGRIN RH19 . 14 B4
Santa Cruz Dr LGNY BN23 . 197 M7
Sanyhils Av BRI BN1 .... 145 M7
Saunders Cl HAS TN34 .. 5 J6
  UCK TN22 ............ 76 A6
Saunders Hl BRI BN1 ... 146 D7
Saunders Park Vw ROTT BN2 . 169 J5
Saunders Rd SBGH/RUST TN4 . 19 L1
Saunders Wy RYE TN31 . 119 G4 🗖
Savill Rd HWH RH16 ... 49 K6
Sawyers Cl BURH RH15 . 97 K5
Saxby Cl LGNY BN23 ... 197 L5
Saxby Rd BEXW TN39 ... 183 G2
  BURH RH15 .......... 96 D2
Saxonbury Cl CROW TN6 . 39 M4
Saxon Cl EAST BN21 ... 196 C8
  ROTT BN2 ........... 189 J4
Saxon La SEAF BN25 ... 202 E4
Saxon Ri BEX TN40 .... 183 L2
Saxon Rd HOVE BN3 ... 167 K8
  NEWHV BN9 .......... 9 G3
  RHAS TN35 .......... 163 K3
Saxon Shore Wy HAS TN34 . 5 M6
  RHAS TN35 .......... 142 C6
  RHAS TN35 .......... 163 K5
  RYE TN31 ........... 91 L6
  WSEA TN36 .......... 116 F3
Saxons Cl SLVH TN37 .. 4 A1
Saxonwood Rd BAT TN33 . 137 J4
Sayerland La POLE BN26 . 178 A6
Sayerland Rd POLE BN26 . 177 M7
The Sayers EGRIN RH19 . 13 J5
Scamps Hl HWH RH16 . 49 J8

Scanlon Cl EDN/EASTW BN20 . 196 A3 🗖
Scarborough Rd BRI BN1 .. 168 D5 🗖
Scarletts Cl UCK TN22 .... 76 B7
Schofield Wy LGNY BN23 .. 197 M7
School Cl BURH RH15 .... 96 F4
  STHW BN42 .......... 166 E7 🗖
School Fld RING/NEW BN8 . 126 E2
School Gdns RING/NEW BN8 . 126 D2
School Hl RING/NEW BN8 .. 126 D2
  WSEA TN36 .......... 116 E6
School La CROW TN6 .... 39 J2
  EGRIN RH19 .......... 14 D8
  FROW RH18 .......... 24 F4
  POLE BN26 .......... 178 A7
  POY/PYE BN45 ....... 122 C8
  RHWH RH17 ......... 51 G2
  RYE TN31 ........... 90 A5
  RYE TN31 ........... 91 J5
  UCK TN22 ........... 52 C1
  UCK TN22 ........... 55 H8
  UCK TN22 ........... 78 A8
School Pl BEX TN40 .... 184 A1
School Ri ROTT BN2 .... 169 L8 🗖
  RTWE/PEM TN2 ....... 19 M5 🗖
School Rd HOVE BN3 ... 167 M7
  RHAS TN35 .......... 163 J3
School Ter HAWK TN18 . 47 M4
Schwerte Wy SLVH TN37 . 4 E8
Scotland St ROTT BN2 .. 7 H5
Scotsford Hl MAYF TN20 . 57 L4
Scotsford Rd HTHF TN21 . 80 F5
Scott Rd HOVE BN3 .... 167 M7 🗖
Scotts Acre RYE TN31 .. 118 E3
Scotts Wy RTWE/PEM TN2 . 19 L6
Scraper's Hl RING/NEW BN8 . 130 F6
Scutes Cl HAS TN34 .... 162 F3
Seabeach La LW/ROSE BN22 . 11 K2
Seabourne Rd BEX TN40 . 160 F8
Seafield Cl SEAF BN25 .. 203 H1 🗖
Seafield Rd HOVE BN3 .. 186 B1
Seaford Rd HOVE BN3 .. 167 J8
  LW/ROSE BN22 ....... 11 K1
  NEWHV BN9 .......... 9 L2
Seagrave Cl SEAF BN25 . 192 A8 🗖
Seagrove Wy SEAF BN25 . 192 F6
Searle Av PEAHV BN10 . 190 E8
Sea Rd BEX TN40 ..... 183 K3
  PEV BN24 ........... 198 D1
  RHAS TN35 .......... 165 C1
  RYE TN31 ........... 118 F4
  STLEO TN38 ......... 161 M8
  WSEA TN36 .......... 116 F6
Seasaw Wy ROTT BN2 . 169 M7
Seaside LW/ROSE BN22 . 11 H5
Seaside Rd EAST BN21 . 11 G8
  STLEO TN38 ......... 161 M8
Seaside Wy STLEO TN38 . 161 M8
Seaview Av PEAHV BN10 . 190 E8
  PEAHV BN10 ........ 200 E1
Seaview Rd NEWHV BN9 . 191 M5
  PEAHV BN10 ........ 200 E1
  ROTT BN2 .......... 170 B6
Seaville Dr LGNY BN23 . 197 K6
  PEV BN24 .......... 198 D1
Second Av BEX TN40 . 183 M1
  HOVE BN3 .......... 186 C1
  NEWHV BN9 ......... 8 E4
  RYE TN31 .......... 118 F4
Second Rd PEAHV BN10 . 190 A7 🗖
Sedgebrook Gdns HAS TN34 . 4 E2
Sedgewick Rd BEXW TN39 . 160 C8
  BRI BN1 ........... 146 C8
Sedlescombe Gdns
  STLEO TN38 ........ 162 B4
Sedlescombe Rd North
  BAT TN33 .......... 112 B4
  SLVH TN37 ......... 4 A1
  STLEO TN38 ........ 162 B1
Sedlescombe Rd South
  STLEO TN38 ........ 162 B5
Sefton Cha CROW TN6 . 40 A3
Sefton Rd PTSD BN41 . 166 F3
Sefton Wy CROW TN6 . 40 A3 🗖
Segrave Cl LEW BN7 .. 2 C4
Selba Dr ROTT BN2 ... 169 L2
Selborne Pl HOVE BN3 . 168 C7 🗖
Selborne Rd HOVE BN3 . 168 C8
Selby Ct HWH RH16 .. 71 L3
Selby Gdns UCK TN22 . 102 D1
Selby Ri UCK TN22 ... 102 D1
Selby Rd EAST BN21 . 206 D1
  UCK TN22 .......... 76 D8
Selham Cl BRI BN1 ... 146 E8 🗖
Selham Dr BRI BN1 .. 146 E8
Selhurst Rd ROTT BN2 . 170 E8
Sellbourne Pk RRTW TN3 . 30 C2
Selmeston Cl HAS TN34 . 4 D4
Selmeston Rd ROTT BN2 . 187 M1 🗖
Selmeston Pl ROTT BN2 . 169 M8 🗖
Selmeston Rd EAST BN21 . 196 C7
Selsey Cl BRI BN1 ... 146 E8
Selsfield Cl EAST BN21 . 196 D8
Selsfield Dr ROTT BN2 . 169 K3
Selsfield Rd CRAWE RH10 . 22 A3
  EGRIN RH19 ........ 22 C7
  RHWH RH17 ........ 34 B5
Selwyn Dr EAST BN21 . 10 A3
Selwyn Rd EAST BN21 . 10 A3
Semley Rd BRI BN1 .. 169 G5
  HPPT/KEY BN6 ..... 122 E2
Sempstead La RBTBR TN32 . 87 J3
Senlac Rd NEWHV BN9 . 9 G3
Senlac Wy SLVH TN37 . 162 C1
Sergison Cl HWH RH16 . 71 J1
Sergison Rd HWH RH16 . 71 K1
Setfords Fld RING/NEW BN8 . 99 L5
Sevelands Cl ROTT BN2 . 169 M7 🗖
Seven Acre Cl SLVH TN37 . 162 A1
Sevenoaks Rd LGNY BN23 . 197 K5
Seven Sisters Rd
  LW/ROSE BN22 ...... 196 B3
Seville St ROTT BN2 . 7 J2
Sewell Av BEX TN40 . 183 J1
Seymour St ROTT BN2 . 7 L9
Shaftesbury Pl BRI BN1 . 6 F1 🗖
Shaftesbury Rd BRI BN1 . 6 F1
Shakespeare St HOVE BN3 . 168 A6
Shalesbrook La FROW RH18 . 24 F5

Shalfleet Cl LGNY BN23 ... 197 H3
Shandon Cl RTWE/PEM TN2 . 20 C2
Shanklin Cl ROTT BN2 ... 197 H2
Shanklin Rd ROTT BN2 .. 7 K1
Shannon Cl PEAHV BN10 . 190 A5
Shannon Wy LGNY BN23 . 197 M6
Sharpthorne Crs PTSD BN41 . 167 L4
The Shaw RTWE/PEM TN2 . 20 C4
Sheddingdean Cl BURH RH15 . 97 G2 🗖
Sheen Rd LW/ROSE BN22 . 11 H4
Sheepbell Cl PTSD BN41 . 167 H3
Sheepfair LEW BN7 ..... 2 A3
Sheep Pen La SEAF BN25 . 203 G3
Sheep Pln CROW TN6 ... 39 K7
Sheepsetting La HTHF TN21 . 79 L7
Sheepstreet La BUR/ETCH TN19 . 60 E2
Sheep Wk ROTT BN2 ... 188 F5
Sheepwash La UCK TN22 . 78 C6
Sheerwater Crs HAS TN34 . 162 D2
Sheffield Br UCK TN22 .. 74 B2
Sheffield Mill La UCK TN22 . 51 J6
Sheffield Park Wy
  LW/ROSE BN22 ....... 197 G2
Sheiling Rd CROW TN6 . 39 L3
Shelldale Av PTSD BN41 . 167 H7
Shelldale Crs PTSD BN41 . 167 H7
Shelldale Rd PTSD BN41 . 167 G6
Shelley Cl LEW BN7 .... 2 E6
Shelley Rd EGRIN RH19 . 13 K5 🗖
  HOVE BN3 .......... 167 M7
Shenfield Wy BRI BN1 . 169 H4
Shenstone HWH RH16 . 49 H6
Shepham Av ROTT BN2 . 189 J5
Shepham La POLE BN26 . 178 C7
Shepherd's Cl BEXW TN39 . 182 C2
  NEWHV BN9 ......... 191 H4 🗖
  POLE BN26 ......... 196 F5 🗖
  RING/NEW BN8 ...... 150 E1 🗖
Shepherds Cft BRI BN1 . 168 C3
Shepherdsgrove La
  EGRIN RH19 ........ 14 F1
Shepherd's Hl HRTF TN7 . 25 K5
Shepherds Md BURH RH15 . 96 F2 🗖
Shepherd St STLEO TN38 . 4 A9
Shepherds Wk CROW TN6 . 40 C5 🗖
  HPPT/KEY BN6 ....... 122 E1
  RTWE/PEM TN2 ...... 20 D2 🗖
Shepherds Wy RHAS TN35 . 164 E2
  RING/NEW BN8 ...... 99 J7
  RING/NEW BN8 ...... 150 J1
  UCK TN22 .......... 102 C1
Sheppard Wy PTSD BN41 . 167 G3
Sheppeys HWH RH16 . 71 K4
Sheppey Wk HAIL BN27 . 155 G5
The Shepway SEAF BN25 . 203 H2
Sheraton Cl EAST BN21 . 10 D8
Sherbourne Cl HOVE BN3 . 167 K3
Sherbourne Rd HOVE BN3 . 167 K3
Sherbourne Wy HOVE BN3 . 167 K3
Sheridan Cl EGRIN RH19 . 13 J5
Sheridan Ter HOVE BN3 . 168 A6
Sheriff's La CROW TN6 . 41 J8
Sheringham Cl RBTBR TN32 . 86 E4
Sherman Br POLE BN26 . 176 C7
Sherrington Rd ROTT BN2 . 170 F6
Sherwood Cl HAS TN34 . 5 H3
Sherwood Dr HWH RH16 . 71 J1
Sherwood Gn HAIL BN27 . 155 H8 🗖
Sherwood Pl RRTW TN3 . 18 E5 🗖
Sherwood Ri SEAF BN25 . 202 F2
Sherwood Rd
  RTWE/PEM TN2 ...... 20 D2 🗖
  SEAF BN25 ......... 202 F2
Shinewater La LGNY BN23 . 197 H5
Shingle Cl STLEO TN38 . 138 E7
Shingle Rd SHOR BN43 . 166 B6
Shipley La BEXW TN39 . 182 D4
Shipley Mill Cl PEV BN24 . 197 H1
Shipley Rd ROTT BN2 . 170 E7
Ship St BRI BN1 ..... 6 D7
  EGRIN RH19 ........ 13 L6
  NEWHV BN9 ........ 8 F7
Shirlea Vw BAT TN33 . 137 L2
Shirley Av HOVE BN3 . 168 B4
Shirley Cl SHOR BN43 . 166 C6
Shirley Dr HOVE BN3 . 168 C5
  SLVH TN37 ......... 162 B3
Shirley Gdns SBGH/RUST TN4 . 19 J2 🗖
Shirley Gv SBGH/RUST TN4 . 19 K1
Shirley Rd HOVE BN3 . 168 C6
Shirleys HPPT/KEY BN6 . 123 L4
Shirley St HOVE BN3 . 168 B7
Short Brow SEAF BN25 . 203 C2 🗖
Short Brow Cl
  LW/ROSE BN22 ..... 196 B3 🗖
Shortdean Pl EAST BN21 . 206 D2 🗖
Shortgate La RING/NEW BN8 . 129 G4
Shortgate Rd ROTT BN2 . 169 M2
Shortlands Cl
  LW/ROSE BN22 ..... 196 C5 🗖
Shovelstrode La EGRIN RH19 . 14 E4
Showfields Rd RTWE/PEM TN2 . 19 M5
The Shrublands BEXW TN39 . 182 E3
Shrub La WADH TN5 . 60 B1
Sicklehatch La HTHF TN21 . 106 A4
Sidcup Cl LGNY BN23 . 197 K4 🗖
Sidehill Dr PTSD BN41 . 166 F4
Sidley Gn BEXW TN39 . 160 C7
Sidley Rd LW/ROSE BN22 . 11 K2
Sidley St BEXW TN39 . 160 B7
Sidney Cl RTWE/PEM TN2 . 19 L6
Silchester Rd STLEO TN38 . 4 B1
Sillwood Pl BRI BN1 . 6 A6
Sillwood Rd BRI BN1 . 6 A6
Sillwood St BRI BN1 . 6 A6
Silva Cl BEX TN40 . 161 G8
Silvan Rd STLEO TN38 . 161 L3 🗖
Silver Birches HWH RH16 . 72 A2
Silverdale Av HOVE BN3 . 168 D7
Silverdale La HAWK TN18 . 63 H2
Silverdale Rd BURH RH15 . 97 H4
  EDN/EASTW BN20 ... 206 D5
  HOVE BN3 ......... 168 D7
Silverhill Av SLVH TN37 . 162 C2

Silverlands Rd SLVH TN37 . 162 B4
Silvester Rd BEX TN40 . 183 J1
Simons Cl CROW TN6 . 40 A5 🗖
Singleton Mill Rd PEV BN24 . 197 J1
Singleton Rd BRI BN1 . 146 A8
Singleton Wy BURH RH15 . 97 J5
Six Bells Ms RYE TN31 . 88 C1
Skinner Cl BAT TN33 . 136 C7
Skinner's La BAT TN33 . 136 C7
Skyline Vw PEAHV BN10 . 190 D4
The Slade RRTW TN3 . 33 G3
Sleepers Stile Rd WADH TN5 . 32 D5
Slider's La UCK TN22 . 50 F8
The Slides STLEO TN38 . 161 M3
Slimbridge Rd BURH RH15 . 96 F3
Slindon Av PEAHV BN10 . 190 D8
Slindon Crs LGNY BN23 . 197 L5 🗖
Slinford Cl ROTT BN2 . 7 M7
Slip Mill Rd HAWK TN18 . 47 L4
Sliverick's La HTHF TN21 . 108 F7
Sloe La POLE BN26 . 194 A3
Slonk Hill Rd SHOR BN43 . 166 A4
Slugwash La RHWH RH17 . 98 B1
Smeatons La WSEA TN36 . 143 H1
Smith Cl BAT TN33 . 159 H1
Smithy's Cl SLVH TN37 . 162 C1 🗖
The Smithy UCK TN22 . 76 B8
Smolletts EGRIN RH19 . 13 J6 🗖
Smugglers Cl POLE BN26 . 193 M3
Smugglers La CROW TN6 . 39 K1
Smugglers Wy RHAS TN35 . 164 F2
Snape La WADH TN5 . 43 L5
Snape Vw WADH TN5 . 43 M2
Snatt's Rd UCK TN22 . 76 C5
Snednore LEW BN7 . 171 M1
Snowdon Cl LGNY BN23 . 197 K3
Snowdrop La HWH RH16 . 72 C2
Snowflakes La HWH RH16 . 49 K8
Solomon's La RBTBR TN32 . 111 J2
Solway Av BRI BN1 . 145 M7
Somerhill Av HOVE BN3 . 168 D7
Somerhill Rd HOVE BN3 . 168 D8
Somerset St ROTT BN2 . 7 J7 🗖
Somerville Cl LGNY BN23 . 197 L7 🗖
Somerville Gdns
  SBGH/RUST TN4 . 19 M2
Sompting Cl ROTT BN2 . 169 M7 🗖
Soper's La HAWK TN18 . 47 K2
Sorrel Cl LGNY BN23 . 197 J3 🗖
Sorrel Dr LGNY BN23 . 197 J3
Southall Av ROTT BN2 . 169 K4
Southampton Cl LGNY BN23 . 197 M6 🗖
Southampton St ROTT BN2 . 7 H4
South Av EDN/EASTW BN20 . 206 B1
  HPPT/KEY BN6 . 122 A1
  ROTT BN2 . 7 J6
South Bank HPPT/KEY BN6 . 122 E3
Southbourne Rd
  LW/ROSE BN22 . 197 J8
South Brooks Rd LYDD TN29 . 120 E6
South Cliff BEXW TN39 . 182 E4
  EDN/EASTW BN20 . 206 F6
South Cliff Av BEXW TN39 . 182 E4
  EDN/EASTW BN20 . 206 F5 🗖
South Cliffe LEW BN7 . 3 J6
South Cl BURH RH15 . 96 E3
  HAIL BN27 . 155 H8
  PEAHV BN10 . 180 F8
South Coast Rd PEAHV BN10 . 189 L6
  ROTT BN2 . 189 K6
Southcourt Av BEXW TN39 . 182 E4
Southdown Av BRI BN1 . 169 G5
  EDN/EASTW BN20 . 196 A3
  HAS TN34 . 163 H3
  PEAHV BN10 . 190 D7
  PTSD BN41 . 167 J6 🗖
Southdown Cl HWH RH16 . 71 K4
  NEWHV BN9 . 8 C5
Southdown Pl BRI BN1 . 169 G5 🗖
Southdown Rd BRI BN1 . 169 G5
  EDN/EASTW BN20 . 196 B3
  NEWHV BN9 . 8 D6
  PTSD BN41 . 167 G4
  SEAF BN25 . 202 F3
  STHW BN42 . 166 E7
South Downs LEW BN7 . 124 F1 🗖
South Downs Rd LEW BN7 . 3 H3
South Downs Wy
  EDN/EASTW BN20 . 206 B3
  HPPT/KEY BN6 . 123 J7
  LEW BN7 . 148 A6
  LEW BN7 . 170 F2
  POLE BN26 . 194 E3
  POY/PYE BN45 . 122 E8
  RING/NEW BN8 . 173 K6
  RING/NEW BN8 . 193 J1
  SEAF BN25 . 204 A3
South Dr BURH RH15 . 96 E3
Southerden Cl HAIL BN27 . 155 J7
Southern Av POLE BN26 . 178 B8
Southern Rd LW/ROSE BN22 . 196 F4
Southfield POLE BN26 . 195 M1
Southfields WADH TN5 . 31 M8
Southfields Rd EAST BN21 . 10 C6
South Gv RTW TN1 . 20 A4 🗖
Southgrove EGRIN RH19 . 13 L7
Southlands Av BEXW TN39 . 160 A7
Southlands Rd BEXW TN39 . 160 A7
South La HTHF TN21 . 108 C4
  NEWHV BN9 . 9 G3
South Lodge Cl BURH RH15 . 96 F2 🗖
South Lynn Dr EAST BN21 . 10 C3
Southmead Cl MAYF TN20 . 57 K3
Southmount ROTT BN2 . 169 H5
Southon Cl PTSD BN41 . 166 F4
Southover High St LEW BN7 . 2 E7
Southover Pl ROTT BN2 . 7 G3
Southover Rd LEW BN7 . 2 F7
  ROTT BN2 . 7 G3
Southridge Ri CROW TN6 . 39 L6
Southridge Rd CROW TN6 . 39 L6
South Rd BRI BN1 . 168 E5
  HAIL BN27 . 155 G8
  HWH RH16 . 71 L2
  NEWHV BN9 . 9 G3
  RHWH RH17 . 98 C2

South Rough *RING/NEW* BN8 ...... 74 C8
South St *BRI* BN1 ...................... 6 D7
  *BRI* BN1 .............................. 147 J8
  *CROW* TN6 .......................... 39 M5
  *CROW* TN6 .......................... 41 H7
  *EAST* BN21 .......................... 10 D7
  *HPPT/KEY* BN6 ................... 123 K3
  *LEW* BN7 ................................ 3 J6
  *LYDD* TN29 ......................... 95 J8
  *MAYF* TN20 ......................... 57 H4
  *PTSD* BN41 ........................ 167 G5
  *RHWH* RH17 ........................ 70 E1
  *RING/NEW* BN8 ................. 129 M2
  *SEAF* BN25 ......................... 202 E4
  *SLVH* TN37 ............................ 4 B8
South Ter *HAS* TN34 .................. 5 C5
South Undercliff *RYE* TN31 ...... 117 J1
South Vw *HPPT/KEY* BN6 ......... 122 E6
South View *BUR/ETCH* TN19 ... 61 M3
Southview *CROW* TN6 ............... 39 L5
  *SHOR* BN43 ....................... 166 C7
  *STHW* BN42 ...................... 166 E5
Southview Dr *UCK* TN22 ........... 76 C6
South View Rd *CROW* TN6 ........ 39 L5
Southview Rd *PEAHV* BN10 ..... 190 C6
  *STHW* BN42 ...................... 166 E6
South View Wy *WADH* TN5 ........ 31 M8
Southwater Cl *ROTT* BN2 ........... 7 L5
Southwater Rd *SLVH* TN37 ......... 4 A6
Southway *BURH* RH15 ............... 96 D3
South Wy *LEW* BN7 ..................... 2 A5
  *NEWHV* BN9 .......................... 9 C3
  *SEAF* BN25 ........................ 203 J5
Southwick Cl *EGRIN* RH19 ....... 13 K4
Southwick Sq *STHW* BN42 ...... 166 E7
Southwick St *STHW* BN42 ....... 166 E7
Southwood Cl *STLEO* TN38 ..... 162 B5
South Woodlands *BRI* BN1 ..... 168 E2
Southwood Rd
  *SBGH/RUST* TN4 ................ 19 H1
Sovereign Cl *HAS* TN34 .......... 163 G2
  *SEAF* BN25 ........................ 203 G1
The Spaldings *STLEO* TN38 ..... 161 L5
The Sparrows *PEAHV* BN10 ..... 190 D5
Sparrow Wy *HPPT/KEY* BN6 ...... 96 D3
Spatham La *HPPT/KEY* BN6 ..... 123 M3
Speldhurst Rd *RRTW* TN3 ......... 18 F1
Spencer Av *HOVE* BN3 ............ 167 K3
Spencer Rd *EAST* BN21 ........... 10 E8
Spences Fld *LEW* BN7 ................ 3 J3
Spences La *LEW* BN7 ................. 3 H3
Spicers Cl *BURH* RH15 .............. 96 F1
Spindlewood Dr *BEXW* TN39 ... 182 C1
Spinnals Gv *STHW* BN42 ......... 166 D7
Spinney Cl *CRAWE* RH10 ......... 12 C6
  *HPPT/KEY* BN6 ................... 122 C1
The Spinneys *HTHF* TN21 ........ 80 B8
  *LEW* BN7 ................................ 3 J4
The Spinney *BAT* TN33 ........... 137 M5
  *BEXW* TN39 ...................... 182 D3
  *HAS* TN34 ............................. 4 E4
  *HOVE* BN5 ......................... 168 C5
  *HPPT/KEY* BN6 ................... 122 F1
  *RBTBR* TN32 ....................... 84 F3
  *RHWH* RH17 ........................ 48 D7
Spital Rd *LEW* BN7 ..................... 2 C6
Spithurst Rd *RING/NEW* BN8 ... 100 E7
Spotted Cow La *UCK* TN22 ....... 77 L1
Spout HI *CROW* TN6 .................. 41 K5
Spray Hl *RRTW* TN3 ................... 33 H2
Spray's La *BAT* TN33 ............... 139 H2
Springate Rd *STHW* BN42 ....... 166 F6
Spring Cl *EDN/EASTW* BN20 ... 196 B5
Springett Av *RING/NEW* BN8 ... 150 D1
Springfield *EGRIN* RH19 .......... 13 K2
Springfield Av *PEAHV* BN10 ... 189 M6
Springfield Cl *CROW* TN6 ......... 40 B4
  *PEV* BN24 ......................... 179 M8
Springfield Rd *BEX* TN40 ......... 160 C8
  *BRI* BN1 ............................. 169 C6
  *LW/ROSE* BN22 ................... 11 H3
  *RRTW* TN3 ......................... 18 C7
  *STLEO* TN38 ...................... 162 B5
Springfields *WADH* TN5 ........... 45 L5
Springfield Valley Rd
  *STLEO* TN38 ...................... 162 B5
Spring Gdns *BRI* BN1 ................. 6 E6
  *LEW* BN7 .............................. 3 C5
Springhead *RTWE/PEM* TN2 ... 20 D1
Springhead Wy *CROW* TN6 ...... 39 L6
Spring Hl *RYE* TN31 .................. 65 H7
Spring La *BEXW* TN39 ............. 182 C1
  *BUR/ETCH* TN19 .................. 59 J6
  *HPPT/KEY* BN6 ................... 122 E6
  *HWH* RH16 ........................... 49 H5
  *UCK* TN22 ............................ 78 F1
Spring Lodge Cl *LGNY* BN23 ... 197 L4
Spring Meadow *FROW* RH18 .... 24 F5
Springside Wk *STLEO* TN38 .... 161 M5
Spring St *BRI* BN1 ...................... 6 B6
  *SLVH* TN37 ............................ 4 A4
Spring Wy *EGRIN* RH19 ............ 14 A2
Springwood Rd *HTHF* TN21 ...... 79 M6
Spruce Cl *LW/ROSE* BN22 ..... 196 D4
Spur Rd *POLE* BN26 ................ 196 B1
Spurway Pk *POLE* BN26 .......... 196 B1
Squab La *HAIL* BN27 ............... 156 A2
The Square *PEV* BN24 ............. 180 F8
Squires Cl *CRAWE* RH10 .......... 12 A6
Squirrel Cl *BEXW* TN39 .......... 182 C1
Squirrel Wy *RTWE/PEM* TN2 ... 20 E1
Stablefield *RHAS* TN35 ........... 139 L2
Stables La *EAST* BN21 ............. 10 E6
Stafford Rd *BRI* BN1 ................... 6 B1
  *RTWE/PEM* TN2 .................. 20 E1
  *SEAF* BN25 ....................... 202 F3
Stafford Wy *HPPT/KEY* BN6 ... 123 C3
Stainsby St *SLVH* TN37 .............. 4 B7
Stalkers La *RING/NEW* BN8 .... 104 D8
Stanam Rd *RTWE/PEM* TN2 ..... 21 L1
Stanbridge Wy *RHWH* RH17 .... 34 A7
Standard Hill Cl *BAT* TN33 ..... 135 M8
Standean Cl *BRI* BN1 .............. 146 D8
Standen Cl *EGRIN* RH19 .......... 13 G3
Standen St *SBGH/RUST* TN4 .... 20 A1
Standgrove Pl *RHWH* RH17 ..... 34 A7
Stanford Av *BRI* BN1 .............. 169 C6
  *HPPT/KEY* BN6 ................... 122 E2

Stanford Cl *HOVE* BN3 ............ 168 C5
  *HPPT/KEY* BN6 ................... 122 E2
Stanford Rd *BRI* BN1 .............. 168 E6
Stanhope Rd *RTW* TN1 ............. 20 C1
Stanley Rd *PTSD* BN41 ........... 166 F2
Stanley Rd *BRI* BN1 .................. 6 E2
  *HAS* TN34 ............................ 4 F5
  *LW/ROSE* BN22 .................. 11 H3
  *PEAHV* BN10 ...................... 190 B5
  *PTSD* BN41 ....................... 167 G6
  *RTW* TN1 ............................. 20 B1
Stanley St *ROTT* BN2 ................. 7 H6
Stanmer Av *ROTT* BN2 ............ 189 K3
Stanmer Dr *LW/ROSE* BN22 ... 196 D5
Stanmer Park Rd *BRI* BN1 ...... 169 G4
Stanmer St *BRI* BN1 ............... 169 H4
Stanmer Vls *BRI* BN1 .............. 169 H3
Stansfield Rd *LEW* BN7 .............. 2 D4
Stanstead Crs *ROTT* BN2 ........ 170 F8
Stansted Rd *LW/ROSE* BN22 ... 10 F3
Staplefield Dr *ROTT* BN2 ........ 169 M3
Stapley Rd *HOVE* BN3 ............. 167 K6
Starfield *CROW* TN6 ................. 39 L5
Star La *MAYF* TN20 ................. 57 H4
  *POLE* BN26 ........................ 193 M3
  *UCK* TN22 ........................... 78 B8
Starling Cl *HPPT/KEY* BN6 ...... 96 C3
Star Rd *EAST* BN21 .................. 10 A4
Starr's Green La *BAT* TN33 ..... 137 M3
Starrs Md *BAT* TN33 ............... 137 M3
Starvecrow La *RYE* TN31 ........ 89 H8
Starwell Cl *HAS* TN34 ............. 162 D3
Station Ap *BAT* TN33 .............. 137 L3
  *BRI* BN1 ............................. 147 H8
  *BUR/ETCH* TN19 .................. 61 J5
  *HAS* TN34 ............................ 4 F6
  *HPPT/KEY* BN6 ................... 122 E2
  *HTHF* TN21 ......................... 80 A7
  *LW/ROSE* BN22 ................. 196 F5
  *MAYF* TN20 ......................... 56 F4
  *RHWH* RH17 ........................ 35 G7
  *RYE* TN31 ........................... 91 H8
  *SEAF* BN25 ........................ 202 E3
  *SLVH* TN37 ............................ 4 B7
Station Cl *CROW* TN6 ................ 41 J5
  *LEW* BN7 ........................... 124 E1
Station Rd *BAT* TN33 .............. 138 A8
  *BAT* TN33 ........................... 160 F1
  *BEX* TN40 .......................... 183 J2
  *BRI* BN1 ............................. 168 D3
  *BUR/ETCH* TN19 .................. 61 M3
  *BURH* RH15 ......................... 96 F4
  *CRAWE* RH10 ...................... 12 B6
  *CROW* TN6 .......................... 39 L5
  *EGRIN* RH19 ........................ 13 K5
  *EGRIN* RH19 ........................ 23 G8
  *FROW* RH18 ......................... 24 F3
  *HAIL* BN27 ......................... 155 H7
  *HAIL* BN27 ......................... 155 G6
  *HAS* TN34 ............................ 5 G6
  *HRTF* TN7 ........................... 27 H1
  *HTHF* TN21 ......................... 80 A7
  *LEW* BN7 .............................. 3 G8
  *LEW* BN7 ............................. 98 E8
  *LYDD* TN29 ......................... 95 J7
  *MAYF* TN20 ......................... 56 F4
  *NEWHV* BN9 ...................... 191 M5
  *POLE* BN26 ........................ 178 A8
  *RBTBR* TN32 ....................... 85 G3
  *RHWH* RH17 ........................ 50 C1
  *RING/NEW* BN8 .................. 73 L7
  *RRTW* TN3 ......................... 18 C7
  *RYE* TN31 ........................... 65 H6
  *SEAF* BN25 ........................ 202 B2
  *STHW* BN42 ...................... 166 E4
  *UCK* TN22 ........................ 101 K6
  *WADH* TN5 .......................... 31 J8
  *WADH* TN5 .......................... 59 L1
  *WSEA* TN36 ....................... 116 E5
Station St *BRI* BN1 ..................... 6 E4
  *EAST* BN21 .......................... 10 D6
  *LEW* BN7 .............................. 3 F5
Staveley Rd *EDN/EASTW* BN20 206 E6
Steellands Rd *RRTW* TN3 ........ 18 C7
Steep Hill Brede La *RYE* TN31 113 K4
Steep Rd *CROW* TN6 ................ 40 C8
Steine Gdns *ROTT* BN2 ............... 6 F6
Steine La *BRI* BN1 ..................... 6 E7
Steine St *ROTT* BN2 .................. 6 F8
The Stennings *EGRIN* RH19 ..... 13 J3
Stephens Cl *RING/NEW* BN8 ... 150 D1
Stephenson Dr *EGRIN* RH19 .... 13 M8
Stephens Rd *BRI* BN1 ............. 169 H4
Stevens Cl *BEXW* TN39 .......... 160 C7
Stevenson Cl *LGNY* BN23 ...... 197 L3
Stevenson Rd *ROTT* BN2 ........... 7 K7
  *SLVH* TN37 ....................... 162 B3
Stewards Inn La *LEW* BN7 ........ 2 F7
Steyne Cl *SEAF* BN25 ............. 202 F4
Steyne Rd *SEAF* BN25 ............ 202 E4
Steyning Av *HOVE* BN3 ........... 167 M3
  *PEAHV* BN10 ...................... 190 C7
Steyning Cl *SEAF* BN25 .......... 203 J4
Steyning Rd *SEAF* BN25 ......... 188 F5
  *SEAF* BN25 ........................ 203 J4
The Stiles *HAIL* BN27 .............. 155 J7
Stirling Av *SEAF* BN25 ............ 203 J2
Stirling Cl *BURH* RH15 ............. 97 J2
  *SEAF* BN25 ........................ 203 J3
Stirling Court Rd *BURH* RH15 ... 97 J2
Stirling Pl *HOVE* BN3 ............... 168 A4
Stirling Wy *EGRIN* RH19 .......... 14 B3
Stock Dl *RHAS* TN35 ............... 164 F2
Stockland La *UCK* TN22 ........... 55 H8
Stockleigh Rd *STLEO* TN38 ....... 4 A7
Stocks Meadow *BAT* TN33 ..... 159 H1
Stocks Rd *TENT* TN30 .............. 67 L3
Stockwell Rd *EGRIN* RH19 ...... 13 L8
Stoddards La *RYE* TN31 ........... 88 L1
Stoke Cl *SEAF* BN25 ............... 203 H3
Stoke Manor Cl *SEAF* BN25 ... 203 H3
Stonebeach Ri *STLEO* TN38 ... 138 F7
Stone Br *TENT* TN30 ................. 69 H4
Stonebridge La *UCK* TN22 ..... 103 M1
Stonecott Cl *CROW* TN6 ........... 39 M6
Stonecroft Cl *HOVE* BN3 ........ 167 L2
Stonecross La *HWH* RH16 ........ 49 K3
Stone Cross Rd *CROW* TN6 ..... 39 M8

Stonecross Rd *ROTT* BN2 ....... 169 M2
Stone Cross Rd *WADH* TN5 ..... 44 A3
Stonedene Cl *FROW* RH18 ....... 25 H4
Stonefield Rd *HAS* TN34 ............ 5 H5
Stonefield Wy *BURH* RH15 ...... 96 F1
Stonegate Cl *LW/ROSE* BN22 197 G2
Stonegate Rd *WADH* TN5 ........ 44 C5
Stonegate Wy *HTHF* TN21 ....... 80 B6
Stoneham Cl *LEW* BN7 ............... 2 F1
Stoneham Rd *HOVE* BN3 ........ 167 M5
Stonehouse Dr *BAT* TN33 ...... 138 F5
  *STLEO* TN38 ...................... 162 A4
Stonehurst Ct *ROTT* BN2 .......... 7 K4
Stonehurst La *MAYF* TN20 ....... 56 A6
  *UCK* TN22 ............................ 55 J8
Stoneleigh Av *BRI* BN1 ........... 145 M8
Stoneleigh Cl *BRI* BN1 ............ 145 M8
  *EGRIN* RH19 ........................ 13 M4
Stonelink Cl *STLEO* TN38 ....... 138 F7
Stonepark Dr *FROW* RH18 ....... 25 G4
Stone Pit La *HAWK* TN18 ......... 64 E1
Stonepound Rd
  *HPPT/KEY* BN6 ................... 122 C2
Stone Quarry Rd *RHWH* RH17 .. 36 D7
Stonery Cl *PTSD* BN41 ........... 167 G4
Stonery Rd *PTSD* BN41 .......... 167 G4
Stonestile La *RHAS* TN35 ....... 139 L3
Stone St *BRI* BN1 ....................... 6 B6
  *HAS* TN34 ............................ 5 H6
  *RTW* TN1 ............................. 20 B2
Stonewall Park Rd *RRTW* TN3 ... 18 F3
Stonewood Cl *SEAF* BN25 ...... 203 J2
Stoney La *SHOR* BN43 ............ 166 C6
Stonhouse Dr *STLEO* TN38 ... 162 B3
Storrington Cl *HOVE* BN3 ....... 167 L4
Straight Half Mile *UCK* TN22 ... 76 B1
Strand *RYE* TN31 ..................... 117 H1
Strand Hl *WSEA* TN36 ............ 116 F7
Strand Meadow
  *BUR/ETCH* TN19 .................. 60 B7
The Strand *ROTT* BN2 ............. 188 A3
Stratford St *RTW* TN1 ............... 20 C1
Strathfield Cl *HWH* RH16 ........ 71 M2
Strawberry Cl *RRTW* TN3 ........ 19 L6
Strawberry Flds *RYE* TN31 ...... 65 G7
Stream La *BAT* TN33 ............... 112 B4
  *HAWK* TN18 ....................... 47 M7
  *RHAS* TN35 ........................ 142 M3
Stream Pk *EGRIN* RH19 ........... 13 G3
Stream Pit La *HAWK* TN18 ....... 64 B1
Streamside Cl *HAS* TN34 ........ 162 E3
Streat Bostall *HPPT/KEY* BN6 ... 124 C7
Streatfield Gdns *HTHF* TN21 ... 79 M6
Streatfield Rd *HTHF* TN21 ....... 79 M6
  *UCK* TN22 ........................... 76 B7
Streat La *HPPT/KEY* BN6 ......... 98 C6
  *HPPT/KEY* BN6 ................... 124 C5
Streele La *UCK* TN22 ............... 77 K5
Streele Vw *UCK* TN22 .............. 76 D6
Street End La *HTHF* TN21 ........ 80 D6
  *MAYF* TN20 ......................... 80 F2
Streetlands *BAT* TN33 ............. 112 A5
Street La *RHWH* RH17 .............. 34 A6
The Street *BAT* TN33 ............... 112 A6
  *HPPT/KEY* BN6 ................... 123 M6
  *LEW* BN7 ........................... 171 L1
  *RING/NEW* BN8 ................. 174 B2
  *TENT* TN30 .......................... 67 K4
  *TENT* TN30 .......................... 69 G1
  *UCK* TN22 ......................... 103 H1
Stringer Wy *BRI* BN1 ............... 168 F3
The Stringwalk *HAIL* BN27 ..... 155 J7
Stroma Gdns *HAIL* BN27 ........ 154 F4
Strood Ga *RHWH* RH17 ............ 98 C1
Strood Rd *SLVH* TN37 ................ 4 A7
Stuart Av *EAST* BN21 .............. 196 C8
Stuart Cl *RTWE/PEM* TN2 ........ 19 M6
Stuart Wy *EGRIN* RH19 ........... 13 M6
Stubb La *RYE* TN31 ................. 114 B5
Studdens La *HAIL* BN27 ......... 133 K5
Sturdee Cl *LGNY* BN23 ........... 197 M7
Sudeley Pl *ROTT* BN2 ................. 7 M9
Sudeley St *ROTT* BN2 ................ 7 L8
Sudeley Ter *ROTT* BN2 ............... 7 L8
Suffolk Cl *BEXW* TN39 ............ 160 C7
Suffolk St *HOVE* BN3 .............. 167 M6
Sugar La *RHWH* RH17 ............. 37 L5
Sugworth Cl *HWH* RH16 .......... 48 D7
Sullington Cl *ROTT* BN2 .......... 169 M2
Sullington Wy *SHOR* BN43 ..... 166 A6
Sumach Cl *LW/ROSE* BN22 ... 196 E4
Summer Cl *PTSD* BN41 ........... 167 G7
Summerdale Rd *HOVE* BN3 .... 167 K4
Summerdown Cl
  *EDN/EASTW* BN20 ............. 206 D3
Summerdown La
  *EDN/EASTW* BN20 ............. 205 J5
Summerdown Rd
  *EDN/EASTW* BN20 ............. 206 C3
Summerfields *SLVH* TN37 ......... 4 C6
Summerfields Av *HAIL* BN27 ... 155 G6
Summerheath Rd *HAIL* BN27 ... 155 H6
Summer Hl *STLEO* TN38 ......... 162 A6
Summerhill Cl *HWH* RH16 ........ 48 F7
Summerhill Dr *HWH* RH16 ....... 48 F7
Summerhill Gra *HWH* RH16 ..... 48 F7
Summerhill La *HWH* RH16 ....... 48 F7
Summerlands Rd
  *LW/ROSE* BN22 ................. 196 B4
Summersdeane *STHW* BN42 ... 166 F5
Summervale Rd
  *SBGH/RUST* TN4 ................ 19 K5
Sumners *RHWH* RH17 .............. 34 A7
Sunningdale Cl *BEX* TN40 ...... 183 L1
  *HAIL* BN27 ......................... 155 G5
  *SEAF* BN25 ........................ 203 G4
Sunningdale Dr *STLEO* TN38 ... 161 M7
Sunninghill Av *HOVE* BN3 ....... 167 L4
Sunninghill Cl *HOVE* BN3 ....... 167 L4
Sunny Av *CRAWE* RH10 ........... 12 A6
Sunnybrooke Cl *UCK* TN22 ..... 76 D7
Sunnycroft Cl *RHWH* RH17 ..... 72 E4
Sunnydale Av *BRI* BN1 ........... 146 A8
Sunnydale Cl *BRI* BN1 ............ 146 B8
Sunnyhill Cl *CRAWE* RH10 ...... 12 A6
Sunnyside Rd *SBGH/RUST* TN4 .. 19 J2

Sunnywood Dr *HWH* RH16 ...... 71 K3
Sunset Cl *PEAHV* BN10 .......... 190 B5
  *PEV* BN24 ......................... 180 E8
Sunstar La *POLE* BN26 ........... 177 L8
Sun St *LEW* BN7 ......................... 2 F5
Sunview Av *PEAHV* BN10 ....... 190 D8
Surrenden Cl *BRI* BN1 ............ 168 F2
Surrenden Crs *BRI* BN1 .......... 168 F1
Surrenden Holt *BRI* BN1 ......... 168 F1
Surrenden Pk *BRI* BN1 ............ 169 G2
Surrenden Rd *BRI* BN1 ........... 168 F1
Surrey Cl *RTWE/PEM* TN2 ....... 19 M6
Surrey Rd *SEAF* BN25 ............ 202 C2
Surrey St *BRI* BN1 ...................... 6 C4
Susans Cl *RING/NEW* BN8 ..... 130 A1
Susan's Rd *EAST* BN21 ............ 10 E5
Sussex Av *HAIL* BN27 ............. 155 H6
Sussex Border Pth *BRI* BN1 ... 144 F4
  *EGRIN* RH19 ........................ 12 D7
  *EGRIN* RH19 ........................ 14 A5
  *EGRIN* RH19 ........................ 24 A1
  *PTSD* BN41 ....................... 144 A5
  *RHWH* RH17 ........................ 35 K6
  *RTW* TN1 ............................. 17 K2
  *TENT* TN30 .......................... 67 K7
  *WADH* TN5 .......................... 31 K6
  *WADH* TN5 .......................... 42 F1
  *WADH* TN5 .......................... 46 A2
Sussex Cl *BEXW* TN39 ........... 182 F1
  *HAIL* BN27 ......................... 155 H6
  *RTWE/PEM* TN2 .................. 20 C5
Sussex Gdns
  *EDN/EASTW* BN20 ............. 205 J5
  *HWH* RH16 ........................... 72 B3
Sussex Ms *RTWE/PEM* TN2 ..... 20 A4
Sussex Pl *ROTT* BN2 .................. 7 G6
Sussex Rd *HOVE* BN3 ............. 186 B1
  *HWH* RH16 ........................... 71 L3
  *STLEO* TN38 ...................... 162 A8
Sussex Sq *ROTT* BN2 .............. 187 L2
Sussex St *ROTT* BN2 ................. 7 G6
Sussex Wy *BURH* RH15 ............ 96 E1
  *PEAHV* BN10 ...................... 189 M7
Sutherland Av *BEXW* TN39 ..... 183 G3
Sutherland Cl *BEXW* TN39 ..... 182 F2
Sutherland Rd *ROTT* BN2 .......... 7 K7
  *RTW* TN1 ............................. 20 B4
Sutton Av *PEAHV* BN10 .......... 190 B7
  *SEAF* BN25 ........................ 203 G4
Sutton Av North *PEAHV* BN10 .. 190 B6
Sutton Cl *ROTT* BN2 ............... 170 E5
Sutton Croft La *SEAF* BN25 .... 202 E3
Sutton Dro *SEAF* BN25 ........... 202 E2
Sutton Park Rd *SEAF* BN25 .... 202 E3
Sutton Pl *BEX* TN40 ............... 183 L2
Sutton Rd *EAST* BN21 .............. 10 E6
  *SEAF* BN25 ........................ 202 F3
The Suttons *RYE* TN31 ........... 118 F5
  *STLEO* TN38 ...................... 161 M4
Swaines Wy *HTHF* TN21 .......... 80 A8
Swainham La *BAT* TN33 .......... 161 G3
Swainsthorpe Cl *HWH* RH16 ... 71 M3
Swallow Bank *STLEO* TN38 ... 161 M4
Swallow Cl *LGNY* BN23 .......... 197 H4
Swallow Ct *UCK* TN22 ........... 102 D1
Swallow Dr *BAT* TN33 ............. 137 M2
The Swallows *PEAHV* BN10 ... 190 B5
Swamp Rd *LYDD* TN29 ............ 95 G2
Swanborough Dro *LEW* BN7 .. 169 M7
Swanborough Hollow
  *LEW* BN7 ........................... 172 A2
Swanborough Pl *ROTT* BN2 ... 169 M7
Swan Cottages *TENT* TN30 ..... 67 K3
Swanley Cl *LGNY* BN23 .......... 197 J4
Swann Cl *BURH* RH15 .............. 97 K3
Swannee Cl *PEAHV* BN10 ...... 190 D5
Swan Rd *HAIL* BN27 ............... 155 J8
Swansbrook La *HTHF* TN21 .... 131 K5
Swans Ghyll *FROW* RH18 ........ 24 E3
Swan St *TENT* TN30 .................. 67 H3
Swan Ter *HAS* TN34 ................... 5 K6
Swaylands Av *CROW* TN6 ....... 39 M7
Sweethaws La *CROW* TN6 ...... 39 J8
Sweetings La *RTW* TN3 ............ 32 D5
Sweetlands *HPPT/KEY* BN6 ... 123 H1
Swife La *HTHF* TN21 ................. 81 J3
Swift Cl *CROW* TN6 .................. 39 K5
  *HPPT/KEY* BN6 ..................... 96 D3
  *UCK* TN22 .......................... 102 D1
Swinburne Av *LW/ROSE* BN22 .. 196 B3
Swynford Dr *STLEO* TN38 ...... 161 M1
Sybron Wy *CROW* TN6 ............ 40 D6
Sycamore Cl *BEXW* TN39 ...... 182 C1
  *HTHF* TN21 ......................... 80 B8
  *LW/ROSE* BN22 ................. 196 D3
  *LYDD* TN29 ......................... 95 K7
  *PTSD* BN41 ....................... 167 J3
  *ROTT* BN2 .......................... 170 E4
  *SEAF* BN25 ........................ 203 J3
  *STLEO* TN38 ...................... 162 A5
Sycamore Ct *UCK* TN22 .......... 76 D6
Sycamore Dr *EGRIN* RH19 ...... 14 A5
  *HAIL* BN27 ......................... 155 H6
The Sycamores *PEAHV* BN10 . 190 D5
Sydney Cl *STLEO* TN38 ......... 162 B3
Sydney Little Rd *STLEO* TN38 .. 161 K2
Sydney Rd *HWH* RH16 .............. 48 E8
  *LW/ROSE* BN22 .................. 11 G5
Sydney St *BRI* BN1 ..................... 6 E5
Sylvan Cl *HWH* RH16 ............... 72 B2
Sylvester Wy *HOVE* BN3 ........ 167 J3
Symbister Rd *PTSD* BN41 ...... 167 J7
Syresham Gdns *HWH* RH16 .... 71 L2

## T

Tackleway *HAS* TN34 ................ 5 L6
Taddington Rd *LW/ROSE* BN22 . 11 J3
Tainter's Brook *UCK* TN22 ....... 76 E6
Talbot Crs *BEXW* TN39 ........... 146 D8
Talbot Pk *RTWE/PEM* TN2 ....... 20 D1
Talbot Rd *HAWK* TN18 ............. 47 M6
Talbot Ter *LEW* BN7 ................... 2 F5
Tall Ash Dr *SLVH* TN37 ........... 162 C2
Tamarack Cl *LW/ROSE* BN22 .. 196 D4
Tamar Cl *PEV* BN24 ................. 197 G1
Tamplin Ter *ROTT* BN2 ............... 7 G2
Tamworth Rd *HOVE* BN3 ......... 167 M7
Tandridge Rd *LGNY* BN23 ...... 197 M5
Tandridge Rd *HOVE* BN3 ......... 167 L8
Tangier La *RRTW* TN3 ............... 20 B8
Tangle Oak *EGRIN* RH19 .......... 12 E2
Tanglewood Coppice
  *BEXW* TN39 ...................... 182 E3
Tangmere Cl *BEXW* TN39 ....... 182 E3
Tangmere Rd *BRI* BN1 ............ 146 A8
Tanhouse La *RYE* TN31 ............ 89 M4
Tanners Brook *LEW* BN7 ............ 3 C7
Tanners Fld *RHWH* RH17 .......... 98 A1
Tanners Wy *CROW* TN6 ........... 40 A5
Tanyard *HAWK* TN18 ................ 64 B1
Tanyard Av *EGRIN* RH19 ......... 14 A6
Tanyard La *RHWH* RH17 .......... 51 J2
  *WSEA* TN36 ....................... 116 E6
Tapsell's La *WADH* TN5 ............ 43 J1
Tarner Rd *ROTT* BN2 .................. 7 H6
Tarragon Wy *SHOR* BN43 ....... 166 C5
Tarring Cl *NEWHV* BN9 ........... 191 K4
Tas Combe Wy
  *EDN/EASTW* BN20 ............. 196 A4
Tate Crs *BURH* RH15 ............... 96 F1
Taunton Rd *ROTT* BN2 ............ 169 M5
Taunton Wy *ROTT* BN2 ............ 170 A5
Tavistock Down *BRI* BN1 ........ 169 J4
Taylor Cl *STLEO* TN38 ............ 161 M2
Tea Garden La *RRTW* TN3 ........ 19 H5
Teal Ct *STLEO* TN38 ................ 161 L3
Teg Cl *PTSD* BN41 .................. 167 J4
Telegraph St *ROTT* BN2 ............. 7 K8
Telford Rd *STLEO* TN38 .......... 162 A1
Telham Cl *HAS* TN34 ............... 163 G1
Telham La *BAT* TN33 ............... 137 L5
Telscombe Cliffs Wy
  *PEAHV* BN10 ...................... 189 M7
Telscombe Pk *PEAHV* BN10 ... 190 C4
  *LGNY* BN23 ....................... 197 M4
  *PEAHV* BN10 ...................... 190 C4
Temple Gdns *HOVE* BN3 ........... 6 A4
Temple Gv *BURH* RH15 ............ 96 D2
Temple St *BRI* BN1 ..................... 6 A6
Tenantry Down Rd *ROTT* BN2 .. 169 L7
Tenantry Rd *ROTT* BN2 ........... 169 K6
Tennis Cl *HAIL* BN27 ............... 155 H7
Tennis Rd *HOVE* BN3 .............. 167 L8
Tennyson Ri *EGRIN* RH19 ........ 13 J5
Tenterden Cl *LGNY* BN23 ....... 197 K4
Tenterden Ri *HAS* TN34 ............. 4 D1
Terminus Av *BEXW* TN39 ........ 182 F3
Terminus Pl *BRI* BN1 ................. 6 D3
Terminus Rd *BEXW* TN39 ....... 183 G3
  *BRI* BN1 ................................ 6 D3
  *EAST* BN21 .......................... 10 F6
  *BRI* BN1 ................................ 6 D4
Terminus St *BRI* BN1 .................. 6 D4
Terrace Rd *SLVH* TN37 ............... 4 C6
Thackeray Cl *LGNY* BN23 ...... 197 L3
Thakeham Cl *BEX* TN40 .......... 161 G8
Thames Cl *ROTT* BN2 ................. 7 H6
Thanet Wy *HAS* TN34 ................ 4 E2
Thatchers Cl *BURH* RH15 ......... 97 K5
The Thatchings *POLE* BN26 ... 196 A1
Theobalds *HAWK* TN18 ............ 47 M4
Theobalds Gn *HTHF* TN21 ...... 106 A1
Theobalds Rd *BURH* RH15 ....... 71 J8
Third Av *HOVE* BN3 ................. 186 B1
  *NEWHV* BN9 ........................ 8 E5
Third Rd *PEAHV* BN10 ............ 190 A7
Third St *RRTW* TN3 .................. 18 B8
Thirlmere Rd *SBGH/RUST* TN4 .. 19 K1
Thomas Brassey Cl
  *SLVH* TN37 ....................... 162 B1
Thomas St *LEW* BN7 .................. 3 J4
  *SBGH/RUST* TN4 ................ 20 A1
Thomas Turner Dr
  *RING/NEW* BN8 .................. 130 A1
Thompson Rd *BRI* BN1 ............ 169 J5
  *NEWHV* BN9 ...................... 191 M4
Thornbank Crs *BEXW* TN39 ... 182 F3
Thornbush Crs *PTSD* BN41 .... 167 H3
Thorndean Rd *ROTT* BN2 ........ 169 K3
Thorne Crs *BEXW* TN39 .......... 159 L5
Thornfield Gdns
  *RTWE/PEM* TN2 .................. 20 F1
Thornhill Av *BRI* BN1 ............... 146 A7
Thornhill Cl *HOVE* BN3 ........... 167 L4
Thornhill Ri *PTSD* BN41 .......... 167 G2
Thornhill Wy *PTSD* BN41 ....... 167 G2
The Thorns *RHAS* TN35 ........... 141 G6
Thornwell Rd *POLE* BN26 ....... 176 F7
Thornwood Cl
  *LW/ROSE* BN22 ................. 196 E4
Thorny Cl *HTHF* TN21 ............... 80 A8
Three Leg Cross Rd *WADH* TN5 .. 45 K3
Three Oaks La *WADH* TN5 ....... 31 J7
Thurrock Cl
  *EDN/EASTW* BN20 ............. 196 B2
Thyme Cl *SHOR* BN43 ............ 166 C5
Thyssel La *RYE* TN31 ................ 65 H8
Tibbs Mill La *UCK* TN22 ........... 54 E5
Ticehurst Av *BEXW* TN39 ........ 181 M1
Ticehurst Rd *ROTT* BN2 ........... 187 M1
Tichborne St *BRI* BN1 ................ 6 C4
Tickerage La *UCK* TN22 ............ 77 M8
Tidebrook Gdns *LGNY* BN23 ... 197 M4
Tideswell Rd *EAST* BN21 .......... 10 E5
Tidy St *BRI* BN1 ......................... 6 E5
Tilbury Pl *ROTT* BN2 ................... 7 H5
Tilbury Wy *ROTT* BN2 ................. 7 H5
Tile Barn Cl *UCK* TN22 ........... 101 K6
Tile Barn Rd *STLEO* TN38 ...... 161 M2
Tilehurst Dr *HAIL* BN27 .......... 155 G6
Tilekiln La *RHAS* TN35 ............ 163 L2
Tilers Cl *BURH* RH15 ................ 97 K3
Tilgate Cl *EAST* BN21 .............. 196 D7
  *ROTT* BN2 ............................ 7 L5
Tilgate Dr *BEXW* TN39 ............ 182 D3
Tilley La *HAIL* BN27 ................. 157 K1
Tillingham Av *RYE* TN31 ......... 117 H1
Tillingham La *RYE* TN31 ........... 89 M8
  *RYE* TN31 .......................... 116 B1
Tillingham Vw *RYE* TN31 ........ 114 A2

**Tillingham Wy** *PEV* BN24 197 G1
**Tillstone Cl** *ROTT* BN2 169 K4 2
**Tillstone St** *ROTT* BN2 7 H7
**Tilsmore Cnr** *HTHF* TN21 79 M7
**Tilsmore Rd** *HTHF* TN21 79 M7
**Tiltwood Dr** *CRAWE* RH10 12 C5
**Timberlaine Rd** *PEV* BN24 198 C2
**Timberley Rd** *LW/ROSE* BN22 196 D5
**Timbers Ct** *HAIL* BN27 155 J7 3
**Timber Yard Cottages** *LEW* BN7 3 J6
**Tindal Cl** *BURH* RH15 97 K3 3
**Tinker's La** *UCK* TN22 78 E2
*WADH* TN5 45 K3
**Tintern Cl** *BRI* BN1 169 H5
*LW/ROSE* BN22 196 D3
**Tisbury Rd** *HOVE* BN3 168 C8
**Titchfield Cl** *BURH* RH15 97 K5
**Tithe Barn Fld** *WSEA* TN36 141 M1 2
**Tithe Orch** *EGRIN* RH19 12 E2
**Titian Rd** *HOVE* BN3 167 M7
**Tiverton Dr** *BEX* TN40 183 L1
**Tivoli Crs** *BRI* BN1 168 D5
**Tivoli Crs North** *BRI* BN1 168 D4
**Tivoli Pl** *BRI* BN1 168 D4
**Tivoli Rd** *BRI* BN1 168 D4
**Tolhurst La** *WADH* TN5 45 G5
**Tolkien Rd** *LGNY* BN23 197 L4
**Tollgate** *PEAHV* BN10 190 B5
**Tollgates** *BAT* TN33 137 H2
**Toll La** *UCK* TN22 52 F5
**Tollwood Pk** *CROW* TN6 40 B5
**Tollwood Rd** *CROW* TN6 40 B6
**Toll Wood Rd** *HTHF* TN21 105 M7
**Tompset's Bank** *FROW* RH18 24 F6
**Tomtits La** *FROW* RH18 24 E5
**Tonbridge Wy** *RYE* TN31 118 E4 2
**Tongdean Av** *HOVE* BN3 168 C3
**Tongdean La** *BRI* BN1 168 D2
**Tongdean Ri** *BRI* BN1 168 C2
**Tongdean Rd** *HOVE* BN3 168 B3
**Top Cross Rd** *BEX* TN40 161 G7
**Top Dr** *UCK* TN22 53 G8
**Top Rd** *EGRIN* RH19 34 F1
*TENT* TN30 68 E3
**Torcross Cl** *ROTT* BN2 169 L5
**Torfield Rd** *EAST* BN21 10 B4
**Toronto Ter** *LEW* BN7 2 F5
*ROTT* BN2 7 H5
**Torrance Cl** *HOVE* BN3 167 M5 2
**Tor Rd** *PEAHV* BN10 190 C4
**Tor Rd West** *PEAHV* BN10 190 B4
**Totland Rd** *ROTT* BN2 7 L2
**Tottington Wy** *SHOR* BN43 166 B5 4
**Tott Yew Rd** *EDN/EASTW* BN20 196 A2
**Tourney Rd** *LYDD* TN29 121 H1
**Tovey Cl** *EAST* BN21 196 D8
**Tower Cl** *EGRIN* RH19 13 L4
*PEV* BN24 180 F8
**Towergate** *BRI* BN1 168 E4
**Tower Ride** *UCK* TN22 76 D5
**Tower Rd** *ROTT* BN2 7 J4
*STLEO* TN38 4 A4
**Tower Rd West** *STLEO* TN38 162 B6
**Towerscroft Av** *SLVH* TN37 162 B1
**Tower St** *HTHF* TN21 80 B6
*RYE* TN31 91 J8 2
**Tower Vw** *UCK* TN22 76 D6 2
**Town Hl** *RRTW* TN3 33 G2
**Trafalgar Cl** *PEAHV* BN10 190 C5 3
*STLEO* TN38 138 F7
**Trafalgar Ct** *BRI* BN1 6 F4 2
**Trafalgar Ga** *ROTT* BN2 187 M3
**Trafalgar La** *BRI* BN1 6 E5
**Trafalgar Pl** *BRI* BN1 6 E4 2
**Trafalgar St** *BRI* BN1 6 E4
**Tram Rd** *RYE* TN31 118 A4
**Transit Rd** *NEWHV* BN9 9 H4
**Travellers La** *RHAS* TN35 163 J2
**Treblers Rd** *CROW* TN6 40 D7
**Tredcroft Rd** *HOVE* BN3 168 B4
**Treemans Rd** *RHWH* RH17 50 B4
**Tree Tops Cl** *ROTT* BN2 170 E6
**Tremola Av** *ROTT* BN2 189 H4
**Trenches Rd** *CROW* TN6 39 M5
**Treyford Cl** *ROTT* BN2 170 E5
**Triangle Rd** *HWH* RH16 71 L3
**The Triangle**
*EDN/EASTW* BN20 196 A3 4
**Trinity Cl** *RTWE/PEM* TN2 20 D2
**Trinity Fld** *RING/NEW* BN8 127 L8
**Trinity Pl** *EAST* BN21 10 F7
**Trinity Rd** *HPPT/KEY* BN6 96 A8
**Trinity St** *HAS* TN34 4 F7
*ROTT* BN2 7 H2
**Trinity Trees** *EAST* BN21 10 F7
**Tristan Gdns** *SBGH/RUST* TN4 19 K2 2
**Troon Cl** *SEAF* BN25 192 A8 3
**Trossachs Cl** *LGNY* BN23 197 K3
**Troy Cl** *CROW* TN6 40 A5 4
**Truleigh Cl** *ROTT* BN2 170 F7
**Truleigh Dr** *PTSD* BN41 167 G2
**Truleigh Wy** *SHOR* BN43 166 A5
**Truman Dr** *STLEO* TN38 138 F8
**Trumpet La** *HAIL* BN27 134 B4
**Tubwell La** *CROW* TN6 40 D7
*HTHF* TN21 105 M4
**Tudor Av** *STLEO* TN38 162 A7
**Tudor Cl** *EGRIN* RH19 13 M7 4
*HOVE* BN3 167 M4
*SEAF* BN25 202 D2
**Tudor Ct** *RTWE/PEM* TN2 19 L5 3
**Tudor Gdns** *BURH* RH15 96 F2 4
**Tudor Wk** *UCK* TN22 103 H1
**Tugwell Rd** *LW/ROSE* BN22 196 F4
**Tumulus Rd** *ROTT* BN2 189 J4
**Tunbridge Wells Rd** *CROW* TN6 41 L8
*MAYF* TN20 56 F1
**Tunnel Rd** *RTW* TN1 20 B1
**Turkey La** *BURH* RH15 97 H3 3
**Turkey Rd** *BEXW* TN39 159 K7
**Turk's Br** *HTHF* TN21 58 E6
**Turnberry Cl** *STLEO* TN38 161 M7
**Turnberry Dr** *HAIL* BN27 155 G6
**Turner Cl** *BEX* TN40 183 K1
*LGNY* BN23 197 K5 4
**Turner Ct** *EGRIN* RH19 14 A3
**Turners Green La** *WADH* TN5 31 M8
**Turners Green Rd** *WADH* TN5 31 M7
**Turner's Hill Rd** *EGRIN* RH19 23 G1
**Turners Mill Cl** *HWH* RH16 48 D7 4
**Turners Mill Rd** *HWH* RH16 48 D8
**Turners Wy** *BURH* RH15 96 F2 3
**Turnpike Cl** *PEAHV* BN10 190 C6
*RING/NEW* BN8 128 A7
**Turton Cl** *ROTT* BN2 7 L7
**Tutts Barn La** *LW/ROSE* BN22 10 D2
**Tuxford Rd** *SBGH/RUST* TN4 19 H1
**Twineham Cl** *ROTT* BN2 169 M7
**Twineham Rd** *EAST* BN21 196 D7
**Twitten Cl** *STHW* BN42 166 E7 4
**Twitten La** *EGRIN* RH19 12 E2
**The Twitten** *BURH* RH15 97 H2 4
*CROW* TN6 39 L5
*STHW* BN42 166 E7
**Twyford Crs** *SLVH* TN37 162 C2
**Twyford Rd** *BRI* BN1 146 D8
**Twyfords** *CROW* TN6 39 L5 3
**Twyhurst Ct** *EGRIN* RH19 13 K3 3
**Tye Cl** *ROTT* BN2 189 K6
**Tyedean Rd** *PEAHV* BN10 189 M6
**Tye Hill Rd** *POLE* BN26 176 F2
**Tye Vw** *PEAHV* BN10 190 A5 4
**Tyler's Gn** *RHWH* RH17 71 H2
**Tylers La** *UCK* TN22 52 E5
**Tyndale Av** *BEXW* TN39 182 C3

## U

**Uckfield Cl** *ROTT* BN2 169 M8
**Uckfield Rd** *CROW* TN6 39 H8
*RING/NEW* BN8 127 H7
**Uckham La** *BAT* TN33 111 L8
**Udimore Rd** *RYE* TN31 114 B2
*RYE* TN31 116 E2
**Undercliff** *STLEO* TN38 4 A9
**Underdown Rd** *STHW* BN42 166 E6
**Underhill** *UCK* TN22 76 B1
**Underhill La** *HPPT/KEY* BN6 122 E6
**Under Rd** *HAIL* BN27 156 B3
**Underwood Cl** *CRAWE* RH10 12 B6 3
**Union Cl** *HAIL* BN27 155 H4
**Union Rd** *ROTT* BN2 7 G3
**Union St** *BRI* BN1 6 D7
*STLEO* TN38 4 A8
**Upland Rd** *EDN/EASTW* BN20 206 B3
**Uplands Cl** *BEXW* TN39 159 M8
*UCK* TN22 76 C5
**Uplands Pk** *HTHF* TN21 80 E5
**Uplands Rd** *BRI* BN1 169 J4
**Upper Abbey Rd** *ROTT* BN2 7 L8
**Upper Av** *EAST* BN21 10 F4
*LW/ROSE* BN22 10 E3
**Upper Bannings Rd** *ROTT* BN2 189 L3
**Upper Bedford St** *ROTT* BN2 7 J8
**Upper Belgrave Rd** *SEAF* BN25 202 F1
**Upper Bevendean Av**
*ROTT* BN2 169 L5
**Upper Broomgrove Rd**
*HAS* TN34 163 H3
**Upper Carlisle Rd**
*EDN/EASTW* BN20 206 C6
**Upper Chalvington Pl**
*ROTT* BN2 187 L1
**Upper Church Rd** *SLVH* TN37 162 B2
**Upper Chyngton Gdns**
*SEAF* BN25 203 H1 4
**Upper Cl** *FROW* RH18 24 F4
**Upper Cumberland Wk**
*RTW* TN1 20 B5
**The Upper Dr** *HOVE* BN3 168 C6
**Upper Duke's Dr**
*EDN/EASTW* BN20 206 D7
**Upper Gardner St** *BRI* BN1 6 E5
**Upper Glen Rd** *SLVH* TN37 162 A1
**Upper Gloucester Rd** *BRI* BN1 6 D5 3
**Upper Greenwoods La**
*HTHF* TN21 81 H8
**Upper Grosvenor Rd**
*SBGH/RUST* TN4 20 B1
**Upper Hamilton Rd** *BRI* BN1 6 B1
**Upper Hollingdean Rd**
*BRI* BN1 169 H5
**Upper Horsebridge Rd**
*HAIL* BN27 155 G3
**Upper King's Dr**
*EDN/EASTW* BN20 196 B5
**Upper Kingston La**
*STHW* BN42 166 D5
**Upper Lake** *BAT* TN33 137 K2
**Upper Lewes Rd** *ROTT* BN2 7 G2
**Upper Market St** *HOVE* BN3 186 D1 3
**Upper Maze Hl** *STLEO* TN38 162 B6
**Upper Nellington** *RRTW* TN3 19 H2
**Upper North St** *BRI* BN1 6 B5
**Upper Park Pl** *ROTT* BN2 7 H6
**Upper Park Rd** *SLVH* TN37 4 B3
**Upper Profit** *RRTW* TN3 19 G3
**Upper Ratton Dr**
*EDN/EASTW* BN20 196 B6
**Upper Rock Gdns** *ROTT* BN2 7 H8
**Upper St James's St** *ROTT* BN2 7 H8
**Upper St Johns Rd** *BURH* RH15 97 G3
**Upper Sea Rd** *BEX* TN40 183 K2
**Upper Sherwood Rd**
*SEAF* BN25 202 F2
**Upper Shoreham Rd**
*STHW* BN42 166 D5
**Upper South Rd** *SLVH* TN37 4 A4
**Upper Station Rd** *HTHF* TN21 80 A7
**Upper Stephens** *RRTW* TN3 19 G3
**Upper Stoneham**
*RING/NEW* BN8 149 M2
**Upper St** *EDN/EASTW* BN20 205 H6
**Upper Sudeley St** *ROTT* BN2 7 L8 1
**Upperton Gdns** *EAST* BN21 10 D5
**Upperton La** *EAST* BN21 10 C5
**Upperton Rd** *EAST* BN21 10 A4
**Upper Valley Rd** *NEWHV* BN9 8 C5
**Upper Wellington Rd** *ROTT* BN2 7 J2
**Upper Winfield Av** *BRI* BN1 145 M8
**Upper Wish Hl**
*EDN/EASTW* BN20 196 B6
**Upton Av** *STHW* BN42 166 E5
**Upton Quarry** *RRTW* TN3 18 F3 4
**Upwick Rd** *EDN/EASTW* BN20 206 C3

## V

**Vale Av** *BRI* BN1 145 L7
*RTW* TN1 20 A3 5
**Valebridge Cl** *BURH* RH15 71 J8 1
**Valebridge Dr** *BURH* RH15 97 J1 2
**Valebridge Rd** *BURH* RH15 97 J1
**Vale Cl** *SEAF* BN25 203 G2
**Vale Gdns** *PTSD* BN41 167 H7
**Valence Rd** *LEW* BN7 2 C5
**Valentine Dr** *BURH* RH15 96 E2
**Valerie Cl** *PTSD* BN41 167 H4
**Vale Rd** *BAT* TN33 137 H1
*HAWK* TN18 47 M3
*HWH* RH16 71 K4
*MAYF* TN20 57 H4
*PTSD* BN41 167 J7
*ROTT* BN2 189 K3
*RTW* TN1 20 A3
*SEAF* BN25 202 F2
*SLVH* TN37 4 A1
**The Vale** *ROTT* BN2 188 E1
**Vale View Rd** *HTHF* TN21 80 B8 3
**Vallance Cl** *BURH* RH15 96 E2
**Vallance Gdns** *HOVE* BN3 168 A8
**Vallance Rd** *HOVE* BN3 168 A8
**Valley Cl** *BRI* BN1 168 C2
*NEWHV* BN9 8 D2
**Valley Dene** *NEWHV* BN9 8 D4
**Valley Dr** *BRI* BN1 168 C2
*SEAF* BN25 203 G1
**Valley Ri** *SEAF* BN25 202 F2
**Valley Rd** *CROW* TN6 39 M5
*LEW* BN7 2 B8
*NEWHV* BN9 8 B4
*PEAHV* BN10 190 C4
*PTSD* BN41 167 G4
*SBGH/RUST* TN4 19 K2
**Valley Side Rd** *HAS* TN34 163 J3
**Valley View Cl** *CROW* TN6 39 M5
**Val Prinseps Rd** *PEV* BN24 198 C2
**Vanguard Wy** *CROW* TN6 38 F7
*EGRIN* RH19 14 F1
*POLE* BN26 175 M4
*RING/NEW* BN8 130 F4
*SEAF* BN25 203 G5
*UCK* TN22 54 C6
*UCK* TN22 104 A3
**Varndean Cl** *BRI* BN1 168 E3
**Varndean Dr** *BRI* BN1 168 E3
**Varndean Gdns** *BRI* BN1 168 E3
**Varndean Holt** *BRI* BN1 168 F3
**Varndean Rd** *BRI* BN1 168 E3
**Vega Cl** *HAIL* BN27 155 K7
**Ventnor Cl** *LGNY* BN23 197 H2
**Ventnor Vls** *HOVE* BN3 168 B8
**Venture Cl** *BEX* TN40 183 M2
**Verbania Wy** *EGRIN* RH19 14 B5
**Verdant Cl** *HAS* TN34 4 D5
**Vere Rd** *BRI* BN1 6 F1
**Vermont Rd** *SBGH/RUST* TN4 19 J2 2
**Vernon Av** *PEAHV* BN10 190 D8
*ROTT* BN2 170 C5
**Vernon Cl** *LGNY* BN23 197 L7 6
**Vernon Rd** *UCK* TN22 76 D8
**Vernons Rd** *RING/NEW* BN8 74 C7
**Vernon Ter** *BRI* BN1 6 B4
**Veronica Wy** *ROTT* BN2 7 H8
**Verulam Pl** *SLVH* TN37 4 E8
**Viaduct Rd** *BRI* BN1 6 E2
**Vian Av** *LGNY* BN23 197 M8
**Vicarage Cl** *NEWHV* BN9 191 L4 2
*RING/NEW* BN8 150 C1
*SEAF* BN25 202 F3
**Vicarage Dr** *EDN/EASTW* BN20 206 D3
**Vicarage La** *BUR/ETCH* TN19 82 A3
*EDN/EASTW* BN20 206 D3 6
*HAIL* BN27 132 A8
*HAIL* BN27 155 J6
*RHAS* TN35 139 K3
*RHWH* RH17 72 F3
*ROTT* BN2 188 F5 1
**Vicarage Rd** *BUR/ETCH* TN19 82 A3
*CRAWE* RH10 12 A7
*EDN/EASTW* BN20 206 D3
*HAIL* BN27 155 J7
*HAS* TN34 5 J4
**Vicarage Ter** *ROTT* BN2 188 F5 2
**Vicarage Wy** *BUR/ETCH* TN19 62 A3
*RING/NEW* BN8 150 D1
**Victor Cl** *SEAF* BN25 202 D1
**Victoria Av** *BURH* RH15 96 E3 2
*PEAHV* BN10 190 C8
*RHAS* TN35 163 J2
**Victoria Cl** *BURH* RH15 96 E3 3
*POLE* BN26 177 M7
**Victoria Dr** *EAST* BN21 206 C1
*EDN/EASTW* BN20 196 B8
*EDN/EASTW* BN20 206 C2
**Victoria Gdns** *BURH* RH15 96 E4
*EDN/EASTW* BN20 206 C2 1
**Victoria Gv** *HOVE* BN3 168 C8 2
**Victoria Pl** *BRI* BN1 6 B5 1
**Victoria Rd** *BEXW* TN39 183 H2
*BRI* BN1 6 B5
*BURH* RH15 96 E4
*CROW* TN6 40 C6
*EDN/EASTW* BN20 206 B1 3
*HAIL* BN27 155 J7
*HAIL* BN27 157 H1
*HWH* RH16 71 M3
*MAYF* TN20 57 G3
*POLE* BN26 177 M7
*PTSD* BN41 167 H6
*RTW* TN1 20 B2 9
*SLVH* TN37 4 C8
*STHW* BN42 166 D7
**Victoria St** *BRI* BN1 6 B5
**Victoria Wy** *BURH* RH15 96 F4
*EGRIN* RH19 13 M7
*WSEA* TN36 143 G1
**Victory Ms** *ROTT* BN2 188 A3
**View Bank** *RHAS* TN35 163 K4
**View Rd** *PEAHV* BN10 190 C6
**Viking Cl** *SEAF* BN25 192 A8
**The Village Barn** *BRI* BN1 145 L7
**Village Ms** *BEXW* TN39 182 C2
**The Village** *EDN/EASTW* BN20 206 D6
**Village Wy** *BRI* BN1 147 J8
**Villa Rd** *SLVH* TN37 4 C8
**Villiers Cl** *ROTT* BN2 170 E6
**Vincent Cl** *LGNY* BN23 197 M7 5
**Vinehall Cl** *HAS* TN34 163 G1
**Vinehall Rd** *RBTBR* TN32 85 L8
**Vine Lands** *LYDD* TN29 95 H8
**The Vineries** *BURH* RH15 97 K3
*LGNY* BN23 197 K4 10
**Vines Cross Rd** *HTHF* TN21 106 A6
*ROTT* BN2 169 M7
**Vine Sq** *LW/ROSE* BN22 197 K8
**Vine St** *BRI* BN1 6 F5
**Vineyard La** *WADH* TN5 45 H4
**Virgin's Cft** *BAT* TN33 111 K8
**Virgin's La** *BAT* TN33 111 K8
**Vowels La** *EGRIN* RH19 22 D4

## W

**Wade Cl** *LGNY* BN23 197 M7
**Wadhurst Cl** *LW/ROSE* BN22 196 F4
*SLVH* TN37 162 B1
**Wadhurst La** *BAT* TN33 136 E1
**Wadhurst Ri** *ROTT* BN2 187 M1
**Wadhurst Rd** *CROW* TN6 42 F3
*RRTW* TN3 30 C5
*WADH* TN5 30 F6
**Wadlands Brook Rd**
*EGRIN* RH19 13 K1
**Wagg Cl** *EGRIN* RH19 14 A5
**Waghorns La** *UCK* TN22 78 C1
**Wainwright Cl** *STLEO* TN38 161 K3
**Wainwright Rd** *BEXW* TN39 183 H2
**Waite Cl** *LEW* BN7 3 H3
**Waites La** *RHAS* TN35 164 E1
**Wakefield Rd** *ROTT* BN2 7 G1
**Wakehurst La** *RHWH* RH17 34 A6
**Waldegrave Rd** *BRI* BN1 168 F4
**Waldegrave St** *HAS* TN34 5 H5
**Waldene Cl** *HAS* TN34 5 H1
**Waldron Av** *BRI* BN1 146 D8
**Waldron Cl** *LW/ROSE* BN22 196 D6
**Waldron Rd** *RING/NEW* BN8 130 A1
**Waldron Thorns** *HTHF* TN21 80 A8
**Waldshut Rd** *LEW* BN7 2 B2
**Walesbeech Rd** *ROTT* BN2 189 K6
**Walker Cl** *LGNY* BN23 197 M7
**Wallace Cl** *RTWE/PEM* TN2 20 A6
**Wallands Crs** *LEW* BN7 2 E4
**The Walled Gdn** *UCK* TN22 76 D2 1
**Wall Hill Rd** *FROW* RH18 24 D1
**Wallis Av** *LGNY* BN23 197 L7
**Wallis Cl** *CROW* TN6 40 A5 3
**Wallis Pl** *LGNY* BN23 197 L6
**Wallis Wy** *BURH* RH15 96 E2 3
**Wallsend Rd** *PEV* BN24 180 B8
**Walmer Crs** *ROTT* BN2 170 A5
**Walmer Rd** *SEAF* BN25 203 J2
**Walnut Cl** *BRI* BN1 168 E3
*HTHF* TN21 80 B8
**Walnut Pk** *HWH* RH16 72 B2 3
**Walnut Tree Wk**
*EDN/EASTW* BN20 196 B6
**Walnut Wk** *POLE* BN26 178 A8
**Walpole Rd** *ROTT* BN2 7 K8
**Walpole Ter** *ROTT* BN2 7 L7
**Walshes Rd** *CROW* TN6 40 A7
**Walsingham Cl**
*LW/ROSE* BN22 196 D3 7
**Walsingham Rd** *HOVE* BN3 167 M8
**Walton Bank** *BRI* BN1 169 L1
**Walton Cl** *SLVH* TN37 162 C1 12
**Walton Pk** *BEXW* TN39 182 F2
**Wanderdown Cl** *ROTT* BN2 188 E2
**Wanderdown Dr** *ROTT* BN2 188 E2
**Wanderdown Rd** *ROTT* BN2 188 D2
**Wanderdown Wy** *ROTT* BN2 188 E2
**Wannock Av**
*EDN/EASTW* BN20 195 M3
**Wannock Cl** *BEX* TN40 161 G8
**Wannock Dr** *POLE* BN26 195 M1
**Wannock Gdns**
*EDN/EASTW* BN20 195 M3
*POLE* BN26 195 M3
**Wannock La** *EDN/EASTW* BN20 195 M3
**Wannock Rd** *LW/ROSE* BN22 11 L2
*POLE* BN26 195 M1
**Warbleton Cl** *ROTT* BN2 187 L1
**Warburton Cl** *EAST* BN21 196 C6 1
*EGRIN* RH19 14 A5 1
*UCK* TN22 76 D6 3
**Ward Cl** *WADH* TN5 43 L1
**Wardsbrook Rd** *WADH* TN5 45 K7
**Ward's La** *WADH* TN5 44 E3
**Ward Wy** *BEXW* TN39 160 A8
**Warelands** *BURH* RH15 96 F5
**Warenne Rd** *HOVE* BN3 167 J3
**Wares Fld** *UCK* TN22 102 D2
**Wares Rd** *UCK* TN22 102 D2
**Warleigh Rd** *BRI* BN1 6 F1
**Warmdene Av** *BRI* BN1 145 M8 1
**Warmdene Cl** *BRI* BN1 168 F1 1
**Warmdene Rd** *BRI* BN1 145 M8
**Warmdene Wy** *BRI* BN1 145 M8
**Warminster Rd** *PEV* BN24 198 D1
**Warnham Gdns** *BEXW* TN39 182 D4
**Warnham Ri** *BRI* BN1 169 G1
**Warren Av** *ROTT* BN2 170 C5
**Warren Cl** *CROW* TN6 39 K4
*EDN/EASTW* BN20 205 H5
*EDN/EASTW* BN20 206 C6
*EGRIN* RH19 12 E3
*HTHF* TN21 78 F8
*LEW* BN7 2 C7
*ROTT* BN2 170 B6 3
*STLEO* TN38 161 L6
**Warren Dr** *LEW* BN7 2 B7
**Warren Farm La** *RRTW* TN3 29 G2
**Warren Gdn** *CROW* TN6 39 L4 2
**Warren Hl** *EDN/EASTW* BN20 206 A5
**Warren La** *EDN/EASTW* BN20 205 H5
*HTHF* TN21 79 G6
*RING/NEW* BN8 73 L6
**Warren Rdg** *CROW* TN6 39 K4 3
*RRTW* TN3 30 C3
**Warren Ri** *ROTT* BN2 170 B6
**Warren Rd** *CROW* TN6 39 J5
*RHAS* TN35 164 C2
*ROTT* BN2 169 L7
*ROTT* BN2 170 C6
**The Warren** *BURH* RH15 97 J5
*MAYF* TN20 57 J4
*WADH* TN5 45 L5
**Warren Wy** *PEAHV* BN10 190 A5
*RING/NEW* BN8 73 M6
*ROTT* BN2 170 D6
**Warrenwood** *RING/NEW* BN8 74 A6
**Warr Gn** *LEW* BN7 2 C2
**Warrior Cl** *PTSD* BN41 167 H4
**Warrior Gdns** *SLVH* TN37 4 B7
**Warrior Sq** *SLVH* TN37 4 B8
**Warrs Hill La** *RING/NEW* BN8 73 L5
**Wartling Cl** *STLEO* TN38 161 M3
**Wartling Dr** *BEXW* TN39 181 M1
**Wartling Rd** *HAIL* BN27 157 K6
*LW/ROSE* BN22 11 K1
**Warwick Cl** *HAIL* BN27 155 J3 2
**Warwick Pk** *RTWE/PEM* TN2 20 B5
**Warwick Rd** *BEXW* TN39 182 F1
*RTW* TN1 20 A4
*SEAF* BN25 202 E3 4
**Washington Av** *STLEO* TN38 138 F8
**Washington Rd** *HWH* RH16 71 M1
**Washington St** *ROTT* BN2 7 H4
**Washwell La** *WADH* TN5 43 M3
**Watchbell La** *RYE* TN31 117 J1 6
**Watchbell St** *RYE* TN31 117 H1
**Waterbury Hl** *RHWH* RH17 35 H8
**Waterdown Rd** *SBGH/RUST* TN4 19 K5
**Waterdyke Av** *STHW* BN42 166 E7 5
**Waterfield** *RTWE/PEM* TN2 20 A7
**Waterford Cl** *PEAHV* BN10 190 C4
**Watergate** *BEXW* TN39 160 B6
**Watergate La** *LEW* BN7 2 F6
**Waterhall Rd** *BRI* BN1 145 J8
**Waterloo Cl** *STLEO* TN38 138 F7
**Waterloo Pl** *LEW* BN7 3 G5 3
**Waterloo Sq** *POLE* BN26 194 A3
**Waterloo St** *HOVE* BN3 186 D1
**Watermen's Cl** *HAS* TN34 162 E3
**Watermill Cl** *BEXW* TN39 160 B6
*POLE* BN26 196 A1
**Watermill Dr** *STLEO* TN38 161 K3
**Watermill La** *BEXW* TN39 160 B6
*RHAS* TN35 141 J5
*RYE* TN31 88 D3
**Waters Cottages** *WADH* TN5 44 A2
**Waterside** *EGRIN* RH19 14 B5
**Waterside Cl** *HAS* TN34 163 H3
**Waterworks Rd** *HAS* TN34 5 H5
*LW/ROSE* BN22 10 F3
**Watling Cl** *STHW* BN42 166 E7 6
**Wattle's Wish** *BAT* TN33 111 J8
**Watts Cl** *WADH* TN5 43 M2
**Watts La** *EAST* BN21 10 A4
**Watts' Palace La** *RYE* TN31 87 K6
**Waverley Crs** *BRI* BN1 169 H5
**Waverley Gdns** *PEV* BN24 198 D1
**Wayfaring Down** *POLE* BN26 195 K3
**Wayfield Av** *HOVE* BN3 167 L5
**Wayfield Cl** *HOVE* BN3 167 M5 3
**Wayford Cl** *LGNY* BN23 197 K4 11
**Wayland Av** *BRI* BN1 168 C2
**Wayland Hts** *BRI* BN1 168 C2
**Wayside** *BRI* BN1 145 K8
*EDN/EASTW* BN20 205 H6 1
**Wayside Wk** *HTHF* TN21 79 M8
**Weald Av** *HOVE* BN3 167 M5
**Weald Cl** *LEW* BN7 2 E4 1
*RING/NEW* BN8 126 E2 3
**Wealden** *BUR/ETCH* TN19 60 B7
**Wealden Cl** *CROW* TN6 39 M3
**Wealden Pk** *LW/ROSE* BN22 196 C4
**Wealden Wy** *BEXW* TN39 159 J8
*HWH* RH16 71 K2
**Weald Ri** *HWH* RH16 71 L5
**Weald Rd** *BURH* RH15 96 E3 4
**The Weald** *EGRIN* RH19 13 M3
**Weald Vw** *RBTBR* TN32 86 E5
*RING/NEW* BN8 126 D2
*WADH* TN5 31 M8
**Wealdview Rd** *HTHF* TN21 79 L7
**Wealdway** *CROW* TN6 38 C4
*EDN/EASTW* BN20 195 L5
*EDN/EASTW* BN20 206 A3
*HAIL* BN27 131 J5
*HAIL* BN27 153 M7
*HRTF* TN7 17 G8
*HRTF* TN7 26 F6
*HTHF* TN21 131 L6
*POLE* BN26 176 E1
*POLE* BN26 194 E2
*RING/NEW* BN8 103 M7
*RING/NEW* BN8 129 M1
*UCK* TN22 38 C6
*UCK* TN22 53 J2
*UCK* TN22 76 E2
*UCK* TN22 103 L2
**Weatherby Cl** *EAST* BN21 196 C6
**Weavers Cl** *BURH* RH15 97 K5
**Weavers La** *POLE* BN26 193 M3
**Weavers Rock La** *HTHF* TN21 106 C1
**Wedderburn Rd**
*EDN/EASTW* BN20 196 B6
**Week La** *RING/NEW* BN8 150 D4
**Welbeck Av** *HOVE* BN3 167 L8
*STLEO* TN38 162 A7 2
**Welbeck Cl** *BURH* RH15 97 K2
*LW/ROSE* BN22 196 D3 8
**Welbeck Dr** *BURH* RH15 97 J1
**Welesmere Rd** *ROTT* BN2 189 G3
**The Welkin** *HWH* RH16 49 G6
**Welland Cl** *CROW* TN6 40 A7
**Wellcombe Crs**
*EDN/EASTW* BN20 206 D7
**Weller Rd** *SBGH/RUST* TN4 19 J2
**Wellesley Cl** *BEXW* TN39 182 D3
*CROW* TN6 39 K5
**Wellesley Rd** *EAST* BN21 10 F5

Wellfield *EGRIN* RH19 .... 14 C7
Wellgreen La *LEW* BN7 .... 171 M1
Wellhouse La *BURH* RH15 .... 97 H7
Well House Pl *LEW* BN7 .... 2 E6 ②
Wellingham La
  *RING/NEW* BN8 .... 127 G7
Wellington Cottages *HAWK* TN18 47 L2
Wellington Ms *HAS* TN34 .... 5 H6
Wellington Pk *SEAF* BN25 .... 203 C3
Wellington Pl *HAS* TN34 .... 5 J6
Wellington Rd *HAS* TN34 .... 5 J6
  *NEWHV* BN9 .... 191 L4
  *PEAHV* BN10 .... 190 E8 ②
  *PTSD* BN41 .... 167 H8
  *ROTT* BN2 .... 7 H2
Wellington Sq *HAS* TN34 .... 5 H7
Wellington St *LEW* BN7 .... 3 G5
  *ROTT* BN2 .... 7 J3
Wellington Town Rd
  *EGRIN* RH19 .... 13 K3
Wellis Gdns *STLEO* TN38 .... 162 A6
Wellsbourne Rd *PEV* BN24 .... 197 G1
Wells Cl *EDN/EASTW* BN20 .. 206 C6 ①
  *LEW* BN7 .... 98 E8
  *RTW* TN1 .... 20 A3 ②
Wells Lea *EGRIN* RH19 .... 13 K3
Wells Meadow *EGRIN* RH19 .. 13 K3 ①
Wendale Dr *PEAHV* BN10 .... 190 D4
Wenthill Cl *EDN/EASTW* BN20 .. 205 H5
Went Hill Gdns *LW/ROSE* BN22 .. 196 B3
Went Hill Pk *SEAF* BN25 .... 203 G3 ②
Went La *EDN/EASTW* BN20 .. 205 J5 ②
Went Wy *EDN/EASTW* BN20 .. 205 H6
Wentworth Cl *BEX* TN40 .... 183 M1
  *HAIL* BN27 .... 154 F5
Wentworth St *ROTT* BN2 .... 7 G8
Wentworth Wy *STLEO* TN38 .. 161 M6
Westaway Dr *BEXW* BN39 .... 183 G2
West Beeches Rd *CROW* TN6 .. 40 A4
Westbourne Gdns *HOVE* BN3 .. 168 A8
Westbourne Pl *HOVE* BN3 .... 168 A8
Westbourne St *HOVE* BN3 .... 168 A7
Westbourne Vls *HOVE* BN3 .... 167 M8
Westbrook La *RHAS* TN35 .... 139 L1
Westbrook Wy *STHW* BN42 .... 166 F7
West Cl *POLE* BN26 .... 178 B7
  *POLE* .... 193 M3
West Common *HWH* RH16 .... 48 F7
West Common Dr *HWH* RH16 .. 49 G7
Westcourt Dr *BEXW* BN39 .... 182 F3
Westdean Av *NEWHV* BN9 .... 8 B7
West Dean Ri *SEAF* BN25 .... 203 G2
Westdene Cl *SLVH* TN37 .... 139 J8 ①
Westdene Dr *BRI* BN1 .... 168 C1
Westdown La *BUR/ETCH* TN19 .. 82 A3
Westdown Rd *BEXW* BN39 .... 183 G1
Westdown Rd *SEAF* BN25 .... 202 D2
West Dr *ROTT* BN2 .... 7 H6
West End *HAIL* BN27 .... 133 L8
Westergate Rd *ROTT* BN2 .... 169 L2
Westerham Rd *LGNY* BN23 .... 197 K5
Westerleigh Cl *STLEO* TN38 .... 162 A6
Western Av *HAWK* TN18 .... 47 M4
  *POLE* BN26 .... 178 B8
Western Rd *BEX* TN40 .... 183 J3
  *BURH* RH15 .... 96 E3
  *CROW* TN6 .... 40 C3
  *HAIL* BN27 .... 155 G6
  *HAWK* TN18 .... 47 M4
  *HWH* RH16 .... 71 M3
  *LEW* BN7 .... 2 C6
  *LW/ROSE* BN22 .... 11 G3
  *NEWHV* BN9 .... 8 B7
  *RING/NEW* BN8 .... 74 C7
  *RTW* TN1 .... 20 C1
  *SLVH* TN37 .... 4 B7
  *WADH* TN5 .... 31 M8
Western St *BRI* BN1 .... 186 D1
Western Ter *BRI* BN1 .... 6 A6
Westfield Av *ROTT* BN2 .... 189 K3
Westfield Av North *ROTT* BN2 .. 189 K3
Westfield Av South *ROTT* BN2 .. 189 K3
Westfield Cl *BRI* BN1 .... 169 G2
  *MAYF* TN20 .... 56 B8
  *POLE* BN26 .... 178 A7 ②
Westfield Ct *POLE* BN26 .. 178 A7 ②
Westfield Crs *BRI* BN1 .... 169 G1
Westfield La *SLVH* TN37 .... 139 H7
Westfield Ri *ROTT* BN2 .... 189 K3
Westfield Rd *EAST* BN21 .... 196 D8
West Furlong La
  *HPPT/KEY* BN6 .... 122 A1
West Ga *LEW* BN7 .... 98 E8
Westgate St *LEW* BN7 .... 2 E6
Westham Cl *BEXW* BN39 .. 182 E3 ③
Westham Dr *PEV* BN24 .... 180 F8
West Hi *EGRIN* RH19 .... 13 K6
Westhill Dr *BURH* RH15 .... 96 E3
West Hill Rd *BRI* BN1 .... 6 C4
  *STLEO* TN38 .... 162 A8
West Hill St *BRI* BN1 .... 6 C4
West Hoathly Rd *EGRIN* RH19 ... 23 J3
Westlands Rd *HWH* RH16 .... 72 B1
West La *EGRIN* RH19 .... 13 K6
West Leigh *EGRIN* RH19 .... 13 M7
Westmeston Av *ROTT* BN2 .... 189 H4
Westminster Cl
  *LW/ROSE* BN22 .... 196 D3
Westminster Crs *HAS* TN34 .... 163 G2
Westmoreland Cl *STLEO* TN38.. 161 M3
Westmount Cl *STHW* BN42 .. 166 D6 ②
West Pde *BEXW* BN39 .... 183 G4
West Park Crs *BURH* RH15 .... 96 D2
Westpoint *RING/NEW* BN8 .... 74 C7
West Rd *CRBK* TN17 .... 33 M3
  *PTSD* BN41 .... 167 G7
West St *BRI* BN1 .... 6 D7
  *BURH* RH15 .... 96 E2
  *EAST* BN21 .... 10 D7
  *EGRIN* RH19 .... 13 L6
  *HAS* TN34 .... 5 K7
  *HPPT/KEY* BN6 .... 123 J3
  *LEW* BN7 .... 3 G5
  *MAYF* TN20 .... 57 G5
  *POLE* BN26 .... 193 M2
  *PTSD* BN41 .... 167 J7

*ROTT* BN2 .... 188 F5
*RYE* TN31 .... 117 J1
*SEAF* BN25 .... 202 E4 ②
West Street La *HTHF* TN21 .... 105 M4
West Ter *EAST* BN21 .... 10 D7
  *HAIL* BN27 .... 133 L8
West Undercliff *RYE* TN31 .... 117 G1
West Vw *HAS* TN34 .... 5 M2
  *HWH* RH16 .... 49 H8
  *SEAF* BN25 .... 202 E4 ②
West View Gdns *EGRIN* RH19 .. 13 L6
Westville Rd *BEXW* BN39 .... 183 G2
West Wy *HOVE* BN3 .... 167 K4
Westway Cl *PTSD* BN41 .. 166 E2 ②
Westway Gdns *PTSD* BN41 .... 166 E2
Westwood Rd *SBGH/RUST* TN4... 19 H1
Wharf Rd *EAST* BN21 .... 10 D6
Whatlington Rd *BAT* TN33 .... 111 L8
Whatlington Wy *STLEO* TN38 .. 161 K4
Wheatfield Cl *SLVH* TN37 .. 162 C1 ③
Wheatfield Wy *ROTT* BN2 .... 169 M3
Wheatland Cl *PEAHV* BN10 .. 190 B4 ②
Wheatsheaf Cl *BURH* RH15 .... 96 E1
Wheatsheaf Gdns *LEW* BN7 .... 3 K4
Wheatsheaf La *RHWH* RH17 .... 48 A3
Wheelers La *RHAS* TN35 .... 139 K3
Wheelers Wy *EGRIN* RH19 .... 12 E3
Wheel La *RHAS* TN35 .... 139 K3
Wheelwright Cl
  *LW/ROSE* BN22 .... 196 D2
Wheelwright La *BURH* RH15 .... 97 K5
Whichelo Pl *ROTT* BN2 .... 7 J4
Whin Croft Pk *CROW* TN6 .... 39 K6
Whippingham Rd *ROTT* BN2 .... 7 K1
Whippingham St *ROTT* BN2 .... 7 K1
Whipping Post La *ROTT* BN2 .. 188 F5 ③
Whitbread Cl *LGNY* BN23 .. 197 H2 ③
White Bear Pas
  *SBGH/RUST* TN4 .... 20 A4 ⑤
Whitebread La *RYE* TN31 .... 65 K6
Whitecross St *BRI* BN1 .... 6 F4
Whitefriars Rd *HAS* TN34 .... 5 K3
Whitegates Cl *RING/NEW* BN8 .. 99 K7 ①
Whitegates La *WADH* TN5 .... 31 J6
Whitehawk Cl *ROTT* BN2 .... 169 L8
Whitehawk Crs *ROTT* BN2 .... 187 L1
Whitehawk Hill Rd *ROTT* BN2 ... 7 L8
Whitehawk Rd *ROTT* BN2 .... 169 M7
Whitehawk Wy *ROTT* BN2 .... 169 M8
White Hl *LEW* BN7 .... 2 F5
White Hill Av *BEXW* BN39 .... 182 E2
Whitehill Cl *CROW* TN6 .... 39 M5
White Hill Dr *BEXW* BN39 .... 182 E2
Whitehill Rd *CROW* TN6 .... 39 M6
Whitehouse Av *BEXW* BN39.. 160 B7
Whitehouse La *HTHF* TN21 .... 105 G3
Whitelot Cl *STHW* BN42 .... 166 E5
Whitelot Wy *STHW* BN42 .... 166 E4
White Rock Gdns *HAS* TN34..... 4 F7
Whiterock Pl *STHW* BN42 .... 166 E7
White Rock Rd *SLVH* TN37 .... 4 E8
White's Cl *HPPT/KEY* BN6 .... 96 A7
White St *ROTT* BN2 .... 7 G7
  *POLE* BN26 .... 193 M5
Whitethorn Dr *BRI* BN1 .... 168 D2
White Wy *LEW* BN7 .... 172 B5
  *POLE* BN26 .... 193 M5
Whiteway Cl *SEAF* BN25 .... 192 E8
Whiteway Rd *ROTT* BN2 .... 7 K1
Whitfeld La *RING/NEW* BN8 .... 126 C8
Whitley Rd *LW/ROSE* BN22 .... 11 H3
Whittingehame Gdns *BRI* BN1 .. 168 F3
Whittington's Wy *HAS* TN34 .... 163 H2
Whittlewood Cl *STLEO* TN38 .. 161 L4
Whybourne Crest
  *RTWE/PEM* TN2 .... 20 D5
Whydown Hi *BAT* TN33 .... 112 F6
Whydown Rd *BEXW* BN39 .... 159 H6
The Wickets *BURH* RH15 .... 96 F1
Wickham Av *BEXW* BN39 .... 182 E3
Wickham Cl *HWH* RH16 .... 48 E7
Wickham Dr *HPPT/KEY* BN6 .. 122 E1
Wickham Gdns *SBGH/RUST* TN4... 19 K1
Wickham Hl *HPPT/KEY* BN6 .. 122 C2
Wickham La *RING/NEW* BN8 .. 125 L4
Wickham Rock La *WSEA* TN36 .. 142 D1
Wickham Wy *HWH* RH16 .... 48 E7
Wickhurst Cl *PTSD* BN41 .... 166 F4
Wickhurst Ri *PTSD* BN41 .... 166 F3
Wickhurst Rd *PTSD* BN41 .... 166 F4
Wicklands Av *ROTT* BN2 .... 189 K5
Wick St *RING/NEW* BN8 .... 174 C1
Widbury Rd *RRTW* TN3 .. 18 F3 ②
Widdicombe Wy *ROTT* BN2 .. 169 H5
Wigmore Cl *BRI* BN1 .... 169 H5
Wilbury Av *HOVE* BN3 .... 168 C6
Wilbury Crs *HOVE* BN3 .... 168 D7
Wilbury Gdns *HOVE* BN3 .... 168 C6
Wilbury Gv *HOVE* BN3 .... 168 C7
Wilbury Rd *HOVE* BN3 .... 168 C7
Wilbury Vls *HOVE* BN3 .... 168 C7
Wilby Av *STHW* BN42 .... 166 E5
Wilderness Gdns *RYE* TN31 .... 65 G7
Wilderness La *UCK* TN22 .... 78 C2
Wilderness Pk *CROW* TN6 .... 39 L4
Wilderness Ri *EGRIN* RH19 .... 14 A1
Wilderness Rd *HPPT/KEY* BN6.. 96 A8
The Wilderness *HWH* RH16 .... 49 H6
Wilderwick Rd *EGRIN* RH19 .... 14 A1
Wild Park Cl *ROTT* BN2 .... 169 L3
Wildwood *LGNY* BN23 .. 197 J2 ⑦
Wilfrid Rd *HOVE* BN3 .... 167 K6
Wilkinson Cl *ROTT* BN2 .... 188 F3
Wilkins Wy *SEAF* BN25 .... 202 C8
Wilkins Wy *BEX* TN40 .... 160 F8
Willard Cl *LW/ROSE* BN22 .... 197 G8
Willetts Fld *RING/NEW* BN8 .. 130 E6
Willetts La *RRTW* TN3 .... 17 J2
William Allen La *HWH* RH16 .... 49 H6
  *HWH* .... 72 B1
William Rd *STLEO* TN38 .... 161 L7
Williams Rd *SHOR* BN43 .... 166 B8
William St *PTSD* BN41 .... 167 H7
  *ROTT* BN2 .... 7 G6
  *SBGH/RUST* TN4 .... 20 A1
Willingdon Av *BEXW* BN39 .... 182 A1
  *STLEO* TN38 .... 162 A1
Willingdon Cl
  *EDN/EASTW* BN20 .. 196 B5 ②

*STLEO* TN38 .... 162 A1
Willingdon Ct
  *EDN/EASTW* BN20 .... 196 A3 ②
Willingdon Dro *LGNY* BN23 .... 197 H5
  *LW/ROSE* BN22 .... 197 G5
Willingdon La *POLE* BN26 .... 195 J7
Willingdon Park Dr
  *LW/ROSE* BN22 .... 196 D4
Willingdon Rd *EAST* BN21 .. 196 C8 ②
  *EAST* BN21 .... 206 D2
  *LW/ROSE* BN22 .... 196 C5
  *ROTT* BN2 .... 169 L5
Willingdon Wy
  *LW/ROSE* BN22 .... 196 B4 ②
  *STLEO* TN38 .... 162 A1 ①
Willingford La
  *BUR/ETCH* TN19 .... 82 C4
Willoughby Crs
  *LW/ROSE* BN22 .... 197 J8
Willow Av *HAIL* BN27 .... 155 H5
Willow Bank *RBTBR* TN32 .... 85 H3
Willowbed Wk *HAS* TN34 .... 162 E1
Willowbrook Wy
  *HPPT/KEY* BN6 .... 123 G3 ②
Willow Cl *BUR/ETCH* TN19 .... 61 H6
  *EGRIN* RH19 .... 13 K3
  *HTHF* TN21 .... 80 B6
  *ROTT* BN2 .... 170 E6
Willow Dr *BEXW* TN39 .... 182 C1
  *POLE* BN26 .... 196 A1
  *SEAF* BN25 .... 203 J3
Willow End *HAS* TN34 .... 162 F2
Willowfield Rd *LW/ROSE* BN22.. 11 H5
Willowfield Sq *LW/ROSE* BN22 .. 11 H5
Willow La *WSEA* TN36 .... 117 H8
Willowmead *CROW* TN6 .... 39 L6
Willow Md *RBTBR* TN32 .... 85 H3 ①
Willow Ms *EGRIN* RH19 .... 13 M6
Willow Pk *HWH* RH16 .... 72 B2
Willow Rdg *CRAWE* RH10 .... 22 A3
Willows Ri *UCK* TN22 .... 103 H1
The Willows *BURH* RH15 .... 97 H1
  *RING/NEW* BN8 .... 126 E1
Willow Stream Cl *RHAS* TN35 ... 140 E3
Willow Tree Rd *RTWE/PEM* TN2.. 19 L5
Willow Wk *NEWHV* BN9 .... 8 E2
Willow Wy *HPPT/KEY* BN6 .... 96 A6
Wilmington Cl *BRI* BN1 .... 169 G1
  *HPPT/KEY* BN6 .... 122 F3
Wilmington Pde *BRI* BN1 .. 168 F1 ②
Wilmington Rd *HAS* TN34 .... 163 G3
  *NEWHV* BN9 .... 8 C6
  *SEAF* BN25 .... 202 C8
Wilmington Sq *EAST* BN21 .... 10 E9
Wilmington St *POLE* BN26 .... 194 F1
Wilmington Wy *BRI* BN1 .... 168 F1
  *HWH* RH16 .... 72 A1
Wilmot Rd *SHOR* BN43 .... 166 C6
Wilson Av *ROTT* BN2 .... 187 M2
Wilson Gv *UCK* TN22 .... 76 A7
Wilton Av *LW/ROSE* BN22 .... 196 F3
Wilton Rd *BEX* TN40 .... 183 J3
Winceby Cl *BEXW* TN39 .... 182 E4
Winchcombe Rd
  *LW/ROSE* BN22 .... 10 F4
Winchelsea Cl *SEAF* BN25 .. 203 J1 ②
Winchelsea La *RHAS* TN35 .... 163 L1
  *RYE* TN31 .... 115 M4
Winchelsea Rd *LW/ROSE* BN22 .. 197 K8
  *RHAS* TN35 .... 140 F3
  *RYE* TN31 .... 117 H1
Winchester St *BRI* BN1 .... 6 E1
Winchester Wy
  *LW/ROSE* BN22 .... 196 B4
Wincombe Rd *BRI* BN1 .... 168 D5 ②
Windermere Crs
  *LW/ROSE* BN22 .... 11 J1
Windermere Rd *HWH* RH16.... 71 M1
Winding St *HAS* TN34 .... 5 K6
Windlesham Av *HOVE* BN3 .... 6 A4
Windlesham Cl *PTSD* BN41 .... 167 G5
Windlesham Gdns *BRI* BN1 .... 6 A4
Windlesham Rd *BRI* BN1 .... 6 A4
Windmill Av *HPPT/KEY* BN6.... 122 F3
Windmill Cl *EAST* BN21 .... 196 C8
  *HAS* TN34 .... 167 M4
  *HTHF* TN21 .... 80 B6
Windmill Dr *BRI* BN1 .... 145 J8
  *BURH* RH15 .... 97 G2
Windmill Gn *PEV* BN24 .... 197 H1
Windmill La *EDN/EASTW* BN20 .. 205 C5
  *EGRIN* RH19 .... 13 K3
  *EGRIN* RH19 .... 14 C7
  *WADH* TN5 .... 32 C6
  *WADH* TN5 .... 43 K2
Windmill Pl *POLE* BN26 .... 196 A2
Windmill Rd *POLE* BN26 .... 196 A1
  *STHW* BN42 .... 166 E5
  *STLEO* TN38 .... 162 B4
Windmill St *ROTT* BN2 .... 7 H6
  *RTWE/PEM* TN2 .... 20 C3 ③
Windmill Ter *ROTT* BN2 .... 7 H5
Windmill Vw *BRI* BN1 .... 146 A8
Windmill Wy *WSEA* TN36 .... 117 H7 ②
Windover Crs *LEW* BN7 .... 2 A4
Windover Wy *LW/ROSE* BN22 . 196 B3 ②
Windsor Cl *HOVE* BN3 .... 168 A3
  *HWH* RH16 .... 71 L4
  *SEAF* BN25 .... 192 B8
Windsor Ct *CROW* TN6 .... 40 C6
Windsor Pl *CROW* TN6 .... 40 C6
  *EGRIN* RH19 .... 14 A6 ②
Windsor Rd *BEXW* BN39 .... 183 H2
  *CROW* TN6 .... 40 C6
  *HAIL* BN27 .... 155 H8
  *STLEO* TN38 .... 162 B3
Windsor St *BRI* BN1 .... 6 D6
Windsor Wy *POLE* BN26 .... 178 A7
  *WSEA* TN36 .... 143 C2
Windward Quay *LGNY* BN23 .... 197 M6
Wineham Wy *BEX* TN40 .... 183 M2
Winfield Av *BRI* BN1 .... 145 M8
Winfield Cl *BRI* BN1 .... 168 F1 ③
  *PTSD* BN41 .... 167 G2
Wingate Cl *STLEO* TN38 .. 162 A5 ③
Wingle Tye Rd *BURH* RH15.... 97 G6
Winkhurst Wy *BURH* RH15 .... 97 K5
Winkney Rd *LW/ROSE* BN22 .. 196 F3

Winscote Cl *CROW* TN6 .... 39 K5 ②
Winston Crs *LGNY* BN23 .. 197 K7 ②
Winston Dr *BEXW* TN39 .... 159 H6
Winstone Scott Av *RRTW* TN3 .. 18 E2 ②
  *LEW* BN7 .... 2 B8
Winterbourne Cl *HAS* TN34 .... 4 D5
Winterbourne La *LEW* BN7 .... 2 C7
Winterbourne La *LEW* BN7 .... 2 B8
Winterbourne Ms *LEW* BN7 .... 2 C8
Winterton Wy *SHOR* BN43 .... 166 B8
Winton Av *BRI* BN1 .... 189 J4
Winton St *POLE* BN26 .... 193 M2
Wisden Av *BURH* RH15 .... 96 E1
Wiseacre *RRTW* TN3 .... 33 C3
Wish Hi *EDN/EASTW* BN20 .... 196 B5
Wishing Tree Cl *STLEO* TN38 .. 161 M4
Wishing Tree La *STLEO* TN38 .. 161 M4
Wishing Tree Rd *STLEO* TN38 .. 161 M4
Wishing Tree Rd North
  *STLEO* TN38 .... 162 A2
Wish Rd *EAST* BN21 .... 10 E7
  *HOVE* BN3 .... 167 L8
Wish Ward *RYE* TN31 .... 117 H1 ③
Wiston Rd *ROTT* BN2 .... 169 M7
Wiston Wy *ROTT* BN2 .... 169 M7
Withdean Av *BRI* BN1 .... 168 D4
Withdean Cl *BRI* BN1 .... 168 D3
Withdean Court Av *BRI* BN1 .. 168 D3
Withdean Crs *BRI* BN1 .... 168 D3
Withdean Ri *BRI* BN1 .... 168 D3
Withdean Rd *BRI* BN1 .... 168 D4
Witherenden Rd *MAYF* TN20.... 57 L5
Withy Bush *BURH* RH15 .... 96 E2 ②
  *BURH* RH15 .... 96 E1 ①
Withyham Av *ROTT* BN2 .... 189 J6
Withyham Cl *LW/ROSE* BN22.. 196 F5
Withyham Rd *BEXW* BN39 .... 182 C4
  *RRTW* TN3 .... 18 A8
Withypitts *CRAWE* RH10 .... 22 A3
Withypitts East *CRAWE* RH10 .. 22 A3
Wittersham La *RYE* TN31 .... 91 H1
Wittersham Rd *CRBK* TN17 .... 66 D2
  *RYE* TN31 .... 68 A6
  *RYE* TN31 .... 91 H1
  *TENT* TN30 .... 67 H1
Wivelsfield Rd *HWH* RH16 .... 71 L4
  *ROTT* BN2 .... 189 J3
Woburn Cl *HAIL* BN27 .... 155 C5
Woburn Pl *BRI* BN1 .... 169 M1
Woburn Wy *LW/ROSE* BN22 .. 196 D3
Wode Rd *BAT* TN33 .... 159 C3
Wolfe Cl *CROW* TN6 .... 40 A6
Wolseley Rd *BRI* BN1 .... 146 D8
  *PTSD* BN41 .... 167 G6
Wolstonbury Rd *HOVE* BN3 .... 6 A2
Wolstonbury Wy *BURH* RH15 .. 97 G4 ②
Wolverstone Dr *BRI* BN1 .... 169 J4
Woodbourne Av *BRI* BN1 .... 168 F2
Woodbrook Rd *HAS* TN34 .... 162 F3
Woodbury Av *EGRIN* RH19 .... 14 B6
Woodbury Cl *EGRIN* RH19 .... 14 B6
Woodbury Park Gdns
  *SBGH/RUST* TN4 .... 20 A1
Woodbury Park Rd
  *SBGH/RUST* TN4 .... 20 A1
Woodcombe *HAS* TN34 .... 162 F2
Woodcote Rd *FROW* RH18 .... 24 E4
Woodcrest Rd *BURH* RH15 .... 96 F5
Woodcroft *BURH* RH15 .... 96 F1 ①
Woodcroft Dr *EAST* BN21 .... 196 C8
Woodgate Meadow *LEW* BN7 .. 98 C7
Woodgate Rd *LW/ROSE* BN22.. 11 H1
Woodhams Cl *BAT* TN33 .... 137 L2
Woodhouse Rd *HOVE* BN3 .... 167 L7
Woodland Av *BURH* RH15 .... 97 J2
  *HOVE* BN3 .... 168 B2
  *LW/ROSE* BN22 .... 196 C6
Woodland Cl *BURH* RH15 .... 97 J2 ①
  *HOVE* BN3 .... 168 B4 ①
Woodland Dr *CRAWE* RH10 .... 12 B6
  *HOVE* BN3 .... 168 B3
Woodland Ms *HTHF* TN21 .... 80 B8 ②
Woodland Ri *BEX* TN40 .... 183 L2
Woodlands *HOVE* BN3 .... 168 C4
Woodlands Cl *CRAWE* RH10 .... 12 B7
  *HAIL* BN27 .... 155 J4
  *HPPT/KEY* BN6 .... 122 F2 ①
  *HTHF* TN21 .... 106 B1
  *PEAHV* BN10 .. 190 B5 ⑪
  *UCK* TN22 .... 76 D6
Woodlands Rd *EGRIN* RH19 .... 14 A2
  *HPPT/KEY* BN6 .... 122 F2
  *HWH* RH16 .... 71 M2
The Woodlands *BRI* BN1 .... 168 E1
  *HAS* TN34 .... 162 E1
Woodlands Wy *HAS* TN34 .... 139 L8 ①
Woodland Vale Rd *STLEO* TN38 .. 4 A5
Woodland Vw *TENT* TN30 .... 67 L2
Woodland Wk *ROTT* BN2 .... 188 D2
Woodland Wy *BAT* TN33 .... 160 F2
  *BRI* BN1 .... 168 F2
  *CROW* TN6 .... 39 M6
  *HTHF* TN21 .... 80 B3 ①
  *RHAS* TN35 .... 164 E1
Wood La *HAIL* BN27 .... 157 L3
Woodleigh Rd *BURH* RH15.... 97 J2
Woodpecker Crs
  *HPPT/KEY* BN6 .... 96 D3
Woodpecker Dr *HAIL* BN27 .... 155 C6
Woodpecker Rd *LGNY* BN23 .... 197 H4
Woodpecker Wy *UCK* TN22 .... 102 D1
Wood Ride *HWH* RH16 .... 71 K3
Woodridge Cl *HWH* RH16 .... 72 A3 ②
Woodruff Av *HOVE* BN3 .... 168 C4
Woodsgate Av *BEX* TN40 .... 160 C8
  *BEXW* TN39 .... 160 C8
Woodsgate Pk *BEXW* BN39 .... 160 A8
Woods Hill Cl *EGRIN* RH19 .... 14 D8
Woods Hill La *EGRIN* RH19 .... 14 D8
Woodside *CROW* TN6 .... 39 L4
Woodside Av *BRI* BN1 .... 168 C2
Woodside Rd *SBGH/RUST* TN4 .. 19 K2
Woodside Wy *HAIL* BN27 .... 178 A2
Woodspring Cl *SLVH* TN37 .... 162 B1
Woodstock Rd *BEXW* TN39 .... 159 J8
Wood St *EGRIN* RH19 .... 13 K5
  *RTW* TN1 .... 20 B2

Woodview *BRI* BN1 .... 146 D8
Woodville Rd *BEXW* TN39 .... 183 H3
Woodward Cl *LGNY* BN23 .. 197 L7 ⑦
Woodwards Cl *BURH* RH15 .. 97 H5 ②
Woolven Cl *BURH* RH15 .... 96 E5
Worcester Vls *HOVE* BN3 .... 167 J7
Wordsworth Dr *LGNY* BN23 .... 197 L4
Wordsworth Ri *EGRIN* RH19 .. 13 J5 ②
Wordsworth St *HOVE* BN3 .... 168 A7
Workhouse La *WSEA* TN36 .... 141 M1
Worsham La *BEX* TN40 .... 160 F7
Worsted La *EGRIN* RH19 .... 14 D8
Wray Cl *EGRIN* RH19 .... 14 D8
Wren Cl *HTHF* TN21 .... 80 A7
Wren Ct *BAT* TN33 .... 137 M2 ③
  *STLEO* TN38 .... 162 A2
Wrestwood Av *LW/ROSE* BN22.. 196 C5
Wrestwood Rd *BEX* TN40 .... 160 D8
Wrotham Cl *HAS* TN34 .... 162 E1
  *LGNY* BN23 .... 197 K5 ⑤
Wroxham Rd *LGNY* BN23 .... 197 H2
Wyatts La *RHWH* RH17 .... 50 D1
Wyberlye Rd *BURH* RH15 .... 97 G2
Wybourne Ri *RTWE/PEM* TN2.... 20 B5
Wychperry Rd *HWH* RH16 .... 71 K1
Wychurst Gdns *BEX* TN40 .... 160 D8
Wykeham Rd *HAS* TN34 .... 4 C3
Wykeham Wy *BURH* RH15 .... 97 J4 ⑥
Wyndham St *ROTT* BN2 .... 7 H8
Wynlea Cl *CRAWE* RH10 .... 12 A6
Wynnes Ms *HOVE* BN3 .. 168 A7 ②
The Wyshe *POY/PYE* BN45 .... 122 C8
Wythwood *HWH* RH16 .... 71 L5

# Y

Yardley St *BRI* BN1 .... 6 E1
Yates Cl *RYE* TN31 .... 119 G4
Yeomans *RING/NEW* BN8 .... 128 A7
Yew La *EGRIN* RH19 .... 13 H3
Yew Tree Cl *HAS* TN34 .... 139 L4
  *HTHF* TN21 .... 80 A8 ①
  *RING/NEW* BN8 .... 127 M7
Yewtree La *CROW* TN6 .... 41 K6
Yielding's Cl *EAST* BN21 .. 206 D1 ②
York Av *EGRIN* RH19 .... 14 A6
  *HOVE* BN3 .... 6 A4
York Gdns *HAS* TN34 .... 5 G7
York Gv *BRI* BN1 .... 6 C2
York Hl *BRI* BN1 .... 6 F4
York Pl *BRI* BN1 .... 6 F4
York Rd *BEX* TN40 .... 184 A1
  *EAST* .... 10 D7
  *HOVE* BN3 .... 6 A5
  *PEAHV* BN10 .... 190 B4
  *RTW* TN1 .... 20 A2
  *SLVH* TN37 .... 4 B7
York Vls *BRI* BN1 .... 6 C2
Youngsmere Cl *BRI* BN1 .... 146 B8 ③

Abbotsford School
 *BURH* RH15 ............... 70 F8
A B C Cinema
 *HAS* TN34 ..................... 5 G7
A B C Cinema
 *RTW* TN1 ..................... 20 A3
Adur District Council
 *STHW* BN42 ............ 166 E7
Aids Positive
 Underground Theatre
 *ROTT* BN2 ..................... 7 J7
Albion Doctors Surgery
 *ROTT* BN2 ..................... 7 G4
Aldrington House Hospital
 *HOVE* BN3 ............... 167 M8
Alfriston County
 Primary School
 *POLE* BN26 ............. 193 M3
The Alfriston Gallery
 *POLE* BN26 ............. 194 A3
All Saints Hospital
 *EDN/EASTW* BN20 .. 206 E7
All Saints Infant School
 *BEXW* TN39 ............. 160 B7
All Saints Junior School
 *RHAS* TN35 ............. 163 J4
Alwin Gallery
 *SBGH/RUST* TN4 ....... 20 A4
Amberstone Hospital
 *HAIL* BN27 ............... 132 D8
Amberstone Hospital
 *HAIL* BN27 ............... 155 L2
Ambulance Station
 *LW/ROSE* BN22 ......... 10 F4
The Arden Foot & Health Clinic
 *ROTT* BN2 ..................... 6 F7
Arndale Shopping Centre
 *EAST* BN21 ............... 10 E6
Art Gallery
 *BRI* BN1 ....................... 6 E5
Arthur Blackman Clinic
 *SLVH* TN37 ............. 162 B2
Ashdown Forest Health Centre
 *FROW* RH18 ............... 24 E3
The Ashdown Hospital
 *HWH* RH16 ............... 48 D8
Ashwyn Business Centre
 *BURH* RH15 ............... 97 G1
Assembly Hall Theatre
 *RTWE/PEM* TN2 ........ 20 B3
The Audrey Wickens
 School of Music
 *EAST* BN21 ............... 10 A5
The Avenue Surgery
 *BURH* RH15 ............... 96 F4
Bad Apple Theatre Co
 *RTW* TN1 ..................... 20 C2
Baldwins Hill CP School
 *EGRIN* RH19 ............. 13 J3
Balfour Junior School
 *BRI* BN1 ................... 169 G3
Bandstand
 *EAST* BN21 ............... 11 G8
Barclays Business Centre
 *HTHF* TN21 ............... 80 A6
Barcombe Primary School
 *RING/NEW* BN8 ....... 126 D1
Bartholomews Tutorial College
 *BRI* BN1 ....................... 6 E7
Barton School
 *STLEO* TN38 ............ 162 B5
Battle Abbey
 Preparatory School
 *BEX* TN40 ................ 183 L1
Battle Abbey School
 *BAT* TN33 ................ 137 K2
Battle Hospital
 *BAT* TN33 ................ 137 G2
Battle & Langton School
 *BAT* TN33 ................ 137 J2
Battle Museum
 *BAT* TN33 ................ 137 K2
Beacon Community College
 *CROW* TN6 ................ 40 A4
Beacon Community College
 *CROW* TN6 ................ 40 B3
Beckley Gallery
 *RYE* TN31 .................. 89 J2
Beckley School
 *RYE* TN31 .................. 89 G2
Beeching Park Industrial Estate
 *BEXW* TN39 ............. 183 H2
Bellerbys College
 *HOVE* BN3 ............... 168 C7
Bellerbys College Mayfield
 *WADH* TN5 ................ 43 J2
Bell Tower Industrial Estate
 *ROTT* BN2 ............... 187 M2
Belmont Surgery
 *WADH* TN5 ................ 44 A2
Benfield County Junior School
 *PTSD* BN41 .............. 167 J6
Benfield Valley Golf Course
 *PTSD* BN41 .............. 167 J3
Bentley Wildfowl &
 Motor Museum
 *RING/NEW* BN8 ....... 128 F2
Bethany House Surgery
 *HAIL* BN27 ............... 155 J5
Bevendean County
 Primary School
 *ROTT* BN2 ............... 169 M5
Bexhill Amateur Athletic Club
 *BEXW* TN39 ............. 183 H1
Bexhill C of E Primary
 Junior School
 *BEX* TN40 ................ 183 J2
Bexhill College
 *BEXW* TN39 ............. 160 A7
Bexhill Costume Museum
 *BEX* TN40 ................ 183 K2
Bexhill High School
 *BEXW* TN39 ............. 183 H1
Bexhill Hospital
 *BEX* TN40 ................ 160 C8
Bexhill Leisure Centre
 *BEXW* TN39 ............. 183 H1

Bexhill Sailing Club
 *BEX* TN40 ................ 183 K3
Bexhill Squash Rackets Club
 *BEX* TN40 ................ 183 L2
The Birman Gallery
 *HWH* RH16 ................ 49 H6
The Bishop Bell C of E School
 *LGNY* BN23 .............. 197 L5
Bishops Down CP School
 *SBGH/RUST* TN4 ...... 19 L1
Blackboys C of E School
 *UCK* TN22 .................. 78 A8
Blackwell CP School
 *EGRIN* RH19 ............. 13 L3
Blatchington Mill School
 *HOVE* BN3 ............... 168 A5
Bodiam Castle (Nt)
 *RBTBR* TN32 .............. 63 M6
Bodiam Manor School
 *RBTBR* TN32 .............. 63 L6
Bodiam Primary School
 *RBTBR* TN32 .............. 63 L6
Boltons Clinic
 *MAYF* TN20 ................ 56 B8
Boltons Clinic
 *STLEO* TN38 ............ 162 B5
Booth Museum of
 Natural History
 *BRI* BN1 ................... 168 E6
Bourne County Primary School
 *LW/ROSE* BN22 ......... 11 G4
Bowden House School
 *SEAF* BN25 .............. 202 E2
Brambletye School
 *EGRIN* RH19 ............. 24 C1
Braybon Business Park
 *BURH* RH15 ............... 96 E4
Brede County Primary School
 *RYE* TN31 ................ 114 B2
Bridge Road Business Park
 *HWH* RH16 ................ 48 E7
Brighton Business Centre
 *BRI* BN1 ....................... 6 F2
Brighton Business Centre
 *BRI* BN1 ................... 168 F6
The Brighton Centre
 *BRI* BN1 ....................... 6 C7
Brighton College
 *ROTT* BN2 ..................... 7 K7
Brighton College of Technology
 *BRI* BN1 ....................... 6 F4
Brighton College of Technology
 *HOVE* BN3 ............... 167 L6
Brighton College of Technology
 *HOVE* BN3 ............... 168 B8
Brighton College of Technology
 *ROTT* BN2 ..................... 7 G3
Brighton County Court
 *ROTT* BN2 ..................... 6 F6
Brighton Fishing Museum
 *BRI* BN1 ....................... 6 D8
Brighton Framing Gallery
 *ROTT* BN2 ..................... 7 K8
Brighton General Hospital
 *ROTT* BN2 ..................... 7 M3
Brighton & Hove Council
 *BRI* BN1 ....................... 6 F3
Brighton & Hove Council
 *BRI* BN1 ................... 146 B8
Brighton & Hove Council
 *HOVE* BN3 ............... 167 M5
Brighton & Hove Council
 *HOVE* BN3 ............... 168 B7
Brighton & Hove Council
 *HOVE* BN3 ............... 168 C8
Brighton & Hove Council
 *PTSD* BN41 .............. 167 J6
Brighton & Hove Council
 *PTSD* BN41 .............. 167 G5
Brighton & Hove Council
 *ROTT* BN2 ..................... 7 K2
Brighton & Hove Council
 *ROTT* BN2 ............... 169 L3
Brighton & Hove Girls
 Day School
 *BRI* BN1 ....................... 6 A5
Brighton & Hove Golf Course
 *HOVE* BN3 ............... 144 E8
Brighton & Hove High Schools
 *BRI* BN1 ....................... 6 A4
Brighton & Hove Islamic
 Centre & Mosque
 *HOVE* BN3 ..................... 6 B2
Brighton & Hove Progressive
 Synagogue
 *HOVE* BN3 ............... 168 D8
Brighton Hove &
 Sussex Sixth Form College
 *HOVE* BN3 ..................... 6 B1
Brighton Library & Museum
 *BRI* BN1 ....................... 6 E6
Brighton Media Centre
 *BRI* BN1 ....................... 6 D7
Brighton Municipal Market
 *ROTT* BN2 ..................... 6 F5
Brighton Racecourse
 *ROTT* BN2 ............... 170 A6
Brighton Rugby Club
 *BRI* BN1 ................... 145 H8
Brighton Technical College
 *BRI* BN1 ....................... 6 D1
Brighton Youth Centre
 *ROTT* BN2 ..................... 7 H7
Broad Oak Primary School
 *HTHF* TN21 ................ 80 F4
Broadwater CP School
 *RTWE/PEM* TN2 ........ 19 M6
Broadway Surgery
 *ROTT* BN2 ............... 187 M2
The Brook Health Centre
 *CROW* TN6 ................ 40 C5
Broomham School
 *RHAS* TN35 .............. 141 G3
Bross Estate
 *NEWHV* BN9 ................ 9 H1
Buchanan Hospital
 *STLEO* TN38 ............ 162 B5

Buckingham Middle School
 *SHOR* BN43 .............. 166 A6
Burfield Park Industrial Estate
 *HAIL* BN27 ............... 155 G7
Burgess Hill Clinic
 *BURH* RH15 ............... 96 F4
Burgess Hill School
 *BURH* RH15 ............... 97 H4
Burgess Hill Town Football Club
 *BURH* RH15 ............... 97 H1
Burrswood Medical Centre
 *RRTW* TN3 .................. 18 A6
Burwash School
 *BUR/ETCH* TN19 ........ 60 B8
Buxted C of E Primary School
 *UCK* TN22 .................. 76 F3
Camber Castle
 *RYE* TN31 ................ 117 J4
Cambridge Gardens College
 *HAS* TN34 ..................... 4 F7
Campion Gallery
 *RYE* TN31 ................ 117 H1
Cardinal Newman School
 *HOVE* BN3 ............... 168 D6
Carlton Hill CP School
 *ROTT* BN2 ..................... 7 G6
Castledean School
 *BRI* BN1 ................... 169 H4
Castledown County
 Primary School
 *HAS* TN34 ..................... 5 K3
Catsfield C of E Primary School
 *BAT* TN33 ................ 136 E6
Causeway Secondary School
 *LW/ROSE* BN22 ....... 197 G3
The Cavendish School
 *EAST* BN21 ............... 206 D1
Centenary Industrial Estate
 *BRI* BN1 ................... 169 H5
The Central Hove Surgery
 *HOVE* BN3 ............... 168 B8
Central Library
 *EAST* BN21 ............... 10 C6
Chailey Comprehensive School
 *RING/NEW* BN8 ......... 99 K7
Chailey Heritage
 Clinical Services
 *RING/NEW* BN8 ......... 73 J7
Chailey Heritage School
 *RING/NEW* BN8 ......... 73 J7
Chantry CP School
 *BEX* TN40 ................ 183 J1
Charlwoods Industrial Estate
 *EGRIN* RH19 ............. 13 L3
Charter Medical Centre
 *HOVE* BN3 ............... 168 D7
Charters Ancaster School
 *BEX* TN40 ................ 183 L1
Chaucer Industrial Estate
 *POLE* BN26 ............. 178 D8
Chiddingly CP School
 *RING/NEW* BN8 ....... 130 E6
Chiddingly Cricket Club
 *RING/NEW* BN8 ....... 130 E5
Child Clinic
 *ROTT* BN2 ..................... 6 F6
Churchfields Industrial Estate
 *STLEO* TN38 ............ 161 K2
Churchill Square
 Shopping Centre
 *BRI* BN1 ....................... 6 C7
Churchwood Primary School
 *STLEO* TN38 ............ 161 M3
Churchwood Surgery
 *STLEO* TN38 ............ 161 M2
Cinema
 *EAST* BN21 ............... 10 F6
Cinque Ports Surgery
 *RYE* TN31 .................. 91 H8
Circe Health & Beauty Clinic
 *UCK* TN22 .................. 76 C7
Civic Centre
 *SHOR* BN43 .............. 166 A7
Clairmonte Galleries
 *BRI* BN1 ....................... 6 E6
Clanricarde Medical Centre
 *RTW* TN1 ..................... 20 A3
Claremont CP School
 *RTWE/PEM* TN2 ........ 20 B4
Claverham Community College
 *BAT* TN33 ................ 137 G2
Clermont C P U School
 *BRI* BN1 ................... 168 E4
Cliffe Business Centre
 *LEW* BN7 ..................... 3 J6
Cliffe Industrial Estate
 *LEW* BN7 ..................... 3 L8
Club House
 *EDN/EASTW* BN20 .. 206 A4
Cofe Primary School
 *MAYF* TN20 ................ 57 H3
Coghurst Hall County Primary
 *RHAS* TN35 .............. 140 C6
Coldean Junior & Infant School
 *BRI* BN1 ................... 146 D8
Community Mental
 Health Centre
 *BURH* RH15 ............... 97 G2
The Congress Theatre
 *EAST* BN21 ............... 10 E9
Conquest Hospital
 *HAS* TN34 ................ 139 K8
Conway Court Clinic
 *HOVE* BN3 ............... 168 B6
Cooden Beech Golf Club
 *BEXW* TN39 ............. 182 B4
Coombe Road County
 Primary School
 *ROTT* BN2 ............... 169 K5
The Corner Gallery
 *HWH* RH16 ................ 49 H6

Cornerstones Independent School
 *HOVE* BN3 ............... 168 D8
Corn Exchange Theatre
 *BRI* BN1 ....................... 6 E6
The Cottage Clinic
 *BEX* TN40 ................ 183 J3
Cottage Surgery
 *PEAHV* BN10 ............ 190 C8
Cottesmore St Marys RC Primary
 School
 *HOVE* BN3 ............... 168 D6
Count Primary School
 *BURH* RH15 ............... 97 J5
County Hall
 *LEW* BN7 ..................... 3 H5
County Middle School
 *STHW* BN42 ............ 166 F6
County Primary School
 *BRI* BN1 ................... 169 H4
County Primary School
 *RING/NEW* BN8 ....... 129 J8
Court Meadow School
 *RHWH* RH17 .............. 48 A6
Cradle Hill CP School
 *SEAF* BN25 .............. 203 G1
The Craftsman Gallery
 *HPPT/KEY* BN6 ........ 123 K3
Crawley Down C of E
 Infant School
 *CRAWE* RH10 ............ 12 B6
Crawley Down C of E School
 *CRAWE* RH10 ............ 12 B6
Crawley Down Health Centre
 *CRAWE* RH10 ............ 12 A6
Cross In Hand C of E
 Primary School
 *HTHF* TN21 ................ 79 M7
Crowborough Beacon Golf Club
 *CROW* TN6 ................ 39 K6
Crowborough War
 Memorial Hospital
 *CROW* TN6 ................ 39 L5
Crowhurst School
 *BAT* TN33 ................ 160 F1
Crown Court
 *HOVE* BN3 ............... 168 D8
Crown Prosecution Service
 *EAST* BN21 ............... 10 E4
Cumnor House School
 *RHWH* RH17 .............. 51 H1
The Cyril Richings Business
 Centre
 *SHOR* BN43 .............. 166 A7
Dale Hill Hotel & Golf Club
 *WADH* TN5 ................ 45 M5
Dallington School
 *HTHF* TN21 .............. 108 D3
Davigdor County Infants School
 *HOVE* BN3 ............... 168 D7
Denton County Primary School
 *NEWHV* BN9 ............ 191 L5
Devonshire Park Cricket Ground
 *EAST* BN21 ............... 10 E9
Devonshire Park Theatre
 *EAST* BN21 ............... 10 E9
Ditchling Gallery
 *HPPT/KEY* BN6 ........ 123 J3
Ditchling Health Centre
 *HPPT/KEY* BN6 ........ 123 K3
Ditchling Museum
 *HPPT/KEY* BN6 ........ 123 J3
Ditchling Primary School
 *HPPT/KEY* BN6 ........ 123 K3
Dolphin House Clinic for Adults
 *BRI* BN1 ....................... 6 E6
Dolphin Leisure Centre
 *HWH* RH16 ................ 48 D8
Douglas Moat Practice
 *SBGH/RUST* TN4 ...... 20 A4
Downland Medical Centre
 *POLE* BN26 ............. 178 A8
Downlands School
 *HPPT/KEY* BN6 ........ 122 F3
Downs County First School
 *BRI* BN1 ................... 169 G6
Downs Junior School
 *BRI* BN1 ................... 169 G6
Downs Leisure Centre
 *SEAF* BN25 .............. 203 G2
Downs Park School
 *PTSD* BN41 .............. 167 H4
Downs Special School
 *EDN/EASTW* BN20 .. 206 B2
Downs View School
 *ROTT* BN2 ............... 170 C6
The Dr Jan De Winter Clinic for
 Cancer Prevention Advice
 *BRI* BN1 ....................... 6 E6
Drusillas Zoo Park
 *POLE* BN26 ............. 176 B8
DSS
 *EAST* BN21 ............... 10 D5
DSS
 *ROTT* BN2 ..................... 7 G7
Dudley Infants School
 *RHAS* TN35 ................ 5 M3
Dunnings Squash Club
 *EGRIN* RH19 ............. 13 L8
Durgates Industrial Estate
 *WADH* TN5 ................ 43 L1
The Eastbourne Clinic
 *EDN/EASTW* BN20 .. 10 C8
Eastbourne College
 *EAST* BN21 ............... 10 D8
Eastbourne College
 *EDN/EASTW* BN20 .. 10 C8
Eastbourne College of Arts &
 Technology
 *EAST* BN21 ............... 196 E7
Eastbourne County Court
 *EAST* BN21 ............... 10 C5
Eastbourne District
 General Hospital
 *EAST* BN21 ............... 196 E7
Eastbourne Downs Golf Club
 *EDN/EASTW* BN20 .. 206 A4

Eastbourne & Hailsham
 Magistrates Court
 *EAST* BN21 ............... 10 C7
Eastbourne Health Authority
 *EAST* BN21 ............... 10 E3
Eastbourne Hospitals N H S Trust
 *EAST* BN21 ............... 10 E4
Eastbourne Pier
 *LW/ROSE* BN22 ......... 11 H7
Eastbourne Rugby Football Club
 *LW/ROSE* BN22 ....... 196 D6
Eastbourne Saffrons Sports Club
 *EAST* BN21 ............... 10 B8
Eastbourne Sovereign
 Sailing Club Ltd
 *LW/ROSE* BN22 ......... 11 L3
Eastbourne United Football Club
 *LW/ROSE* BN22 ......... 11 L1
East Court
 *EGRIN* RH19 ............. 13 M4
East Grinstead Health Clinic
 *EGRIN* RH19 ............. 13 L4
East Grinstead Sports Club
 *EGRIN* RH19 ............. 23 J1
East Hoathly C of E School
 *RING/NEW* BN8 ....... 129 M1
East Hoathly Surgery
 *RING/NEW* BN8 ....... 130 A1
East Sussex Brighton &
 Hove Health Auth
 *LEW* BN7 ..................... 3 H4
East Sussex County Council
 *BRI* BN1 ....................... 6 E6
East Sussex County Council
 *HOVE* BN3 ............... 167 L3
East Sussex County Council
 *HTHF* TN21 ................ 80 C6
East Sussex County Council
 *LEW* BN7 ..................... 2 D6
East Sussex County Council
 *LEW* BN7 ..................... 3 H4
East Sussex County Council
 *LEW* BN7 ..................... 3 J9
East Sussex County Council
 *NEWHV* BN9 ................ 8 E4
East Sussex County Council
 *NEWHV* BN9 ................ 8 F3
East Sussex County Council
 *PEAHV* BN10 ............ 190 E8
East Sussex County Council
 *PEAHV* BN10 ............ 190 C7
East Sussex County Council
 *POLE* BN26 ............. 178 A8
East Sussex County Council
 *ROTT* BN2 ............... 169 L8
East Sussex County Council
 *SEAF* BN25 .............. 202 E7
East Sussex County
 Music School
 *LEW* BN7 ..................... 2 F7
East Sussex Health Authority
 *NEWHV* BN9 ................ 9 G2
East Sussex National Golf Club
 *UCK* TN22 ................ 102 D6
Eaton Place Surgery
 *ROTT* BN2 ..................... 7 M9
E F International School of
 English
 *SLVH* TN37 ................. 4 B7
Elm Grove CP School
 *ROTT* BN2 ..................... 7 K2
Elphinstone Junior School
 *HAS* TN34 ..................... 5 J1
Emerson College
 *FROW* RH18 ............... 25 H3
Enterprise Shopping Centre
 *EAST* BN21 ............... 10 D6
Escotts County Primary School
 *EGRIN* RH19 ............. 14 A5
Esperance Private Hospital
 *EAST* BN21 ............... 10 F8
Etchingham C of E
 rimary School
 *BUR/ETCH* TN19 ........ 61 K4
Eversfield Hospital
 *STLEO* TN38 ............ 162 A8
Evolution Health Centre
 *BRI* BN1 ....................... 6 B5
Fairfax Gallery
 *RTW* TN1 ..................... 20 A4
Fairfield Surgery
 *BUR/ETCH* TN19 ........ 60 A8
Fairlight County Primary School
 *ROTT* BN2 ..................... 7 J1
Faques Gallery
 *ROTT* BN2 ..................... 7 J8
Felbridge CP School
 *EGRIN* RH19 ............. 12 F2
Felix Gallery
 *LEW* BN7 ..................... 3 G5
Fermor School
 *CROW* TN6 ................ 40 A4
Ferryfield Industrial Estate
 *NEWHV* BN9 ................ 9 J4
Filching Manor
 *POLE* BN26 ............. 195 K4
Filsham Valley
 Secondary School
 *STLEO* TN38 ............ 161 M7
Firle C of E School
 *RING/NEW* BN8 ....... 174 A2
Firle Place
 *RING/NEW* BN8 ....... 174 C3
The Firs Surgery
 *HTHF* TN21 ................ 79 L6
The Fishermans Museum
 *HAS* TN34 ..................... 5 M7
Fishersgate First School
 *PTSD* BN41 .............. 167 G7
Five Ashes Primary School
 *MAYF* TN20 ................ 56 B8
Fletching C of E School
 *UCK* TN22 .................. 74 F3
The Fold School
 *HOVE* BN3 ............... 167 K7
Fonthill Lodge School
 *EGRIN* RH19 ............. 13 J8

Fordcombe C of E
  Primary School
  *RRTW* TN3................... 18 B1
Forest Row Business Park
  *FROW* RH18 ................ 24 F3
Forest Row C of E Infant
  School
  *FROW* RH18 ................ 24 F4
Fort
  *NEWHV* BN9 .................. 9 H8
Foxhill Surgery
  *PEAHV* BN10 .............. 190 B5
Framfield C of E School
  *UCK* TN22 ................... 77 H8
Frant C of E School
  *RRTW* TN3................... 30 B2
Freda Gardham Cp School
  *RYE* TN31 ................... 91 K8
The Gallery
  *BEXW* TN39 ............... 183 H3
The Gallery
  *BRI* BN1 ...................... 6 C6
The Gallery
  *HOVE* BN3 ................. 168 A7
Gattons Cp School
  *BURH* RH15 ............... 96 E3
Gemini Business Centre
  *HOVE* BN3 ................. 168 A6
George Street Gallery
  *ROTT* BN2 ................... 6 F7
Georgian House
  Business Centre
  *ROTT* BN2 ................... 6 F7
Gerald Dale Motor
  Sports Centre
  *STLEO* TN38 .............. 161 M1
Glebe CP School
  *STHW* BN42 .............. 166 D7
Glennys Estate
  *LW/ROSE* BN22 .......... 11 J2
Glynde Palace
  *RING/NEW* BN8 ......... 150 F7
Goldsmith Leisure Centre
  *CROW* TN6 ................ 39 M2
Goldstone Junior School
  *HOVE* BN3 ................. 167 L5
The Good Start School
  *POY/PYE* BN45 ......... 144 C1
Graham Gallery
  *SBGH/RUST* TN4......... 20 A3
Graham Whitehouse Practice
  *BURH* RH15 ............... 96 E2
Granary Business Centre
  *HAIL* BN27 ............... 131 M8
Grays County Infants School
  *NEWHV* BN9 .............. 9 G5
Great Walstead School
  *HWH* RH16 ................ 49 M8
Greenfield School
  *FROW* RH18 ................ 24 C5
Green Street Clinic
  *EAST* BN21 .............. 206 C2
Grosvenor Medical Centre
  *RTW* TN1 ................... 20 A2
Grovelands County
  Primary School
  *HAIL* BN27 ............... 155 C5
Grove Park School
  *CROW* TN6 ................. 39 L5
The Grove School
  *STLEO* TN38 ............. 161 M5
Guestling School
  *RHAS* TN35 .............. 141 G6
Guestling Surgery
  *RHAS* TN35 .............. 141 G6
Hailsham School
  *HAIL* BN27 ............... 155 H6
Hailsham Town Council
  *HAIL* BN27 ............... 155 J7
Hailsham Whitehouse Cp School
  *HAIL* BN27 ............... 155 H6
Halsford Park Primary School
  *EGRIN* RH19 .............. 13 H4
Ham Business Centre
  *SHOR* BN43 .............. 166 A7
Hamilton Lodge School
  *ROTT* BN2 ................... 7 L7
Hammerwood Park
  *EGRIN* RH19 .............. 15 J4
Hampden Park Infants School
  *LW/ROSE* BN22 ........ 196 E4
Hampden Park Secondary
  School
  *LW/ROSE* BN22 ........ 196 E4
Hampden Park Sports Centre
  *LW/ROSE* BN22 ........ 196 D4
Hamsey CP School
  *RING/NEW* BN8 ........ 126 A6
Hangleton County
  Junior & Infant School
  *HOVE* BN3 ................. 167 L4
Hankham CP School
  *PEV* BN24 ................. 179 H6
Hapstead Business Centre
  *RHWH* RH17 .............. 34 B6
Harden Road Industrial Estate
  *LYDD* TN29 ................ 95 K7
Harlands CP School
  *RHWH* RH17 .............. 48 D7
Harlands Farm County
  Primary School
  *UCK* TN22 ................. 102 D1
Harvington Business Park
  *LW/ROSE* BN22 ........ 196 F6
Hassocks County Infant School
  *HPPT/KEY* BN6........... 122 F2
Hassocks Golf Club
  *HPPT/KEY* BN6........... 122 E1
Hasting Medical Centre
  *HAS* TN34 .................. 5 G6
Hastings Castle
  *HAS* TN34 .................. 5 J6
Hastings College of Arts &
  Technology
  *HAS* TN34 .................. 5 K3
Hastings College of Arts &
  Technology
  *STLEO* TN38 ............. 162 B8

Hastings Education College
  *STLEO* TN38 ............. 161 M7
Hastings Golf Club
  *BAT* TN33 ................. 138 F6
Hastings Indoor Market
  *HAS* TN34 .................. 5 H7
Hastings Museum & Art Gallery
  *HAS* TN34 .................. 4 E7
Hastings & St Leonards
  Sailing Club
  *STLEO* TN38 ............... 4 A9
Hastings & St Leonards
  Sailing Club
  *STLEO* TN38 ............. 162 B8
Hastings Town Football Club
  *STLEO* TN38 ............. 163 G2
Hawkes Farm CP School
  *HAIL* BN27 ............... 155 H4
Hawkhurst C of E
  Primary School
  *HAWK* TN18............... 47 M6
Hawkhurst Squash Club
  *HAWK* TN18............... 47 L4
Haywards Heath College
  *HWH* RH16 ................ 48 D8
Haywards Heath Football Club
  *HWH* RH16 ................ 72 A1
Haywards Heath Golf Club
  *HWH* RH16 ................ 48 F5
Haywards Heath Hospital
  *HWH* RH16 ................ 71 J1
Hazel Cottage Clinic
  *ROTT* BN2 ................ 170 C6
Hazel Court School
  *LGNY* BN23 .............. 197 H3
Heathfield C of E Primary School
  *HTHF* TN21 ............... 80 D8
Heathfield School
  *HTHF* TN21 ............... 80 E7
Helenswood Lower School
  *SLVH* TN37 .............. 139 K7
Helenswood Upper School
  *HAS* TN34 ................ 163 G2
Hellingly CP School
  *HAIL* BN27 ............... 154 F1
Hellingly Hospital
  *HAIL* BN27 ............... 155 K1
Herbert Hone Clinic
  *ROTT* BN2 ................... 7 G2
Herne School
  *CROW* TN6 ................ 39 M6
Herons Dale School
  *SHOR* BN43 .............. 166 C5
Herstmonceux Castle
  *HAIL* BN27 ............... 157 H5
Herstmonceux C of E School
  *HAIL* BN27 ............... 156 E1
Hesketh Gallery &
  Potters Supplies
  *LEW* BN7 ................... 3 G6
Heyworth County Primary
  School
  *HWH* RH16 ................ 71 L1
High Beech Hotel &
  Country Club
  *STLEO* TN38 ............. 138 F8
Highfield Business Park
  *STLEO* TN38 ............. 161 K2
Highfield County Junior School
  *LW/ROSE* BN22 ........ 196 F6
High Hurstwood C of E School
  *UCK* TN22 ................. 54 A5
Highwoods Golf Club Ltd
  *BEXW* TN39 ............. 159 H2
Hillcrest School
  *RHAS* TN35 .............. 163 L1
Hillside School
  *PTSD* BN41 ............... 167 H4
Hippodrome Bingo
  *BRI* BN1 ...................... 6 D7
Hoddern County Junior School
  *PEAHV* BN10 ............ 190 B6
Hollington Junior School
  *STLEO* TN38 ............. 162 A2
Hollington Lodge Country Club
  *SLVH* TN37 .............. 139 G7
Holmbush County
  Infants School
  *SHOR* BN43 .............. 166 C5
Holmewood House School
  *RRTW* TN3.................. 19 L4
Homecare Business Centre
  *LEW* BN7 ................... 3 J6
Home Farm Business Centre
  *BRI* BN1 ................... 169 K3
Homeopathic Hospital
  *RTW* TN1 ................... 20 A3
Horsted Keynes C of E School
  *RHWH* RH17 .............. 35 J8
Hospital
  *HAWK* TN18............... 47 K4
Hove Business Centre
  *HOVE* BN3 ................. 168 B6
Hove General Hospital
  *HOVE* BN3 ................. 168 A7
Hove Medical Centre
  *HOVE* BN3 ................. 167 K4
Hove Metal Galleries
  *BRI* BN1 ...................... 6 C3
Hove Park Upper School
  *HOVE* BN3 ................. 168 A5
Hove Polyclinic
  *HOVE* BN3 ................. 167 M5
Hove Rugby Football Club
  *HOVE* BN3 ................. 168 B5
How We Lived Then
  Museum of Shops
  *EAST* BN21 ................ 10 E7
Hubbard School
  *EGRIN* RH19 .............. 13 L5
Hurstpierpoint College
  *HPPT/KEY* BN6........... 96 B6
Hurstwood Park Hospital
  *HWH* RH16 ................ 72 A4
The Hutchinson Gallery
  *HWH* RH16 ................ 71 L1
Ice Rink
  *BRI* BN1 ...................... 6 D6

Icklesham Primary School
  *WSEA* TN36 .............. 115 L8
Iford & Kingston C of E School
  *LEW* BN7 ................. 171 M1
Imberhorne School
  *EGRIN* RH19 .............. 13 H4
The Imber Sports Centre
  *EGRIN* RH19 .............. 13 K3
Independent Business Park
  *EGRIN* RH19 .............. 13 G3
The Indooer Market
  *HAS* TN34 .................. 5 G7
Indoor Market
  *SLVH* TN37 ................. 4 B8
Inglesea School
  *STLEO* TN38 ............. 161 M2
Inside Out Theatre Co Ltd
  *SLVH* TN37 ................. 4 A5
International Lawn
  Tennis Centre
  *EAST* BN21 ................ 10 E8
Jarvis Brook Cp School
  *CROW* TN6 ................ 40 C7
Jempsons Trading Estate
  *RYE* TN31 ................. 117 H1
Kent & Sussex Hospital
  *SBGH/RUST* TN4......... 20 A3
King Offa CP School
  *BEXW* TN39 ............. 183 H1
Kings Manor School
  *SHOR* BN43 .............. 166 D6
Kingston Buci School
  *SHOR* BN43 .............. 166 A6
Kingswood Surgery
  *RTWE/PEM* TN2 ......... 20 C3
Knoll Business Centre
  *HOVE* BN3 ................. 167 K6
Lamberhurst Surgery
  *RRTW* TN3.................. 33 G1
Langney CP School
  *LGNY* BN23 .............. 197 L5
Langney Shopping Centre
  *LGNY* BN23 .............. 197 J3
Langney Sports Club
  *LGNY* BN23 .............. 197 M3
Langton Green Cp School
  *RRTW* TN3.................. 18 E2
Lansdowne Road Clinic
  *RTW* TN1 ................... 20 B2
Law Courts
  *ROTT* BN2 ................... 7 G6
Lawn Tennis Club
  *EAST* BN21 ................ 10 E8
Leap Cross Small
  Business Centre
  *HAIL* BN27 ............... 155 G4
Lewes Business Centre
  *LEW* BN7 ................... 2 F4
Lewes Castle & Museums
  *LEW* BN7 ................... 2 F6
Lewes District Council
  *LEW* BN7 ................... 3 G7
Lewes District Council
  *NEWHV* BN9 .............. 8 F2
Lewes District Council
  *SEAF* BN25 .............. 202 E3
Lewes Gallery
  *LEW* BN7 ................... 2 F7
Lewes Grammar School
  *LEW* BN7 ................... 2 E6
Lewes Leisure Centre
  *LEW* BN7 ................... 3 J8
Lewes Little Theatre
  *LEW* BN7 ................... 3 G5
Lewes Magistrates Court
  *LEW* BN7 ................... 3 H6
Lewes Natural Health Centre
  *LEW* BN7 ................... 3 J5
Lewes Sports Club
  *LEW* BN7 ................. 149 H1
Lewes Tertiary College
  *LEW* BN7 ................... 3 H1
Lewes Victoria Hospital
  *LEW* BN7 ................... 2 B5
Lewes Wallands Cp School
  *LEW* BN7 ................... 2 B3
Lexden Lodge Industrial Estate
  *CROW* TN6 ................ 40 D6
Life Boat Museum
  *EAST* BN21 ................ 10 F9
Lindfield Infant School
  *HWH* RH16 ................ 49 G7
Lindfield Junior School
  *HWH* RH16 ................ 49 H7
Lindfield Medical Centre
  *HWH* RH16 ................ 49 H6
Lindfield School
  *LW/ROSE* BN22 ........ 196 A4
Liongate Clinic
  *SBGH/RUST* TN4......... 20 A1
Little Common Primary School
  *BEXW* TN39 ............. 182 D2
Little Horsted School
  *UCK* TN22 ................. 102 C5
Little Ridge School
  *SLVH* TN37 .............. 162 C1
Little Ridge Surgery
  *SLVH* TN37 .............. 162 C1
Little Theatre
  *SEAF* BN25 .............. 202 E4
London Meed CP School
  *BURH* RH15 ............... 97 G5
Longhill School
  *ROTT* BN2 ................ 188 E2
Longley Industrial Estate
  *BRI* BN1 ...................... 6 E2
Lower Glen Surgery
  *SLVH* TN37 .............. 162 B2
L T C International College
  *EAST* BN21 ................ 10 B8
Lydd County Primary School
  *LYDD* TN29 ................ 95 J8
Lydd Town Council
  *LYDD* TN29 ................ 95 J8
Malthouse Business Park
  *RYE* TN31 ................. 90 C4
Manor CP School
  *UCK* TN22 ................. 76 D6

Manor Farm Business Centre
  *POY/PYE* BN45 ......... 144 D1
Manor Field Cp School
  *BURH* RH15 ............... 97 J2
Manor House Hospital
  *HOVE* BN3 ................. 168 A7
Manor Oak Surgery
  *HTHF* TN21 ............... 105 M7
Manor Park Medical Centre
  *POLE* BN26 ............... 177 M8
Marefield Leisure Centre
  *UCK* TN22 ................. 76 A2
Maresfield Bonners School
  *UCK* TN22 ................. 76 B2
Marine Clinic
  *ROTT* BN2 ................ 189 G5
Mark Cross C of E School
  *CROW* TN6 ................ 42 A3
Market Place
  *HOVE* BN3 ................. 97 G4
Marlborough House School
  *HAWK* TN18............... 47 L4
Marshlands CP School
  *HAIL* BN27 ............... 155 K6
Martins Oak Surgery
  *BAT* TN33 ................. 137 K2
Mayfield Gallery
  *MAYF* TN20 ............... 57 H3
Maynards Green Cp School
  *HTHF* TN21 ............... 106 A4
The Meadows Surgery
  *BURH* RH15 ............... 96 D2
The Mead School
  *RTWE/PEM* TN2 ......... 20 A5
Meads Surgery
  *EGRIN* RH19 .............. 13 L7
The Meads Surgery
  *UCK* TN22 ................. 76 C7
The Medical Centre
  *PEV* BN24 ................. 198 D1
Meeching Valley Cp School
  *NEWHV* BN9 .............. 8 C3
Megabowl
  *BEX* TN40 ................ 184 A2
Memorial Art Gallery
  *HAS* TN34 .................. 5 G7
Mercateria Business Centre
  *STLEO* TN38 ............... 4 A9
Meridian CP School
  *PEAHV* BN10 ............ 190 C5
Meridian Leisure Centre
  *PEAHV* BN10 ............ 190 C7
Meridian Surgery
  *PEAHV* BN10 ............ 190 B6
The Mews Clinic
  *EAST* BN21 ................ 10 A4
Michael Hall School
  *FROW* RH18 ................ 24 D5
Michelham Priory
  *HAIL* BN27 ............... 154 B7
Middle Street Primary School
  *BRI* BN1 ...................... 6 D7
Mid Sussex Golf Club
  *HPPT/KEY* BN6........... 124 A1
Mile Oak Clinic
  *PTSD* BN41 ............... 166 F3
Mile Oak Junior School
  *PTSD* BN41 ............... 166 F3
Millbrook Business Park
  *CROW* TN6 ................ 40 D6
Mill Green Industrial Estate
  *HWH* RH16 ................ 48 E8
Mill View Hospital
  *HOVE* BN3 ................. 167 L5
Moatfield Surgery
  *EGRIN* RH19 .............. 13 L4
Moira House School
  *EDN/EASTW* BN20 .... 206 D5
Morley Street Health Centre
  *ROTT* BN2 ................... 7 G5
The Mosque
  *STLEO* TN38 ............... 4 A8
Motcombe County
  Infant School
  *EAST* BN21 .............. 206 C1
Moulsecoomb Clinic
  *ROTT* BN2 ................ 169 L3
Moulsecoomb County
  Junior School
  *ROTT* BN2 ................ 169 L3
Mountfield & Whatlington
  C of E Primary Sch
  *RBTBR* TN32 ............... 85 K7
Mount Pleasant Hospital
  *SLVH* TN37 .............. 162 A2
Mount School
  *WADH* TN5 ................ 31 H8
Mowden School
  *HOVE* BN3 ................. 168 D5
Museum of Local History
  *HAS* TN34 .................. 5 K6
Netherfield C of E
  Primary School
  *BAT* TN33 ................. 110 C4
Nevill Golf Club
  *RTWE/PEM* TN2 ......... 20 D7
Newhaven Flea Market
  *NEWHV* BN9 .............. 8 F4
Newhaven Health Centre
  *NEWHV* BN9 .............. 9 G3
Newhaven Town Council
  *NEWHV* BN9 .............. 9 G4
Newick Health Centre
  *RING/NEW* BN8 ......... 74 D7
Newick House Special School
  *BURH* RH15 ............... 97 J5
Newick School
  *RING/NEW* BN8 ......... 74 C8
Newlands Health Clinic
  *HWH* RH16 ................ 71 L2
Newlands Preparatory School
  *SEAF* BN25 .............. 203 H2
Newlands Senior School
  *SEAF* BN25 .............. 203 G2
New Life School
  *EGRIN* RH19 .............. 13 K4
Newmans Loner School
  *HOVE* BN3 ................. 168 D6

Ninfield C of E School
  *BAT* TN33 ................. 159 H1
Northbourne Medical Centre
  *SHOR* BN43 .............. 166 A6
Northease Manor School
  *LEW* BN7 ................. 172 C5
Northfield Business Park
  *HAIL* BN27 ............... 154 A2
Northiam Primary School
  *RYE* TN31 ................. 88 B1
Northlands Wood Cp School
  *HWH* RH16 ................ 72 B2
Northlands Wood Surgery
  *HWH* RH16 ................ 72 B2
Nutley Primary School
  *UCK* TN22 ................. 52 C2
Oakmeads Community School
  *BURH* RH15 ............... 97 G4
Oathall Community College
  *HWH* RH16 ................ 48 F8
Ocklynge County Junior School
  *EAST* BN21 .............. 196 C8
Odeon Cinema
  *BRI* BN1 ...................... 6 C7
Old Grammar School
  *LEW* BN7 ................... 2 D5
Old Grammar School
  *LEW* BN7 ................... 2 E6
The Old Museum
  *RYE* TN31 ................. 88 F4
Old Salehurst School
  *RBTBR* TN32 ............... 85 H1
Old Town Surgery
  *SEAF* BN25 .............. 202 E4
Old Town Art Gallery
  *HAS* TN34 .................. 5 K6
The Open University
  *EGRIN* RH19 .............. 13 L5
Ore Business Park
  *HAS* TN34 .................. 5 M1
Our Lady of Lourdes School
  *ROTT* BN2 ................ 188 F4
Ovingdean Hall School
  *ROTT* BN2 ................ 188 D2
Palace Pier
  *ROTT* BN2 ................... 6 F9
Park College Eastbourne
  *EAST* BN21 .............. 196 D7
Parklands Junior & Infant
  School
  *LW/ROSE* BN22 ........ 196 D5
Park Mead School
  *HAIL* BN27 ............... 154 A6
Parkside County Primary
  School
  *HTHF* TN21 ............... 106 C1
Park View Leisure Centre
  *HOVE* BN3 ................. 167 L7
Pashley Down County
  Infant School
  *EDN/EASTW* BN20 .... 206 B2
Patcham Cp School
  *BRI* BN1 ................... 145 M8
Patcham First School
  *BRI* BN1 ................... 145 L8
Patcham High School
  *BRI* BN1 ................... 145 M8
Patcham House School
  *BRI* BN1 ................... 145 L8
The Pavilion Clinic
  *BRI* BN1 ...................... 6 B6
Pavilion Theatre
  *BRI* BN1 ...................... 6 E6
Paxton Business Centre
  *HOVE* BN3 ................. 167 K6
Peacehaven Infant School
  *PEAHV* BN10 ............ 190 B7
Peacehaven Sports Centre
  *PEAHV* BN10 ............ 190 D7
Peacehaven Town Council
  *PEAHV* BN10 ............ 190 C6
Peacock Industrial Estate
  *HOVE* BN3 ................. 168 D7
Peasmarsh C of E
  Primary School
  *RYE* TN31 ................. 90 B5
Pebsham Primary School
  *BEX* TN40 ................ 184 A1
Pells C of E Infant School
  *LEW* BN7 ................... 2 D4
Pells Primary School
  *LEW* BN7 ................... 2 F5
Penns Gallery
  *EAST* BN21 ................ 10 D7
Peter Gladwin School
  *PTSD* BN41 ............... 167 G4
Pevensey Bay Sailing Club
  *PEV* BN24 ................. 198 C4
Pevensey Castle
  *PEV* BN24 ................. 180 B8
Pevensey & Westham
  C of E Primary School
  *PEV* BN24 ................. 180 A8
Philpots Manor School
  *EGRIN* RH19 .............. 34 C1
Phoenix Industrial Estate
  *LEW* BN7 ................... 3 G4
Phoenix Industrial Estate
  *LEW* BN7 ................... 3 H5
The Picture House
  *UCK* TN22 ................. 76 C7
The Piltdown Golf Club
  *UCK* TN22 ................. 75 L4
Playden School
  *RYE* TN31 ................. 91 J4
Plumpton New Primary School
  *LEW* BN7 ................. 124 F1
Polegate CP School
  *POLE* BN26 ............... 178 D2
Polegate Town Council Office
  *POLE* BN26 ............... 195 M1
Police Station and
  Magistrates Court
  *RTW* TN1 ................... 20 B2
Portfolio Studio Gallery
  *BRI* BN1 ...................... 6 E7
Portland Business Park
  *HOVE* BN3 ................. 167 K7

Portland Industrial Estate
*HOVE* BN3 .................... 167 L6
Portland Road Industrial Estate
*HOVE* BN3 .................... 167 K6
Portland Surgery
*HOVE* BN3 .................... 167 M7
Portslade Community College
*PTSD* BN41 .................... 167 G3
Portslade Community College
*PTSD* BN41 .................... 167 G5
Portslade Community College
*STHW* BN42 .................... 166 F4
Portslade Health Centre
*PTSD* BN41 .................... 167 H7
Practice
*SBGH/RUST* TN4 .................... 20 A4
Premier Gallery
*EAST* BN21 .................... 10 D7
Preston Furniture Gallery
*BRI* BN1 .................... 168 F4
Preston Park Clinic
*BRI* BN1 .................... 169 G5
Preston Park Surgery
*BRI* BN1 .................... 169 G6
Priest House
*EGRIN* RH19 .................... 22 E8
Prince Regent Swimming
Complex
*BRI* BN1 .................... 6 F6
The Princes Royal Hospital
*HWH* RH16 .................... 71 M4
Prinnys Antique Gallery
*BRI* BN1 .................... 6 D7
Priory Hill Shopping Centre
*HAS* TN34 .................... 5 G6
Priory School
*LEW* BN7 .................... 3 H8
Punnetts Town School
*HTHF* TN21 .................... 81 H8
Queensdown School
*BRI* BN1 .................... 169 J3
Queens Park County
Primary School
*ROTT* BN2 .................... 7 J7
Queen Victoria Hospital
N H S Trust
*EGRIN* RH19 .................... 13 M3
Quintin Medical Centre
*HAIL* BN27 .................... 155 J3
Ranalah Estate
*NEWHV* BN9 .................... 9 H1
Ratton County Secondary
School
*EAST* BN21 .................... 196 C7
Red Lake CP School
*RHAS* TN35 .................... 163 K2
Regent Business Centre
*BURH* RH15 .................... 96 E4
Rich Industrial Estate
*NEWHV* BN9 .................... 191 L5
Ringmer Business Centre
*RING/NEW* BN8 .................... 127 M8
Ringmer CP School
*RING/NEW* BN8 .................... 150 E1
Ringmer Football Club
*RING/NEW* BN8 .................... 150 D1
Ringmer Parish Council
*RING/NEW* BN8 .................... 150 D1
River Lodge Surgery
*LEW* BN7 .................... 3 H5
Riverside Industrial Estate
*LEW* BN7 .................... 3 G4
Robertsbridge Community
College
*RBTBR* TN32 .................... 84 F2
Roborough Day Hospital
*EAST* BN21 .................... 10 E4
Robsack Infant School
*STLEO* TN38 .................... 161 L4
Rock & Bowl Bowling Alley
*EGRIN* RH19 .................... 13 L5
Rocks Park CP School
*UCK* TN22 .................... 76 B6
Rockys Leisure Centre
*HAS* TN34 .................... 4 F8
Rodmell Primary School
*LEW* BN7 .................... 172 E5
Roebuck House Surgery
*HAS* TN34 .................... 5 L5
Roedean School
*ROTT* BN2 .................... 188 C3
Rose Hill School
*SBGH/RUST* TN4 .................... 19 L1
Roselands County Infants School
*LW/ROSE* BN22 .................... 11 H1
Rother District Council
*BAT* TN33 .................... 137 J1
Rotherfield CP School
*CROW* TN6 .................... 41 H6
Rotherfield Surgery
*CROW* TN6 .................... 41 H6
Rottingdean Football Club
*ROTT* BN2 .................... 188 F3
Rottingdean Primary School
*ROTT* BN2 .................... 189 G4
Rottingdean Surgery
*ROTT* BN2 .................... 188 E3
Royal Alexandra Hospital
*BRI* BN1 .................... 6 C4
Royal Ashdown Forest Golf Club
*FROW* RH18 .................... 25 G5
Royal Eastbourne Golf Club
*EAST* BN21 .................... 10 A7
Royal Eastbourne Golf Club
*EDN/EASTW* BN20 .................... 206 D4
Royal George Clinic
*BURH* RH15 .................... 96 E3
Royal Hippodrome Theatre
*EAST* BN21 .................... 11 G6
Royal Pavilion
*BRI* BN1 .................... 6 F6
Royal Sussex County Hospital
N H S Trust
*ROTT* BN2 .................... 7 L8
Royal Victoria Place
Shopping Centre
*RTW* TN1 .................... 20 B2

Rudyard Kipling Primary School
*ROTT* BN2 .................... 170 E7
Rugby Club
*EGRIN* RH19 .................... 23 J1
Rusthall Medical Centre
*SBGH/RUST* TN4 .................... 19 H2
Rutherfords Business Park
*BAT* TN33 .................... 112 F4
Rye Art Gallery
*RYE* TN31 .................... 117 J1
Rye Bay Club House
*WSEA* TN36 .................... 143 G1
Rye Castle Museum
*RYE* TN31 .................... 117 J1
Rye Community Clinic
*RYE* TN31 .................... 117 H1
Rye Football & Cricket Club
*RYE* TN31 .................... 91 J8
Rye Golf Club
*RYE* TN31 .................... 118 B3
Rye Harbour Sailing Club
*RYE* TN31 .................... 118 A3
Rye Industrial Estate
*RYE* TN31 .................... 117 K2
Sackville School
*EGRIN* RH19 .................... 14 A5
Sacred Heart School
*RTWE/PEM* TN2 .................... 20 E2
Sacred Heart School
*WADH* TN5 .................... 43 K1
St Andrews C of E Infant School
*LW/ROSE* BN22 .................... 197 J8
St Andrews C of E School
*HOVE* BN3 .................... 168 B8
St Andrews Market
*HAS* TN34 .................... 5 H6
St Andrews School
*EDN/EASTW* BN20 .................... 206 D7
St Andrews Surgery
*LEW* BN7 .................... 3 G7
St Annes Special School
*LEW* BN7 .................... 2 D7
St Aubyns School
*ROTT* BN2 .................... 189 G5
St Barnabas C of E
Primary School
*BRI* BN1 .................... 6 E3
St Bartholomews C of E Primary
School
*RTW* TN1 .................... 20 B1
St Bedes School
*EDN/EASTW* BN20 .................... 206 E7
St Bedes School
*HAIL* BN27 .................... 153 M6
St Bernadettes First
Middle Va School
*BRI* BN1 .................... 168 E4
St Christophers School
*HOVE* BN3 .................... 168 A7
St Dominics Gallery
*HPPT/KEY* BN6 .................... 123 J3
St Faith Clinic
*ROTT* BN2 .................... 187 L2
St Georges School
*RTWE/PEM* TN2 .................... 21 G1
St Giles College
*EDN/EASTW* BN20 .................... 206 F5
St James's Junior & Infant School
*RTWE/PEM* TN2 .................... 20 C2
St Johns Church School
*CROW* TN6 .................... 39 J2
St Johns Infant School
*SBGH/RUST* TN4 .................... 20 A1
St Johns Residential School
*ROTT* BN2 .................... 7 L7
St John the Baptist RC
Primary School
*ROTT* BN2 .................... 7 M6
St Josephs R C Primary School
*HWH* RH16 .................... 71 L2
St Josephs RC School
*LW/ROSE* BN22 .................... 11 J2
St Leonards C of E Primary School
*STLEO* TN38 .................... 162 A7
St Leonards Football Club
*HAS* TN34 .................... 163 G3
St Lukes Junior & Infant School
*ROTT* BN2 .................... 7 K5
St Lukes Swimming Pool
*ROTT* BN2 .................... 7 K4
St Marks C of E Primary School
*ROTT* BN2 .................... 187 L1
St Marks C of E Primary School
*SBGH/RUST* TN4 .................... 19 K5
St Marks C of E Primary School
*UCK* TN22 .................... 78 C1
St Martins C of E Primary School
*ROTT* BN2 .................... 7 J1
St Martins C of E Primary School
*ROTT* BN2 .................... 169 J6
St Mary Magdalene School
*BEX* TN40 .................... 160 E8
St Mary Magdalene School
*BRI* BN1 .................... 6 B6
St Marys C of E School
*EGRIN* RH19 .................... 13 K4
St Marys Primary Catholic School
*CROW* TN6 .................... 39 M4
St Marys RC School
*PTSD* BN41 .................... 167 H7
St Marys School
*BEX* TN40 .................... 160 E8
St Marys School
*HTHF* TN21 .................... 106 A5
St Mary the Virgin School
*HRTF* TN7 .................... 26 D2
St Michaels Cp School
*HRTF* TN7 .................... 27 H1
St Nicholas & St. Mary School
*SHOR* BN43 .................... 166 A6
St Pancras RC Primary School
*LEW* BN7 .................... 2 C6
St Pauls C of E Infant School
*RRTW* TN3 .................... 19 H2
St Pauls C of E Junior School
*SBGH/RUST* TN4 .................... 19 H2
St Pauls C of E School
*BRI* BN1 .................... 6 D5

St Pauls RC Comprehensive School
*HWH* RH16 .................... 71 M1
St Pauls School
*SLVH* TN37 .................... 4 C4
St Peters C of E School
*RHWH* RH17 .................... 34 A6
St Peters County Infant School
*PTSD* BN41 .................... 167 H8
St Peters Medical Centre
*BRI* BN1 .................... 6 F3
St Peters Primary School
*RING/NEW* BN8 .................... 99 L2
St Peters Primary School
*RTWE/PEM* TN2 .................... 20 C3
St Peters RC School
*EGRIN* RH19 .................... 13 J5
St Peters R C School
*SHOR* BN43 .................... 166 A6
St Phillips R C Primary School
*UCK* TN22 .................... 102 C1
St Richards School
*BEX* TN40 .................... 183 L2
St Thomas A Becket RC
Infants School
*EAST* BN21 .................... 10 D2
St Thomas A Becket RC
Junior School
*EAST* BN21 .................... 10 D1
St Thomas C of E Primary School
*RTRW* TN3 .................... 18 C8
St Thomas C of E Primary School
*WSEA* TN36 .................... 116 F7
St Vincent School
*STLEO* TN38 .................... 161 M4
St Wilfrids C of E School
*HWH* RH16 .................... 72 A1
St Wilfrids RC School
*BURH* RH15 .................... 97 G4
Salehurst C of E Primary School
*RBTBR* TN32 .................... 85 H2
Saltdean County Primary School
*ROTT* BN2 .................... 189 J4
Salvation Army
*LW/ROSE* BN22 .................... 11 G5
Sandhurst CP School
*HAWK* TN18 .................... 64 C1
Sandown School
*RHAS* TN35 .................... 163 J2
Saxonborough Surgery
*CROW* TN6 .................... 39 M4
Saxon Mount School
*STLEO* TN38 .................... 161 M7
The Seaford Business Centre
*SEAF* BN25 .................... 202 E3
Seaford CP School
*SEAF* BN25 .................... 202 E2
Seaford Day Hospital
*SEAF* BN25 .................... 202 F3
Seaford Golf Club
*SEAF* BN25 .................... 192 F8
Seaford Head
Community College
*SEAF* BN25 .................... 202 F4
Seaford Head
Community College
*SEAF* BN25 .................... 203 G4
Seaford Head Lower School
*SEAF* BN25 .................... 202 F4
Seaford Health Centre
*SEAF* BN25 .................... 202 E3
Seaford Sports & Leisure Centre
*SEAF* BN25 .................... 202 E3
Sea Life Centre
*ROTT* BN2 .................... 6 F8
Sea Road Surgery
*BEX* TN40 .................... 183 K3
Seaside Medical Centre
*LW/ROSE* BN22 .................... 11 H4
Secondary School
*ROTT* BN2 .................... 169 L8
Sedlescombe C of E School
*BAT* TN33 .................... 112 E5
Sedlescombe Golf Club
*BAT* TN33 .................... 138 E1
The Seven Dials Medical Centre
*BRI* BN1 .................... 6 C4
Shankill Surgery
*RHAS* TN35 .................... 163 K2
Sheddindean Business Centre
*BURH* RH15 .................... 96 F1
Sheddingdean First School
*BURH* RH15 .................... 97 G1
Sheila Cashin Gallery
*BRI* BN1 .................... 6 C5
Sheriffs Gallery
*HAIL* BN27 .................... 155 J7
The Ship Street Surgery
*EGRIN* RH19 .................... 13 L6
Shoe Gallery
*LEW* BN7 .................... 3 G6
Shoreham Beach
County First School
*SHOR* BN43 .................... 166 A8
Shoreham College
*SHOR* BN43 .................... 166 D7
Shoreham Football Club
*PTSD* BN41 .................... 167 H7
Sidley Primary School
*BEXW* TN39 .................... 160 C8
Sidley Sports Club
*BEXW* TN39 .................... 160 C7
Sidley Surgery
*BEXW* TN39 .................... 160 B7
Silverhill Natural Health Centre
*STLEO* TN38 .................... 162 B4
Silver Springs Medical Practice
*SLVH* TN37 .................... 4 B5
Simpsons Industrial Estate
*RYE* TN31 .................... 117 J3
Skippers Hill Manor Preparatory
School
*MAYF* TN20 .................... 56 B6
Snowhill Business Centre
*CRAWE* RH10 .................... 12 A2
Somerhill County Junior School
*HOVE* BN3 .................... 168 D8
Southdown Business Park
*LEW* BN7 .................... 3 J3

South Downs Health Clinic
*BRI* BN1 .................... 6 D4
South Malling Primary School
*LEW* BN7 .................... 3 H2
Southover C of E Primary School
*LEW* BN7 .................... 2 E7
Southover C of E Primary School
*LEW* BN7 .................... 2 F8
South Saxon Howe Surgery
*STLEO* TN38 .................... 161 L7
Southway County Junior School
*HPPT/KEY* BN6 .................... 96 D3
Southwick Business Centre
*PTSD* BN41 .................... 166 E8
Southwick Manor Hall
County First School
*STHW* BN42 .................... 166 F7
Spinney School
*HTHF* TN21 .................... 105 K3
Springfield Industrial Estate
*HAWK* TN18 .................... 47 M3
Springfield Industrial Estate
*RHWH* RH17 .................... 97 M1
Squash Club
*EAST* BN21 .................... 10 C8
Squires Farm Industrial Estate
*UCK* TN22 .................... 103 L5
Stafford County Junior School
*LW/ROSE* BN22 .................... 197 G8
Stanford Junior School
*BRI* BN1 .................... 6 C1
Stanley Deason Leisure Centre
*ROTT* BN2 .................... 187 M1
Staplecross School
*RBTBR* TN32 .................... 86 E4
Stevenson Gallery
*RYE* TN31 .................... 117 H1
Stewart Gallery
*BEX* TN40 .................... 183 J3
Stone Cross CP School
*PEV* BN24 .................... 197 G1
Stonegate C of E Primary School
*WADH* TN5 .................... 59 M1
Stonelands School of
Ballet & Theatre
*HOVE* BN3 .................... 168 B8
Summerfields Business Centre
*SLVH* TN37 .................... 4 C5
Summerfield Sports Centre
*HAS* TN34 .................... 4 D6
Sussex County Cricket Club
*HOVE* BN3 .................... 168 C7
Sussex Eye Hospital
*ROTT* BN2 .................... 7 L8
Sussex House Industrial Estate
*HOVE* BN3 .................... 167 M6
Sussex Nuffield Hospital
*HOVE* BN3 .................... 167 M8
Sussex Nuffield Hospital
*ROTT* BN2 .................... 170 C6
Sussex Private Clinic
*STLEO* TN38 .................... 162 B6
The Sussex Toy & Model Museum
*BRI* BN1 .................... 6 D4
Sussex University
*LEW* BN7 .................... 3 J4
Sutton Industrial Park
*WSEA* TN36 .................... 117 G7
Swan Barn Business Centre
*HAIL* BN27 .................... 155 K8
Sydney West Sports Centre
*BURH* RH15 .................... 97 G2
Synagogue
*BRI* BN1 .................... 6 D7
Synagogue
*EAST* BN21 .................... 10 F6
TA Centre
*LW/ROSE* BN22 .................... 11 H4
Tavistock & Summerhill School
*HWH* RH16 .................... 48 F7
Teacher Training School
*HAS* TN34 .................... 5 K4
Telscombe Cliffs Primary School
*PEAHV* BN10 .................... 190 A6
Temple Grove with
St Nicholas School
*UCK* TN22 .................... 53 L3
Tennis Club
*CROW* TN6 .................... 39 L4
Theatre Royal
*BRI* BN1 .................... 6 E6
Thomas Peacocke
Community College
*RYE* TN31 .................... 91 H8
Ticehurst Clinic
*HOVE* BN3 .................... 168 A8
Ticehurst C of E Primary School
*WADH* TN5 .................... 45 K6
Tideway School
*NEWHV* BN9 .................... 8 D6
Tilling Green School
*RYE* TN31 .................... 117 G1
Tobias School of Art
*EGRIN* RH19 .................... 13 L8
Tollgate Junior School
*LGNY* BN23 .................... 197 K7
Torfield School
*HAS* TN34 .................... 5 L4
Towner Art Gallery & Local
History Museum
*EDN/EASTW* BN20 .................... 206 D3
Town Hall
*BRI* BN1 .................... 6 E8
Town Hall
*EAST* BN21 .................... 10 C7
Town Hall
*HOVE* BN3 .................... 168 B8
Town Hall
*RTW* TN1 .................... 20 A2
Tree Tops Tree Surgery
*STLEO* TN38 .................... 161 M3
Trinity Theatre & Arts Association
*RTW* TN1 .................... 20 A2
Tunbridge Wells Borderers Sports
Club
*RTWE/PEM* TN2 .................... 20 A6
Tunbridge Wells Centre
*RTW* TN1 .................... 20 A2

Tunbridge Wells Golf Club
*SBGH/RUST* TN4 .................... 19 L3
Tunbridge Wells Hockey Club
*RTW* TN1 .................... 20 B5
Tunbridge Wells Independent
Hospital
*RRTW* TN3 .................... 18 B3
Tunbridge Wells Museum &
Art Gallery
*SBGH/RUST* TN4 .................... 20 A2
Tunbridge Wells Nuffield Hospital
*RTWE/PEM* TN2 .................... 20 D3
Turners Hill C of E School
*CRAWE* RH10 .................... 22 A3
Uckfield Civic Centre
*UCK* TN22 .................... 76 C7
Uckfield Community Hospital
*UCK* TN22 .................... 76 D8
Uckfield Community School
*UCK* TN22 .................... 76 D6
Uckfield Holy Cross School
*UCK* TN22 .................... 76 C7
Uckfield Rugby Football Club
*UCK* TN22 .................... 76 E6
Uckfield Sports Centre
*UCK* TN22 .................... 76 C7
University of Brighton
*BRI* BN1 .................... 146 E8
University of Brighton
*BRI* BN1 .................... 170 A1
University of Brighton
*EAST* BN21 .................... 10 C4
University of Brighton
*EDN/EASTW* BN20 .................... 10 A9
University of Brighton
*EDN/EASTW* BN20 .................... 206 D7
University of Brighton
*EDN/EASTW* BN20 .................... 206 D5
University of Brighton
*ROTT* BN2 .................... 6 F6
University of Brighton
*ROTT* BN2 .................... 169 J4
University of Sussex
*BRI* BN1 .................... 147 H7
Uplands Community College
*WADH* TN5 .................... 43 M2
Uplands School
*BRI* BN1 .................... 169 J4
Utopia Leisure Centre
*UCK* TN22 .................... 76 D6
Vals Swim School
*BEXW* TN39 .................... 160 B6
Varndean College
*BRI* BN1 .................... 168 F3
Varndean High School
*BRI* BN1 .................... 169 G3
Venture Industrial Park
*STLEO* TN38 .................... 162 A4
Vicarage Field Surgery
*HAIL* BN27 .................... 155 J6
Virgin Cinemas
*LGNY* BN23 .................... 197 M5
Virgin Cinemas
*ROTT* BN2 .................... 187 L3
Wadhurst Business Park
*WADH* TN5 .................... 31 H1
Wadhurst C of E Primary School
*WADH* TN5 .................... 43 M1
Warden Park School
*RHWH* RH17 .................... 71 G1
Warrior Square Surgery
*SLVH* TN37 .................... 4 B9
Waterhall Golf Course
*BRI* BN1 .................... 145 H7
Wayfield Clinic
*BRI* BN1 .................... 168 E4
Wealden College
*CROW* TN6 .................... 39 M6
Wealden District Council
*HAIL* BN27 .................... 155 J6
Wealden Industrial Estate
*CROW* TN6 .................... 40 C6
Websters Gallery
*BRI* BN1 .................... 11 G6
Welfare Clinic
*HOVE* BN3 .................... 167 L4
Wellington Square
Medical Centre
*HAS* TN34 .................... 5 H7
Wellshurst Golf & Country Club
*HAIL* BN27 .................... 132 A4
Westdene Primary School
*BRI* BN1 .................... 168 C1
Westerleigh School
*STLEO* TN38 .................... 162 A6
Western Road Primary School
*LEW* BN7 .................... 2 C6
Westham Medical Centre
*PEV* BN24 .................... 198 A1
West Hoathly School
*EGRIN* RH19 .................... 22 E8
West Hove Middle School
*HOVE* BN3 .................... 167 L7
West Pier (Under Repair)
*BRI* BN1 .................... 6 B8
West Rise Junior & Infant
School
*LGNY* BN23 .................... 197 J4
West St Leonards County
Primary School
*STLEO* TN38 .................... 161 M6
West Sussex County Council
*SHOR* BN43 .................... 166 B7
West Terrace Clinic
*EAST* BN21 .................... 10 D7
Wheel Park Farm Industrial
Estate
*RHAS* TN35 .................... 139 K2
The White Gallery
*HOVE* BN3 .................... 168 C8
Whitehawk Clinic
*ROTT* BN2 .................... 187 M1
The Whitehawk College
*EAST* BN21 .................... 10 E6
Whitehawk Infant School
*ROTT* BN2 .................... 169 L8
Whitehawk Junior School
*ROTT* BN2 .................... 169 L8

Whitehill County Infant School
*CROW* TN6 .............................. **40** A5
White Rock Theatre
*HAS* TN34 .............................. **4** E8
William Parker Lower School
*HAS* TN34 .............................. **162** D2
William Parker Upper School
*HAS* TN34 .............................. **162** D2
Willingdon CP School
*EDN/EASTW* BN20 .................... **196** A3

Willingdon Golf Club
*EDN/EASTW* BN20 .................... **196** B7
Willingdon School
*POLE* BN26 .............................. **195** M2
Willingdon Trees Primary School
*LW/ROSE* BN22 ....................... **196** D3
The Willow Surgery
*ROTT* BN2 .............................. **169** M5
Windmills County Junior School
*HPPT/KEY* BN6......................... **122** F3

Window Gallery
*BRI* BN1.............................. **6** C3
Window Gallery
*BRI* BN1.............................. **6** D7
Winifred Lee Health Centre
*LW/ROSE* BN22 ..................... **11** K1
Winter Gardens
*EAST* BN21 .............................. **10** E9
Wish Tower Puppet Museum
*EAST* BN21 .............................. **207** G5

Wish Valley Surgery
*HAWK* TN18.............................. **47** M6
Wittersham Primary School
*TENT* TN30 .............................. **67** K4
Woodingdean Primary School
*ROTT* BN2 .............................. **170** C6
Workshop Gallery
*EAST* BN21 .............................. **10** F5
Worthing & Southlands Hospitals
N H S Trust
*SHOR* BN43.............................. **166** B6

Wych Cross Place
*FROW* RH18 .............................. **36** C2
Yeowart Business Centre
*UCK* TN22 .............................. **76** B8
YMCA
*BRI* BN1.............................. **6** E5

## Page 19

**K2**
1 Rusthall Gra
2 Tristan Gdns

**K5**
1 Nottidge Rd

## Page 20

**A2**
1 Belgrave Rd
2 Clarence Rw
3 Culverden St
4 Dudley Rd
5 Grosvenor Wk
6 Hanover Rd
7 Lime Hill Rd
8 Mount Ephraim Rd
9 Rock Villa Rd

**A3**
1 Clanricarde Gdns
2 Clarence Rd
3 Lonsdale Gdns
4 Rosehill Wk
5 Vale Av
6 Wells Cl

**A4**
1 Berkeley Rd
2 Castle St
3 Cumberland Yd
4 Grove Av
5 Little Mount Sion
6 Market St
7 The Pantiles
8 South Gv
9 Sussex Ms
10 White Bear Pas

**A5**
1 Broad Gv
2 Clarendon Cl

**B1**
1 Hill St
2 Mercer St
3 Norman Rd
4 St Barnabas' Cl
5 St Stephons Ct

**B2**
1 Calverley Rd
2 The Ferns
3 Garden Rd
4 Garden St
5 Lansdowne Sq
6 Monson Rd
7 Monson Wy
8 Newton Rd
9 Victoria Rd

**B3**
1 Calverley Park Crs
2 Camden Hl
3 Camden Pk
4 Catherine Pl
5 Guildford Rd
6 Meadow Hill Rd
7 Mount Pleasant Av

**B4**
1 Cambridge Gdns
2 Clifton Pl
3 Farmcombe Cl
4 Grecian Rd
5 Madeira Pk
6 Norfolk Rd

**B5**
1 Beau Nash Wy

**B6**
1 Elphick's Pl

**C1**
1 Chandos Rd
2 Fairfield Av
3 Stanhope Rd

**C2**
1 Carlton Crs
2 Concord Cl
3 Ferndale Cl
4 Lansdowne Rd

**C3**
1 Bucklers Cl
2 Calverley Ct
3 Cambridge St
4 Oakfield Court Rd
5 Park St
6 Prince's St
7 St Peter's St
8 Windmill St

**C4**
1 Camden Hl
2 Hollyshaw Cl

**C6**
1 Cypress Gv

**D1**
1 Andrews Cl
2 Brendon Cl
3 Pinewood Rd

**D2**
1 Shepherds Wk
2 Sherwood Rd

**D4**
1 Camden Pk
2 Hawkenbury Cl
3 Polesden Rd
4 Rookley Cl

**D5**
1 Hawkenbury Mead

**E1**
1 Bracken Cl

## Page 80

**B8**
1 Ashdown Pl
2 The Avenue
3 Coppice Vw
4 Hawthorne Cl
5 Oakleigh Dr
6 Prospect Rd
7 The Spinneys
8 Vale View Rd
9 Woodland Ms
10 Woodland Wy

## Page 96

**E2**
1 Baylis Crs
2 Pannett
3 Wallis Wy
4 Withy Bush

**F3**
1 Commercial Rd
2 London Rd
3 Orchard Wy

## Page 97

**J5**
1 Bough Beeches
2 Hambrook
3 Kirdford Cl
4 Lurgashall
5 Pendean

## Page 149

**J3**
1 Hoopers Cl
2 Mealla Cl
3 Peckham Cl

---

**J5**
1 Banks Castle
2 Castle Ditch La
3 Paddock Rd
4 Precincts Castle
5 Queen Anne's Cl
6 Sackville St
7 St Peters Pl
8 Well House Pl

**K5**
1 Albion St
2 Eastgate Whf
3 Edward St
4 Little East St
5 Market La
6 Phoenix Pl
7 St Andrew's La
8 St Nicholas La
9 Spring Gdns
10 Waterloo Pl
11 Wellington St

**L5**
1 Brooks La
2 Farncombe Rd
3 Morris Rd
4 Rusbridge La
5 Thomas St

## Page 155

**G8**
1 Blacksmiths Copse
2 Oaklands Wy

**H3**
1 Beckenham Cl
2 Hawkstown Cl
3 Hawkstown Gdns

**J3**
1 Pembroke Cl
2 Warwick Cl

## Page 162

**A2**
1 Beauchamp Rd
2 Edward Ter
3 Meadow Cl
4 Northampton Wy

**B2**
1 Battle Crs
2 Bellingham Cl
3 Clarendon Cl
4 Hollinghurst Rd

**C1**
1 Anvil Ct
2 Folkington Gdns
3 Glyndebourne Gdns
4 Harvest Wy
5 Highlea Cl
6 Laleham Cl
7 Lullington Gdns
8 Martingale Cl
9 Pentland Cl
10 The Ridings
11 Smithy's Cl
12 Walton Cl
13 Wheatfield Ct

**C6**
1 Anglesea Ter
2 De Cham Rd

**C7**
1 Cardiff Rd
2 Cross St
3 Ellenslea Rd
4 Hatherley Rd
5 The Lawn
6 Rothsay Rd
7 Station Ap
8 Terrace Rd
9 Union St

**C8**
1 Harold Ms
2 Market St
3 Mercatoria
4 Mews Rd
5 Saxon St
6 Shepherd St
7 Stanhope Pl

**D1**
1 Honeysuckle Cl
2 Oasthouse Cl

**D2**
1 Richborough Cl

**D5**
1 Selmeston Cl

**D6**
1 De Cham Av
2 St Catherine's Cl
3 Summerfields

**D7**
1 The Cloisters
2 Prince's Rd
3 St Paul's Pl
4 Victoria Rd

**E1**
1 Cloverlea

**E4**
1 Hole Farm Cl

**E5**
1 Piltdown Cl

**E6**
1 Braybrooke Ter
2 Cornwallis Ter
3 Hillyglen Cl
4 Hopgarden Cl
5 Linton Crs
6 Station Ap

**E7**
1 Claremont
2 Dorset Pl
3 Prospect Pl
4 Robertson St
5 Schwerte Wy
6 White Rock Gdns

**F4**
1 Hughenden Pl

**F6**
1 Brook St
2 Castle Hill Pas
3 Cornwallis St
4 Elford St
5 Middle St
6 Portland Pl
7 Station Rd
8 Stonefield Rd
9 Stone St
10 Waldegrave St
11 Wellington Ms
12 Wellington Sq

**F7**
1 Castle Gdns
2 Castle St
3 Harold Pl
4 Queen's Rd
5 Robertson Pas
6 Robertson Ter
7 Wellington Pl
8 York Gdns

## Page 163

**G6**
1 Alpine Rd
2 Castledown Av
3 Exmouth Pl
4 Gordon Rd
5 Swan Ter

---

**G7**
1 Cutter La
2 East St
3 Pelham Crs
4 Shell La
5 Sun La

**H5**
1 The Glebe

**J4**
1 High Bank Cl
2 Richmond St

**K4**
1 Hawthorn Rd

## Page 166

**B5**
1 Berberis Cl
2 Marjoram Pl
3 New Barn Cl
4 Tottington Wy

**G7**
1 The Cotswolds
2 Green Cl
3 School Cl
4 Twitten Cl
5 Waterdyke Av
6 Watling Cl

## Page 167

**H4**
1 Blackthorn Cl
2 Brackenbury Cl
3 Cornford Cl
4 Foredown Cl
5 Highways
6 Meadow Cl

**H6**
1 Bampfield St
2 Barnes Rd
3 Buckler St

**H7**
1 Church St
2 St Aubyn's Crs

**L4**
1 Ashlings Wy
2 Storrington Cl
3 Sunninghill Cl
4 Thornhill Rd

**M3**
1 Findon Cl
2 Midhurst Wk
3 Nutley Cl

**M4**
1 Fallowfield Cl

**M5**
1 Acacia Av
2 Torrance Cl
3 Wayfield Cl

**M7**
1 Mainstone Rd
2 Scott Rd

## Page 168

**A3**
1 Elizabeth Cl
2 Queen Caroline Cl
3 Sandringham Cl

**A7**
1 Wynnes Ms

**B4**
1 Woodland Cl

**B7**
1 Haddington St
2 Malvern St
3 Monmouth St

**B8**
1 Kings Ms
2 Norton Cl

**C3**
1 Barrowfield Cl

**C7**
1 Eaton Gv
2 Selborne Rd

**C8**
1 St John's Pl
2 Victoria Gv

**D1**
1 Deneside
2 Downside

**D3**
1 Blackthorn Cl

**D5**
1 Scarborough Rd
2 Wincombe Cl

**D6**
1 Burton Vls

**D8**
1 Farm Ms
2 Lansdowne Ms

**E1**
1 Grangeways

**E4**
1 Cumberland Dr

**E5**
1 Miller's Rd

**E6**
1 Port Hall Av
2 Port Hall Ms

**E7**
1 Belmont
2 Caburn Rd
3 Chanctonbury Rd
4 Wolstonbury Rd

**E8**
1 Victoria Pl

**F1**
1 Warmdene Cl
2 Wilmington Pde
3 Winfield Cl

**F3**
1 Mulberry Cl

**F7**
1 Russell Crs
2 Terminus Pl

**F8**
1 Buckingham St
2 Clifton St
3 Guildford St
4 Kew St
5 Mount Zion Pl
6 North Rd
7 Railway St
8 Surrey St
9 Terminus St
10 Upper Gloucester Rd

## Page 169

**G4**
1 Hollingbury Ter

**G5**
1 St Andrew's Rd
2 Southdown Pl

**G6**
1 Ditchling Ri

---

**G7**
1 Belmont St
2 Kingsbury Rd
3 Kingsbury St
4 Marshalls Rw
5 New England St
6 Oxford Ct
7 Oxford St
8 Queen's Pl

**G8**
1 Blackman St
2 Cheltenham Pl
3 Gloucester Pl
4 Kensington Gdns
5 Kensington St
6 Pelham Sq
7 Robert St
8 St George's Ms
9 St George's Pl
10 Station St
11 Trafalgar Ct
12 Trafalgar Pl
13 Upper Gardner St
14 Vine St
15 Whitecross St

**H3**
1 Brentwood Cl

**H4**
1 Fountains Cl
2 Quarry Bank Rd
3 Stanmer St

**H6**
1 Aberdeen Rd
2 Caledonian Rd
3 Edinburgh Rd
4 Round Hill Rd
5 Round Hill St
6 St Mary Magdalene St

**H7**
1 Hanover Crs
2 Newport St
3 St Martin's St

**H8**
1 Ashton Ri
2 Lincoln Cottages
3 Phoenix Ri
4 Richmond Pde
5 Sussex Ri
6 Windmill Ter

**J4**
1 Barrow Cl

**J5**
1 Liphook Cl

**J6**
1 Bembridge St
2 Fairlight Pl
3 Inverness Rd
4 Newmarket Rd
5 Pevensey Rd
6 St Leonard's Rd
7 Whippingham St

**J7**
1 Bernard Pl
2 Coronation St
3 Cromwell St
4 Normanton St

**J8**
1 Barn Field Gdns
2 Barry Wk
3 Beaufort Ter
4 Stonehurst Ct

**K4**
1 Culpepper Cl
2 Tillstone Cl

**K5**
1 Borrow King Cl
2 Canfield Rd

**L1**
1 Arlington Crs
2 Ashbumham Cl

**L3**
1 Broadfields
2 Broadfields Rd

**L7**
1 Haybourne Cl

**L8**
1 Exceat Cl
2 School Ri

**M7**
1 Pulborough Cl
2 Sevelands Cl
3 Sompting Cl
4 Swanborough Pl

**M8**
1 Horsham Cl
2 Pett Cl
3 Selmeston Pl

## Page 186

**D1**
1 Brunswick Ms
2 Brunswick St West
3 Chapel Ms
4 Donkey Ms
5 Ivy Pl
6 Lansdowne Sq
7 Lower Market St
8 Upper Market St

**E1**
1 Bedford Pl
2 Bedford Sq
3 Hampton St
4 Little Western St
5 Norfolk Buildings
6 Norfolk Ms
7 Queensbury Ms
8 Sillwood Pl
9 Sillwood Rd
10 Spring St
11 Western St
12 Western Ter

**F1**
1 Cannon Pl
2 Crown St
3 Marlborough Ms
4 Marlborough St
5 Middle St
6 Portland St
7 Regent Rw
8 Russell Pl
9 Russell Rd
10 St Margaret's Pl
11 Ship St
12 Upper North St
13 Windsor St

## Page 187

**G1**
1 Bartholomews
2 Bond St
3 Brighton Pl
4 Dorset St
5 East St
6 Gardner St
7 Grand Parade Ms
8 Jew St
9 King Pl
10 King St
11 Kingswood St
12 Market St
13 Marlborough Pl
14 Meeting House La
15 New Rd
16 Nile St
17 North Pl
18 North St
19 Old Steine
20 Orange Rw
21 Palace Pl
22 Pavilion Buildings
23 Pavilion Pde
24 Pavilion St
25 Prince Albert St
26 Prince's Pl
27 Prince's St
28 Regent St
29 St James's St
30 Steine Gdns
31 Steine La
32 Tichborne St
33 Union St
34 William St

**H1**
1 Carlton Pl
2 Cavendish St
3 Dorset Pl
4 Egremont Pl
5 George St
6 Grosvenor St
7 Mighell St
8 Mount Pleasant
9 Nelson Rw
10 St James's Street Ms
11 St John's Pl
12 Tilbury Pl
13 Upper Park Pl
14 White St

**H2**
1 Atlingworth St
2 Camelford St
3 Charlotte St
4 Grafton St
5 Lower Rock Gdns
6 Madeira Pl
7 Margaret St
8 Marine Gdns
9 New Steine
10 Wentworth St
11 Wyndham St

**J2**
1 Bloomsbury Pl
2 Bloomsbury St
3 Marine Terrace Ms
4 Royal Crescent Ms
5 Telegraph St

**K2**
1 Belgrave Pl
2 Chapel Ter
3 Chesham Pl
4 Chichester Pl
5 Clarendon Ter
6 Eastern Ter
7 Eastern Terrace Ms
8 Kemp Town Pl
9 Millfield Cottages
10 Percival Ter
11 St Mary's Sq
12 Seymour Sq
13 Seymour St
14 Sudeley Ter
15 Upper Sudeley St

**L2**
1 Eastern Rd

**L5**
1 De Courcel Rd

## Page 190

**A6**
1 Park View Ri

**B5**
1 Canada Cl
2 Carey Down
3 Chatsworth Pk
4 The Compts
5 The Dewpond
6 Kings Cl
7 Lulham Cl
8 The Martins
9 Sunset Cl
10 The Swallows
11 Woodlands Cl

## Page 191

**H7**
1 Hawthorn Ri
2 Hazel Cl
3 Lapierre Rd
4 Lewry Cl

**J8**
1 Northdown Cl

**K4**
1 Glynde Cl
2 Iford Cl
3 Tarring Cl

**K5**
1 Cottage Cl
2 St Martins Crs

## Page 196

**B2**
1 Thurrock Cl

**D5**
1 Holland Cl

## Page 197

**G8**
1 Filder Cl

**H1**
1 Lavender Cl

**J2**
1 Borrowdale Cl
2 Buttermere Wy
3 Coniston Rd
4 Elmwood Cl
5 Elmwood Gdns
6 Middleham Wy
7 Wildwood

**J3**
1 Cleveland Cl
2 Harebell Cl
3 Magdalen Cl
4 Milfoil Dr
5 Sorrel Cl

**J4**
1 Robin Cl

**K4**
1 Appledore Cl
2 Barming Cl
3 Bathford Cl
4 Chilham Cl
5 Close Three
6 Close Twentyfive
7 Close Two
8 Lydd Cl
9 Sidcup Cl
10 The Vineries
11 Wayford Cl

---

**K5**
1 Gainsborough Crs
2 Goudhurst Cl
3 Lawrence Cl
4 Turner Cl
5 Wrotham Cl

**L3**
1 Close Eight
2 Close Eleven
3 Close Five
4 Close Fourteen
5 Close Seven
6 Close Six
7 Goldsmith Cl
8 Lambert Rd
9 Stevenson Cl

**L4**
1 Close Eighteen
2 Close Fifteen
3 Close Four
4 Close Ten
5 Close Twelve
6 Close Twentyfour
7 Spring Lodge Cl

**L8**
1 Cook Av
2 Nelson Dr
3 Palliser Cl

**M6**
1 Athelstan Cl
2 Canute Cl
3 Falmouth Cl
4 Finistere Av
5 Hengist Cl
6 Leeward Quay
7 Plymouth Cl
8 Rockall Av
9 Southampton Cl

**M7**
1 Ayscue Cl
2 Boscawen Cl
3 Cornwallis Cl
4 Rodney Cl
5 Vincent Cl

**M8**
1 Pound Cl
2 Royal Sovereign Vw

## Page 202

**D2**
1 Berwick Cl
2 Birling Cl

**E3**
1 Croft Ct
2 Richmond Ter
3 Sutton Croft La
4 Warwick Rd

**E4**
1 Chatham Pl
2 Church La
3 Mallett Cl
4 Pelham Yd
5 West St

**F2**
1 Blatchington Cl
2 Esher Cl
3 Homefield Cl
4 Northcliffe Cl
5 Pinewood Cl

## Page 203

**G3**
1 Aquila Pk
2 Went Hill Pk

**H1**
1 Hillside Av
2 Landsdown Rd
3 Seafield Cl
4 Upper Chyngton Gdns

**J3**
1 Barcombe Cl
2 Buckthorn Cl
3 Elm Cl
4 Findon Cl
5 Ladycross Cl
6 Romney Cl
7 Rowan Cl
8 Stirling Cl
9 Sycamore Cl

**J4**
1 Fairways Cl
2 Mark Cl
3 Newick Cl
4 Poynings Cl
5 Steyning Cl

## Page 206

**D2**
1 Bay Pond Rd
2 Brodie Pl
3 Gore Park Av
4 Old Motcombe Ms
5 Prospect Gdns
6 Shortdean Pl

**D6**
1 Coltstocks Rd
2 Meads Brow

**E5**
1 Ascham Pl
2 Beristede Cl
3 Collington Cl
4 Gaudick Cl
5 Naomi Cl
6 St Vincents Pl

**F5**
1 Fitzgerald Cl
2 Old Wish Rd
3 South Cliff Av

## Page 207

**G5**
1 Carlisle Rd
2 Howard Sq
3 Lascelles Ter
4 Regency Ms
5 Wilmington Gdns
6 Wilmington Sq

**H2**
1 Albion Rd
2 Beltring Ter
3 Chawbrook Rd
4 Havelock Rd
5 Hoad Rd
6 Neville Rd
7 Oxford Rd
8 St George's Rd
9 Sheen Rd
10 Springfield Rd
11 Stanley Rd
12 Willowfield Rd

**H3**
1 Burfield Rd
2 Cavendish Pl
3 Colonade Rd
4 Leaf Hall Rd
5 Lion La
6 Marine Rd
7 Queen's Colonnade Gdns
8 St Aubyn's Rd
9 Willowfield Sq